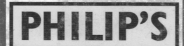

STREET ATLAS
Berkshire

First published in 1990 by

Philip's, a division of
Octopus Publishing Group Ltd
2-4 Heron Quays, London E14 4JP
An Hachette Livre UK Company

Third colour edition 2004
Third impression 2007
BERCB

ISBN-10   0-540-08492-1 (hardback)
ISBN-13   978-0-540-08492-0 (hardback)
ISBN-10   0-540-08493-X (spiral)
ISBN-13   978-0-540-08493-7 (spiral)

© Philip's 2005

OS Ordnance Survey®

This product includes mapping data licensed
from Ordnance Survey® with the permission of
the Controller of Her Majesty's Stationery Office.
© Crown copyright 2005. All rights reserved.
Licence number 100011710.

No part of this publication may be reproduced,
stored in a retrieval system or transmitted in any
form or by any means, electronic, mechanical,
photocopying, recording or otherwise, without
the permission of the Publishers and the
copyright owner.

To the best of the Publishers' knowledge, the
information in this atlas was correct at the time
of going to press. No responsibility can be
accepted for any errors or their consequences.

The representation in this atlas of a road, track
or path is no evidence of the existence of a right
of way.

Ordnance Survey and the OS Symbol are
registered trademarks of Ordnance Survey, the
national mapping agency of Great Britain.

Printed by Toppan, China

Contents

III   **Key to map symbols**

IV   **Key to map pages**

VI   **Route planning**

VIII   **Administrative and Postcode boundaries**

1   **Street maps** at 3½ inches to 1 mile

154   **Index** of towns and villages

156   **Index** of streets, hospitals, industrial estates, railway stations, schools, shopping centres and universities and places of interest

Digital Data

The exceptionally high-quality mapping found in this atlas is available as digital data in TIFF format, which is easily convertible to other bitmapped (raster) image formats.

The index is also available in digital form as a standard database table. It contains all the details found in the printed index together with the National Grid reference for the map square in which each entry is named.

For further information and to discuss your requirements, please contact james.mann@philips-maps.co.uk

Motorway with junction number		◆	Ambulance station
Primary route – dual/single carriageway		◆	Coastguard station
A road – dual/single carriageway		◆	Fire station
B road – dual/single carriageway		◆	Police station
Minor road – dual/single carriageway		✚	Accident and Emergency entrance to hospital
Other minor road – dual/single carriageway		H	Hospital
Road under construction		+	Place of worship
Tunnel, covered road		i	Information Centre (open all year)
Rural track, private road or narrow road in urban area		P	Parking
Gate or obstruction to traffic (restrictions may not apply at all times or to all vehicles)		P&R	Park and Ride
Path, bridleway, byway open to all traffic, road used as a public path		PO	Post Office
Pedestrianised area		Ⓧ	Camping site
DY7 Postcode boundaries		Caravan site	
County and unitary authority boundaries		▶	Golf course
Railway, tunnel, railway under construction		✕	Picnic site
Tramway, tramway under construction		Prim Sch	Important buildings, schools, colleges, universities and hospitals
Miniature railway		River Medway	Water name
Walsall Railway station			River, weir, stream
Private railway station			Canal, lock, tunnel
London Underground station			Water
Tram stop, tram stop under construction			Tidal water
Bus, coach station			Woods

Acad	Academy	Inst	Institute	Recn Gd	Recreation Ground		Built up area
Allot Gdns	Allotments	Ct	Law Court			*Church*	Non-Roman antiquity
Cemy	Cemetery	L Ctr	Leisure Centre	Resr	Reservoir		
C Ctr	Civic Centre	LC	Level Crossing	Ret Pk	Retail Park	ROMAN FORT	Roman antiquity
CH	Club House	Liby	Library	Sch	School		
Coll	College	Mkt	Market	Sh Ctr	Shopping Centre		
Crem	Crematorium	Meml	Memorial	TH	Town Hall/House	◀ 87	
Ent	Enterprise	Mon	Monument	Trad Est	Trading Estate		Adjoining page indicators
Ex H	Exhibition Hall	Mus	Museum	Univ	University	▼ 58	
Ind Est	Industrial Estate	Obsy	Observatory	W Twr	Water Tower		
IRB Sta	Inshore Rescue Boat Station	Pal	Royal Palace	Wks	Works		
		PH	Public House	YH	Youth Hostel		

■ The small numbers around the edges of the maps identify the 1 kilometre National Grid lines

■ The dark grey border on the inside edge of some pages indicates that the mapping does not continue onto the adjacent page

The scale of the maps on the pages numbered in blue is 5.52 cm to 1 km • 3½ inches to 1 mile • 1: 18103

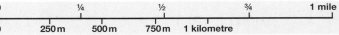

0		¼		½		¾		1 mile
0	250 m		500 m		750 m	1 kilometre		

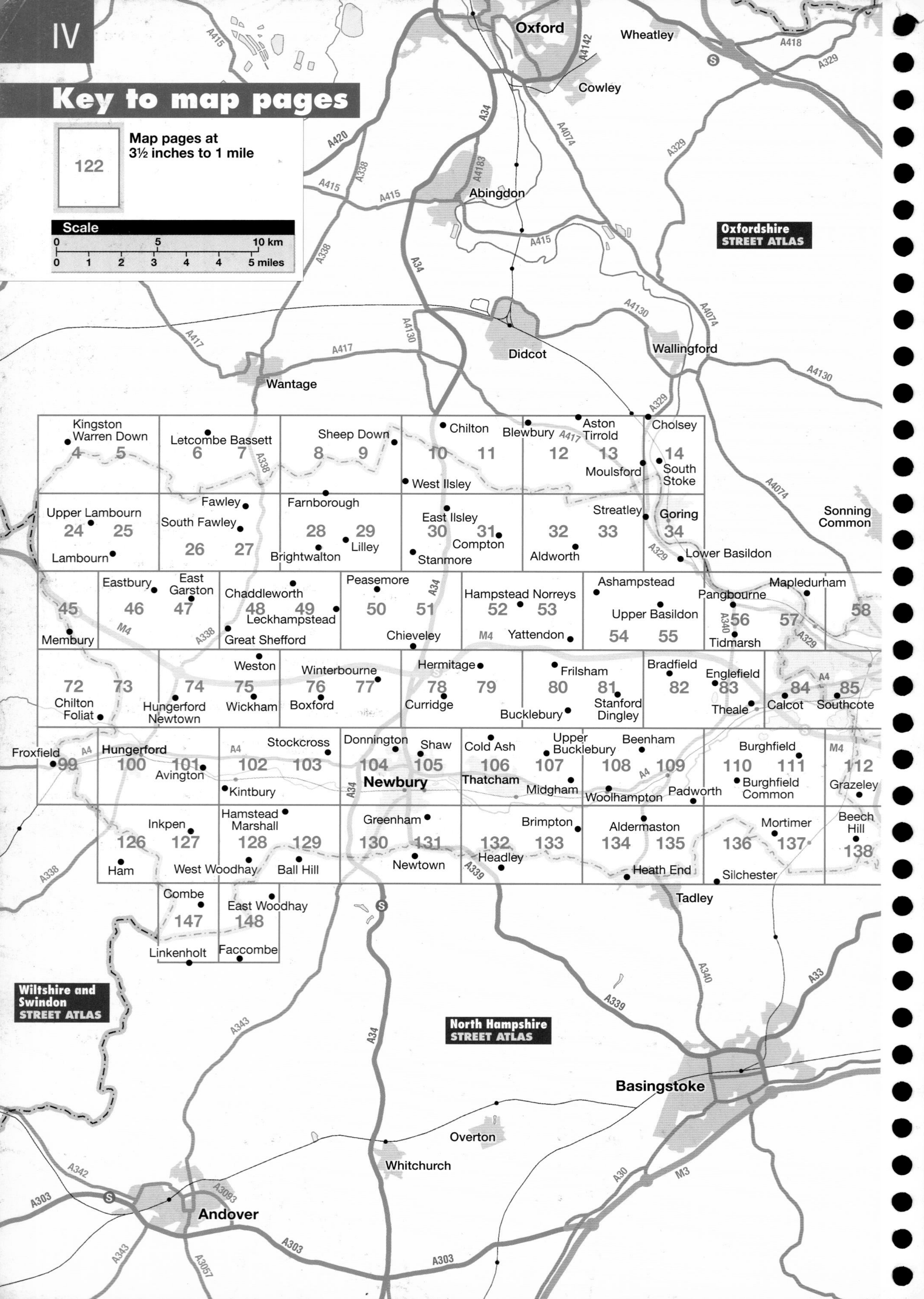

IV

Key to map pages

Map pages at
3½ inches to 1 mile

122

Scale

0   5   10 km
0   1   2   3   4   4   5 miles

Oxfordshire STREET ATLAS

Oxford
Wheatley
Cowley
Abingdon
Wallingford
Sonning Common
Didcot
Wantage

Kingston Warren Down 4	5	Letcombe Bassett 6	7	Sheep Down 8	9	Chilton 10	11	Blewbury 12	Aston Tirrold 13	Cholsey 14

West Ilsley
Moulsford
South Stoke

Upper Lambourn 24	25	Fawley 26	South Fawley 27	Farnborough 28	29 Lilley	East Ilsley 30	31 Compton	32	Streatley 33	Goring 34

Lambourn
Brightwalton
Stanmore
Aldworth
Lower Basildon

Eastbury 45	46	East Garston 47	Chaddleworth 48	49 Leckhampstead	Peasemore 50	51	Hampstead Norreys 52	53	Ashampstead 54	Upper Basildon 55	Mapledurham 58

Membury
Great Shefford
Chieveley
Yattendon
Pangbourne 56
Tidmarsh 57

72	73	Weston 74	75 Wickham	Winterbourne 76	77	Hermitage 78	79	Frilsham 80	81	Bradfield 82	Englefield 83	84	85

Chilton Foliat
Hungerford Newtown
Boxford
Curridge
Bucklebury
Stanford Dingley
Theale
Calcot
Southcote

Froxfield

99	Hungerford 100	101	Stockcross 102	103	Donnington 104	Shaw 105	Cold Ash 106	Upper Bucklebury 107	108	Beenham 109	Burghfield 110	111	112

Avington
Kintbury
Newbury
Thatcham
Midgham
Woolhampton
Padworth
Burghfield Common
Grazeley

Inkpen 126	127	Hamstead Marshall 128	129	Greenham 130	131	132	Brimpton 133	Aldermaston 134	135	Mortimer 136	137	Beech Hill 138

Ham
West Woodhay
Ball Hill
Newtown
Headley
Heath End
Silchester

Combe 147	East Woodhay 148

Linkenholt
Faccombe

Wiltshire and Swindon STREET ATLAS

Tadley

North Hampshire STREET ATLAS

Basingstoke
Overton
Whitchurch
Andover

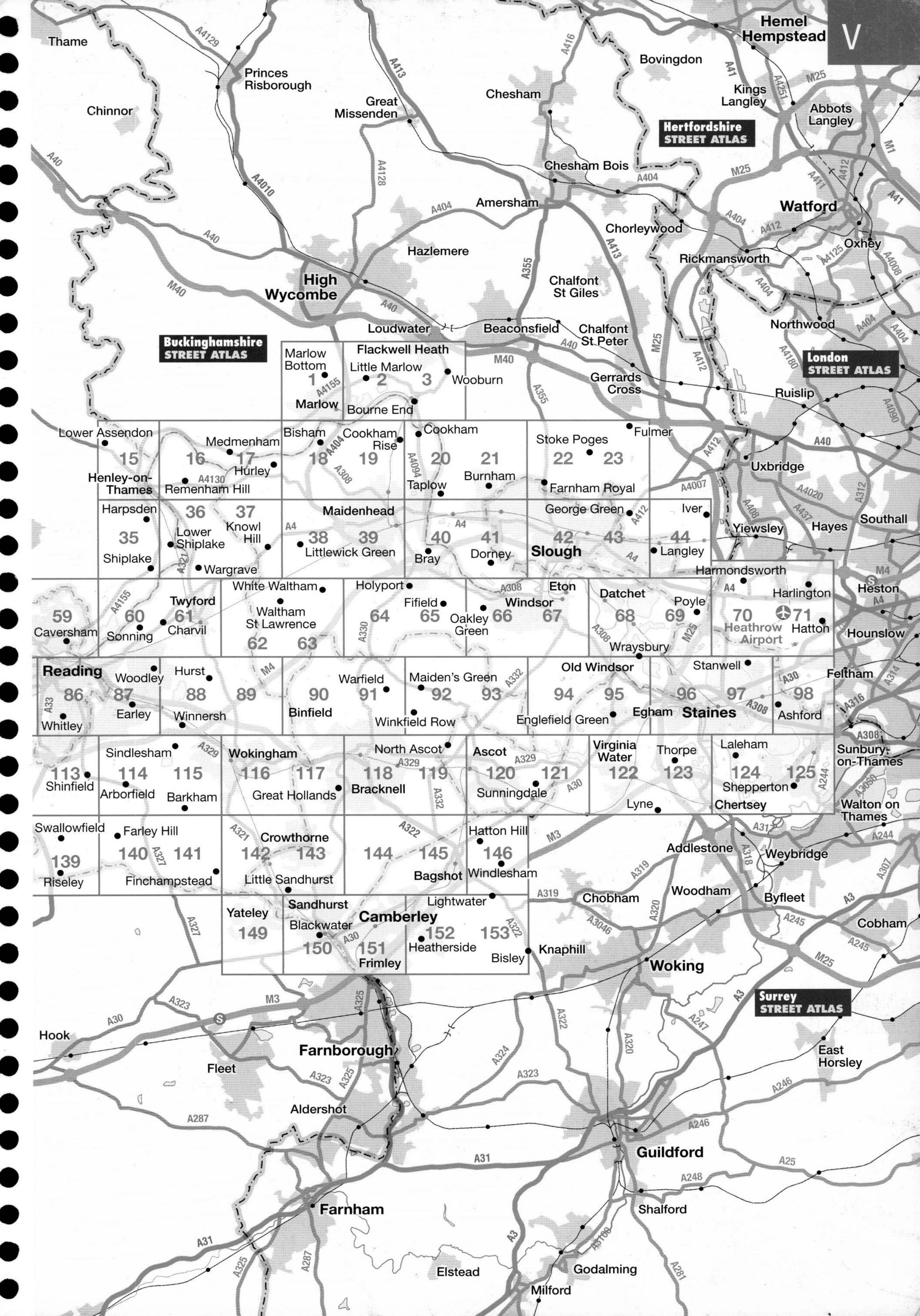

Thame

Chinnor

Princes Risborough

Great Missenden

Chesham

Chesham Bois

Amersham

Bovingdon

Kings Langley

Abbots Langley

Hemel Hempstead

Hertfordshire STREET ATLAS

Watford

Oxhey

Chorleywood

Rickmansworth

Northwood

Hazlemere

High Wycombe

Loudwater

Beaconsfield

Chalfont St Giles

Chalfont St Peter

Gerrards Cross

Ruislip

Uxbridge

Hayes

Southall

London STREET ATLAS

Buckinghamshire STREET ATLAS

Marlow Bottom **1**

Flackwell Heath

Little Marlow **2**

3

Wooburn

Marlow

Bourne End

Fulmer

Lower Assendon

Medmenham

Bisham

Cookham Rise

Cookham

Stoke Poges

Henley-on-Thames **15**

16

Hurley **17**

18

19

Taplow **20**

Burnham **21**

22

23

Farnham Royal

George Green

Iver

Harpsden

Remenham Hill

Maidenhead

Yiewsley

35

Shiplake

36

Lower Shiplake

Knowl Hill **37**

38

Littlewick Green

39

Bray **40**

Dorney **41**

Slough **42**

43

Langley **44**

Wargrave

Harmondsworth

Heston

Caversham **59**

Sonning **60**

Twyford **61** Charvil

White Waltham

Waltham St Lawrence **62**

63

Holyport

64

Fifield

65

Oakley Green

Windsor **66**

Eton

67

Datchet **68**

Poyle **69**

Harlington

70 Heathrow Airport

71 Hatton

Hounslow

Reading

Woodley

Hurst

Whitley **86**

Earley **87**

88

Winnersh

89

90

Warfield **91**

Winkfield Row

Maiden's Green **92**

93

Englefield Green **94**

Old Windsor

95

Egham

Stanwell

96

97

Staines

Feltham

Ashford **98**

Sunbury-on-Thames

Sindlesham

Wokingham

North Ascot

Ascot

Virginia Water

Thorpe

Laleham

Shinfield **113**

Arborfield **114**

Barkham **115**

116

117

Great Hollands

118

Bracknell

119

120

Sunningdale **121**

122

123

Lyne

Shepperton **124**

Chertsey

125

Walton on Thames

Swallowfield

Farley Hill

Crowthorne

Hatton Hill

Addlestone

Weybridge

Riseley **139**

140

141

Finchampstead

Little Sandhurst

142

143

144

145

146 Windlesham

Bagshot

Woodham

Byfleet

Cobham

Chobham

Sandhurst

Lightwater

Yateley

Blackwater

Camberley

149

150

151

Frimley

152 Heatherside

153

Bisley

Knaphill

Woking

Surrey STREET ATLAS

Hook

Farnborough

Fleet

East Horsley

Aldershot

Guildford

Farnham

Shalford

Elstead

Milford

Godalming

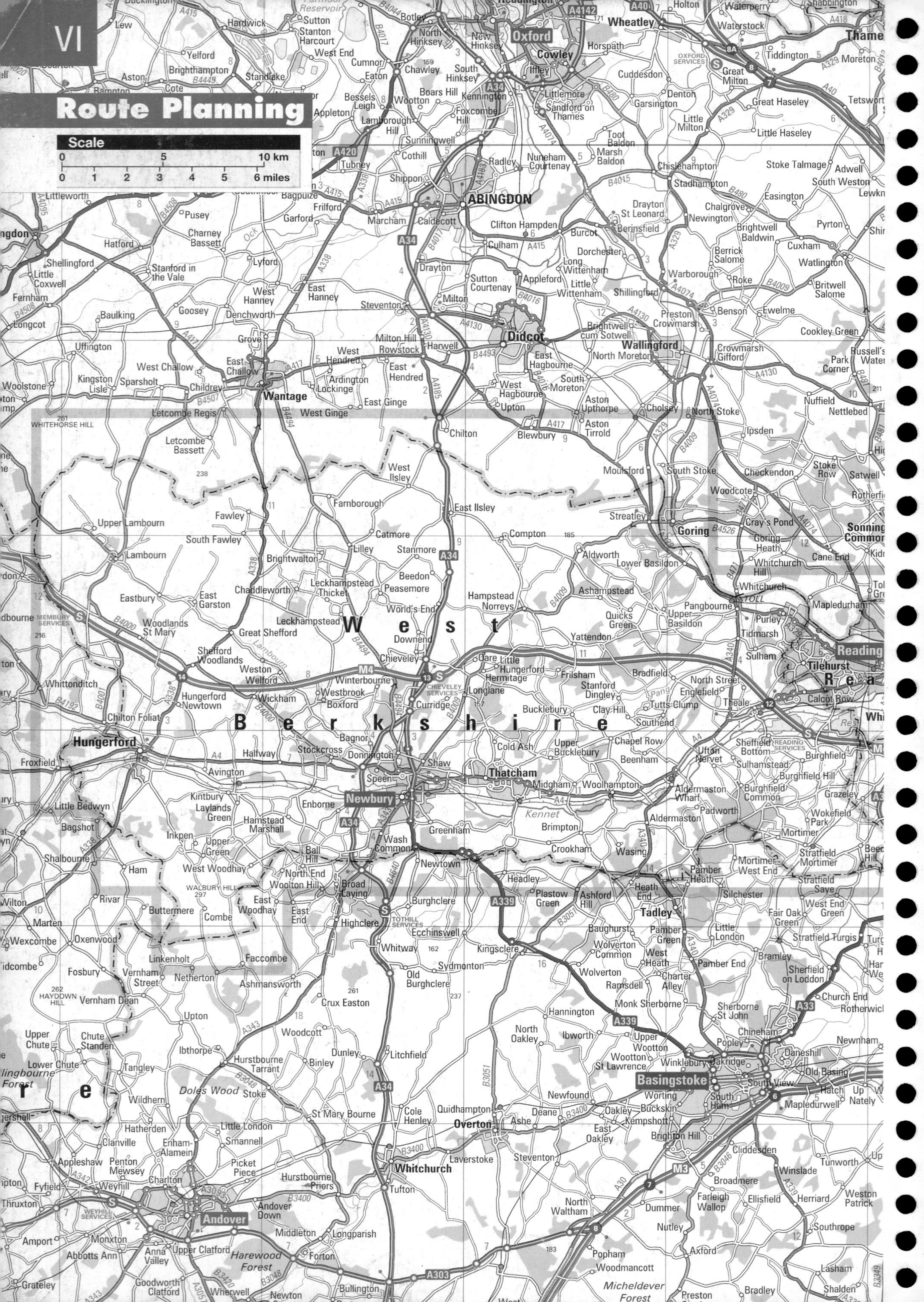

VI
Route Planning
Scale
0 5 10 km
0 1 2 3 4 5 6 miles
Lew
Hardwick
Sutton
Stanton Harcourt
Botley
North Hinksey
New Hinksey
Oxford
A4142
Wheatley
Holton
Waterperry
Waterstock
Thame
Yelford
West End
Cumnor
Eaton
Chawley
South Hinksey
Cowley
Iffley
Horspath
Cuddesdon
Great Milton
Tiddington
Moreton
Aston
Brighthampton
Standlake
Cote
Bampton
Bessels Leigh
Appleton
Wootton
Boars Hill
Kennington
A34
Littlemore
Sandford on Thames
Denton
Garsington
Great Haseley
Tetsworth
Lamborough Hill
Foxcombe Hill
Sunningwell
Little Milton
Little Haseley
Toot Baldon
Marsh Baldon
Tubney
Cothill
Radley
Nuneham Courtenay
Chislehampton
Stoke Talmage
Adwell
Shippon
Stadhampton
South Weston
Lewknor
Littleworth
Bagpuize
Frilford
Marcham
Caldecott
ABINGDON
Drayton St Leonard
Chalgrove
Easington
Newington
Pusey
Garford
Clifton Hampden
Burcot
Berinsfield
Brightwell Baldwin
Pyrton
Faringdon
Charney Bassett
Hatford
Culham
Dorchester
Berrick Salome
Cuxham
Watlington
Shellingford
Little Coxwell
Stanford in the Vale
Lyford
Drayton
Long Wittenham
Warborough
Roke
Fernham
West Hanney
East Hanney
Sutton Courtenay
Appleford
Little Wittenham
Shillingford
Britwell Salome
Longcot
Baulking
Goosey
Denchworth
Steventon
Milton
Benson
Ewelme
Preston Crowmarsh
Uffington
Grove
Milton Hill
Rowstock
Harwell
Didcot
Brightwell cum Sotwell
Wallingford
Cookley Green
West Challow
East Challow
West Hendred
East Hendred
Ardington
Lockinge
North Moreton
Crowmarsh Gifford
Russell's Water
Park Corner
Kingston Lisle
Sparsholt
Woolstone
Childrey
Wantage
East Hagbourne
West Hagbourne
South Moreton
Upton
Aston Upthorpe
Aston Tirrold
Cholsey
North Stoke
Nuffield
Nettlebed
Letcombe Regis
West Ginge
East Ginge
Whitehorse Hill
Chilton
Blewbury
Ipsden
Letcombe Bassett
West Ilsley
Moulsford
South Stoke
Checkendon
Stoke Row
Satwell
Woodcote
Rotherfield
Farnborough
East Ilsley
Streatley
Goring
Cray's Pond
Sonning Common
Upper Lambourn
Fawley
South Fawley
Catmore
Compton
Goring Heath
Lambourn
Brightwalton
Lilley
Stanmore
Aldworth
Lower Basildon
Whitchurch Hill
Cane End
Chaddleworth
Leckhampstead Thicket
Beedon
Peasemore
Ashampstead
Whitchurch
Eastbury
East Garston
World's End
Hampstead Norreys
Pangbourne
Mapledurham
Membury Services
Woodlands St Mary
Leckhampstead
Quicks Green
Upper Basildon
Purley
Great Shefford
West
Downend
Yattendon
Tidmarsh
Shefford Woodlands
Weston
Welford
Chieveley
Oare
Little Hungerford
Hermitage
Frilsham
Bradfield
Sulham
Reading
Tilehurst
Whittonditch
Winterbourne
Chieveley Services
Stanford Dingley
North Street
Englefield
Hungerford Newtown
Wickham
Westbrook
Boxford
Curridge
Longlane
Bucklebury
Clay Hill
Tutts Clump
Theale
Calcot Row
Chilton Foliat
Berkshire
Southend
Hungerford
Bagnor
Cold Ash
Upper Bucklebury
Chapel Row
Froxfield
Halfway
Stockcross
Donnington
Shaw
Beenham
Ufton Nervet
Sheffield Bottom
Reading Services
Burghfield
Avington
Speen
Thatcham
Midgham
Woolhampton
Sulhamstead
Burghfield Hill
Kintbury
Laylands Green
Enborne
Newbury
Aldermaston Wharf
Burghfield Common
Grazeley
Little Bedwyn
Hamstead Marshall
Kennet
Brimpton
Padworth
Wokefield Park
Bagshot
Inkpen
Upper Green
Wash Common
Greenham
Aldermaston
Mortimer
Shalbourne
Ball Hill
Crookham
Wasing
Stratfield Mortimer
Ham
West Woodhay
North End
Newtown
Headley
Mortimer West End
Walbury Hill
Woolton Hill
Broad Laying
Plastow Green
Ashford Hill
Heath End
Pamber Heath
Silchester
Stratfield Saye
Rivar
Buttermere
East Woodhay
East End
Burghclere
Tadley
West End Green
Wilton
Combe
Highclere
Tothill Services
Fair Oak Green
Marten
Baughurst
Pamber Green
Little London
Stratfield Turgis
Wexcombe
Oxenwood
Ecchinswell
Wolverton Common
Linkenholt
Faccombe
Whitway
Kingsclere
West Heath
Pamber End
Bramley
Fosbury
Vernham Street
Netherton
Sydmonton
Wolverton
Charter Alley
Sherfield on Loddon
Haydown Hill
Vernham Dean
Ashmansworth
Old Burghclere
Ramsdell
Church End
Crux Easton
Monk Sherborne
Sherborne St John
Rotherwick
Upton
Hannington
Upper Chute
Chute Standen
Woodcott
North Oakley
Ibworth
Upper Wootton
Chineham
Newnham
Ibthorpe
Dunley
Litchfield
Wootton St Lawrence
Popley
Daneshill
Hurstbourne Tarrant
Binley
Winklebury
Oakridge
Old Basing
Lower Chute
Tangley
Basingstoke
South View
Hatch
Up Nately
Doles Wood
Stoke
Newfound
Worting
South Ham
Mapledurwell
Wildhern
Quidhampton
Cole Henley
Deane
Oakley
Buckskin
Kempshott
St Mary Bourne
Overton
Ashe
East Oakley
Brighton Hill
Hatherden
Little London
Smannell
Clanville
Enham-Alamein
Laverstoke
Steventon
Cliddesden
Winslade
Tunworth
Appleshaw
Penton Mewsey
Picket Piece
Whitchurch
Charlton
Weyhill
Hurstbourne Priors
Broadmere
Fyfield
Farleigh Wallop
Ellisfield
Herriard
Weston Patrick
Thruxton
Weyhill Services
Andover
Andover Down
Tufton
North Waltham
Dummer
Amport
Monxton
Anna Valley
Upper Clatford
Middleton
Longparish
Nutley
Southrope
Abbotts Ann
Harewood Forest
Forton
Popham
Axford
Woodmancott
Grateley
Goodworth Clatford
Wherwell
Newton
Bullington
Micheldever Forest
Preston
Bradley
Lasham
Shalden
A303
M3
M4
A4
A339
A33
A343
A34

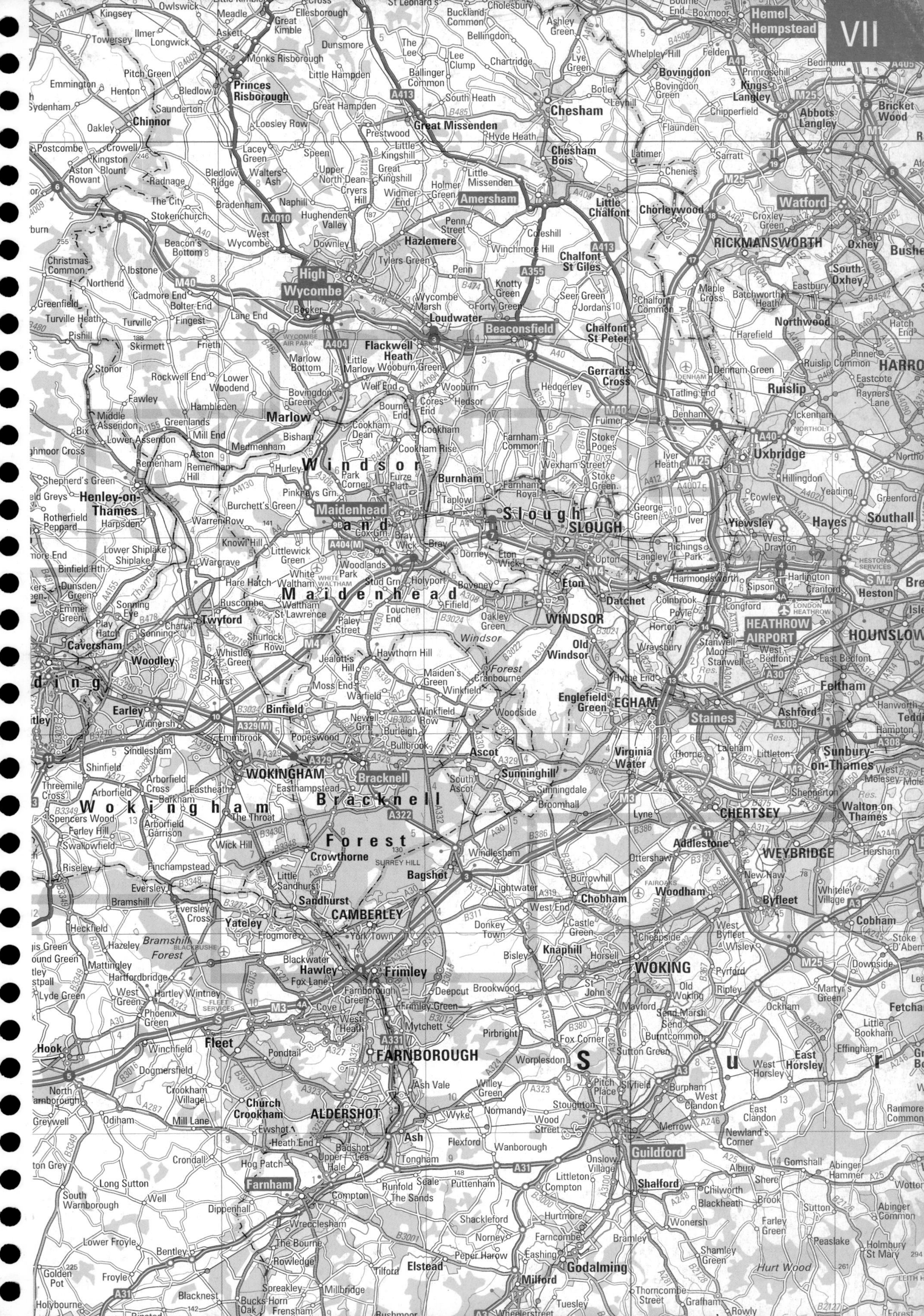
VII
Hemel Hempstead
Kingsey
Owlswick
Meadle
Great Kimble
Ellesborough
St Leonard's
Buckland Common
Cholesbury
Ashley Green
Bourne End
Boxmoor
Towersey
Ilmer
Longwick
Askett
Monks Risborough
Dunsmore
The Lee
Lee Clump
Bellingdon
Chartridge
Lye Green
Whelpley Hill
Felden
Bovingdon
Bovingdon Green
Primrose Hill
Kings Langley
Bedmond
Emmington
Henton
Bledlow
Princes Risborough
Little Hampden
Ballinger Common
Botley
Ley Hill
Chipperfield
Abbots Langley
Bricket Wood
Sydenham
Chinnor
Saunderton
Great Hampden
South Heath
Chesham
Flaunden
Oakley
Loosley Row
Great Missenden
Hyde Heath
Prestwood
Postcombe
Crowell
Kingston Blount
Aston Rowant
Lacey Green
Speen
Little Kingshill
Chesham Bois
Latimer
Sarratt
Chenies
Radnage
Bledlow Ridge
Walters Ash
Upper North Dean
Great Kingshill
Cryers Hill
Widmer End
Holmer Green
Little Missenden
Amersham
Little Chalfont
Chorleywood
Watford
The City
Stokenchurch
Bradenham
Naphill
Hughenden Valley
Penn Street
Coleshill
Croxley Green
Oxhey
Bushey
Beacon's Bottom
West Wycombe
Downley
Hazlemere
Winchmore Hill
Chalfont St Giles
RICKMANSWORTH
South Oxhey
Christmas Common
Ibstone
High Wycombe
Tylers Green
Penn
Knotty Green
Seer Green
Jordans
Maple Cross
Batchworth Heath
Eastbury
Northend
Cadmore End
Bolter End
Fingest
Lane End
Booker
Wycombe Marsh
Loudwater
Forty Green
Chalfont Common
Northwood
Greenfield
Turville Heath
Turville
Pishill
Skirmett
Frieth
WYCOMBE AIR PARK
Flackwell Heath
Beaconsfield
Chalfont St Peter
Harefield
Hatch End
Stonor
Rockwell End
Lower Woodend
Marlow Bottom
Little Marlow
Wooburn Green
Gerrards Cross
Denham Green
Pinner
Ruislip Common
HARROW
Fawley
Hambleden
Bovingdon Green
Well End
Wooburn
Cores End
Bourne End
Hedsor
Hedgerley
Tatling End
Ruislip
Eastcote
Rayners Lane
Middle Assendon
Lower Assendon
Greenlands
Mill End
Marlow
Bisham
Cookham Dean
Cookham
Farnham Common
Fulmer
Denham
Ickenham
NORTHOLT
Bix
Medmenham
Cookham Rise
Stoke Poges
Uxbridge
Northolt
Remenham
Aston
Remenham Hill
Hurley
Windsor
Park Corner
Furze Platt
Burnham
Wexham Street
Iver Heath
Hillingdon
Shepherd's Green
Henley-on-Thames
Pinkneys Grn.
Farnham Royal
Stoke Green
Cowley
Yeading
Greenford
Rotherfield Greys
Rotherfield Peppard
Harpsden
Burchett's Green
Maidenhead
Taplow
Slough
SLOUGH
George Green
Iver
Yiewsley
Hayes
Southall
Warren Row
Cox Grn.
Bray Wick
Bray
Dorney
Eton Wick
Upton
Langley
Richings Park
West Drayton
Knowl Hill
Littlewick Green
Lower Shiplake
Shiplake
Wargrave
Woodlands Park
White Waltham
Eton
HESTON SERVICES
Binfield Hth
Hare Hatch
Stud Grn
Holyport
Boveney
Harmondsworth
Harlington
Cranford
Heston
Dunsden Green
Emmer Green
Sonning Eye
Ruscombe
Waltham St Lawrence
Touchen End
Fifield
Oakley Green
Datchet
Colnbrook
Sipson
Longford
LONDON HEATHROW
Sonning
Charvil
Twyford
Paley Street
WINDSOR
Poyle
Horton
HEATHROW AIRPORT
HOUNSLOW
Caversham
Woodley
Shurlock Row
Whistley Green
Windsor
Old Windsor
Wraysbury
Stanwell Moor
Stanwell
West Bedfont
East Bedfont
Hawthorn Hill
Jealott's Hill
Forest
Cranbourne
Hurst
Moss End
Maiden's Green
Winkfield
Hythe End
Feltham
Reading
Earley
Winnersh
Binfield
Warfield
Englefield Green
EGHAM
Ashford
Hanworth
Newell Grn.
Winkfield Row
Woodside
Staines
Emmbrook
Popeswood
Burleigh
Bullbrook
Ascot
Virginia Water
Thorpe
Laleham
Littleton
Sunbury-on-Thames
Sindlesham
Shinfield
Arborfield
Arborfield Cross
WOKINGHAM
Bracknell
Easthampstead
South Ascot
Sunninghill
Sunningdale
Broomhall
Shepperton
West Molesey
Threemile Cross
Eastheath
Barkham
Wokingham
The Throat
Forest
Walton-on-Thames
Spencers Wood
Farley Hill
Arborfield Garrison
Lyne
CHERTSEY
Swallowfield
Wick Hill
Crowthorne
SURREY HILL
Windlesham
Addlestone
WEYBRIDGE
Hersham
Riseley
Finchampstead
Little Sandhurst
Bagshot
Ottershaw
Burrowhill
Lightwater
New Haw
Eversley
Bramshill
Eversley Cross
Sandhurst
West End
Chobham
FAIROAKS
Woodham
Byfleet
Whiteley Village
CAMBERLEY
Yateley
Frogmore
York Town
Donkey Town
Castle Green
Cheapside
West Byfleet
Cobham
Heckfield
Hazeley
Bramshill Forest
BLACKBUSHE
Bisley
Knaphill
Horsell
Wisley
Stoke D'Abernon
Mattingley
Hartfordbridge
Blackwater
Hawley
Frimley
Fox Lane
Deepcut
Brookwood
WOKING
Pyrford
Downside
Lyde Green
West Green
Hartley Wintney
FLEET SERVICES
Farnborough Green
Frimley Green
St John's
Old Woking
Ripley
Martyr's Green
Phoenix Green
Cove
West Heath
Mytchett
Mayford
Send Marsh
Send
Ockham
Fetcham
Hook
Winchfield
Fleet
Pondtail
FARNBOROUGH
Pirbright
Fox Corner
Burntcommon
Little Bookham
Effingham
Dogmersfield
Worplesdon
Sutton Green
West Horsley
East Horsley
North Warnborough
Crookham Village
Church Crookham
ALDERSHOT
Ash Vale
Willey Green
Pitch Place
Stoughton
Slyfield
Burpham
West Clandon
East Clandon
Ranmore Common
Greywell
Odiham
Mill Lane
Ewshot
Wyke
Normandy
Wood Street
Merrow
Heath End
Ash
Flexford
Wanborough
Newland's Corner
Crondall
Hog Patch
Badshot Lea
Upper Hale
Tongham
Guildford
Onslow Village
Albury
Gomshall
Abinger Hammer
Wotton
Farnham
Long Sutton
Well
Runfold
Seale
Puttenham
Littleton
Compton
Shalford
Chilworth
Shere
South Warnborough
Dippenhall
The Sands
Blackheath
Brook
Sutton
Abinger Common
Wrecclesham
Shackleford
Hurtmore
Wonersh
Farley Green
Lower Froyle
The Bourne
Norney
Farncombe
Bramley
Peaslake
Holmbury St Mary
Bentley
Rowledge
Peper Harow
Eashing
Godalming
Shamley Green
Golden Pot
Froyle
Tilford
Elstead
Milford
Hurt Wood
Blacknest
Spreakley
Millbridge
Bucks Horn Oak
Frensham
Rushmoor
Wheelerstreet
Tuesley
Thorncombe Street
Grafham
Rowly
Holybourne
Binsted
Forest
LEITH HILL
M25
M40
M4
M3
A404
A413
A4010
A355
A40
A329(M)
A4
A322
A30
A31
A3
A331
A404(M)
Thames

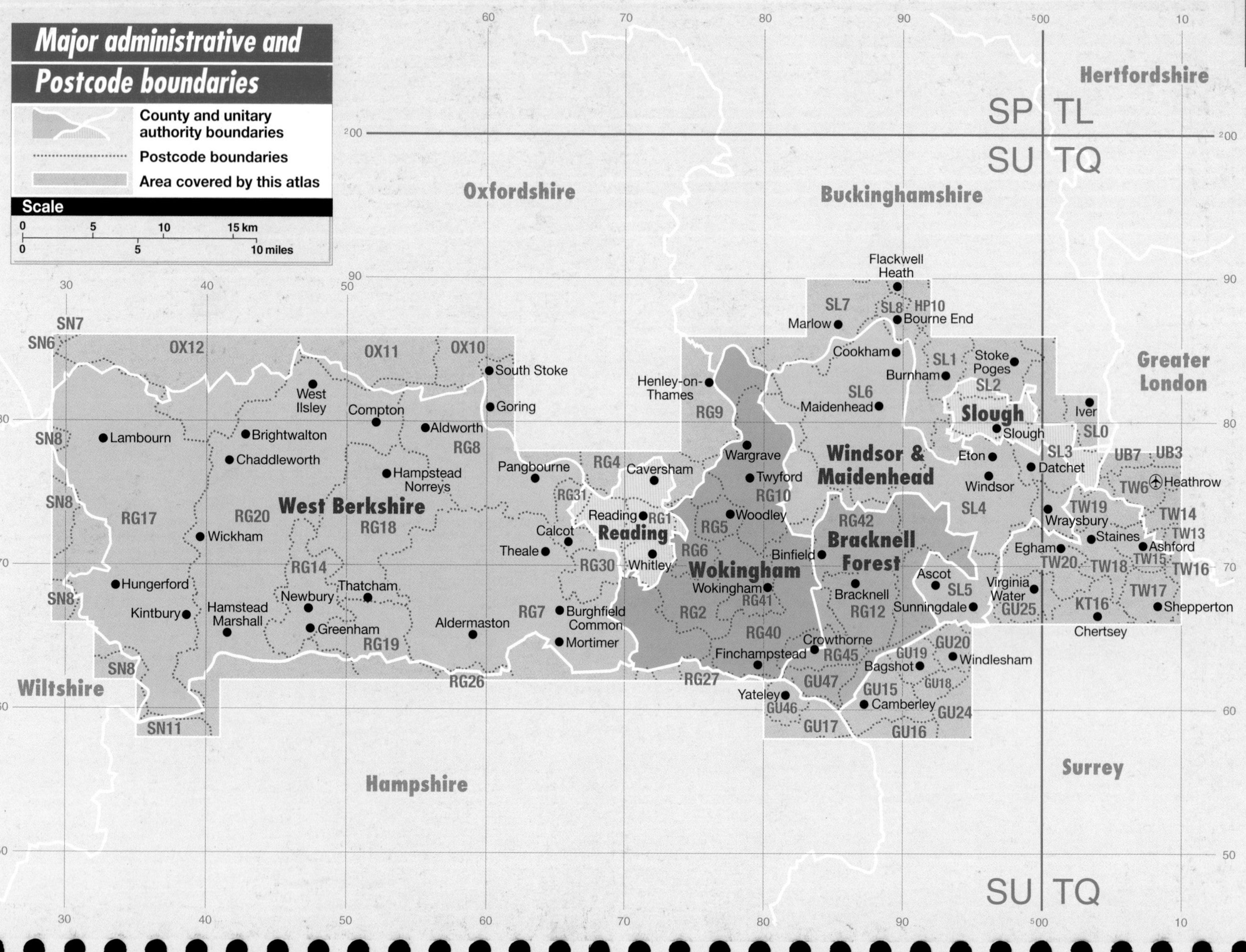

Major administrative and Postcode boundaries

County and unitary authority boundaries

Postcode boundaries

Area covered by this atlas

Scale

0   5   10   15 km

0   5   10 miles

Hertfordshire

SP | TL

SU | TQ

Greater London

Buckinghamshire

Slough

Windsor & Maidenhead

Bracknell Forest

Wokingham

Reading

West Berkshire

Oxfordshire

Surrey

SU | TQ

Hampshire

Wiltshire

UB7 · UB3

Heathrow

TW6

TW14
TW13
TW15
TW3
Ashford
TW17
TW16
Shepperton

TW19
Wraysbury
Staines
TW18
TW20
KT16
Chertsey

Iver
SL0
SL3
Datchet
Slough
Egham
Virginia Water
GU25

Stoke Poges
SL2
Eton
Windsor
SL4
SL5
Sunningdale
GU20
Windlesham

Flackwell Heath
SL8
HP10
Bourne End
SL1
Burnham
Ascot
GU19
GU18
Bagshot
GU24

Cookham
SL6
Maidenhead
RG42
Bracknell
RG12
Crowthorne
RG45
GU15
Camberley
GU16

SL7
Marlow
Binfield
RG41
Finchampstead
GU47
GU46
GU17

Wargrave
Twyford
RG10
Woodley
Wokingham
RG40
Yateley

RG9
RG5
RG6
RG2
RG27

Henley-on-Thames
Caversham
RG1
Reading
Whitley
RG30

RG4
Burghfield Common
Mortimer

South Stoke
Goring
RG31
Calcot
Theale
RG7
Aldermaston
RG26

OX10
Aldworth
RG8
Hampstead Norreys

OX11
Compton
RG18
RG14
Thatcham
RG19

West Ilsley
Brightwalton
Chaddleworth
Newbury
Greenham

RG20
Wickham
Hamstead Marshall
SN11

OX12
Lambourn
Hungerford
Kintbury
SN8

RG17
SN8

SN7
SN6
SN8
SN8

200
200

10
90
80
70
60
50

500

90
80
70
60
50

40
30

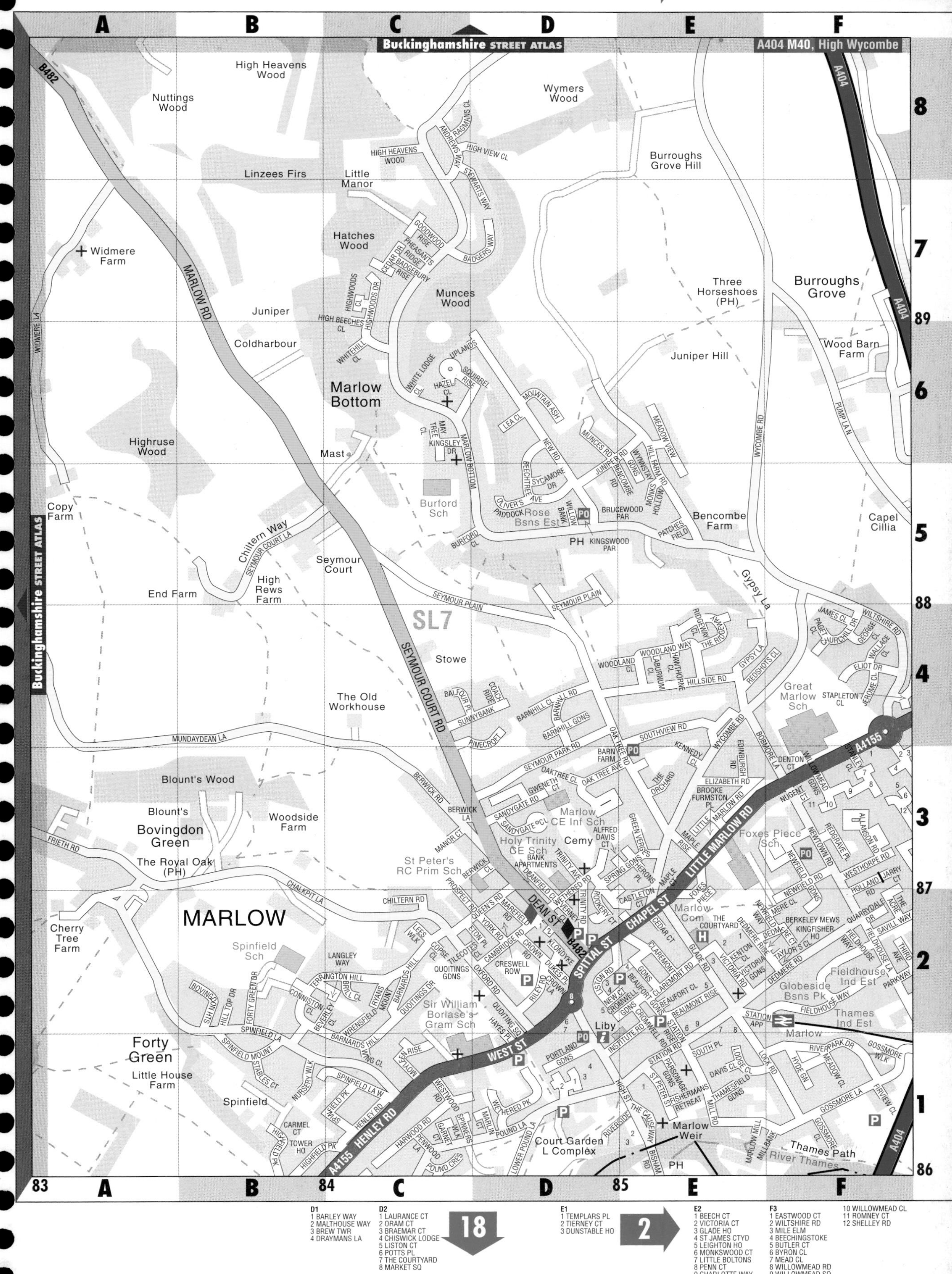

D1
1 BARLEY WAY
2 MALTHOUSE WAY
3 BREW TWR
4 DRAYMANS LA

D2
1 LAURANCE CT
2 ORAM CT
3 BRAEMAR CT
4 CHISWICK LODGE
5 LISTON CT
6 POTTS PL
7 THE COURTYARD
8 MARKET SQ

E1
1 TEMPLARS PL
2 TIERNEY CT
3 DUNSTABLE HO

E2
1 BEECH CT
2 VICTORIA CT
3 GLADE HO
4 ST JAMES CTYD
5 LEIGHTON HO
6 MONKSWOOD CT
7 LITTLE BOLTONS
8 PENN CT
9 CHARLOTTE WAY

F3
1 EASTWOOD CT
2 WILTSHIRE RD
3 MILE ELM
4 BEECHINGSTOKE
5 BUTLER CT
6 BYRON CL
7 MEAD CL
8 WILLOWMEAD RD
9 WILLOWMEAD SQ

10 WILLOWMEAD CL
11 ROMNEY CT
12 SHELLEY RD

1

Buckinghamshire STREET ATLAS

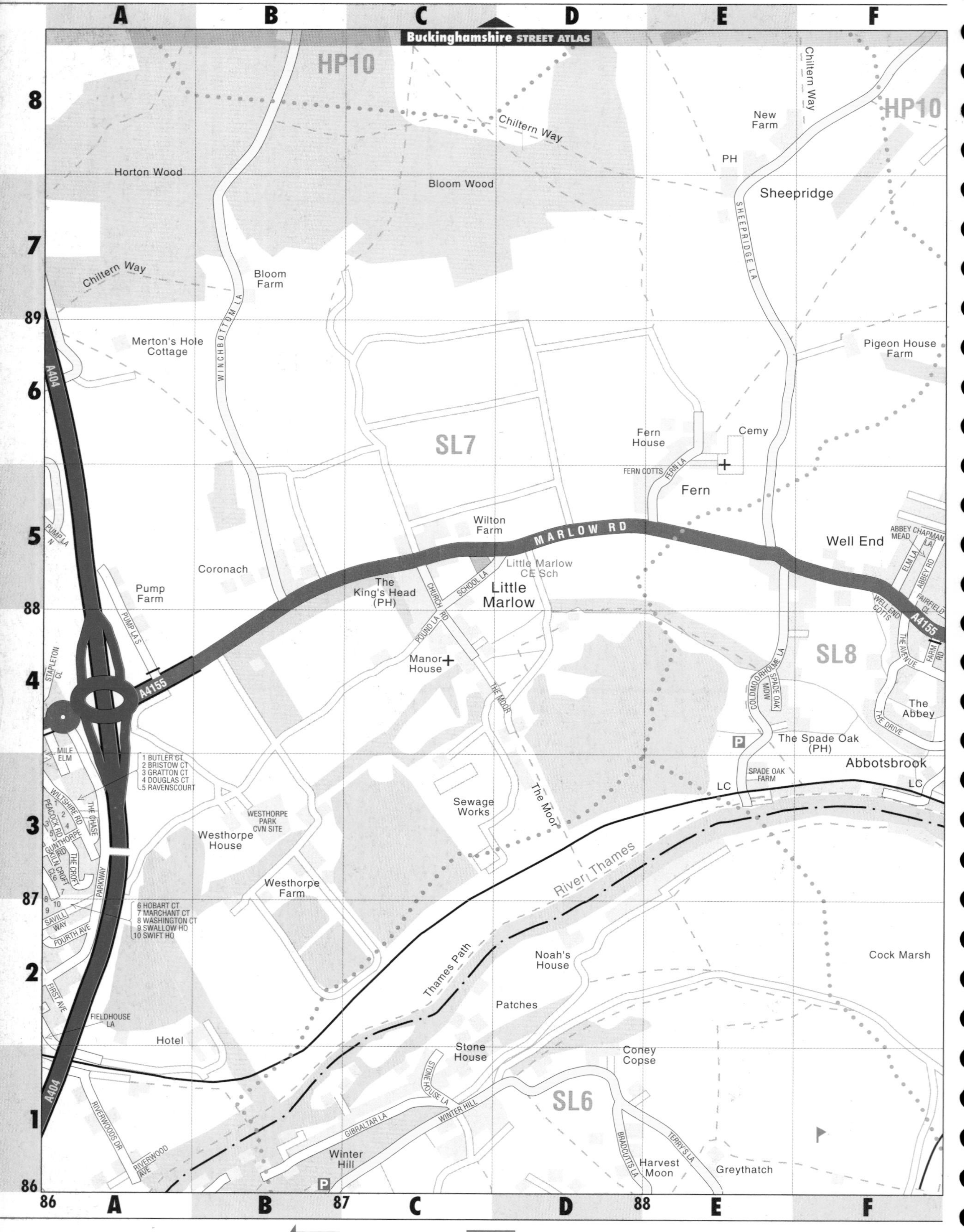
HP10
Chiltern Way
Horton Wood
Bloom Wood
New Farm
PH
Sheepridge
SHEEPRIDGE LA
Bloom Farm
WINCHBOTTOM LA
Merton's Hole Cottage
Pigeon House Farm
A404
SL7
Fern House
Cemy
FERN COTTS
FERN LA
Fern
Wilton Farm
MARLOW RD
Well End
PUMP LA N
Coronach
Pump Farm
The King's Head (PH)
CHURCH
SCHOOL LA
Little Marlow CE Sch
Little Marlow
ABBEY MEAD
CHAPMAN LA
ELM LA
ABBEY RD
FAIRFIELD CL
WELL END COTTS
A4155
POUND LA
RD
PUMP LAS
Manor House
THE MOOR
STAPLETON CL
SL8
COLDMOORHOLME LA
SPADE OAK MDW
THE AVENUE
FARM RD
The Abbey
THE DRIVE
The Spade Oak (PH)
Abbotsbrook
MILE ELM
1 BUTLER CT
2 BRISTOW CT
3 GRATTON CT
4 DOUGLAS CT
5 RAVENSCOURT
SPADE OAK FARM
LC
WILTSHIRE RD
PEACOCK RD
THE CHASE
GUNTHORPE RD
KILN CROFT CL
THE CROFT
WESTHORPE PARK CVN SITE
Sewage Works
The Moor
Westhorpe House
River Thames
Westhorpe Farm
PARKWAY
SAVILL WAY
FOURTH AVE
6 HOBART CT
7 MARCHANT CT
8 WASHINGTON CT
9 SWALLOW HO
10 SWIFT HO
Thames Path
Noah's House
Cock Marsh
FIRST AVE
FIELDHOUSE LA
Patches
Hotel
Stone House
Coney Copse
STONE HOUSE LA
WINTER HILL
SL6
RIVERWOODS DR
GIBRALTAR LA
BRADCUTTS LA
TERRY'S LA
RIVERWOOD AVE
Winter Hill
Harvest Moon
Greythatch
A B C D E F
8 7 6 5 4 3 2 1
89 88 87 86

1
19

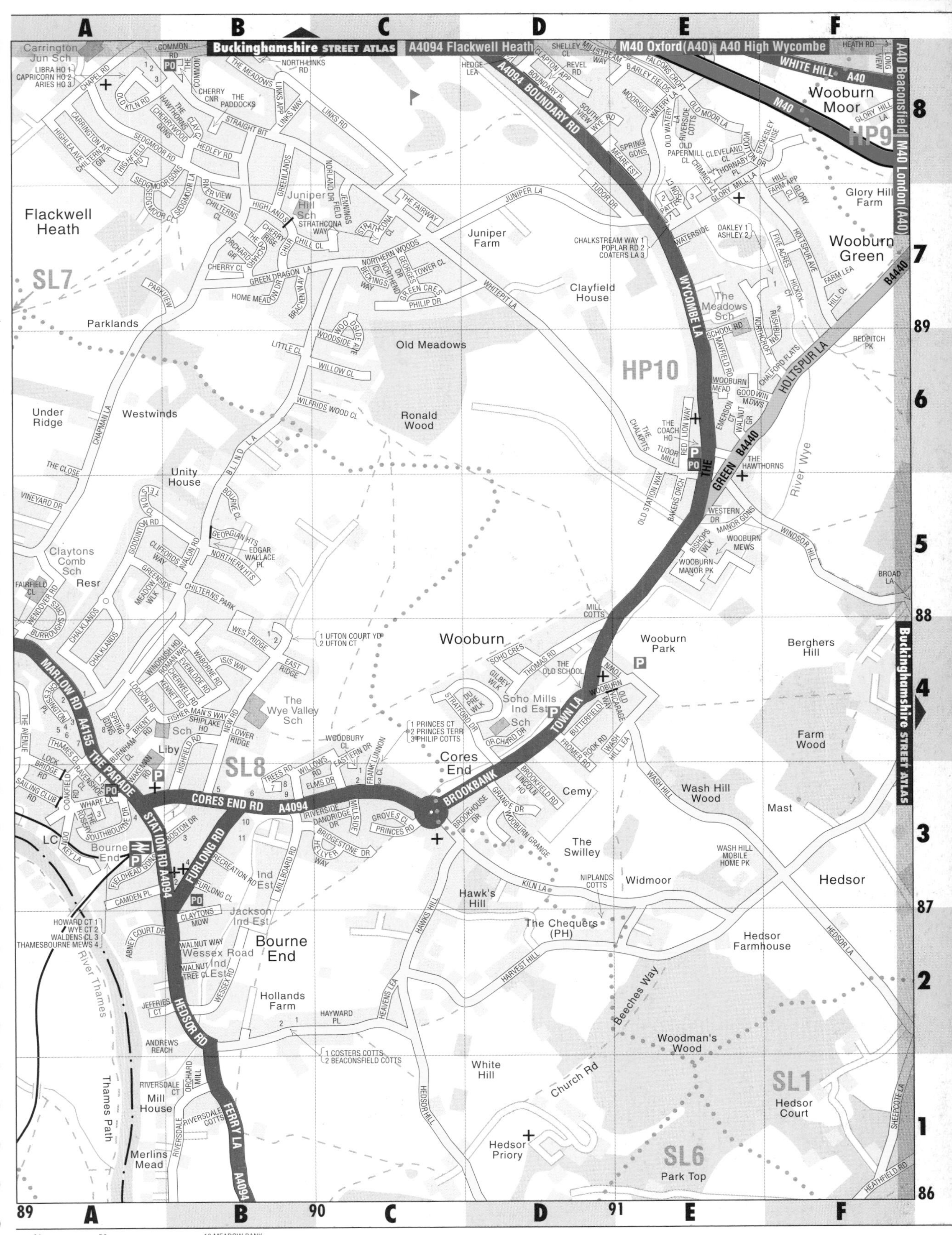

A4094 Flackwell Heath   M40 Oxford(A40) A40 High Wycombe

Flackwell Heath

SL7

HP9

Wooburn Moor

Wooburn Green

89

6

Glory Hill Farm

HP10

Juniper Farm

Clayfield House

Old Meadows

Ronald Wood

Wooburn

Wooburn Park

Berghers Hill

88

Farm Wood

SL8

Cores End

Bourne End

BROOKBANK

Cemy

Wash Hill Wood

Mast

Hedsor

3

Widmoor

The Swilley

Hawk's Hill

The Chequers (PH)

Hedsor Farmhouse

87

Bourne End

Hollands Farm

White Hill

Beeches Way

Woodman's Wood

SL1

Hedsor Court

SL6

Park Top

86

A4
1 ROWAN HO
2 CRESSINGTON CT
3 COKERS CT
4 RUSSELL HO
5 RAY HO
6 GRANT HO
7 PARADE CT
8 ORCHARD HO
9 BAILEY HO

B3
1 BOURNE END BSNS CTR
2 ALFRED CT
3 EGHAMS CT
4 HYLAND HO
5 FARRIER CT
6 MOUNT PLEASANT COTTS
7 SYCAMORE CL
8 THE WILLOWS
9 THE MAPLES

10 MEADOW BANK
11 THE COURTYARD

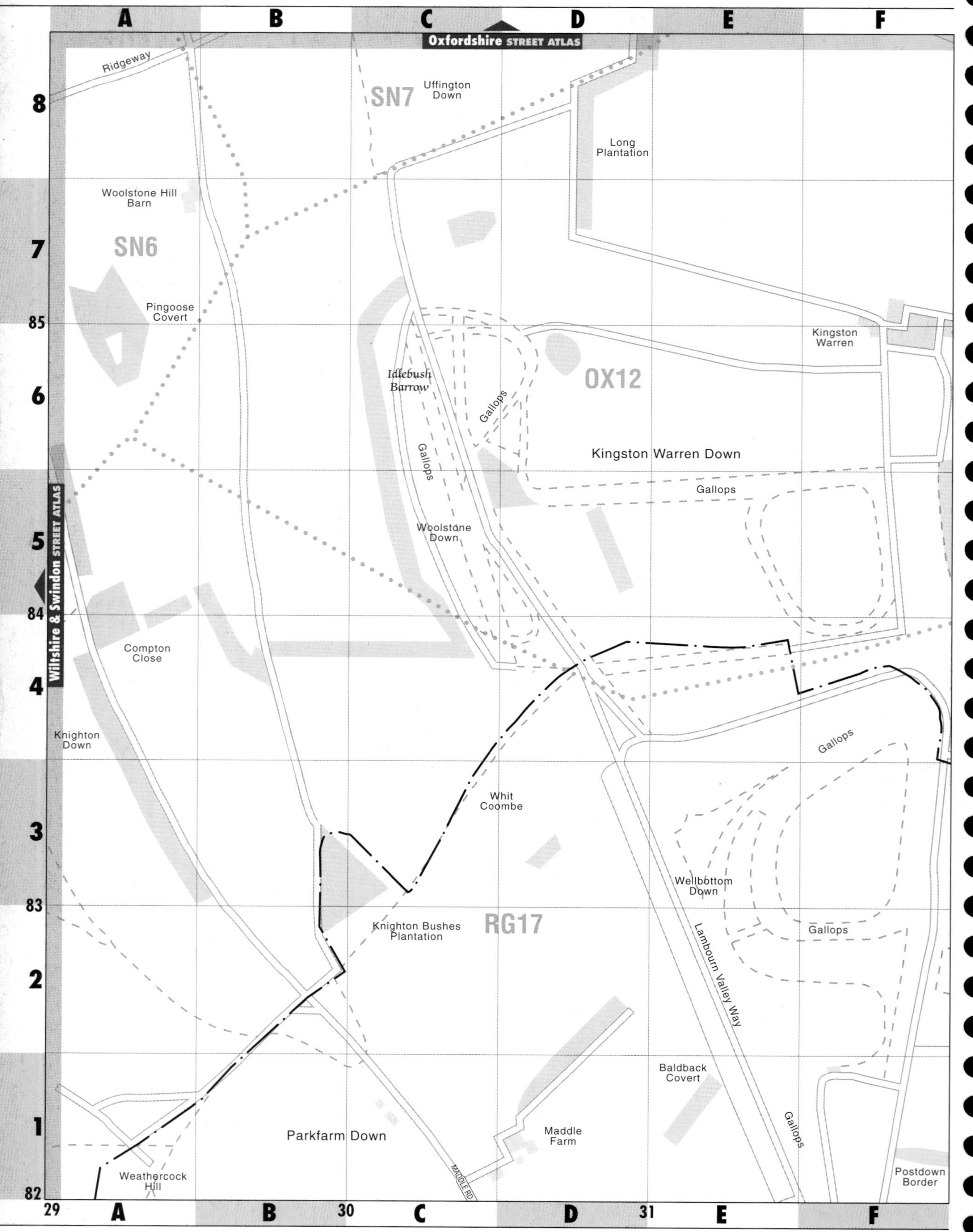

Wiltshire & Swindon STREET ATLAS

SN7

Uffington Down

Ridgeway

Long Plantation

Woolstone Hill Barn

SN6

Kingston Warren

Pingoose Covert

Idlebush Barrow

OX12

Gallops

Gallops

Kingston Warren Down

Gallops

Gallops

Woolstone Down

Compton Close

Knighton Down

Gallops

Whit Coombe

Wellbottom Down

Gallops

Knighton Bushes Plantation

RG17

Gallops

Lambourn Valley Way

Baldback Covert

Gallops

Parkfarm Down

Maddle Farm

MADDLE RD

Weathercock Hill

Postdown Border

A
B
C
D
E
F
Oxfordshire STREET ATLAS
Hillbarn Clump
Ridgeway
Rubblepit Plantation
8
Pigtrough Bottom
B4001
Old Plantation
Hill Barn
7
Gallops
Down Barn
Gallops
85
Mast
Hackpen Hill
Radio Station
6
OX12
Sparsholt Firs
Scary Hill
Sparsholt Down
Gallops
Moss Hill
5
Gallop
Faringdon Down Gallop
Green Down
Eastmanton Down
84
Crog Hill
4
Westcot Down
Boundary Covert
Long Barrow
Pit Down
3
Old Warren
83
Sevenbarrows House
2
Seven Barrows
RG17
Gallops
Gallops
Faringdon Road Down
Long Covert
Post Down
Crow Down
1
Postdown Farm
Sheepdrove Farm
Croker's Hole
Wormhill Bottom
B4001
82
32
A
B
33
C
D
34
E
F

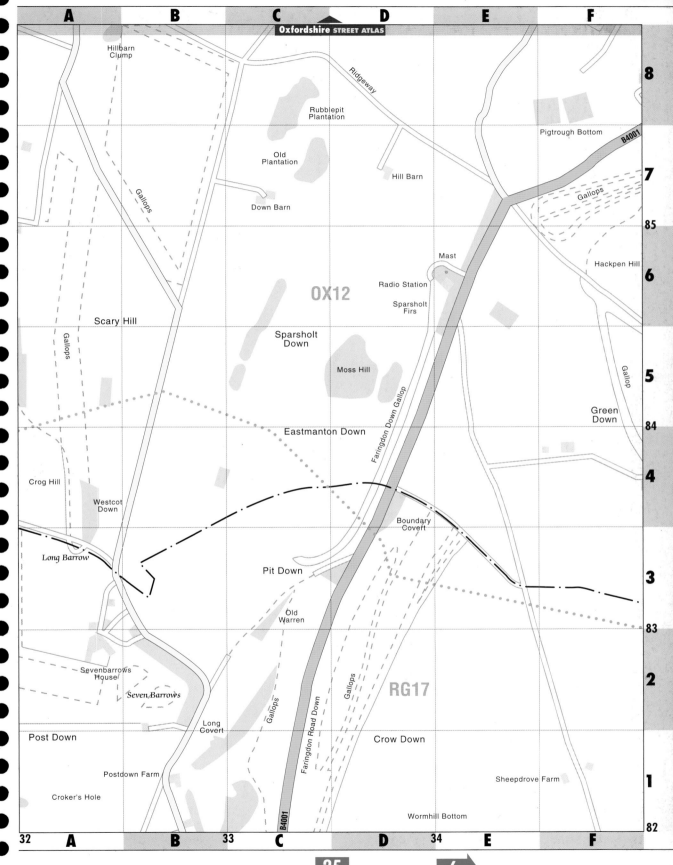

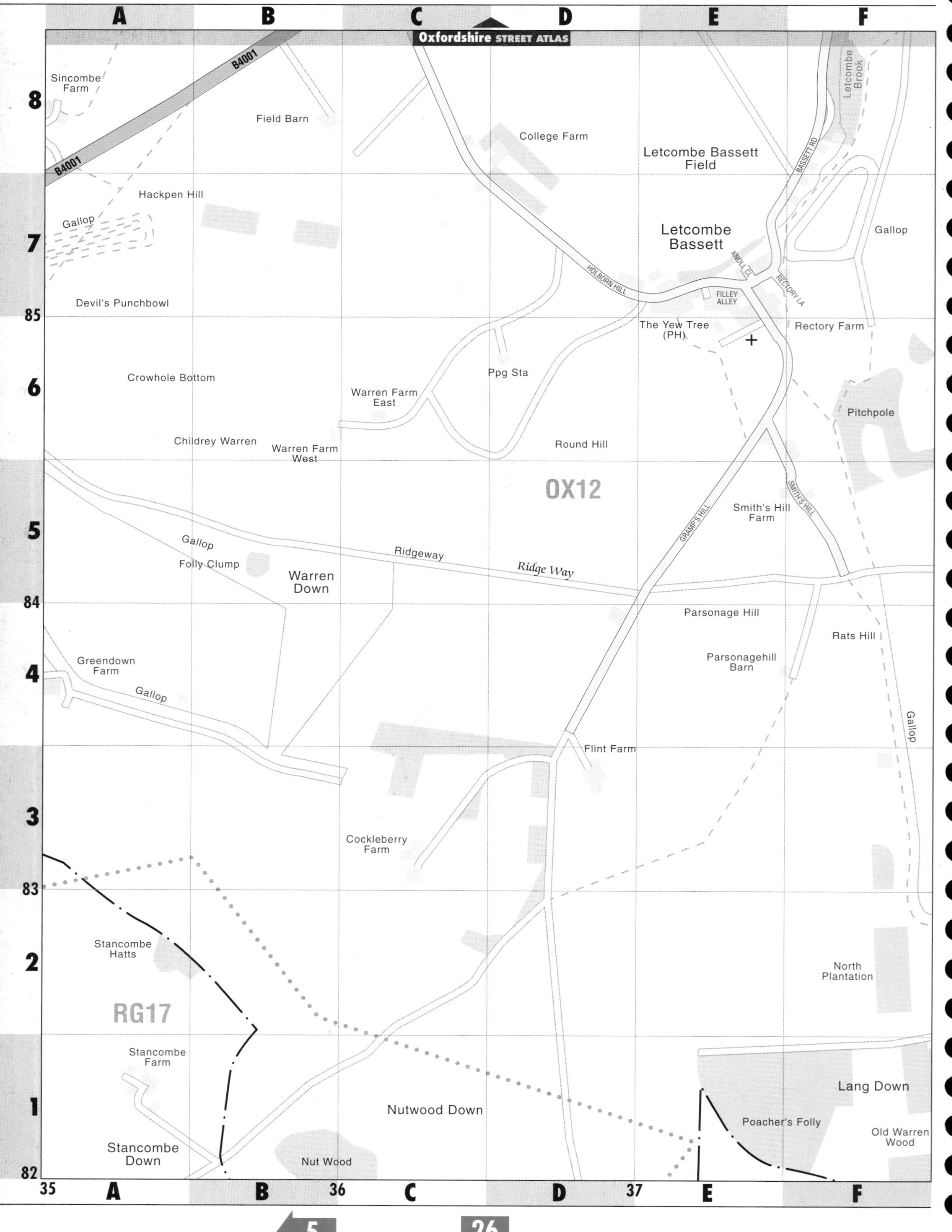

A   B   C   D   E   F

8

Sincombe
Farm

B4001

Field Barn

College Farm

Letcombe Bassett
Field

Letcombe
Brook

BASSETT RD

B4001

7

Gallop

Hackpen Hill

Letcombe
Bassett

KNOLL CL

RECTORY LA

Gallop

85

Devil's Punchbowl

HOLBORN HILL

FILLEY
ALLEY

The Yew Tree
(PH)

+

Rectory Farm

6

Crowhole Bottom

Ppg Sta

Warren Farm
East

Round Hill

Pitchpole

Childrey Warren

Warren Farm
West

OX12

Smith's Hill
Farm

GRAMP'S HILL

SMITH'S HILL

5

Gallop

Folly Clump

Warren
Down

Ridgeway

Ridge Way

84

Parsonage Hill

Rats Hill

4

Greendown
Farm

Gallop

Parsonagehill
Barn

Gallop

Flint Farm

3

Cockleberry
Farm

83

2

Stancombe
Hatts

North
Plantation

RG17

1

Stancombe
Farm

Lang Down

Poacher's Folly

Old Warren
Wood

Nutwood Down

82

Stancombe
Down

Nut Wood

35   A   B   36   C   D   37   E   F

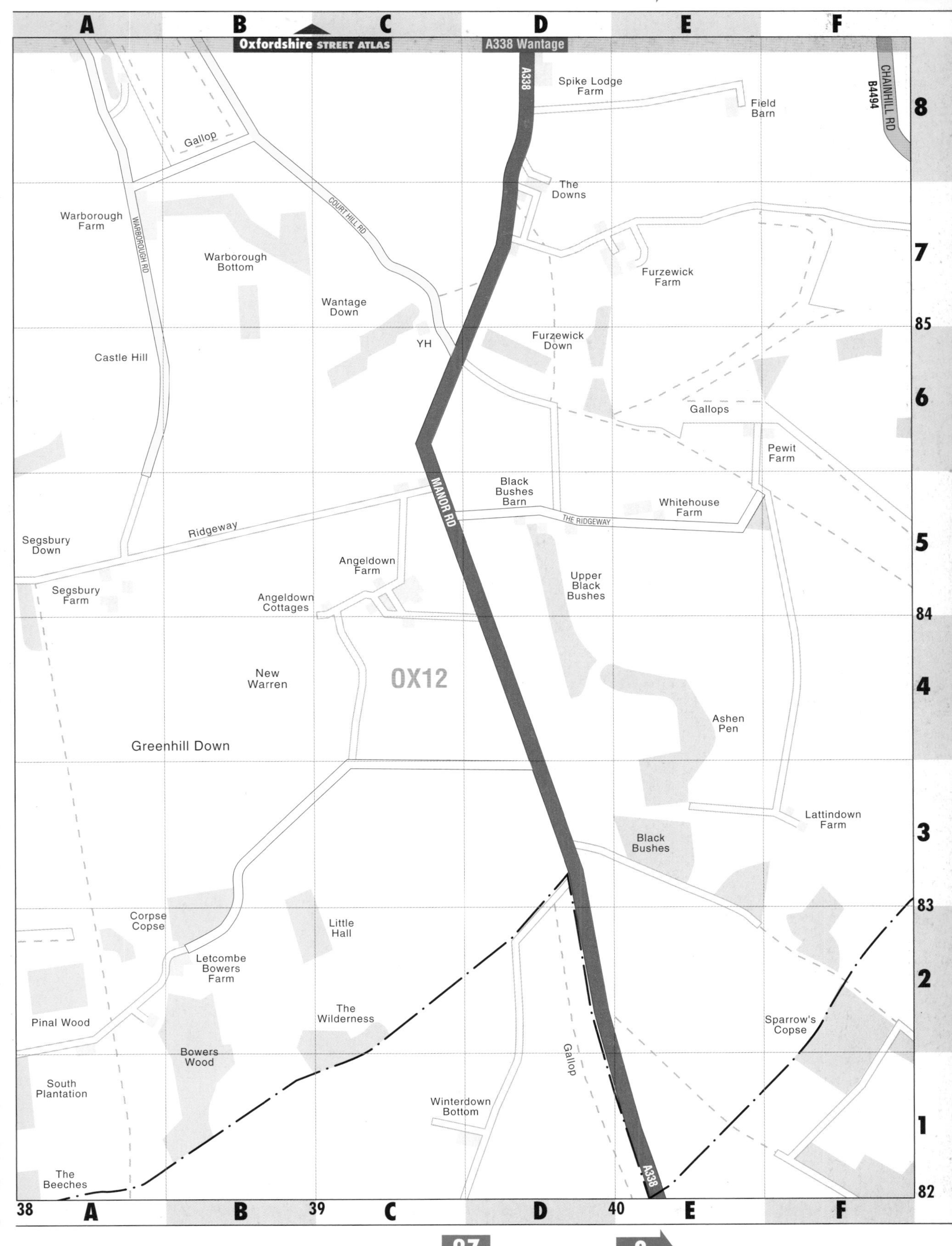

Oxfordshire STREET ATLAS

A338 Wantage

CHAINHILL RD
B4494

Spike Lodge Farm

Field Barn

The Downs

Warborough Farm

COURT HILL RD

WARBOROUGH RD

Furzewick Farm

Gallop

Warborough Bottom

Wantage Down

Furzewick Down

YH

Castle Hill

Gallops

Pewit Farm

Black Bushes Barn

THE RIDGEWAY

Whitehouse Farm

Segsbury Down

Ridgeway

MANOR RD

Angeldown Farm

Upper Black Bushes

Segsbury Farm

Angeldown Cottages

New Warren

OX12

Ashen Pen

Greenhill Down

Lattindown Farm

Black Bushes

Corpse Copse

Little Hall

83

Letcombe Bowers Farm

Sparrow's Copse

Pinal Wood

The Wilderness

Bowers Wood

Gallop

South Plantation

Winterdown Bottom

The Beeches

A338

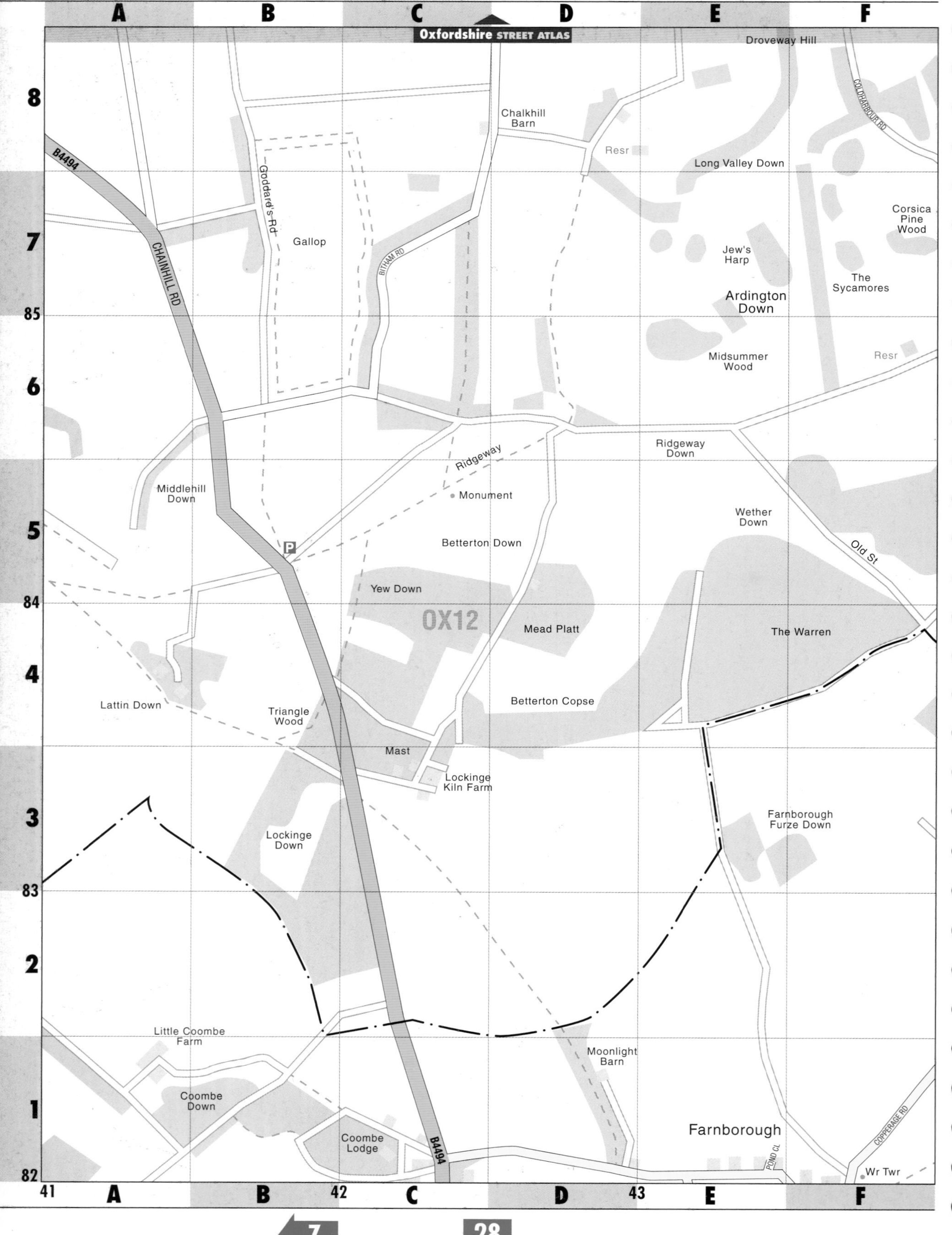

A B C D E F

8

Droveway Hill

Chalkhill Barn

Long Valley Down

7

Resr

Corsica Pine Wood

B4494

Goddard's Rd

Gallop

Jew's Harp

The Sycamores

85

BITHAM RD

Ardington Down

CHAINHILL RD

6

Midsummer Wood

Resr

Ridgeway

Ridgeway Down

Middlehill Down

Monument

Wether Down

Old St

5

P

Betterton Down

84

Yew Down

OX12

Mead Platt

The Warren

4

Betterton Copse

Lattin Down

Triangle Wood

Mast

Lockinge Kiln Farm

Farnborough Furze Down

3

Lockinge Down

83

Moonlight Barn

2

Little Coombe Farm

Coombe Down

1

Coombe Lodge

B4494

Farnborough

POND CL

COPPERAGE RD

COLDHARBOUR RD

Wr Twr

82

41 A 42 B C 43 D E F

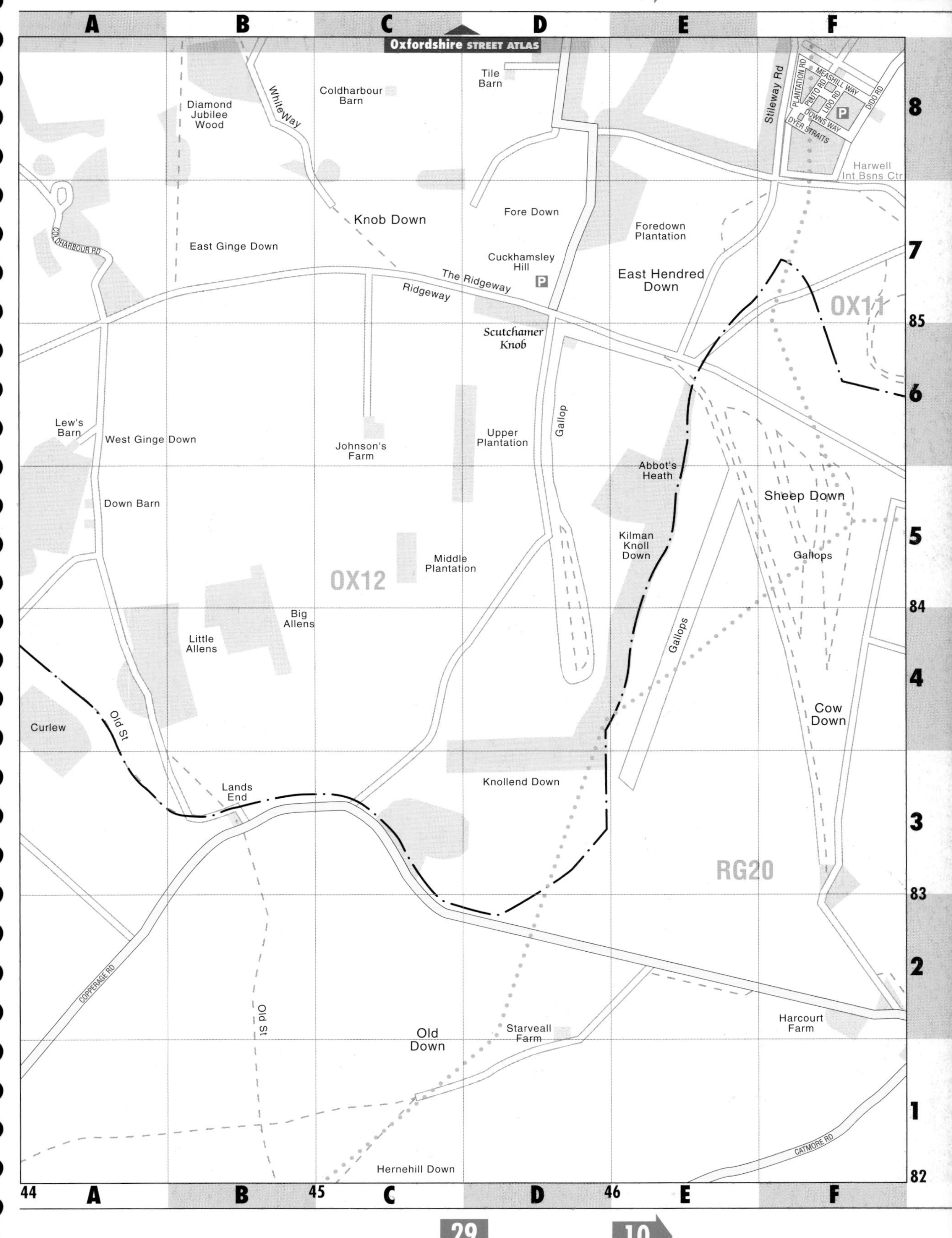

Oxfordshire STREET ATLAS

Stilleway Rd
Harwell Int Bsns Ctr
MEASHILL WAY
PLANTATION RD
PITTO RD
LIDO RD
DUDD RD
DOWNS WAY
DYER STRAITS

Tile Barn
Diamond Jubilee Wood
Coldharbour Barn
WhiteWay
Knob Down
Fore Down
Foredown Plantation
East Ginge Down
Cuckhamsley Hill
East Hendred Down
COLDHARBOUR RD
The Ridgeway
Ridgeway
Scutchamer Knob
OX11
Lew's Barn
West Ginge Down
Johnson's Farm
Upper Plantation
Gallop
Abbot's Heath
Sheep Down
Down Barn
Kilman Knoll Down
Gallops
OX12
Middle Plantation
Cow Down
Big Allens
Little Allens
Gallops
Curlew
Old St
Lands End
Knollend Down
RG20
Old St
Old Down
Starveall Farm
Harcourt Farm
Hernehill Down
COPPERAGE RD
CATMORE RD

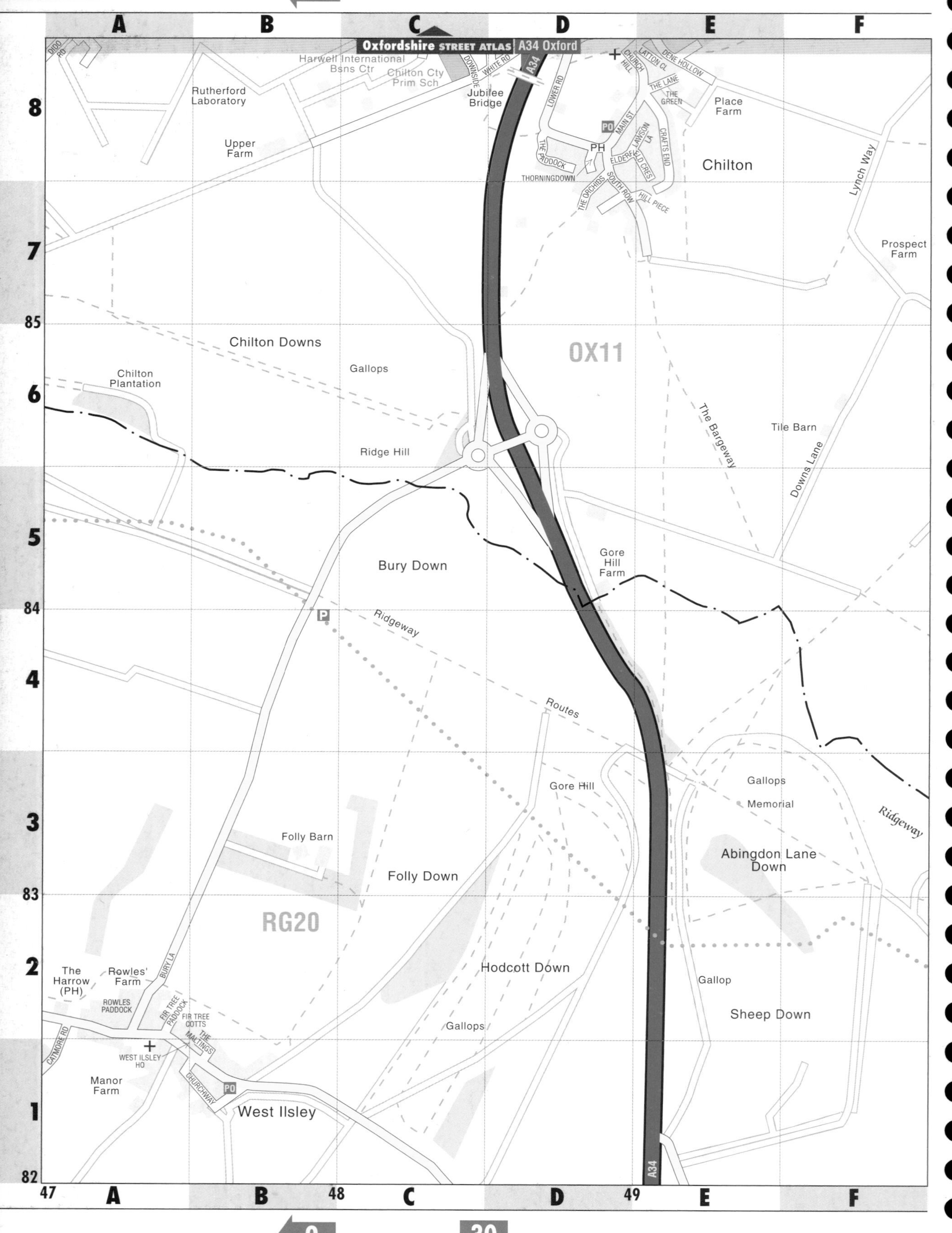

Oxfordshire STREET ATLAS A34 Oxford

Rutherford Laboratory

Harwell International Bsns Ctr

Chilton Cty Prim Sch

Upper Farm

Jubilee Bridge

Chilton

Place Farm

Prospect Farm

Chilton Downs

Gallops

OX11

Chilton Plantation

The Bargeway

Tile Barn

Downs Lane

Ridge Hill

Gore Hill Farm

Bury Down

Ridgeway

Routes

Gore Hill

Gallops

Memorial

Abingdon Lane Down

Ridgeway

Folly Barn

RG20

Folly Down

Hodcott Down

The Harrow (PH)

Rowles' Farm

ROWLES PADDOCK

Gallop

Sheep Down

WEST ILSLEY HO

Gallops

Manor Farm

West Ilsley

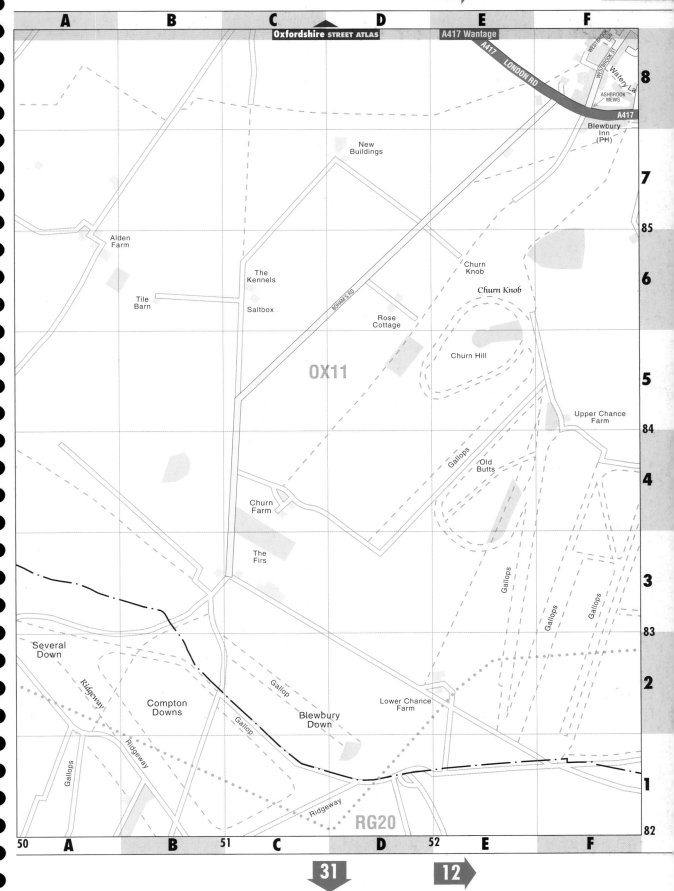

Oxfordshire STREET ATLAS

A417 Wantage

A417 LONDON RD

WESTBROOK GN
WESTBROOK ST
Watery La

ASHBROOK MEWS

A417

Blewbury Inn (PH)

New Buildings

Alden Farm

The Kennels

Tile Barn

Saltbox

BOHAM'S RD

Rose Cottage

Churn Knob

Churn Knob

Churn Hill

OX11

Upper Chance Farm

Gallops

Old Butts

Churn Farm

The Firs

Gallops

Gallops

Gallops

Gallops

Several Down

Ridgeway

Gallop

Compton Downs

Gallop

Blewbury Down

Lower Chance Farm

Gallops

Ridgeway

Ridgeway

RG20

11

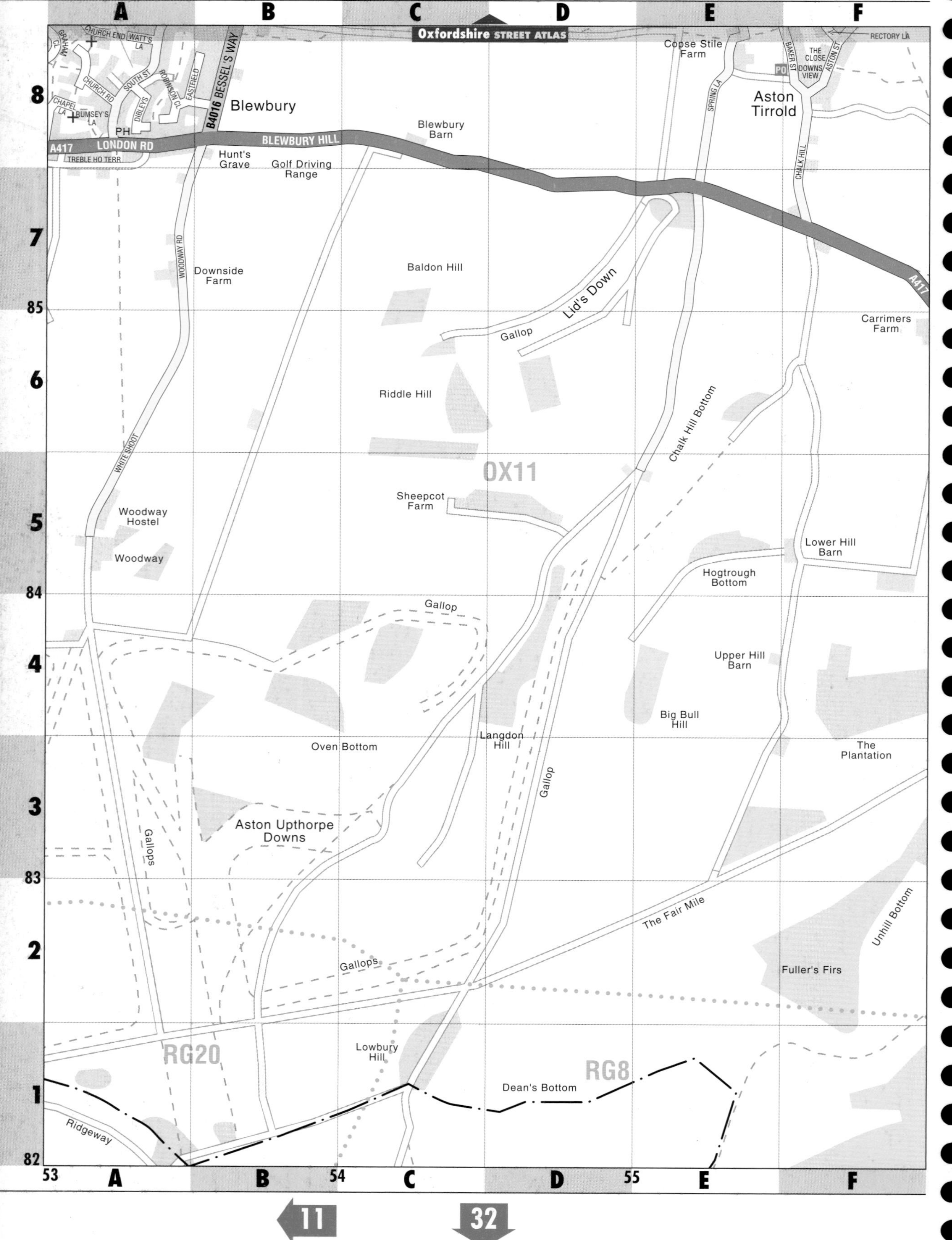

Oxfordshire STREET ATLAS
Blewbury
B4016 BESSEL'S WAY
A417 LONDON RD
BLEWBURY HILL
TREBLE HO TERR
CHURCH END
WATT'S LA
CHURCH RD
SOUTH ST
DIBLEYS
ROBINSON CL
EASTFIELD
CHAPEL LA
RUMSEY'S LA
GRAHAM CL
PH
Hunt's Grave
Golf Driving Range
Blewbury Barn
Copse Stile Farm
Aston Tirrold
SPRING LA
BAKER ST
THE CLOSE
DOWNS VIEW
ASTON ST
RECTORY LA
PO
CHALK HILL
WOODWAY RD
Downside Farm
Baldon Hill
Lid's Down
Gallop
A417
Carrimers Farm
Riddle Hill
WHITE SHOOT
Chalk Hill Bottom
OX11
Sheepcot Farm
Woodway Hostel
Woodway
Lower Hill Barn
Hogtrough Bottom
Gallop
Upper Hill Barn
Big Bull Hill
Langdon Hill
Oven Bottom
The Plantation
Gallop
Aston Upthorpe Downs
Gallops
The Fair Mile
Unhill Bottom
Gallops
Fuller's Firs
RG20
Lowbury Hill
RG8
Dean's Bottom
Ridgeway
A B C D E F
8 7 85 6 5 84 4 3 83 2 1 82
53 54 55

11
32

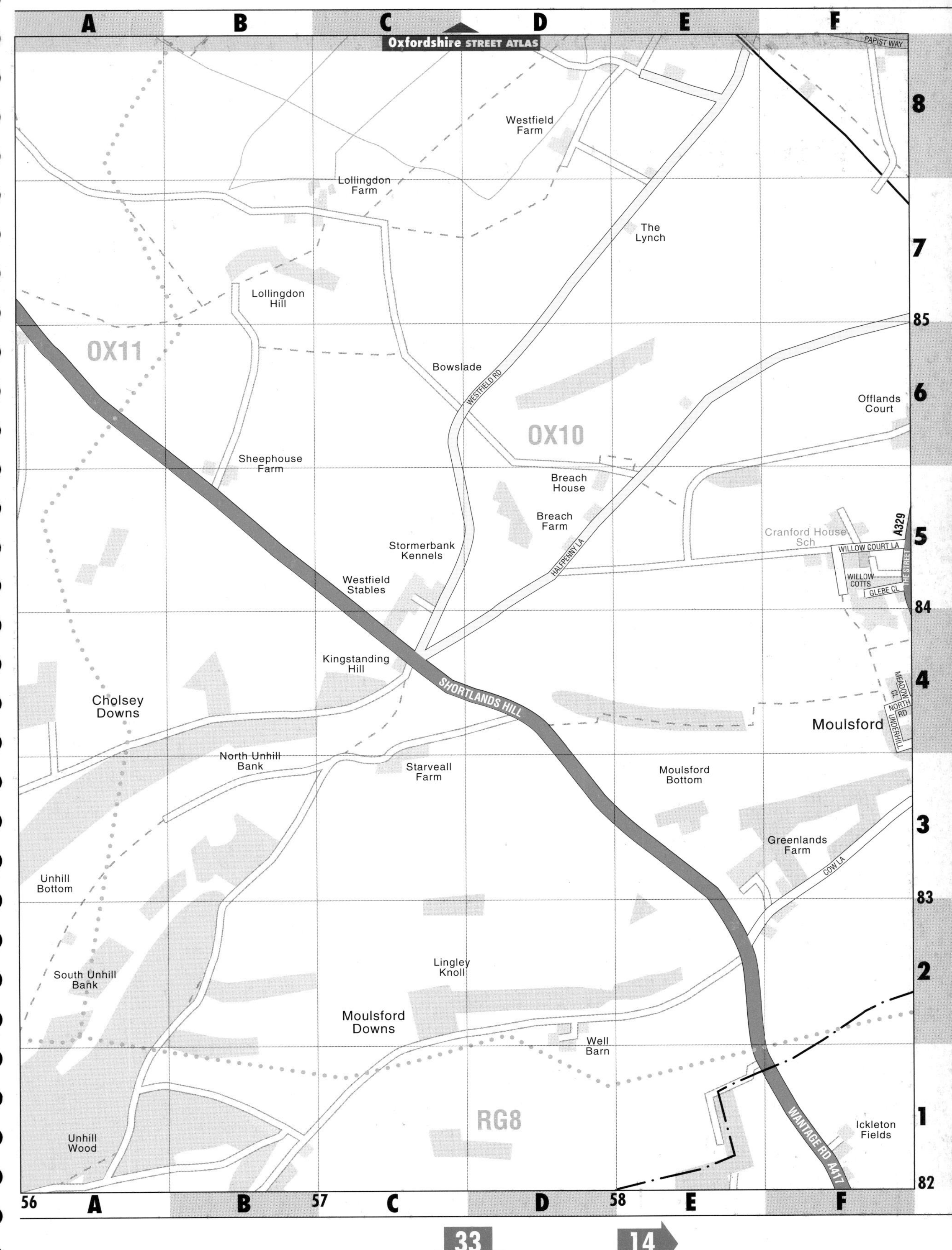

A   B   C   D   E   F

Oxfordshire STREET ATLAS

8

Westfield
Farm

Lollingdon
Farm

The
Lynch

7

Lollingdon
Hill

85

OX11

Bowslade

WESTFIELD RD

6

OX10

Offlands
Court

Sheephouse
Farm

Breach
House

Cranford House
Sch

A329

Stormerbank
Kennels

Breach
Farm

HALFPENNY LA

WILLOW COURT LA

5

Westfield
Stables

WILLOW
COTTS

THE STREET

GLEBE CL

84

Kingstanding
Hill

SHORTLANDS HILL

MEADOW CL

NORTH
UNDERHILL RD

4

Cholsey
Downs

Moulsford

North Unhill
Bank

Starveall
Farm

Moulsford
Bottom

Greenlands
Farm

COW LA

3

Unhill
Bottom

83

Lingley
Knoll

2

South Unhill
Bank

Moulsford
Downs

Well
Barn

WANTAGE RD A417

RG8

Ickleton
Fields

1

Unhill
Wood

A417

82

56   A   B   57   C   D   58   E   F

PAPIST WAY

13

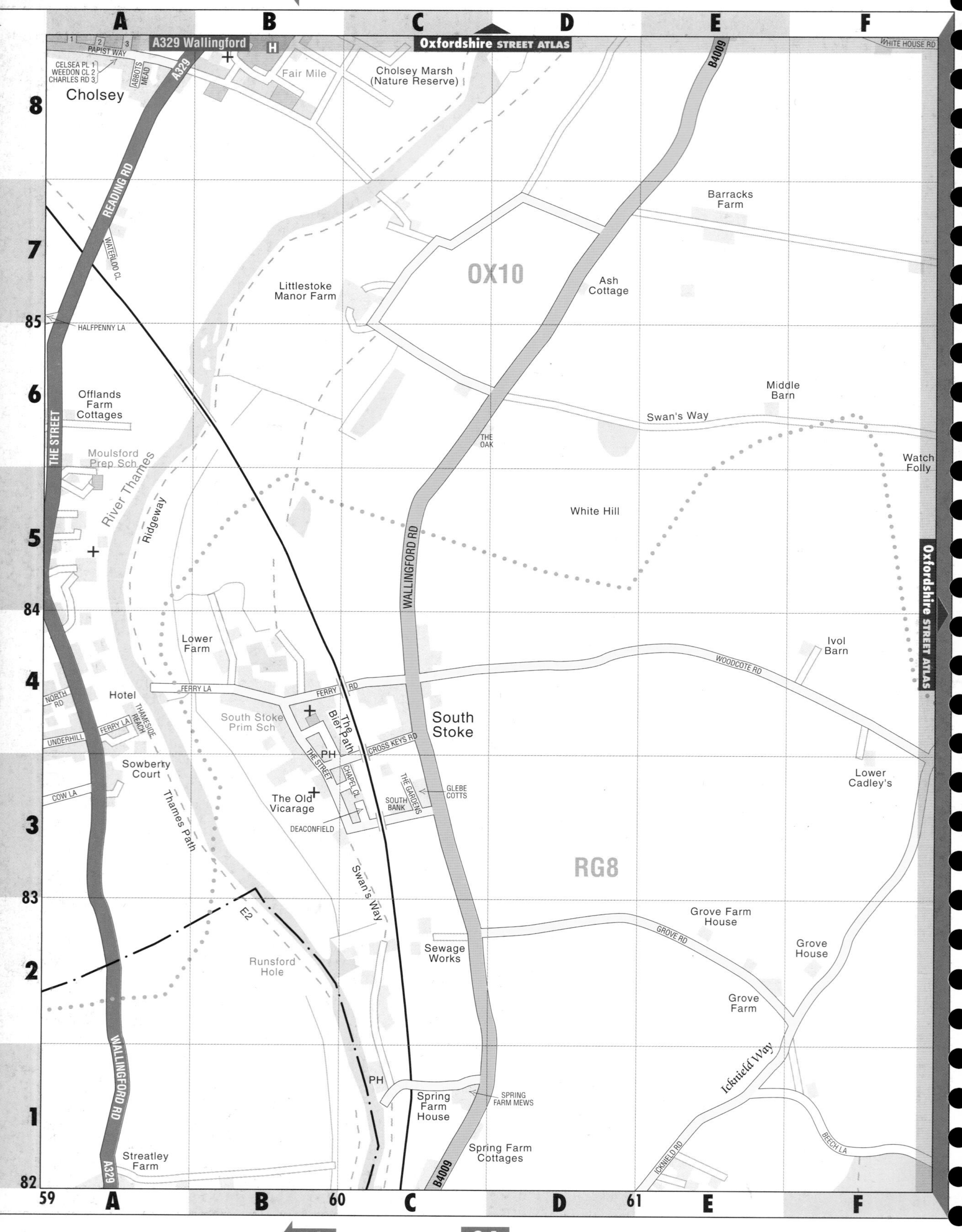
A329 Wallingford
Oxfordshire STREET ATLAS
PAPIST WAY
CELSEA PL 1
WEEDON CL 2
CHARLES RD 3
ABBOTS MEAD
Cholsey
Fair Mile
Cholsey Marsh
(Nature Reserve)
B4009
WHITE HOUSE RD
READING RD
A329
Barracks
Farm
WATERLOO CL
OX10
Littlestoke
Manor Farm
Ash
Cottage
HALFPENNY LA
Offlands
Farm
Cottages
Middle
Barn
Swan's Way
THE STREET
THE OAK
Watch
Folly
Moulsford
Prep Sch
River Thames
Ridgeway
White Hill
WALLINGFORD RD
Lower
Farm
Ivol
Barn
WOODCOTE RD
FERRY LA
FERRY RD
Hotel
NORTH RD
THAMESIDE REACH
FERRY LA
UNDERHILL
South Stoke
Prim Sch
The Bier Path
South
Stoke
CROSS KEYS RD
PH
THE STREET
CHAPEL CL
Sowberry
Court
THE GARDENS
GLEBE COTTS
SOUTH BANK
COW LA
The Old
Vicarage
DEACONFIELD
Lower
Cadley's
Thames Path
Swan's Way
RG8
E2
Grove Farm
House
GROVE RD
Sewage
Works
Grove
House
Runsford
Hole
Grove
Farm
Icknield Way
PH
WALLINGFORD RD
Spring
Farm
House
SPRING
FARM MEWS
BEECH LA
Spring Farm
Cottages
Streatley
Farm
A329
B4009
ICKNIELD RD
A B C D E F
8 7 85 6 5 84 4 3 83 2 1 82
59 60 61

13
34

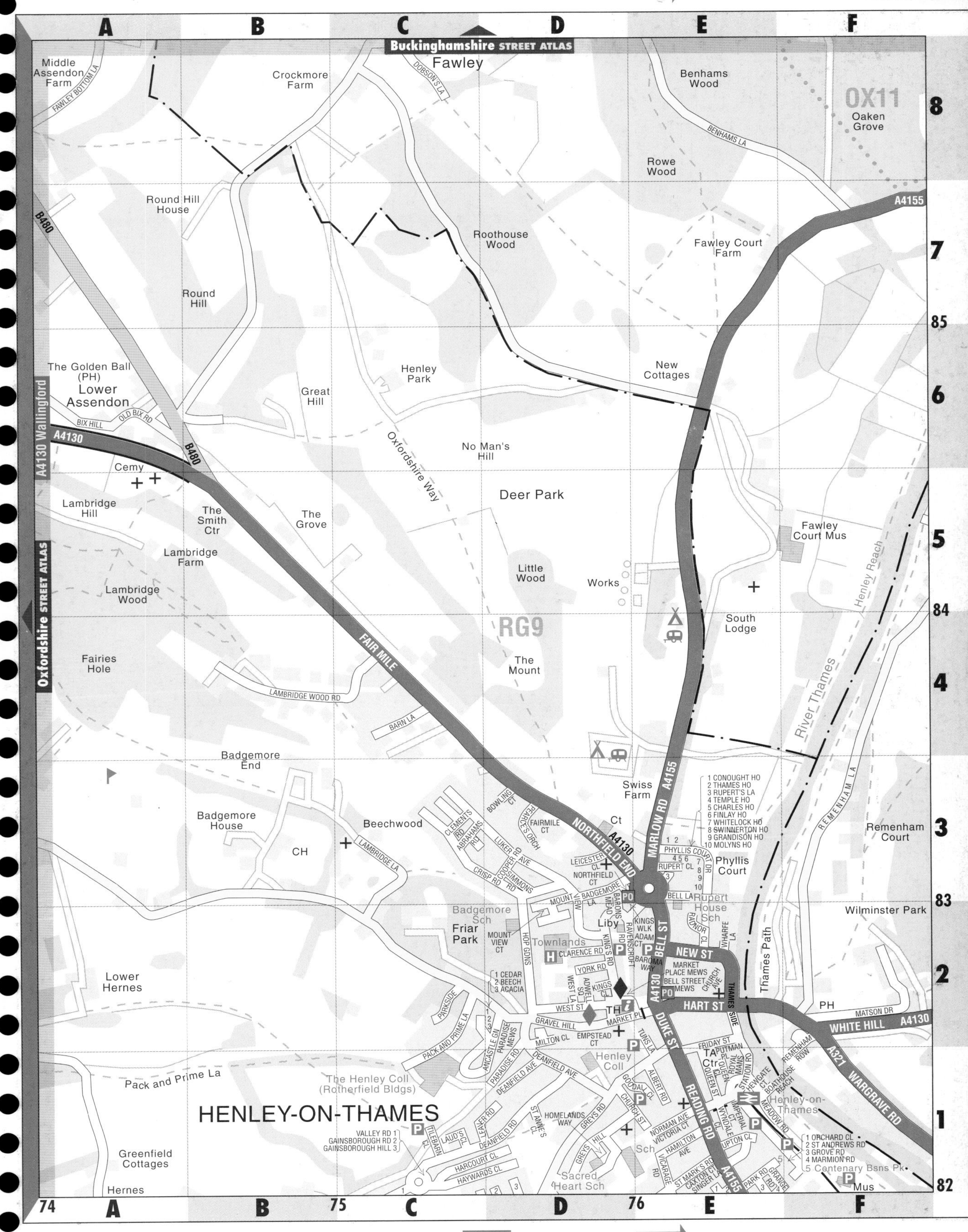

Buckinghamshire STREET ATLAS

Fawley

Middle Assendon Farm

Crockmore Farm

Benhams Wood

OX11
Oaken Grove

A4155

Round Hill House

Roothouse Wood

Fawley Court Farm

Round Hill

Henley Park

New Cottages

The Golden Ball (PH)
Lower Assendon

Great Hill

Oxfordshire Way

No Man's Hill

Fawley Court Mus

Cemy

Lambridge Hill

The Smith Ctr

The Grove

Deer Park

Henley Reach

Lambridge Farm

RG9

Little Wood

Works

South Lodge

Lambridge Wood

Fairies Hole

FAIR MILE

The Mount

River Thames

LAMBRIDGE WOOD RD

BARN LA

Badgemore End

Swiss Farm

Remenham Court

Badgemore House

Beechwood

LAMBRIDGE LA

CH

Ct

MARLOW RD

1 CONOUGHT HO
2 THAMES HO
3 RUPERT'S LA
4 TEMPLE HO
5 CHARLES HO
6 FINLAY HO
7 WHITELOCK HO
8 SWINNERTON HO
9 GRANDISON HO
10 MOLYNS HO

Wilminster Park

Badgemore Sch

Friar Park

Townlands

Liby

Rupert House Sch

Lower Hernes

1 CEDAR
2 BEECH
3 ACACIA

NEW ST

HART ST

PH

MATSON DR

WHITE HILL A4130

Henley Coll

A321 WARGRAVE RD

Pack and Prime La

The Henley Coll (Rotherfield Bldgs)

HENLEY-ON-THAMES

Henley-on-Thames

Greenfield Cottages

VALLEY RD 1
GAINSBOROUGH RD 2
GAINSBOROUGH HILL 3

Sacred Heart Sch

1 ORCHARD CL
2 ST ANDREWS RD
3 GROVE RD
4 MARMION RD
5 Centenary Bsns Pk

Mus

Hernes

15

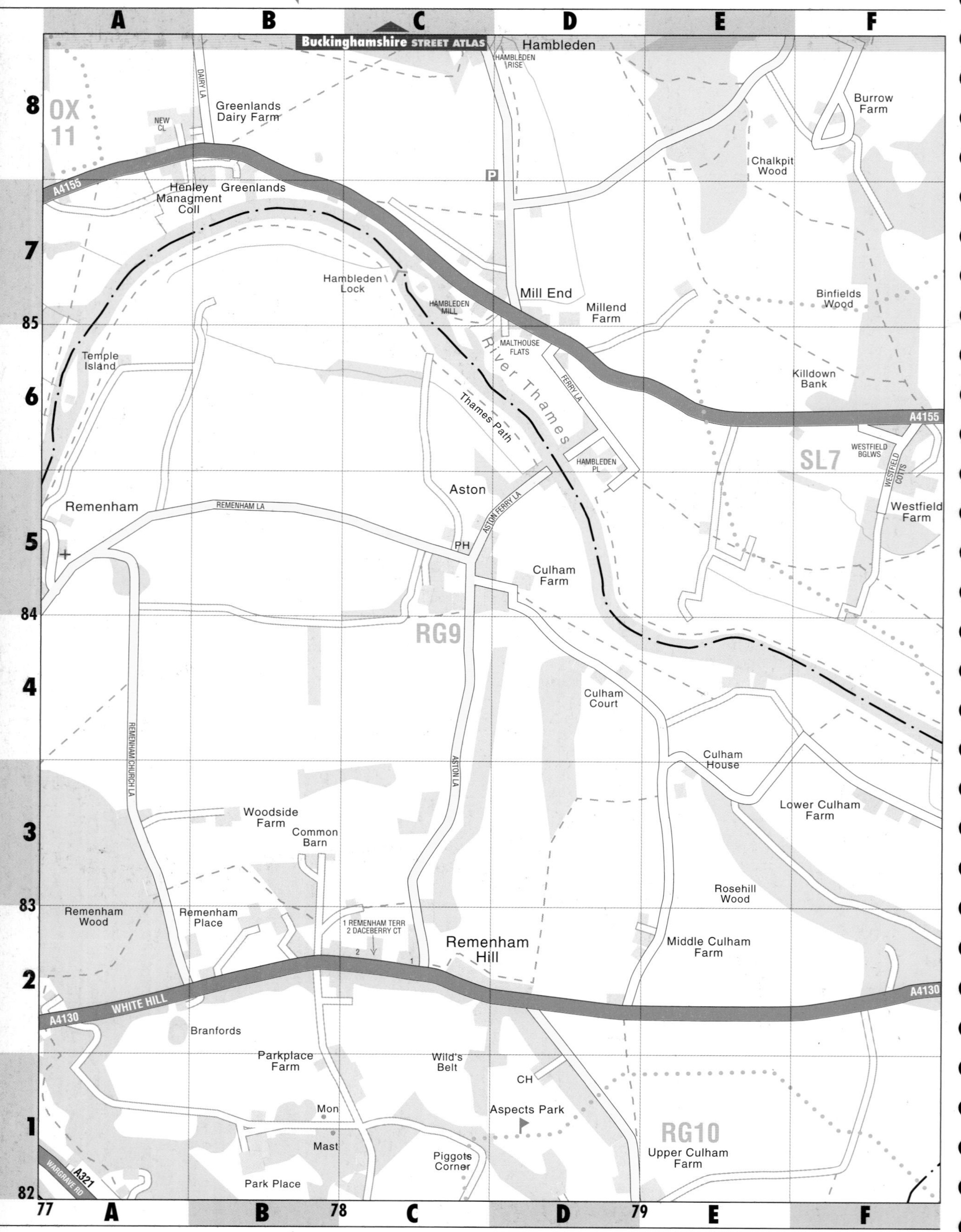

A
B
C
D
E
F
Buckinghamshire STREET ATLAS
Hambleden
HAMBLEDEN RISE
8
OX 11
DAIRY LA
NEW CL
Greenlands Dairy Farm
Burrow Farm
Chalkpit Wood
P
A4155
Henley Managment Coll
Greenlands
7
Hambleden Lock
HAMBLEDEN MILL
Mill End
Millend Farm
Binfields Wood
85
MALTHOUSE FLATS
River Thames
FERRY LA
Temple Island
Killdown Bank
6
Thames Path
A4155
WESTFIELD BGLWS
SL7
HAMBLEDEN PL
WESTFIELD COTTS
Aston
Remenham
REMENHAM LA
ASTON FERRY LA
Westfield Farm
5
PH
Culham Farm
84
RG9
4
Culham Court
REMENHAM CHURCH LA
ASTON LA
Culham House
Lower Culham Farm
3
Woodside Farm
Common Barn
Rosehill Wood
83
Remenham Wood
Remenham Place
1 REMENHAM TERR
2 DACEBERRY CT
Remenham Hill
Middle Culham Farm
2
WHITE HILL
A4130
A4130
Branfords
Parkplace Farm
Wild's Belt
CH
1
Mon
Aspects Park
RG10
Mast
Piggots Corner
Upper Culham Farm
A321
WARGRAVE RD
Park Place
82
77
78
79

15
36

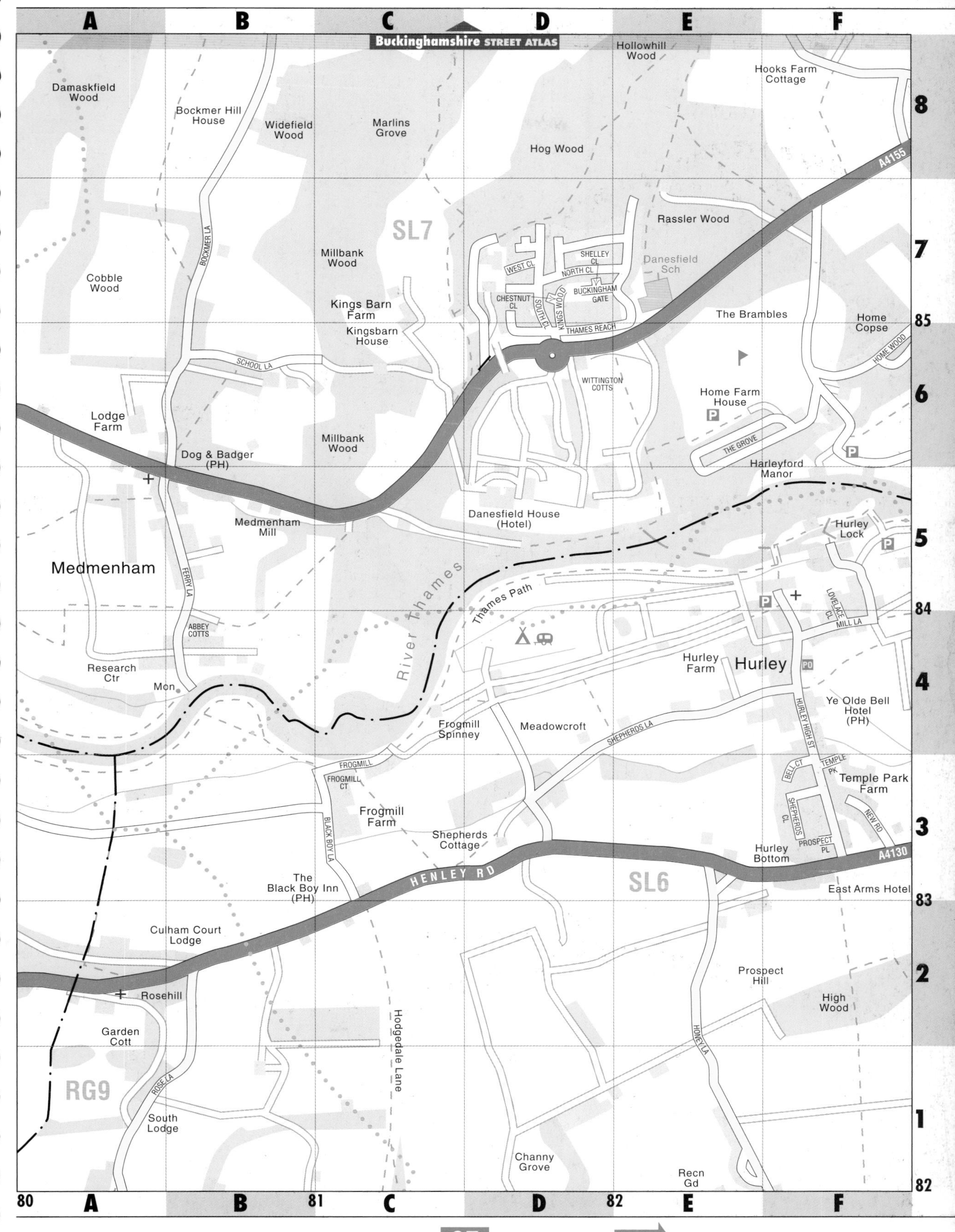

Buckinghamshire STREET ATLAS

A **B** **C** **D** **E** **F**

Damaskfield Wood

Bockmer Hill House

Widefield Wood

Marlins Grove

Hollowhill Wood

Hooks Farm Cottage

8

Hog Wood

A4155

SL7

Cobble Wood

Millbank Wood

Rassler Wood

Danesfield Sch

7

WEST CL

NORTH CL

SHELLEY CL

Kings Barn Farm

CHESTNUT CL

SOUTH CL

BUCKINGHAM GATE

The Brambles

Home Copse

85

Kingsbarn House

THAMES REACH

HOME WOOD

6

SCHOOL LA

WITTINGTON COTTS

Home Farm House

Lodge Farm

Millbank Wood

P

THE GROVE

P

Dog & Badger (PH)

Harleyford Manor

Hurley Lock

5

Medmenham Mill

Danesfield House (Hotel)

P

LOVELACE CL

MILL LA

84

Medmenham

FERRY LA

River Thames

Thames Path

P

Hurley Farm

Hurley

PO

4

ABBEY COTTS

Hurley High St

Ye Olde Bell Hotel (PH)

Research Ctr

Mon

Frogmill Spinney

Meadowcroft

SHEPHERDS LA

BELL CT

TEMPLE PK

Temple Park Farm

3

FROGMILL CT

Frogmill Farm

Shepherds Cottage

SHEPHERDS CL

PROSPECT PL

NEW RD

A4130

BLACK BOY LA

HENLEY RD

SL6

Hurley Bottom

East Arms Hotel

83

The Black Boy Inn (PH)

Culham Court Lodge

Prospect Hill

High Wood

2

HONEY LA

Rosehill

Garden Cott

ROSE LA

RG9

South Lodge

Hodgedale Lane

Channy Grove

Recn Gd

1

82

80 **A** **B** **81** **C** **D** **82** **E** **F**

17
1

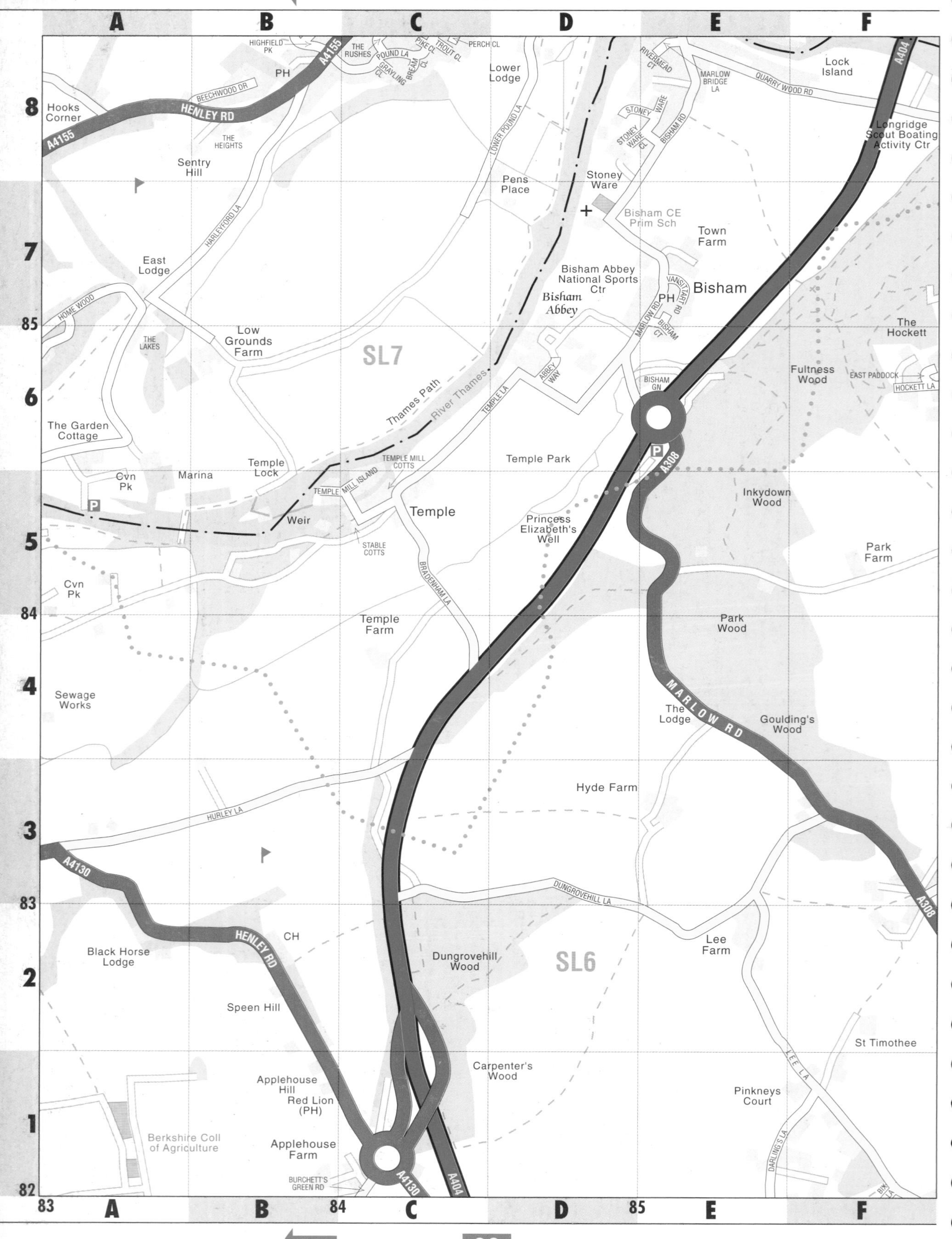
A
B
C
D
E
F
8
7
85
6
5
84
4
3
83
2
1
82
83
84
85
HIGHFIELD PK
THE RUSHES
POUND LA
PIKE CL
TROUT CL
PERCH CL
GRAYLING CL
BREAM CL
A4155
PH
Lower Lodge
RIVERMEAD CT
MARLOW BRIDGE LA
QUARRY WOOD RD
Lock Island
A404
BEECHWOOD DR
HENLEY RD
A4155
Hooks Corner
THE HEIGHTS
Sentry Hill
LOWER POUND LA
STONEY WARE
STONEY WARE CL
BISHAM RD
Longridge Scout Boating Activity Ctr
Pens Place
Stoney Ware
Bisham CE Prim Sch
Town Farm
HARLEYFORD LA
East Lodge
Bisham Abbey National Sports Ctr
Bisham Abbey
VANSITTART RD
PH
Bisham
HOME WOOD
THE LAKES
Low Grounds Farm
SL7
MARLOW RD
BISHAM CT
The Hockett
Fultness Wood
EAST PADDOCK
HOCKETT LA
ABBEY WAY
BISHAM GN
Thames Path
River Thames
TEMPLE LA
The Garden Cottage
P
A308
Temple Park
Temple Lock
TEMPLE MILL COTTS
Cvn Pk
Marina
TEMPLE MILL ISLAND
Temple
Inkydown Wood
P
Weir
Princess Elizabeth's Well
STABLE COTTS
Park Farm
Cvn Pk
BRADENHAM LA
Temple Farm
Park Wood
Sewage Works
MARLOW RD
The Lodge
Goulding's Wood
Hyde Farm
HURLEY LA
A4130
DUNGROVEHILL LA
A308
CH
Lee Farm
HENLEY RD
Black Horse Lodge
Dungrovehill Wood
SL6
Speen Hill
St Timothee
Carpenter's Wood
Applehouse Hill
Red Lion (PH)
LEE LA
Pinkneys Court
Berkshire Coll of Agriculture
Applehouse Farm
DARLING'S LA
BURCHETT'S GREEN RD
A4130
A404
BIX LA

17
38

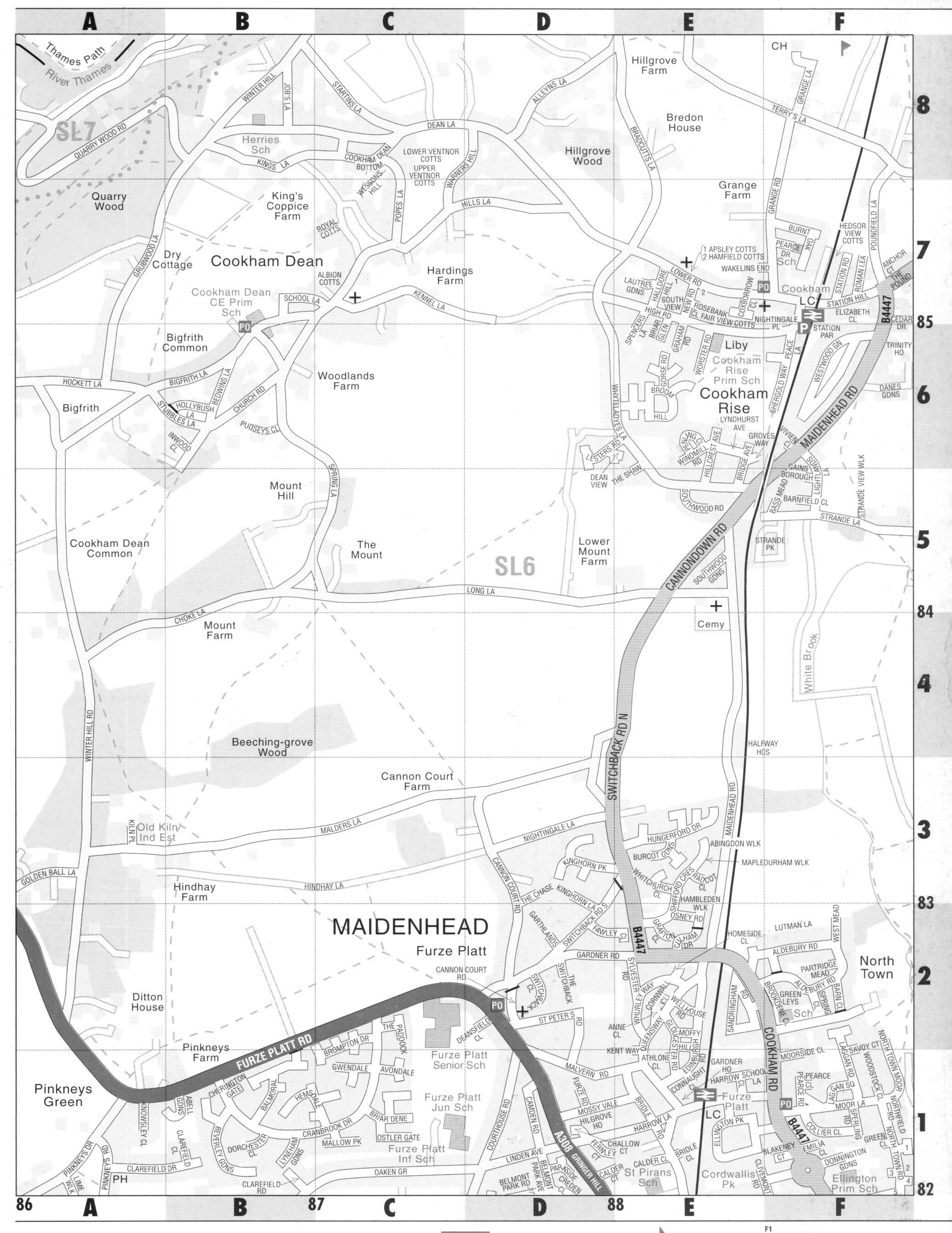

F1
1 NORTH TOWN CL
2 ALYSON CT
3 NORTH GN
4 NORTH TOWN MEAD
5 NORTHDEAN

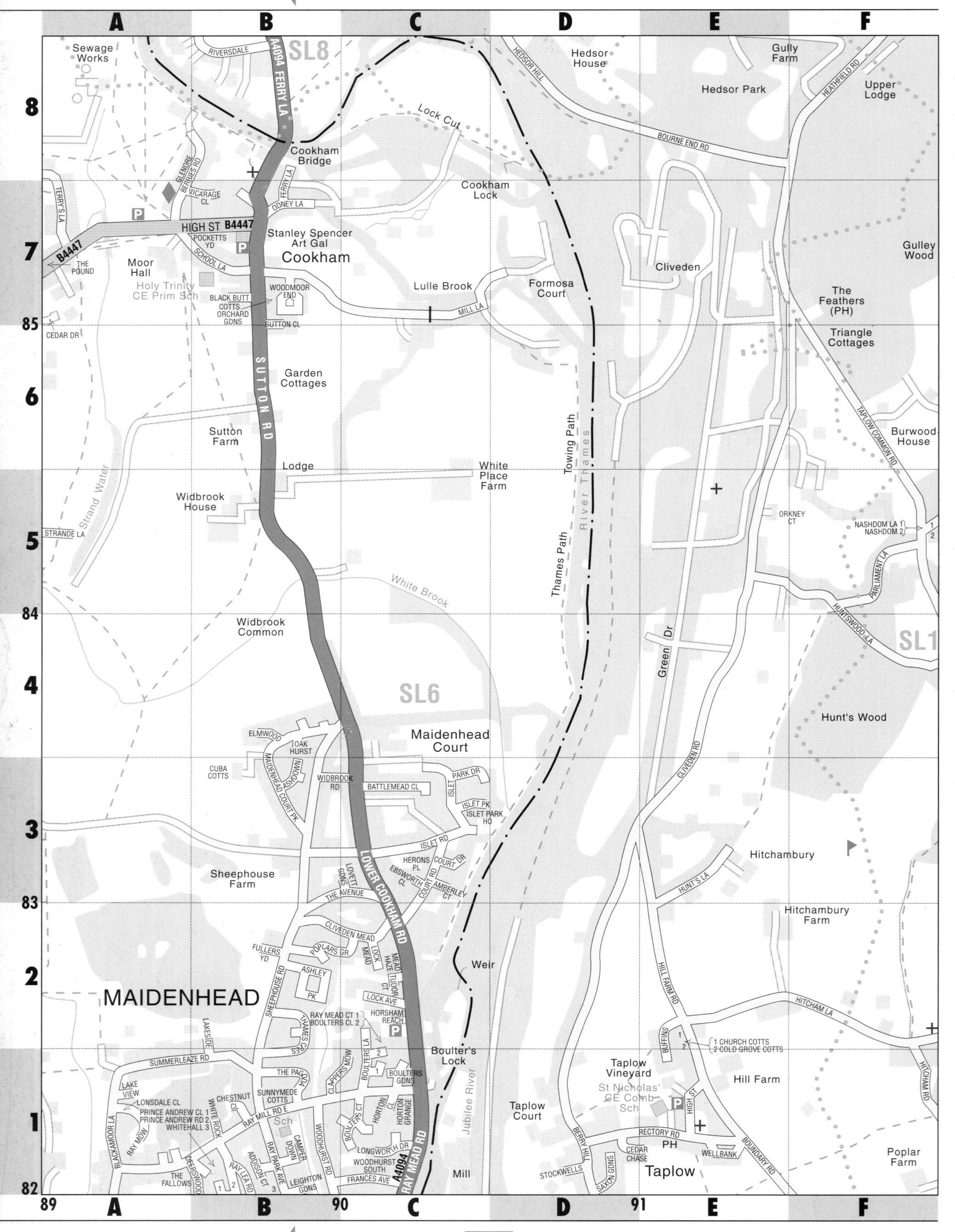
19
3
A
B
C
D
E
F
8
7
85
6
5
84
4
3
83
2
1
82
89
90
91
SL8
SL6
SL1
Sewage Works
RIVERSDALE
A4094 FERRY LA
Lock Cut
HEDSOR HILL
Hedsor House
Gully Farm
Hedsor Park
HEATHFIELD RD
Upper Lodge
BOURNE END RD
Cookham Bridge
GLENORE
BERRIES RD
VICARAGE CL
FERRY LA
ODNEY LA
TERRY'S LA
Cookham Lock
HIGH ST B4447
POCKETTS YD
SCHOOL LA
Stanley Spencer Art Gal
Cookham
B4447
THE POUND
Moor Hall
Holy Trinity CE Prim Sch
BLACK BUTT COTTS
ORCHARD GDNS
WOODMOOR END
SUTTON CL
Lulle Brook
MILL LA
Formosa Court
Cliveden
Gulley Wood
The Feathers (PH)
Triangle Cottages
CEDAR DR
SUTTON RD
Garden Cottages
Sutton Farm
Lodge
White Place Farm
Towing Path
River Thames
TAPLOW COMMON RD
Burwood House
Widbrook House
Strand Water
ORKNEY CT
NASHDOM LA 1
NASHDOM 2
STRANDE LA
Thames Path
White Brook
PARLIAMENT LA
HUNTSWOOD LA
Widbrook Common
Green Dr
Hunt's Wood
ELMWOOD
OAK HURST
Maidenhead Court
CUBA COTTS
MAIDENHEAD COURT PK
ASHDOWN
WIDBROOK RD
BATTLEMEAD CL
PARK DR
ISLET
ISLET PK
ISLET PARK HO
CLIVEDEN RD
ISLET RD
HERONS PL
COURT DR
Hitchambury
Sheephouse Farm
LOVETT GDNS
EBSWORTH CL
COURT RD
AMBERLEY CT
HUNT'S LA
THE AVENUE
LOWER COOKHAM RD
Hitchambury Farm
CLIVEDEN MEAD
FULLERS YD
POPLARS GR
MEAD
LOCK MEAD
HAZE MEAD
Weir
ASHLEY PK
SHEEPHOUSE RD
TUDOR CT
LOCK AVE
HILL FARM RD
MAIDENHEAD
HITCHAM LA
RAY MEAD CT 1
BOULTERS CL 2
HORSHAM REACH
THAMES CL
LAKESIDE
BUFFINS
1 CHURCH COTTS
2 COLD GROVE COTTS
BOULTERS LA
Boulter's Lock
SUMMERLEAZE RD
THE PAGODA
CLAPPERS MDW
BOULTERS GDNS
Taplow Vineyard
Hill Farm
HITCHAM RD
LAKE VIEW
CHESTNUT CL
SUNNYMEDE COTTS
St Nicholas' CE Comb Sch
LONSDALE CL
PRINCE ANDREW CL 1
PRINCE ANDREW RD 2
WHITEHALL 3
WHITE ROCK
RAY MILL RD E
Sch
BOULTERS CT
HORTON CL
HORTON GRANGE
Jubilee River
Taplow Court
HIGH ST
BLACKAMOOR LA
RAY MDW
CAMPER DOWN
WOODHURST RD
LONGWORTH DR
RECTORY RD
BERRY HILL
PH
BOUNDARY RD
Poplar Farm
DEERSWOOD
RAY LEA RD
ADDISON CT
RAY PARK AVE
WOODHURST SOUTH
A4094
RAY MEAD RD
CEDAR CHASE
WELLBANK
THE FALLOWS
LEIGHTON GDNS
FRANCES AVE
Mill
STOCKWELLS
SAXON GDNS
Taplow
19
40

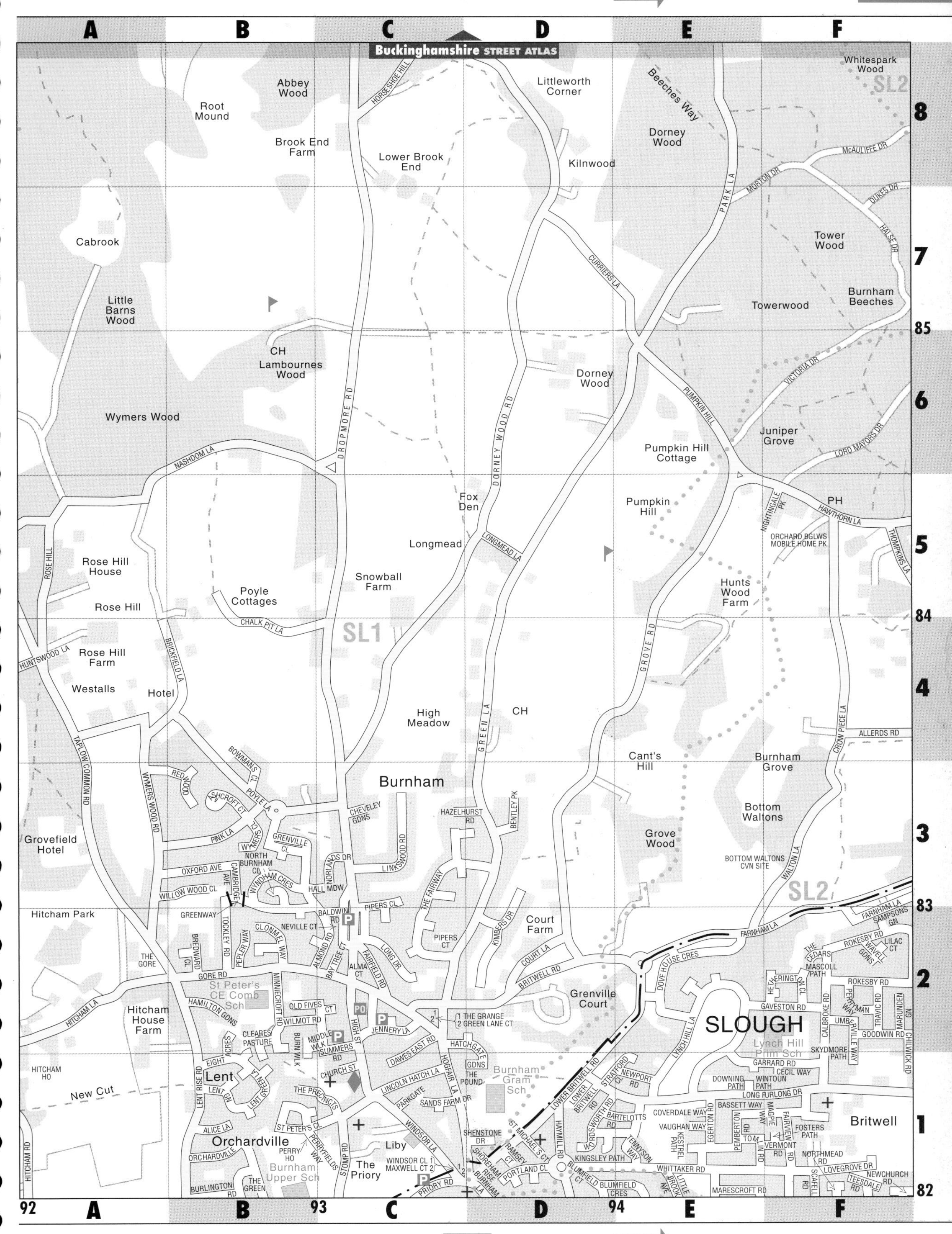

Buckinghamshire STREET ATLAS

A B C D E F

SL2

8

Whitespark Wood

Root Mound
Abbey Wood
Littleworth Corner
Beeches Way

Cabrook
Brook End Farm
Lower Brook End
Kilnwood
Dorney Wood

McAULIFFE DR
DUKES DR
HALSE DR
Tower Wood

7

Little Barns Wood
CURRIERS LA
Towerwood
Burnham Beeches

PARK LA

85

CH Lambournes Wood
MORTON DR
PUMPKIN HILL
Dorney Wood

6

Wymers Wood
VICTORIA DR
LORD MAYORS DR
Juniper Grove

NASHDOM LA
DROPMORE RD
DORNEY WOOD RD
Pumpkin Hill Cottage
PH

NIGHTINGALE PK
HAWTHORN LA
ORCHARD BGLWS MOBILE HOME PK

5

Rose Hill House
Fox Den
Pumpkin Hill
THOMPKINS LA

ROSE HILL
Poyle Cottages
Longmead
Snowball Farm
LONGMEAD LA
Hunts Wood Farm

84

Rose Hill
CHALK PIT LA
SL1

4

Rose Hill Farm
HUNTSWOOD LA
BRICKFIELD LA
Hotel
GROVE RD

Westalls
High Meadow
GREEN LA
CH
Cant's Hill
Burnham Grove
CROWN PIECE LA
ALLERDS RD

TAPLOW COMMON RD
ROSE HILL

3

Grovefield Hotel
BOWMANS CT
POYLE LA
Burnham
Grove Wood
Bottom Waltons
SL2

WYMERS WOOD RD
REDWOOD
PINK LA
GRENVILLE CL
Hazelhurst RD
BENTLEY PK
BOTTOM WALTONS CVN SITE
WALTON LA

Hitcham Park
ASHCROFT CT
NORTH BURNHAM CL
WYNDHAM CRES
LINKSWOOD RD
THE FAIRWAY
KINBROOK DR
Court Farm
FARNHAM LA
SAMPSONS GN
LILAC CT

83

OXFORD AVE
CAMBRIDGE AVE
HALL MDW
PIPERS CL
COURT LA
FARNHAM RD
ROKESBY RD
WENTWORTH AVE

THE GORE
WILLOW WOOD CL
GREENWAY
NEVILLE CT
BALDWIN RD
PIPERS CT
BRITWELL RD
DOVE HOUSE CRES
THE CEDARS
MASCOLL PATH
ROKESBY RD

2

GORE RD
TOCKLEY RD
CLONMEL WAY
BAY TREE CT
ALMA CT
LONG LA
Grenville Court
CALBROKE RD
GAVESTON RD
MARUNDEN
CHILWICK RD

Hitcham House Farm
BREDWARD CL
PEPPLER WAY
ALMOND RD
FAIRFIELD RD
SLOUGH
HETHERINGTON CL
PERRYMAN WAY
TRAVIC RD
GOODWIN RD

HITCHAM LA
HAMILTON GDNS
MINNIECROFT RD
OLD FIVES CT
WILMOT RD
JENNERY LA
2 GREEN LANE CT
1 THE GRANGE
HATCHGATE GDNS
Lynch Hill Prim Sch
DOWNING PATH
WINTOUN PATH
UMBERLEY
SKYDMORE PATH

HITCHAM HO
CLEARES PASTURE
BURN WLK
SUMMERS RD
PO
DAWES EAST RD
HOGARTH LA
THE POUND
Burnham Gram Sch
LOWER BRITWELL RD
NEWPORT RD
CECIL WAY
GARRARD RD
FAIRVIEW AVE

1

New Cut
LENT RISE RD
LENT
LENT GRN
ALICE LA
CHURCH ST
LINCOLN HATCH LA
PARKGATE
SANDS FARM DR
STAFFORD RD
LOWER BRITWELL RD
BARTELOTTS RD
Coverdale WAY
VAUGHAN WAY
BASSETT WAY
PEMBERTON RD
EGERTON RD
MAPLE
KESTREL PATH
Britwell
FOSTERS PATH
LONG FURLONG DR

ST PETER'S CL
WINDSOR LA
Liby
SHENSTONE DR
ST MICHEL'S CT
RAMSBY
KINGSLEY PATH
TENNYSON WAY
LILIAN RD
VERMONT RD
NORTHMEAD
LOVEGROVE RD
NEWCHURCH RD

Orchardville
ORCHARDVILLE
PERRYFIELDS
STOMP RD
THE PRECINCTS
The Priory
WINDSOR CL 1
MAXWELL CT 2
PRIORY RD
PORTLAND CL
BLUMFIELD CRES
BLUMFIELD CT
WHITTAKER RD
MARESCROFT RD
CHAPELS
TEESDALE RD

BURLINGTON RD
THE GREEN
Burnham Upper Sch

82

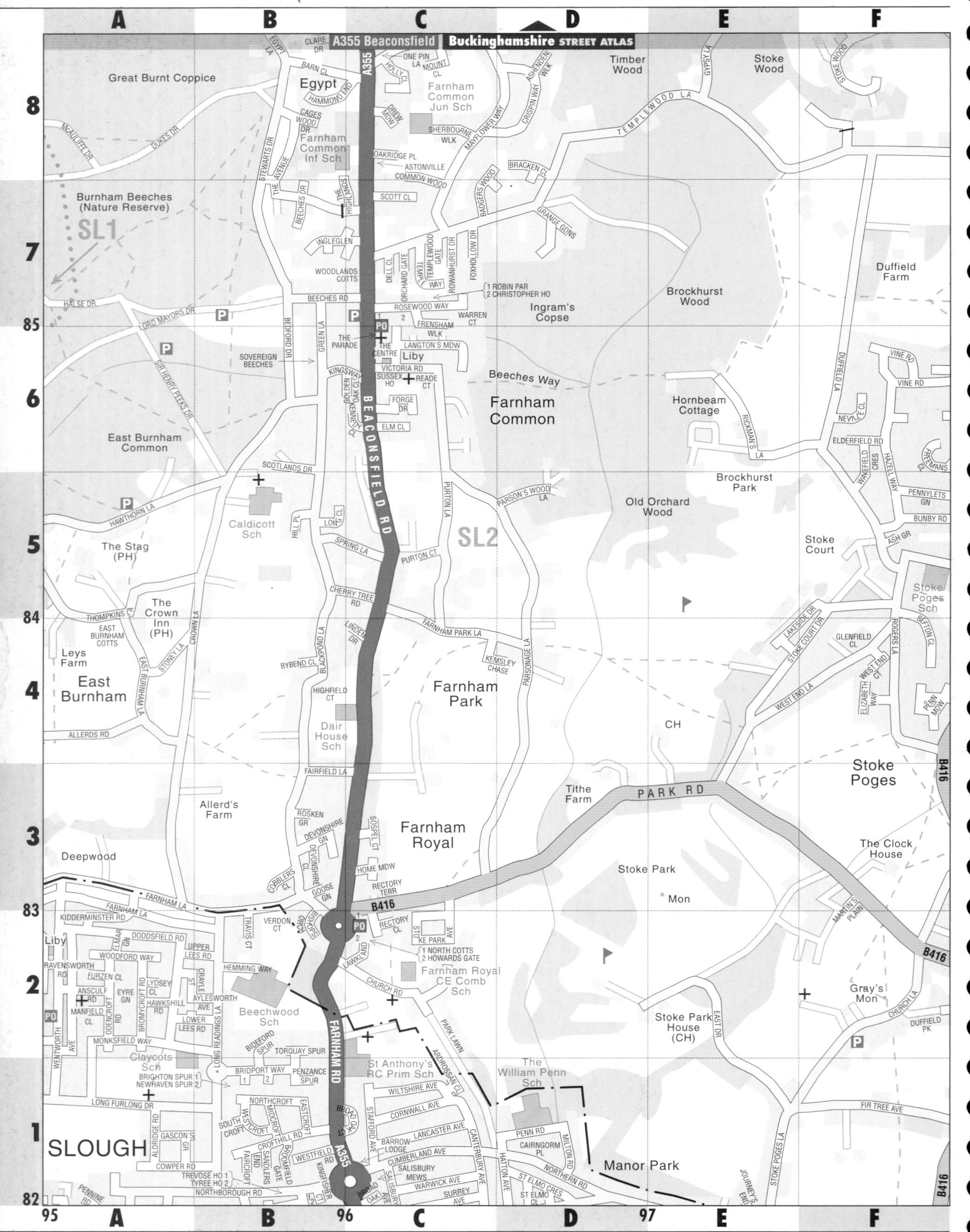

A355 Beaconsfield | **Buckinghamshire** STREET ATLAS

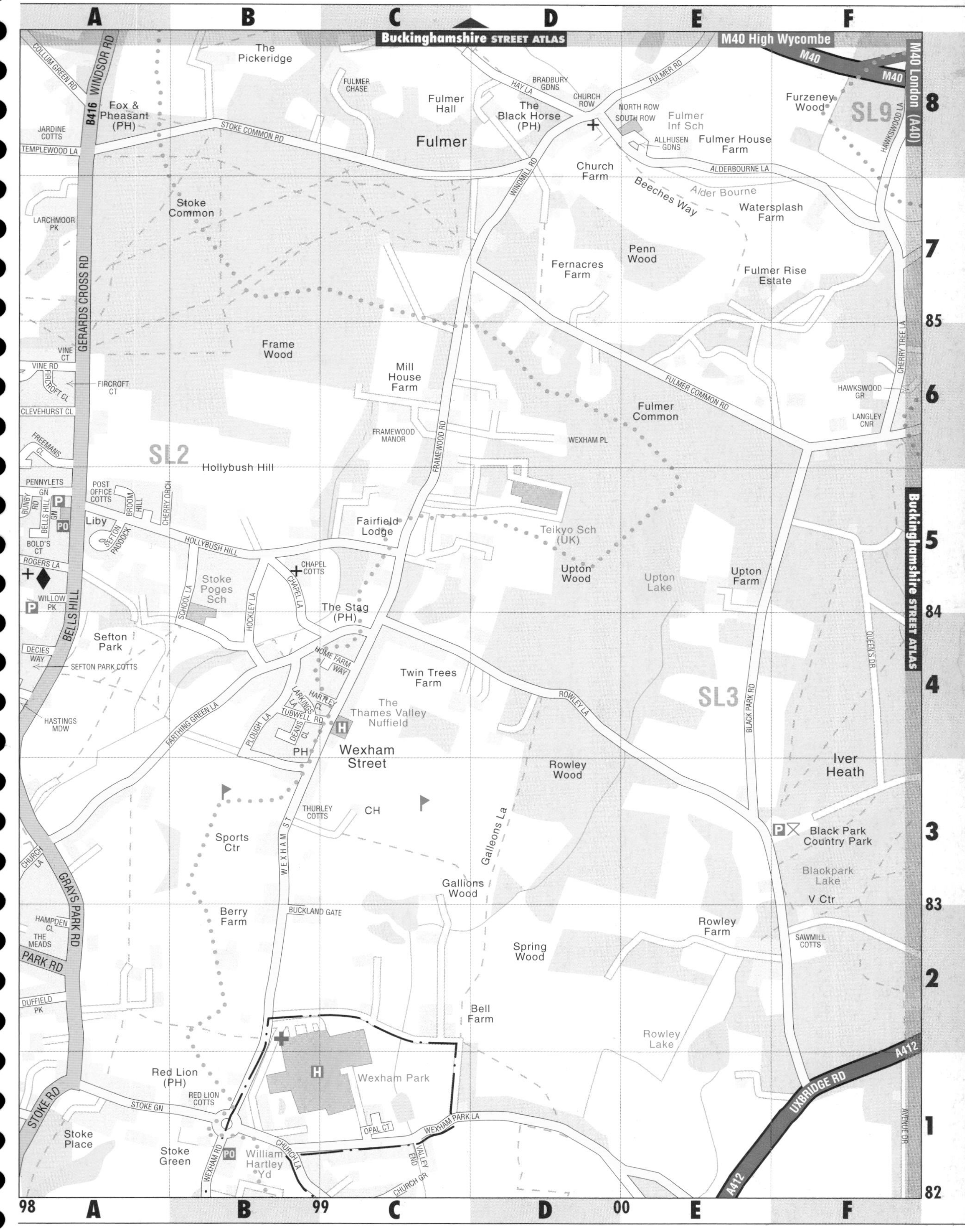

Buckinghamshire STREET ATLAS

M40 High Wycombe

M40 London (A40)

SL9

Collum Green Rd

WINDSOR RD

B416

The Pickeridge

Fulmer Chase

Fulmer Hall

Bradbury Gdns

Hay La

Church Row

North Row

South Row

Furzeney Wood

Fox & Pheasant (PH)

Jardine Cotts

STOKE COMMON RD

The Black Horse (PH)

Fulmer

Fulmer Inf Sch

Allhusen Gdns

Fulmer House Farm

Templewood La

Larchmoor Pk

Stoke Common

Church Farm

Alder Bourne

Beeches Way

ALDERBOURNE LA

Watersplash Farm

GERARDS CROSS RD

Vine Ct

Vine Rd

Fircroft Cl

FIRCROFT CT

Fernacres Farm

Penn Wood

Fulmer Rise Estate

Cherry Tree La

Hawkswood Gr

Clevehurst Cl

Frame Wood

Mill House Farm

FULMER COMMON RD

Fulmer Common

Langley Cnr

Freemans Cl

SL2

Framewood Manor

FRAMEWOOD RD

WEXHAM PL

Pennylets Gn

Bury Rd

Bells Hill

P

Post Office Cotts

Broom Hill

Cherry Orch

Hollybush Hill

Bold's Ct

PO

Liby

HOLLYBUSH HILL

SCHOOL LA

Fairfield Lodge

Teikyo Sch (UK)

Upton Lake

Upton Farm

Rogers La

Sefton Paddock

CHAPEL COTTS

Chapel La

HOCKLEY LA

Upton Wood

WILLOW PK

P

Stoke Poges Sch

The Stag (PH)

Decies Way

Sefton Park

HOME FARM WAY

Twin Trees Farm

The Thames Valley Nuffield

ROWLEY LA

SL3

SEFTON PARK COTTS

HARTLEY

LANDING CL

TUBWELL CL

DEANS CL

H

Rowley Wood

Iver Heath

Hastings Mdw

PLOUGH LA

PH

Wexham Street

FARTHING GREEN LA

THURLEY COTTS

CH

Galleons La

P

Black Park Country Park

Church La

GRAY'S PARK RD

Sports Ctr

WEXHAM ST

Rowley Wood

Blackpark Lake

V Ctr

Hampden Cl

The Meads

Berry Farm

BUCKLAND GATE

Gallions Wood

Spring Wood

Rowley Farm

SAWMILL COTTS

PARK RD

Duffield Pk

Bell Farm

Rowley Lake

Stoke Rd

Red Lion (PH)

RED LION COTTS

H

Wexham Park

UXBRIDGE RD

A412

Stoke Place

STOKE GN

PO

William Hartley Yd

OPAL CT

WEXHAM PARK LA

A412

AVENUE DR

Stoke Green

WEXHAM RD

CHURCH LA

OLD WEXHAM RD

CHURCH GR

QUEEN'S DR

BLACK PARK RD

FULMER RD

WINDMILL RD

Hollybush Hill

Buckinghamshire STREET ATLAS

98 99 00

82 83 84 85 1 2 3 4 5 6 7 8

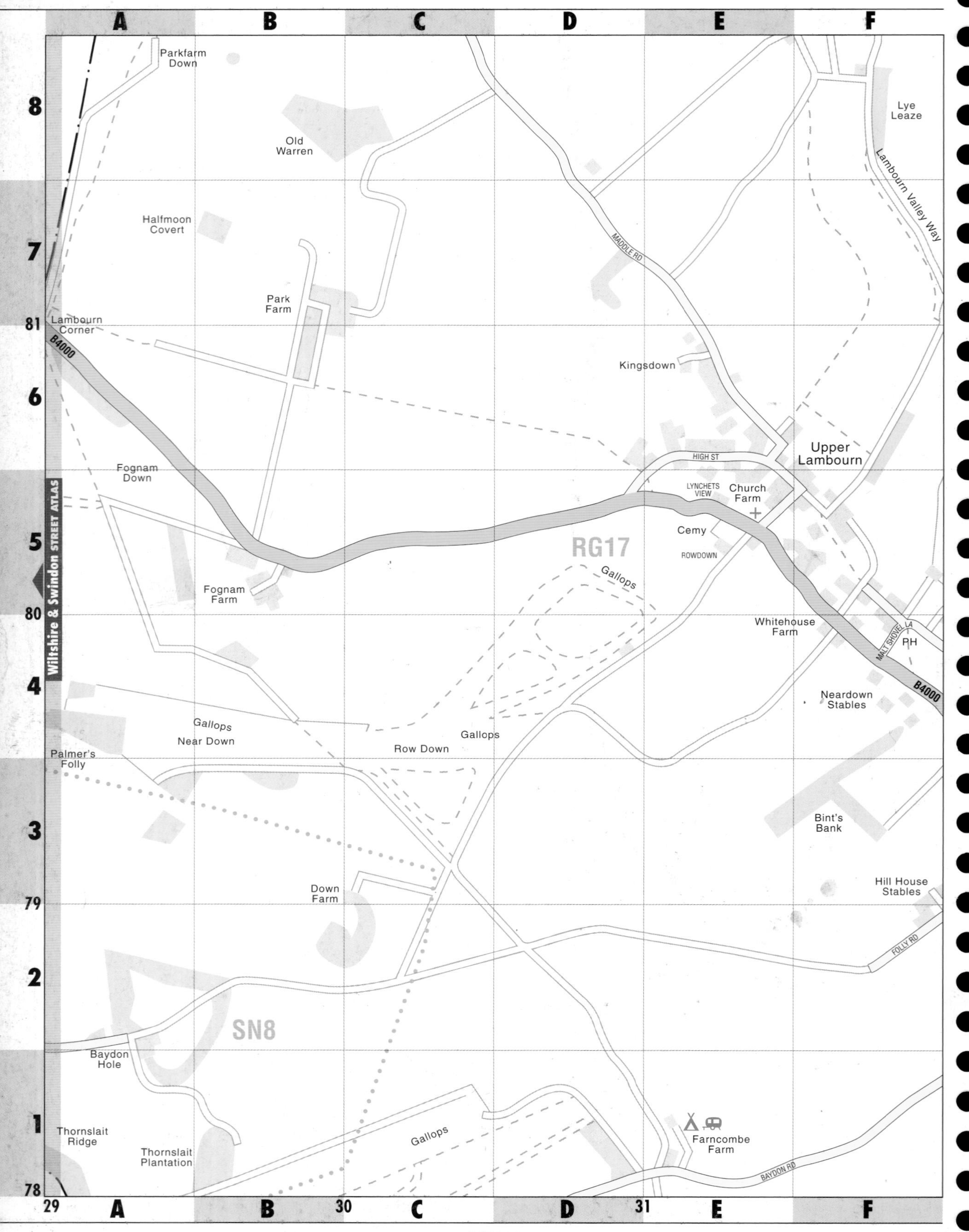

A B C D E F

8

Parkfarm Down

Old Warren

Lye Leaze

Lambourn Valley Way

7

Halfmoon Covert

MADDLE RD

81

Park Farm

Lambourn Corner

B4000

Kingsdown

6

Fognam Down

Upper Lambourn

HIGH ST

LYNCHETS VIEW

Church Farm

5

RG17

Cemy

ROWDOWN

Gallops

Fognam Farm

80

Whitehouse Farm

MALT SHOVEL LA

PH

B4000

4

Gallops

Near Down

Palmer's Folly

Gallops

Row Down

Gallops

Neardown Stables

3

Bint's Bank

79

Down Farm

Hill House Stables

FOLLY RD

2

SN8

Baydon Hole

1

Thornslait Ridge

Thornslait Plantation

Gallops

Farncombe Farm

BAYDON RD

78

29 A B 30 C D 31 E F

Wiltshire & Swindon STREET ATLAS

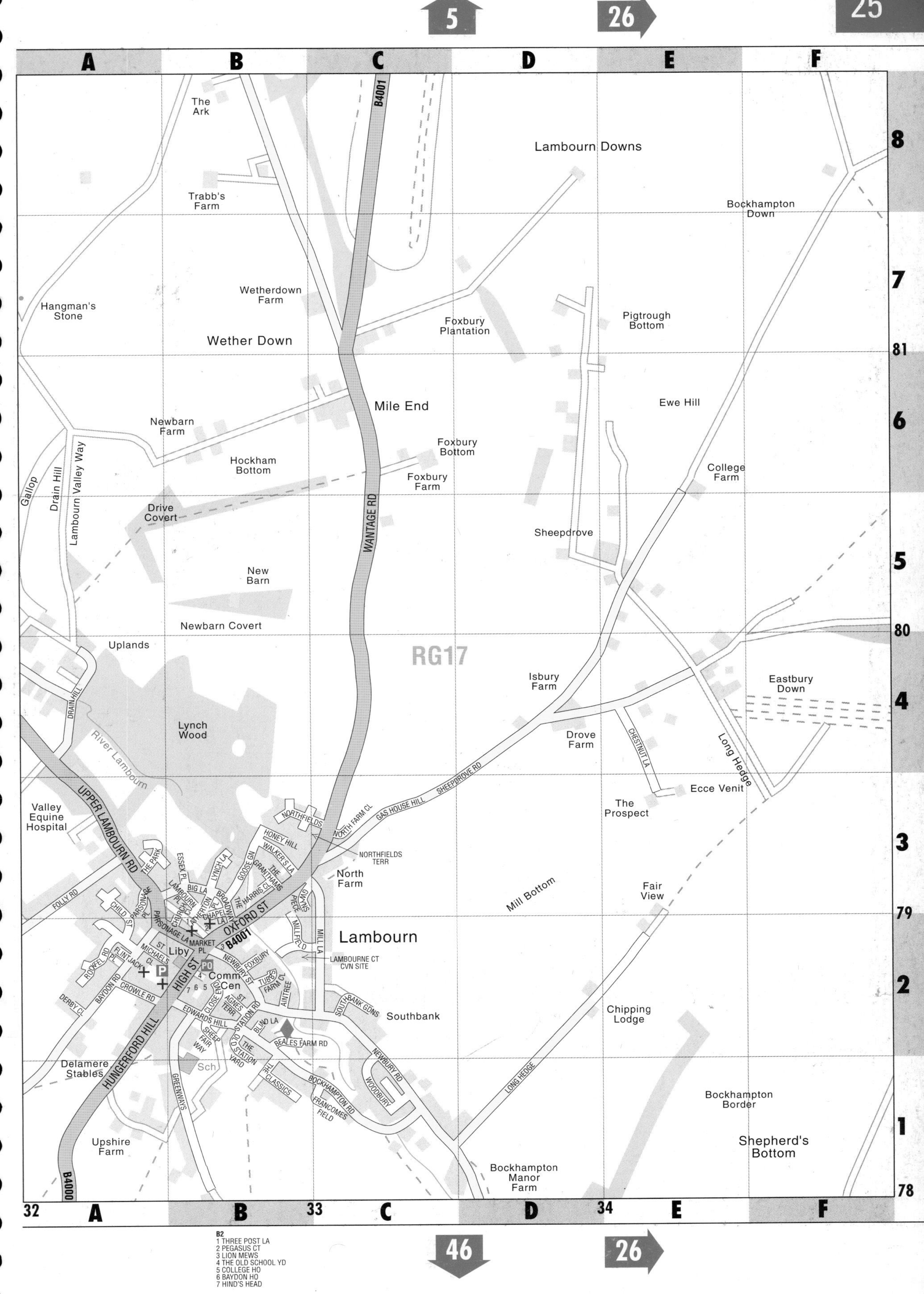

B2
1 THREE POST LA
2 PEGASUS CT
3 LION MEWS
4 THE OLD SCHOOL YD
5 COLLEGE HO
6 BAYDON HO
7 HIND'S HEAD

25
6

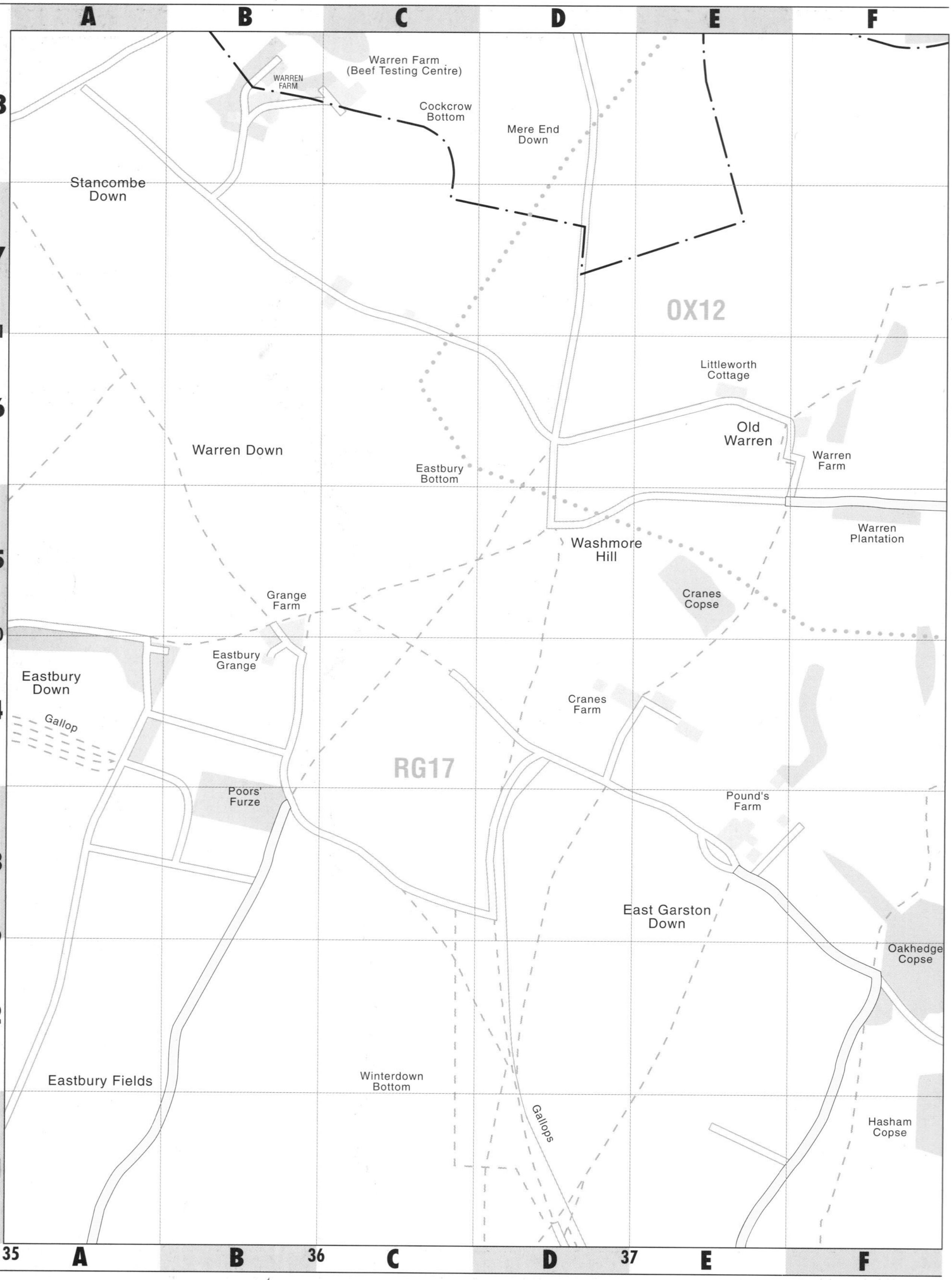

A B C D E F

8

7

81

6

5

80

4

3

79

2

1

78

35 A B 36 C D 37 E F

Warren Farm
(Beef Testing Centre)

WARREN
FARM

Cockcrow
Bottom

Mere End
Down

Stancombe
Down

OX12

Littleworth
Cottage

Old
Warren

Warren
Farm

Warren Down

Eastbury
Bottom

Warren
Plantation

Washmore
Hill

Grange
Farm

Cranes
Copse

Eastbury
Down

Eastbury
Grange

Gallop

Cranes
Farm

Poors'
Furze

RG17

Pound's
Farm

East Garston
Down

Oakhedge
Copse

Eastbury Fields

Winterdown
Bottom

Gallops

Hasham
Copse

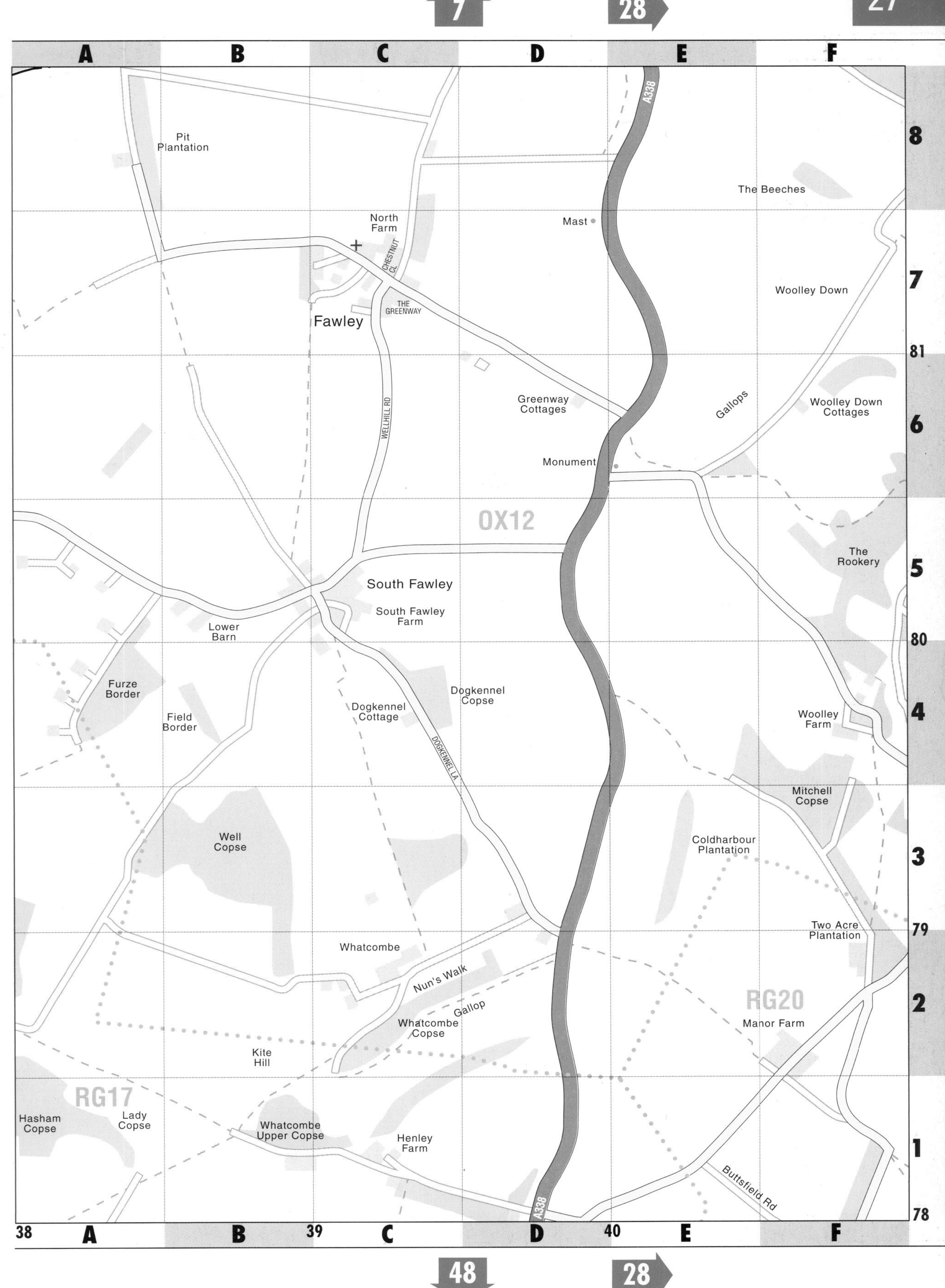
7
28
A
B
C
D
E
F
Pit Plantation
North Farm
CHESTNUT CL
THE GREENWAY
Fawley
A338
Mast
The Beeches
Woolley Down
Greenway Cottages
Gallops
Woolley Down Cottages
WELLHILL RD
Monument
OX12
The Rookery
South Fawley
South Fawley Farm
Lower Barn
Furze Border
Field Border
Dogkennel Cottage
Dogkennel Copse
DOGKENNEL LA
Woolley Farm
Mitchell Copse
Well Copse
Coldharbour Plantation
Two Acre Plantation
Whatcombe
Nun's Walk
Gallop
RG20
Manor Farm
Whatcombe Copse
Kite Hill
RG17
Hasham Copse
Lady Copse
Whatcombe Upper Copse
Henley Farm
Buttsfield Rd
8
7
81
6
5
80
4
3
79
2
1
78
38
39
40
48
28

27
8

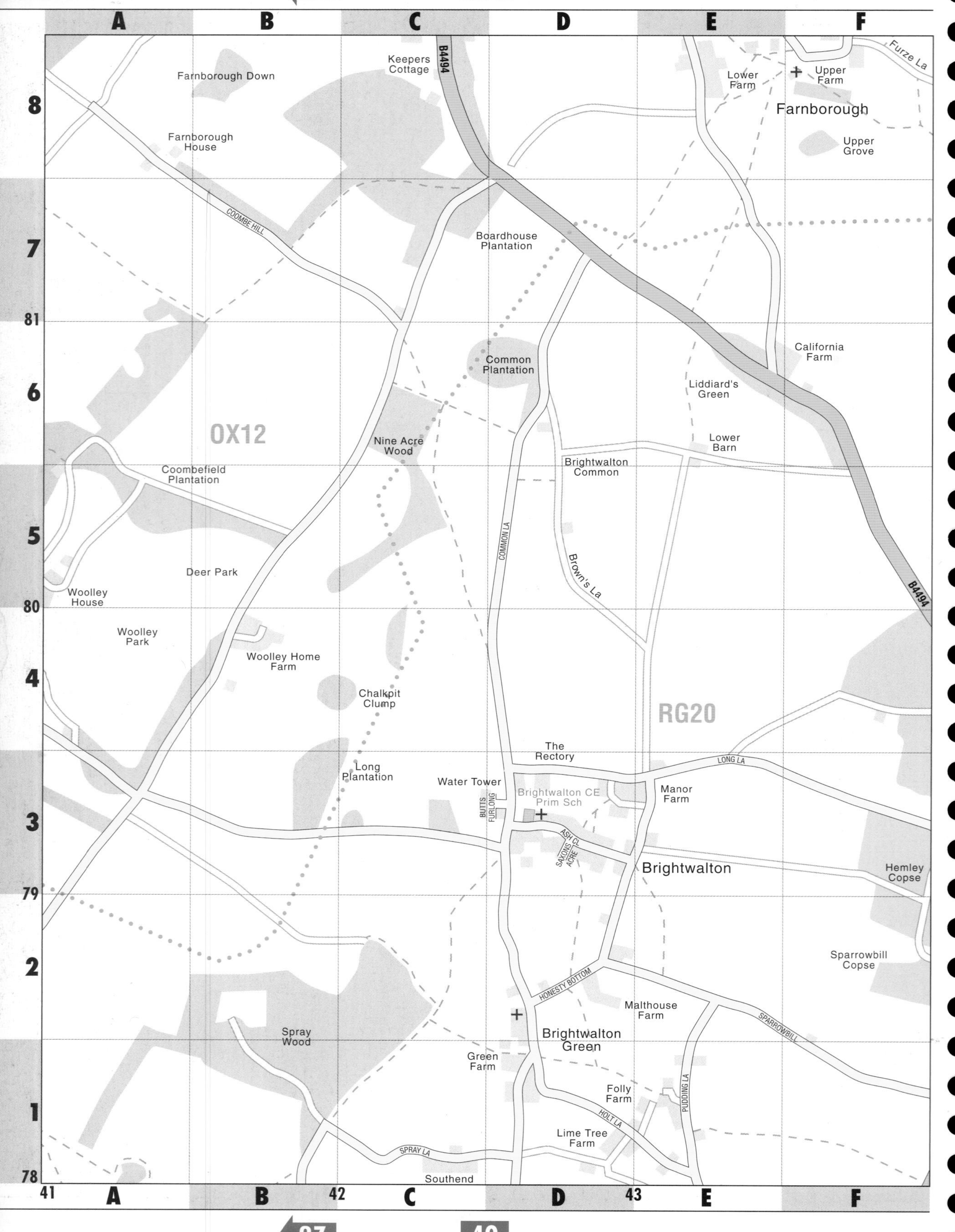
A
B
C
D
E
F
8
7
81
6
5
80
4
3
79
2
1
78
41
42
43
Farnborough Down
Keepers Cottage
B4494
Lower Farm
Upper Farm
Furze La
Farnborough
Upper Grove
Farnborough House
COOMBE HILL
Boardhouse Plantation
Common Plantation
California Farm
Liddiard's Green
OX12
Nine Acre Wood
Lower Barn
Brightwalton Common
Coombefield Plantation
COMMON LA
Brown's La
Deer Park
Woolley House
B4494
Woolley Park
Woolley Home Farm
Chalkpit Clump
RG20
The Rectory
LONG LA
Long Plantation
Water Tower
Brightwalton CE Prim Sch
Manor Farm
BUTTS FURLONG
ASH CL
SAXONS ACRE
Brightwalton
Hemley Copse
Sparrowbill Copse
HONESTY BOTTOM
Malthouse Farm
SPARROWBILL
Spray Wood
Brightwalton Green
Green Farm
Folly Farm
PUDDING LA
HOLT LA
Lime Tree Farm
SPRAY LA
Southend

27
49

9
30

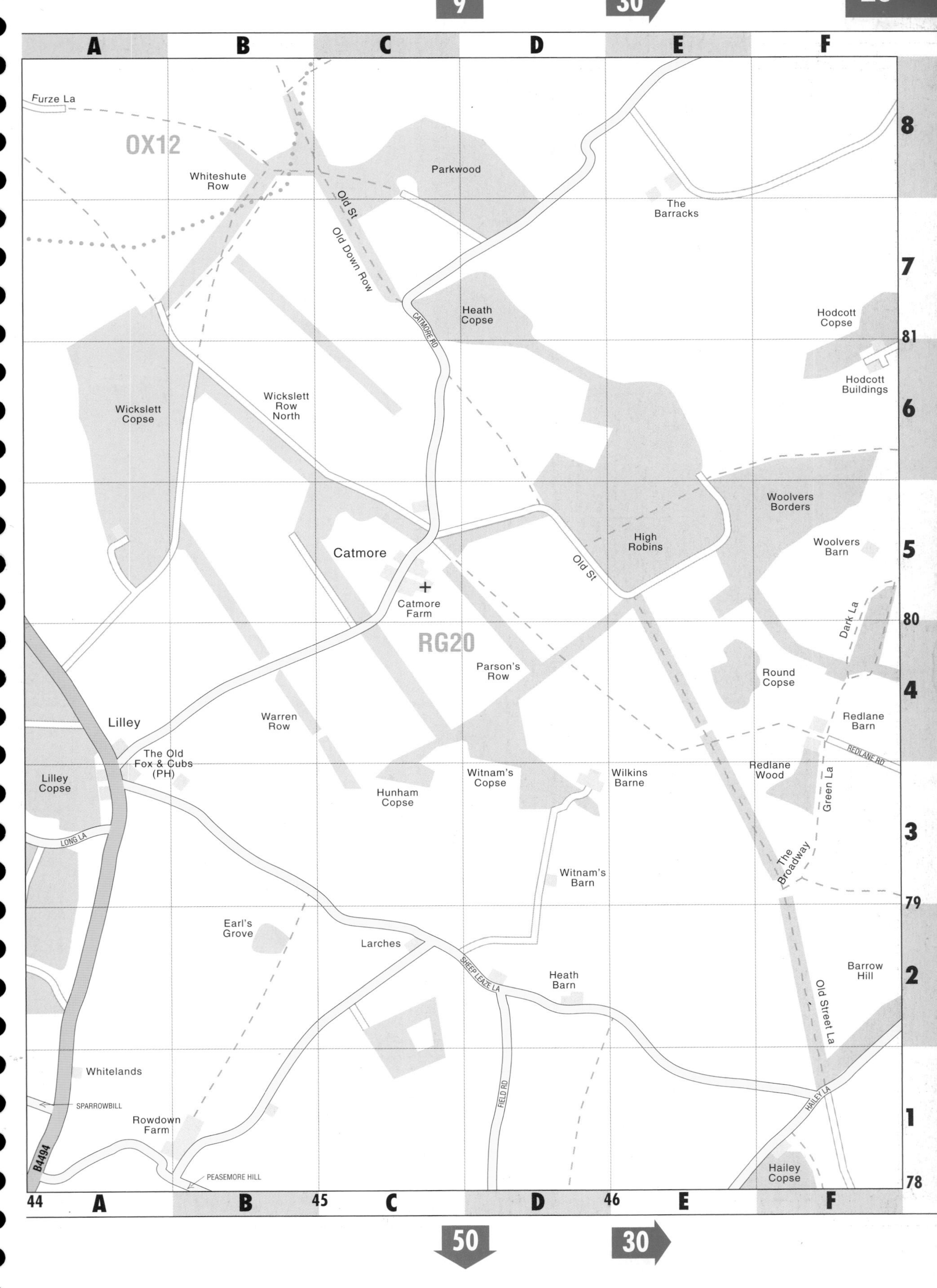
A
B
C
D
E
F
Furze La
OX12
Whiteshute Row
Parkwood
Old St
Old Down Row
The Barracks
Heath Copse
CATMORE RD
Hodcott Copse
Hodcott Buildings
Wickslett Copse
Wickslett Row North
Woolvers Borders
Woolvers Barn
High Robins
Catmore
Catmore Farm
Old St
Dark La
RG20
Parson's Row
Round Copse
Lilley
Warren Row
Redlane Barn
The Old Fox & Cubs (PH)
REDLANE RD
Lilley Copse
Witnam's Copse
Wilkins Barne
Redlane Wood
Hunham Copse
Green La
LONG LA
The Broadway
Witnam's Barn
Earl's Grove
Larches
SHEEP LEAZE LA
Heath Barn
Barrow Hill
Old Street La
FIELD RD
Whitelands
SPARROWBILL
HAILEY LA
Rowdown Farm
B4494
PEASEMORE HILL
Hailey Copse
8
7
81
6
5
80
4
3
79
2
1
78
44
45
46

50
30

29 10

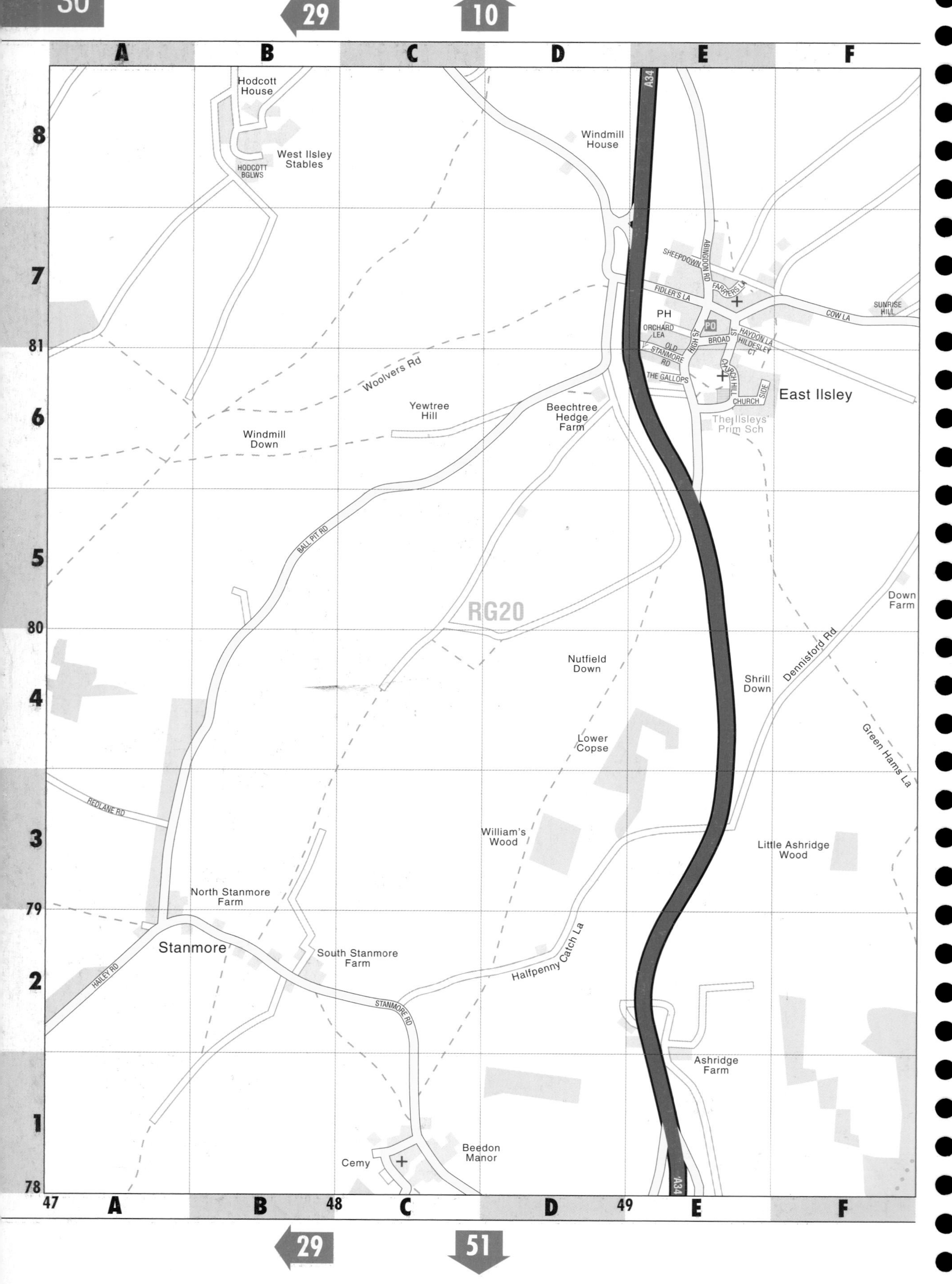
A B C D E F
8
7
81
6
5
80
4
3
79
2
1
78
47 48 49
Hodcott House
West Ilsley Stables
HODCOTT BGLWS
Windmill House
A34
SHEEPDOWN
ABINGDON RD
FARRIERS LA
FIDLER'S LA
PH
PO
ORCHARD LEA
OLD STANMORE RD
HIGH ST
BROAD ST
HAYDON LA
HILDESLEY CT
CHURCH HILL
CHURCH SIDE
THE GALLOPS
COW LA
SUNRISE HILL
East Ilsley
The Ilsleys' Prim Sch
Woolvers Rd
Yewtree Hill
Beechtree Hedge Farm
Windmill Down
BALL PIT RD
RG20
Down Farm
Nutfield Down
Shrill Down
Dennisford Rd
Green Hams La
Lower Copse
REDLANE RD
William's Wood
Little Ashridge Wood
North Stanmore Farm
Stanmore
South Stanmore Farm
HAILEY RD
Halfpenny Catch La
STANMORE RD
Ashridge Farm
Cemy
Beedon Manor

29 51

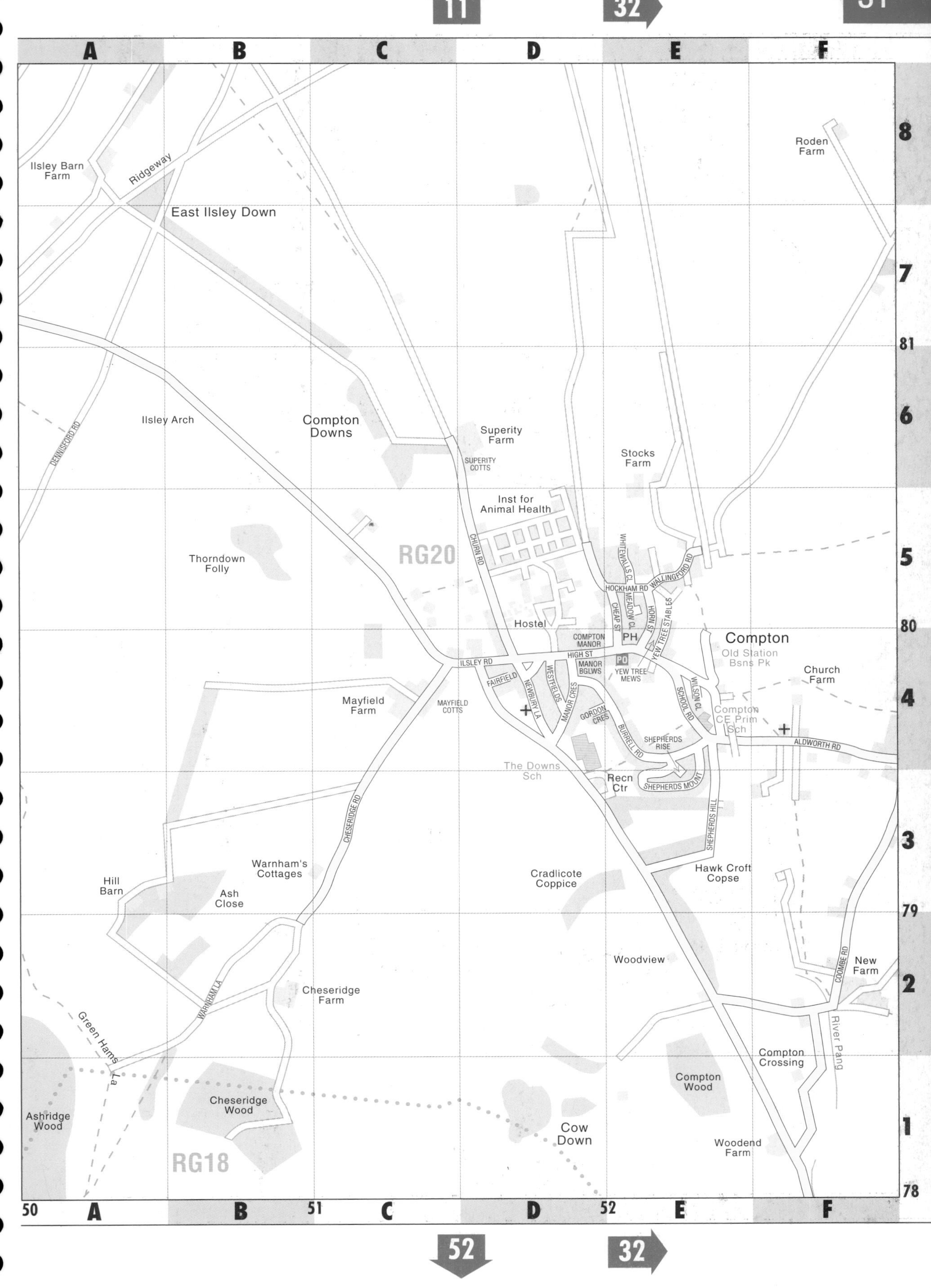

A B C D E F

Ilsley Barn Farm
Ridgeway
East Ilsley Down
DENNISFORD RD
Ilsley Arch
Compton Downs
Superity Farm
SUPERITY COTTS
Roden Farm
Stocks Farm
Inst for Animal Health
Thorndown Folly
RG20
CHURN RD
Hostel
WHITEWALLS CL
HOCKHAM RD
WALLINGFORD RD
HIGH ST
CHEAP ST
YEW TREE STABLES
Compton
Old Station Bsns Pk
PH
Compton Manor
MANOR BGLWS
PO
YEW TREE MEWS
Church Farm
Mayfield Farm
Mayfield Cotts
ILSLEY RD
FAIRFIELD
NEWBURY LA
WESTHILLS
MANOR CRES
GORDON CRES
SCHOOL RD
WILSON CL
Compton CE Prim Sch
ALDWORTH RD
The Downs Sch
BURRELL RD
SHEPHERDS RISE
Recn Ctr
SHEPHERDS MOUNT
SHEPHERDS HILL
CHESERIDGE RD
Warnham's Cottages
Ash Close
Hill Barn
Cradlicote Coppice
Hawk Croft Copse
COOMBE RD
New Farm
River Pang
WARNHAM LA
Cheseridge Farm
Green Hams La
Woodview
Compton Crossing
Ashridge Wood
Cheseridge Wood
RG18
Cow Down
Compton Wood
Woodend Farm

8
7
81
6
5
80
4
79
3
2
1
78

50   51   52
A B C D E F

A B C D E F

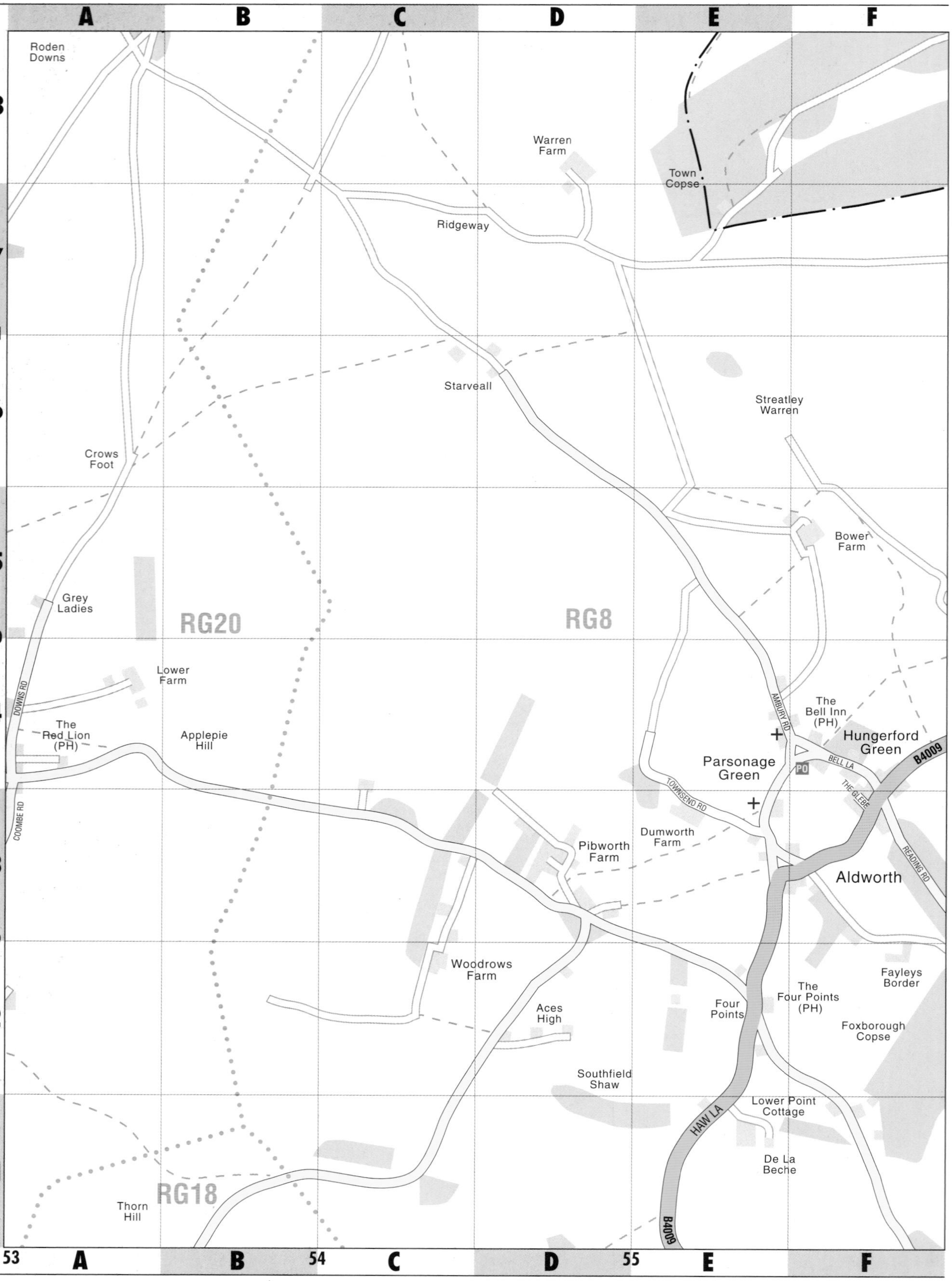

8

Roden
Downs

Warren
Farm

Town
Copse

7

Ridgeway

81

Starveall

Streatley
Warren

6

Crows
Foot

5

Grey
Ladies

Bower
Farm

RG20

RG8

80

Lower
Farm

4

DOWNS RD

The
Red Lion
(PH)

Applepie
Hill

AMBURY RD

The
Bell Inn
(PH)

Hungerford
Green

B4009

Parsonage
Green

BELL LA

PO

THE GLEBE

COOMBE RD

TOWNSEND RD

READING RD

3

Pibworth
Farm

Dumworth
Farm

Aldworth

79

Woodrows
Farm

Fayleys
Border

2

Aces
High

Four
Points

The
Four Points
(PH)

Foxborough
Copse

Southfield
Shaw

Lower Point
Cottage

HAW LA

1

RG18

Thorn
Hill

De La
Beche

B4009

78

53 A B 54 C D 55 E F

13
34

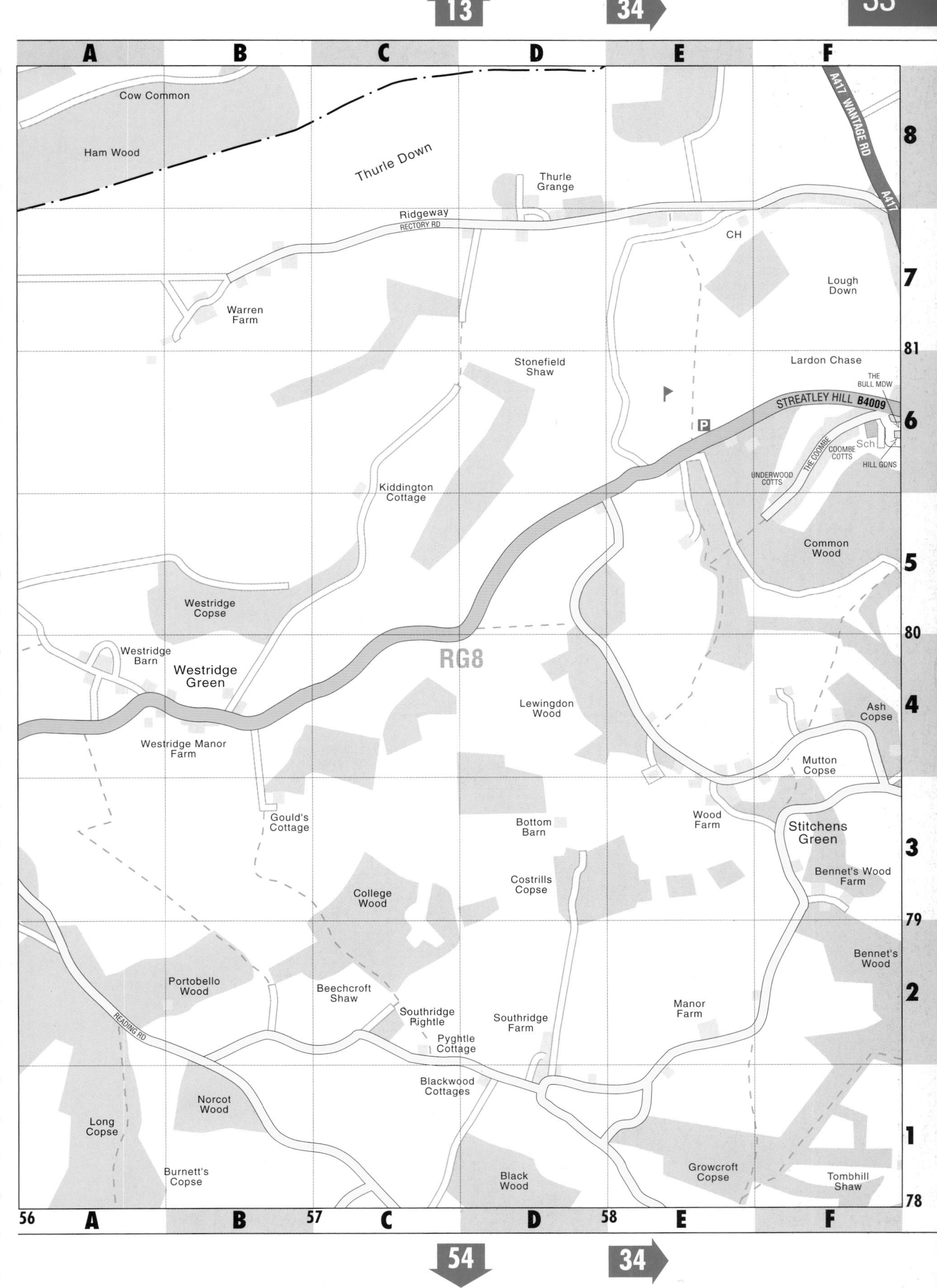
A
B
C
D
E
F
Cow Common
Ham Wood
Thurle Down
Thurle Grange
A417 WANTAGE RD
A417
8
Ridgeway
RECTORY RD
CH
7
Lough Down
Warren Farm
81
Stonefield Shaw
Lardon Chase
THE BULL MDW
STREATLEY HILL B4009
6
Sch
COOMBE COTTS
THE COOMBE
HILL GDNS
UNDERWOOD COTTS
Kiddington Cottage
Common Wood
5
Westridge Copse
80
Westridge Barn
Westridge Green
RG8
Lewingdon Wood
Ash Copse
4
Westridge Manor Farm
Mutton Copse
Gould's Cottage
Bottom Barn
Wood Farm
Stitchens Green
3
Costrills Copse
Bennet's Wood Farm
College Wood
79
Bennet's Wood
Portobello Wood
Beechcroft Shaw
Southridge Pightle
Southridge Farm
Manor Farm
2
READING RD
Pyghtle Cottage
Blackwood Cottages
Norcot Wood
Long Copse
1
Burnett's Copse
Black Wood
Growcroft Copse
Tombhill Shaw
78
56
57
58

54
34

33
14

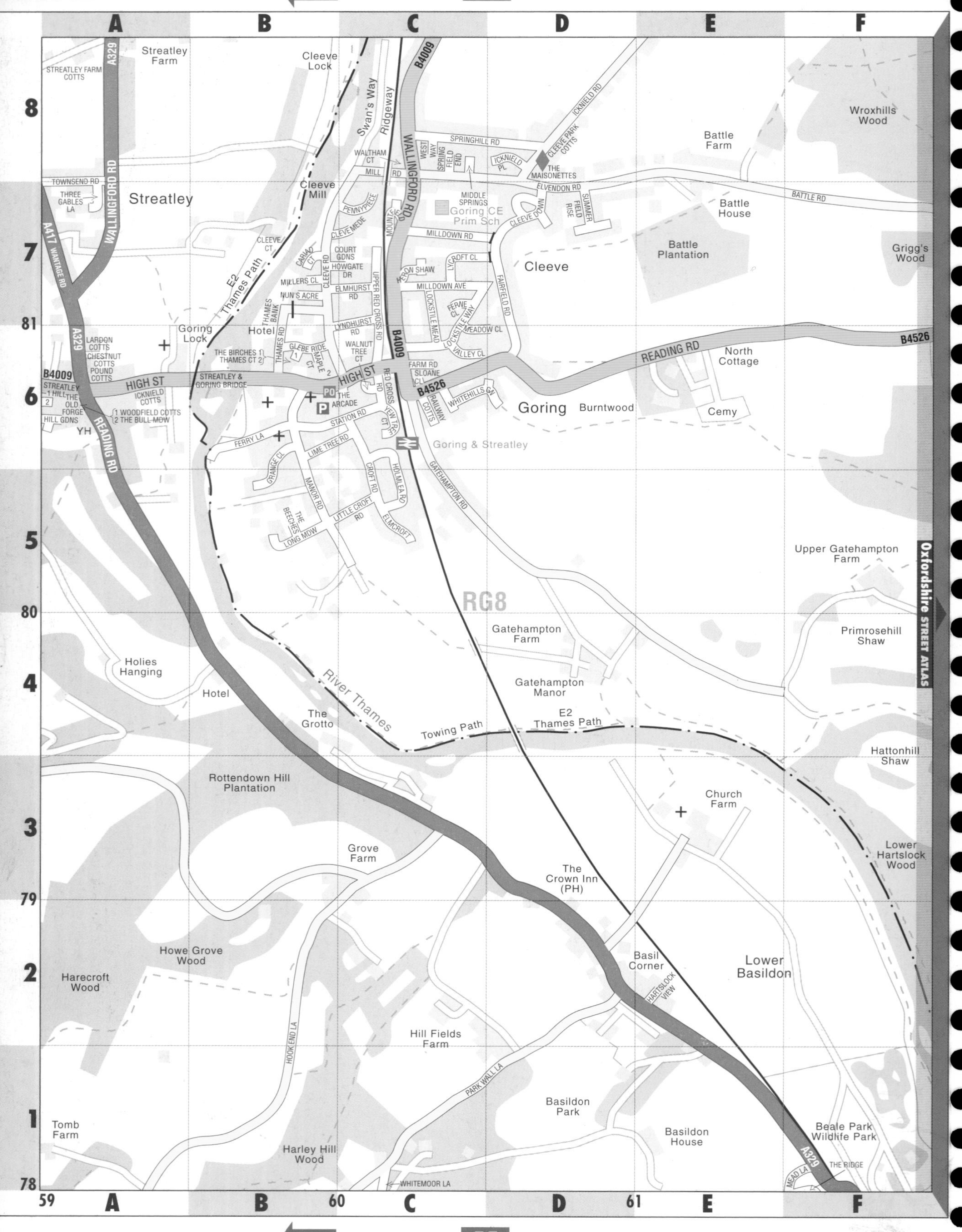
A
B
C
D
E
F
8
7
81
6
5
80
4
3
79
2
1
78
59
60
61
Streatley Farm
STREATLEY FARM COTTS
A329
Cleeve Lock
B4009
Swan's Way
Ridgeway
ICKNIELD RD
Wroxhills Wood
Battle Farm
SPRINGHILL RD
CLEEVE PARK COTTS
WALTHAM CT
WALLINGFORD RD
THE MAISONETTES
TOWNSEND RD
THREE GABLES LA
Streatley
Cleeve Mill
MIDDLE SPRINGS
ELVENDON RD
BATTLE RD
Battle House
Goring CE Prim Sch
CLEEVE DOWN
PENNYPIECE
CLEEVE MEDE
MILLDOWN RD
SUMMERFIELD RISE
A417 WANTAGE RD
CLEEVE CT
COURT GDNS
HOWGATE DR
Battle Plantation
Grigg's Wood
E2 Thames Path
LYCROFT CL
Cleeve
MILLERS CL
HERON SHAW
MILLDOWN AVE
NUN'S ACRE
ELMHURST RD
LOCKSTILE MEAD
FERNE CL
FAIRFIELD RD
UPPER RED CROSS RD
Goring Lock
THAMES BANK
Hotel
LYNDHURST RD
LOCKSTILE WAY
MEADOW CL
LARDON COTTS
CHESTNUT COTTS
POUND COTTS
THE BIRCHES
THAMES CT
GLEBE RIDE
WALNUT TREE CT
VALLEY CL
READING RD
North Cottage
B4526
B4009
HIGH ST
STREATLEY & GORING BRIDGE
HIGH ST
FARM RD
SLOANE CL
B4526
WHITEHILLS GN
STREATLEY HILL
THE OLD FORGE
ICKNIELD COTTS
THE ARCADE
PO
P
RED CROSS RD
RAILWAY COTTS
Goring
Burntwood
Cemy
HILL GDNS
1 WOODFIELD COTTS
2 THE BULL MDW
YH
READING RD
STATION RD
YEW TREE CT
FERRY LA
LIME TREE RD
Goring & Streatley
GRANGE CL
CROFT RD
HOLMLEA RD
GATEHAMPTON RD
MANOR RD
THE BEECHES
LONG MDW
LITTLE CROFT RD
ELMCROFT
Upper Gatehampton Farm
RG8
Oxfordshire STREET ATLAS
Gatehampton Farm
Primrosehill Shaw
Holies Hanging
Hotel
River Thames
Gatehampton Manor
The Grotto
Towing Path
E2 Thames Path
Hattonhill Shaw
Rottendown Hill Plantation
Church Farm
Lower Hartslock Wood
Grove Farm
The Crown Inn (PH)
Howe Grove Wood
Basil Corner
Lower Basildon
Harecroft Wood
HARTSLOCK VIEW
HOOK END LA
Hill Fields Farm
PARK WALL LA
Basildon Park
Tomb Farm
Basildon House
Beale Park Wildlife Park
Harley Hill Wood
A329
THE RIDGE
MEAD LA
WHITEMOOR LA

33
55

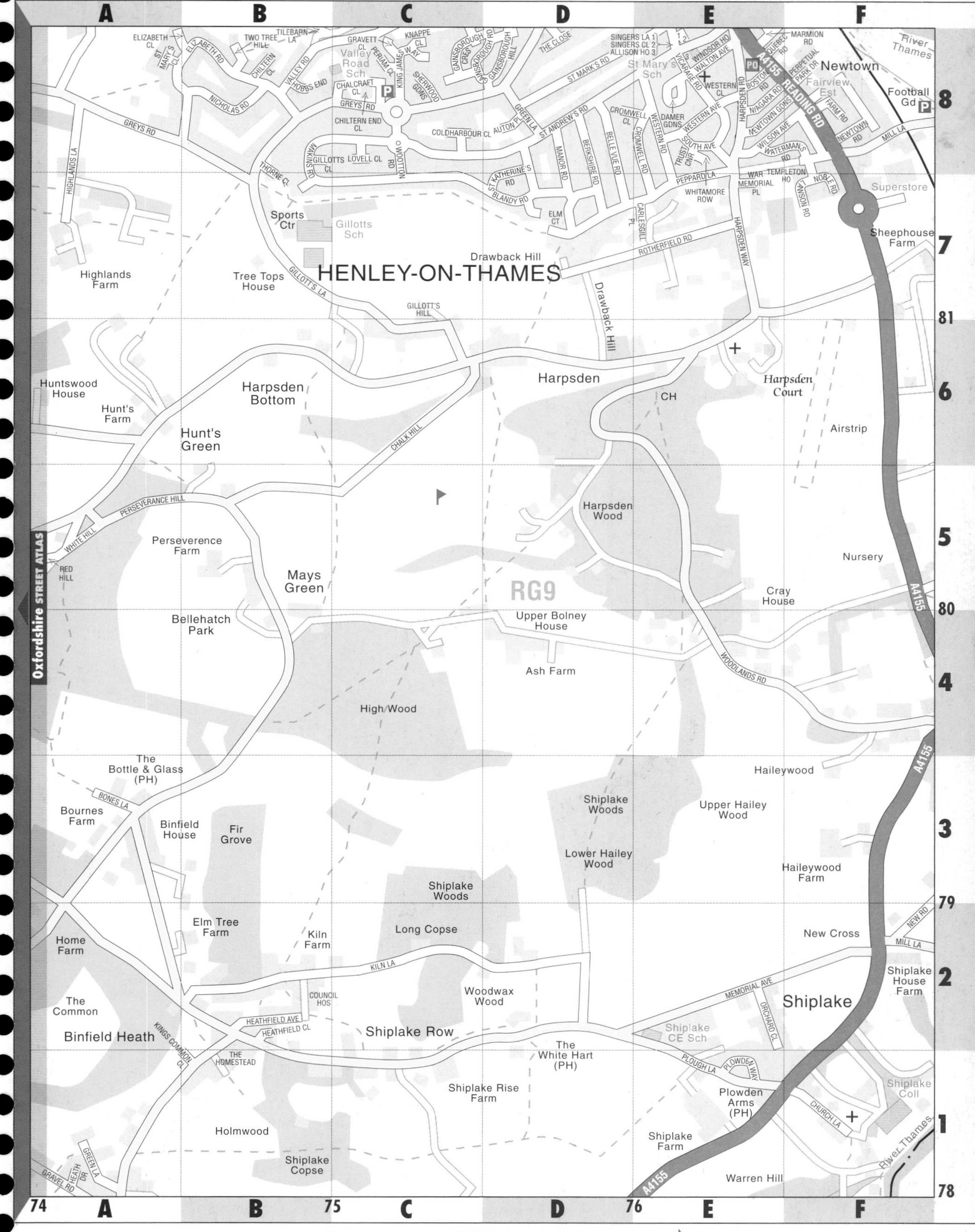

HENLEY-ON-THAMES

Highlands Farm

Huntswood House

Hunt's Farm

Hunt's Green

Harpsden Bottom

Tree Tops House

Drawback Hill

Harpsden

Harpsden Court

Airstrip

Perseverence Farm

Harpsden Wood

Nursery

Mays Green

RG9

Cray House

Bellehatch Park

Upper Bolney House

Ash Farm

High Wood

Haileywood

The Bottle & Glass (PH)

Bournes Farm

Binfield House

Fir Grove

Shiplake Woods

Upper Hailey Wood

Lower Hailey Wood

Haileywood Farm

Shiplake Woods

New Cross

Elm Tree Farm

Kiln Farm

Long Copse

Shiplake House Farm

Home Farm

Woodwax Wood

Shiplake

The Common

Binfield Heath

Shiplake Row

Shiplake CE Sch

Shiplake Coll

The White Hart (PH)

Plowden Arms (PH)

Shiplake Rise Farm

Holmwood

Shiplake Farm

Warren Hill

Shiplake Copse

Sports Ctr

Gillotts Sch

Valley Road Sch

St Mary's Sch

Newtown

Fairview Est

Football Gd

Superstore

Sheephouse Farm

River Thames

A4155 READING RD

A4155

Oxfordshire STREET ATLAS

35
16

A B C D E F

Mill Bank
MARSH MILLS
MILL LA
WARGRAVE RD
A321
Happy Valley
Temple Combe
Temple Coombe Farm
Hatchgate House
White Cottages
Cockpole Green
ASHLEY HILL PL
GOULDERS COTTS
PH
WARREN ROW RD
Kenton's Corner Cottage
The Druids Temple
Passage Grave
Thames Path
Sheephouse Farm
HATCH GATE LA
Hatchgate Farm
KENTON'S LA
Worley's Farm
Crazies Hill CE Prim Sch
Crazies Hill
Lower Bolney Farm
Penny's La
Hennerton House
Fairman's Wood
Bolney Court
CH
Hennerton Backwater
RG9
BOLNEY LA
BOLNEY RD
Kilnpits
Wargrave Marsh
Gibstroude Farm
Maplecroft
Highfield Farm
Lower Rivermead Farm
RG10
Spring Meadows Bsns Ctr
MANOR WOOD GATE
NORTHFIELD AVE
NURSERY CL
BRAMPTON CHASE
NORTHFIELD RD
LC
BASMORE LA
River Thames
A4155
BOLNEY TREVOR DR
QUARRY LA
LASHBROOK RD
STATION RD
Shiplake
WILLOW LA
Lower Shiplake
BROCKS WAY
OAKS RD
LOWES CL
Lashbrook
Towing Path
The Woodclyffes
THE CHESTNUTS
BADGERS WLK
THE CRESCENT
LASHBROOK MEAD
WESTFIELD CRES
BASKERVILLE LA
CROWSLEY RD
NEW RD
MILL RD
Lash Brook
Wargrave Manor
White Gables
Lashbrook House
THE SPUR
THE COPSE
RIDGEWAY
BLAKES RD
DUNNOCK WAY
NEWALLS RISE
RYECROFT CL
FIDLERS WLK
HIGHFIELD PK
HANOVER GDNS
FIELD END
THE BOTHY
THE VINERY
WARGRAVE HILL
THE WALLED GDN
CHILTERN MANOR
HILL LANDS
MILL LA
QUEEN'S COTTS
PO
HIGH ST
BACKSIDEANS
DARK LA
LANGHAMS WAY
PURFIELD DR
VICTORIA RD
RECREATION RD
EAST VIEW RD
EAST VIEW CL
Upper Wargrave
ELIZABETH CT
AUTUMN WLK
McCRAE'S WLK
FERRY LA
CHURCH ST
Liby
B477
SCHOOL LA
HAMILTON RD
EMMA LA
CLIFTON RISE
Thames Path
WATERMANS WAY
SPRING WLK
BAYLISS RD
BRAYBROOKE RD
BRAYBROOKE GDNS
SILVERDALE RD
BEVERLEY GDNS
SCHOOL HILL
STATION RD
Wargrave
Cemy
Robert Piggott CE Inf Sch
MARKET PL
Phillimore's Island
Borough Lake
LODDON DR
River Loddon
Wargrave
Robert Piggott CE Jun Sch
MUMBERY HILL
B477

8 7 81 6 5 80 4 3 79 2 1 78
77 78 79

A B C D E F

35
61

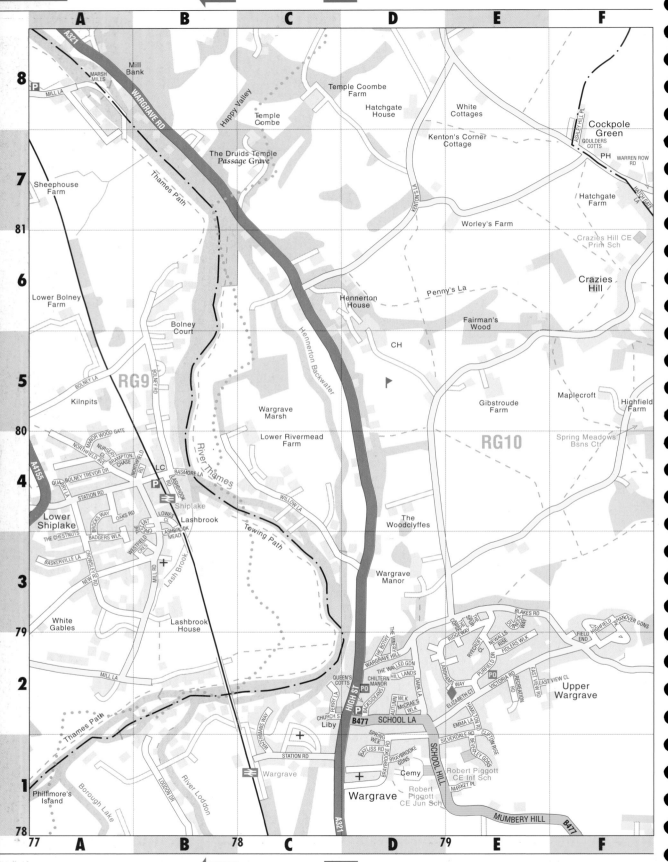

17
38

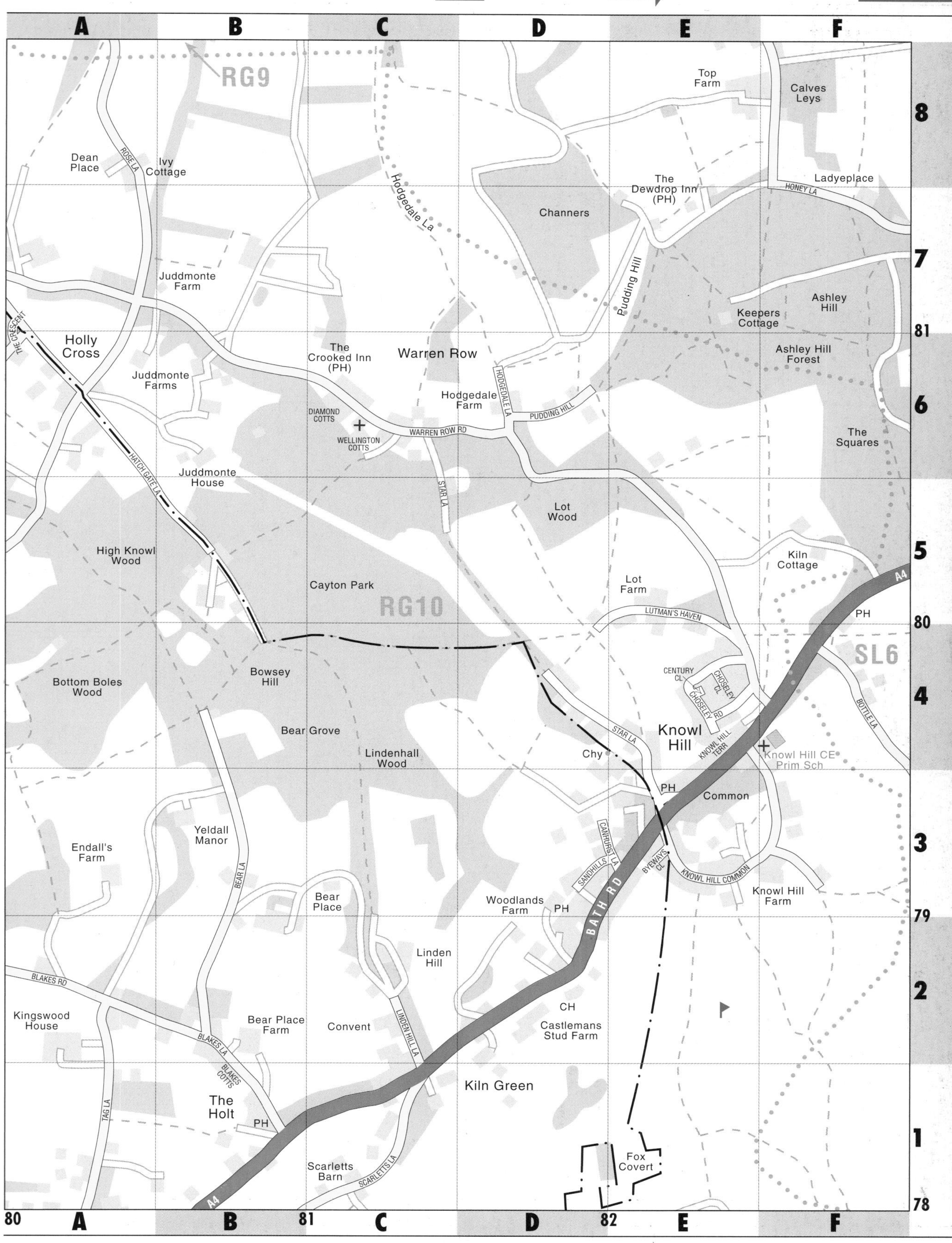
A
B
C
D
E
F
RG9
Top Farm
Calves Leys
Dean Place
ROSE LA
Ivy Cottage
Hodgedale La
The Dewdrop Inn (PH)
Ladyeplace
HONEY LA
Channers
Pudding Hill
Juddmonte Farm
Ashley Hill
Keepers Cottage
THE CRESCENT
Holly Cross
The Crooked Inn (PH)
Warren Row
Ashley Hill Forest
Juddmonte Farms
HODGEDALE LA
Hodgedale Farm
PUDDING HILL
DIAMOND COTTS
WELLINGTON COTTS
WARREN ROW RD
The Squares
HATCH GATE LA
Juddmonte House
STAR LA
Lot Wood
High Knowl Wood
Kiln Cottage
Cayton Park
Lot Farm
RG10
A4
PH
LUTMAN'S HAVEN
SL6
Bottom Boles Wood
Bowsey Hill
CENTURY CL
CHOSELEY CL
CHOSELEY RD
BOTTLE LA
Bear Grove
Lindenhall Wood
STAR LA
Knowl Hill
KNOWL HILL TERR
Chy
Knowl Hill CE Prim Sch
PH
Common
Yeldall Manor
Endall's Farm
CANHURST LA
BYEWAYS CL
KNOWL HILL COMMON
SANDHILLS
BEAR LA
Bear Place
Knowl Hill Farm
Woodlands Farm
PH
BATH RD
Linden Hill
BLAKES RD
CH
Kingswood House
Bear Place Farm
Convent
Castlemans Stud Farm
BLAKES LA
LINDEN HILL LA
BLAKES COTTS
Kiln Green
The Holt
TAG LA
PH
Fox Covert
Scarletts Barn
SCARLETTS LA
A4
8
7
81
6
5
80
4
3
79
2
1
78
80
81
82

62
38

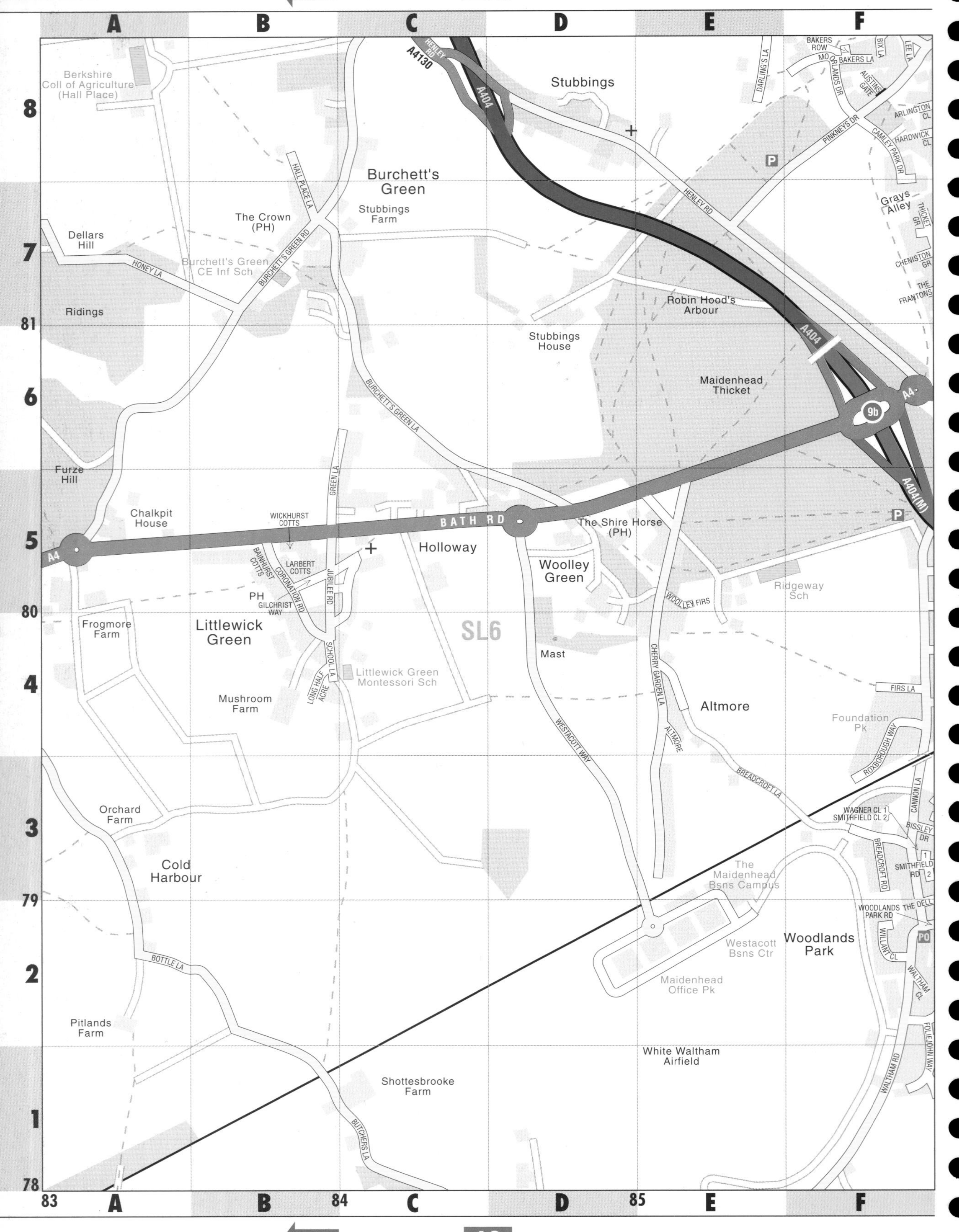
A
B
C
D
E
F
8
7
81
6
5
80
4
3
79
2
1
78
83
84
85
Berkshire Coll of Agriculture (Hall Place)
Stubbings
Burchett's Green
The Crown (PH)
Stubbings Farm
Dellars Hill
Burchett's Green CE Inf Sch
Ridings
Robin Hood's Arbour
Stubbings House
Maidenhead Thicket
Grays Alley
Furze Hill
Chalkpit House
The Shire Horse (PH)
Holloway
Woolley Green
Ridgeway Sch
Frogmore Farm
Littlewick Green
SL6
Mast
Mushroom Farm
Littlewick Green Montessori Sch
Altmore
Foundation Pk
Orchard Farm
Cold Harbour
The Maidenhead Bsns Campus
Westacott Bsns Ctr
Woodlands Park
Maidenhead Office Pk
Pitlands Farm
White Waltham Airfield
Shottesbrooke Farm
A4
A4130
A404
A404(M)
HENLEY RD
BATH RD
HALL PLACE LA
BURCHETT'S GREEN RD
BURCHETT'S GREEN LA
HONEY LA
GREEN LA
WICKHURST COTTS
BAINHURST COTTS
LARBERT COTTS
CORONATION RD
JUBILEE RD
GILCHRIST WAY
PH
SCHOOL LA
LONG HALF ACRE
WESTACOTT WAY
CHERRY GARDEN LA
ALTMORE
WOOLLEY FIRS
FIRS LA
BREADCROFT LA
ROXBOROUGH WAY
BOTTLE LA
BUTCHERS LA
DARLING'S LA
BAKERS ROW
BAKERS LA
MOORLANDS DR
BIX LA
LEE LA
AUSTINS GATE
PINKNEYS DR
ARLINGTON CL
CAMLEY PARK DR
HARDWICK CL
THICKET GR
CHENISTON GR
THE FRANTONS
CANNON LA
WAGNER CL 1
SMITHFIELD CL 2
BISSLEY DR
BREADCROFT RD
SMITHFIELD RD
WOODLANDS PARK RD
THE DELL
WILLANT CL
WALTHAM CL
WALTHAM RD
FOLIEJOHN WAY
PO
P
9b

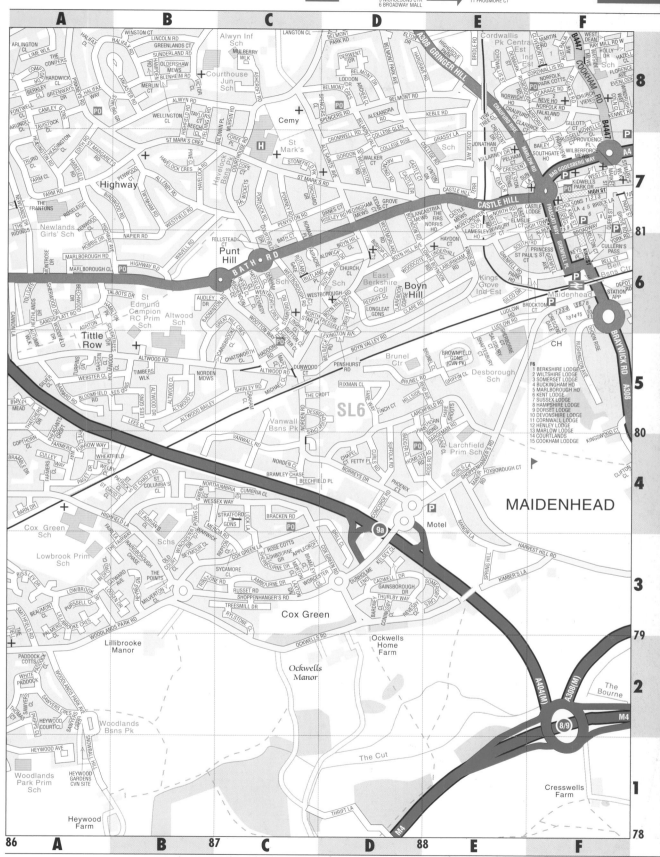

19

40

F7
1 HIGH ST MALL
2 WHITE HART RD
3 QUEENS WLK MALL
4 KINGS WLK
5 NICHOLSONS CTR
6 BROADWAY MALL

F7
7 BROCK LA MALL
8 QUEEN'S LA
9 REGENT CT
10 OLD POST OFFICE LA
11 FROGMORE CT

F8
1 CORDWALLIS EST
2 SUFFOLK CT

39

MAIDENHEAD

SL6

39
20

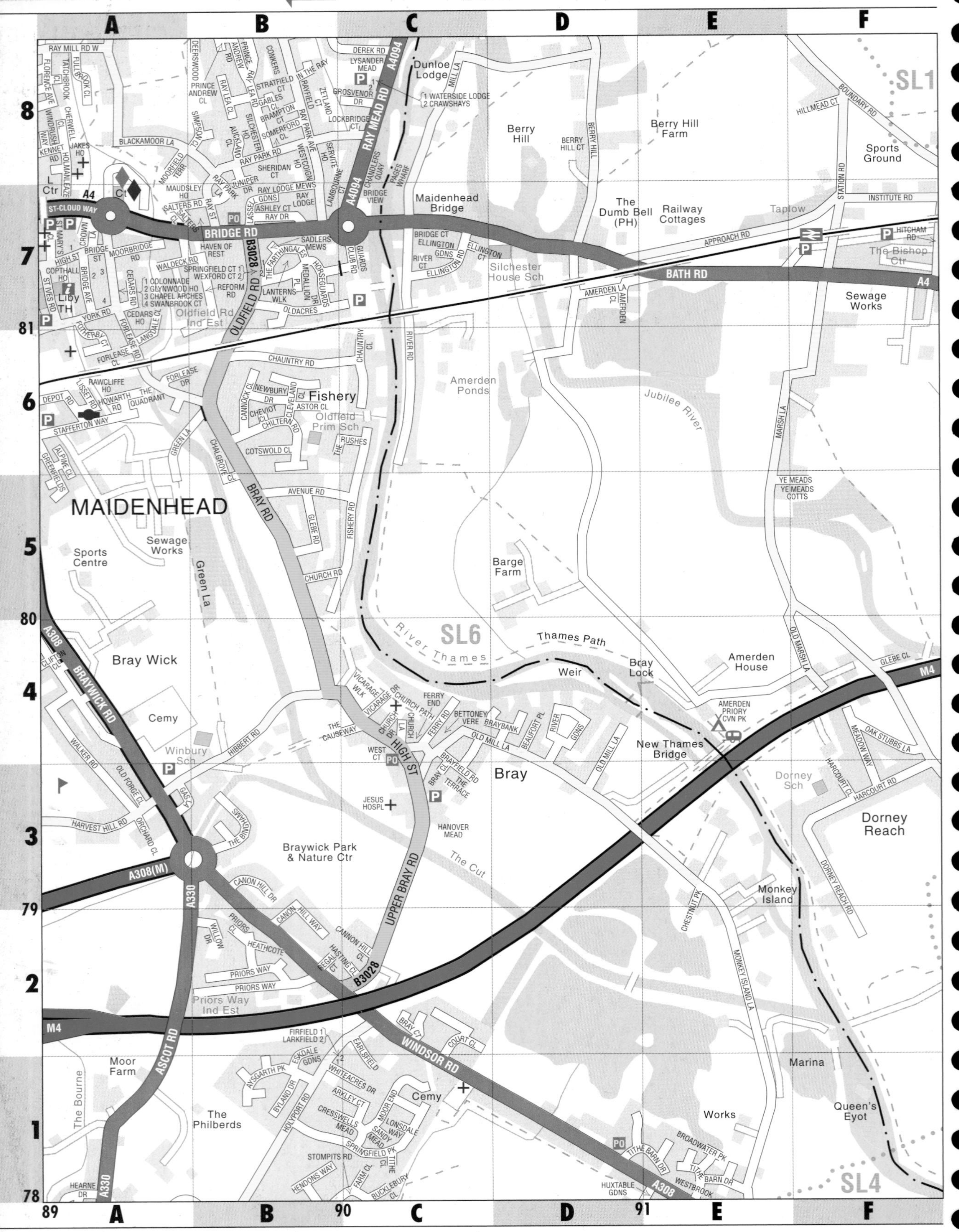
A
B
C
D
E
F
8
7
81
6
5
80
4
3
79
2
1
78
89
90
91
RAY MILL RD W
FLORENCE AVE
TATCHBROOK CL
FULLBROOK CL
CROWN LA
WINDRUSH WAY
CHERWELL CL
KENNET RD
HOLMANLEAZE
JAKES HO
BLACKAMOOR LA
L Ctr
Ct
A4
ST-CLOUD WAY
MOORFIELD TERR
MAUDSLEY HO
SALTERS RD
RAY PARK LA
RAY ST
DERWOOD
ANDREW RD
PRINCE ANDREW CL
SIMPSON CL
RAY LEA CL
RAY LEA RD
PRINCE
CONKERS
STRATFIELD CT
GABLES CL
BRAMPTON CT
SOMERFORD CL
AUCKLAND CL
SILCHESTER HO
IN THE RAY
RAYFIELD
ZETLAND CT
RAY PARK AVE
WESTCOIGN HO
SERUITE HO
LAMBOURNE CT
RAY PARK RD
SHERIDAN CT
JUNIPER DR
RAY LODGE MEWS
RAY LODGE
GDNS
ASHLEY CT
RAY DR
DEREK RD
LYSANDER MEAD
GROSVENOR DR
LOCKBRIDGE CT
RAY MEAD RD
A4094
CHANDLERS QUAY
PAGES WHARF
BRIDGE VIEW
1 WATERSIDE LODGE
2 CRAWSHAYS
Dunloe Lodge
MILL LA
Maidenhead Bridge
BRIDGE RD
B3028
HAVEN OF REST
SADLERS MEWS
THE FARTHINGALES
HORSEGUARDS DR
MEDALLION PL
GUARDS CLUB RD
LANTERNS WLK
OLDACRES
SPRINGFIELD CT 1
WEXFORD CT 2
REFORM RD
WALDECK RD
1 COLONNADE
2 GLYNWOOD HO
3 CHAPEL ARCHES
4 SWANBROOK CT
Oldfield Rd Ind Est
OLDFIELD RD
MOORBRIDGE RD
BRIDGE ST
BRIDGE AVE
ST MARY'S CL
HIGH ST
COPTHALL HO
ST IVES RD
Liby
TH
YORK RD
CEDARS RD
CEDARS HO
FOTHERBY CT
FORLEASE RD
FORLEASE CL
LANGDALE CL
BRIDGE CT
ELLINGTON GDNS
RIVER CT
ELLINGTON RD
ELLINGTON CT
Silchester House Sch
Berry Hill
BERRY HILL CT
BERRY HILL
Berry Hill Farm
The Dumb Bell (PH)
Railway Cottages
Taplow
APPROACH RD
BATH RD
A4
AMERDEN LA
AMERDEN CL
SL1
BOUNDARY RD
HILLMEAD CT
Sports Ground
STATION RD
INSTITUTE RD
HITCHAM RD
The Bishop Ctr
Sewage Works
CHAUNTRY RD
CHAUNTRY CL
RIVER RD
RAWCLIFFE HO
LISSET RD
HOWARTH RD
THE QUADRANT
FORLEASE DR
DEPOT RD
STAFFERTON WAY
NEWBURY DR
CANNOCK CL
CLEVELAND CL
CHEVIOT CL
CHILTERN RD
ASTOR CL
Fishery
Oldfield Prim Sch
THE RUSHES
COTSWOLD CL
Amerden Ponds
Jubilee River
MARSH LA
GREEN LA
CHALGROVE CL
ALPINE CL
GREENFIELDS
MAIDENHEAD
BRAY RD
AVENUE RD
GLEBE RD
FISHERY RD
YE MEADS
YE MEADS COTTS
Sports Centre
Sewage Works
Green La
Barge Farm
CHURCH RD
A308
CLIFTON CL
BRAYWICK RD
Bray Wick
SL6
River Thames
Thames Path
Weir
Bray Lock
Amerden House
OLD MARSH LA
GLEBE CL
M4
VICARAGE WLK
VICARAGE DR
CHURCH PATH
CHURCH LA
CHURCH DR
FERRY END
FERRY RD
BETTONEY VERE
BRAYBANK
BEAUFORT PL
RIVER GDNS
OLD MILL LA
AMERDEN PRIORY CVN PK
New Thames Bridge
OAK STUBBS LA
MEADOW WAY
Cemy
THE CAUSEWAY
HIBBERT RD
WEST CT
PO
HIGH ST
BRAYFIELD RD
BRAY CL
THE TERRACE
Bray
Dorney Sch
HARCOURT CL
HARCOURT RD
Winbury Sch
WALKER RD
OLD FORGE CL
GAS LA
THE BRAMBLES
JESUS HOSPL
HANOVER MEAD
Dorney Reach
HARVEST HILL RD
ORCHARD CL
THE BINGHAMS
Braywick Park & Nature Ctr
The Cut
A308(M)
A330
CANON HILL DR
CANON HILL WAY
UPPER BRAY RD
DORNEY REACH RD
CHESTNUT PK
Monkey Island
PRIORS CL
WILLOW DR
HEATHCOTE
CANNON HILL CL
HASTING CL
REGAL CT
B3028
PRIORS WAY
MONKEY ISLAND LA
Priors Way Ind Est
M4
FIRFIELD 1
LARKFIELD 2
BRAY CT
COURT CL
WINDSOR RD
Moor Farm
ASCOT RD
ESKDALE GDNS
EARLSFIELD
AYSGARTH PK
WHITEACRES DR
BYLAND DR
ARKLEY CT
HOLYPORT RD
CRESSWELLS MEAD
MOOR END
LONSDALE WAY
SANDY MEAD
Cemy
Marina
The Bourne
The Philberds
Works
Queen's Eyot
SPRINGFIELD PK
TITHE CL
STOMPITS RD
HENDONS WAY
FARM CL
BUCKLEBURY CL
BROADWATER PK
TITHE BARN DR
TITHE BARN DR
WESTBROOK
HUXTABLE GDNS
A308
HEARNE DR
A330
SL4

39
65

21
42

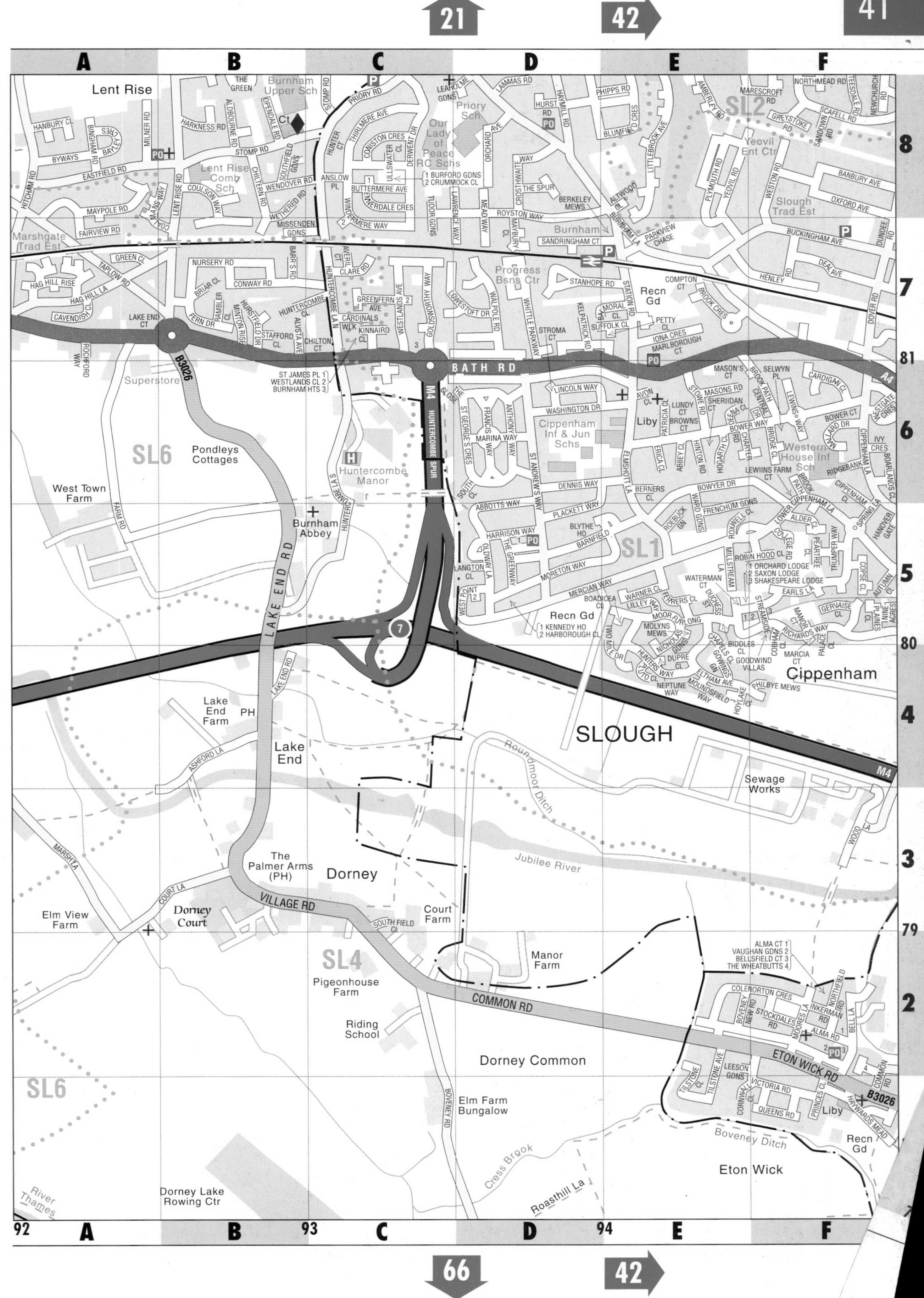
A
B
C
D
E
F
8
7
81
6
5
80
4
3
79
2
92
93
94
Lent Rise
Burnham Upper Sch
Priory Sch
Our Lady of Peace RC Schs
SL2
Yeovil Ent Ctr
Lent Rise Comb Sch
Slough Trad Est
Marshgate Trad Est
Burnham
Progress Bsns Ctr
Recn Gd
BATH RD
A4
B3026
M4
HUNTERCOMBE SPUR
Superstore
SL6
Pondleys Cottages
West Town Farm
Huntercombe Manor
Burnham Abbey
Cippenham Inf & Jun Schs
Liby
Western House Inf Sch
SL1
Recn Gd
LAKE END RD
Lake End Farm
PH
Lake End
SLOUGH
Cippenham
Roundmoor Ditch
Sewage Works
Jubilee River
The Palmer Arms (PH)
Dorney
VILLAGE RD
Elm View Farm
Dorney Court
Court Farm
SL4
Pigeonhouse Farm
Manor Farm
COMMON RD
Riding School
Dorney Common
ETON WICK RD
SL6
Elm Farm Bungalow
BOVENEY RD
Cress Brook
Boveney Ditch
Roasthill La
Eton Wick
Recn Gd
River Thames
Dorney Lake Rowing Ctr

66
42

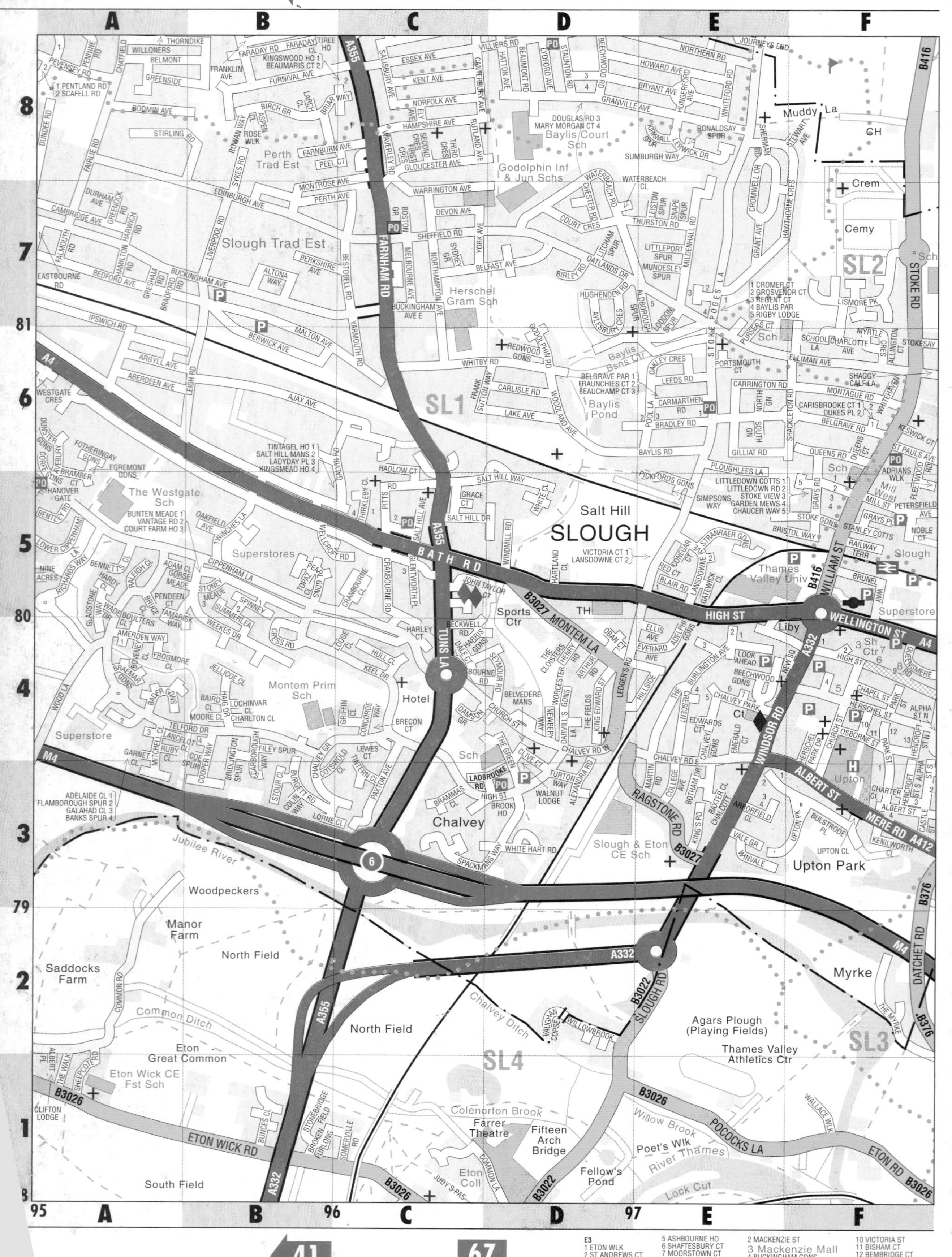

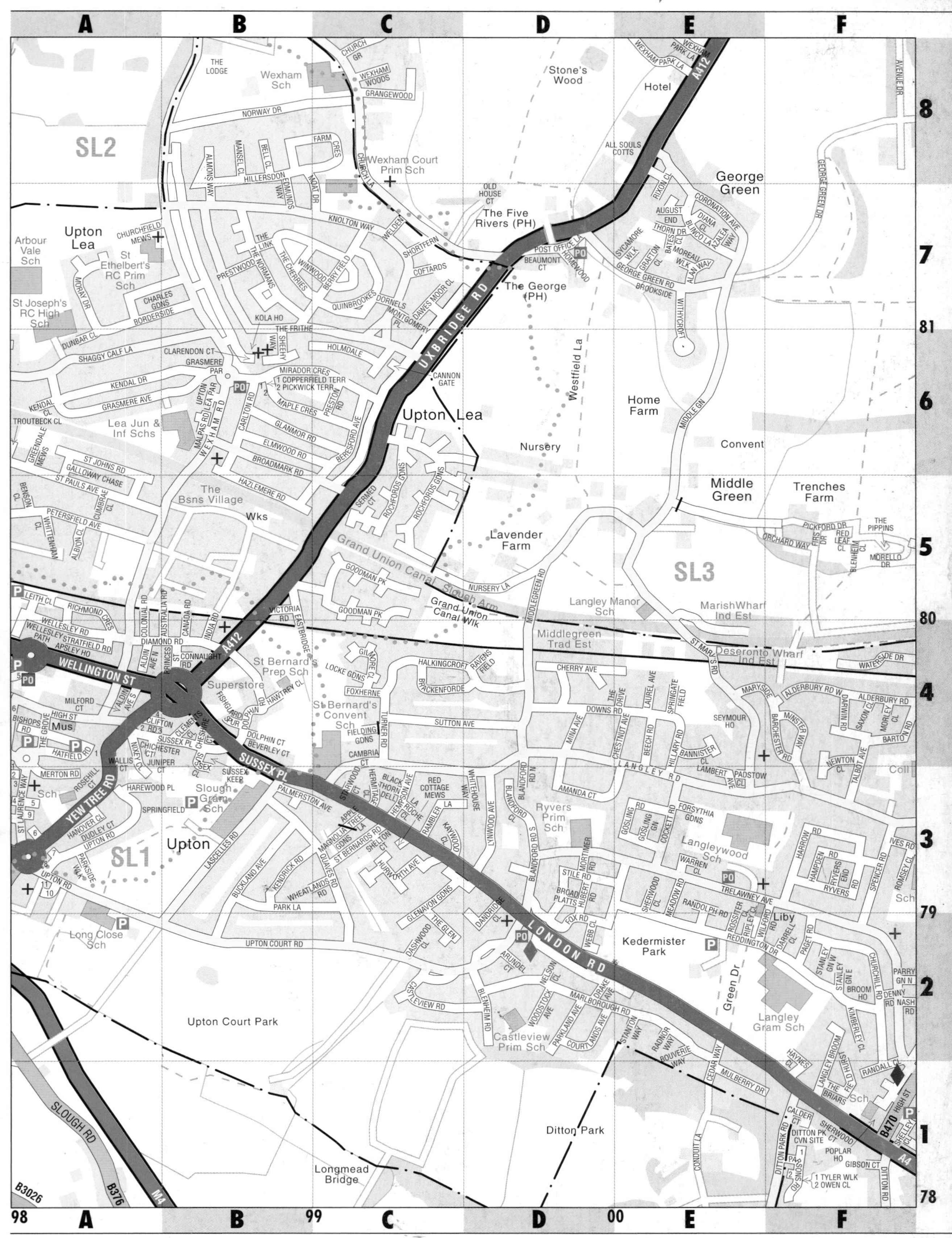

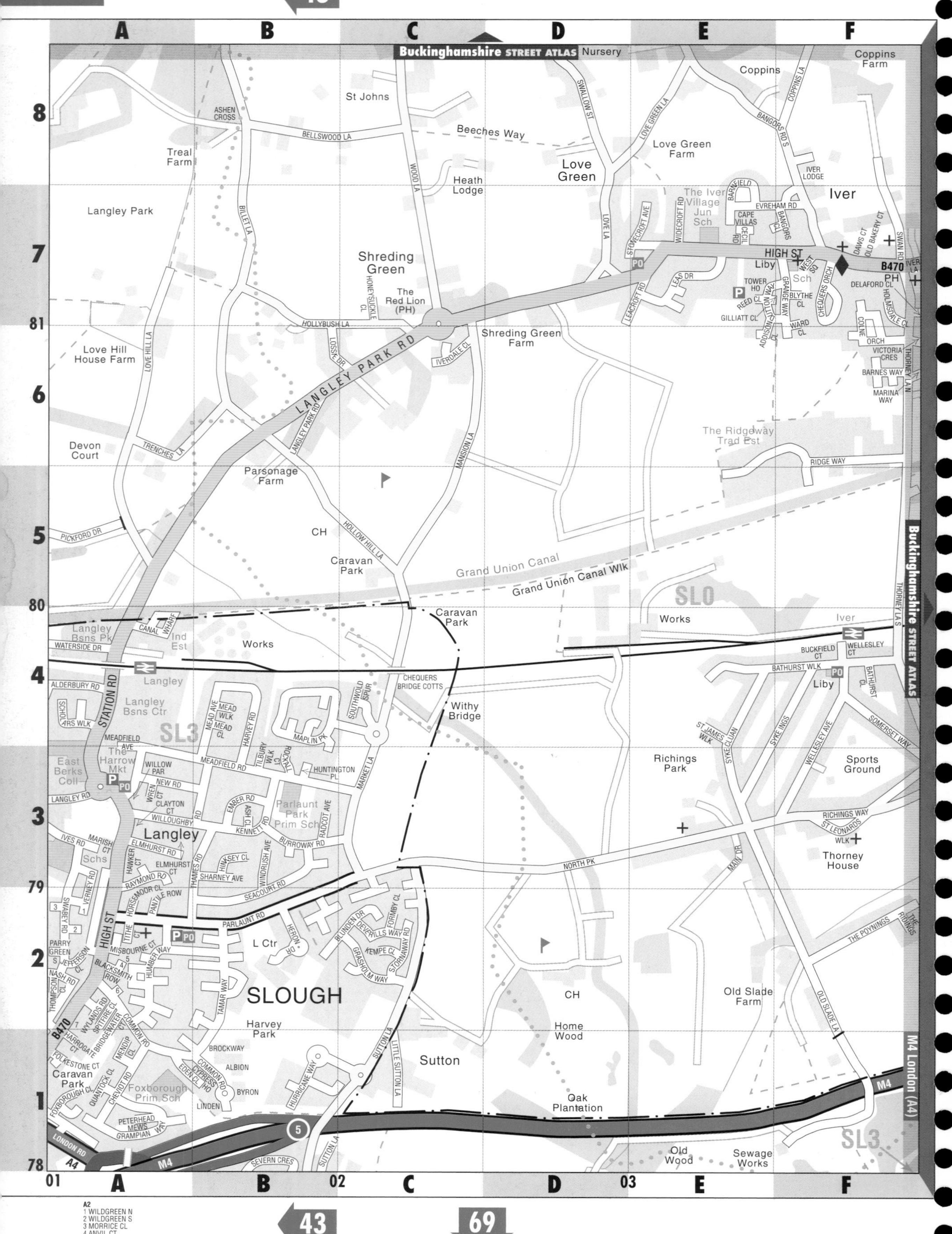

24
46

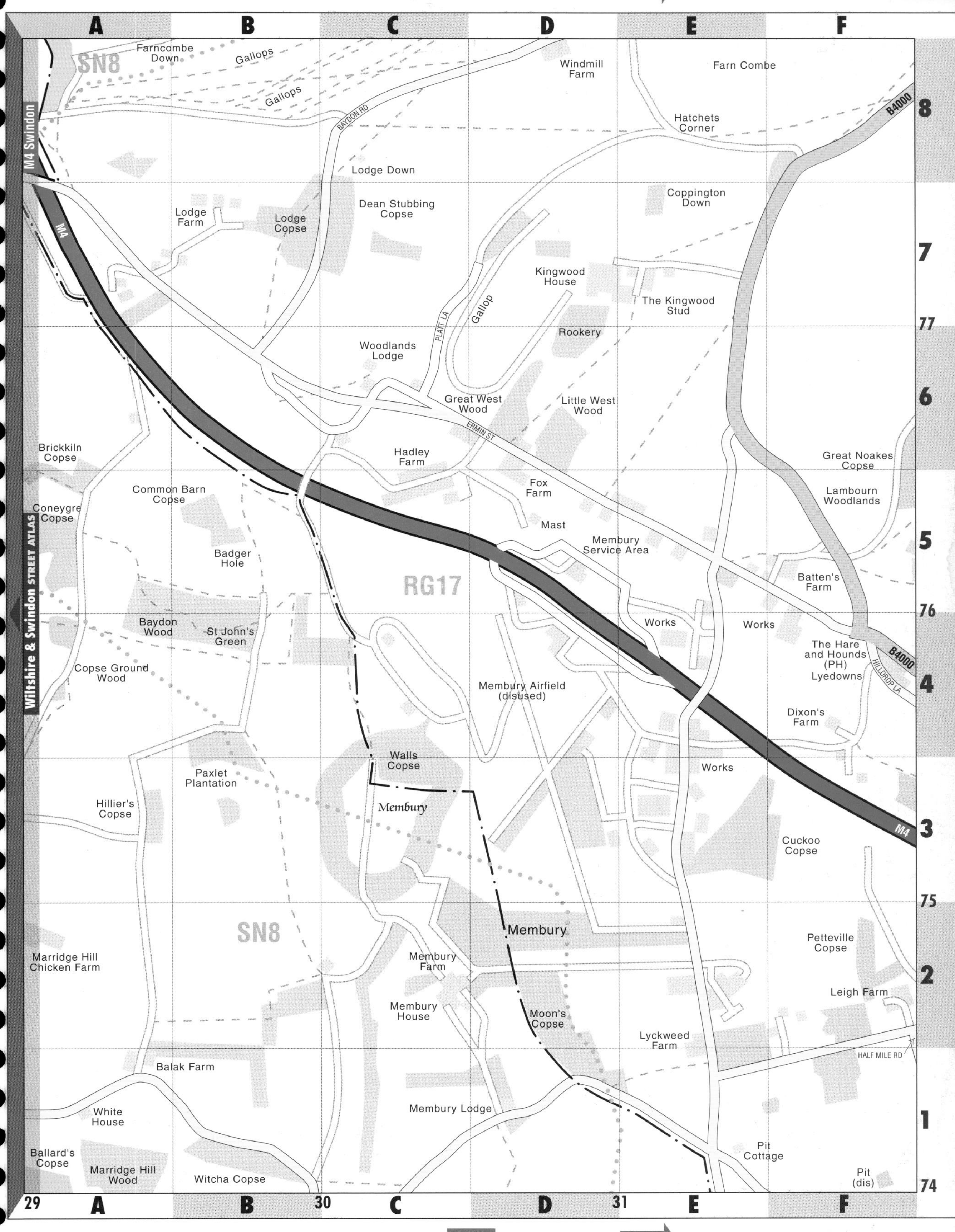
A
B
C
D
E
F
SN8
Farncombe Down
Gallops
Gallops
Windmill Farm
Farn Combe
Hatchets Corner
B4000
8
M4 Swindon
BAYDON RD
Lodge Down
Coppington Down
Lodge Farm
Lodge Copse
Dean Stubbing Copse
M4
7
Kingwood House
The Kingwood Stud
Gallop
PLATT LA
Rookery
77
Woodlands Lodge
Great West Wood
Little West Wood
6
ERMIN ST
Hadley Farm
Brickkiln Copse
Great Noakes Copse
Lambourn Woodlands
Common Barn Copse
Fox Farm
Coneygre Copse
Mast
Wiltshire & Swindon STREET ATLAS
Membury Service Area
5
Badger Hole
Batten's Farm
RG17
Baydon Wood
St John's Green
Works
Works
76
The Hare and Hounds (PH)
Lyedowns
B4000
HILLDROP LA
Copse Ground Wood
Membury Airfield (disused)
4
Dixon's Farm
Walls Copse
Works
Paxlet Plantation
Hillier's Copse
Membury
M4
3
Cuckoo Copse
75
SN8
Membury
Petteville Copse
Marridge Hill Chicken Farm
Membury Farm
2
Leigh Farm
Membury House
Moon's Copse
Lyckweed Farm
HALF MILE RD
Balak Farm
White House
Membury Lodge
1
Pit Cottage
Ballard's Copse
Marridge Hill Wood
Witcha Copse
Pit (dis)
74
29
30
31

72
46

45
25

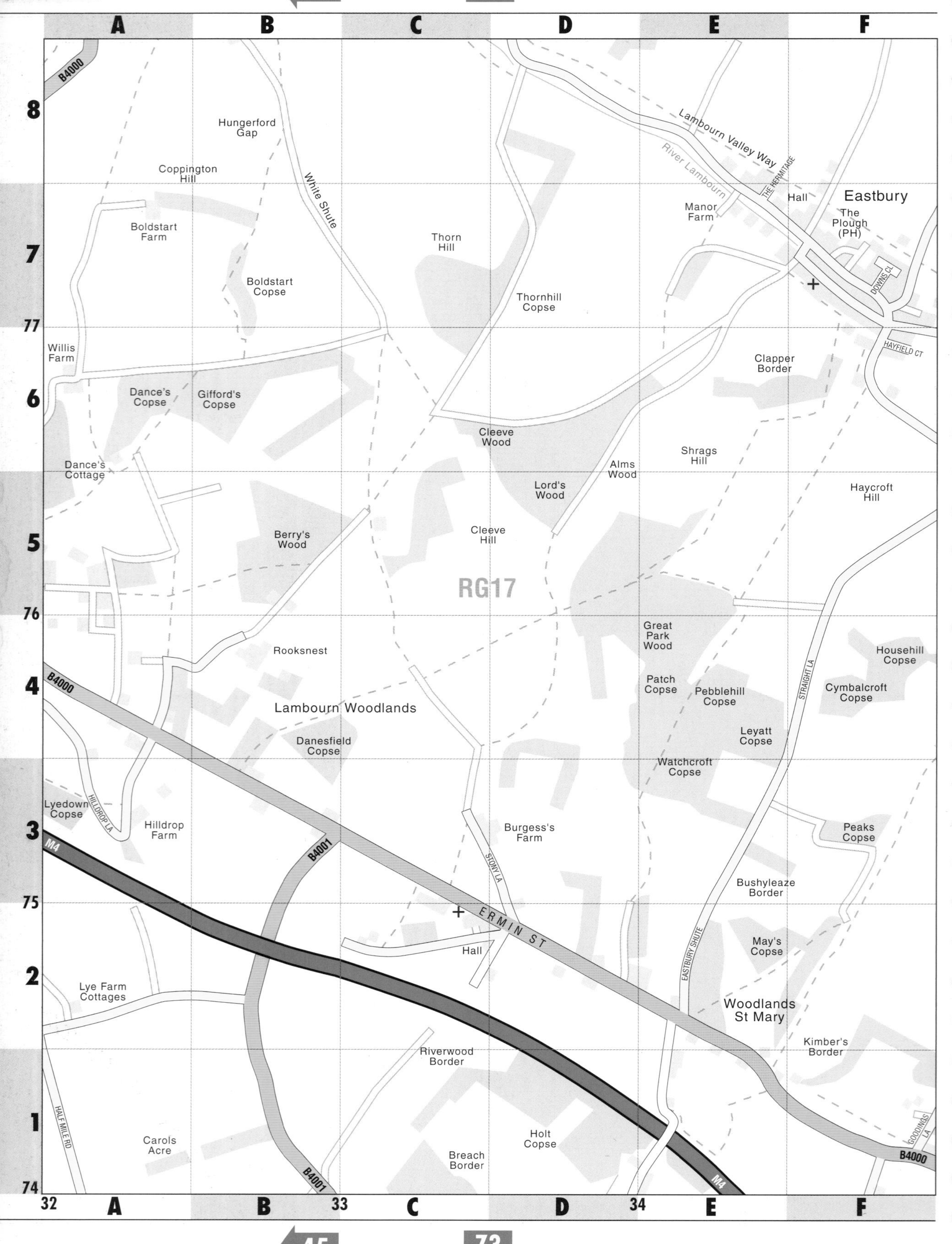
A
B
C
D
E
F
8
7
77
6
5
76
4
3
75
2
1
74
32
33
34
B4000
Hungerford Gap
Coppington Hill
White Shute
Lambourn Valley Way
River Lambourn
THE HERMITAGE
Hall
Eastbury
The Plough (PH)
Manor Farm
DOWNS CL
Boldstart Farm
Boldstart Copse
Thorn Hill
Thornhill Copse
Willis Farm
Clapper Border
HAYFIELD CT
Dance's Copse
Gifford's Copse
Cleeve Wood
Dance's Cottage
Shrags Hill
Alms Wood
Lord's Wood
Haycroft Hill
Berry's Wood
Cleeve Hill
RG17
Great Park Wood
Rooksnest
Househill Copse
Patch Copse
Pebblehill Copse
Cymbalcroft Copse
STRAIGHT LA
Lambourn Woodlands
Leyatt Copse
Danesfield Copse
Watchcroft Copse
Lyedown Copse
HILLDROP LA
Hilldrop Farm
Burgess's Farm
Peaks Copse
M4
B4001
STONY LA
Bushyleaze Border
ERMIN ST
EASTBURY SHUTE
May's Copse
Hall
Lye Farm Cottages
Woodlands St Mary
Kimber's Border
Riverwood Border
HALF MILE RD
GOODINGS LA
Holt Copse
Carols Acre
Breach Border
B4000
B4001
M4

45
73

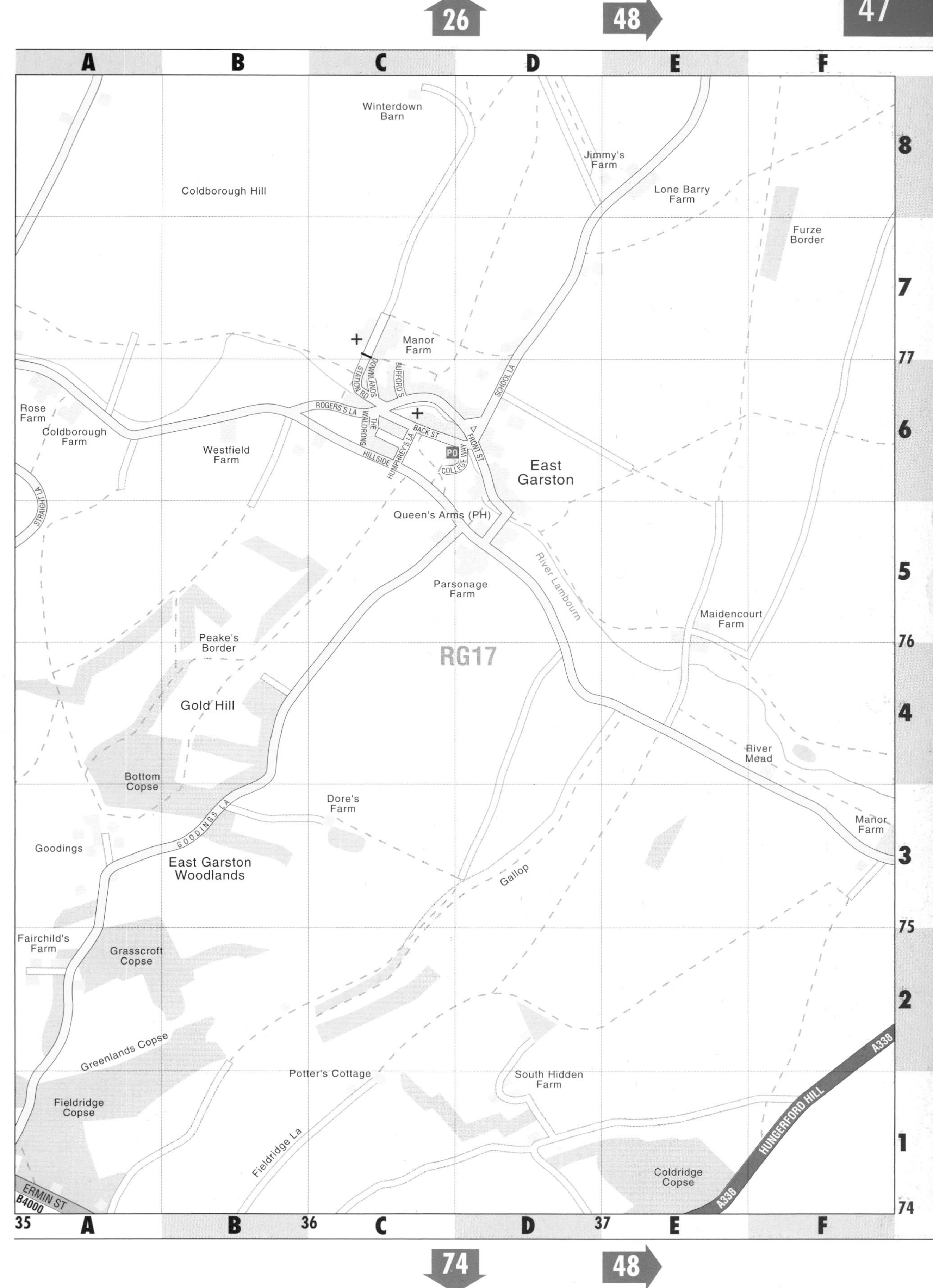

A B C D E F

8

Winterdown
Barn

Coldborough Hill

Jimmy's
Farm

Lone Barry
Farm

Furze
Border

7

77

Manor
Farm

Rose
Farm

Coldborough
Farm

ROGERS'S LA.

STATION RD.

DOWNLANDS

BURFORD'S

SCHOOL LA.

6

Westfield
Farm

THE WALDRONS

HILLSIDE

JIMMY'S LA.

BACK ST.

COLLEGE WAY

PO

FRONT ST.

East
Garston

Queen's Arms (PH)

River Lambourn

Maidencourt
Farm

5

76

Parsonage
Farm

Peake's
Border

RG17

Gold Hill

River
Mead

4

Bottom
Copse

GOODINGS LA.

Dore's
Farm

Manor
Farm

3

Goodings

East Garston
Woodlands

Gallop

75

Fairchild's
Farm

Grasscroft
Copse

2

Greenlands Copse

Potter's Cottage

South Hidden
Farm

A338

HUNGERFORD HILL

Fieldridge
Copse

Fieldridge La

Coldridge
Copse

A338

1

ERMIN ST

B4000

74

35 A 36 B C 37 D E F

47 27

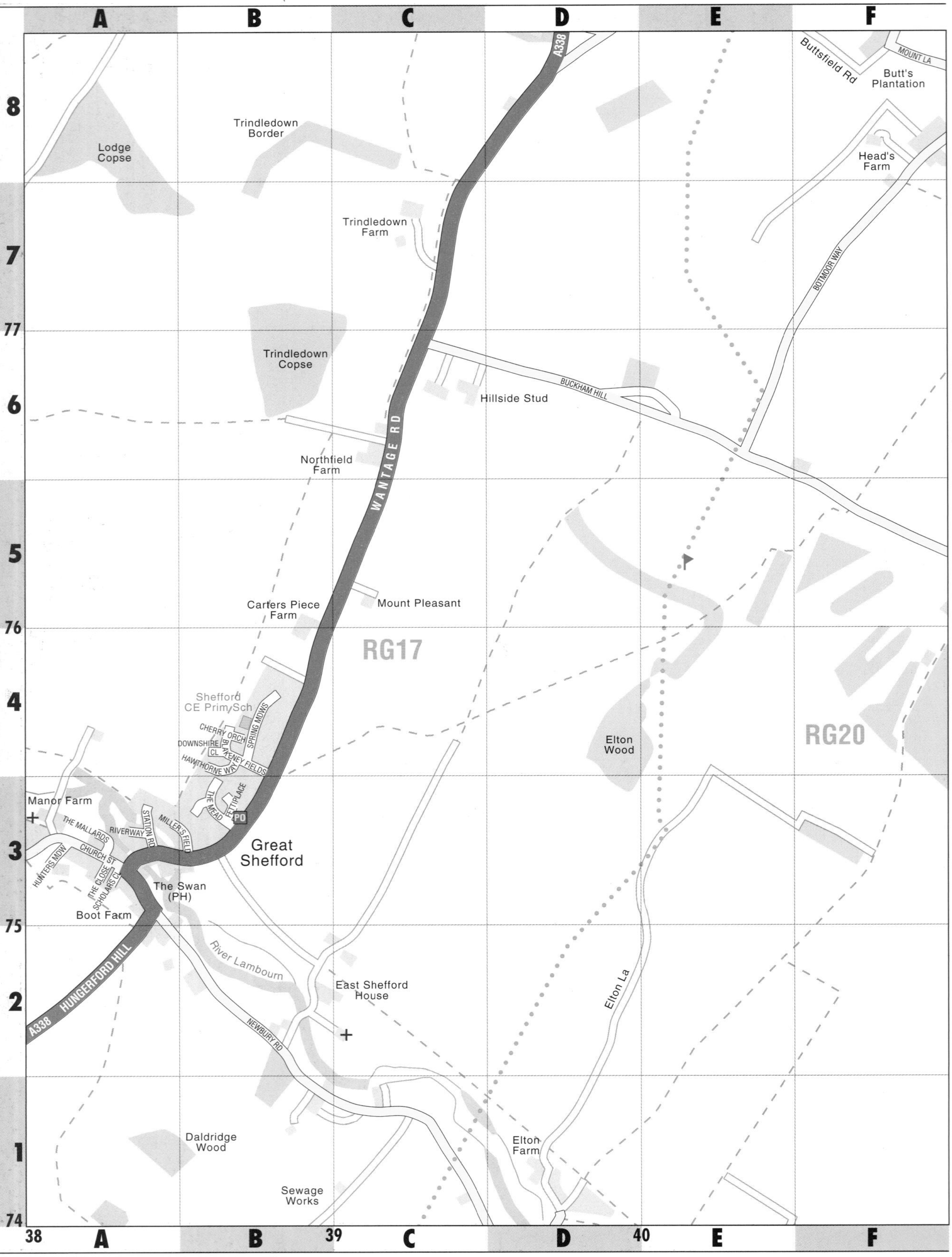

A B C D E F

8

7

77

6

5

76

4

76

3

75

2

1

74

Lodge Copse

Trindledown Border

Trindledown Farm

Trindledown Copse

Buttsfield Rd

Butt's Plantation

MOUNT LA

Head's Farm

BOTTMOOR WAY

A338

WANTAGE RD

Northfield Farm

Hillside Stud

BUCKHAM HILL

Carters Piece Farm

Mount Pleasant

RG17

Shefford CE Prim Sch

CHERRY ORCH

SPRING MDWS

DOWNSHIRE CL

KEENEY FIELDS

HAWTHORNE WAY

THE MEAD

MILLER'S FIELD

Manor Farm

THE MALLARDS

Riverway

STATION RD

HUNTERS MDW

CHURCH ST

THE CLOSE

SCHOLARS CL

Boot Farm

The Swan (PH)

A338 HUNGERFORD HILL

Great Shefford

River Lambourn

NEWBURY RD

East Shefford House

Elton Wood

RG20

Elton La

Daldridge Wood

Sewage Works

Elton Farm

38 A B 39 C D 40 E F

28
50

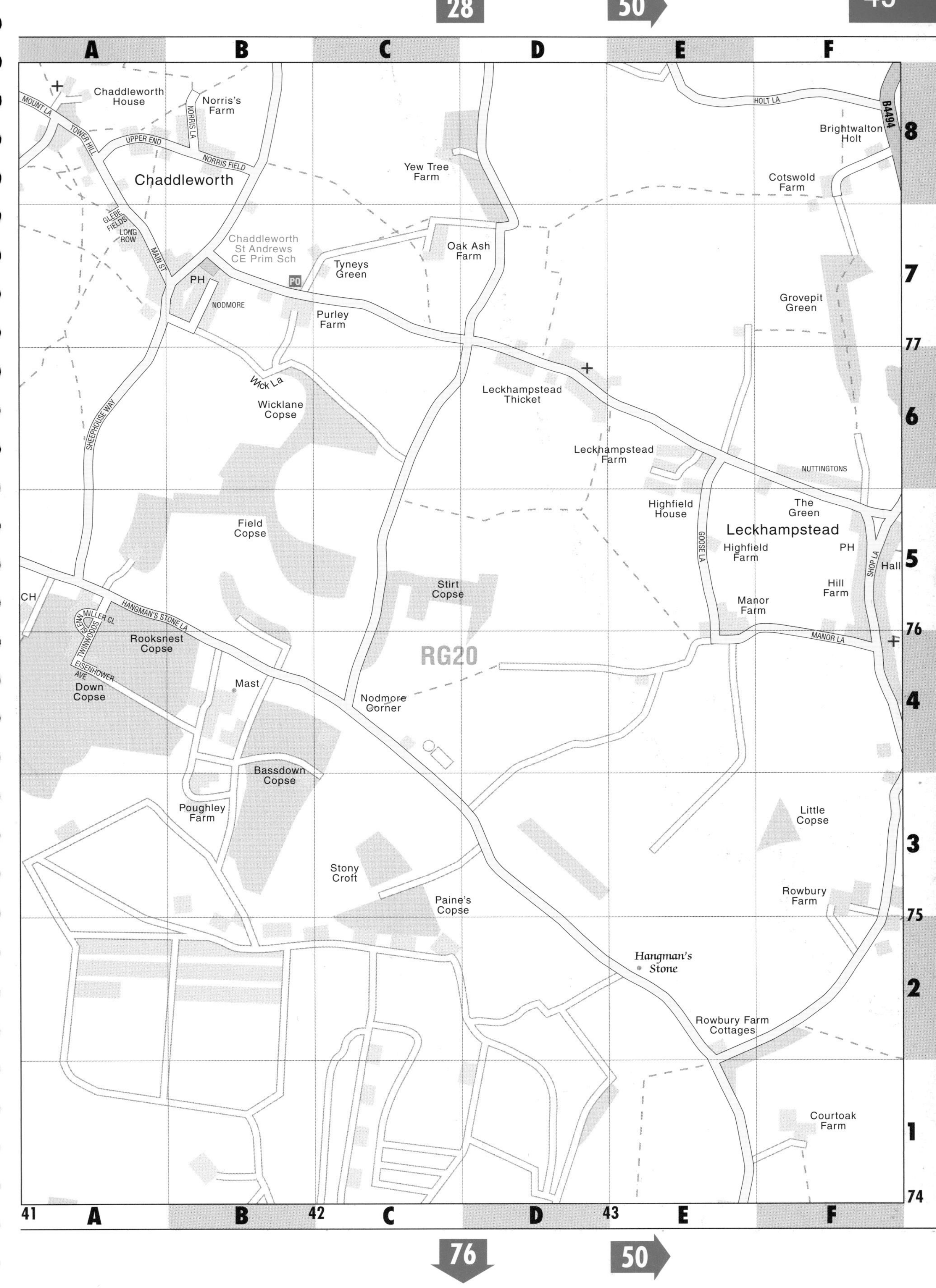
A
B
C
D
E
F
Chaddleworth House
Norris's Farm
MOUNT LA
TOWER HILL
UPPER END
NORRIS LA
NORRIS FIELD
Chaddleworth
GLEBE FIELDS
LONG ROW
MAIN ST
Chaddleworth St Andrews CE Prim Sch
PH
PO
NODMORE
Yew Tree Farm
Oak Ash Farm
Tyneys Green
Purley Farm
HOLT LA
B4494
Brightwalton Holt
Cotswold Farm
Grovepit Green
Wick La
Wicklane Copse
SHEEPHOUSE WAY
Leckhampstead Thicket
Leckhampstead Farm
NUTTINGTONS
Highfield House
The Green
Leckhampstead
GOOSE LA
Highfield Farm
PH
SHOP LA
Hall
Hill Farm
Manor Farm
MANOR LA
Field Copse
Stirt Copse
CH
HANGMAN'S STONE LA
MILLER CL
GLEN
TWINWOODS
EISENHOWER AVE
Rooksnest Copse
Down Copse
Mast
RG20
Nodmore Corner
Bassdown Copse
Poughley Farm
Little Copse
Stony Croft
Paine's Copse
Rowbury Farm
Hangman's Stone
Rowbury Farm Cottages
Courtoak Farm
8
7
77
6
5
76
4
3
75
2
1
74
41
42
43

76
50

49
29

A B C D E F

8
4
7
77
6

5
76
4
2
3
75
2
1
74

B4494

PEASEMORE HILL

Eastley Copse

Eastley House

Nightingale Farm

Egypt

Windmill Place

Hillgreen House

Bushy Leaze

Hillgreen

Chapel Farm

Prior's Wood

RG20

Ward's Copse

Pope's Wood

Green La

Penclose Wood

WEST VIEW

HILLGREEN LA

PH

HATT CL

BOLTON ROW

MEADS CL

Peasemore

Prince's Farm

PRINCE'S LA

PALMER CL

FIELD RD

Drake's Farm

THE ROOKERY

Widows' Farm

Peasemore House

MUD LA

HAILEY LA

Hailey Copse

Little Hailey Copse

Lower Hailey Copse

Old Street La

Old Street La

Woods Folly Bungalow

Gidley Farm

Gidley Copse

New Rd

Chapel Wood

North Heath Farm

North Heath

Hazelhanger Farm

GIDLEY LA

SCHOOL RD

Blue Boar Inn (PH)

B4494

44 A B 45 C B D 46 E F

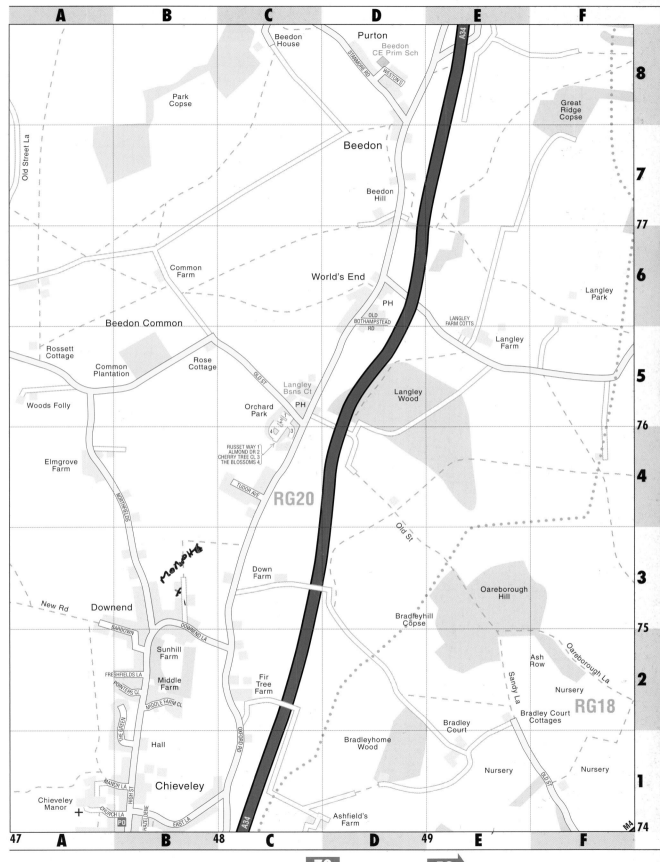

A B C D E F

8

7

77

6

5

76

4

3

75

2

1

74

Old Street La

Park Copse

Beedon House

Purton

Beedon CE Prim Sch

STANMORE RD

WESTON'S

A34

Great Ridge Copse

Beedon

Common Farm

Beedon Hill

World's End

Langley Park

Beedon Common

PH

OLD BOTHAMPSTEAD RD

Langley Farm Cotts

Langley Farm

Rossett Cottage

Common Plantation

Rose Cottage

Rose Cottage

OLD ST

Langley Bsns Ct

Langley Wood

Langley Farm

Woods Folly

Orchard Park

PH

RUSSET WAY 1
ALMOND DR 2
CHERRY TREE CL 3
THE BLOSSOMS 4

Elmgrove Farm

TUDOR AVE

RG20

NORTHFIELDS

Old St

Oareborough Hill

Down Farm

Bradleyhill Copse

New Rd

Downend

BARDOWN

DOWNEND LA

Sunhill Farm

Ash Row

Oareborough La

Nursery

FRESHFIELDS LA

Middle Farm

POINTERS CL

MIDDLE FARM CL

Fir Tree Farm

Sandy La

RG18

Bradley Court Cottages

THE GREEN

Hall

OXFORD RD

Bradleyhome Wood

Bradley Court

Nursery

OLD ST

Nursery

MANOR LA

HIGH ST

CHURCH LA

HAZELDENE

Chieveley Manor

Chieveley

EAST LA

A34

Ashfield's Farm

M4

47 A 48 B C 48 D 49 E F

51
31

A B C D E F

8
7
77
6
5
76
4
3
75
2
1
74

Perborough Castle
RG20
Floodcross Cottage
Banterwick Farm
Northfield Row
Little Ridge Copse
Ramsworth Cottages
Milkhill Farm
Uplands
Green Hams La
Allen's Row
River Pang
New Copse
Five Ways
THE OLD SCHOOL
STATION HILL
WATER ST
WEST VIEW COTTS
HILLCREST
Middle Barn
SCOTTALLS LA
THE CLOSE
THE CUTTINGS
PENDALS CL
Hampstead Norreys
Oakhouse Farm
Laycroft Wood
B4009
NEWBURY HILL
CHURCH ST
Oakhouse Cottages
Hampstead Norreys CE Prim Sch
Bothampstead Farm
Hollingsworth
RG18
Park Wood
Westbrook Copse
Bothampstead
Trumpletts Farm
Malthouse
Down Wood
New Cottages
Hatchgate Cottages
The Thatched Cottage
Eling
Elingpark Copse
Eling Farm
Four Elms
Pimbus Shaw
EVERINGTON LA
OAREBOROUGH LA
Sand Pit
Common Barn Cottages
Heather Piece
Spring Plantation
Everington Hill
M4
B4009
Newhouse Farm
Furze Hill
M4

50 A B 51 C D 52 E F

51
79

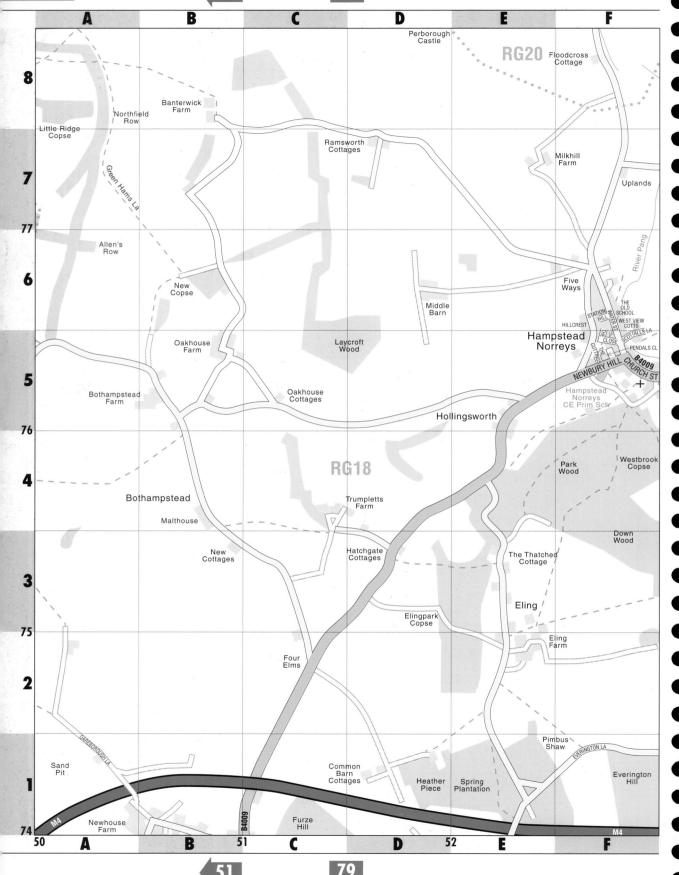

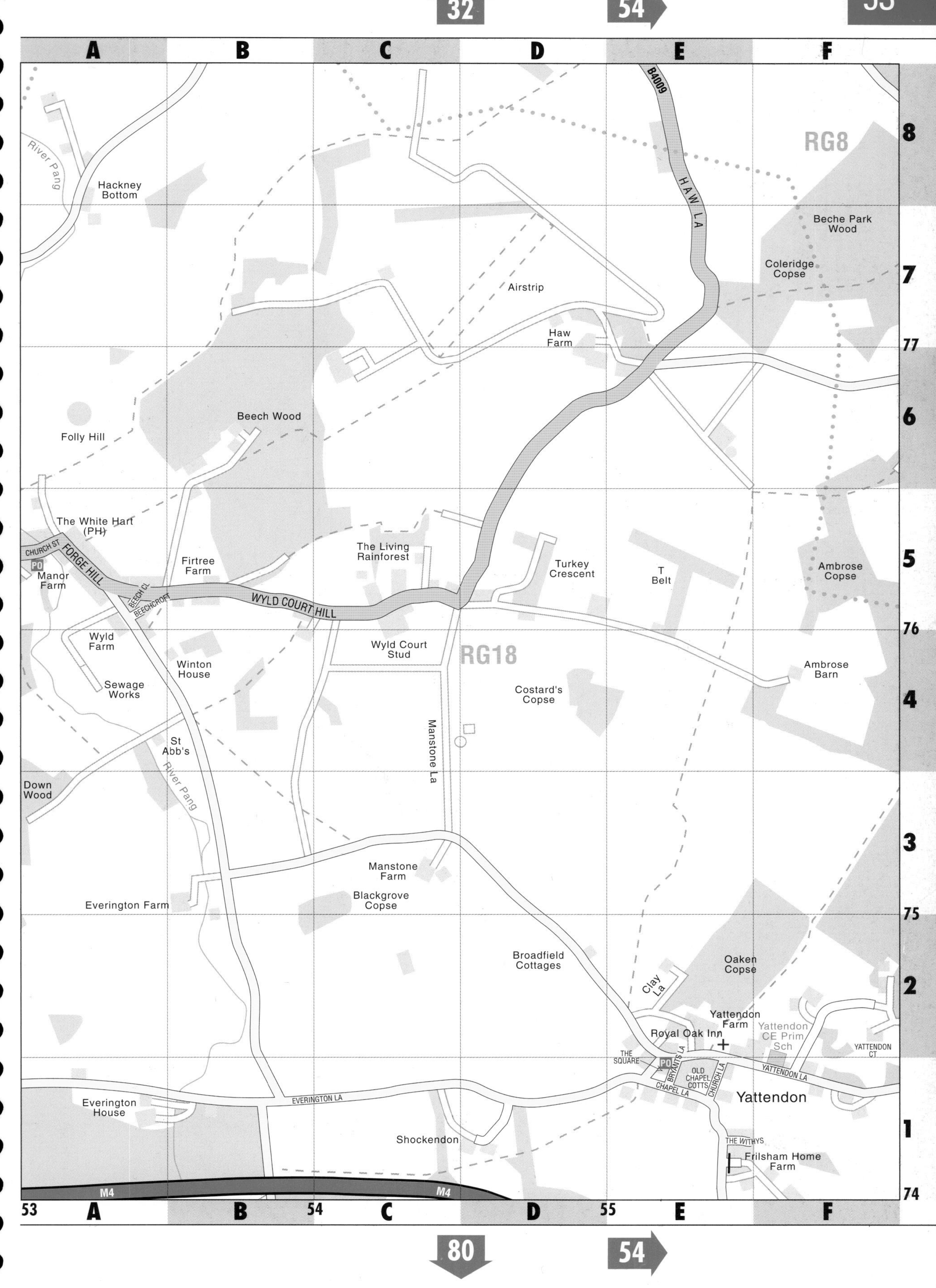

A B C D E F

8

River Pang

Hackney Bottom

Beche Park Wood

B4009

RG8

H A W   L A

Coleridge Copse

7

77

Airstrip

Haw Farm

6

Beech Wood

Folly Hill

The White Hart (PH)

CHURCH ST
PO
Manor Farm

FORGE HILL

BEECH CL.
BEECHCROFT

Firtree Farm

The Living Rainforest

WYLD COURT HILL

The Living Rainforest

Turkey Crescent

T Belt

Ambrose Copse

5

76

Wyld Farm

Winton House

Sewage Works

Wyld Court Stud

RG18

Costard's Copse

Ambrose Barn

4

St Abb's

River Pang

Manstone La

Down Wood

3

75

Everington Farm

Manstone Farm

Blackgrove Copse

Broadfield Cottages

Oaken Copse

Clay La

Yattendon Farm

Yattendon CE Prim Sch

2

Royal Oak Inn

YATTENDON CT

THE SQUARE

PO

BRYANTS LA

OLD CHAPEL COTTS

CHURCH LA

YATTENDON LA

Everington House

EVERINGTON LA

CHAPEL LA

Yattendon

1

Shockendon

THE WITHYS

Frilsham Home Farm

M4

M4

74

A B C D E F

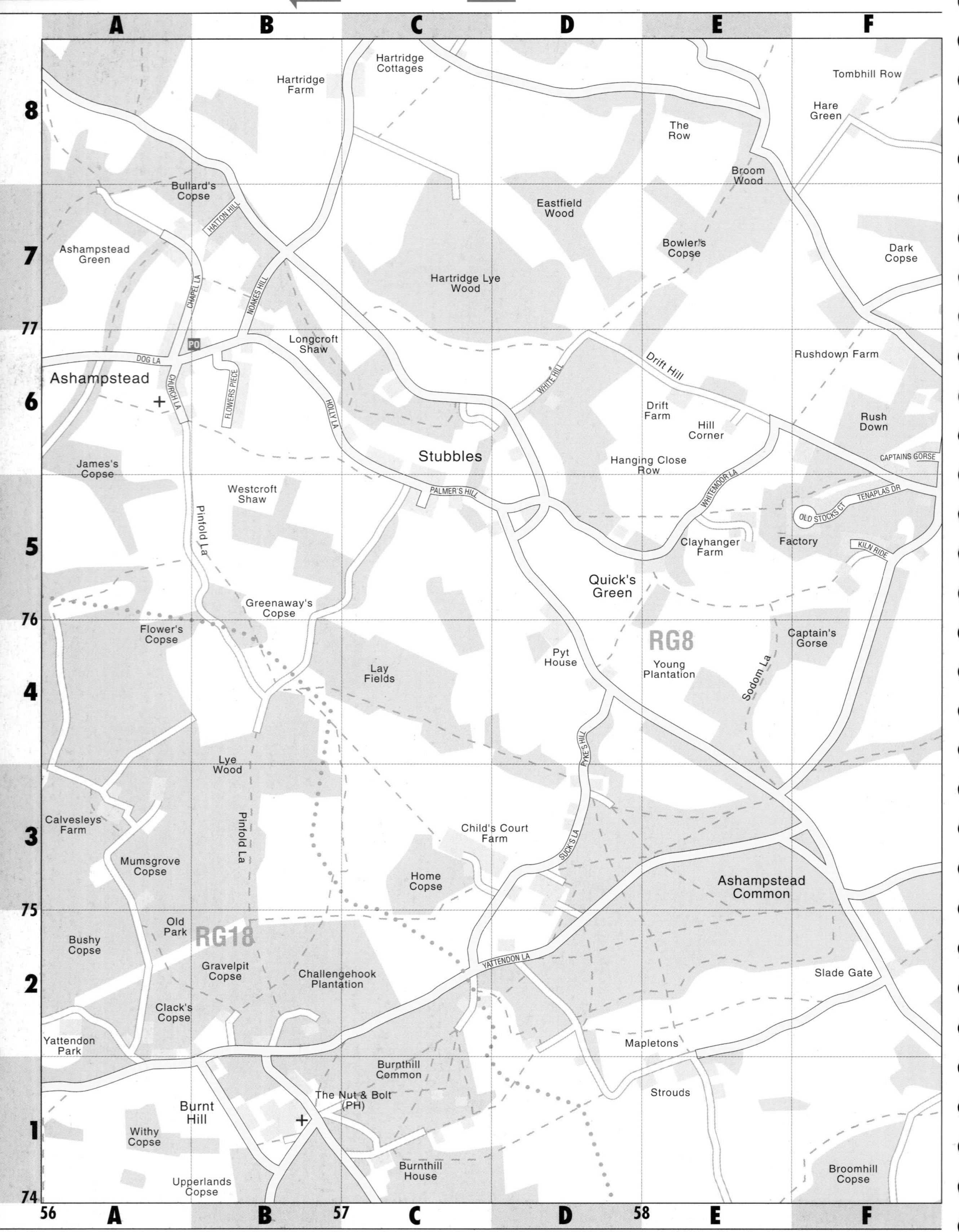
8
7
77
6
5
76
4
3
75
2
1
74
56
57
58
Hartridge Cottages
Hartridge Farm
Tombhill Row
Hare Green
The Row
Broom Wood
Bullard's Copse
HATTON HILL
Eastfield Wood
Ashampstead Green
Bowler's Copse
Dark Copse
Hartridge Lye Wood
CHAPEL LA
NOAKES HILL
PO
Longcroft Shaw
Rushdown Farm
DOG LA
Drift Hill
Ashampstead
WHITE HILL
CHURCH LA
FLOWERS PIECE
HOLLY LA
Drift Farm
Hill Corner
Rush Down
Stubbles
James's Copse
Hanging Close Row
CAPTAINS GORSE
Westcroft Shaw
PALMER'S HILL
WHITEMOOR LA
TENAPLAS DR
OLD STOCKS CT
Pinfold La
Clayhanger Farm
Factory
KILN RIDE
Quick's Green
Greenaway's Copse
Flower's Copse
RG8
Captain's Gorse
Pyt House
Lay Fields
Young Plantation
Sodom La
PYKE'S HILL
Lye Wood
Calvesleys Farm
Child's Court Farm
SUCK'S LA
Mumsgrove Copse
Pinfold La
Home Copse
Ashampstead Common
Old Park
RG18
Bushy Copse
YATTENDON LA
Gravelpit Copse
Challengehook Plantation
Slade Gate
Clack's Copse
Yattendon Park
Mapletons
Burnthill Common
The Nut & Bolt (PH)
Strouds
Burnt Hill
Withy Copse
Burnthill House
Broomhill Copse
Upperlands Copse

A B C D E F

34
56

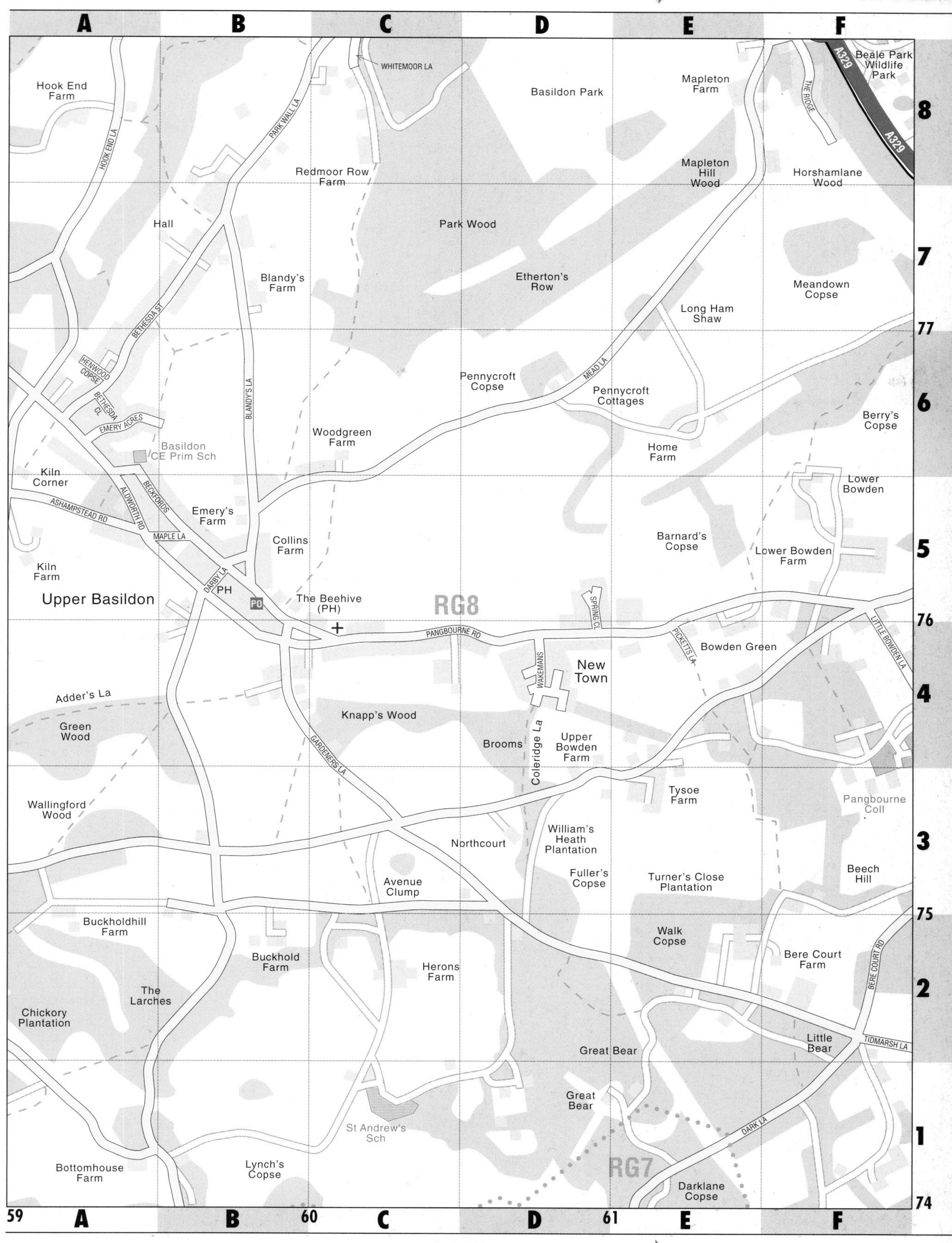
A
B
C
D
E
F
Hook End Farm
HOOK END LA
PARK WALL LA
WHITEMOOR LA
Basildon Park
Mapleton Farm
THE RIDGE
A329
Beale Park Wildlife Park
Redmoor Row Farm
Mapleton Hill Wood
Horshamlane Wood
Hall
Park Wood
Blandy's Farm
Etherton's Row
Meandown Copse
BETHESDA ST
Long Ham Shaw
HENWOOD COPSE
BLANDY'S LA
Pennycroft Copse
MEAD LA
Pennycroft Cottages
BETHESDA CL
EMERY ACRES
Woodgreen Farm
Home Farm
Berry's Copse
Basildon CE Prim Sch
Kiln Corner
Lower Bowden
ASHAMPSTEAD RD
ALDWORTH RD
BECKFORDS
Emery's Farm
MAPLE LA
Barnard's Copse
Collins Farm
Kiln Farm
Lower Bowden Farm
DARBY LA
PH
Upper Basildon
PO
The Beehive (PH)
RG8
SPRING CL
LITTLE BOWDEN LA
PANGBOURNE RD
PICKETTS LA
Bowden Green
WAKEMANS
New Town
Adder's La
Knapp's Wood
Green Wood
Coleridge La
GARDENERS LA
Brooms
Upper Bowden Farm
Tysoe Farm
Wallingford Wood
Pangbourne Coll
William's Heath Plantation
Northcourt
Fuller's Copse
Turner's Close Plantation
Beech Hill
Avenue Clump
Buckholdhill Farm
Walk Copse
Buckhold Farm
Bere Court Farm
BERE COURT RD
Herons Farm
The Larches
Chickory Plantation
Little Bear
TIDMARSH LA
Great Bear
Great Bear
St Andrew's Sch
DARK LA
Bottomhouse Farm
Lynch's Copse
RG7
Darklane Copse
8
7
77
6
5
76
4
3
75
2
1
74
59
60
61

82
56

55

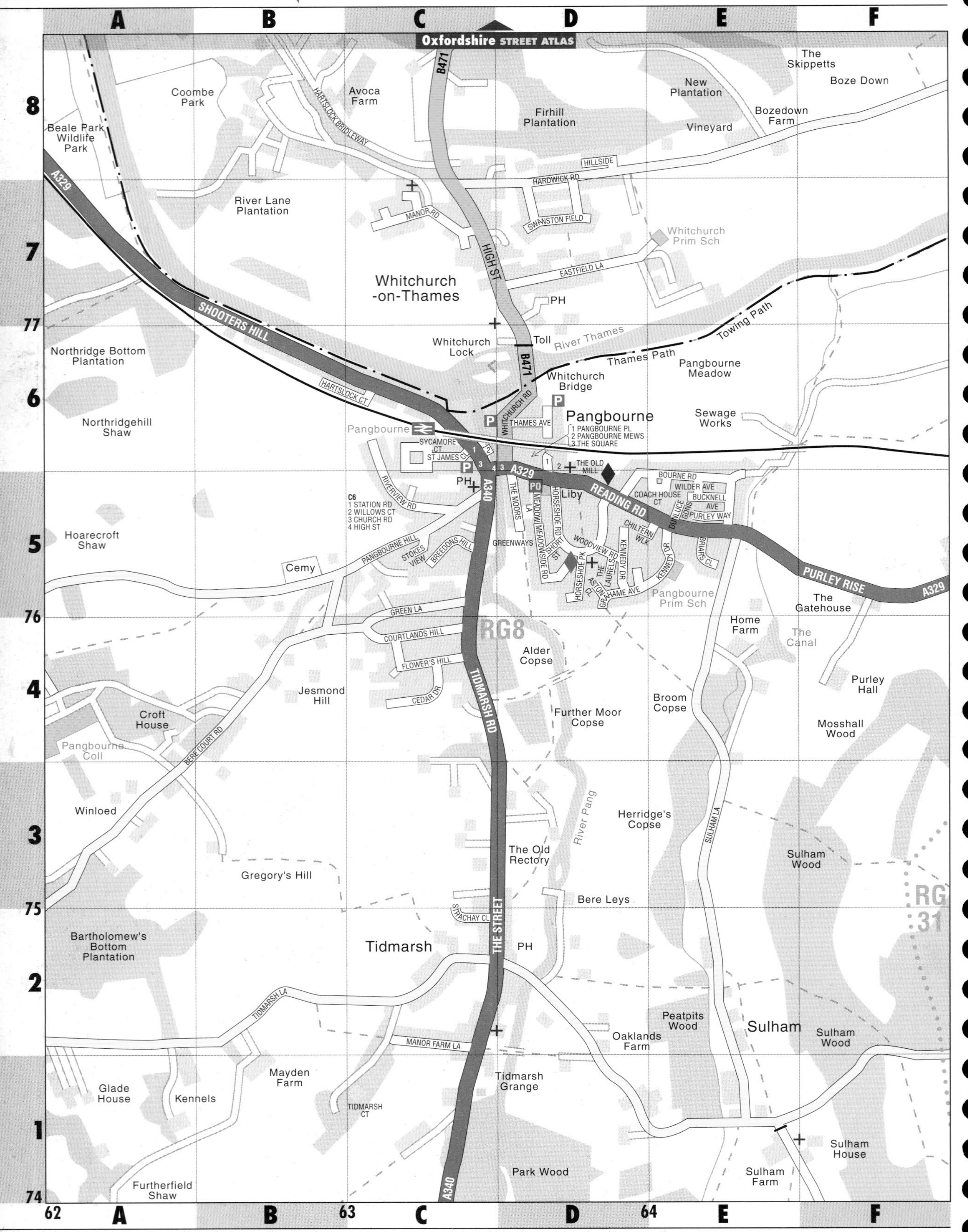

Oxfordshire STREET ATLAS

Whitchurch
-on-Thames

Coombe
Park

Avoca
Farm

Beale Park
Wildlife
Park

River Lane
Plantation

Firhill
Plantation

New
Plantation

The
Skippetts

Boze Down

Bozedown
Farm

Vineyard

Whitchurch
Prim Sch

HARTSLOCK BRIDLEWAY

MANOR RD

HIGH ST

HILLSIDE

HARDWICK RD

SWANSTON FIELD

EASTFIELD LA

A329

SHOOTERS HILL

Northridge Bottom
Plantation

HARTSLOCK CT

PH

Toll

River Thames

Towing Path

Thames Path

Pangbourne
Meadow

Whitchurch
Lock

Whitchurch
Bridge

B471

WHITCHURCH RD

Northridgehill
Shaw

Pangbourne

THAMES AVE

P

P

Sewage
Works

1 Pangbourne Pl
2 Pangbourne Mews
3 The Square

SYCAMORE
CT

ST JAMES CT

P

PH

A329

THE OLD
MILL

BOURNE RD

WILDER AVE

COACH HOUSE
CT

BUCKNELL
AVE

RIVERVIEW RD

A340

THE MOORS

PO

Liby

READING RD

DUNLUCE GDNS

PURLEY WAY

C6
1 STATION RD
2 WILLOWS CT
3 CHURCH RD
4 HIGH ST

Hoarecroft
Shaw

PANGBOURNE HILL

STOKES
VIEW

BREEDONS HILL

MEADOW MEADOWSIDE RD

HORSESHOE RD

WOODVIEW RD

CHILTERN
WLK

KENNEDY DR

KENNEDY DR

THE LAURELS

THE ASH

GRAHAME AVE

Pangbourne
Prim Sch

BRIARS CL

PURLEY RISE

A329

Cemy

Greenways

Home
Farm

The
Gatehouse

GREEN LA

COURTLANDS HILL

RG8

Alder
Copse

The
Canal

Purley
Hall

FLOWER'S HILL

CEDAR DR

Jesmond
Hill

Further Moor
Copse

Broom
Copse

Mosshall
Wood

Croft
House

BERE COURT RD

TIDMARSH RD

Pangbourne
Coll

Winloed

River Pang

Herridge's
Copse

SULHAM LA

Sulham
Wood

RG
31

Gregory's Hill

The Old
Rectory

Bere Leys

Bartholomew's
Bottom
Plantation

STRACHAY CL

THE STREET

PH

Tidmarsh

TIDMARSH LA

MANOR FARM LA

Peatpits
Wood

Oaklands
Farm

Sulham

Sulham
Wood

Sulham
House

Glade
House

Kennels

Mayden
Farm

TIDMARSH
CT

Tidmarsh
Grange

Sulham
Farm

Furtherfield
Shaw

A340

Park Wood

58

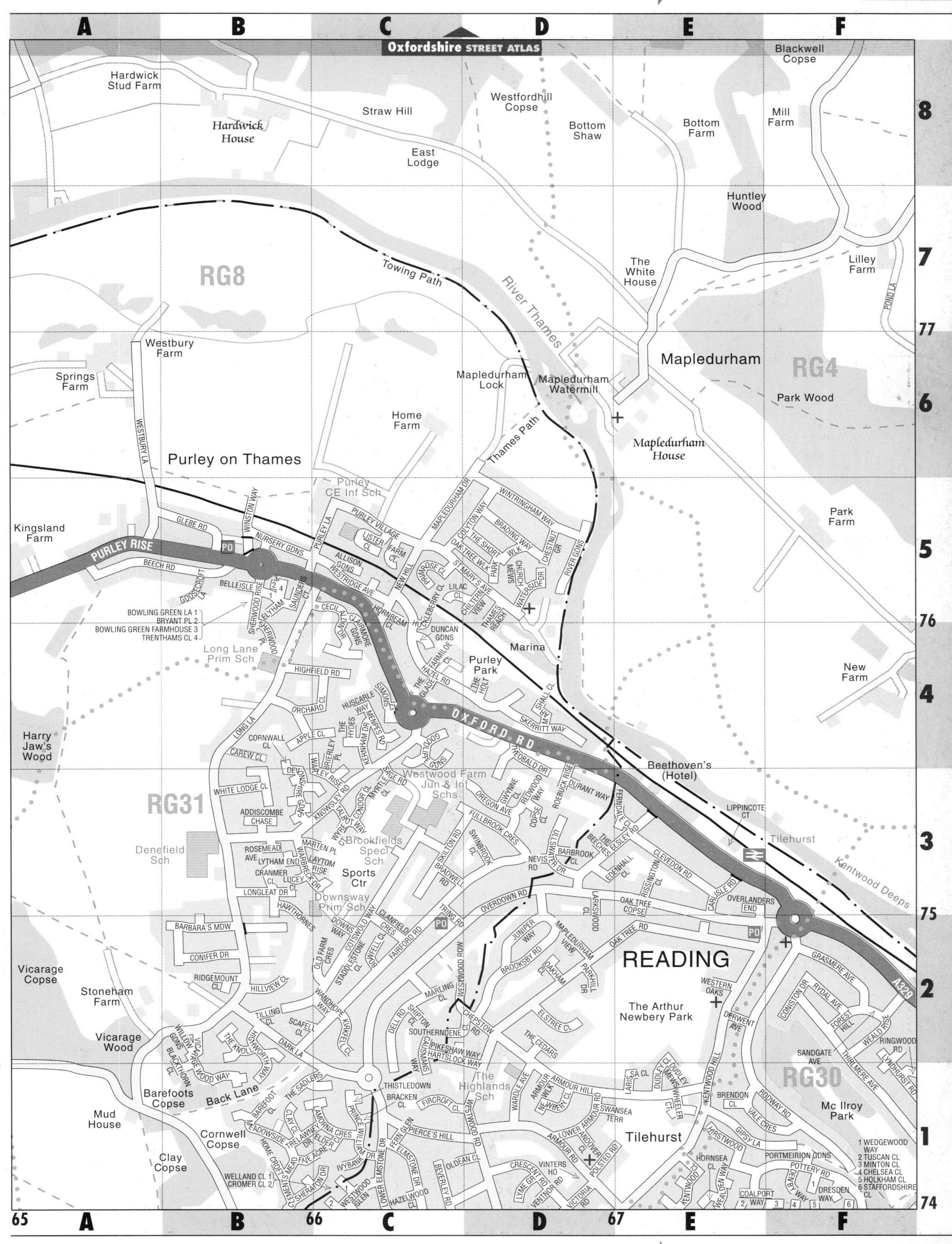
Oxfordshire STREET ATLAS
A
B
C
D
E
F
8
7
77
6
5
76
4
3
75
2
1
74
65
66
67
Hardwick Stud Farm
Hardwick House
Straw Hill
East Lodge
Westfordhill Copse
Bottom Shaw
Bottom Farm
Mill Farm
Blackwell Copse
Huntley Wood
The White House
Lilley Farm
POND LA
RG8
Towing Path
River Thames
Mapledurham
RG4
Park Wood
Westbury Farm
Springs Farm
Mapledurham Lock
Mapledurham Watermill
Home Farm
Thames Path
Mapledurham House
WESTBURY LA
Purley on Thames
Purley CE Inf Sch
Kingsland Farm
Park Farm
PURLEY RISE
GLEBE RD
WINSTON WAY
NURSERY GDNS
PURLEY LA
PURLEY VILLAGE
LISTER CL
FARM CL
MAPLEDURHAM DR
WINTRINGHAM WAY
COLYTON WAY
BRADING WAY
THE SHORT
OAK TREE WLK
PARK WLK
MEWS
CHURCH
WATERSIDE DR
CHESTNUT GR
RIVER GDNS
BEECH RD
BELLEISLE
GOOSECROFT LA
ALLISON GDNS
WESTRIDGE AVE
NEW HILL
PRIMROSE CL
ST MARY'S AVE
LILAC CL
HUCKLEBERRY CL
CHILTERN VIEW
THAMES REACH
BOWLING GREEN LA 1
BRYANT PL 2
BOWLING GREEN FARMHOUSE 3
TRENTHAMS CL 4
SHERWOOD RISE
ELYHAM
SHERWOOD PL
SAUNDERS CT
CECIL ALDIN DR
CLAYMORE GDNS
HORNBEAM CL
DUNCAN GDNS
Marina
Long Lane Prim Sch
HIGHFIELD RD
FARMILOE CL
HAZEL RD
Purley Park
THE HOLT
THE GLADE
SHALL CL
New Farm
LONG LA
ORCHARD CL
HUSCARLE WAY
SIMONS CL
OXFORD RD
SKERRITT WAY
Harry Jaw's Wood
CORNWALL CL
APPLE CL
THE HYDES
KENNHAM DR
MEMPES RD
GOODLIFFE GDNS
CAREW CL
BRIERLEY PL
WAVERLEY RISE
THEOBALD DR
Beethoven's (Hotel)
WHITE LODGE CL
KNOWSLEY RD
CONDOR CL
MYRTLE CL
SAGE RD
Westwood Farm Jun & Inf Schs
GWYNNE CL
REDWOOD WAY
ROEBUCK RISE
DURANT WAY
FERNDALE CL
LIPPINCOTE CT
RG31
ADDISCOMBE CHASE
TALBOT WAY
WYRE CT
OREGON AVE
COPSE WAY
FULLBROOK CRES
THE BEECHES
ELSLEY RD
Tilehurst
Denefield Sch
ROSEMEAD AVE
LYTHAM END
MARTEN PL
LAYTOM RISE
Brookfields Specl Sch
SKILTON RD
SWINBROOK CL
NEVIS RD
ULLSWATER DR
BARBROOK CL
EDENHALL CL
RISSINGTON CL
CLEVEDON RD
Kentwood Deeps
CRANMER CL
LUCEY CL
Sports Ctr
BRADWELL RD
LONGLEAT DR
Downsway Prim Sch
HAWTHORNES
DOWNS WAY
OVERDOWN RD
LARKSWOOD CL
OAK TREE COPSE
CARLISLE RD
OVERLANDERS END
BARBARA'S MDW
OLD FARM CRES
STADDLESTONE CL
COTSWOLD WAY
BOWFELL CL
CLANFIELD CRES
FAIRFORD RD
TRING RD
JUNIPER WAY
MAPLEDURHAM VIEW
OAK TREE RD
CONIFER DR
Vicarage Copse
BROOKSBY RD
OAKHAM CL
PARKHILL DR
READING
GRASMERE AVE
RIDGEMOUNT CL
WESTWOOD ROW
CONISTON DR
RYDAL AVE
A329
Stoneham Farm
HILLVIEW CL
WANDHOPE WAY
KIRKFELL CL
MARLING CL
The Arthur Newbery Park
WESTERN OAKS
FOREST HILL
WEALD RISE
TILLING CL
SCAFELL CL
DELL RD
SHIPTON CL
CHEPSTOW RD
ELSTREE CL
DERWENT AVE
RINGWOOD RD
WILLOW GDNS
VICARAGE WOOD WAY
BLACKTHORN CL
THE KNOLL
HIGHWORTH WAY
DARK LA
SOUTHERNDENE CL
CAUSMANS WAY
PIKESHAW WAY
HARTSLOCK WAY
THE CEDARS
Vicarage Wood
SANDGATE AVE
THIRLMERE AVE
LYNDHURST RD
RG30
Barefoots Copse
Back Lane
BAREFOOT CL
THE SADLERS
THISTLEDOWN
BRACKEN CL
The Highlands Sch
WARDLE AVE
ARMOUR WLK
ARMOUR HILL
NEWBERY CL
LARISSA CL
DUDLEY CL
DUDLEY MEWS
WHEELER CT
KENTWOOD HILL
BRENDON CL
RODWAY RD
VALE CRES
Mc Ilroy Park
Mud House
MEADOWSIDE
CLAY CL
LAMORNA CRES
PRINCE WILLIAM DR
FIRCROFT CL
SWANSEA TERR
Tilehurst
Cornwell Copse
HOME CROFT
TRELAWNEY DR
ELDER CL
YEW ACRE
FERN GLEN
PIERCE'S HILL
WESTWOOD RD
LOWER ARMOUR RD
ANDOVER CL
ARMOUR RD
HIRSTWOOD
GIPSY LA
1 WEDGEWOOD WAY
2 TUSCAN CL
3 MINTON CL
4 CHELSEA CL
5 HOLKHAM CL
6 STAFFORDSHIRE CL
Clay Copse
CLEMENTS MEAD
SHERATON DR
IVYBANK
LOWER ELMSTONE DR
ELMSTONE DR
OLDEAN CL
CRESCENT RD
VINTERS HO
POLSTED RD
HORNSEA CL
PORTMEIRION GDNS
POTTERY RD
WELLAND CL 1
CROMER CL 2
WESTWOOD GLEN
HAZELWOOD CL
BEVERLEY RD
LYME GR
VENTNOR RD
VICTORIA RD
KENTWOOD CL
WEALDEN WAY
COALPORT WAY
DENBY WAY
DRESDEN WAY

84
58

57

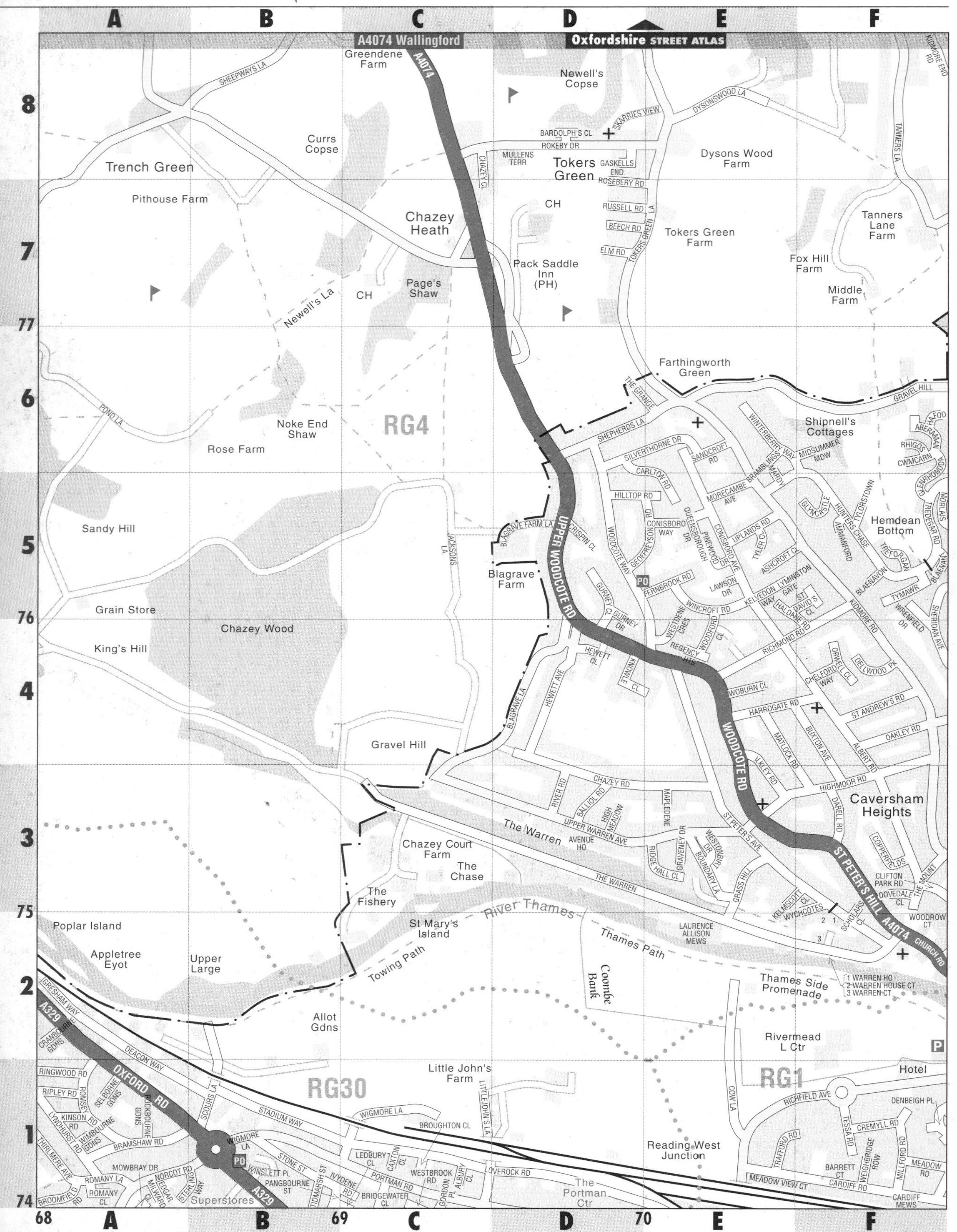

A B C D E F
A4074 Wallingford
Oxfordshire STREET ATLAS
8
7
77
6
5
76
4
3
75
2
1
74
68
69
70
Greendene Farm
A4074
Newell's Copse
SHEEPWAYS LA
SKARRIES VIEW
DYSONSWOOD LA
KIDMORE END RD
BARDOLPH'S CL
ROKEBY DR
Curs Copse
Trench Green
Pithouse Farm
MULLENS TERR
CHAZEY CL
Tokers Green
GASKELLS END
ROSEBERY RD
Dysons Wood Farm
TANNERS LA
CH
RUSSELL RD
BEECH RD
ELM RD
TOKERS GREEN LA
Chazey Heath
Tokers Green Farm
Tanners Lane Farm
Pack Saddle Inn (PH)
Fox Hill Farm
Page's Shaw
Newell's La
CH
Middle Farm
Farthingworth Green
THE GRANGE
GRAVEL HILL
POND LA
Noke End Shaw
RG4
Rose Farm
SHEPHERDS LA
Shipnell's Cottages
WINTERBERRY WAY
MIDSUMMER MDW
HAFOD
ABERAMAN
RHIGOS
CWMCARN
SILVERTHORNE DR
SANDCROFT RD
CARLTON RD
BRAMBLINGS
MARDY
MORECAMBE AVE
HILLTOP RD
GLYNCASTLE
HUNTERS CHASE
TYLORSTOWN
GLENRHONDDA
TREDEGAR RD
MORLAIS
Sandy Hill
CONISBORO WAY
QUEENSBOROUGH DR
CONISBORO AVE
PINEWOOD DR
UPLANDS RD
TYLER CL
AMMANFORD
Hemdean Bottom
BLAGRAVE FARM LA
CRISPIN CL
JACKSONS LA
WOODCOTE WAY
GEOFFREYSON RD
ASHCROFT CL
TREFOREST
UPPER WOODCOTE RD
Blagrave Farm
PO
FERNBROOK RD
LAWSON DR
LYMINGTON GATE
KELVEDON WAY
ST DAVID'S CL
HALDANE RD
BLAENAVON
TYMAWR
BLAENWAY
Grain Store
GURNEY CL
GURNEY DR
WINCROFT RD
WESTDENE CRES
WOODFORD CL
KIDMORE RD
WREMFIELD DR
SHERIDAN AVE
Chazey Wood
King's Hill
HEWETT CL
REGENCY HTS
RICHMOND RD
KNOWLE CL
ORWELL CL
DELWOOD PK
CHELFORD WAY
WOBURN CL
BLAGRAVE LA
HEWETT AVE
HARROGATE RD
ST ANDREW'S RD
OAKLEY RD
MATLOCK RD
BUXTON AVE
ALBERT RD
Gravel Hill
WOODCOTE RD
ILKLEY RD
HIGHMOOR RD
CHAZEY RD
RIVER RD
BALLIOL RD
HIGH MEADOW
MAPLEDENE
Caversham Heights
DARELL RD
The Warren
UPPER WARREN AVE
AVENUE HO
ST PETER'S AVE
GRAVENEY DR
WESTONBIRT DR
BOUNDARY LA
COPPERFIELDS
Chazey Court Farm
The Chase
RIDGE HALL CL
ST PETER'S HILL
CLIFTON PARK RD
THE MOUNT
THE WARREN
GRASS HILL
DOVEDALE CL
The Fishery
KELMSCOTT CL
WYCHCOTES
SCHOLARS CL
WOODROW CT
Poplar Island
River Thames
St Mary's Island
LAURENCE ALLISON MEWS
A4074
CHURCH RD
Appletree Eyot
Upper Large
Thames Path
Towing Path
Coombe Bank
Thames Side Promenade
1 WARREN HO
2 WARREN HOUSE CT
3 WARREN CT
GRESHAM WAY
A329
CRANBOURNE GDNS
Allot Gdns
Rivermead L Ctr
P
DEACON WAY
RINGWOOD RD
OXFORD RD
Little John's Farm
Hotel
RG30
RG1
RIPLEY RD
ROMSEY RD
SELBORNE GDNS
ROCKBOURNE GDNS
SCOURS LA
STADIUM WAY
LITTLEJOHN'S LA
COW LA
RICHFIELD AVE
DENBEIGH PL
KINSON RD
LYNDHURST RD
WIMBOURNE GDNS
WIGMORE LA
BROUGHTON CL
TESSA RD
CREMYLL RD
BRAMSHAW RD
WIGMORE LA
THIRLMERE AVE
PO
STONE ST
LEDBURY CL
CAXTON CL
TRAFFORD RD
WEIGHBRIDGE ROW
MILFORD RD
Reading West Junction
MOWBRAY DR
NORCOT RD
WINSLETT PL
IVYDENE RD
WESTBROOK RD
ALBURY CL
LOVEROCK RD
BARRETT CT
MEADOW RD
ROMANY LA
PANGBOURNE ST
PORTMAN RD
MEADOW VIEW CT
CARDIFF RD
BROOMFIELD RD
ROMANY CL
EDGAR MILWARD CL
STERLING WAY
TIDMARSH ST
BRIDGEWATER CL
GORDON PL
The Portman Ctr
CARDIFF MEWS
Superstores
A329

57
85

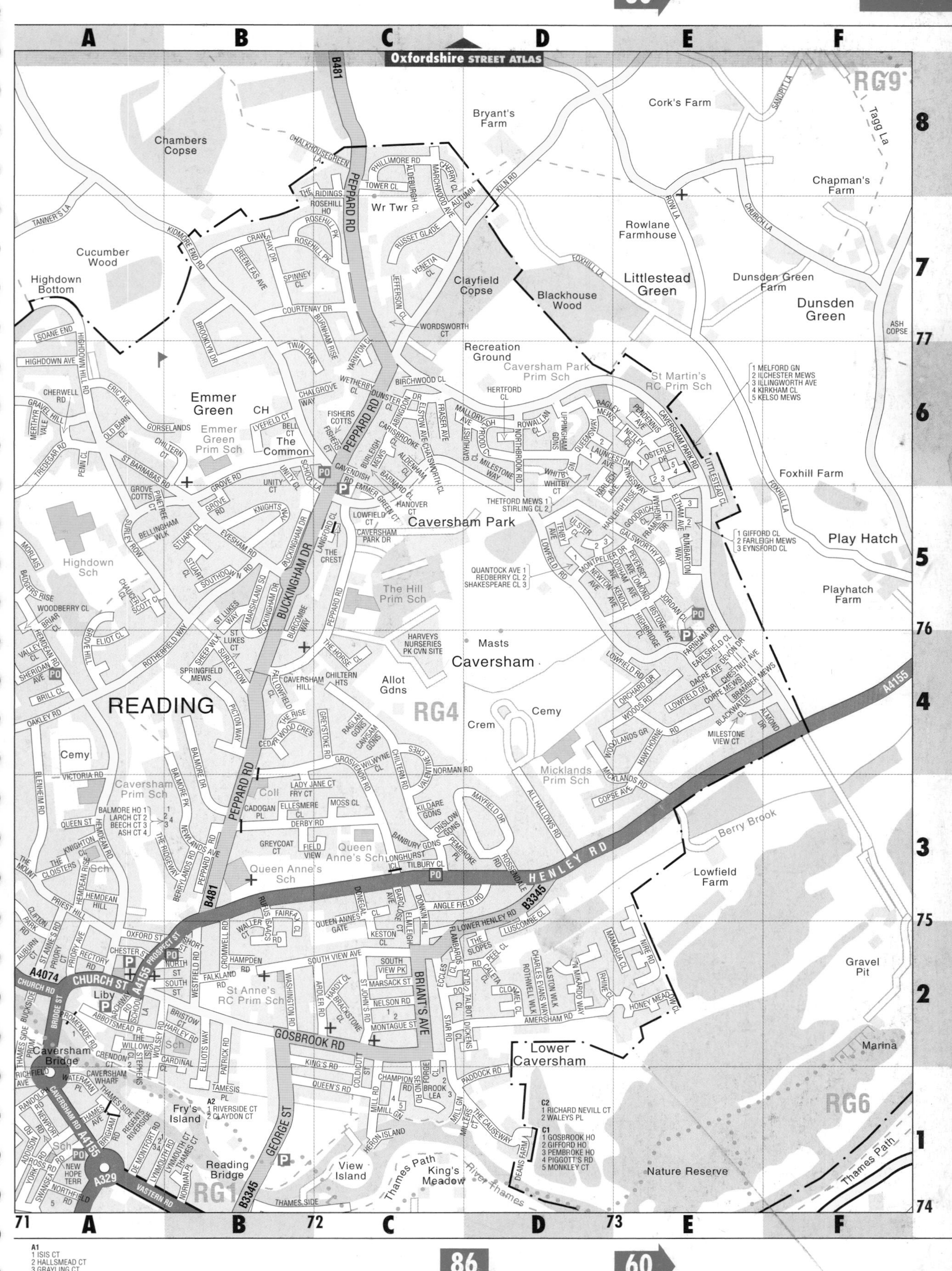

59 35

A B C D E F
8 7 77 6 5 76 4 3 75 2 1 74
RG9
RG10
RG4
RG6
RG5
HAMPSTEAD HILL
A4155
HENLEY RD
SPAN HILL
Hampstead Farm
The Warren
The Lynch
Hallsmead Ait
Bint's Farm
Hampstead Bottom
Round Wood
The Firs
Ash Copse
Spanhill Copse
Dunsden Farmhouse
Dunsden Green
Buck Ait
THAMES DR
Berry Brook
St Patrick's Stream
The Flowing Spring (PH)
St Patrick's Bridge
MILESTONE AVE
Botany Bay
Thames Path
SPRING LA
River Thames
Play Hatch
FOXHILL LA
FOXHILL CL
PLAYHATCH RD
B478
Sonning Eye
BROADMOOR LA
PH
Hotel
Gravel Works
WATERSIDE COTTS
Frizers Farm
Sonning Bridge
Marsh La
Aquatic Research Ctr
Hotel
The Mill at Sonning
Sonning
THAMES ST
CHARVIL LA
THE MEWS
HIGH ST
THE ROBERT PALMER COTTS
PO
Sonning Lock
B4446 PEARSON RD
Sonning Farm
Holme Park
GLEBE GDNS
LITTLE GLEBE
GARDE RD
GLEBE LA
PADDICK CL
Sonning CE Prim Sch
Reading Blue Coat Sch
PARKWAY DR
HAWTHORN WAY
OLD BATH RD
Sports Ground
Sports Ground
SONNING LA
BATH RD
SONNING GATE
HOLMEMOOR DR
SEGRAVE CL
POUND LA
Nature Reserve
CH
WEST CT
Holme Park Farm
HOLME PARK FARM LA
Duffields Bridge
MUSTARD LA
B4446
Thames Valley Bsns Pk
WEST DR
COPSE MEAD
Big Gogs
SONNING MOWS
OLD BATH RD
Buttshill Bridge
HIGHCLIFFE CL
ALDERLEY CL
DUFFIELD RD
SANDFORD DR
RETFORD CL
SOUTH DR
RYECROFT CL
WESTERN AVE
TIVERTON CL
FRAMPTON CL
WILTONSIDE
Willow Bank Jun & Inf Schs
UPPINGHAM DR
ROTHWELL GDNS
BRUNEL DR
WALMER RD
TELFORD CRES
BINGLEY GR
BUTTS HILL RD
MAPLE GROVE
RAVENSBOURNE DR
ROCHESTER AVE
GODSTOW CL
RADCOT CL
WARREN RD
WYNDHAM CRES
HANWOOD CL
LONDON RD
A4
SHEPHERDS HILL
ORACLE PARKWAY
74 75 76

59 87

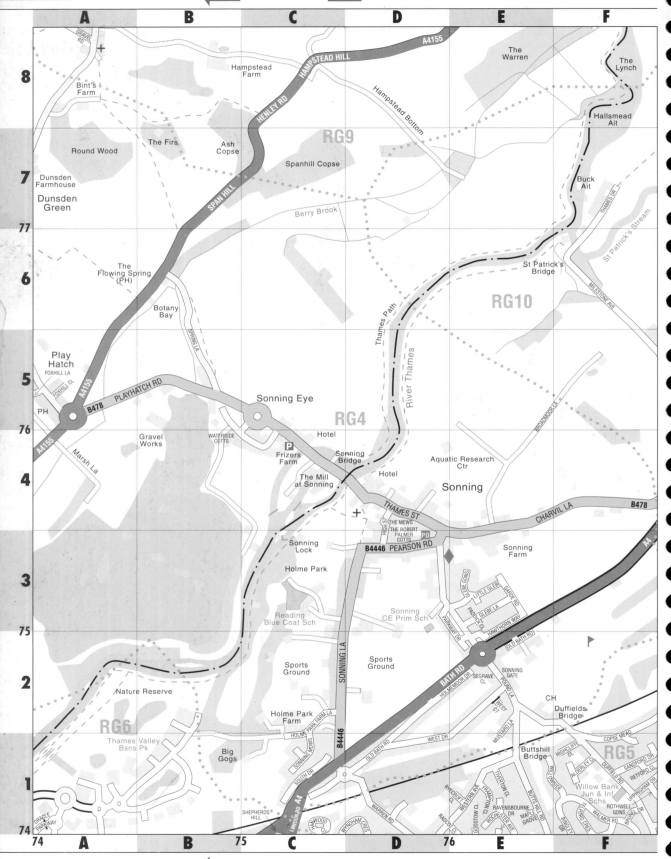

36
62

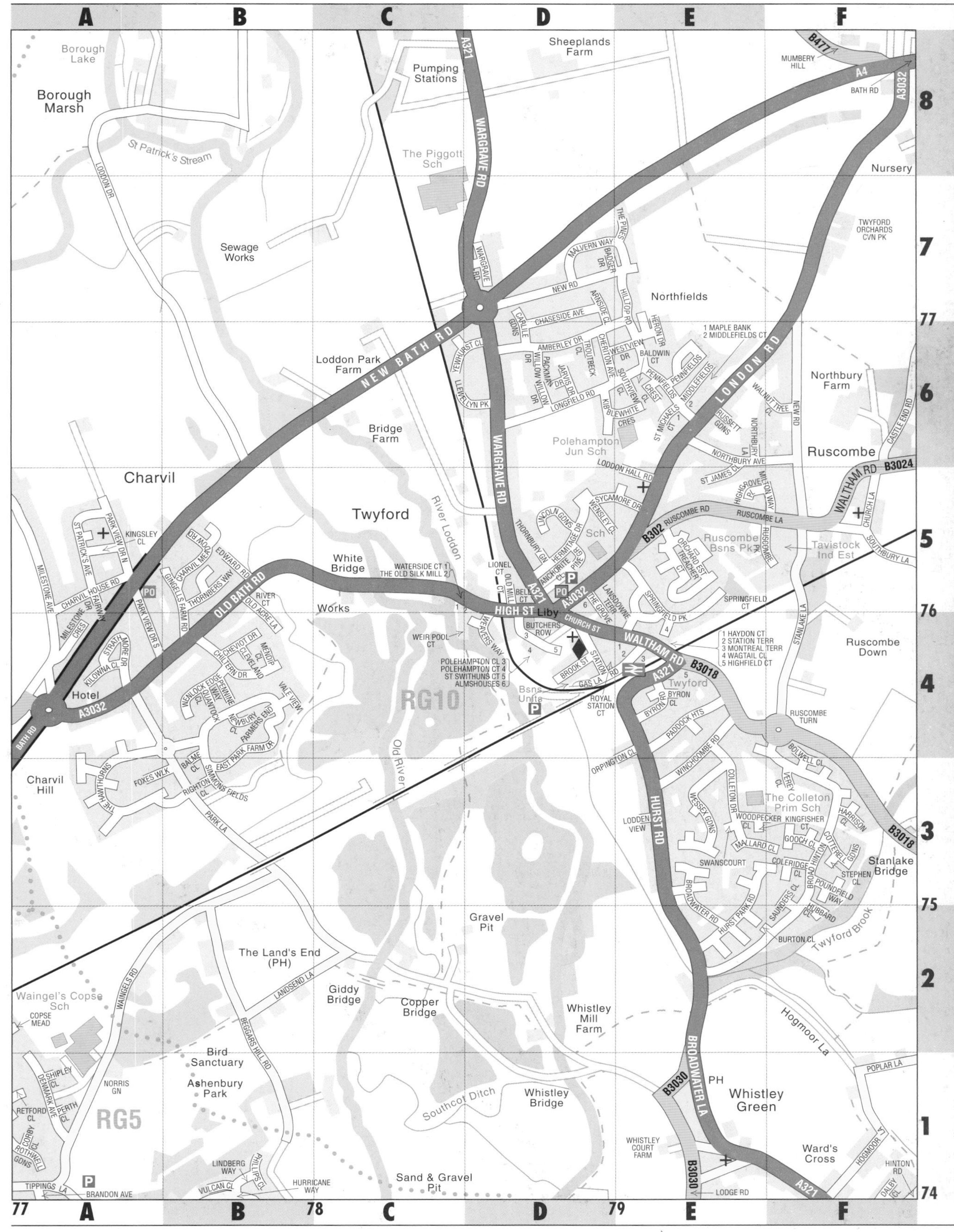
A B C D E F
Borough Lake
Borough Marsh
Sheeplands Farm
Pumping Stations
The Piggott Sch
Sewage Works
St Patrick's Stream
Loddon Park Farm
Bridge Farm
Northfields
Northbury Farm
Polehampton Jun Sch
Ruscombe
Charvil
Twyford
River Loddon
White Bridge
Works
Hotel
Charvil Hill
RG10
Old River
Ruscombe Bsns Pk
Tavistock Ind Est
Ruscombe Down
The Colleton Prim Sch
Stanlake Bridge
Twyford Brook
Gravel Pit
The Land's End (PH)
Giddy Bridge
Copper Bridge
Whistley Mill Farm
Waingel's Copse Sch
Bird Sanctuary
Ashenbury Park
Southcot Ditch
Whistley Bridge
Whistley Green
Ward's Cross
Sand & Gravel Pit
RG5
Hogmoor La
Nursery
Twyford Orchards Cvn Pk
New Bath Rd
Old Bath Rd
Wargrave Rd
London Rd
Waltham Rd
High St
Church St
Hurst Rd
Broadwater La
A4
A321
A3032
B3024
B3018
B3030
B302
B477
77 78 79
74 75 76 77
1 2 3 4 5 6 7 8

88
62

61 37

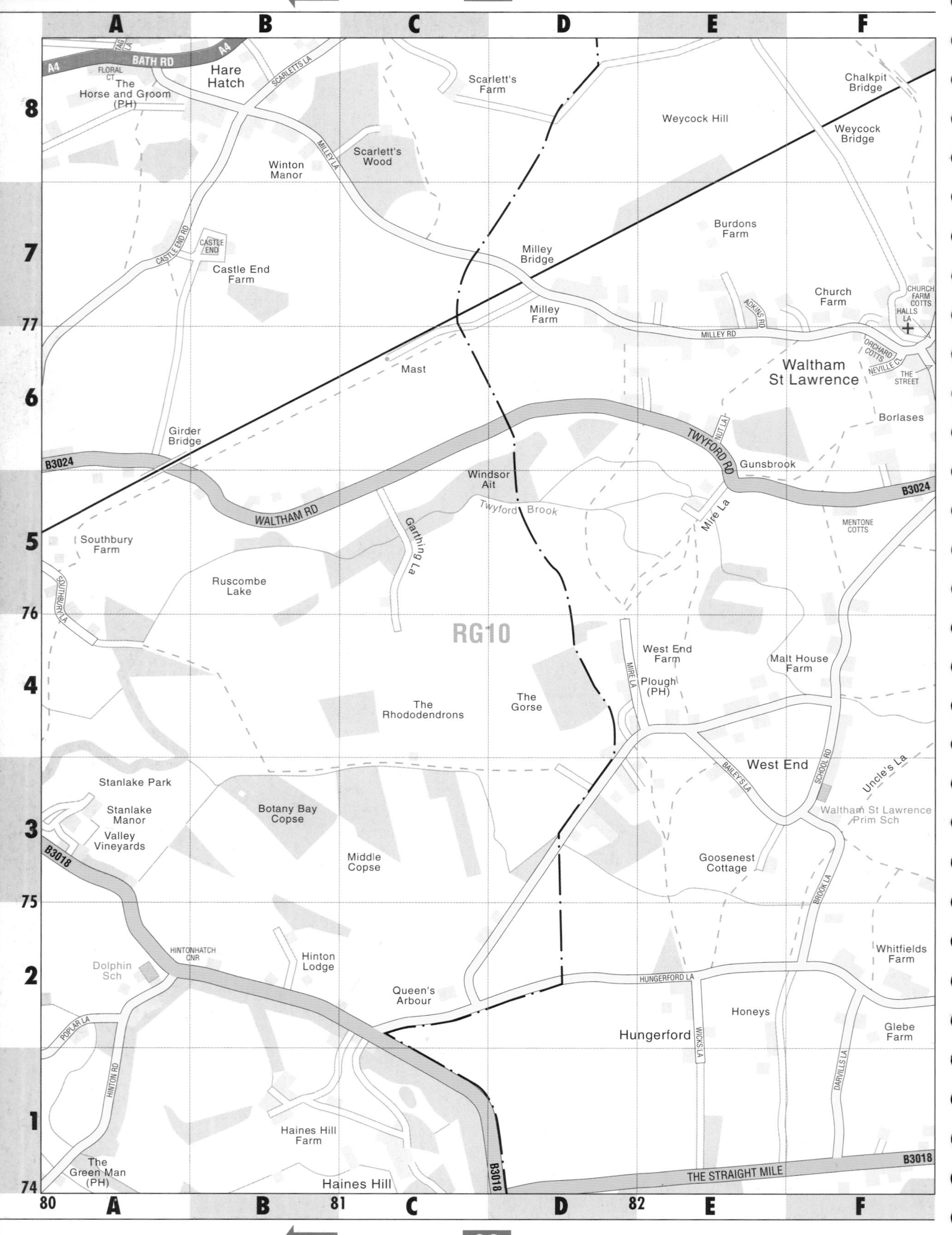
A
B
C
D
E
F
8
7
77
6
5
76
4
3
75
2
1
74
80
81
82
A4
BATH RD
FLORAL CT
The Horse and Groom (PH)
Hare Hatch
SCARLETTS LA
Scarlett's Farm
Weycock Hill
Chalkpit Bridge
Weycock Bridge
Winton Manor
MILLEY LA
Scarlett's Wood
Burdons Farm
CASTLE END RD
CASTLE END
Castle End Farm
Milley Bridge
Milley Farm
Church Farm
ADKINS RD
CHURCH FARM COTTS
HALLS LA
MILLEY RD
ORCHARD COTTS
NEVILLE CL
THE STREET
Waltham St Lawrence
Mast
Borlases
NUT LA
TWYFORD RD
Girder Bridge
B3024
Gunsbrook
Windsor Ait
Twyford Brook
WALTHAM RD
Mire La
Garthing La
MENTONE COTTS
Southbury Farm
SOUTHBURY LA
Ruscombe Lake
RG10
West End Farm
MIRE LA
Plough (PH)
Malt House Farm
The Rhododendrons
The Gorse
Stanlake Park
Botany Bay Copse
West End
BAILEY'S LA
SCHOOL RD
Uncle's La
Stanlake Manor
Valley Vineyards
Waltham St Lawrence Prim Sch
B3018
Middle Copse
Goosenest Cottage
BROOK LA
HINTONHATCH CNR
Hinton Lodge
Dolphin Sch
Whitfields Farm
HUNGERFORD LA
Queen's Arbour
Honeys
POPLAR LA
Hungerford
WICKS LA
Glebe Farm
HINTON RD
DARVILLS LA
Haines Hill Farm
The Green Man (PH)
THE STRAIGHT MILE
Haines Hill

61 89

38
64

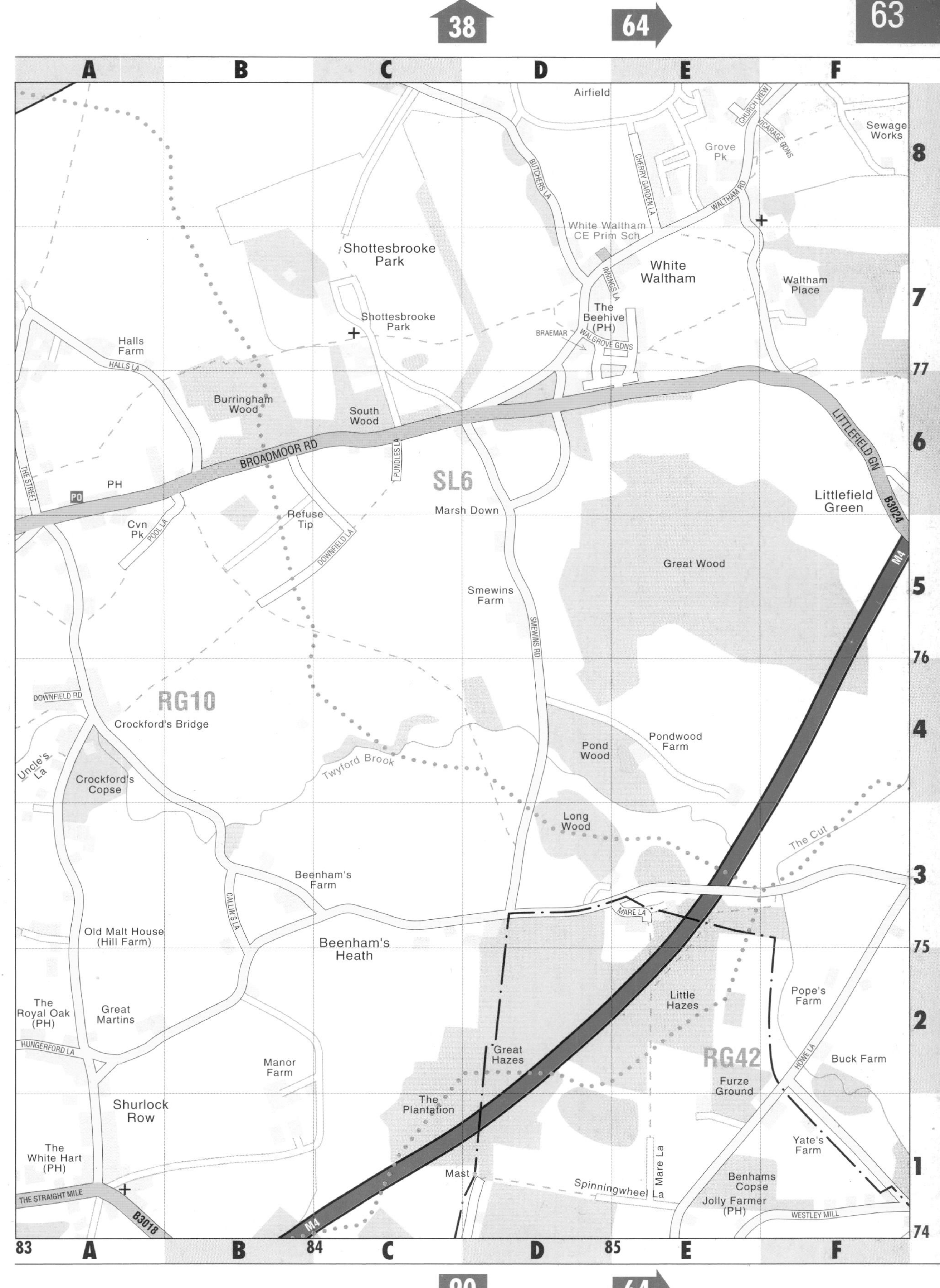
A
B
C
D
E
F
Airfield
Sewage Works
Grove Pk
CHURCH VIEW
VICARAGE GDNS
BUTCHERS LA
CHERRY GARDEN LA
WALTHAM RD
White Waltham CE Prim Sch
Shottesbrooke Park
White Waltham
Waltham Place
INNINGS LA
The Beehive (PH)
BRAEMAR
WALGROVE GDNS
Shottesbrooke Park
Halls Farm
HALLS LA
Burringham Wood
South Wood
BROADMOOR RD
PUNDLES LA
SL6
LITTLEFIELD GN
Littlefield Green
B3024
THE STREET
PH
PO
Cvn Pk
POOL LA
Refuse Tip
DOWNFIELD LA
Marsh Down
Great Wood
M4
Smewins Farm
SMEWINS RD
DOWNFIELD RD
RG10
Crockford's Bridge
Pond Wood
Pondwood Farm
Uncle's La
Crockford's Copse
Twyford Brook
Long Wood
The Cut
Beenham's Farm
CALLIN'S LA
MARE LA
Old Malt House (Hill Farm)
Beenham's Heath
The Royal Oak (PH)
Great Martins
Little Hazes
Pope's Farm
HUNGERFORD LA
Manor Farm
Great Hazes
RG42
HOWE LA
Buck Farm
Furze Ground
Shurlock Row
The Plantation
Yate's Farm
The White Hart (PH)
Mast
Mare La
Spinningwheel La
Benhams Copse
Jolly Farmer (PH)
THE STRAIGHT MILE
B3018
M4
WESTLEY MILL
8
7
77
6
5
76
4
3
75
2
1
74
83
84
85

90
64

63
39

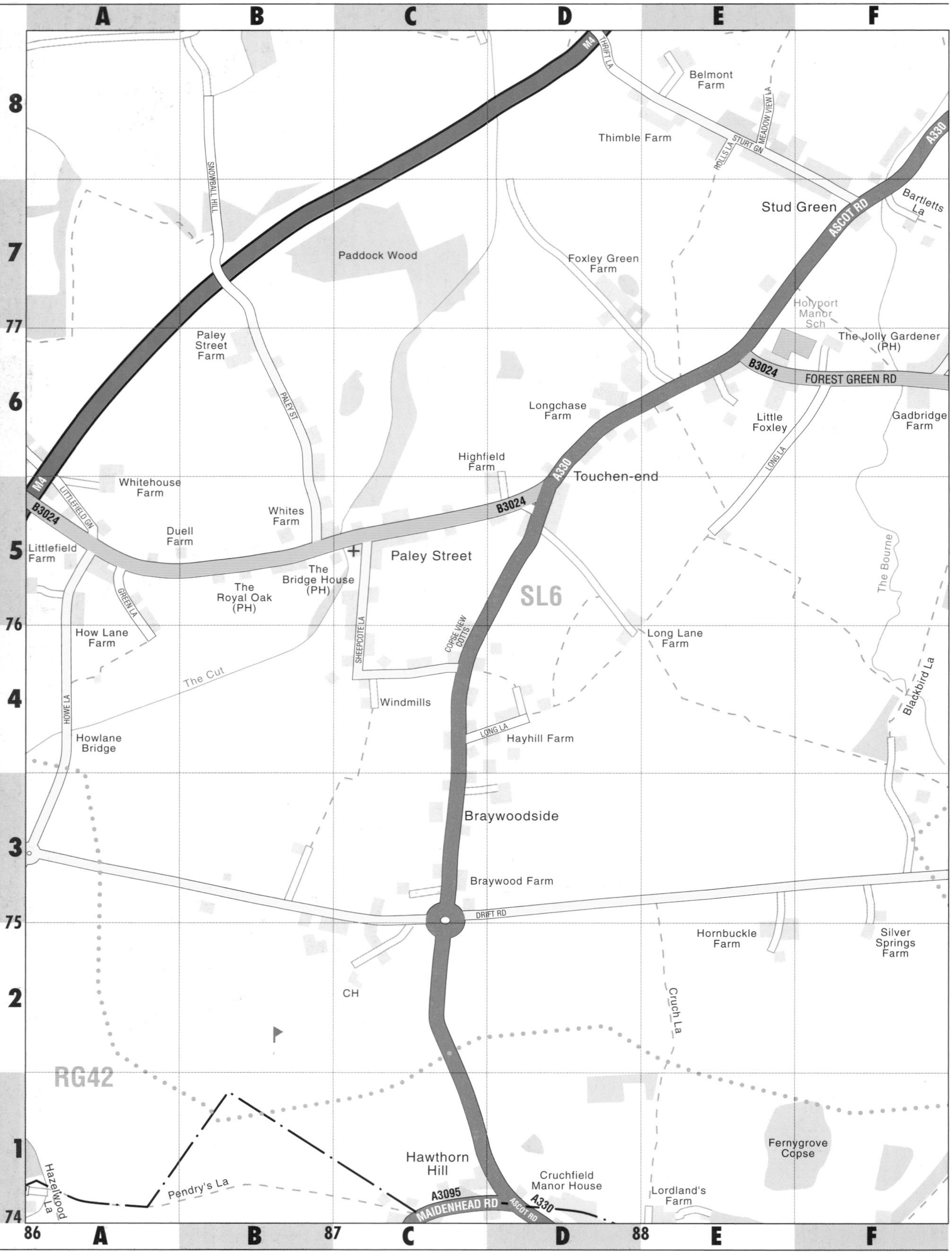

A B C D E F

8

7

77

6

5

76

4

3

75

2

1

74

M4

THRIFT LA

Belmont Farm

Thimble Farm

MEADOW VIEW LA

STURT GN

MILLS LA

A330

ASCOT RD

Stud Green

Bartletts La

Snowball Hill

Paddock Wood

Foxley Green Farm

Holyport Manor Sch

The Jolly Gardener (PH)

B3024

FOREST GREEN RD

Paley Street Farm

PALEY ST

Longchase Farm

Little Foxley

Gadbridge Farm

Highfield Farm

A330

Touchen-end

M4

B3024

Whitehouse Farm

Whites Farm

B3024

LONG LA

Littlefield Farm

LITTLEFIELD GN

Duell Farm

The Royal Oak (PH)

The Bridge House (PH)

Paley Street

SL6

The Bourne

GREEN LA

SHEEPCOTE LA

COPSE VIEW COTTS

Long Lane Farm

How Lane Farm

HOWE LA

The Cut

Windmills

LONG LA

Hayhill Farm

Blackbird La

Howlane Bridge

Braywoodside

Braywood Farm

DRIFT RD

Hornbuckle Farm

Silver Springs Farm

CH

Cruch La

RG42

Fernygrove Copse

Hawthorn Hill

Cruchfield Manor House

Lordland's Farm

Hazelwood La

Pendry's La

A3095

MAIDENHEAD RD

ASCOT RD

A330

86 A 87 B C 88 D E F

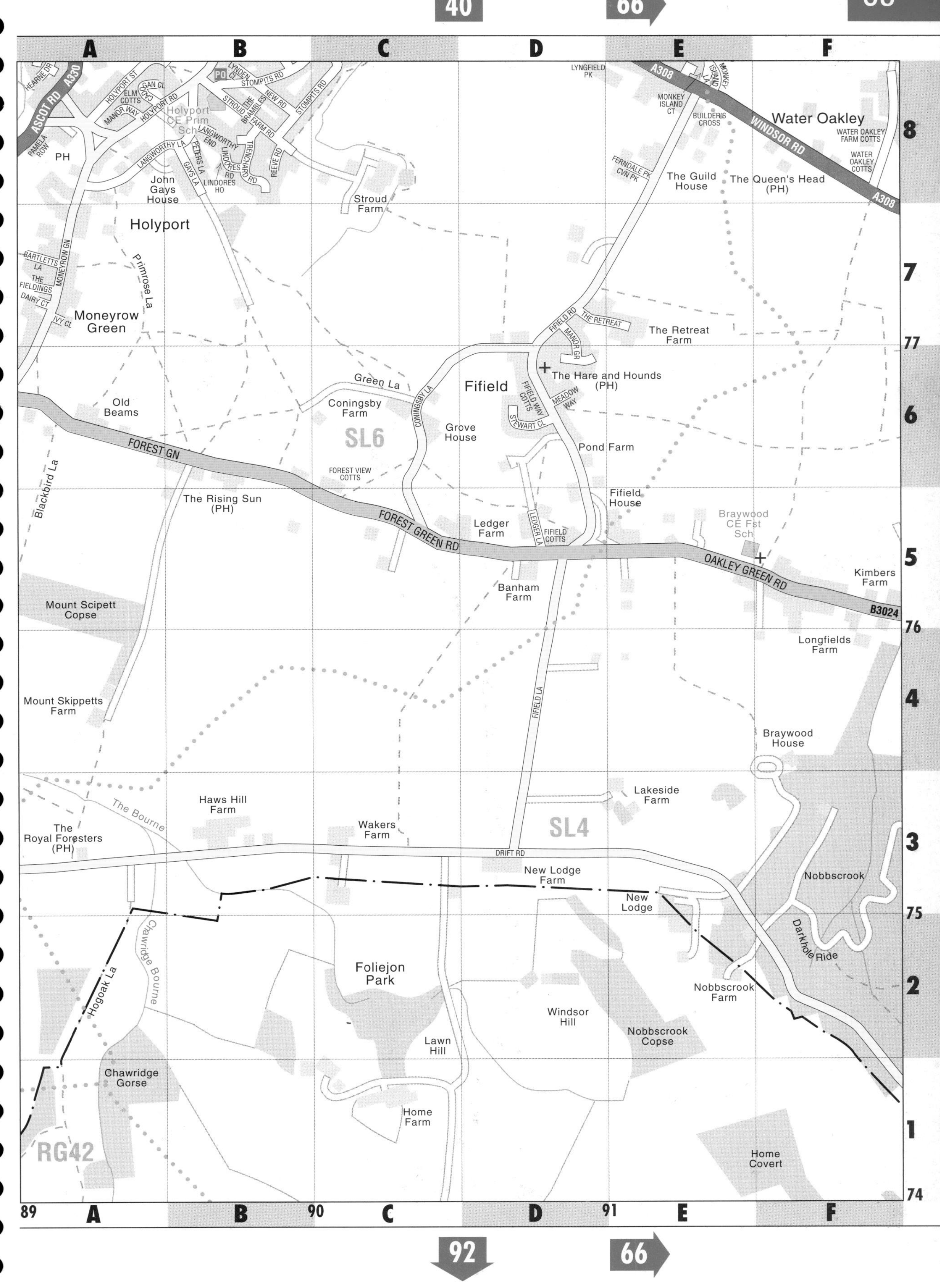

A B C D E F

8

A308

LYNGFIELD PK

MONKEY ISLAND CT

BUILDER'S CROSS

WINDSOR RD

Water Oakley

WATER OAKLEY FARM COTTS

WATER OAKLEY COTTS

A308

HEARNE DR

ASCOT RD A350

PH

PAMELA ROW

HOLYPORT ST

ELM COTTS

GAN CL

HOLYPORT RD

MANOR WAY

MONEYROW GN

PETERS LA

GAYS LA

LINDORES HO

LANGWORTHY LA

Holyport CE Prim Sch

Holyport End

NEW RD

STROUD FARM RD

FRENCHARD RD

STOMPITS RD

REEVE RD

KINDEN CL

PO

WOOD'S RD

Stroud Farm

FERNDALE PK CVN PK

FIFIELD RD

The Guild House

The Queen's Head (PH)

7

BARTLETTS LA

THE FIELDINGS

DAIRY CT

IVY CL

Holyport

Primrose La

John Gays House

Moneyrow Green

MONEYROW GN

THE RETREAT

The Retreat Farm

77

Blackbird La

Old Beams

Green La

Coningsby Farm

CONINGSBY LA

SL6

Fifield

FIFIELD WAY COTTS

MANOR RD

MEADOW WAY

The Hare and Hounds (PH)

Grove House

Pond Farm

6

FOREST GN

The Rising Sun (PH)

FOREST GREEN RD

Ledger Farm

LEDGER LA

STEWART CL

FIFIELD COTTS

Fifield House

Braywood CE Fst Sch

5

Mount Scipett Copse

Banham Farm

OAKLEY GREEN RD

Kimbers Farm

B3024

76

Mount Skippetts Farm

FIFIELD LA

Longfields Farm

4

Braywood House

The Bourne

Haws Hill Farm

Wakers Farm

SL4

Lakeside Farm

Nobbscrook

3

The Royal Foresters (PH)

CHAWRIDGE BOURNE

DRIFT RD

New Lodge Farm

New Lodge

Darkhole Ride

75

HOGOAK LA

Foliejon Park

Windsor Hill

Nobbscrook Farm

Nobbscrook Copse

2

RG42

Chawridge Gorse

Lawn Hill

Home Farm

Home Covert

1

74

65 41

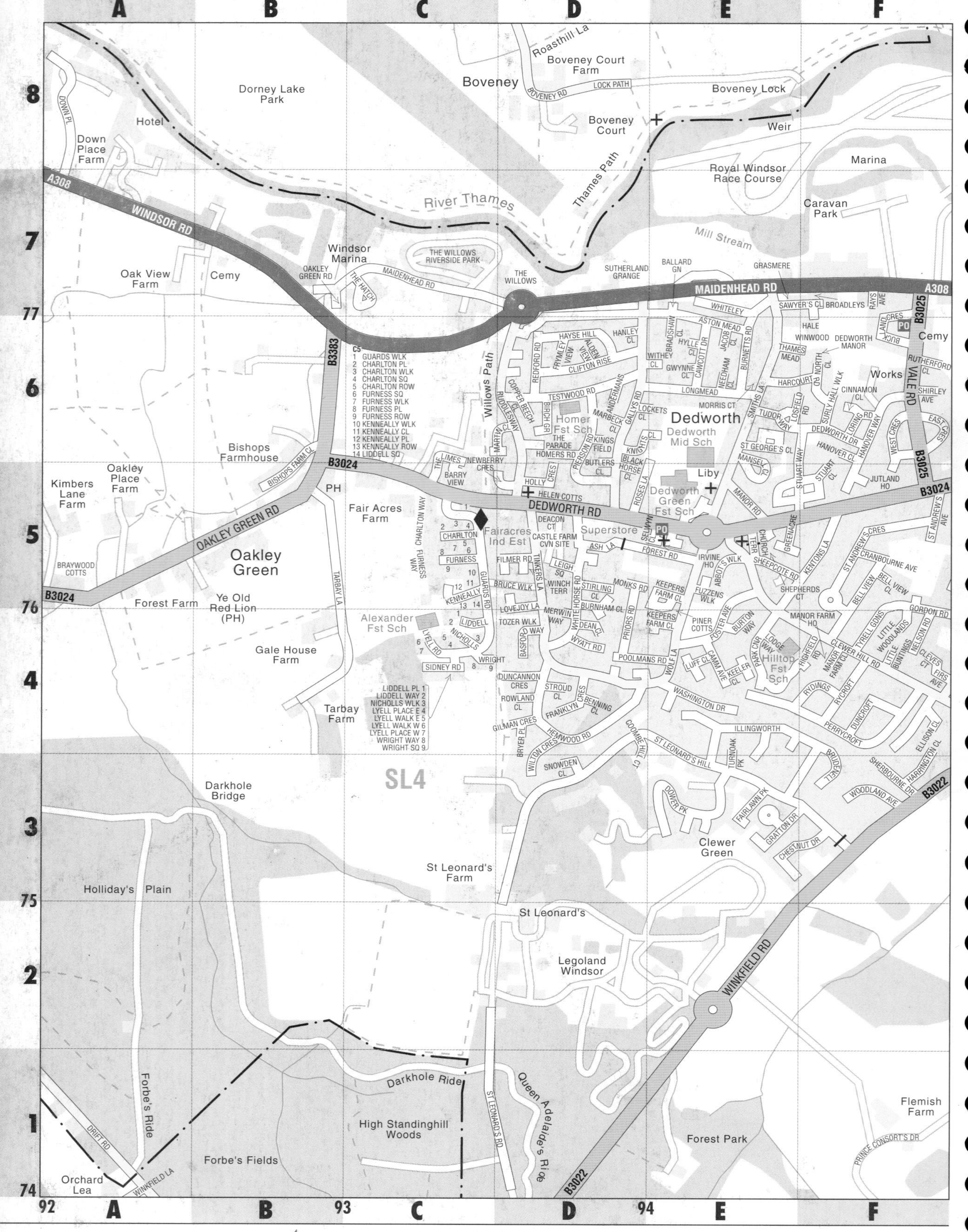
A B C D E F
8 7 77 6 5 76 4 3 75 2 1 74
92 93 94
Dorney Lake Park
Boveney
Roasthill La
Boveney Court Farm
Boveney Lock
Lock Path
Boveney Rd
Boveney Court
Weir
Marina
Royal Windsor Race Course
Caravan Park
Thames Path
River Thames
Mill Stream
Down Pl
Hotel
Down Place Farm
A308
Windsor Rd
Windsor Marina
Oakley Green Rd
The Hatch
Maidenhead Rd
The Willows Riverside Park
The Willows
Sutherland Grange
Ballard Gn
Grasmere
Oak View Farm
Cemy
B3383
Whiteley
Sawyer's Cl
Broadleys
Rays Ave
Land Cres
Buck
PO
B3025
Hale
Winwood
Dedworth Manor
Thames Mead
Rutherford Cl
Shirley Ave
Vale Rd
Works
Hayse Hill
Hanley Cl
Bradshaw
Aston Mead
Withey Cl
Hylle Cl
Cawcott Dr
Jacob Cl
Burnetts Rd
Gwynne Cl
Needham Cl
Frymley View
Alden View
Clifton Rise
Redford Rd
Harcourt
Longmead
Cinnamon Cl
Copper Beech Cl
Ruddlesway
Willows Path
Testwood Rd
Andermans
Marbeck Cl
Gallys Rd
Morris Ct
Smiths La
Tudor Way
Losfield Rd
Surly Hall Wlk
Loring Rd
Hanover Way
East Cres
West Cres
Homer Fst Sch
Birch Gr
Lockets Cl
Dedworth
Dedworth Mid Sch
Dedworth Dr
Hanover Cl
Martin Cl
The Parade
Kings Field
Knights Cl
St George's Cl
Mansel Cl
Stuart Way
Stuart Cl
Jutland Ho
Homers Rd
Pierson Rd
Butlers Cl
Black Horse Cl
Liby
Holly Cres
Roses La
Manor Rd
Dedworth Green Fst Sch
Greenacre
B3024
St Andrew's Ave
The Limes
Newberry Cres
Barry View
Helen Cotts
Dedworth Rd
Deacon Ct
Castle Farm Cvn Site
Selwyn Cl
Superstore
Ash La
Forest Rd
Irvine Ho
Church Terr
Kentons La
St Andrew's Cres
Cranbourne Ave
Bishops Farm Cl
Bishops Farmhouse
Oakley Place Farm
Kimbers Lane Farm
PH
Fair Acres Farm
Charlton Way
Furness Way
Charlton
Furness
Fairacres Ind Est
Filmer Rd
Tinkers La
Leigh Sq
Winch Terr
Stirling Cl
Monks Rd
Keepers Farm Cl
Abbots Wlk
Sheepcote Rd
Shepherds Ct
Bell View
Bell View Cl
Gordon Rd
Oakley Green Rd
Oakley Green
Braywood Cotts
Tarbay La
Guards Rd
Kenneally
Bruce Wlk
Lovejoy La
Burnham Cl
Fuzzens Wlk
Manor Farm Ho
Tyrell Gdns
Little Woodlands
Nelson Rd
Ye Old Red Lion (PH)
Forest Farm
Alexander Fst Sch
Liddell
Tozer Wlk
Merwin Way
White Horse Rd
Dean Cl
Priors Rd
Piner Cotts
Foster Ave
Burton Way
Lodge Way
Park Cnr
Highfield Rd
Clewer Hill Rd
Little Buntings
Cleves Ct
Firs Ave
Basford Way
Wyatt Rd
Manor Farm Cl
Lyell Rd
Nicholls
Wright
Sidney Rd
Gale House Farm
Poolmans Rd
Wolf La
Luff Cl
Camm Ave
Keeler Cl
Hilltop Fst Sch
Rydings
Rycroft
Duncroft
Duncannon Cres
Rowland Cl
Stroud Cl
Benning Cl
Franklyn Cres
Washington Dr
Perrycroft
Ellison Cl
Harrington Cl
Sherbourne Dr
Woodland Ave
B3022
Illingworth
Gilman Cres
Bryer Pl
Wilton Cres
Hemwood Rd
Coombe Hill Ct
St Leonard's Hill
Turnoak Pk
Brudenell
Snowden Cl
Dower Pk
Fairlawn Pk
Gratton Dr
Chestnut Dr
Tarbay Farm
C5
1 Guards Wlk
2 Charlton Pl
3 Charlton Wlk
4 Charlton Sq
5 Charlton Row
6 Furness Sq
7 Furness Wlk
8 Furness Pl
9 Furness Row
10 Kenneally Wlk
11 Kenneally Cl
12 Kenneally Pl
13 Kenneally Row
14 Liddell Sq
Liddell Pl 1
Liddell Way 2
Nicholls Wlk 3
Lyell Place E 4
Lyell Walk E 5
Lyell Walk W 6
Lyell Place W 7
Wright Way 8
Wright Sq 9
SL4
Darkhole Bridge
Clewer Green
St Leonard's Farm
Holliday's Plain
St Leonard's
Legoland Windsor
Winkfield Rd
Darkhole Ride
Queen Adelaide's Ride
St Leonard's Rd
Forbe's Ride
Drift Rd
High Standinghill Woods
Forest Park
Flemish Farm
Prince Consort's Dr
Forbe's Fields
Orchard Lea
Winkfield La

65 93

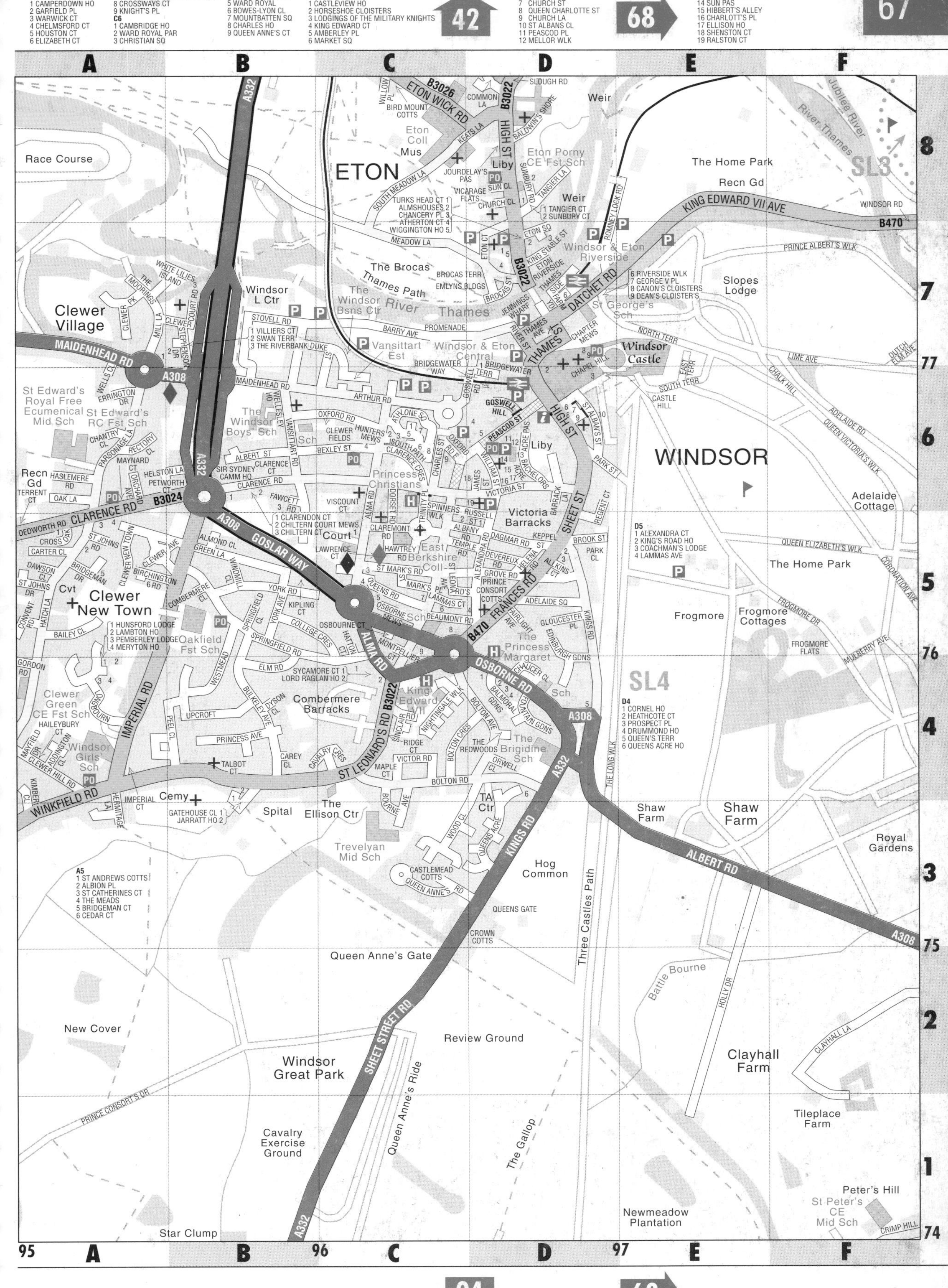

C5
1 CAMPERDOWN HO
2 GARFIELD PL
3 WARWICK CT
4 CHELMSFORD CT
5 HOUSTON CT
6 ELIZABETH CT

7 TRANSCEND OSBOURNE MEWS
8 CROSSWAYS CT
9 KNIGHT'S PL
C6
1 CAMBRIDGE HO
2 WARD ROYAL PAR
3 CHRISTIAN SQ

4 CRESCENT VILLAS
5 WARD ROYAL
6 BOWES-LYON CL
7 MOUNTBATTEN SQ
8 CHARLES HO
9 QUEEN ANNE'S CT

D6
1 CASTLEVIEW HO
2 HORSESHOE CLOISTERS
3 LODGINGS OF THE MILITARY KNIGHTS
4 KING EDWARD CT
5 AMBERLEY PL
6 MARKET SQ

42

D6
7 CHURCH ST
8 QUEEN CHARLOTTE ST
9 CHURCH LA
10 ST ALBANS CL
11 PEASCOD PL
12 MELLOR WLK

68

13 ROYAL FREE CT
14 SUN PAS
15 HIBBERT'S ALLEY
16 CHARLOTT'S PL
17 ELLISON HO
18 SHENSTON CT
19 RALSTON CT

67
43

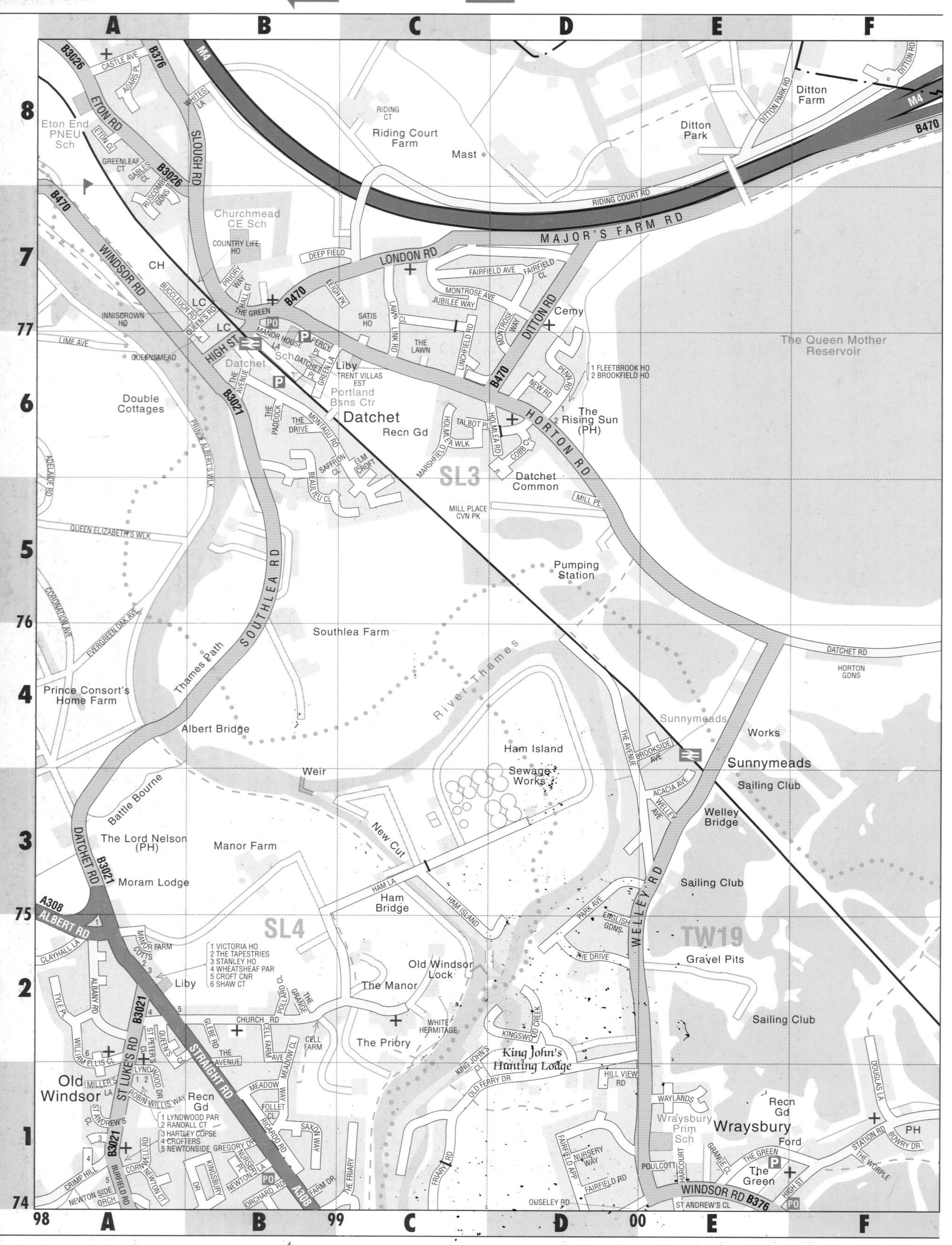
A
B
C
D
E
F
8
7
77
6
5
76
4
3
75
2
1
74
98
99
00
M4
B470
B3026
B376
Eton End PNEU Sch
ETON RD
SLOUGH RD
WHITES LA
Riding Court Farm
Mast
Ditton Park
Ditton Farm
RIDING COURT RD
MAJOR'S FARM RD
Churchmead CE Sch
WINDSOR RD
LONDON RD
DITTON RD
HORTON RD
Cemy
The Queen Mother Reservoir
Datchet
Recn Gd
SL3
Datchet Common
The Rising Sun (PH)
Double Cottages
Pumping Station
Southlea Farm
SOUTHLEA RD
B3021
Thames Path
River Thames
Prince Consort's Home Farm
Albert Bridge
Ham Island
Sewage Works
Weir
New Cut
Battle Bourne
The Lord Nelson (PH)
Manor Farm
Moram Lodge
DATCHET RD
Sunnymeads
Works
Sailing Club
Welley Bridge
WELLEY RD
TW19
Gravel Pits
A308
ALBERT RD
SL4
Ham Bridge
Old Windsor Lock
The Manor
The Priory
Liby
STRAIGHT RD
King John's Hunting Lodge
Old Windsor
Recn Gd
Wraysbury Prim Sch
Wraysbury
The Green
Ford
PH
WINDSOR RD B376
DATCHET RD
HORTON GDNS
1 VICTORIA HO
2 THE TAPESTRIES
3 STANLEY HO
4 WHEATSHEAF PAR
5 CROFT CNR
6 SHAW CT
1 LYNDWOOD PAR
2 RANDALL CT
3 HARTLEY COPSE
4 CROFTERS
5 NEWTONSIDE
1 FLEETBROOK HO
2 BROOKFIELD HO

67
95

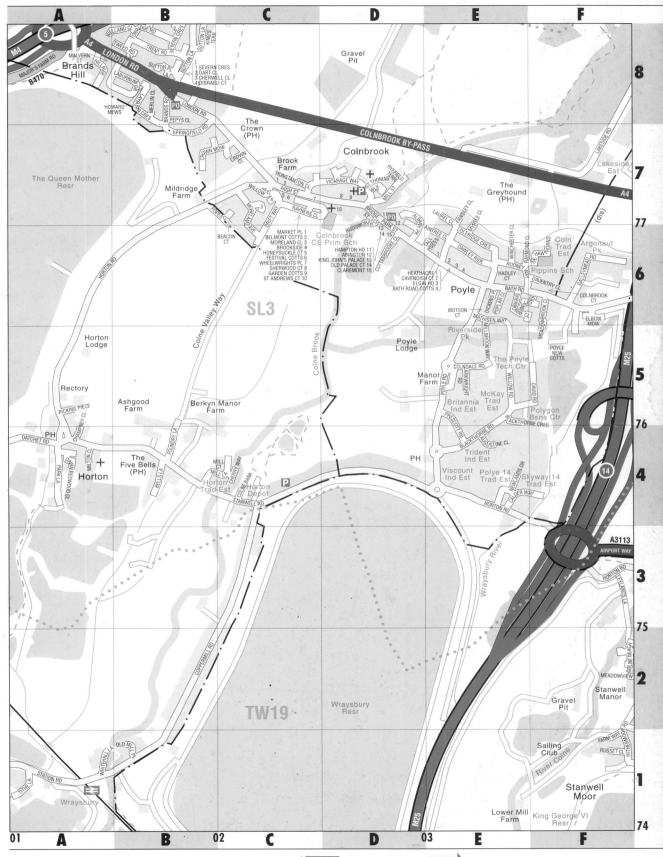
44
70

A B C D E F

8
7
77
6
5
76
4
3
75
2
1
74

M4
5
MALVERN CT
Brands Hill
MAJOR'S FARM RD
B470
HILLSIDE
WELLAND CL
TORRIDGE RD
TWEED RD
TRENT RD
SEVERN CRES
SUTTON LA
KING'S TERR
SUTTON PL
A4 LONDON RD
1 SEVERN CRES
2 DART CL
3 CHERWELL CL
4 DISRAELI CT
LABURNUM GR
LAYBURN CRES
MERLIN CL
BRANDS RD
PO
LONDON RD
HOWARD MEWS
PEPYS CL
SPRINGFIELD RD
CROWN MDW
CROWN CL
The Crown (PH)
Gravel Pit
COLNBROOK BY-PASS
Colnbrook
The Queen Mother Resr
Mildridge Farm
Brook Farm
HUNSTANTON CL
VICARAGE WAY
ST THOMAS WLK
RYEFIELD TERR
MILL ST
WILLOW CL
HIGH ST
POPES CL
MORELAND AVE
DRIFT WAY
RAYNERS CL
BEACON CT
BRIDGE ST
PARK ST
RUDSWORTH CL
Colnbrook CE Prim Sch
MARKET PL 1
BELMONT COTTS 2
MORELAND CL 3
BROOKSIDE 4
HONEYSUCKLE CT 5
FESTIVAL COTTS 6
WHEELWRIGHTS PL 7
SHERWOOD CT 8
GARDEN COTTS 9
ST ANDREWS CT 10
HAMPTON HO 11
ABINGTON 12
KING JOHN'S PALACE 13
OLD PALACE CT 14
CLAREMONT 15
COTTESBROOKE CL
ALBANY PK
AINTREE CL
TALL TREES
LAUREL CL
FAWSLEY CL
MYRTLE CL
COLERIDGE CRES
DAWLEY RIDE
The Greyhound (PH)
A4
Lakeside Est
LAKESIDE RD
(dis)
WINCHESTER CL
RAYMOND CL
THE HAWTHORNS
Coln Trad Est
Argonaut Pk
GALLEYMEAD RD
Pippins Sch
RODNEY WAY
HADLEY CT
DAVENTRY CL
BATH RD
HEATHACRE 1
CAVENDISH CT 2
ELGIN HO 3
BATH ROAD COTTS 4
Poyle
DICKENS PL
POPLAR CL
SHERBORNE CL
MEADOWBROOK CL
COLNBROOK CT
ELBOW MDW
IBOTSON CT
MATHISEN WAY
Riverside Pk
MILLBROOK WAY
Poyle Lodge
POYLE NEW COTTS
SL3
HORTON RD
Colne Valley Way
Colne Brook
Horton Lodge
Manor Farm
COLNDALE RD
ARKWRIGHT RD
The Poyle Tech Ctr
WILLOW RD
DAVID RD
POYLE RD
M25
Rectory
Ashgood Farm
Berkyn Manor Farm
Britannia Ind Est
McKay Trad Est
Polygon Bsns Ctr
PICKINS PIECE
CHAMPNEY CL
PH
DATCHET RD
FOUNDRY LA
PRESCOTT RD
BLACKTHORNE CRES
BLACKTHORNE RD
AUGUSTINE CL
MILTON CL
DAWN REDWOOD CL
PARK LA
Horton
The Five Bells (PH)
BELLS LA
MILL CT
MILL LA
CHERRY WAY
COLNE BANK
Horton Trad Est
Horton Depot
P
Trident Ind Est
PH
Viscount Ind Est
Polye 14 Trad Est
NEWLANDS DR
Skyway 14 Trad Est
CALDER WAY
14
STANWELL RD
HORTON RD
Wraysbury River
A3113
AIRPORT WAY
HORTON RD
LEYLANDS LA
COPPERMILL RD
COLNE REACH
MEADOWVIEW
Stanwell Manor
TW19
Wraysbury Resr
Gravel Pit
OLD MILL PL
WHITEHALL LA
Sailing Club
FARM WAY
HITHERMOOR RD
RUSSET CL
River Colne
STATION RD
TITHE LA
Wraysbury
Stanwell Moor
M25
Lower Mill Farm
King George VI Resr

01 A B 02 C D 03 E F

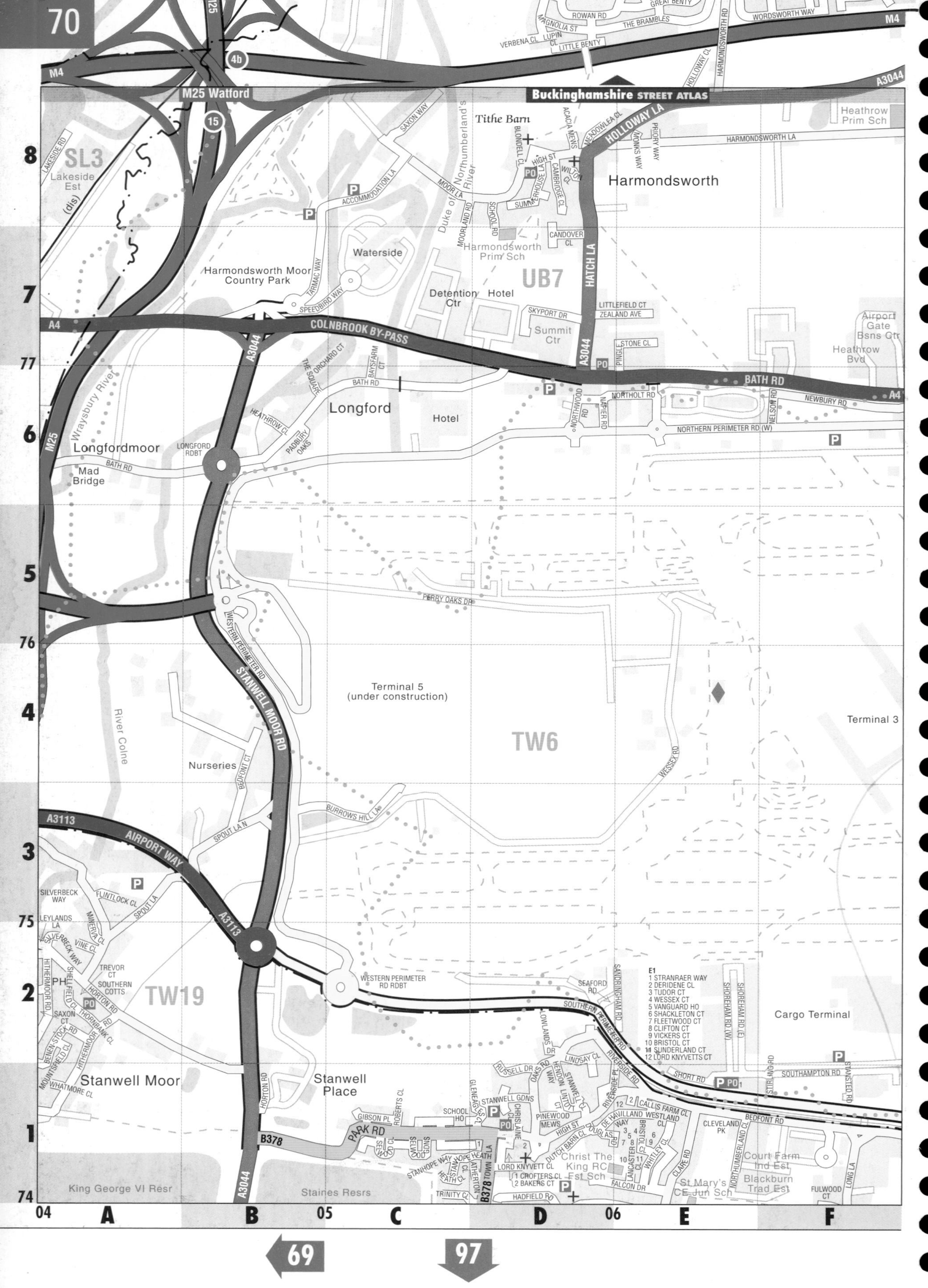

Buckinghamshire STREET ATLAS

M4

M25 Watford

15

SL3
Lakeside Rd
Lakeside Est (dis)

M4

A3044

Heathrow Prim Sch

Tithe Barn

HOLLOWAY LA

Harmondsworth

HARMONDSWORTH LA

SAXON WAY

ACCOMMODATION LA

MOOR LA

Waterside

Duke of Northumberland's River

Harmondsworth Prim Sch

Harmondsworth Moor Country Park

Detention Ctr   Hotel

UB7

HATCH LA

LITTLEFIELD CT
ZEALAND AVE

SKYPORT DR

Summit Ctr

Airport Gate Bsns Ctr

Heathrow Bvd

A4

COLNBROOK BY-PASS

A3044

THE SQUARE

BATH RD

HEATHROW CL

PADBURY OAKS

Hotel

Longford

BATH RD

P   NORTHOLT RD

A4
NEWBURY RD

NORTHERN PERIMETER RD (W)

M25

Wraysbury River

Longfordmoor

BATH RD

Longford RDBT

Mad Bridge

WESTERN PERIMETER RD

STANWELL MOOR RD

PERRY OAKS DR

River Colne

Terminal 5
(under construction)

TW6

Terminal 3

WESSEX RD

Nurseries

BURROWS HILL LA

SPOUT LA N

A3113

AIRPORT WAY

A3113

P
Silverbeck Way   Flintlock Cl   SPOUT LA

LEYLANDS LA

TREVOR CT

TW19

Southern Cotts

PH

SAXON CT   THORNBANK CL

HITHERMOOR RD

HORTON RD

Western Perimeter Rd RDBT

SEAFORD RD

SANDRINGHAM RD

SHOREHAM RD (E)

SOUTHERN PERIMETER RD

E1
1 STRANRAER WAY
2 DERIDENE CL
3 TUDOR CT
4 WESSEX CT
5 VANGUARD HO
6 SHACKLETON CT
7 FLEETWOOD CT
8 CLIFTON CT
9 VICKERS CT
10 BRISTOL CT
11 SUNDERLAND CT
12 LORD KNYVETTS CT

Cargo Terminal

Stanwell Moor

WHATMORE CL

Stanwell Place

GIBSON PL

ROBERTS CL

SCHOOL HO

PARK RD

B378

A3044

HORTON RD

King George VI Resr

Staines Resrs

Stanwell Gdns

CHRISLAINE

PINEWOOD MEWS

HIGH ST

LINDSAY CL

LOWLANDS RD

RIVERSIDE

Christ The King RC Est Sch

St Mary's CE Jun Sch

BEDFONT RD

SOUTHAMPTON RD

Court Farm Ind Est

Blackburn Trad Est

FULWOOD CT

B378

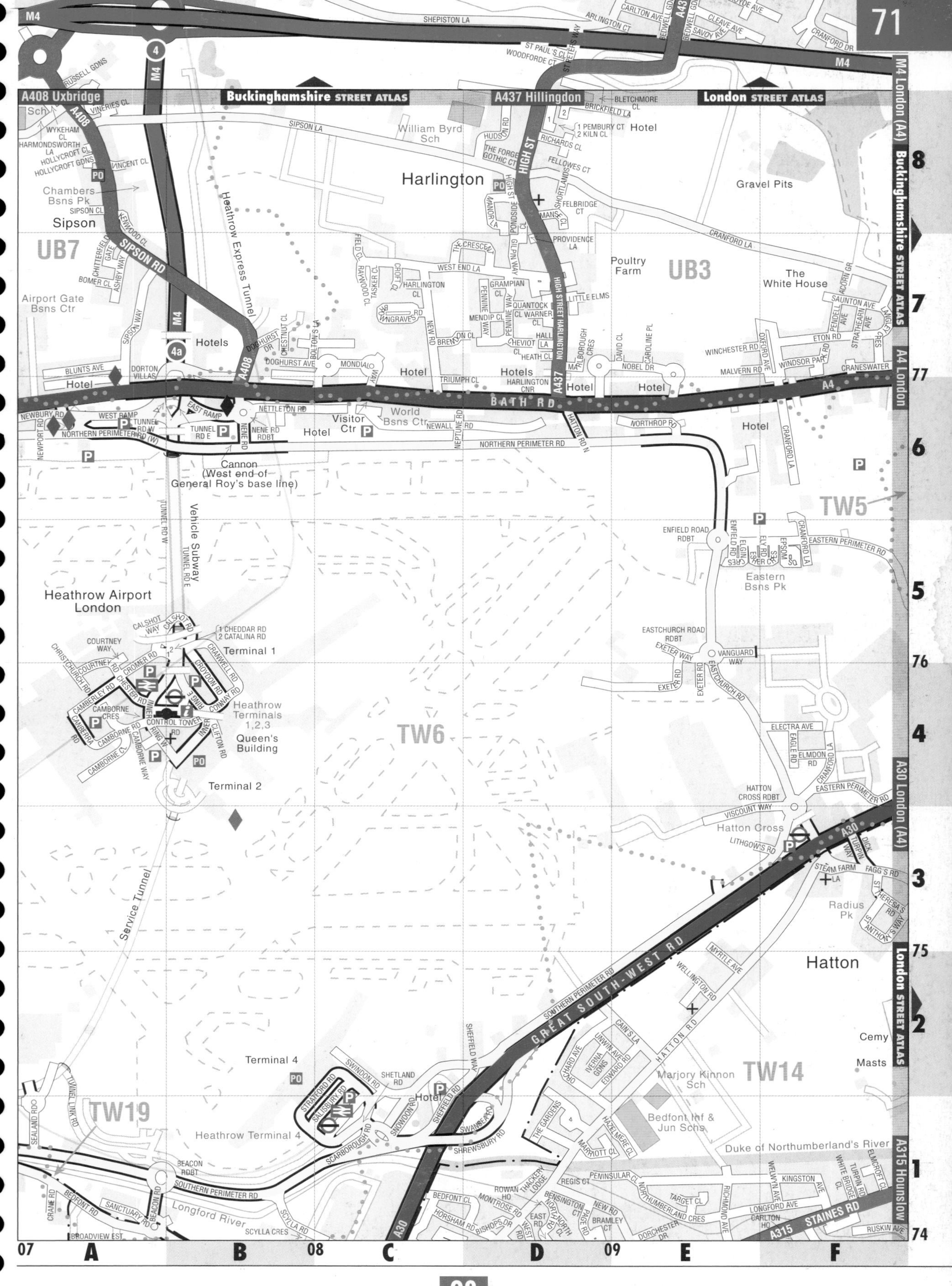
A408 Uxbridge
Buckinghamshire STREET ATLAS
A437 Hillingdon
London STREET ATLAS
M4 London (A4)
Buckinghamshire STREET ATLAS
A4 London
A30 London (A4)
London STREET ATLAS
A315 Hounslow
Harlington
Sipson
UB7
UB3
TW5
TW6
TW14
TW19
Heathrow Airport London
Terminal 1
Terminal 2
Terminal 4
Heathrow Terminals 1,2,3
Queen's Building
Heathrow Terminal 4
Heathrow Express Tunnel
Vehicle Subway
Service Tunnel
Cannon (West end of General Roy's base line)
Gravel Pits
Poultry Farm
The White House
Chambers Bsns Pk
Airport Gate Bsns Ctr
William Byrd Sch
World Bsns Ctr
Visitor Ctr
Eastern Bsns Pk
Hatton Cross
Hatton
Radius Pk
Marjory Kinnon Sch
Bedfont Inf & Jun Schs
Duke of Northumberland's River
Longford River
Cemy
Masts
BATH RD
GREAT SOUTH-WEST RD
NORTHERN PERIMETER RD
SOUTHERN PERIMETER RD
EASTERN PERIMETER RD
SIPSON RD
SIPSON LA
HIGH ST
HIGH STREET HARLINGTON
SHEPISTON LA
CRANFORD LA
HATTON RD
STAINES RD
07 A B 08 C D 09 E F
74 75 76 77

98

45

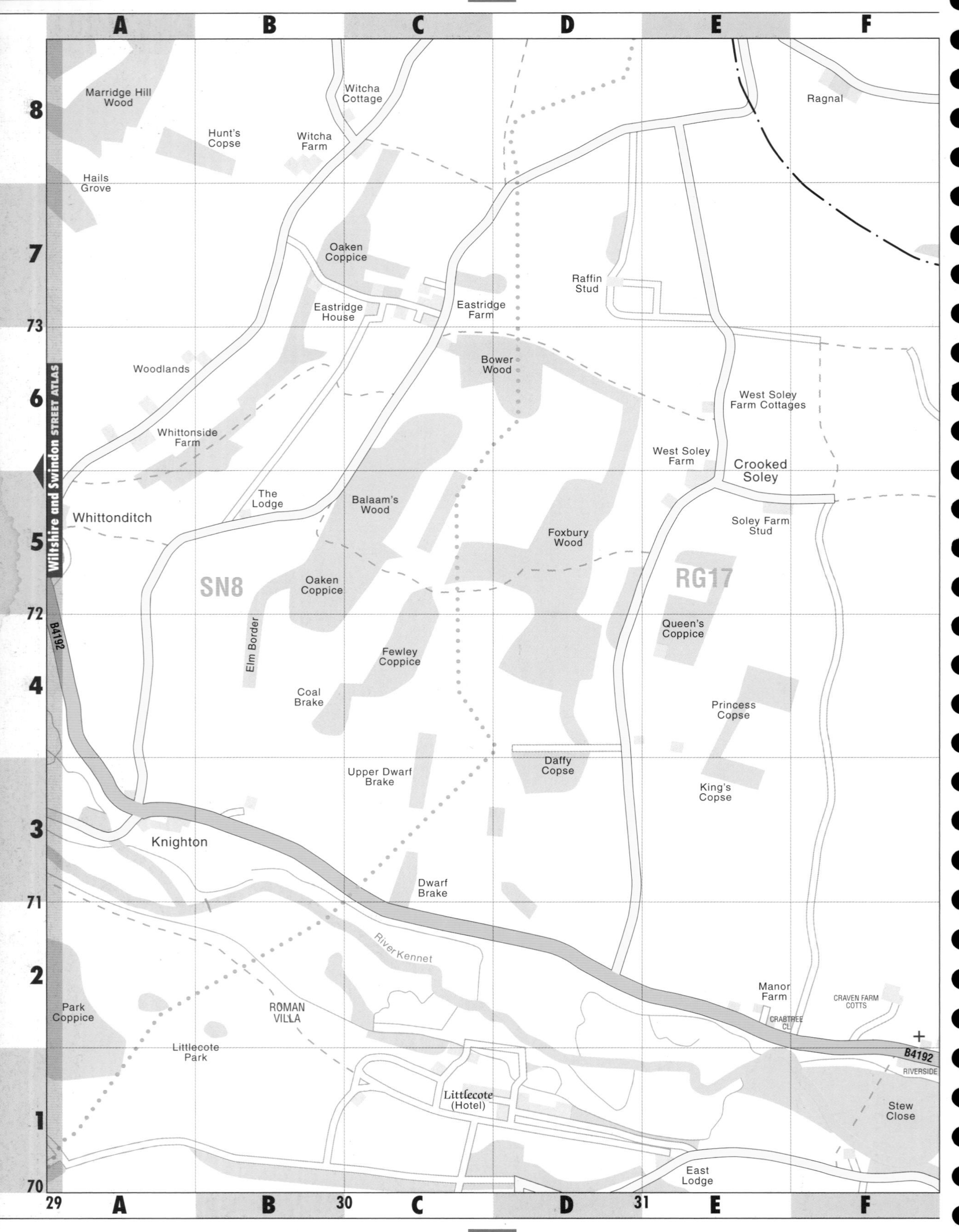
A B C D E F
8
7
73
6
5
72
4
3
71
2
1
70
29 30 31
Wiltshire and Swindon STREET ATLAS
Marridge Hill Wood
Hunt's Copse
Witcha Cottage
Witcha Farm
Ragnal
Hails Grove
Oaken Coppice
Raffin Stud
Eastridge House
Eastridge Farm
Woodlands
Bower Wood
West Soley Farm Cottages
Whittonside Farm
West Soley Farm
Crooked Soley
The Lodge
Balaam's Wood
Whittonditch
Soley Farm Stud
Foxbury Wood
SN8
Oaken Coppice
RG17
B4192
Queen's Coppice
Elm Border
Fewley Coppice
Coal Brake
Princess Copse
Upper Dwarf Brake
Daffy Copse
King's Copse
Knighton
Dwarf Brake
River Kennet
Manor Farm
Park Coppice
ROMAN VILLA
CRAVEN FARM COTTS
CRABTREE CL
Littlecote Park
B4192
RIVERSIDE
Littlecote (Hotel)
Stew Close
East Lodge

99

46
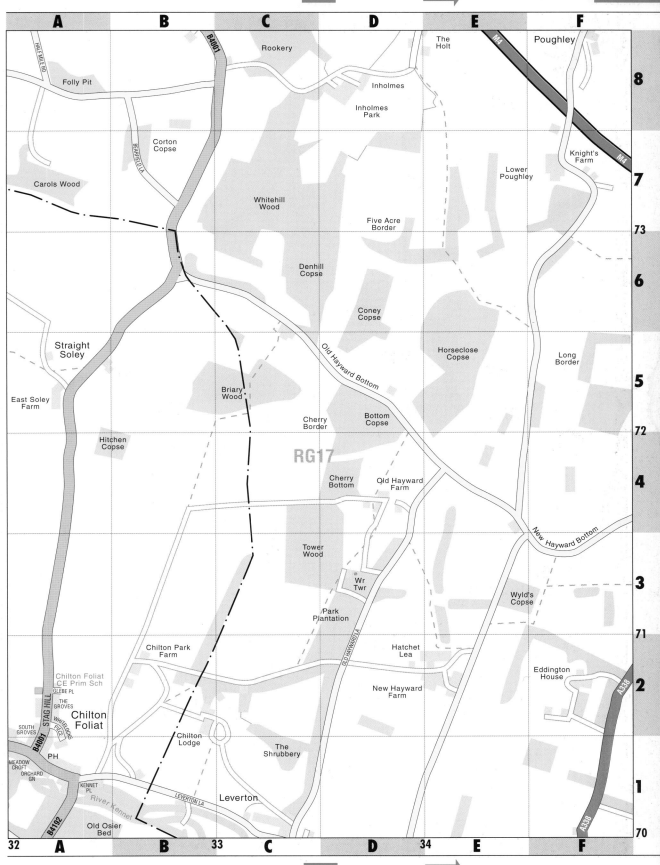
74

A B C D E F

8 7 73 6 5 72 4 3 71 2 1 70

HALF MILE RD
Folly Pit
B4001
Rookery
The Holt
M4
Poughley
Inholmes
Inholmes Park
Corton Copse
BEARFIELD LA
Carols Wood
Whitehill Wood
Knight's Farm
Lower Poughley
Five Acre Border
Denhill Copse
Coney Copse
Straight Soley
Horseclose Copse
Long Border
Old Hayward Bottom
Briary Wood
East Soley Farm
Cherry Border
Bottom Copse
Hitchen Copse
RG17
Cherry Bottom
Old Hayward Farm
New Hayward Bottom
Tower Wood
Wr Twr
Wyld's Copse
Park Plantation
OLD HAYWARD LA
Chilton Park Farm
Hatchet Lea
Eddington House
Chilton Foliat CE Prim Sch
GLEBE PL
New Hayward Farm
A338
STAG HILL
THE GROVES
Chilton Foliat
WHITELOCKS PIECE
SOUTH GROVES
Chilton Lodge
The Shrubbery
PH
MEADOW CROFT
ORCHARD GN
KENNET PL
LEVERTON LA
Leverton
River Kennet
B4192
Old Osier Bed

32 A B 33 C D 34 E F

100
74

73
47

A B C D E F

8

Somercourt

Fisher's Farm

B4000

ERMIN ST

Tommylands Copse

The Pheasant Inn (PH)

B4000

ERMIN ST

B4000

Shefford Woodlands

Templars Farm

7

M4

BARN COTTS

73

A338

Newtown Lodge Farm

BAYDON RD

6

14

Breach Copse

Lovelocks

B4000

North Hidden Farm

Norbin's Wood

M4

5

North Hidden Cottages

72

RG17

4

Wickfield Copse

Windingwood La

Lower Farm

Jeffrey's Border

The Tally-ho (PH)

RADLEY BOTTOM

Hungerford Newtown

Winding Wood

Windingwood Bottom

3

PO

Little Hidden Farm

71

North Denford Farm

A338

2

Dunkin's Copse

Heath Hanger La

Heath Hanger Copse

Stibbs Wood

Three Gate Copse

Radley Farm

1

Great Hidden Farm

The Hassock

70

35 A 36 B C 37 D E F

48
76

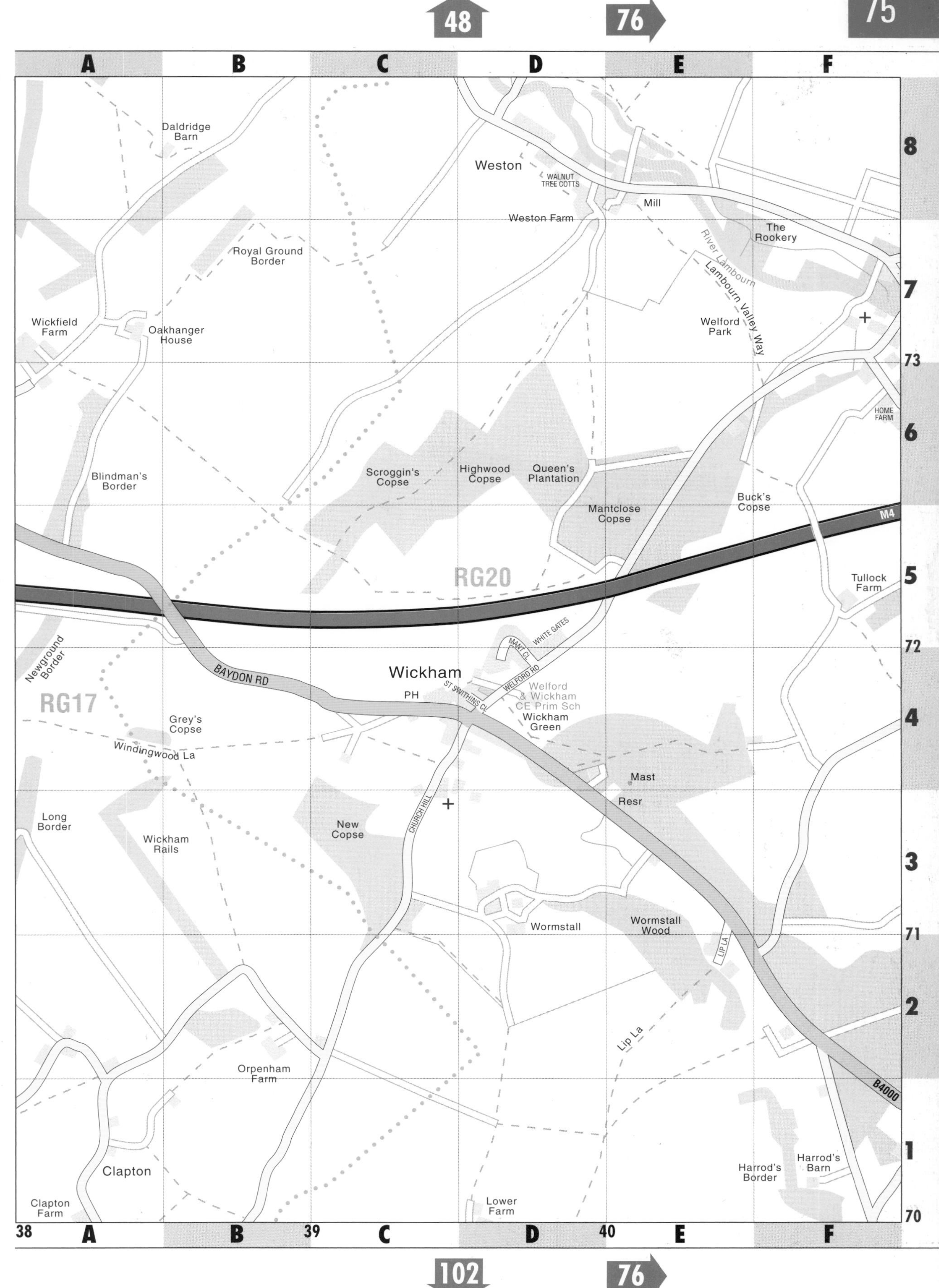
A
B
C
D
E
F
Daldridge Barn
Weston
WALNUT TREE COTTS
Mill
Weston Farm
The Rookery
River Lambourn
Lambourn Valley Way
Royal Ground Border
Wickfield Farm
Oakhanger House
Welford Park
Blindman's Border
Scroggin's Copse
Highwood Copse
Queen's Plantation
Mantclose Copse
Buck's Copse
HOME FARM
M4
RG20
Tullock Farm
Newground Border
WHITE GATES
MANT CL
Wickham
BAYDON RD
RG17
PH
ST SWITHINS CL
WELFORD RD
Welford & Wickham CE Prim Sch
Wickham Green
Grey's Copse
Windingwood La
Mast
Resr
Long Border
Wickham Rails
New Copse
CHURCH HILL
Wormstall
Wormstall Wood
LIP LA
Lip La
Orpenham Farm
B4000
Clapton
Clapton Farm
Lower Farm
Harrod's Border
Harrod's Barn
8
7
73
6
5
72
4
3
71
2
1
70
38
39
40

102
76

75
49

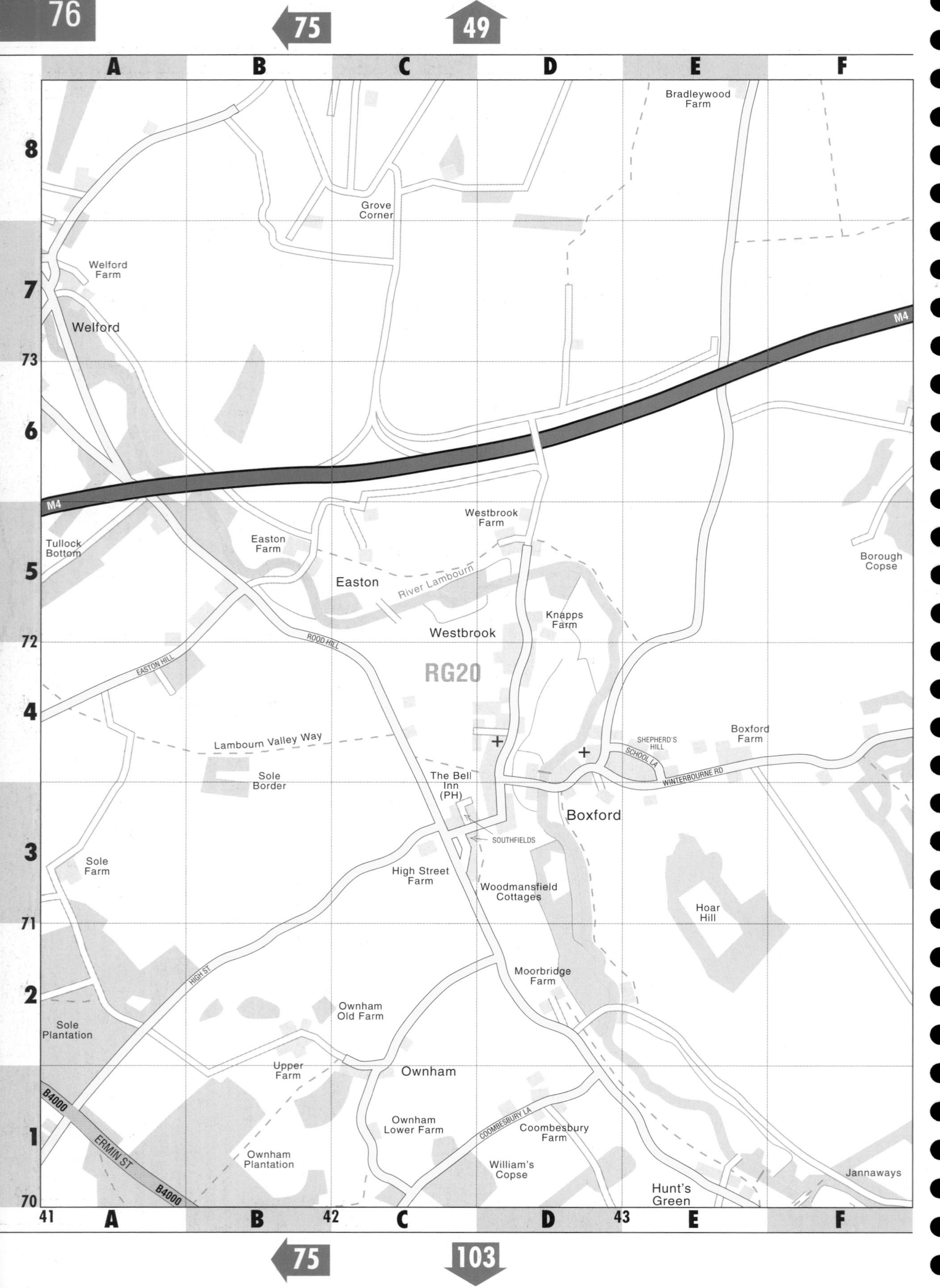
A
B
C
D
E
F
8
7
73
6
5
72
4
3
71
2
1
70
41
42
43
Bradleywood Farm
Grove Corner
Welford Farm
Welford
M4
Tullock Bottom
Easton Farm
Westbrook Farm
Easton
River Lambourn
Westbrook
Knapps Farm
Borough Copse
RG20
ROOD HILL
EASTON HILL
Lambourn Valley Way
SHEPHERD'S HILL
SCHOOL LA
Boxford Farm
WINTERBOURNE RD
Sole Border
The Bell Inn (PH)
Boxford
SOUTHFIELDS
Sole Farm
High Street Farm
Woodmansfield Cottages
Hoar Hill
Moorbridge Farm
HIGH ST
Sole Plantation
Ownham Old Farm
Upper Farm
Ownham
B4000
ERMIN ST
Ownham Lower Farm
COOMBESBURY LA
Coombesbury Farm
Ownham Plantation
William's Copse
Hunt's Green
Jannaways

75
103

50
78

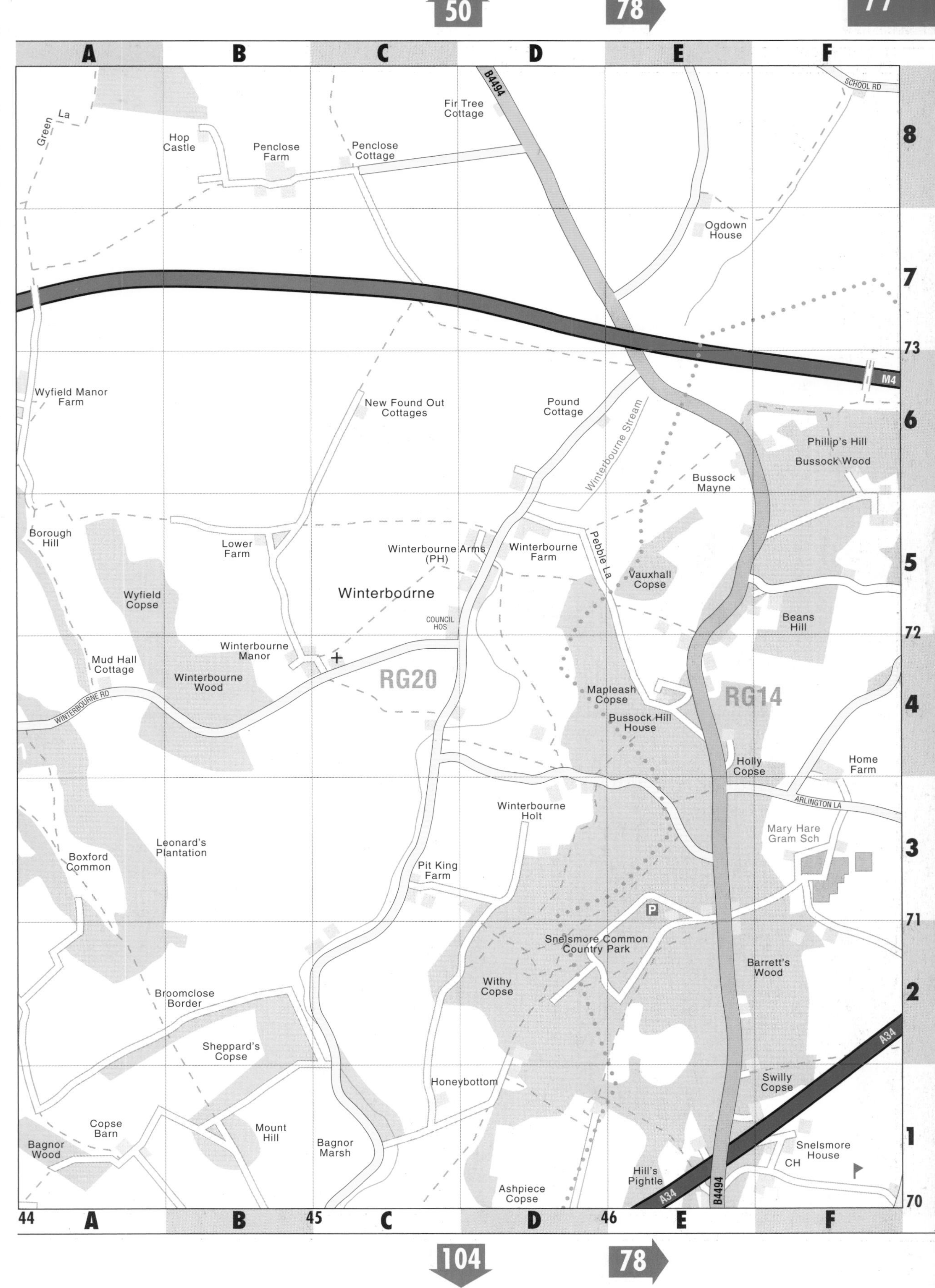
A
B
C
D
E
F
8
7
73
6
5
72
4
3
71
2
1
70
44
45
46
B4494
SCHOOL RD
Fir Tree Cottage
Green La
Hop Castle
Penclose Farm
Penclose Cottage
Ogdown House
M4
Wyfield Manor Farm
New Found Out Cottages
Pound Cottage
Winterbourne Stream
Phillip's Hill
Bussock Wood
Bussock Mayne
Borough Hill
Lower Farm
Winterbourne Arms (PH)
Winterbourne Farm
Pebble La
Vauxhall Copse
Wyfield Copse
Winterbourne
COUNCIL HOS
Beans Hill
Mud Hall Cottage
Winterbourne Manor
RG20
Winterbourne Wood
WINTERBOURNE RD
Mapleash Copse
RG14
Bussock Hill House
Holly Copse
Home Farm
ARLINGTON LA
Winterbourne Holt
Leonard's Plantation
Boxford Common
Mary Hare Gram Sch
Pit King Farm
P
Snelsmore Common Country Park
Barrett's Wood
Withy Copse
Broomclose Border
A34
Sheppard's Copse
Honeybottom
Swilly Copse
Copse Barn
Mount Hill
Bagnor Wood
Bagnor Marsh
Snelsmore House
CH
Hill's Pightle
Ashpiece Copse

104
78

77
51

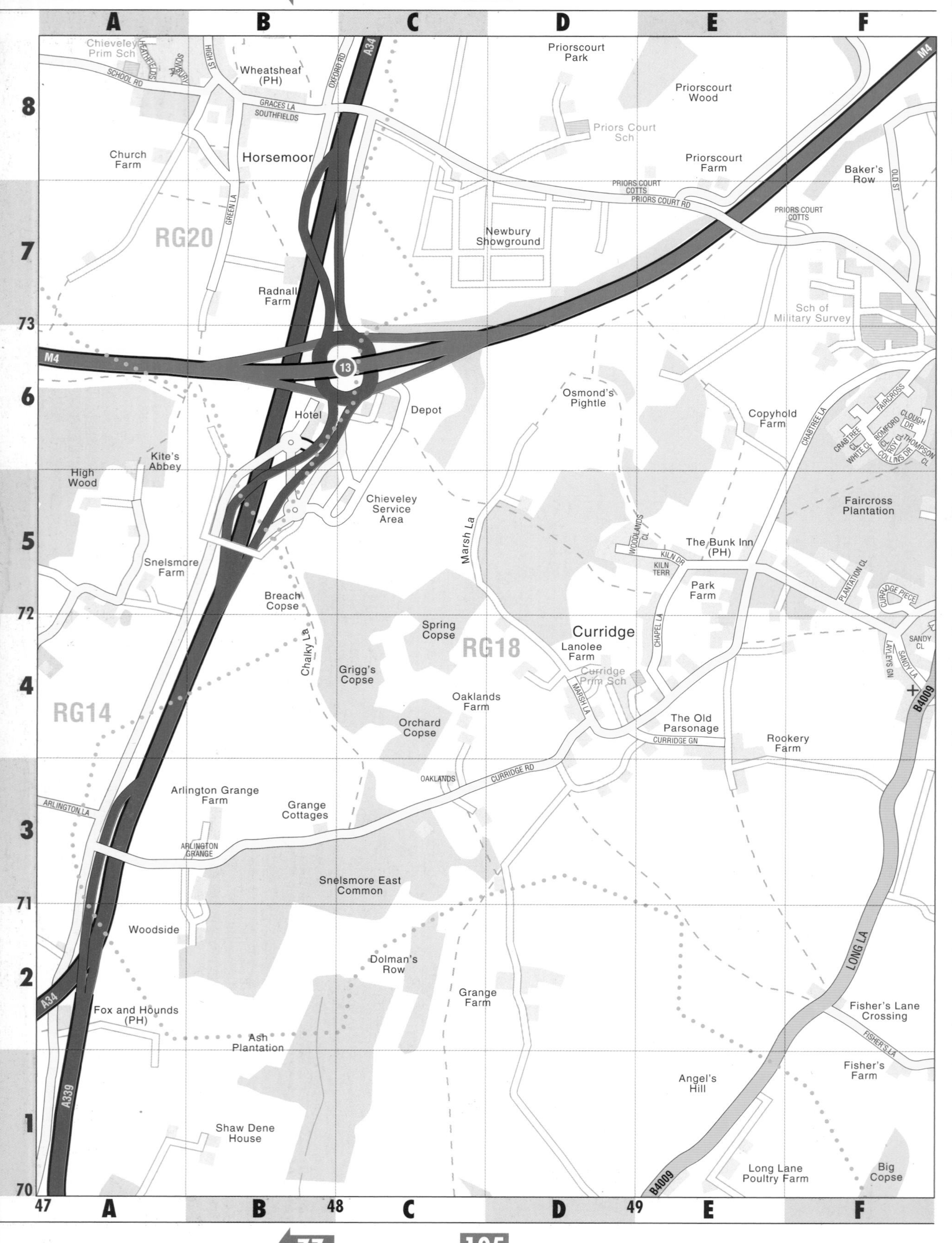
A
B
C
D
E
F
8
7
73
6
5
72
4
3
71
2
1
70
47
48
49
Chieveley Prim Sch
SCHOOL RD
HIGH ST
Wheatsheaf (PH)
OXFORD RD
A34
GRACES LA
SOUTHFIELDS
Priorscourt Park
Priorscourt Wood
Priors Court Sch
M4
Church Farm
Horsemoor
Priorscourt Farm
Baker's Row
OLD ST
PRIORS COURT COTTS
PRIORS COURT RD
GREEN LA
RG20
Newbury Showground
Radnall Farm
Sch of Military Survey
13
Osmond's Pightle
Hotel
Depot
Copyhold Farm
CRABTREE LA
FAIRCROSS
CLOUGH DR
CRABTREE CL
BOMFORD CL
THOMPSON CL
WHITE CL
ROY CL
COLLINS DR
High Wood
Kite's Abbey
Chieveley Service Area
Faircross Plantation
Marsh La
WOODLANDS CL
The Bunk Inn (PH)
KILN DR
KILN TERR
Snelsmore Farm
Park Farm
PLANTATION CL
CURRIDGE PIECE
Breach Copse
Spring Copse
Curridge
Chalky La
RG18
Lanolee Farm
CHAPEL LA
SANDY CL
LAYLEYS GN
SANDY LA
Grigg's Copse
Curridge Prim Sch
MARSH LA
B4009
RG14
Oaklands Farm
The Old Parsonage
Orchard Copse
CURRIDGE GN
Rookery Farm
OAKLANDS
CURRIDGE RD
Arlington Grange Farm
ARLINGTON LA
Grange Cottages
ARLINGTON GRANGE
Snelsmore East Common
Woodside
Dolman's Row
LONG LA
Grange Farm
Fox and Hounds (PH)
Fisher's Lane Crossing
FISHER'S LA
Ash Plantation
Fisher's Farm
Angel's Hill
A339
Shaw Dene House
Long Lane Poultry Farm
Big Copse

77
105

52
80

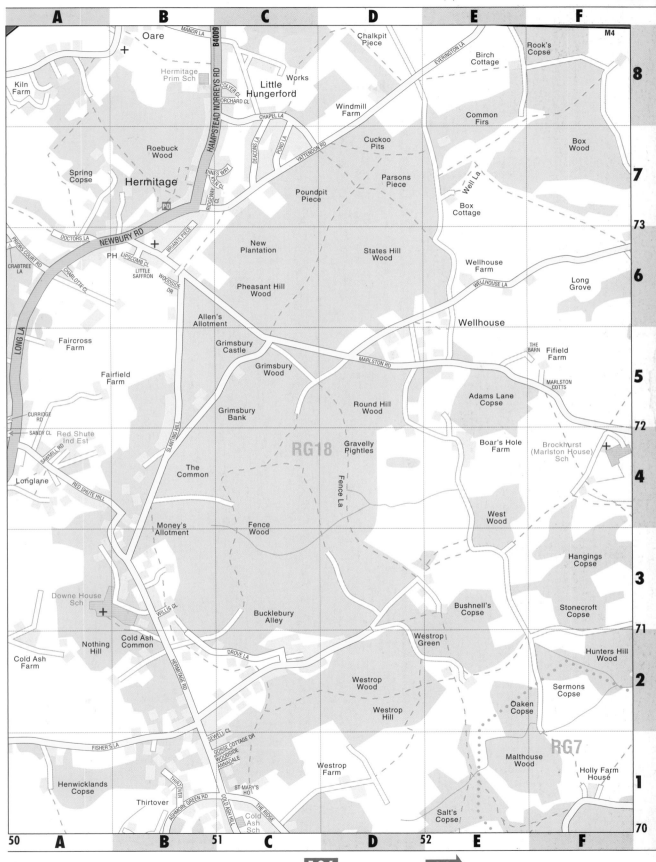
A B C D E F
8 7 6 5 4 3 2 1
73 72 71 70
50 51 52
Oare
MANOR LA
B4009
HAMPSTEAD NORREYS RD
Chalkpit Piece
EVERINGTON LA
Birch Cottage
Rook's Copse
M4
Kiln Farm
Hermitage Prim Sch
COLVER CL
ORCHARD CL
Little Hungerford
Works
Windmill Farm
Common Firs
CHAPEL LA
Box Wood
Roebuck Wood
Cuckoo Pits
DEACONS LA
POND LA
YATTENDON RD
Spring Copse
Hermitage
DINES WAY
Parsons Piece
Well La
RIDGEWAY CL
PO
Poundpit Piece
Box Cottage
DOCTORS LA
NEWBURY RD
BRIANTS PIECE
PRIORS COURT RD
PH
LIPSCOMB CL
LITTLE SAFFRON
CRABTREE LA
CHARLOTTE CL
WOODSIDE DR
New Plantation
States Hill Wood
Wellhouse Farm
WELLHOUSE LA
Long Grove
Pheasant Hill Wood
Allen's Allotment
Wellhouse
LONG LA
Faircross Farm
Grimsbury Castle
THE BARN
Fifield Farm
MARLSTON RD
Grimsbury Wood
MARLSTON COTTS
Fairfield Farm
Adams Lane Copse
Round Hill Wood
Grimsbury Bank
CURRIDGE RD
SANDY CL
Red Shute Ind Est
SAWMILL RD
SLANTING HILL
RG18
Gravelly Pightles
Boar's Hole Farm
Brockhurst (Marlston House) Sch
The Common
Longlane
RED SHUTE HILL
Fence La
West Wood
Money's Allotment
Fence Wood
Hangings Copse
Downe House Sch
WILLIS CL
Bucklebury Alley
Bushnell's Copse
Stonecroft Copse
Nothing Hill
Cold Ash Common
DROVE LA
Westrop Green
Hunters Hill Wood
Cold Ash Farm
HERMITAGE RD
Westrop Wood
Sermons Copse
Westrop Hill
Oaken Copse
SEWELL CL
FISHER'S LA
GORSE COTTAGE DR
WOODSIDE
ANNADALE
RG7
Malthouse Wood
Westrop Farm
Holly Farm House
Henwicklands Copse
THIRTOVER
ST MARY'S HO
ASHMORE GREEN RD
COLD ASH HILL
Thirtover
THE RIDGE
Cold Ash Sch
Salt's Copse

106
80

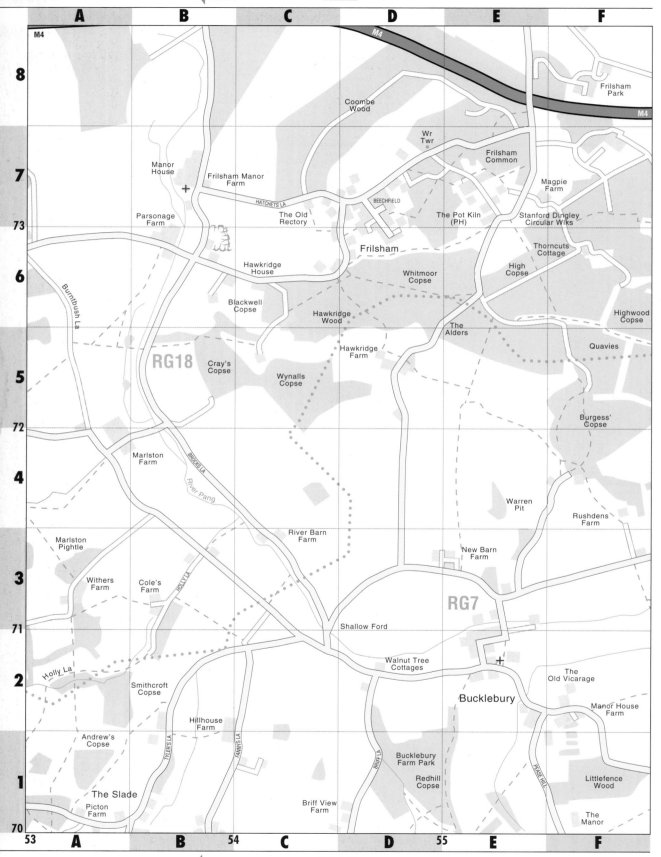

M4

A   B   C   D   E   F

8

Coombe
Wood

Frilsham
Park

M4

7

Manor
House

Frilsham Manor
Farm

Wr
Twr

Frilsham
Common

Magpie
Farm

HATCHETS LA

BEECHFIELD

73

Parsonage
Farm

The Old
Rectory

The Pot Kiln
(PH)

Stanford Dingley
Circular Wlks

Frilsham

Thorncuts
Cottage

6

Hawkridge
House

Whitmoor
Copse

High
Copse

Burnbush La

Blackwell
Copse

Hawkridge
Wood

The
Alders

Highwood
Copse

RG18

Cray's
Copse

Hawkridge
Farm

Quavies

5

Wynalls
Copse

72

Burgess'
Copse

4

Marlston
Farm

BROOKS LA

River Pang

Warren
Pit

Rushdens
Farm

Marlston
Pightle

River Barn
Farm

New Barn
Farm

3

Withers
Farm

Cole's
Farm

HOLLY LA

RG7

71

Shallow Ford

Walnut Tree
Cottages

The
Old Vicarage

Holly La

Smithcroft
Copse

Bucklebury

Manor House
Farm

2

Hillhouse
Farm

TYLERS LA

FANN'S LA

Bucklebury
Farm Park

BRIFF LA

PEASE HILL

Littlefence
Wood

1

Andrew's
Copse

Redhill
Copse

The Slade

Briff View
Farm

The
Manor

Picton
Farm

70

53   A   B   54   C   D   55   E   F

54

82

A B C D E F
8 7 73 6 5 72 4 3 71 2 1 70
56 57 58
Chalkangles Copse
Tanner's Copse
Birchlands Copse
Lambden's Bottom
RG8
Beard's Hill
M4
Gravel Copse
New Fields
Stone Copse
Broomhill Copse
The Gravels
Coxland Cottages
Timber Copse
RG18
Collier's Copse
Cook's Copse
Owlpit Copse
Oxley's Shaw
Hangers Copse
Miram's Copse
SCRATCHFACE LA
Quill Copse
Mazelands Farm
Mazelands Copse
Round Copse
Long Copse
Bradfield House
Rushall Farm
House Leas
New Common
Rushall Manor Farm
Rushall Copse
Mountthill Copse
Manor Farm
Frogmoor Farm
Nightingale's Green
BACK LA
Pangfield Farm
RG7
NEW BLDGS
Severals Farm
Manor Farm
Bradfield Hall
Stanford Dingley
The Bull (PH)
River Pang
Kimberhead Farm
Rotten Row
Bradfield Farm
ROTTEN ROW HILL
Jewell's Farm
The Old Boot Inn (PH)
Jennetshill Wood
CASEY CT
Jennetts Hill
BISHOPS RD
GREEN LA
JENNETTS CL
Jewell's Spring
Tutts Clump
Clay Hill
COCK LA
King's Copse
The Travellers Rest (PH)
Bushnells Green
HUNGERFORD LA
Hillfoot Farm
Acres Farm
HILLFOOT
SOUTH END RD
Nine Elms
St Crispins Farm

108
82

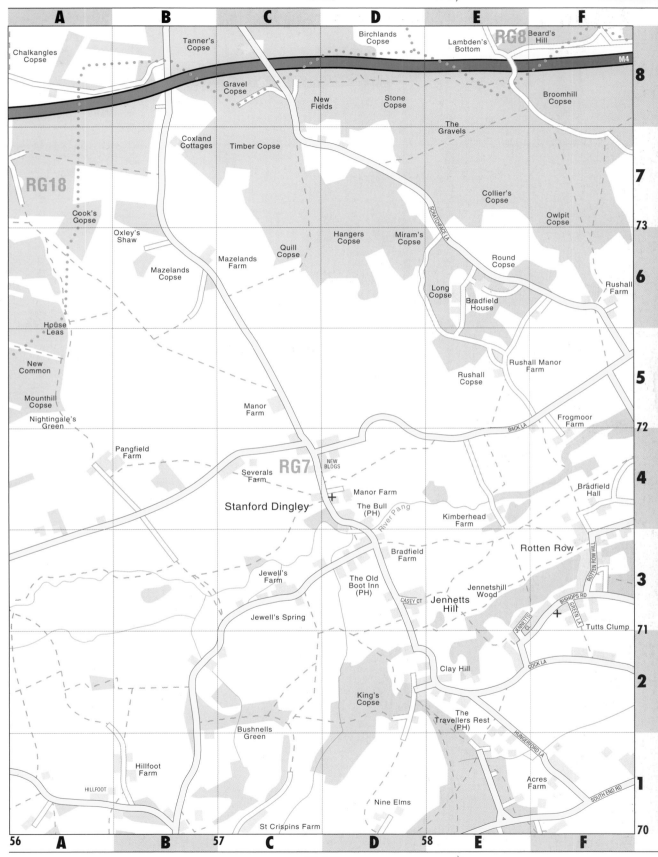

81
55

A　B　C　D　E　F

RG8

M4

RG8

8

Bottingham Shaw

Red Hill

RG8

The Tidmarsh Stud

Maidenhatch Farm

Greathouse Wood

Hewins Wood

Hogmoor Copse

Greathouse Cottages

Hewins Wood Farm

Hewinswood Farm

Barn Elms Farm

DARK LA

7

Maidenhatch Brook

ASHAMPSTEAD RD

Thuja Wood

River Pang

73

Greathouse Wlk

ST ANDREWS CL

BROOK HO

Bradfield Plantation

Home Farm

Sports Ctr

6

Back Lane Plantation

BACK LA

RIVERSIDE

Bradfield Coll

The House on the Hill

Hill Plantation

Bradfield

Old Deerpark Wood

Old Deer Park

5

Folly Bridge

Malthouse Farm

The Old Rectory

72

Sherwood House

Wayland's Copse

RG7

Bennett's Copse

Dainty Land

4

Bradfield Hall Farm

Horse Leas

Bournefield Farm

COMMON HILL

Fisher's Copse

Buscot Gully

WAYLANDS CL

UNION RD

Englefield Common Wood

Copyhold Farm

Ham Copse

3

BISHOPS RD

MARINERS LA

The Bourne

Potash

Berry's Farm

71

Clays Copse

Bradfield CE Prim Sch

THE LACFORDS

ASH RD

Southend Farm

Berry's Shaw

Andrew's Copse

2

COCK LA

PH

Somerwells

NEW WAY

SOUTH END RD

Mayridge Farm

Southend

SANDBROOK CL

HEATH RD

STRETTON CL

Culham Shaw

ADMOOR LA

Cold Hill

WELLINGTON GDNS

STRETTON

Admoor Copse

Ufton Wood

1

PO

Cripps Farm

Holly Copse

LAMBDENS HILL

WEBBS LA

The Lambden's

70

59　A　B　60　C　D　61　E　F

81
109

56
84
A
B
C
D
E
F
8
7
73
6
5
72
4
3
71
2
1
70
62
63
64
RG8
RG31
RG7
River Pang
Hogmoor Bridge
Flobrigham's Copse
Withy Eyot
Moor Copse
A340
Alder Copse
Wigley Copse
Horsemoor Wood
Chalkpit Farm
The Bourne
Horns Copse
CHALKPIT COTTS
Malpas Farm
Pond Farm
Malpas
Sluice Copse
NUNHIDE LA
Nunhide Farm
Dovecot
Beech Hill Wood
PH
North Street
Blossomsend Copse
Englefield
THE STREET
ST MARK'S CL
PO
North Street Farm
Englefield CE Prim Sch
Englefield House
Works
CH
Wickcroft Farm
Theale
Englefield Park (Deer Park)
ENGLEFIELD RD
Cranemoor Lake
Theale CE Prim Sch
Wigmore Wood
Theale Green Com Sch
PARKER'S CNR
Liby
Commerce Pk
Chilton Ent Ctr
Arlington Bsns Pk
WATERSIDE DR
BRUNEL RD
Kennet Weir Bsns Pk
The Markham Ctr Trad Est
Theale
ARROWHEAD RD
Haywards Farm House
A4
M4
12
Kennet and Avon Canal
Mill
Swing Bridge
Gravel Pit Cottages
BOSTOCK LA
WIGMORE LA
BATH RD
Draper's Osier Bed Stream
River Kennet
Milehouse Cottages
110
84

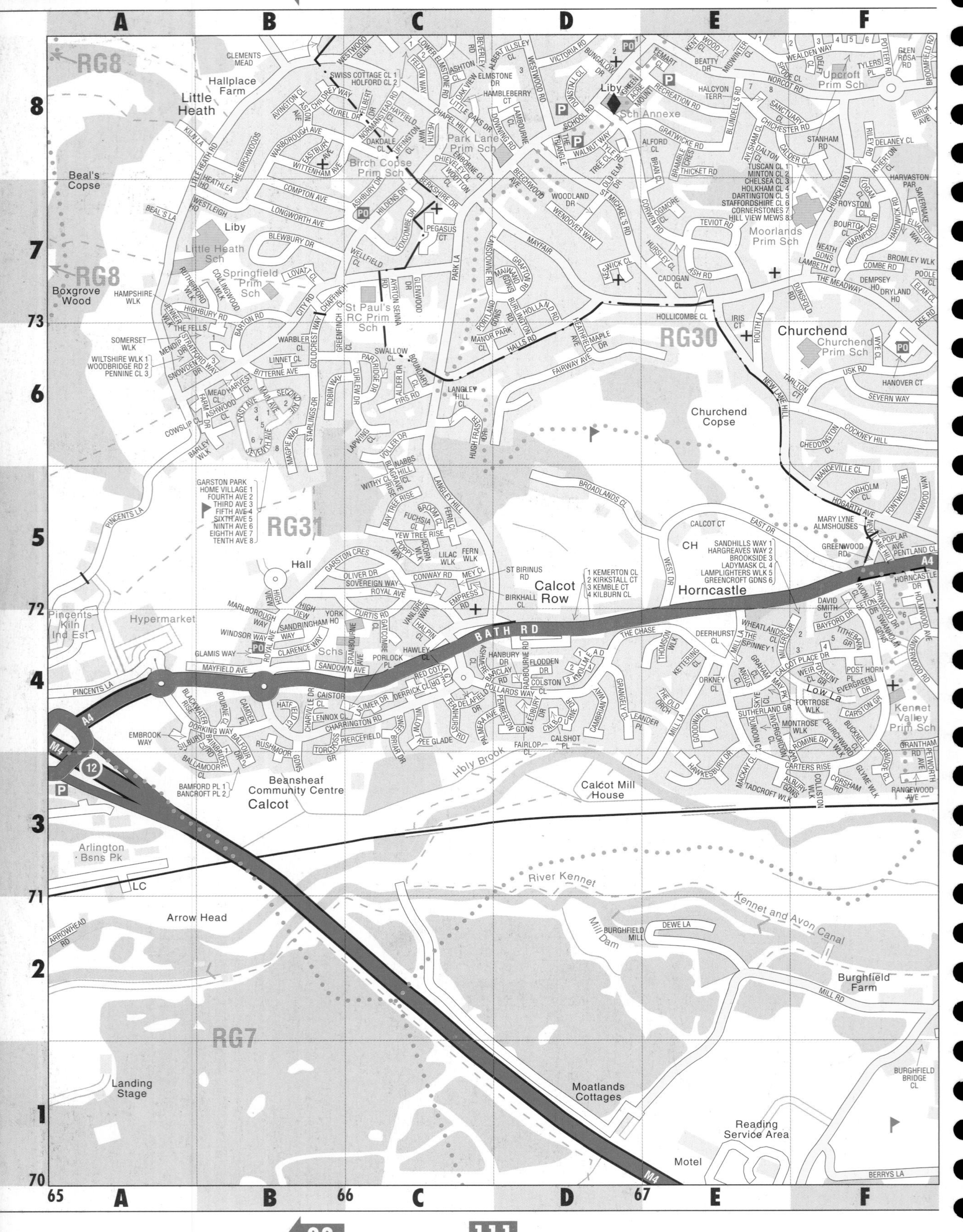

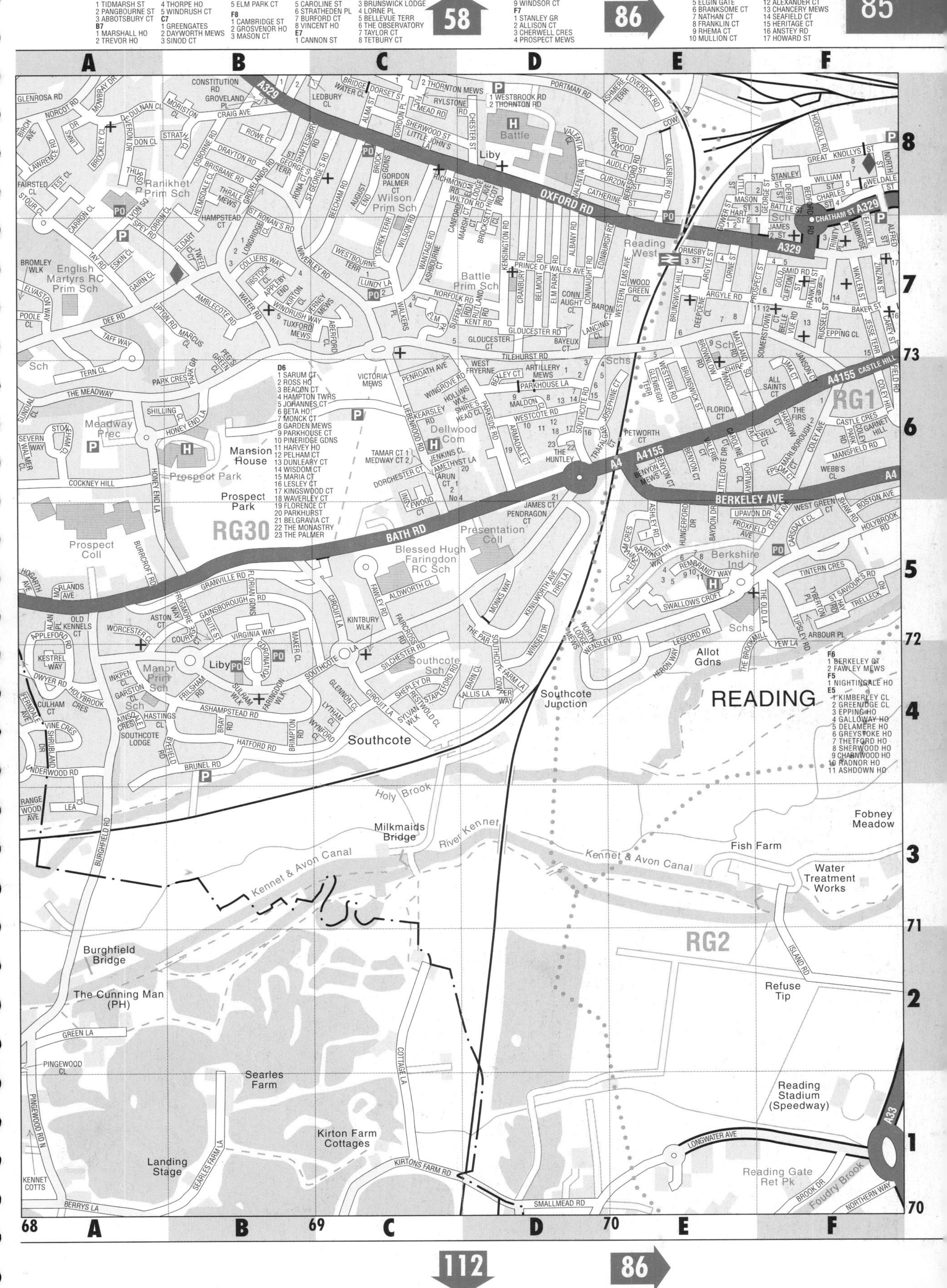

B8
1 TIDMARSH ST
2 PANGBOURNE ST
3 ABBOTSBURY CT
B7
1 MARSHALL HO
2 TREVOR HO
3 FORBURY HO
4 THORPE HO
5 WINDRUSH CT
C7
1 GREENGATES
2 DAYWORTH MEWS
3 SINOD CT
4 QUINN CT
5 ELM PARK CT
F8
1 CAMBRIDGE ST
2 GROSVENOR HO
3 MASON CT
4 MALTHOUSE LA
5 CAROLINE ST
6 STRATHEDEN PL
7 BURFORD CT
8 VINCENT HO
E7
1 CANNON ST
2 FOXGLOVE GDNS
3 BRUNSWICK LODGE
4 LORNE PL
5 BELLEVUE TERR
6 THE OBSERVATORY
7 TAYLOR CT
8 TETBURY CT
58
E7
9 WINDSOR CT
F7
1 STANLEY GR
2 ALLISON CT
3 CHERWELL CRES
4 PROSPECT MEWS
86
F7
5 ELGIN GATE
6 BRANKSOME CT
7 NATHAN CT
8 FRANKLIN CT
9 RHEMA CT
10 MULLION CT
11 NICHOLAS CT
12 ALEXANDER CT
13 CHANCERY MEWS
14 SEAFIELD CT
15 HERITAGE CT
16 ANSTEY RD
17 HOWARD ST
D6
1 SARUM CT
2 ROSS HO
3 BEACON CT
4 HAMPTON TWRS
5 JOHANNES CT
6 BETA HO
7 MONCK CT
8 GARDEN MEWS
9 PARKHOUSE CT
10 PINERIDGE GDNS
11 HARVEY HO
12 PELHAM CT
13 DUNLEARY CT
14 WISDOM CT
15 MARIA CT
16 LESLEY CT
17 KINGSWOOD CT
18 WAVERLEY CT
19 FLORENCE CT
20 PARKHURST
21 BELGRAVIA CT
22 THE MONASTRY
23 THE PALMER
F6
1 BERKELEY CT
2 FAWLEY MEWS
F5
1 NIGHTINGALE HO
E5
1 KIMBERLEY CL
2 GREENIDGE CL
3 EPPING HO
4 GALLOWAY HO
5 DELAMERE HO
6 GREYSTOKE HO
7 THETFORD HO
8 SHERWOOD HO
9 CHARNWOOD HO
10 RADNOR HO
11 ASHDOWN HO
OXFORD RD
BATH RD
BERKELEY AVE
RG30
RG1
RG2
READING
Reading West
Southcote
Southcote Junction
Prospect Park
Mansion House
Battle
Kennet & Avon Canal
River Kennet
Holy Brook
Milkmaids Bridge
Burghfield Bridge
The Cunning Man (PH)
Searles Farm
Kirton Farm Cottages
Landing Stage
Fish Farm
Water Treatment Works
Refuse Tip
Fobney Meadow
Reading Stadium (Speedway)
Reading Gate Ret Pk
Foudry Brook
Allot Gdns
Berkshire Ind
112
86

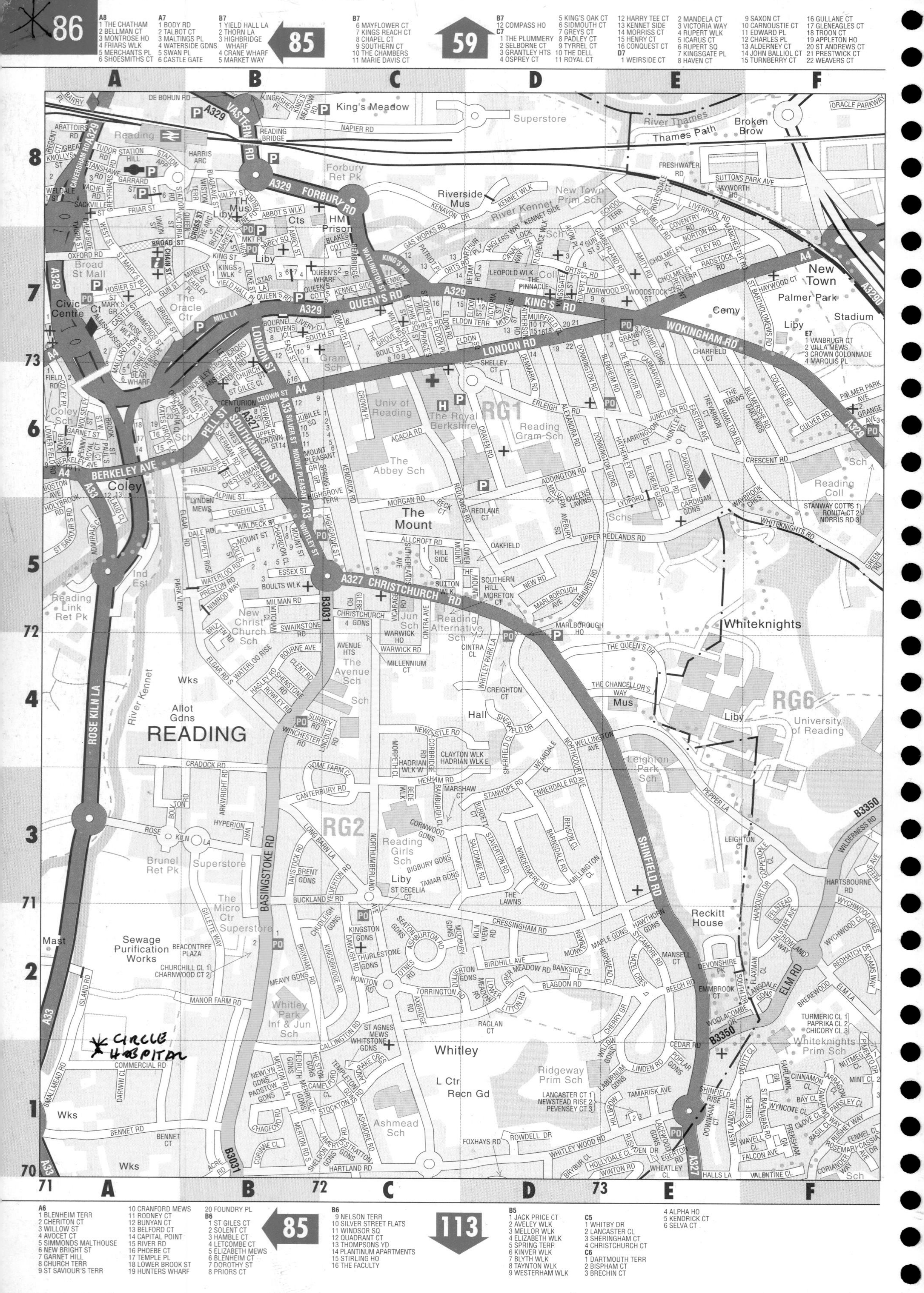

86
A8
1 THE CHATHAM
2 BELLMAN CT
3 MONTROSE HO
4 FRIARS WLK
5 MERCHANTS PL
6 SHOESMITHS CT
A7
1 BODY RD
2 TALBOT CT
3 MALTINGS PL
4 WATERSIDE GDNS
5 SWAN PL
6 CASTLE GATE
B7
1 YIELD HALL LA
2 THORN LA
3 HIGHBRIDGE WHARF
4 CRANE WHARF
5 MARKET WAY
85
B7
6 MAYFLOWER CT
7 KINGS REACH CT
8 CHAPEL CT
9 SOUTHERN CT
10 THE CHAMBERS
11 MARIE DAVIS CT
59
B7
12 COMPASS HO
C7
1 THE PLUMMERY
2 SELBORNE CT
3 GRANTLEY HTS
4 OSPREY CT
5 KING'S OAK CT
6 SIDMOUTH CT
7 GREYS CT
8 PADLEY CT
9 TYRREL CT
10 THE DELL
11 ROYAL CT
12 HARRY TEE CT
13 KENNET SIDE
14 MORRISS CT
15 HENRY CT
16 CONQUEST CT
D7
1 WEIRSIDE CT
2 MANDELA CT
3 VICTORIA WAY
4 RUPERT WLK
5 ICARUS CT
6 RUPERT SQ
7 KINGSGATE PL
8 HAVEN CT
9 SAXON CT
10 CARNOUSTIE CT
11 EDWARD PL
12 CHARLES PL
13 ALDERNEY CT
14 JOHN BALLIOL CT
15 TURNBERRY CT
16 GULLANE CT
17 GLENEAGLES CT
18 TROON CT
19 APPLETON HO
20 ST ANDREWS CT
21 PRESTWICK CT
22 WEAVERS CT
A
B
C
D
E
F
8
7
73
6
5
72
4
3
71
2
1
70
King's Meadow
Superstore
River Thames
Thames Path
Broken Brow
Reading
Forbury Ret Pk
A329
FORBURY RD
Riverside Mus
New Town Prim Sch
River Kennet
HM Prison
Broad St Mall
Civic Centre
The Oracle Ctr
QUEEN'S RD
KING'S RD
A4
New Town
Palmer Park
Stadium
Cemy
WOKINGHAM RD
LONDON RD
LONDON ST
Univ of Reading
The Royal Berkshire
RG1
Reading Gram Sch
The Abbey Sch
The Mount
BERKELEY AVE
Coley
SOUTHAMPTON ST
PELL ST
A33
A327 CHRISTCHURCH RD
Reading Coll
WHITEKNIGHTS RD
Whiteknights
RG6
University of Reading
Leighton Park Sch
Reading Link Ret Pk
Ind Est
New Christ Church Sch
Reading Alternative Sch
The Avenue Sch
READING
Allot Gdns
River Kennet
ROSE KILN LA
Brunel Ret Pk
Superstore
The Micro Ctr Superstore
Sewage Purification Works
BASINGSTOKE RD
B3031
RG2
Reading Girls Sch
SHINFIELD RD
Reckitt House
B3350
ELM RD
Whitley Park Inf & Jun Sch
Whitley
Ridgeway Prim Sch
L Ctr Recn Gd
Ashmead Sch
Whiteknights Prim Sch
CIRCLE HOSPITAL
Wks
71
A
B
72
C
D
73
E
F
A6
1 BLENHEIM TERR
2 CHERITON CT
3 WILLOW ST
4 AVOCET CT
5 SIMMONDS MALTHOUSE
6 NEW BRIGHT ST
7 GARNET HILL
8 CHURCH TERR
9 ST SAVIOUR'S TERR
10 CRANFORD MEWS
11 RODNEY CT
12 BUNYAN CT
13 BELFORD CT
14 CAPITAL POINT
15 RIVER RD
16 PHOEBE CT
17 TEMPLE PL
18 LOWER BROOK ST
19 HUNTERS WHARF
20 FOUNDRY PL
B6
1 ST GILES CT
2 SOLENT CT
3 HAMBLE CT
4 LETCOMBE CT
5 ELIZABETH MEWS
6 BLENHEIM CT
7 DOROTHY ST
8 PRIORS CT
85
B6
9 NELSON TERR
10 SILVER STREET FLATS
11 WINDSOR SQ
12 QUADRANT CT
13 THOMPSONS YD
14 PLANTINUM APARTMENTS
15 STIRLING HO
16 THE FACULTY
113
B5
1 JACK PRICE CT
2 AVELEY WLK
3 MELLOR WLK
4 ELIZABETH WLK
5 SPRING TERR
6 KINVER WLK
7 BLYTH WLK
8 TAYNTON WLK
9 WESTERHAM WLK
C5
1 WHITBY DR
2 LANCASTER CL
3 SHERINGHAM CT
4 CHRISTCHURCH CT
C6
1 DARTMOUTH TERR
2 BISPHAM CT
3 BRECHIN CT
4 ALPHA HO
5 KENDRICK CT
6 SELVA CT

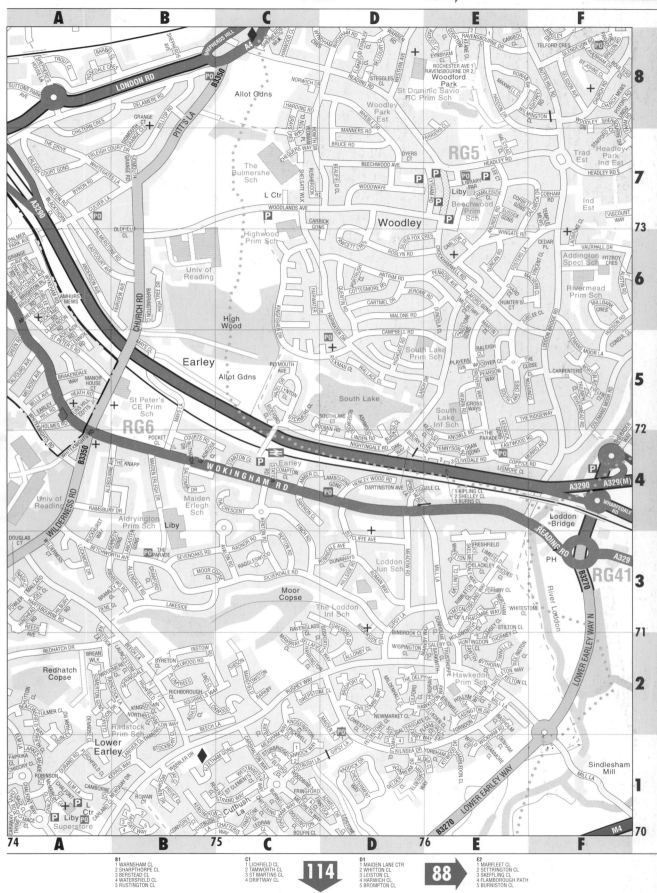

B1
1 WARNSHAM CL
2 SHARPTHORPE CL
3 BERSTEAD CL
4 WATERSFIELD CL
5 RUSTINGTON CL

C1
1 LICHFIELD CL
2 TAMWORTH CL
3 ST MARTINS CL
4 DRIFTWAY CL

D1
1 MAIDEN LANE CTR
2 WHITTON CL
3 LEISTON CL
4 HARWICH CL
5 BROMPTON CL

E2
1 MARFLEET CL
2 SETTRINGTON CL
3 SKEFFLING CL
4 FLAMBOROUGH PATH
5 BURNISTON CL

A3
1 CAVENDISH GDNS
2 BELVEDERE WLK
3 FENCHURCH MEWS
4 RIVERDENE DR
5 BEARWOOD PATH

62
90

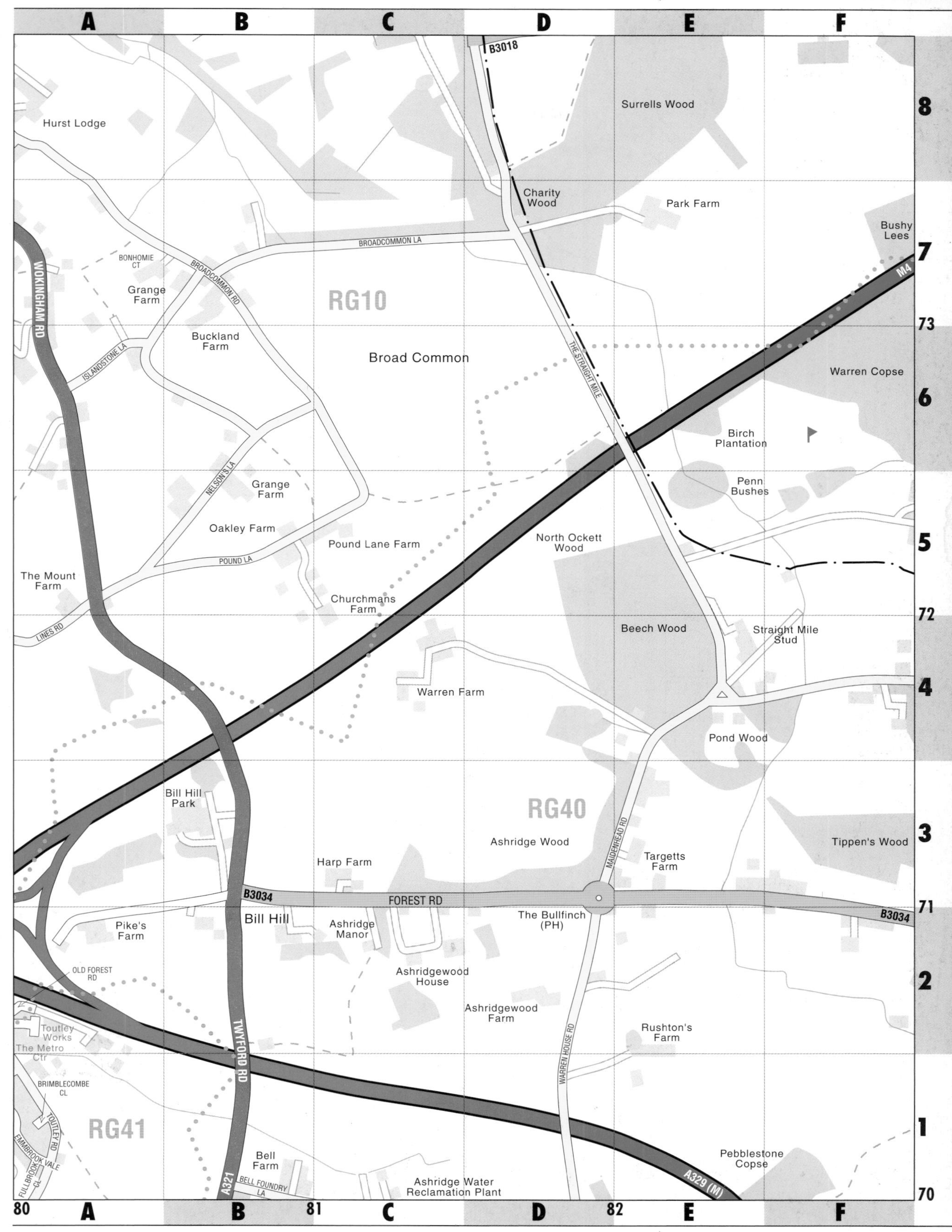
A
B
C
D
E
F
B3018
Surrells Wood
Hurst Lodge
8
Charity Wood
Park Farm
Bushy Lees
BROADCOMMON LA
BONHOMIE CT
BROADCOMMON RD
7
M4
WOKINGHAM RD
Grange Farm
RG10
Buckland Farm
73
ISLANDSTONE LA
Broad Common
THE STRAIGHT MILE
Warren Copse
6
Birch Plantation
NELSON'S LA
Grange Farm
Penn Bushes
Oakley Farm
North Ockett Wood
Pound Lane Farm
5
POUND LA
The Mount Farm
Churchmans Farm
72
LINES RD
Beech Wood
Straight Mile Stud
Warren Farm
4
Pond Wood
Bill Hill Park
RG40
Ashridge Wood
MAIDENHEAD RD
Tippen's Wood
3
Targetts Farm
Harp Farm
B3034
FOREST RD
71
B3034
Bill Hill
Ashridge Manor
The Bullfinch (PH)
Pike's Farm
OLD FOREST RD
Ashridgewood House
2
Ashridgewood Farm
Toutley Works
The Metro Ctr
Rushton's Farm
TWYFORD RD
WARREN HOUSE RD
BRIMBLECOMBE CL
TOUTLEY RD
RG41
1
EMMBROOK VALE
Pebblestone Copse
Bell Farm
FULLBROOK CL
A321
BELL FOUNDRY LA
Ashridge Water Reclamation Plant
A329 (M)
70
80
A
B
81
C
D
82
E
F

116
90

89
63

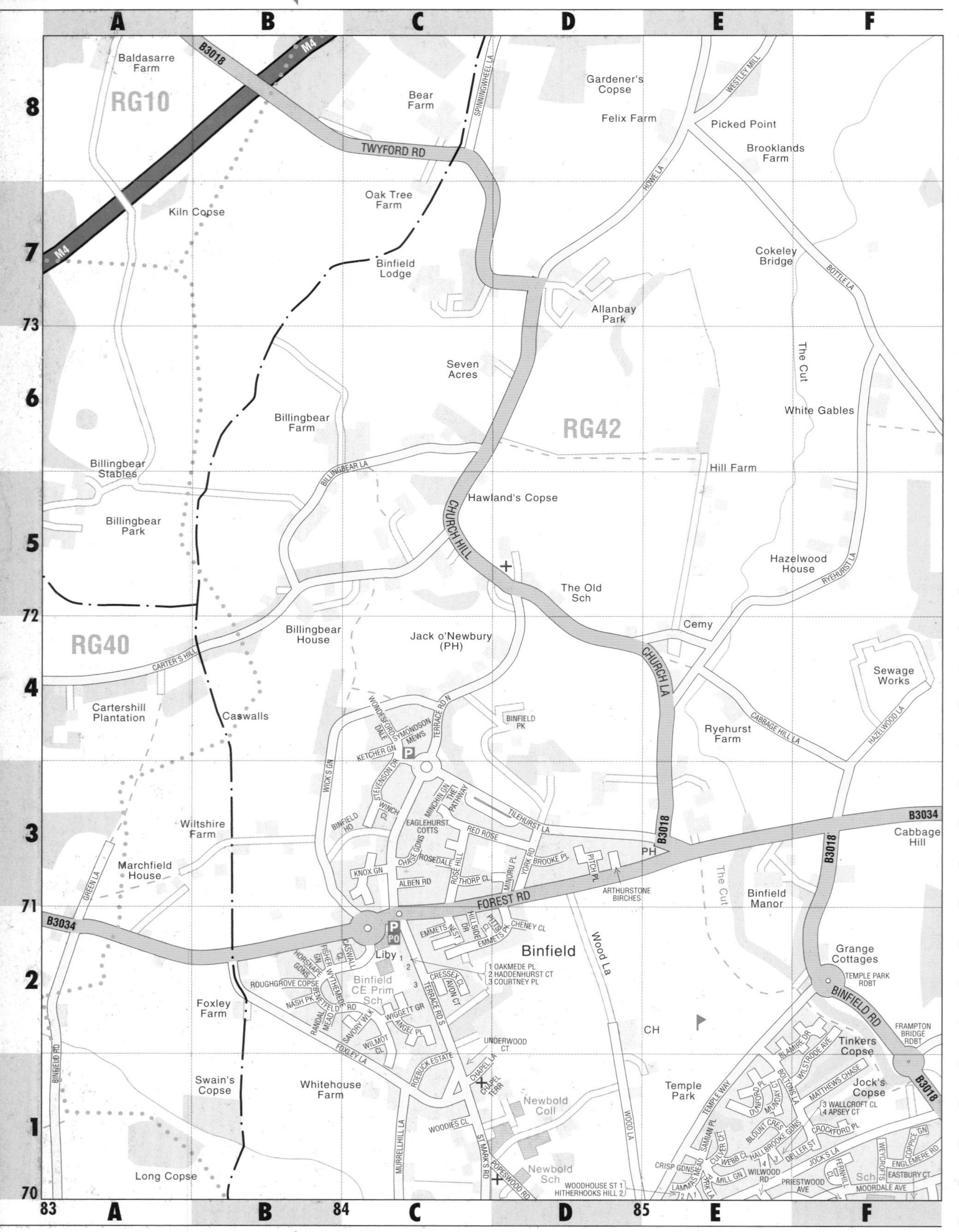

A B C D E F
8
7
73
6
5
72
4
3
71
2
1
70
83 84 85
Baldasarre Farm
RG10
B3018
M4
Bear Farm
SPINNINGWHEEL LA
Gardener's Copse
WESTLEY MILL
Felix Farm
Picked Point
TWYFORD RD
Brooklands Farm
HOWE LA
Oak Tree Farm
Kiln Copse
Cokeley Bridge
Binfield Lodge
BOTTLE LA
Allanbay Park
The Cut
Seven Acres
White Gables
Billingbear Farm
RG42
Billingbear Stables
BILLINGBEAR LA
Hill Farm
Hawland's Copse
Billingbear Park
CHURCH HILL
Hazelwood House
RYEHURST LA
The Old Sch
Cemy
RG40
Billingbear House
Jack o'Newbury (PH)
CHURCH LA
CARTER'S HILL
Sewage Works
Cartershill Plantation
Caswalls
BINFIELD PK
Ryehurst Farm
CABBAGE HILL LA
HAZELWOOD LA
WONDESFORD DALE
SYMONDSON MEWS
TERRACE RD N
KETCHER GN
WICK'S GN
STEVENSON DR
WINCH CL
MINCHIN GN
THE PATHWAY
TILEHURST LA
Wiltshire Farm
BINFIELD HO
EAGLEHURST COTTS
RED ROSE
B3018
PH
B3034
Cabbage Hill
GREEN LA
Marchfield House
KNOX GN
CHASE GDNS
ROSEDALE
ROSE HILL
MINORU PL
YORK RD
BROOKE PL
PITCH PL
The Cut
ALBEN RD
THORP CL
ARTHURSTONE BIRCHES
Binfield Manor
FOREST RD
B3034
EMMETS NEST
HILLSIDE DR
PITTS CL
EMMETS PK
CHENEY CL
Wood La
Grange Cottages
CASWALL CL
HORSNAPE GDNS
FISHER GN
WYTHEMEDE
Liby
Binfield
1 OAKMEDE PL
2 HADDENHURST CT
3 COURTNEY PL
TEMPLE PARK RDBT
ROUGHGROVE COPSE
Binfield CE Prim Sch
CRESSEX CL
AVON CT
BINFIELD RD
Foxley Farm
NASH PK
BENETFIELD RD
RANDALL MEAD
SAVORY WLK
WIGGETT GR
TERRACE RD S
CH
FRAMPTON BRIDGE RDBT
ANGEL PL
WILMOT CL
UNDERWOOD CT
BLAMIRE DR
WILSTRODE AVE
Tinkers Copse
FOXLEY LA
ROEBUCK ESTATE
CHAPEL LA
BINFIELD RD
Swain's Copse
CHAPEL TERR
Temple Park
MATTHEWS CHASE
Jock's Copse
Whitehouse Farm
Newbold Coll
TEMPLE WAY
DYNFORD PL
MUNDAY CT
BOLTONS LA
3 WALLCROFT CL
4 APSEY CT
WOODIES CL
WOOD LA
SAMIAN PL
BLOUNT CRES
HALLBROOKE GDNS
CROCKFORD PL
COPPICE GN
MURRELLHILL LA
ST MARK'S RD
CULVER CT
WEBB CL
DELLER ST
WETCROFTS
ENGLEMERE RD
CRISP GDNS
JOCK'S LA
FERNHILL CL
EASTBURY CT
Long Copse
POPESWOOD RD
Newbold Sch
WOODHOUSE ST 1
HITHERHOOKS HILL 2
LAMMAS MEAD
PARK LA
MILL GN
WILWOOD RD
PRIESTWOOD AVE
Sch
MOORDALE AVE

89
117

64
92

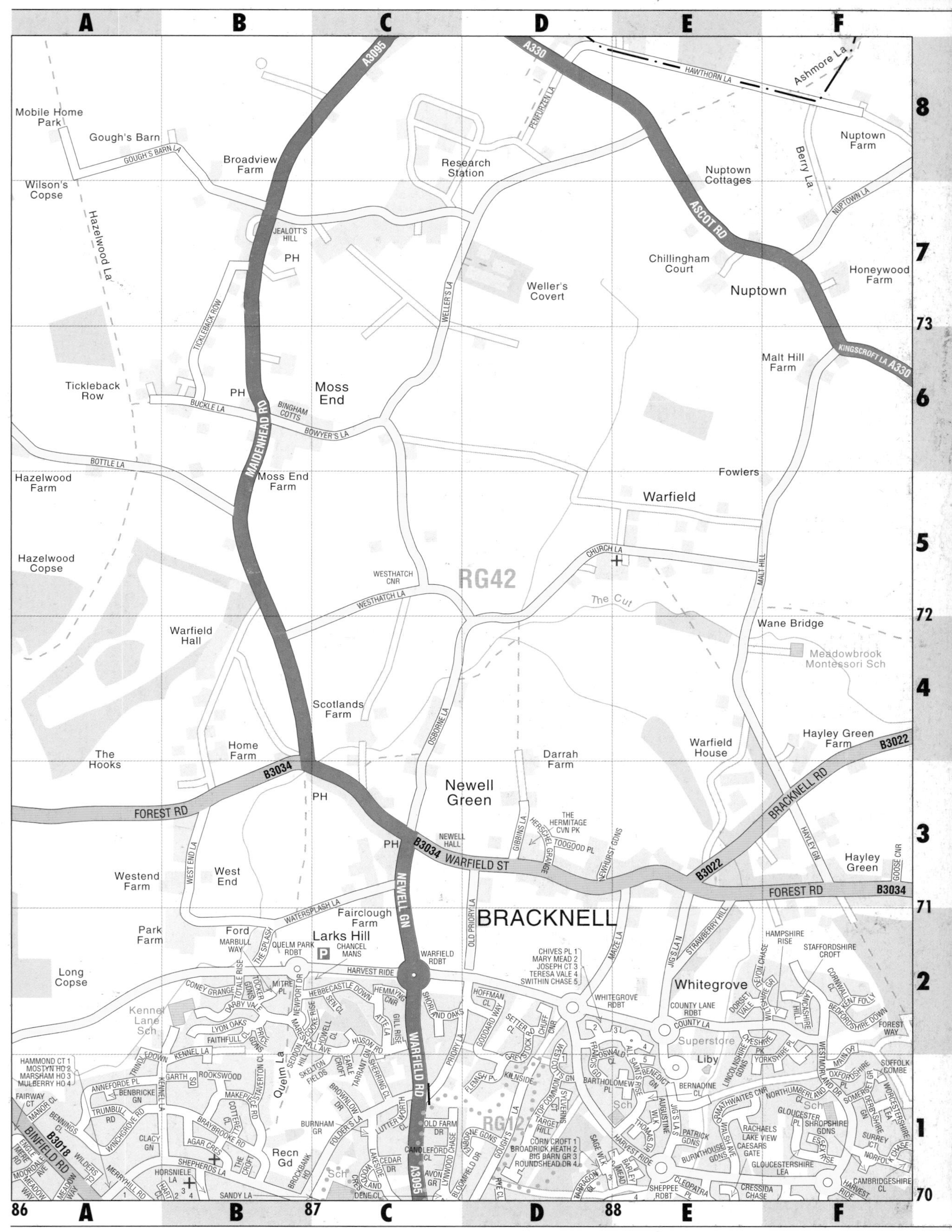
A
B
C
D
E
F
8
7
73
6
5
72
4
3
71
2
1
70
86
87
88
Mobile Home Park
Gough's Barn
GOUGH'S BARN LA
Wilson's Copse
Broadview Farm
Hazelwood La
A3095
A330
PENFURZEN LA
HAWTHORN LA
Ashmore La
Nuptown Farm
Berry La
Research Station
Nuptown Cottages
NUPTOWN LA
ASCOT RD
JEALOTT'S HILL
PH
Chillingham Court
Nuptown
Honeywood Farm
Weller's Covert
WELLER'S LA
TICKLEBACK ROW
KINGSCROFT LA A330
Malt Hill Farm
Tickleback Row
Moss End
BUCKLE LA
MAIDENHEAD RD
BINGHAM COTTS
BOWYER'S LA
BOTTLE LA
Hazelwood Farm
Moss End Farm
Fowlers
Warfield
Hazelwood Copse
CHURCH LA
WESTHATCH CNR
RG42
WESTHATCH LA
MALT HILL
The Cut
Wane Bridge
Warfield Hall
Meadowbrook Montessori Sch
Scotlands Farm
OSBORNE LA
Hayley Green Farm
B3022
The Hooks
Home Farm
Darrah Farm
Warfield House
B3034
Newell Green
BRACKNELL RD
FOREST RD
THE HERMITAGE CVN PK
NEWELL HALL
GIBBINS LA
HERSCHEL GRANGE
TOOGOOD PL
NEWHURST GDNS
HAYLEY GN
Westend Farm
WEST END LA
West End
WARFIELD ST
Hayley Green
GOOSE CNR
NEWELL GN
OLD PRIORY LA
B3034
WATERSPLASH LA
Fairclough Farm
BRACKNELL
MAIZE LA
JIG'S LA N
STRAWBERRY HILL
HAMPSHIRE RISE
STAFFORDSHIRE CROFT
Park Farm
Ford
MARBULL WAY
THE SPLASH
QUELM PARK RDBT
Larks Hill
CHANCEL MANS
WARFIELD RDBT
CHIVES PL 1
MARY MEAD 2
JOSEPH CT 3
TERESA VALE 4
SWITHIN CHASE 5
Long Copse
HARVEST RIDE
Whitegrove
DEVON CHASE
CORNWALL CL
CONEY GRANGE
MITRE PL
HEBBECASTLE DOWN
HEMMYNG CNR
HOFFMAN CL
WHITEGROVE RDBT
COUNTY LANE RDBT
BEDFORDSHIRE DOWN
Kennel Lane Sch
DARBY VALE
NEWPORT DR
LYON OAKS
FAITHFULL CL
SHORLAND OAKS
GODDARD WAY
SETTER CL
COUNTY LA
FOREST WAY
Superstore
CHESHIRE PK
YORKSHIRE PL
KENNEL LA
Quelm La
HUSON RD
ATTE LA
GILL RISE
WARFIELD RD
PRIORY LA
GREYSTOCK RD
OSWALD CL
Liby
LINCOLNSHIRE GDNS
MAIN DR
SUFFOLK COMBE
HAMMOND CT 1
MOSTYN HO 2
MARSHAM HO 3
MULBERRY HO 4
GARTH SQ
ROOKSWOOD
SKELTON FIELDS
FLEMISH PL
KILNSIDE
BARTHOLOMEW PL
BENEDICT GN
BERNADINE CL
NORTHUMBERLAND CL
FAIRWAY
ANNEFORDE PL
BENBRICKE GN
MAKEPIECE RD
BROWNLOW DR
Sch
OXFORDSHIRE PL
WORCESTERSHIRE LEA
TRUMBULL RD
WINCHGROVE RD
BRAYBROOKE RD
BURNHAM GR
OLD FARM DR
RG12
TOP COMMON
AUGUSTINE WLK
THOMAS DR
SMATHWAITES CNR
GLOUCESTER PL
SHROPSHIRE GDNS
BENNINGS CL
CLACY GN
FOLDER'S LA
LUTTERWORTH CL
CORN CROFT 1
BROADRICK HEATH 2
BIG BARN GR 3
ROUNDSHEAD DR 4
PATRICK GDNS
RACHAELS LAKE VIEW
CAESARS GATE
SURREY CT
ESSEX RISE
AGAR CRES
THE CROFT
Recn Gd
CANDLEFORD CL
LYNWOOD CHASE
BLOOMFIELD DR
SAGE WLK
HARVEST RIDE
BURNTHOUSE GDNS
NORFOLK CHASE
B3018
BINFIELD RD
SHEPHERDS LA
HORSNIELE LA
BROCKBANK HO
CEDAR DR
LAKESIDE
AVON GR
GLOUCESTERSHIRE LEA
CAMBRIDGESHIRE CL
MOORDALE AVE
MEADOW WAY
MERRYHILL RD
WILDERS CL
HART CL
SANDY LA
Sch
DENE CL
A3095
TARRAGON CL
SHEPPEE RDBT
CLEOPATRA PL
CRESSIDA CHASE
HARVEST RIDE

118
92

91
65

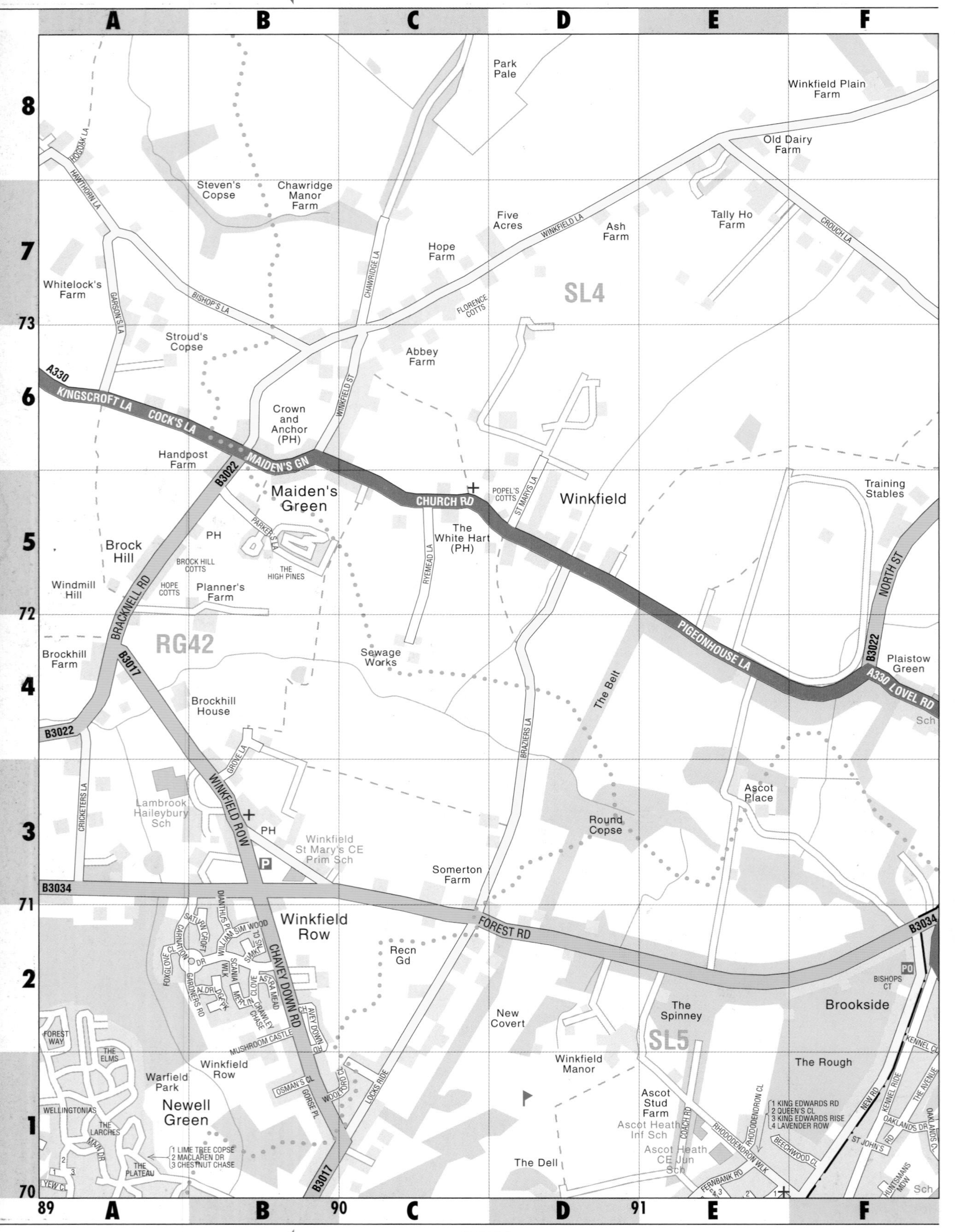
A
B
C
D
E
F
8
7
73
6
5
72
4
3
71
2
1
70
89
90
91
Park Pale
Winkfield Plain Farm
Old Dairy Farm
Steven's Copse
Chawridge Manor Farm
Five Acres
Ash Farm
Tally Ho Farm
Hope Farm
Whitelock's Farm
SL4
Stroud's Copse
Abbey Farm
A330
KINGSCROFT LA
COCK'S LA
MAIDEN'S GN
CHURCH RD
PIGEONHOUSE LA
A330 LOVEL RD
Crown and Anchor (PH)
Handpost Farm
Maiden's Green
Winkfield
Training Stables
The White Hart (PH)
Brock Hill
Windmill Hill
Planner's Farm
THE HIGH PINES
BROCK HILL COTTS
HOPE COTTS
RG42
Brockhill Farm
Sewage Works
Plaistow Green
Brockhill House
The Belt
Lambrook Haileybury Sch
Ascot Place
Round Copse
Winkfield St Mary's CE Prim Sch
Somerton Farm
B3034
FOREST RD
Winkfield Row
Recn Gd
The Spinney
Brookside
New Covert
SL5
The Rough
Winkfield Manor
Warfield Park
Winkfield Row
Newell Green
Ascot Stud Farm
Ascot Heath Inf Sch
Ascot Heath CE Jun Sch
The Dell
1 LIME TREE COPSE
2 MACLAREN DR
3 CHESTNUT CHASE
1 KING EDWARDS RD
2 QUEEN'S CL
3 KING EDWARDS RISE
4 LAVENDER ROW
HOGOAK LA
HAWTHORN LA
GARSON'S LA
BISHOP'S LA
CHAWRIDGE LA
WINKFIELD LA
CROUCH LA
FLORENCE COTTS
WINKFIELD ST
B3022
BRACKNELL RD
B3017
PARKER'S LA
POPEL'S COTTS
ST MARYS LA
RYEMEAD LA
NORTH ST
BRAZIERS LA
GROVE LA
WINKFIELD ROW
CRICKETERS LA
CHAVEY DOWN RD
LOCKS RIDE
MUSHROOM CASTLE
OSMAN'S CL
GORSE PL
WOODFORD CL
AVEY DOWN RD
FOXGLOVE CL
CARNATION DR
GARDNERS RD
SATURN CROFT
DIANTHUS PL
WILLIAM SIM WOOD
SCANIA WLK
CLOVE CL
CRAWLEY CHASE
ASTRA MEAD
FOREST WAY
THE ELMS
WELLINGTONIAS
THE LARCHES
MAIN DR
THE PLATEAU
YEW CL
COACH RD
RHODODENDRON CL
RHODODENDRON WLK
BEECHWOOD CL
FERNBANK RD
BISHOPS CT
KENNEL CL
KENNEL RIDE
NEW RD
THE AVENUE
OAKLANDS DR
ST JOHN'S RD
HUNTSMANS MDW
PO
Sch
PH
P

91
119

66
94

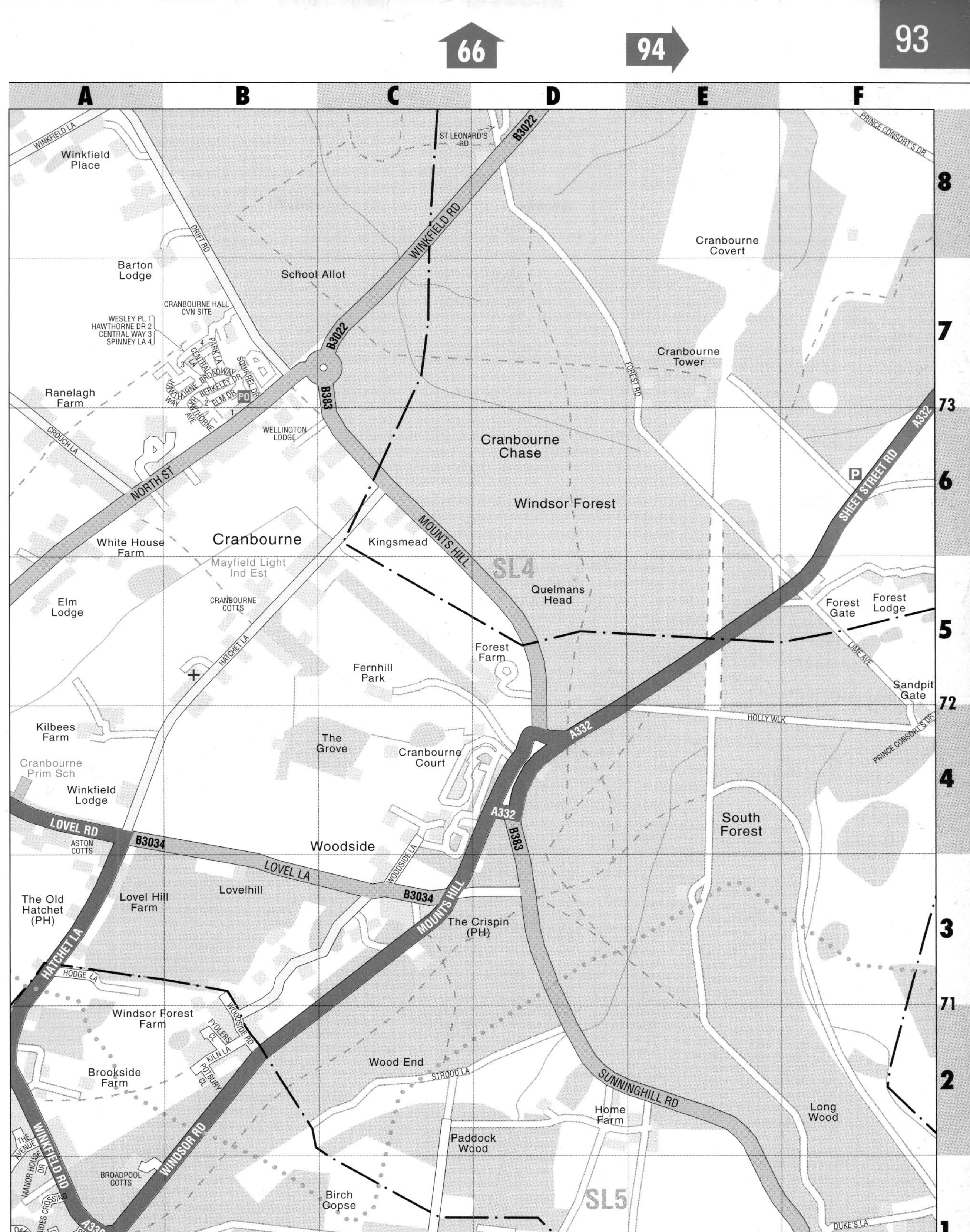
Winkfield Place
Barton Lodge
School Allot
Cranbourne Covert
Cranbourne Tower
Ranelagh Farm
Cranbourne Chase
Windsor Forest
White House Farm
Cranbourne
Mayfield Light Ind Est
Kingsmead
SL4
Quelmans Head
Elm Lodge
Forest Gate
Forest Lodge
Forest Farm
Fernhill Park
Sandpit Gate
Kilbees Farm
The Grove
Cranbourne Court
Cranbourne Prim Sch
Winkfield Lodge
South Forest
Woodside
The Old Hatchet (PH)
Lovel Hill Farm
Lovelhill
The Crispin (PH)
Windsor Forest Farm
Wood End
Brookside Farm
Home Farm
Long Wood
Paddock Wood
Birch Copse
SL5
Otley
Three Castles Path
WINKFIELD RD
NORTH ST
MOUNTS HILL
SHEET STREET RD
LOVEL RD
LOVEL LA
HATCHET LA
WINDSOR RD
SUNNINGHILL RD
HOLLY WLK
FOREST RD
DRIFT RD
CROUCH LA
HODGE LA
WOODSIDE LA
WOODSIDE RD
STROOD LA
DUKE'S LA
LIME AVE
PRINCE CONSORT'S DR
ST LEONARD'S RD
WELLINGTON LODGE
CRANBOURNE HALL CVN SITE
WESLEY PL 1
HAWTHORNE DR 2
CENTRAL WAY 3
SPINNEY LA 4
CRANBOURNE COTTS
ASTON COTTS
BROADPOOL COTTS
B3022
B383
B3034
A332
A330

A B C D E F
8 7 73 6 5 72 4 3 71 2 1 70
92 93 94

120
94

A   B   C   D   E   F

8

Flemish Farm

A332

SHEET STREET RD

Pickleherring
Pond

7

P

Ranger's
Lodge

Beehive
Hill

A332

73

Russel's
Pond

Fiddle
Covert

PRINCE CONSORT'S DR

Battle Bourne

The Gallop

Seymours
Plantation

Rush
Pond

THE LONG WLK

Prince of Wales
Pond

Bear's
Rails

Bear's Rails
Pond

Cemy

BEAR'S RAILS PK

CRIMP HILL

6

Statue
Snow
Hill

Spring
Hill

Cookes Hill

SL4

Three Castles Path

Richardson's
Lawn

RICHARDSON'S LAWN COTTS

PO

THE VILLAGE

QUE...

CLAINE'S CL

5

Isle of
Wight Pond

The
Village

Deepstrood

Royal
Lodge

MAIN GATE
LODGES

BISHOPSGATE RD

The Fox &
Hounds
(PH)

72

Poets
Lawn

Windsor Great Park

Queen Anne's Ride

4

Dark
Wood

The Royal
Fst Sch

Cow
Pond

Bishopsgate

Chapel
Wood

PARK CLOSE
COTTS

DUKE'S LA

MEZEL HILL
COTTS

CUMBERLAND
LODGE

3

Hilton's
Covert

Mezel
Hill

Wilderness

RHODODENDRON RIDE

WICK LA

The Sun
(PH)

Park
Close

71

Square
Covert

The Savill
Gardens

Parkside
House

2

Leiper
Hill

Slans
Hill

Great
Meadow
Pond

Temple
Hill

TW20

P

Obelisk

SL5

Norfolk
Plantation

Norfolk
Farm

Mill
Pond

Statue

Smith's
Lawn

Obelisk
Pond

1

Rosy
Bottom

Polo Gds

70

68
96

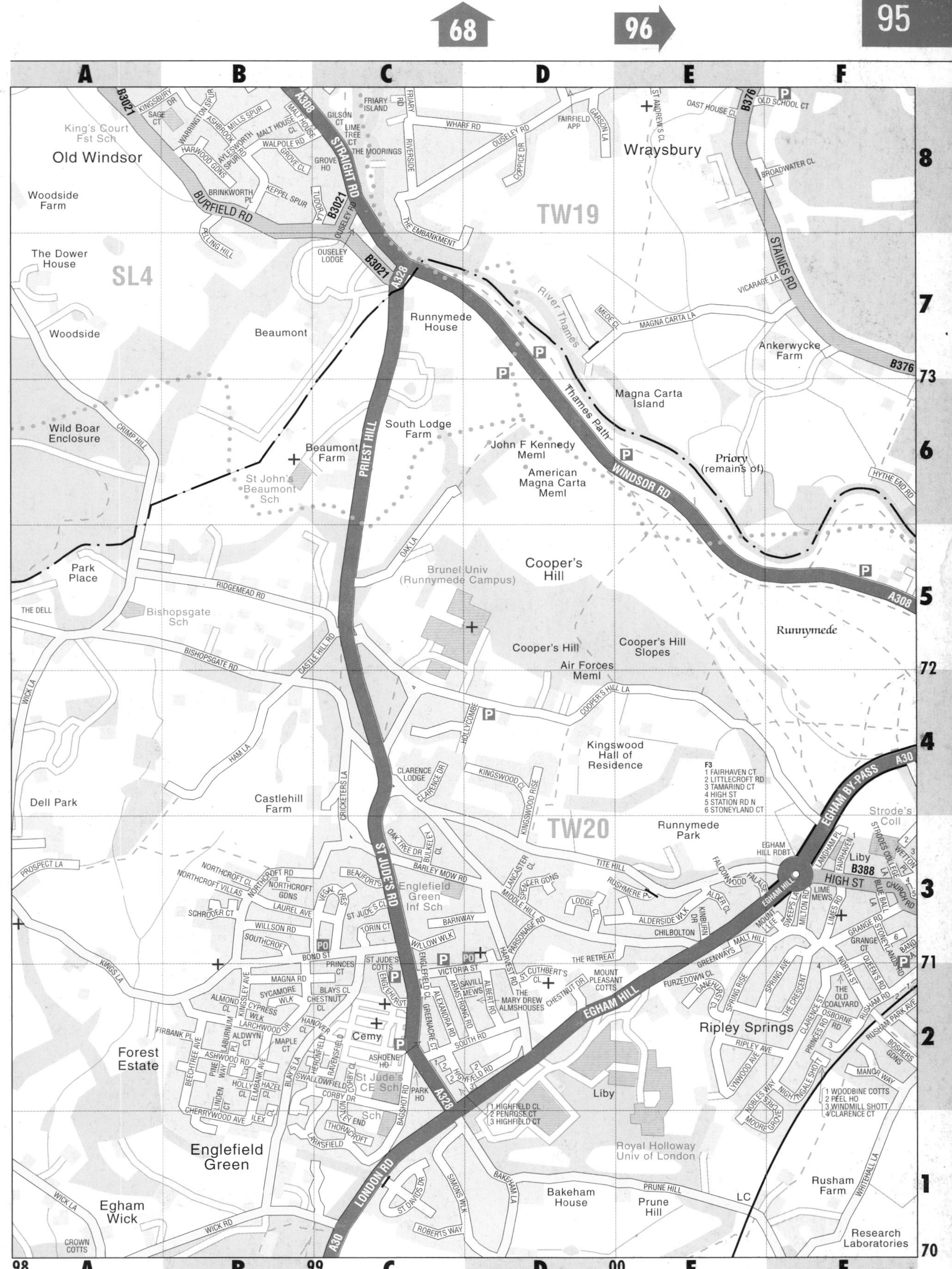
A
B
C
D
E
F
Old Windsor
King's Court Fst Sch
Woodside Farm
The Dower House
SL4
Woodside
Beaumont
Wild Boar Enclosure
Beaumont Farm
St John's Beaumont Sch
Park Place
THE DELL
Bishopsgate Sch
RIDGEMEAD RD
BISHOPSGATE RD
Dell Park
Castlehill Farm
Forest Estate
Englefield Green
Egham Wick
CROWN COTTS
Wraysbury
TW19
Runnymede House
South Lodge Farm
John F Kennedy Meml
American Magna Carta Meml
Magna Carta Island
Ankerwycke Farm
Priory (remains of)
Cooper's Hill
Brunel Univ (Runnymede Campus)
Cooper's Hill Slopes
Air Forces Meml
Runnymede
Kingswood Hall of Residence
TW20
Runnymede Park
Strode's Coll
Liby
Ripley Springs
Royal Holloway Univ of London
Bakeham House
Prune Hill
Rusham Farm
Research Laboratories
Cemy
St Jude's CE Sch
Englefield Green Inf Sch
PRIEST HILL
ST JUDE'S RD
WINDSOR RD
EGHAM HILL
EGHAM BY-PASS
HIGH ST
LONDON RD
STAINES RD
STRAIGHT RD
BURFIELD RD
River Thames
Thames Path
F3
1 FAIRHAVEN CT
2 LITTLECROFT RD
3 TAMARIND CT
4 HIGH ST
5 STATION RD N
6 STONEYLAND CT
1 WOODBINE COTTS
2 PEEL HO
3 WINDMILL SHOTT
4 CLARENCE CT
1 HIGHFIELD CL
2 PENROSE CT
3 HIGHFIELD CT
8
7
73
6
5
72
4
3
71
2
1
70
98
99
00

122
96

A B C D E F

8

7

73

6

5

72

4

3

71

2

1

70

01 A B 02 C D 03 E F

Map labels:

Wraysbury Resr

TW19

Bone Head

Sailing Club

B376

STAINES RD

Hythe End

B376

13

The Moor

Church Lammas

River Colne

Staines Moor

Colne Valley Way

Bonehead Ditch

STAINES

Colne Brook

Maffeking Rd

Sarsby Dr

Feathers La

Bell Weir Cl

Lodge Way

Ferry La

Yeoveney Ct

Berkeley Cl

Moor La

Lammas Cl

STAINES BY-PASS

River Ash

A30

A308 WINDSOR RD

The Island

Hythe End Rd

Yard Mead

Riverside

A30

Hotel

RUNNYMEDE RDBT

A30

WRAYSBURY RD

Queensmead Lake (Resr)

Gloucester Dr

Lammas Dr

Annie

Brides

Manz

Duncroft Manor

Meadow

Vicarage Rd

Victoria Rd

King Acre Ct

Green Pk

Marley Cl

Lammas Cl

Robin Ct

Lark Cl

Westheath Cl

Hawksway

Swallow Cl

Kingfisher

Waters Dr

The Oaks

Runnymede Cres

Fairfield Ave

Mill Mead

London Rd

EGHAM

A30 EGHAM BY-PASS

Strode St

Mandeville Ct

Cedar Ct

B388

THE AVENUE

Green La

Albany Av

WOODHAW

THE GLANTY A308

River Thames

Holm Island

Thames Path

Wks

Wks

Two Rivers Sh Ctr

Binbury Row

Cambria Ct

CHURCH ST

The Maltings

HALES

Goring's Sq

Mustard Mill Rd

Norris Rd

Tilley La

HIGH ST A308

OAST

STATION

Oast House

St George's St

Matthews Cl

The Elmsleigh Ctr

CLARENCE ST

THAMES ST

SOUTH ST

Liby

TH Mus

Aldous Ho 1

Thames Edge Ct 2

Colnebridge Cl 3

Bridge St

B376

Kingsbury Cres

THE CAUSEWAY

River Park Ave

Ind Est

The Green Bsns Ctr

Causeway Est

Lovey St

Gordon Rd

Cumberland Rd

Chandos Rd

Hythe Rd

Superstore

B3376

A320

Glyn Cl

Riverdale Dr

Pine Trees Bsns Pk

LC

Goring Dr

Goring Rd

Beech Lodge

Farm Cl

Monsell Gdns

Coopers Cl

Richmond Rd

Prospect Pl

Gresham Rd

B376

Mus

B388 CHURCH RD

HIGH ST

ARNDALE WAY

Manor Farm Ct

Oasis Mdw

St Nazaire Cl 1

Rhodes Ct 2

Flanders Ct 3

Normandy Wlk 4

Wendover Rd

Hythe Prim Sch

Old School Mews

THORPE RD

St Paul's Rd

Cornwall Way

Bowes Rd

Timsway

St Peter's Rd

TW18

LALEHAM RD

Iffley Ct

Langley Rd

Park La

Heritage Cl

Egham

Sports Ctr

VICARAGE RD

College Ave

Vicarage Ct

Priory

HARCOURT CT

Dugdale Ho

Conifer Cl

Mead Cl

Pooley Green

Windermere Cl 1

Coniston Way 2

Borrowdale Cl 3

Buttermere Way 4

Grasmere Cl 5

Royden Ct 1

Miller's Ct 2

The Magna Carta Sch

Meadow Gdns

Wapshott Rd

Bishops Way

Riverfield Rd

Riverbank

B376

Manorcroft Prim Sch

Rusham Park Ave 1

Braywood Ave 2

TW20

Glenville Farm

LEA RD

THORPE

B3376

Malet Cl

Langton Ave

Knights Cl

Huntingfield Way

Hythe Field Ave

Egham Hythe

Thorpe Lea Prim Sch

CHERTSEY LA

A320

Mayfield Gdns

Barrington Ct

Argosy Gdns

Duncombe

Swandrift

Onslow Lodge

Wythegate

Lodge

Milton Park

New Wickham La

STROUDE RD

Nurseries

Thorpe Lea

Mead Lake Ditch

Clockhouse La W

Clockhouse La E

THE LEA

B388

M25

Park Ave

South Ave

Lacey Rd

Oak Ave

Ferry Ave

A320

PENTON

Wheatsheaf La

Meadway

Avondale Ave

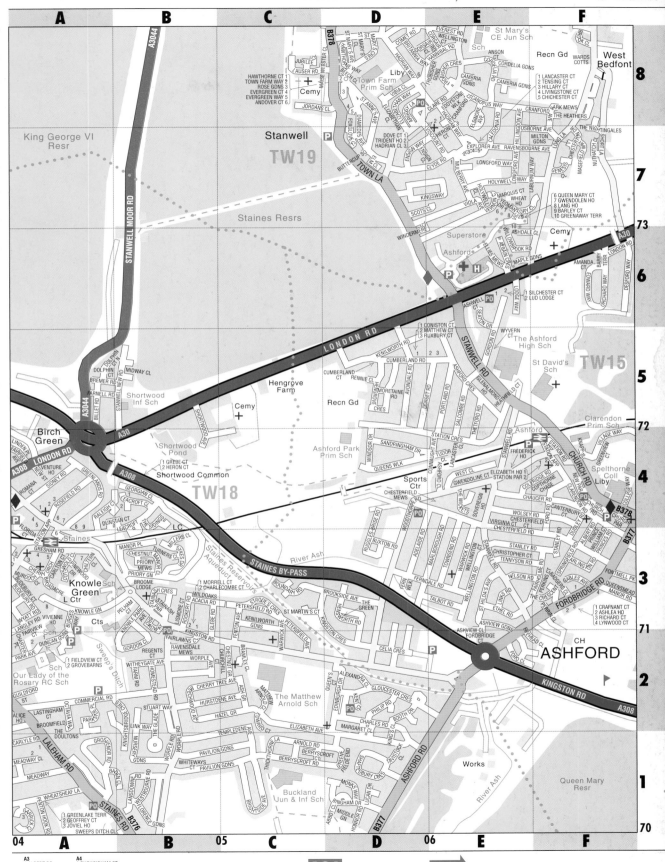

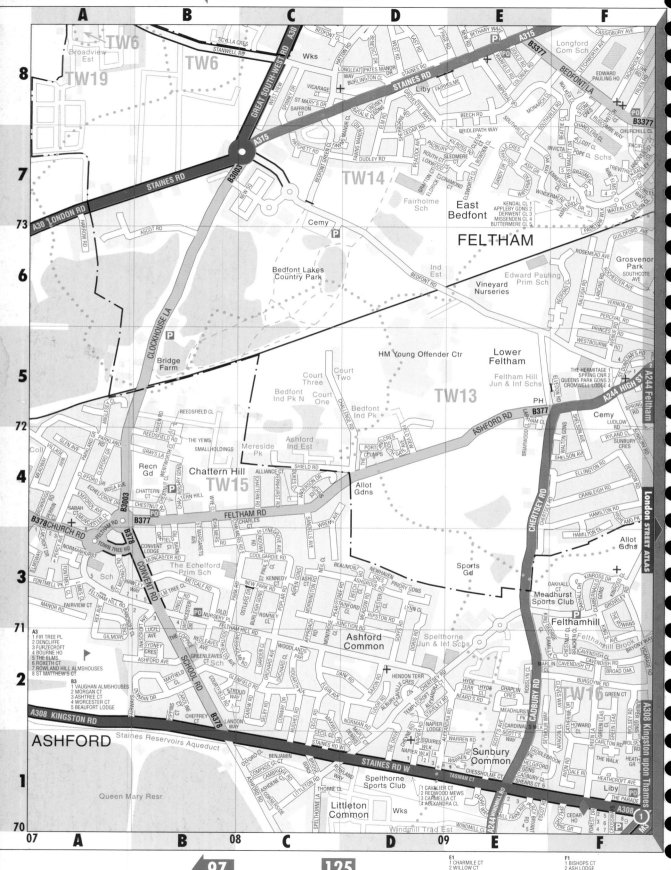

E1
1 CHARMILE CT
2 WILLOW CT
3 CASTLE CL
4 KILLIGREW HO
5 GRANTHAM HO
6 PRINCE ALBERT CT

F1
1 BISHOPS CT
2 ASH LODGE
3 LIME LODGE
4 OAK LODGE
5 ELM CT
6 WILLOW LODGE
7 SYCAMORE LODGE
8 PRISCILLA HO
9 Sunbury Cross Ctr

A3
1 FIR TREE PL
2 DENCLIFFE
3 FURZECROFT
4 BOURNE HO
5 THE ELMS
6 ROXETH CT
7 ROWLAND HILL ALMSHOUSES
8 ST MATTHEW'S CT

B3
1 VAUGHAN ALMSHOUSES
2 MORGAN CT
3 ASHTREE CT
4 WORCESTER CT
5 BEAUFORT LODGE

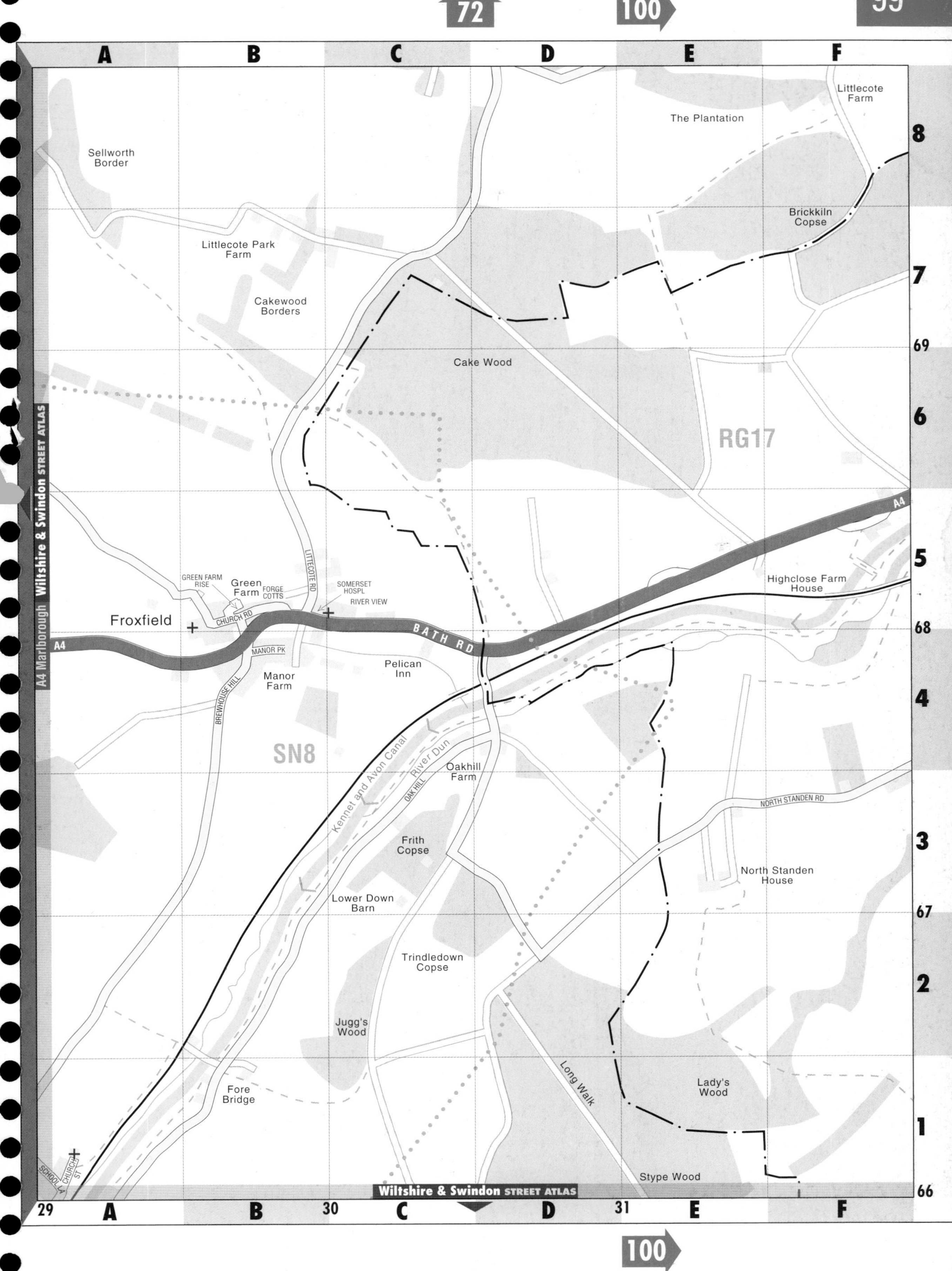
A
B
C
D
E
F
Littlecote Farm
The Plantation
Sellworth Border
8
Brickkiln Copse
Littlecote Park Farm
7
Cakewood Borders
69
Cake Wood
6
RG17
A4
5
LITTLECOTE RD
GREEN FARM RISE
Green Farm
FORGE COTTS
SOMERSET HOSPL
RIVER VIEW
Highclose Farm House
Froxfield
CHURCH RD
BATH RD
68
A4
MANOR PK
Pelican Inn
Manor Farm
BREWHOUSE HILL
4
SN8
Kennet and Avon Canal
River Dun
Oakhill Farm
OAK HILL
NORTH STANDEN RD
3
Frith Copse
North Standen House
Lower Down Barn
67
Trindledown Copse
2
Jugg's Wood
Long Walk
Lady's Wood
Fore Bridge
1
SCHOOL LA
CHURCH ST
Stype Wood
66
29
30
31
A4 Marlborough
Wiltshire & Swindon STREET ATLAS

99
73

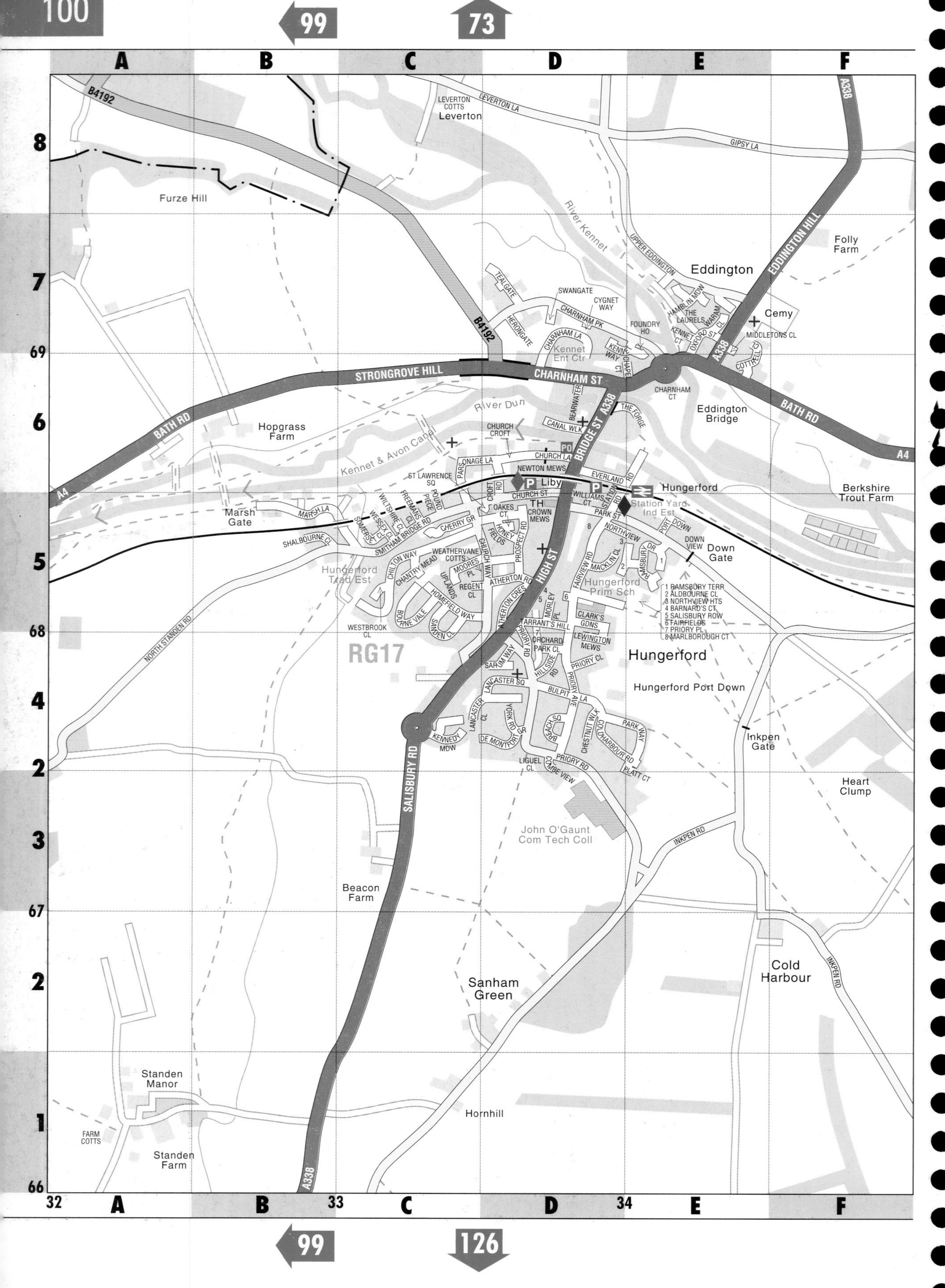
A
B
C
D
E
F
8
7
69
6
5
68
4
3
67
2
1
66
32
33
34
B4192
LEVERTON COTTS
Leverton
LEVERTON LA
GIPSY LA
A338
Furze Hill
River Kennet
Folly Farm
Eddington
UPPER EDDINGTON
EDDINGTON HILL
TEALGATE
SWANGATE
CYGNET WAY
CHARNHAM PK
HAMBLIN MDW
THE LAURELS
WARAM CL
Cemy
HERONGATE
CHARNHAM LA
FOUNDRY HO
KENNET CT
OXFORD ST
MIDDLETONS CL
Kennet Ent Ctr
COTTRELL CL
STRONGROVE HILL
CHARNHAM ST
CHARNHAM CT
BATH RD
Eddington Bridge
BEARWATER
THE FORGE
Hopgrass Farm
River Dun
CHURCH CROFT
CANAL WLK
BRIDGE ST
A4
Kennet & Avon Canal
CHURCH LA
PO
NEWTON MEWS
EVERLAND RD
Hungerford
Berkshire Trout Farm
ST LAWRENCE SQ
Liby
CHURCH ST
TH
WILLIAMS CT
STATION RD
Station Yard Ind Est
Marsh Gate
MARSH LA
POUND PIECE
FREEMANS CL
WILTSHIRE CL
WESSEX CT
SOMERSET CT
OAKES CT
CROWN MEWS
PARK ST
NORTHVIEW
PORT DOWN
DOWN VIEW
Down Gate
SHALBOURNE CL
SMITHAM BRIDGE RD
CHERRY GR
HONEY FIELDS
PROSPECT RD
CHURCH WAY
RAMSBURY DR
CHILTON WAY
WEATHERVANE COTTS
CHANTRY MEAD
MOORES PL
HIGH ST
MACKLIN CL
FAIRVIEW RD
Hungerford Trad Est
REGENT CL
UPLANDS
ATHERTON RD
Hungerford Prim Sch
1 RAMSBURY TERR
2 ALDBOURNE CL
3 NORTHVIEW HTS
4 BARNARD'S CT
5 SALISBURY ROW
6 FAIRFIELDS
7 PRIORY PL
8 MARLBOROUGH CT
HOMEFIELD WAY
ATHERTON CRES
MORLEY PL
CLARK'S GDNS
BOURNE VALE
SANDEN CL
NORTH STANDEN RD
WESTBROOK CL
TARRANT'S HILL
ORCHARD PARK CL
LEWINGTON MEWS
RG17
PRIORY RD
Hungerford
SARUM WAY
HILLSIDE RD
PRIORY CL
LANCASTER SQ
BULPIT LA
PRIORY AVE
Hungerford Port Down
LANCASTER CL
YORK RD
BEACH SQ
CHESTNUT WLK
COLDHARBOUR RD
PARK WAY
KENNEDY MDW
DE MONTFORT GR
Inkpen Gate
LIGUEL CL
COMBE VIEW
PRIORY RD
PLATT CT
SALISBURY RD
Heart Clump
John O'Gaunt Com Tech Coll
INKPEN RD
Beacon Farm
Sanham Green
Cold Harbour
INKPEN RD
Standen Manor
Hornhill
FARM COTTS
Standen Farm

99
126

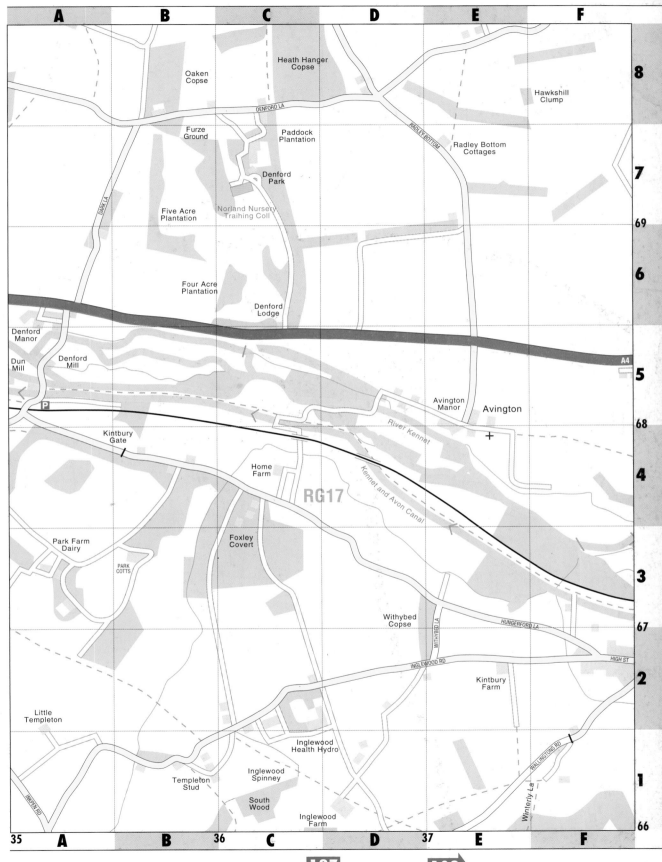

A   B   C   D   E   F

Heath Hanger Copse

Oaken Copse

DENFORD LA

Hawkshill Clump

Furze Ground

Paddock Plantation

Radley Bottom Cottages

RADLEY BOTTOM

Denford Park

Five Acre Plantation

Norland Nursery Traihing Coll

Four Acre Plantation

Denford Lodge

Denford Manor

DARK LA

Dun Mill

Denford Mill

A4

P

Avington Manor

Avington

River Kennet

Kintbury Gate

Home Farm

+

Kennet and Avon Canal

RG17

Park Farm Dairy

Foxley Covert

PARK COTTS

Withybed Copse

WITHYBED LA

HUNGERFORD LA

HIGH ST

Little Templeton

INGLEWOOD RD

Kintbury Farm

Templeton Stud

Inglewood Spinney

Inglewood Health Hydro

WALLINGTONS RD

Winterly La

South Wood

Inglewood Farm

INKPEN RD

35   A   B   36   C   D   37   E   F

8
7
69
6
5
68
4
67
3
2
1
66

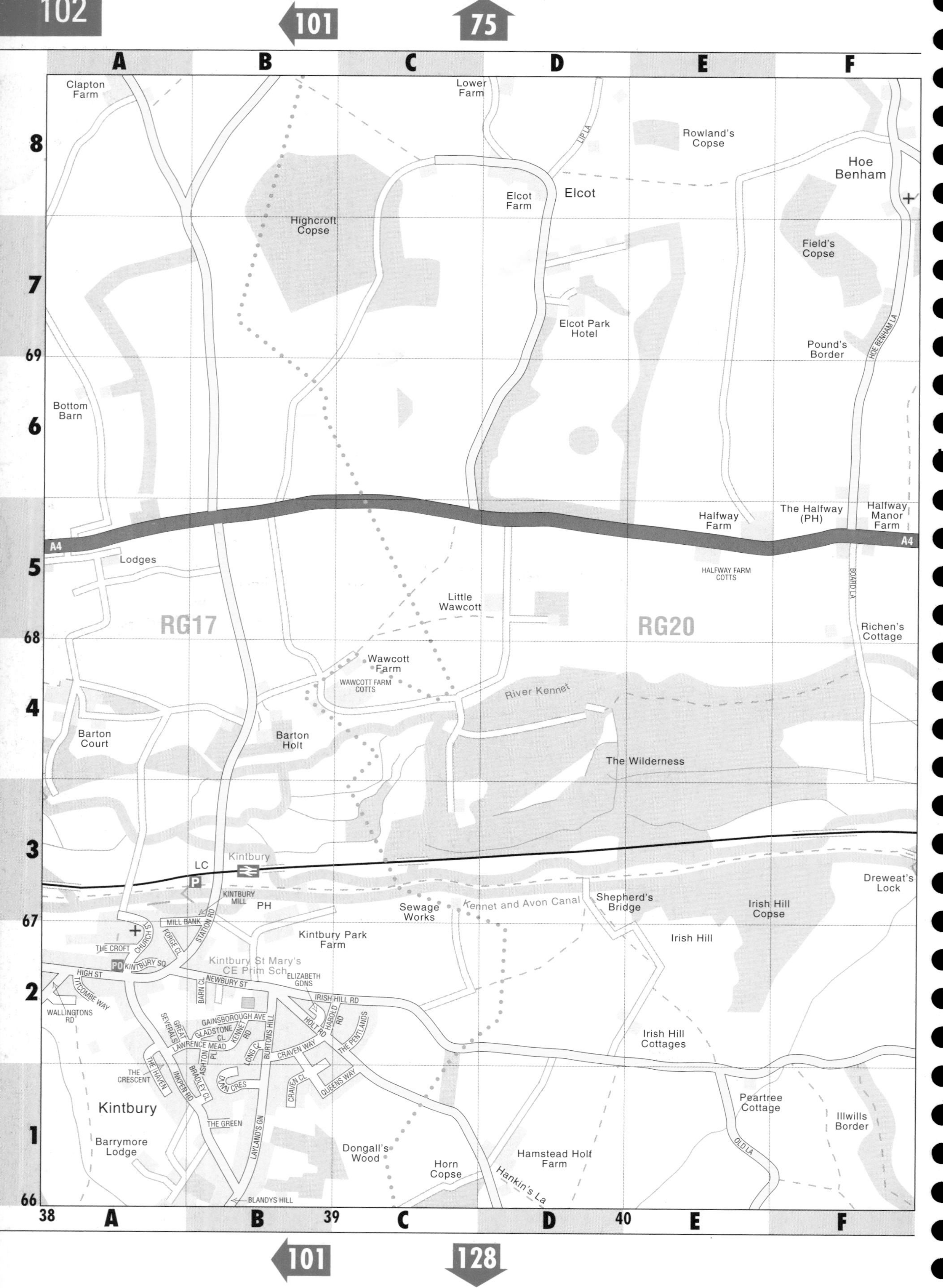

A   B   C   D   E   F

8

Clapton
Farm

Lower
Farm

Rowland's
Copse

Hoe
Benham

Elcot
Farm   Elcot

Highcroft
Copse

7

Field's
Copse

Elcot Park
Hotel

69

Pound's
Border

Bottom
Barn

6

Halfway
Farm   The Halfway
(PH)   Halfway
Manor
Farm

A4   A4

5   Lodges

HALFWAY FARM
COTTS

RG17   Little
Wawcott

RG20   Richen's
Cottage

68

Wawcott
Farm

WAWCOTT FARM
COTTS

4   River Kennet

Barton
Court   Barton
Holt

The Wilderness

3   Kintbury   Dreweat's
Lock

LC

P   Kintbury Mill   PH   Sewage
Works   Kennet and Avon Canal   Shepherd's
Bridge   Irish Hill
Copse

67   MILL BANK

THE CROFT   Kintbury Park
Farm   Irish Hill

PO   KINTBURY SQ
CHURCH   FORGE CL   STATION RD

HIGH ST   BARN CL   NEWBURY ST

Kintbury St Mary's
CE Prim Sch   ELIZABETH
GDNS

2   TITCOMBE WAY   IRISH HILL RD

WALLINGTONS
RD   GAINSBOROUGH AVE
GLADSTONE   CL
GREAT
LAWRENCE MEAD
SEVERALLS
PL   LONG CL
ASHTON   KENNET RD   BURTONS HILL   HOLT RD   HAROLD RD   THE PENTLANDS   Irish Hill
Cottages

THE CRESCENT   BRADLEY CL   THE HAZEL   INKPEN RD   OXEN CRES   CRAVEN CL   CRAVEN WAY   QUEENS WAY   Peartree
Cottage

Illwills
Border

1   Kintbury   THE GREEN   LAYLAND'S GDN   OLD LA

Barrymore
Lodge   Dongall's
Wood   Horn
Copse   Hankin's La   Hamstead Holt
Farm

66   BLANDYS HILL

38   A   B   39   C   D   40   E   F

76
104

A B C D E F
8 7 69 6 5 68 4 3 67 2 1 66
41 42 43
B4000
COOMBESBURY LA
Priddle's Farm
River Lambourn
Huntsgreen Farm
Benham Farm
Wickham Heath
Nalder Plantation
Cecil (old & new)
Woodspeen Farm
ERMIN ST
Shepherd's Farm
Scotch Wood
Nalderhill Copse
Spring Wood
NALDERHILL RD
Pique
Nalderhill House
CHAPEL RD
ROOKSWOOD
CRICKETERS
Stockcross CE Sch
SNAKE LA
HANOVER GN
Stockcross
PO
B4000
Furze Hill
The Dismals
GLEBE LA
Common Wood
Grange Farm
CHURCH RD
BENHAM CHASE
Benham Grange
GRAVEL HILL
Bradford's Farm
Benham Dairy
A4
RG20
Bradford's Gorse
Benham Park
West Meadows
MILKHOUSE RD
Magdalen Plantation
River Kennet
Marsh Benham
Benham Gardens
Red House (PH)
Benham Stud
Hamstead Crossing
Hamstead Lock
Kennet and Avon Canal
Benham Marsh Farm
More Wood
HAMSTEAD MILL
Barnett's Lock
Ivy House
PARK LA
Craven House
Hamstead Park
Enborne Copse
The Mews
Craven Hill

129
104

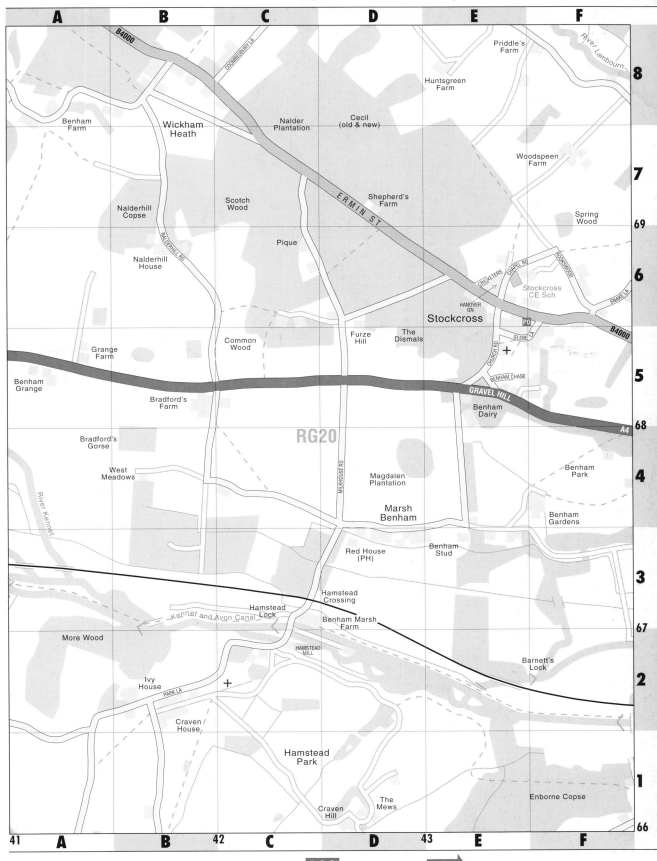

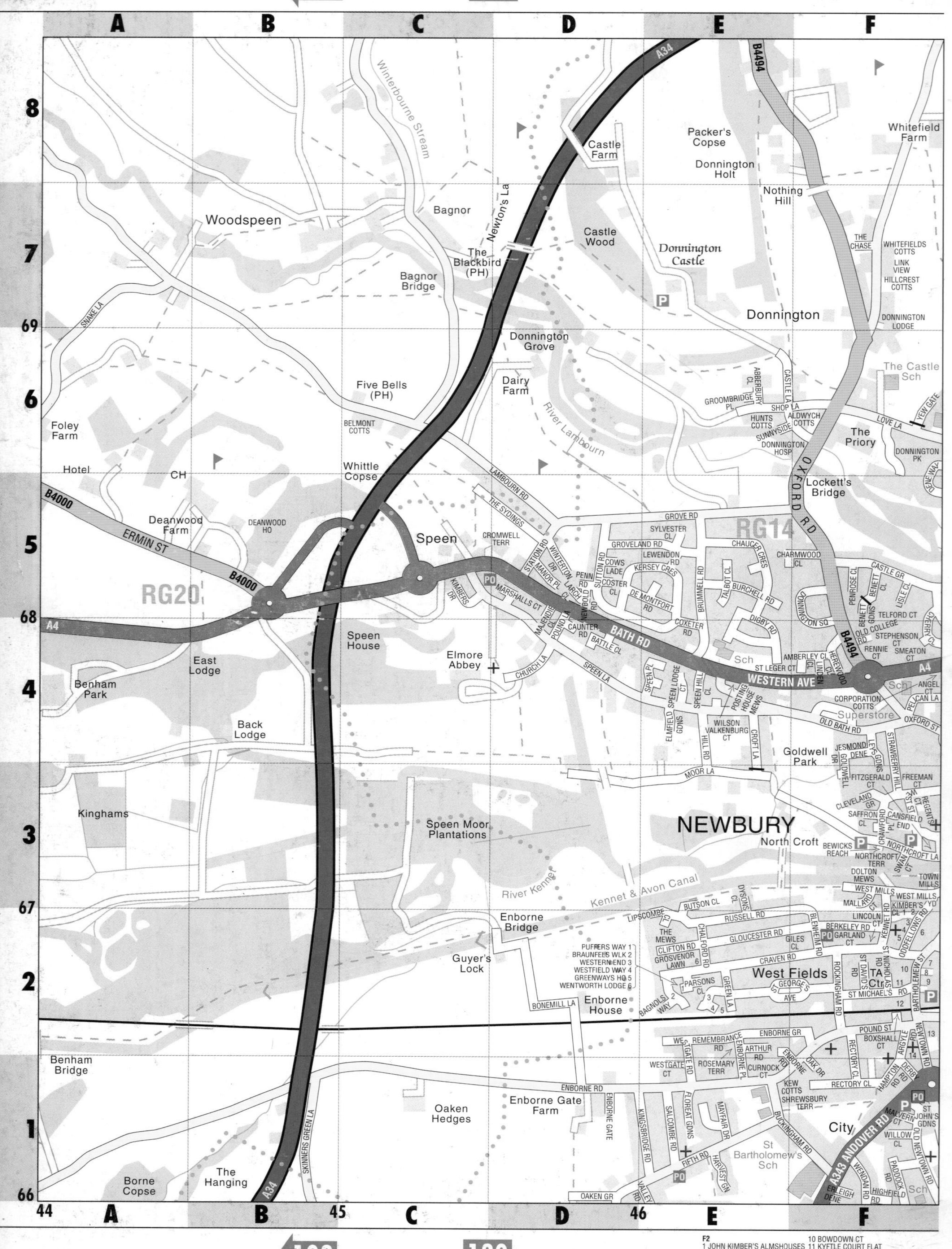

F2
1 JOHN KIMBER'S ALMSHOUSES
2 MULBERRY CT
3 CYPRESS HO
4 BECKET HO
5 FISHER HO
6 CAMPION HO
7 IMPERIAL CT
8 EIGHT BELLS
9 BARTHOLOMEW CT
10 BOWDOWN CT
11 KYFTLE COURT FLAT
12 BARNES TERR
13 LOWER RAYMOND ALMSHOUSES
14 UPPER RAYMOND ALMSHOUSES

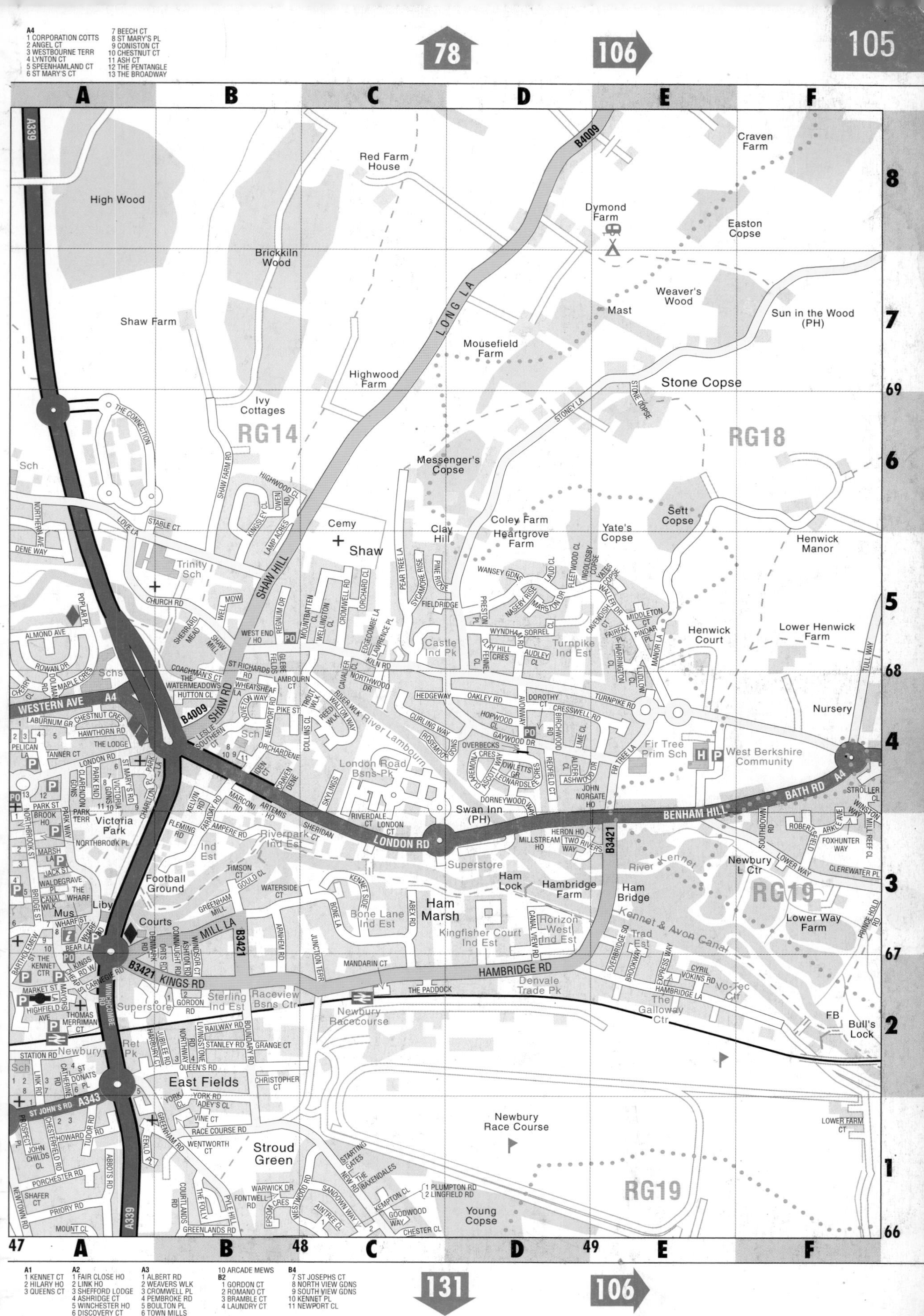

78
106
131
106

105 79

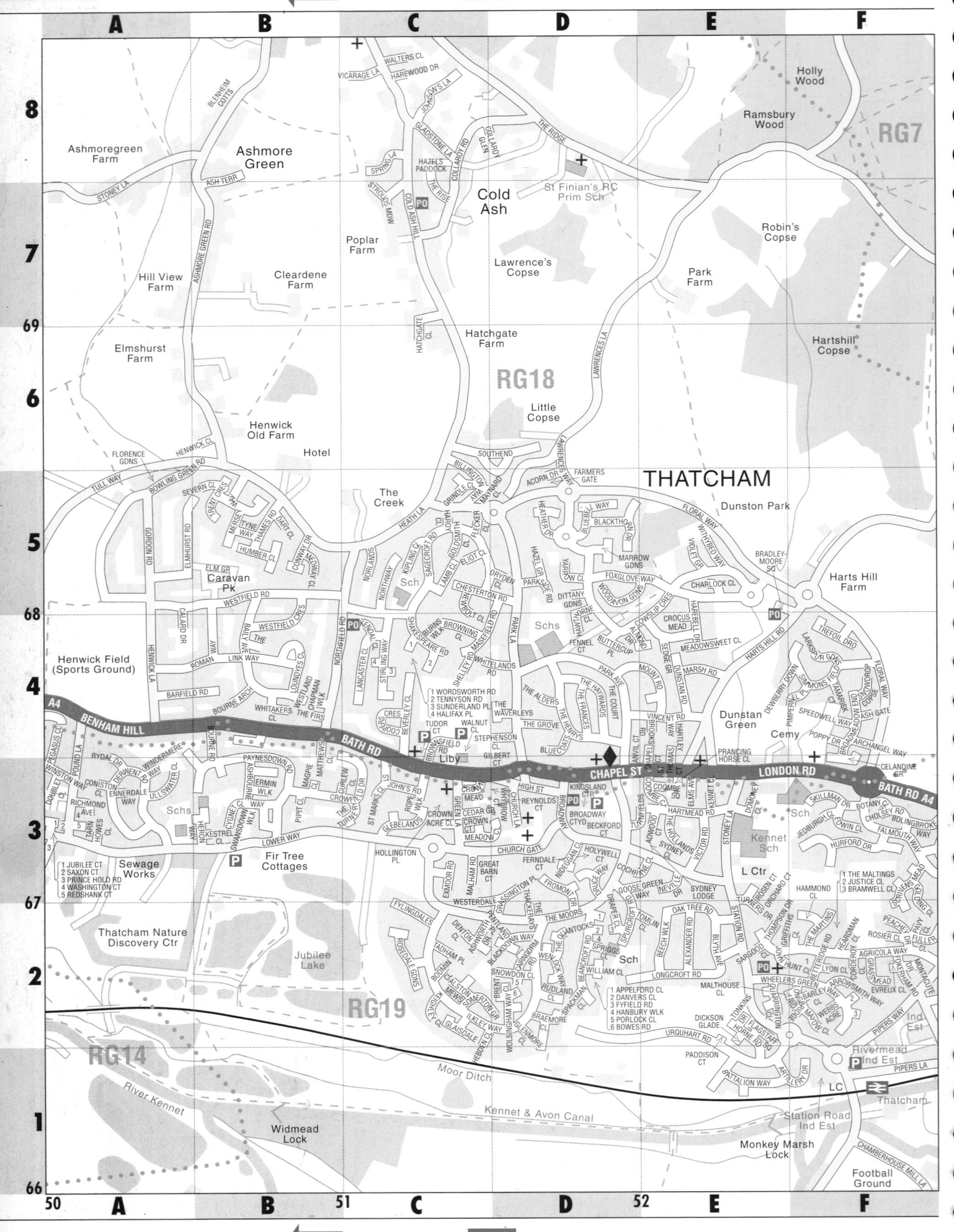
A B C D E F
8
7
69
6
5
68
4
3
67
2
1
66
50 51 52
Ashmoregreen Farm
Ashmore Green
STONEY LA
ASH TERR
BLENHEIM COTTS
ASHMORE GREEN RD
Hill View Farm
Cleardene Farm
Elmshurst Farm
Henwick Old Farm
Hotel
FLORENCE GDNS
HENWICK CL
TULL WAY
BOWLING GREEN RD
VICARAGE LA
WALTERS CL
HAREWOOD DR
JOHNSON'S LA
GLADSTONE LA
SPRING LA
HAZELS PADDOCK
COLLAROY RD
COLLAROY GLEN
THE RISE
STROUDS MDW
COLD ASH HILL
Cold Ash
Poplar Farm
THE RIDGE
St Finian's RC Prim Sch
Lawrence's Copse
Holly Wood
Ramsbury Wood
RG7
Robin's Copse
Park Farm
Hartshill Copse
HATCHGATE CL
Hatchgate Farm
RG18
Little Copse
LAWRENCES LA
SOUTHEND
THATCHAM
Dunston Park
The Creek
Caravan Pk
ELM GR
WESTFIELD RD
Henwick Field (Sports Ground)
BRADLEY-MOORE SQ
Harts Hill Farm
CHARLOCK CL
HARTS HILL RD
Sch
Schs
A4
BENHAM HILL
BATH RD
CHAPEL ST
LONDON RD
BATH RD A4
Liby
1 WORDSWORTH RD
2 TENNYSON RD
3 SUNDERLAND PL
4 HALIFAX PL
Dunstan Green
Cemy
Kennet Sch
L Ctr
1 JUBILEE CT
2 SAXON CT
3 PRINCE HOLD RD
4 WASHINGTON CT
5 REDSHANK CT
Sewage Works
Fir Tree Cottages
1 THE MALTINGS
2 JUSTICE CL
3 BRAMWELL CL
Thatcham Nature Discovery Ctr
Jubilee Lake
RG19
RG14
1 APPELFORD CL
2 DANVERS CL
3 FYFIELD RD
4 HANBURY WLK
5 PORLOCK CL
6 BOWES RD
Rivermead Ind Est
PIPERS LA
Ind Est
Moor Ditch
River Kennet
Kennet & Avon Canal
Widmead Lock
Station Road Ind Est
Monkey Marsh Lock
Thatcham
CHAMBERHOUSE MILL LA
Football Ground
A B C D E F

105 132

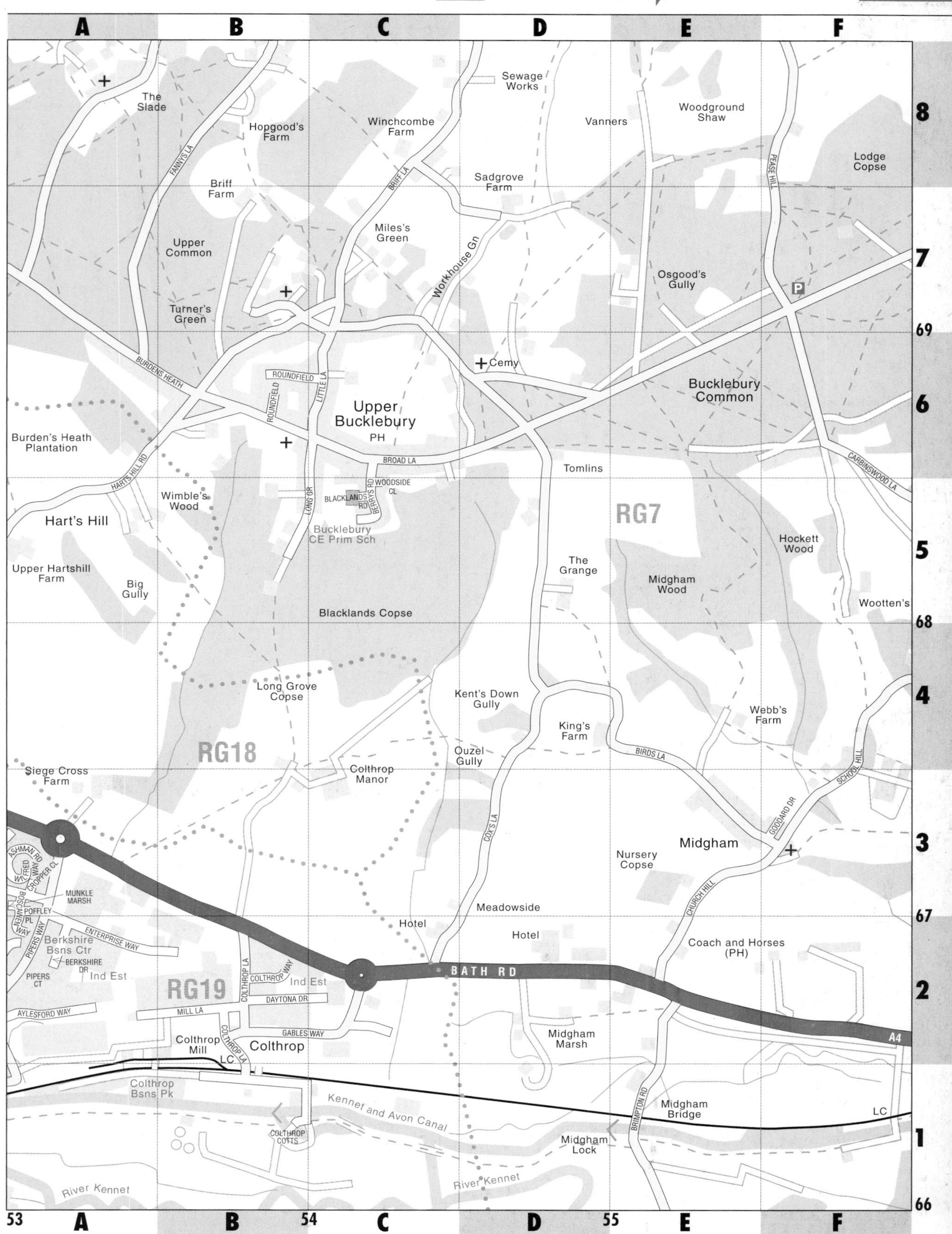

A **B** **C** **D** **E** **F**

The Slade

Hopgood's Farm

Winchcombe Farm

Sewage Works

Vanners

Woodground Shaw

Lodge Copse

8

Briff Farm

Miles's Green

Sadgrove Farm

7

Upper Common

Osgood's Gully

FANNY'S LA

BRIFF LA

PEASE HILL

P

69

Turner's Green

Workhouse Gn

+ Cemy

Bucklebury Common

6

BURDENS HEATH

ROUNDFIELD

LITTLE LA

Upper Bucklebury

PH

Tomlins

CARBINSWOOD LA

Burden's Heath Plantation

HARTS HILL RD

ROUNDFIELD

LONG GR

BROAD LA

WOODSIDE CL

BERRY'S RD

BLACKLANDS RD

RG7

Wimble's Wood

Blacklands

Hockett Wood

5

Hart's Hill

Bucklebury CE Prim Sch

The Grange

Midgham Wood

Wootten's

Upper Hartshill Farm

Big Gully

Blacklands Copse

68

Long Grove Copse

Kent's Down Gully

King's Farm

Webb's Farm

SCHOOL HILL

4

RG18

Colthrop Manor

Ouzel Gully

BIRDS LA

Siege Cross Farm

COX'S LA

GODDARD DR

Midgham

+

3

ASHMAN RD

Nursery Copse

CHURCH HILL

ALFRED WAY

CLOPPER CL

MUNKLE MARSH

67

POFFLEY PL

ENTERPRISE WAY

Meadowside

Coach and Horses (PH)

PIPERS WAY

Berkshire Bsns Ctr

Hotel

Hotel

BERKSHIRE DR

Ind Est

PIPERS CT

RG19

COLTHROP LA

COLTHROP WAY

Ind Est

BATH RD

A4

2

AYLESFORD WAY

MILL LA

DAYTONA DR

Midgham Marsh

BRIMPTON RD

Colthrop Mill

COLTHROP LA

GABLES WAY

Colthrop

LC

Midgham Bridge

LC

Colthrop Bsns Pk

Kennet and Avon Canal

Midgham Lock

1

COLTHROP COTTS

River Kennet

River Kennet

66

53 **A** **B** 54 **C** **D** 55 **E** **F**

A B C D E F

8
Scotland
St Annes Farm
Chapelrow Common
PO
The Blade Bone (PH)
Chapel Row
Beenham Hatch
The Bourne
Gunnells Farm
Hilliers
The Bourne

7
Lower Common
Long Gully
Middle Wood
HATCH LA
PARADISE WAY
PARADISE LA
Ironmongers Copse
Withy Copse
Six Bells (PH)
Awbery's Farm
Beenham Prim Sch

69
Carbins Wood
Copyhold Farm
Greyfield Wood
Beenham
MOUNT PLEASANT
CLAY LA
THE STROUDS
SHIRE COTTS

6
Reading's Gully
Horn's Copse
Kiff Green
High Wood
Old Copse

CARBINSWOOD LA

5
BUCKLEBURY PL
WINDMILL LA
Channel Wood
Douai Abbey (Benedictine)
Ferrises
Oakwood Farm

68
SCHOOL HILL
Midgham Green
RG7
Lodge
Malthouse Farm
Gravelpit Copse

4
Webcroft Copse
Woolhampton C E Prim Sch
Upper Woolhampton
Beenham Lodge

Midgham Park
NEW ROAD HILL
Elstree Sch
PARKSIDE

3
Hallcourt Farm
The Court
Home Farm
Woolhampton Park
Jennings's Copse

67
Great Mounts Copse
ROLAND'S COPSE
VICTOR PL
HILL CRES
WOOLHAMPTON HILL
ORCHARD CL
Inn
A4

2
Gateways
Oxlease Bridge
Midgham
STATION RD
PO
Woolhampton
BATH RD
WATERMILL CT
ANGEL MEAD
P
SUN HILL
RAILSIDE
Rising Sun (PH)
A4

Heales Lock
Kennet & Avon Canal
Woolhampton Lock
Woolhampton Bridge
River Kennet
Swing-bridge
River Enborne
Frouds Bridge Marina

1
Gravel Pit

66
56 A B 57 C D 58 E F

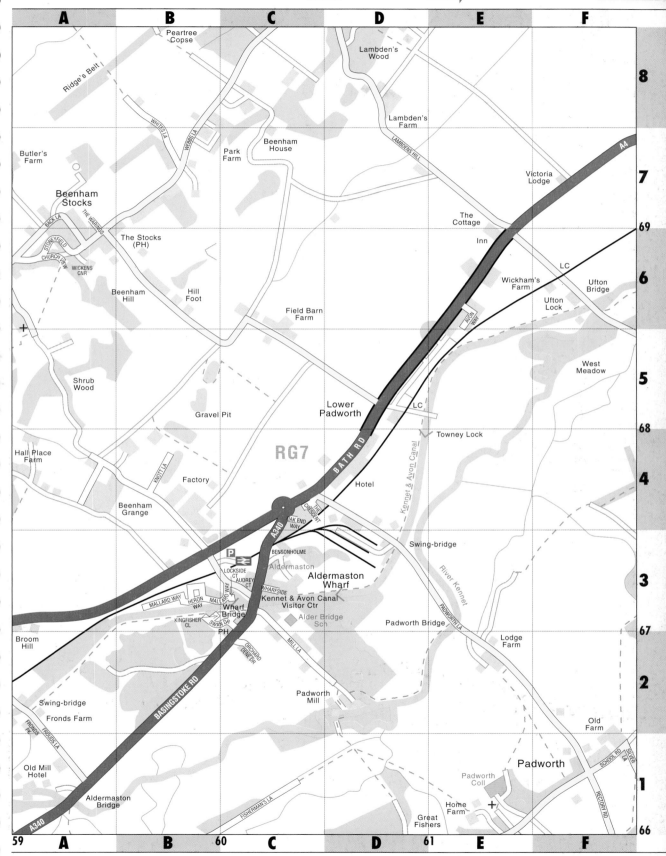
82

110

A B C D E F

Peartree Copse
Lambden's Wood
Ridge's Belt
Lambden's Farm
WHITES LA
WEBBS LA
LAMBDENS HILL
Butler's Farm
Park Farm
Beenham House
A4
Victoria Lodge
Beenham Stocks
BACK LA
THE WARINGS
STONEYFIELD
CHURCH VIEW
WICKENS CNR
The Cottage
The Stocks (PH)
Inn
LC
Wickham's Farm
Ufton Bridge
Ufton Lock
Beenham Hill
Hill Foot
Field Barn Farm
AVON WAY
Shrub Wood
West Meadow
Gravel Pit
Lower Padworth
LC
Towney Lock
Hall Place Farm
RG7
BATH RD
KNOTT LA
Factory
Hotel
Kennet & Avon Canal
Beenham Grange
THE CRESCENT
OAK END WAY
A340
Swing-bridge
BENSONHOLME
Aldermaston
LOCKSIDE CT
AUDREY CT
Aldermaston Wharf
River Kennet
WHARFSIDE
MALLARD WAY
HERON WAY
MALLARD WAY
Kennet & Avon Canal Visitor Ctr
Wharf Bridge
KINGFISHER CL
SWAN DR
Alder Bridge Sch
PH
Padworth Bridge
PADWORTH LA
Broom Hill
ORCHARD DENE DR
MILL LA
Lodge Farm
BASINGSTOKE RD
Padworth Mill
Swing-bridge
Fronds Farm
FRONDS PK
FROUDS LA
Old Farm
Old Mill Hotel
Padworth
SCHOOL RD
SILVER LA
Padworth Coll
RECTORY RD
Aldermaston Bridge
Home Farm
FISHERMAN'S LA
Great Fishers
A340

8 7 69 6 5 68 4 3 67 2 1 66

59 A B 60 C D 61 E F

135

110

109
83

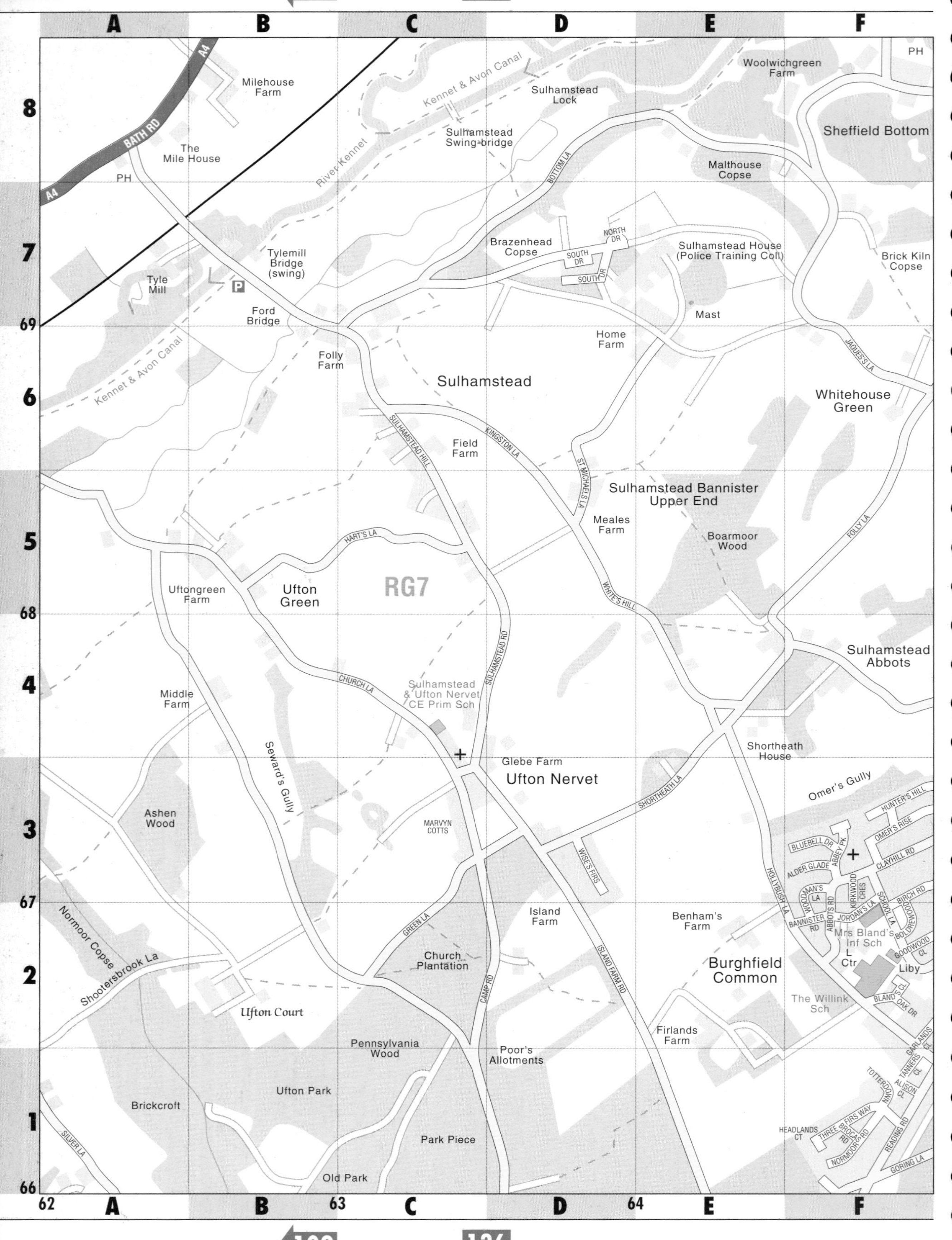
A
B
C
D
E
F
A4
BATH RD
Milehouse Farm
The Mile House
PH
Kennet & Avon Canal
River Kennet
Sulhamstead Lock
Sulhamstead Swing-bridge
Woolwichgreen Farm
PH
Sheffield Bottom
Malthouse Copse
BOTTOM LA
Tylemill Bridge (swing)
Tyle Mill
P
Ford Bridge
Brazenhead Copse
NORTH DR
SOUTH DR
SOUTH DR
Sulhamstead House (Police Training Coll)
Brick Kiln Copse
Mast
Home Farm
Folly Farm
Sulhamstead
JAQUES'S LA
Whitehouse Green
SULHAMSTEAD HILL
KINGSTON LA
Field Farm
ST MICHAEL'S LA
Sulhamstead Bannister Upper End
Meales Farm
Boarmoor Wood
FOLLY LA
HART'S LA
RG7
Uftongreen Farm
Ufton Green
WHITE'S HILL
SULHAMSTEAD RD
Sulhamstead Abbots
CHURCH LA
Sulhamstead & Ufton Nervet CE Prim Sch
Middle Farm
Seward's Gully
Glebe Farm
Ufton Nervet
Shortheath House
SHORTHEATH LA
Omer's Gully
Ashen Wood
MARVYN COTTS
HUNTER'S HILL
OMER'S RISE
BLUEBELL DR
ABBEY PK
ALDER GLADE
CLAYHILL RD
WISE'S FIRS
HOLLYBUSH LA
WOODMAN'S LA
ABBOTS RD
KIRKWOOD CRES
JORDAN'S LA
SCHOOL LA
BIRCH RD
BOLDREWOOD
BANNISTER RD
Mrs Bland's Inf Sch
GOODWOOD CL
L Ctr
Liby
Normoor Copse
Island Farm
Benham's Farm
GREEN LA
Church Plantation
ISLAND FARM RD
Burghfield Common
Shootersbrook La
CAMP RD
Ufton Court
The Willink Sch
BLAND'S CL
OAK DR
Firlands Farm
GARLANDS CL
Pennsylvania Wood
Poor's Allotments
TANNERS CL
ALISON CL
TOTTERDOWN
Ufton Park
Brickcroft
FIRS WAY
HEADLANDS CT
THREE FIRS WAY
BROCAS RD
NORMOOR RD
READING RD
SILVER LA
Park Piece
Old Park
GORING LA
8
7
69
6
5
68
4
3
67
2
1
66
62
63
64

109
136

84
112

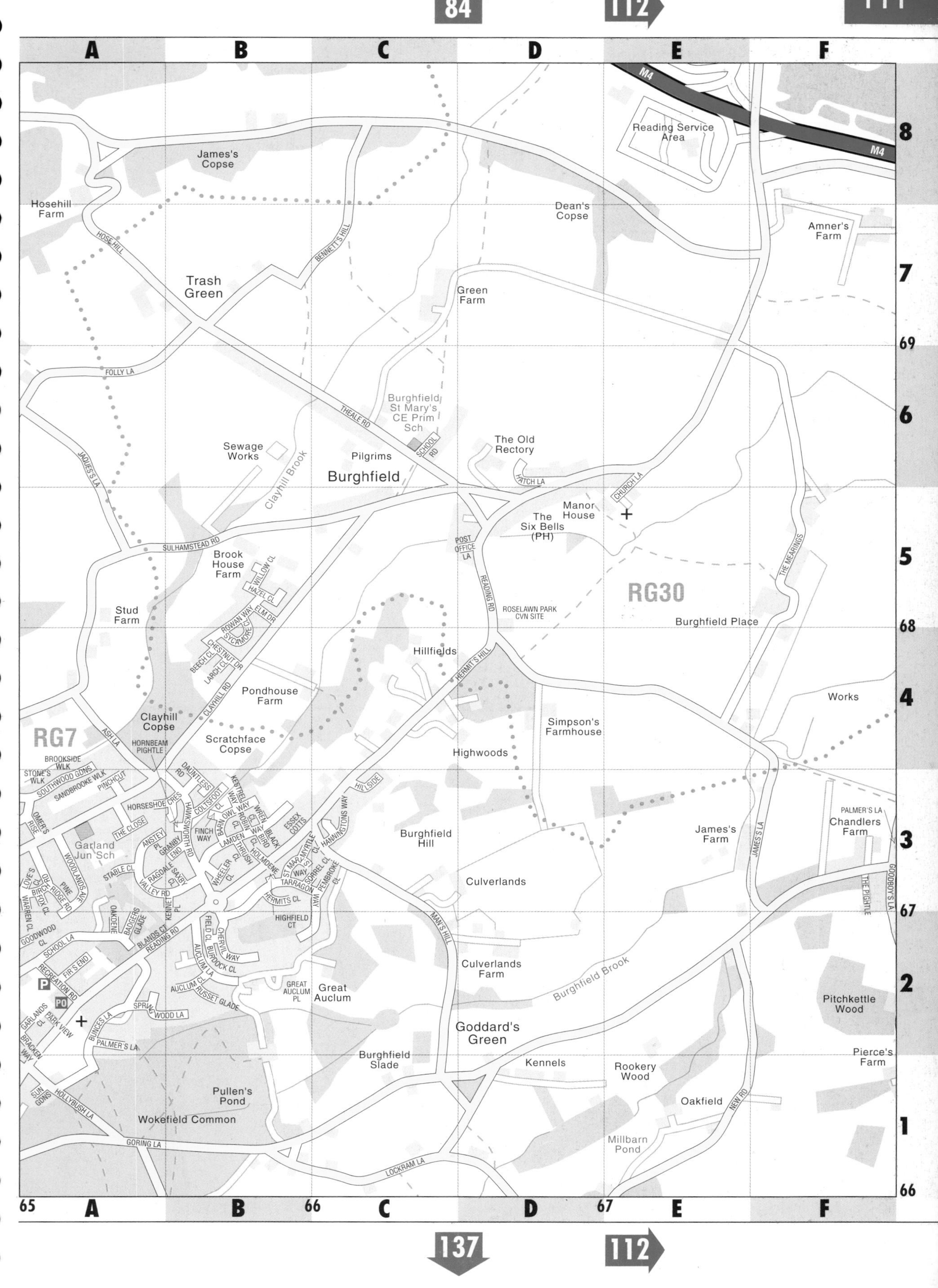
A
B
C
D
E
F
8
7
69
6
5
68
4
3
67
2
1
66
65
66
67
M4
Reading Service Area
James's Copse
Hosehill Farm
HOSE HILL
BENNETT'S HILL
Dean's Copse
Amner's Farm
Trash Green
Green Farm
FOLLY LA
Burghfield St Mary's CE Prim Sch
THEALE RD
SCHOOL RD
The Old Rectory
HATCH LA
CHURCH LA
Sewage Works
Pilgrims
Burghfield
Clayhill Brook
JAQUES'S LA
Manor House
The Six Bells (PH)
POST OFFICE LA
SULHAMSTEAD RD
Brook House Farm
WILLOW CL
HAZEL CL
ELM DR
READING RD
ROSELAWN PARK CVN SITE
RG30
THE MEARINGS
Burghfield Place
Stud Farm
ROWAN WAY
SYCAMORE CL
CHESTNUT DR
BEECH CL
LARCH CL
CLAYHILL RD
Hillfields
HERMIT'S HILL
Pondhouse Farm
Works
RG7
ASH LA
Clayhill Copse
HORNBEAM PIGHTLE
Scratchface Copse
Simpson's Farmhouse
Highwoods
BROOKSIDE WLK
STONE'S WLK
SOUTHWOOD GDNS
SANDBROOKE WLK
PINCHCUT
DAUNTLESS RD
KESTREL WAY
HILLSIDE
HANNINGTONS WAY
HORSESHOE CRES
COLTSFOOT CL
HAWKSWORTH RD
BARN OWL WAY
ROBIN WAY
WREN CL
ESSEX COTTS
OMERS RISE
THE CLOSE
FINCH WAY
LAMDEN
THRUSH
BLACKBIRD
PALMER'S LA
Chandlers Farm
James's Farm
JAMES'S LA
Burghfield Hill
Garland Jun Sch
ANSTEY PL
GRANBY END
RAGDALE
SAXBY CL
HOLMDENE
ST MARY'S WAY
MYRTLE CL
SORREL CL
PEMBROKE CL
TARRAGON WAY
HERMITS CL
WHEELER CL
Culverlands
STABLE CL
VALLEY RD
KENNET PL
LOVE'S CL
BIRCH CL
RIDGE RD
PINE
WOODLANDS AVE
FOX CL
WARREN CL
OAKDENE
BADGERS GLADE
BLANDS CT
GOODWOOD CL
SCHOOL LA
READING RD
FIELD CL
CHERVIL WAY
HIGHFIELD CT
MAN'S HILL
GOODBOY'S LA
THE PIGHTLE
FIR'S END
RECREATION RD
AUCLUM LA
BURDOCK CL
Culverlands Farm
Burghfield Brook
P
PO
AUCLUM CL
RUSSET GLADE
GREAT AUCLUM PL
Great Auclum
Pitchkettle Wood
GARLANDS CL
PARK VIEW
BRACKEN WAY
BUNCES LA
SPRING WOOD LA
PALMER'S LA
Goddard's Green
Burghfield Slade
Kennels
Rookery Wood
Pierce's Farm
SUN GDNS
HOLLYBUSH LA
Pullen's Pond
Oakfield
NEW RD
Wokefield Common
GORING LA
Millbarn Pond
LOCKRAM LA

137
112

111
85

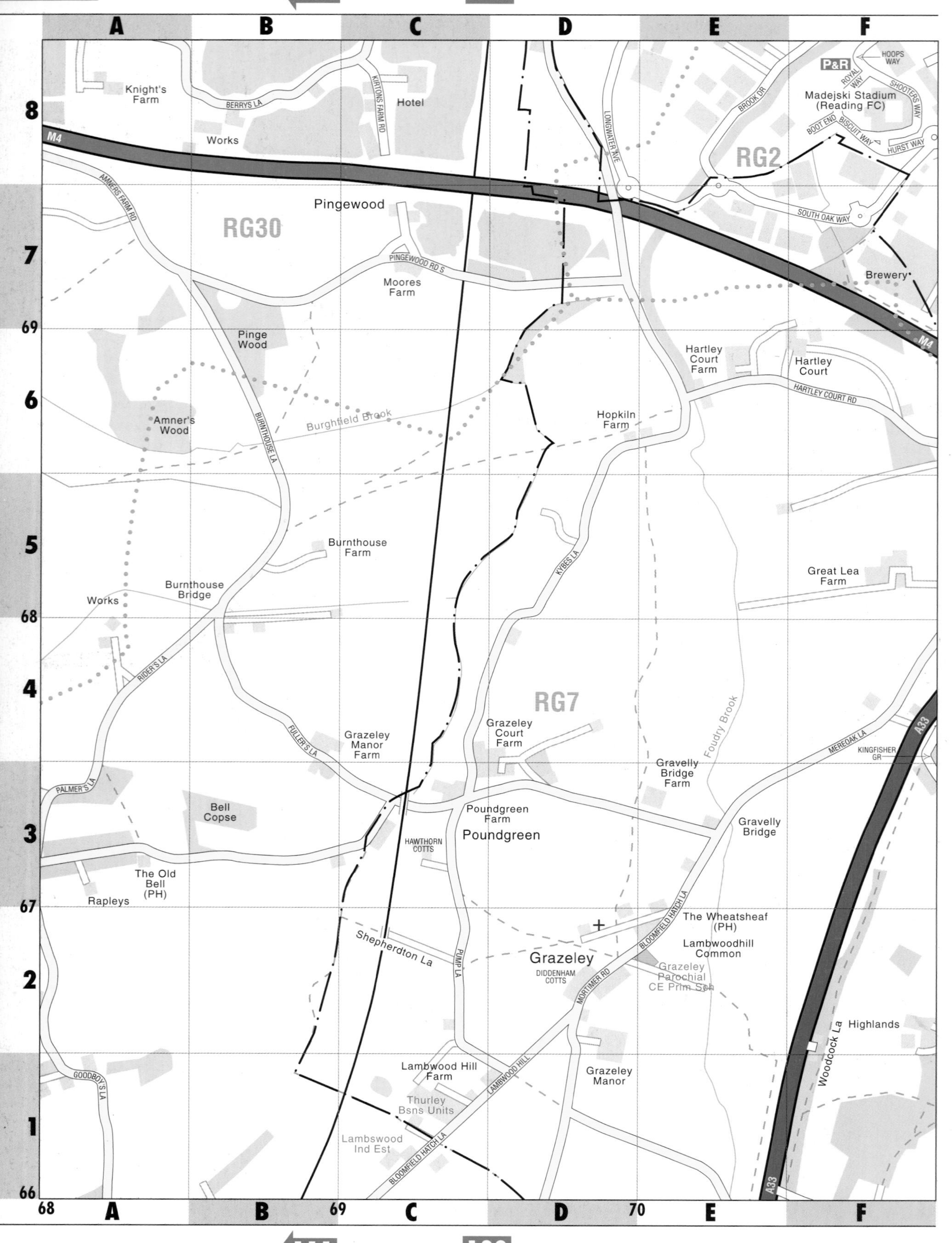
A
B
C
D
E
F
8
7
69
6
5
68
4
3
67
2
1
66
68
69
70
Knight's Farm
BERRYS LA
KIRTONS FARM RD
Hotel
Works
M4
P&R
HOOPS WAY
ROYAL WAY
SHOOTERS WAY
Madejski Stadium (Reading FC)
BROOK DR
LONGWATER AVE
BOOT END
BISCUIT WAY
HURST WAY
RG2
SOUTH OAK WAY
AMNERS FARM RD
Pingewood
RG30
PINGEWOOD RD S
Moores Farm
Brewery
Pinge Wood
Hartley Court Farm
Hartley Court
HARTLEY COURT RD
Amner's Wood
Burghfield Brook
BURNTHOUSE LA
Hopkiln Farm
Burnthouse Farm
KYBES LA
Great Lea Farm
Burnthouse Bridge
Works
RIDER'S LA
RG7
Foudry Brook
A33
FULLER'S LA
Grazeley Manor Farm
Grazeley Court Farm
Gravelly Bridge Farm
MEREOAK LA
KINGFISHER GR
PALMER'S LA
Bell Copse
Poundgreen Farm
Poundgreen
Gravelly Bridge
HAWTHORN COTTS
The Old Bell (PH)
Rapleys
The Wheatsheaf (PH)
BLOOMFIELD HATCH LA
Lambwoodhill Common
Shepherdton La
PUMP LA
Grazeley
DIDDENHAM COTTS
MORTIMER RD
Grazeley Parochial CE Prim Sch
Woodcock La
Highlands
GOODBOY'S LA
Lambwood Hill Farm
LAMBWOOD HILL
Grazeley Manor
Thurley Bsns Units
Lambswood Ind Est
BLOOMFIELD HATCH LA
A33

111
138

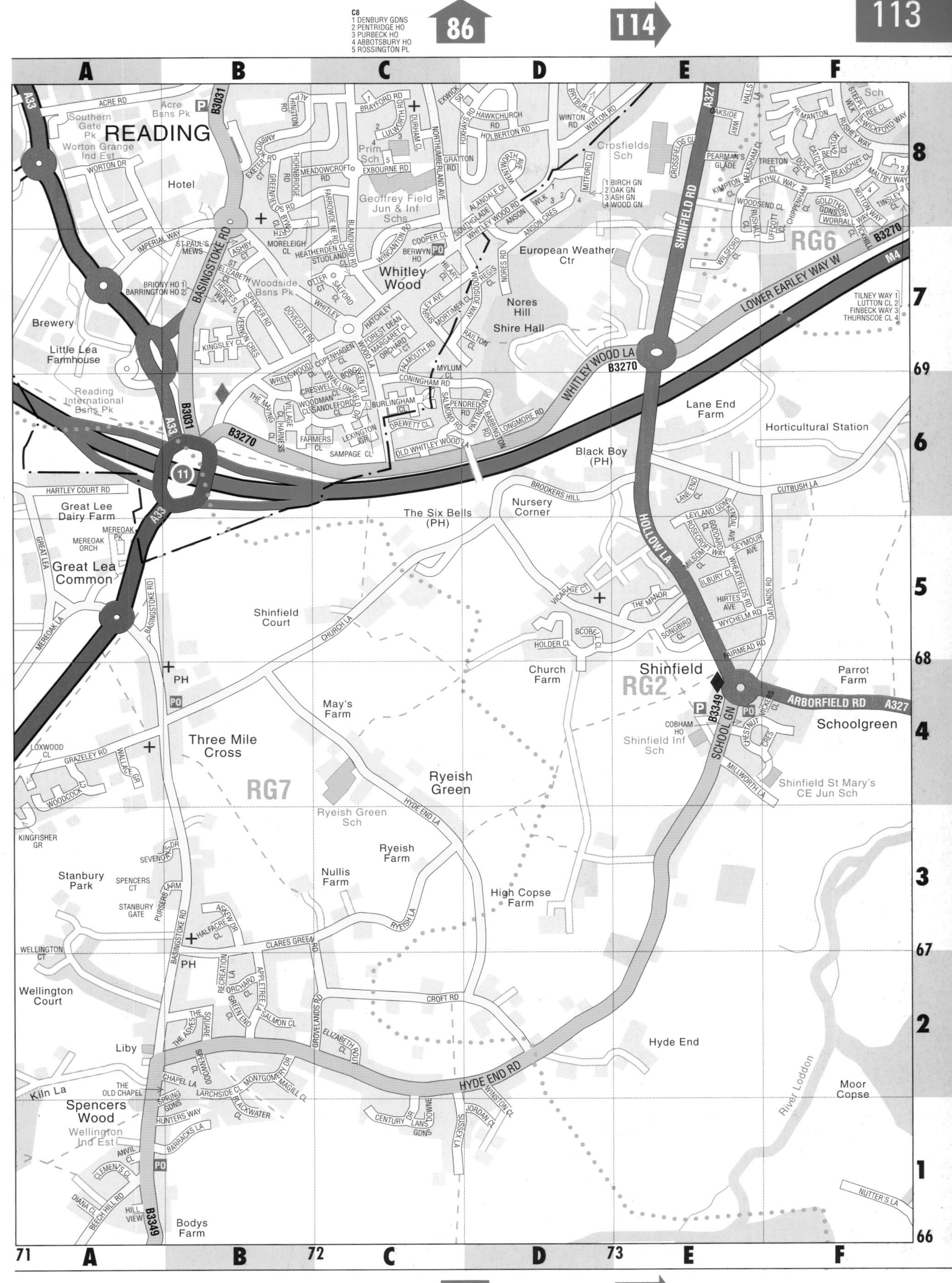

C8
1 DENBURY GDNS
2 PENTRIDGE HO
3 PURBECK HO
4 ABBOTSBURY HO
5 ROSSINGTON PL

86

114

113
87

A **B** **C** **D** **E** **F**

8

CHALFONT WAY
THE SQUARE
TILNEY WAY
RUSHEY
CHAT
CHAT CL
ODELL
ODELL CL
COLMWORTH WAY
BOSHAM
RUSHEY WAY
CUTBUSH CL
PAVENHAM CL
RED HOUSE CL
BRADMORE WAY
BESTON WAY
DANEHILL
GRAFFHAM CL
FAKENHAM CL
MALTBY WAY
PASTURE CL
TURNBRIDGE
WIMBLINGTON
MANEA CL
BOTTISHAM
WARING CL
LEDRAN CL
LITTINGTON
PORTER CL
SONIA CL
CHATTERIS WAY
HARLTON
GREG CL
GREG BASSETT SQ
MERRIFIELD CL
MEREDITH WAY
WYCHAM
LUDSTONE CL
PADDOCK DR
B3270
M4
RG41

LOWER EARLEY WAY

7

B3270
M4
LOWER EARLEY WAY W
1 FELTHORPE CL
2 HEACHAM CL
3 ANSTON CL
4 FINBECK WAY
5 RAINWORTH CL
6 FARNSFIELD CL
1 EBBORN SQ
2 IRVINE WAY
3 STONEA CL
Upperwood House
Upperwood Farm
RG6
St John's Copse
Rushy Mead
CUTBUSH LA
Loader's La
Carter's Hill
JULKES LA
The Holt
Carters Hill Farm
PARKCORNER LA
NEWLANDS COTTS
GIPSY LA
BETTY GROVE LA
B3030

69

6
Shinfield Grange
Oldhouse Farm
River Loddon
Reaearch Centre
The Grove
Barett's La
Copse Barnhill La
MOLE RD

5
Hall Farm
RG2
Carter's Hill La
Newlands
ELLIS'S HILL

68

4
ARBORFIELD RD
A327
Arborfield Bribge
ARBORFIELD GRANGE
CHURCH LA
SINDLESHAM RD
Hazeltons Copse
Sewage Works

3
Rounds Copse
Milkingbarn La
Bridge Farm
Pound Copse
READING RD
Riding Sch
Cross Lanes Farm
WALDEN LANE
Arborfield
The Bull (PH)
Pudding La
B3030
Newland Farm
Cole La
Coombes Inf Sch
Arborfield Newland & Barkham CE Jun Sch
WOOD LA
RG41

67
GREENSWARD LA
B3349
SCHOOL RD
B3349

2
Moor Copse
Nursery
SWALLOWFIELD RD
CHAMBERS GDNS
BRANT'S CL
MELROSE GDNS
PO
ANDREWS CRES
WHITEWELL CL
EMBLEN CRES
HARTS CL
LINK WAY
Arborfield Cross
Langleypond Farm
OAKLANDS CVN PK
LANGLEY COMMON RD
Sch of Electronic Engineering

1
Kenney's Farm
White's Farm
Arborfield Court
Ducks Nest Farm
EVERSLEY RD
FRIXMAN CL
BIGGS LA
Aborfield Garrison

66
NUTTERS LA
Bartlett's Farm
VALON RD
A327
BAIRD RD
HELL RD

74 **A** **B** **75** **C** **D** **76** **E** **F**

88
116
A
B
C
D
E
F
8
7
69
6
5
68
4
3
67
2
1
66
77
78
79
Hatch Farm
Sindlesham
MOLE RD
B3030
KING STREET LA
ST MARY'S RD
NEW RD
Bearwood Prim Sch
Home Farm
WOKINGHAM
The Roundabout
A329
READING RD
Emmbrook Comp Sch
Emmbrook
Walter Arms (PH)
SADLERS END
HOME FARM COTTS
Bearwood Coll
WEST LAWN
Simon's La
Chestnut Ave
Chestnut Park
Superstore
Woose Hill
Smith's Walk
Emm Brook
Bear Wood Lake
BEARWOOD RD
Round Hill
Upper Lake
CH
RG41
Fox Hill
Limmerhill
B3349
HIGHLANDS AVE
Gravelpit Hill
Coombes La
RG2
Ye Olde Leathern Bottel (PH)
Bottel Farm
Folly Court
Ellis's Hill Farm
Barkham Hill
The Coombes
Hayes La
Blagrove Farm
DOLES HILL
BARKHAM RD
Barkham Rectory
Barkham
Mortimers Lodge Farm
Daffield Farm
Hutt's Farm
Coppid Hill
Handpost Farm
SCHOOL RD
Sparks Farm
Edneys Hill Farm
Randall's Farm
Brook Farm
Nashgrove Ride
Barkham Grange
Langley Common
Water Tower
Barkham Square
RG40
Church Farm
Nash Grove
Waverley Sch
The Moors
BARKHAM RIDE
COMMONFIELD LA

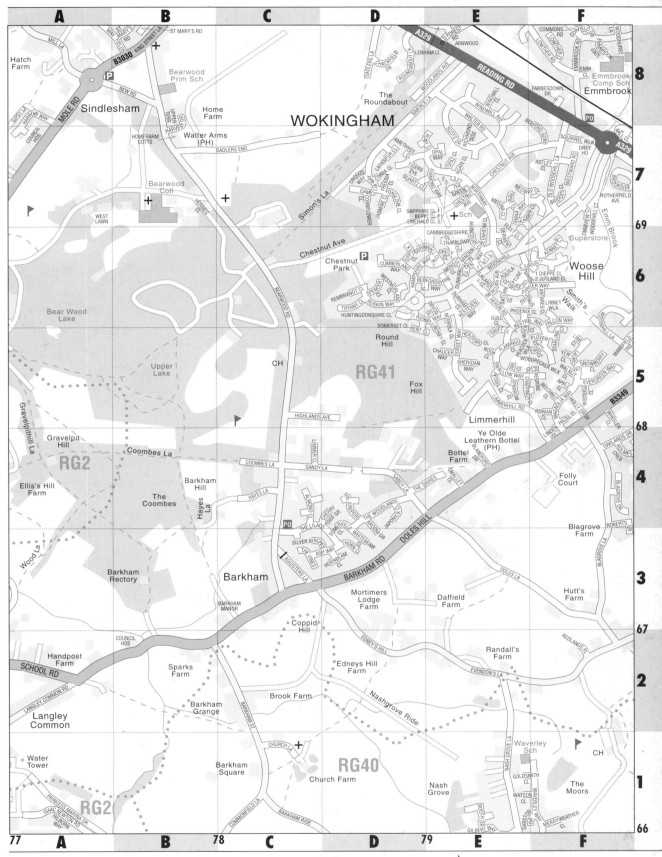

115 89

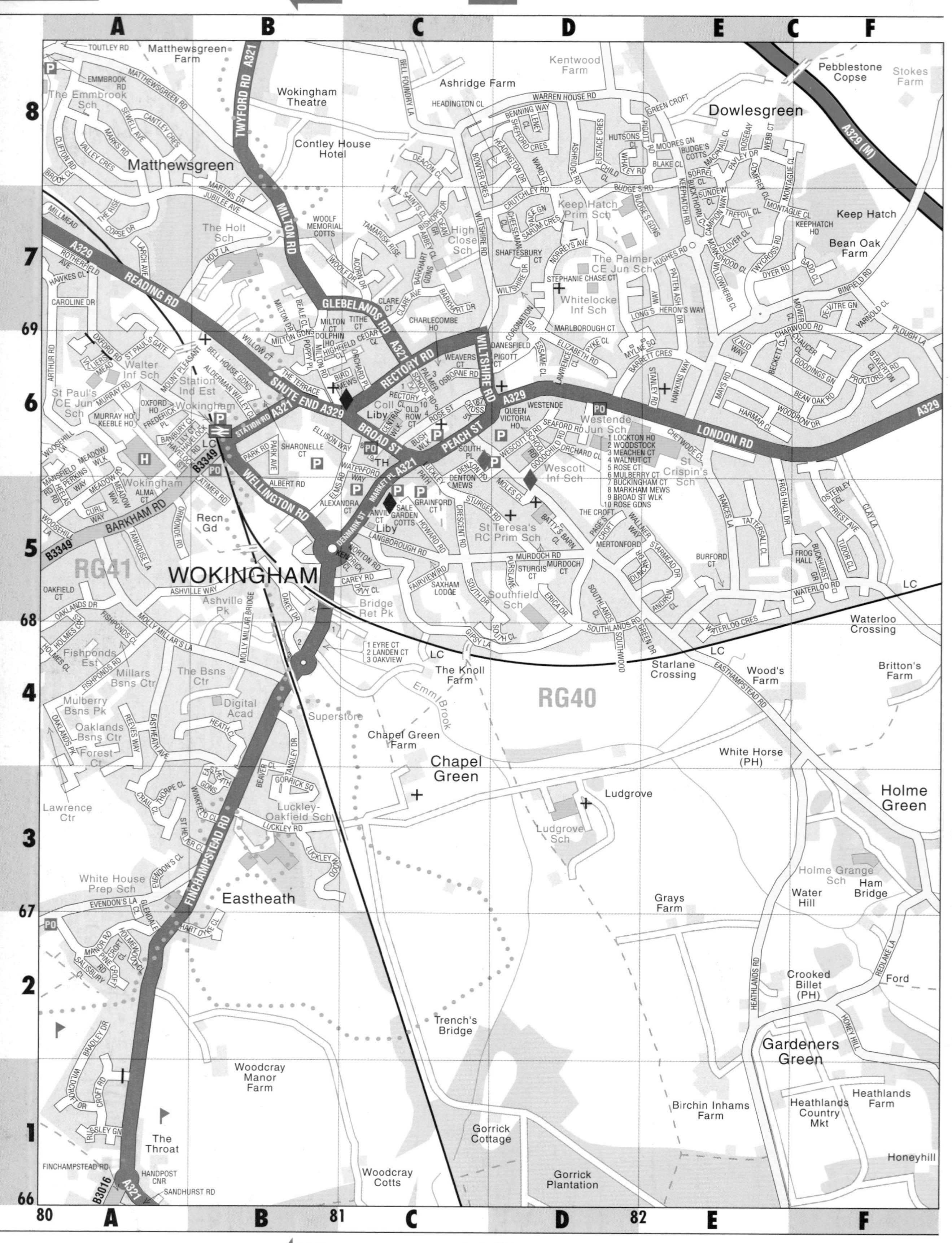
A
B
C
D
E
F
8
7
69
6
5
68
4
3
67
2
1
66
80
81
82
Matthewsgreen Farm
Wokingham Theatre
Ashridge Farm
Kentwood Farm
Pebblestone Copse
Stokes Farm
Dowlesgreen
Contley House Hotel
Matthewsgreen
The Emmbrook Sch
The Holt Sch
High Close Sch
Keep Hatch Prim Sch
Keep Hatch
Bean Oak Farm
The Palmer CE Jun Sch
Whitelocke Inf Sch
Walter Inf Sch
St Paul's CE Jun Sch
Station Ind Est
Wokingham
Westende Jun Sch
St Crispin's Sch
Wescott Inf Sch
St Teresa's RC Prim Sch
Recn Gd
RG41
WOKINGHAM
Ashville Pk
Bridge Ret Pk
Southfield Sch
Waterloo Crossing
The Knoll Farm
Starlane Crossing
Wood's Farm
Britton's Farm
RG40
Fishponds Est
Millars Bsns Ctr
The Bsns Ctr
Digital Acad
Mulberry Bsns Pk
Oaklands Bsns Ctr
Forest Ct
Superstore
Chapel Green Farm
Chapel Green
White Horse (PH)
Holme Green
Ludgrove
Ludgrove Sch
Lawrence Ctr
Luckley-Oakfield Sch
White House Prep Sch
Eastheath
Holme Grange Sch
Water Hill
Ham Bridge
Grays Farm
Crooked Billet (PH)
Ford
Trench's Bridge
Gardeners Green
Woodcray Manor Farm
Birchin Inhams Farm
Heathlands Country Mkt
Heathlands Farm
The Throat
Gorrick Cottage
Gorrick Plantation
Woodcray Cotts
Honeyhill
A329(M)
A329
A321
B3349
B3016
READING RD
LONDON RD
WELLINGTON RD
FINCHAMPSTEAD RD
MILTON RD
TWYFORD RD
WILTSHIRE RD
BARKHAM RD
SHUTE END
BROAD ST
PEACH ST
RECTORY RD
GLEBELANDS RD
EASTHAMPSTEAD RD
1 LOCKTON HO
2 WOODSTOCK
3 MEACHEN CT
4 WALNUT CT
5 ROSE CT
6 MULBERRY CT
7 BUCKINGHAM CT
8 MARKHAM MEWS
9 BROAD ST WLK
10 ROSE GDNS
1 EYRE CT
2 LANDEN CT
3 OAKVIEW

115 142

A B C D E F

8 7 69 6 5 68 4 3 67 2 1 66

Stoke's Farm
Top Copse
Pockets Copse
Binfield
Murrellhill Grange
Popes Manor
Popeswood
RG42
Popeswood Rdbt
Farley Moor
Farley Copse
Priestwood
Meadow Vale Prim Sch
Wokingham Rd
B3408
London Rd
Western Rd
Western Ind Area
The Western Ctr
Enterprise Ct
Downmill Rd
The Bracknell Bsns Ctr
Phoenix Bsns Pk
Hotel
Ski Ctr
Amen Corner
Amen Cnr Bsns Pk
Longshot Ind Est
Longshot La
Coves Farm Wood
Pocket Cl
John Nike Way
Mast
B3408
A329
A329(M)
London Rd
Buttercup Cl
Wainwright Cl
Rose Farm
North View
Moor La
South View
Buckhurst Moors
Berkshire Way
A329
Oldbury
Doncastle Rd
Southern Ind Area
Willoughby Rd
St Annes Dr
Hotel
Peacock Farm
Peacock La
Wykery Copse
RG12
Ellesfield Ave
A3095
Mill La
Big Wood
Peacock Cotts
Northerams (Nature Reserve)
Bilton Ind Est
Lovelace Rd
Mill Pond
West Garden Copse
Big Wood House
Waterloo Rd
BRACKNELL
Wylam
Wroxham
Winscombe
Wheatley
Welbeck
Waverley
Ringmead
Yardley
Wordsworth
Ambassador
Lock's House
Great Hollands Prim Sch
Viking
Abbotsbury
Liby
Appledore
RG40
Easthampstead Park Sch
Great Hollands
Great Hollands Sq
Great Hollands Rd
Con Ctr
Easthampstead Park
Wickham Vale
Vandyke
Cunworth Ct
Halewood
Highfield
Ashbourne
Beedon Dr
Penwood Gdns
Ramsbury Cl
Underwood
Holbeck
Aysgarth
1 Gleneagles Ho
2 Moor Park Ho
3 Muirfield Ho
Turnberry
Carnoustie
Birkdale
Ullswater
Holland Pines
Six Oaks
Easthampstead Rd
Trevelyan
Staplehurst
Tawfield
Ringwood
A3095
Crowthorne Rd
Hanover Gdns
Prescott
Pembroke
West Rd
CH
Cemy
Crem
Wooden Hill Prim Sch
Sylvanus
Spinis
Sutton Court Farm
South Rd
Ringmead
St Margaret Clitherow RC Prim Sch
Old Wokingham Rd
Woodenhill
Southwold
Quintilis
Qualitas
PH
Newlands
Honey Hill
Sarum
Stratfield
A3095
B3430
Nine Mile Ride
Foresters Way

1 Hitherhooks Hill
2 Woodhouse St
3 Campion Ho
4 Bryony Ho
5 Broadlands Ct
6 Hawkswood Ho
7 Hombrook Ho

83 84 85

A B C D E F

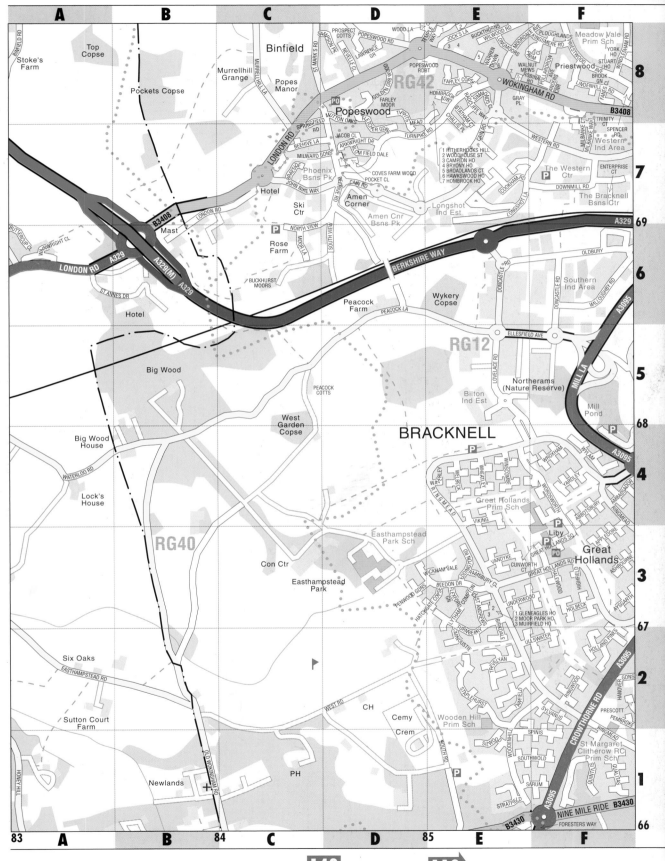

A8
1 PRIESTWOOD SQ
2 SALTIRE GDNS
3 WINDLEBROOK GN
4 APPLETREE PL
5 PORTMAN CL
B8
1 BIRCHETTS CL
2 ASHRIDGE GN
117
91
F5
1 THE WILLOWS
2 THE CEDARS
3 MAPLE CT
4 GREENWOOD
5 THE FIRS
6 LARCHWOOD
7 LAUREL CT
8 CHARLBURY CL
9 HOLTON HEATH
10 BLOXWORTH CL
A
B
C
D
E
F
8
7
69
6
5
68
4
3
67
2
1
66
86
87
88
Priestwood
Playing Field
Sandy Lane Prim Sch
Wick Hill
Big Wood
RG42
Bracknell Coll
Garth Hill Coll
MILLENNIUM WAY
B3408 WOKINGHAM RD
B3018 BINFIELD RD
A3095 WARFIELD RD
Superstore
Arlington Bsns Pk
Arlington Sq
The Arena
The Maxdata Ctr
Bracknell Ent Ctr
Brickfields Ind Pk
The Point (L Ctr)
The Peel Ctr
SKIMPEDHILL LA
A329
Skimpedhill
Liby
Bracknell Coll
Eastern Ind Area
St Joseph's RC Prim Sch
Cemy
Holly Spring Schs
Bullbrook
Clinton's Hill
Lily Hill House
1 GALILEO CT
2 BULLBROOK ROW
3 HIGHCLERE CL
4 LAMBOURNE GR
5 PERRY WAY
LONDON RD
A329
BERKSHIRE WAY
Southern Ind Area
A322
DOWNSHIRE WAY
MILL LA
A3095
Bracknell
CHURCH RD
Ranelagh CE Sch
The Sterling Ctr
Martin's Heron
BRACKNELL
Playing Field
Martin's Heron
B3430
Wildridings
Wildridings Prim Sch
1 WOODPECKERS
2 CROWTHORNE LODGE
3 SPRINGHILL CT
Easthampstead
The Brakenhale Sch
Fox Hill Prim Sch
HOWORTH CT 1
BOVENEY HO 2
BOULTERS HO 3
HEATHERMOUNT 4
HAMBLEDEN CT 5
CLEEVE HO 6
RUSHEY HO 7
CULHAM HO 8
RG12
Harmans Water
Sch Sports Ctr
BAGSHOT RD
Bracknell Sports & L Ctr
1 JACKSON CL
2 LEMINGTON GR
St Michael's CE Prim Sch
Crown Wood Prim Sch
Crown Wood
Forest Park
NEW FOREST RIDE
Swinley Park
Worldsend Hill
CROWTHORNE RD
Hotel
Wilde Theatre
South Hill Park
Birch Hill
Birch Hill Prim Sch
Superstore
1 ATTEBROUCHE CT
2 PAKENHAM RD
3 HORNBY AVE
4 RUSSEL CL
5 BARRY SQ
6 ROBY DR
7 GUERDON PL
Leisure Pool
Tennis Ctr
Three Castles Path
Windsor Ride
The Pines Inf & Jun Schs
Hanworth
B3430
NINE MILE RIDE
Gormoor Farm
The Look Out Discovery Ctr
A322
117
144
F4
1 MULBERRY CT
2 ROWAN
3 LINDEN
4 LYTCHET MINSTER CL
5 STOKEFORD CL
6 FROXFIELD DOWN

92

120

A
B
C
D
E
F
Chavey Down
Warfield Pk
Big Wood
RG42
Pump Rough
North Ascot
Papplewick Sch
PRIORY RD
B3017
LONDON RD
A329
HIGH ST
WINDSOR RD
A332
Ascot Priory
Cemy
Mast
Heathfield Sch
Licensed Victuallers Sch
Hotel
Ascot Race Course
Cvn Pk
The Brackens
Englemere Pond
Heatherwood
CH Hereford House
Englemere Pond Nature Trail
Woodstock
Englemere
Whitmoor Bog
KING'S RIDE
SL5
Sewage Wks
RG12
Three Castles Path
Kings Ride Pk
Green Acres
Passmore's Plantation
Blacksmith's Hill
Icehouse Hill
SWINLEY RD
CROWN COTTS
Swinley Park
Kingsride
Tower Hill
Buttersteep Hill
Blane's Allotment
Bright's Allotment
Buttersteep Allotments
Buttersteep House
BODENS RIDE
BUTTERSTEEP RISE
8
7
69
6
5
68
4
3
67
2
1
66
89
90
91

145
120

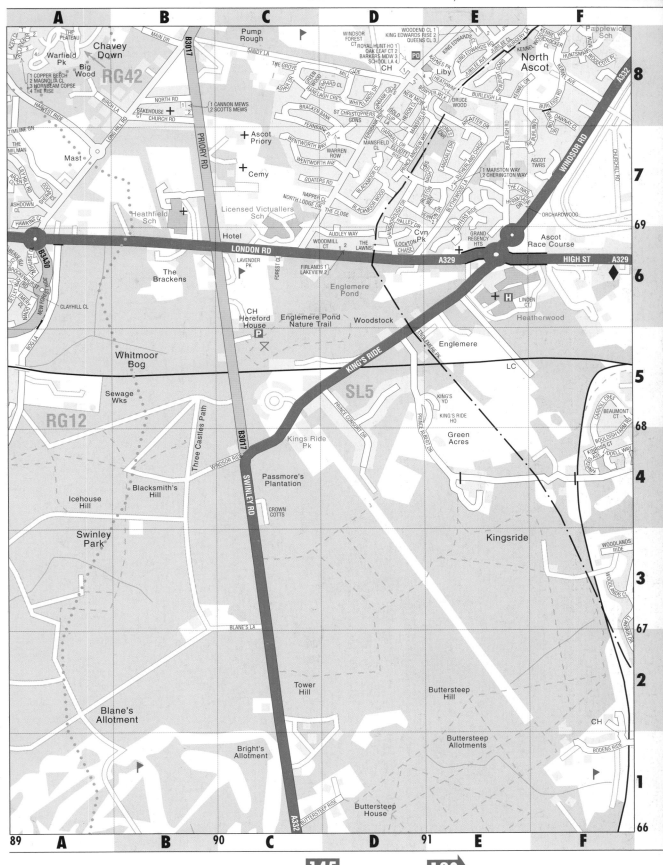

119
93

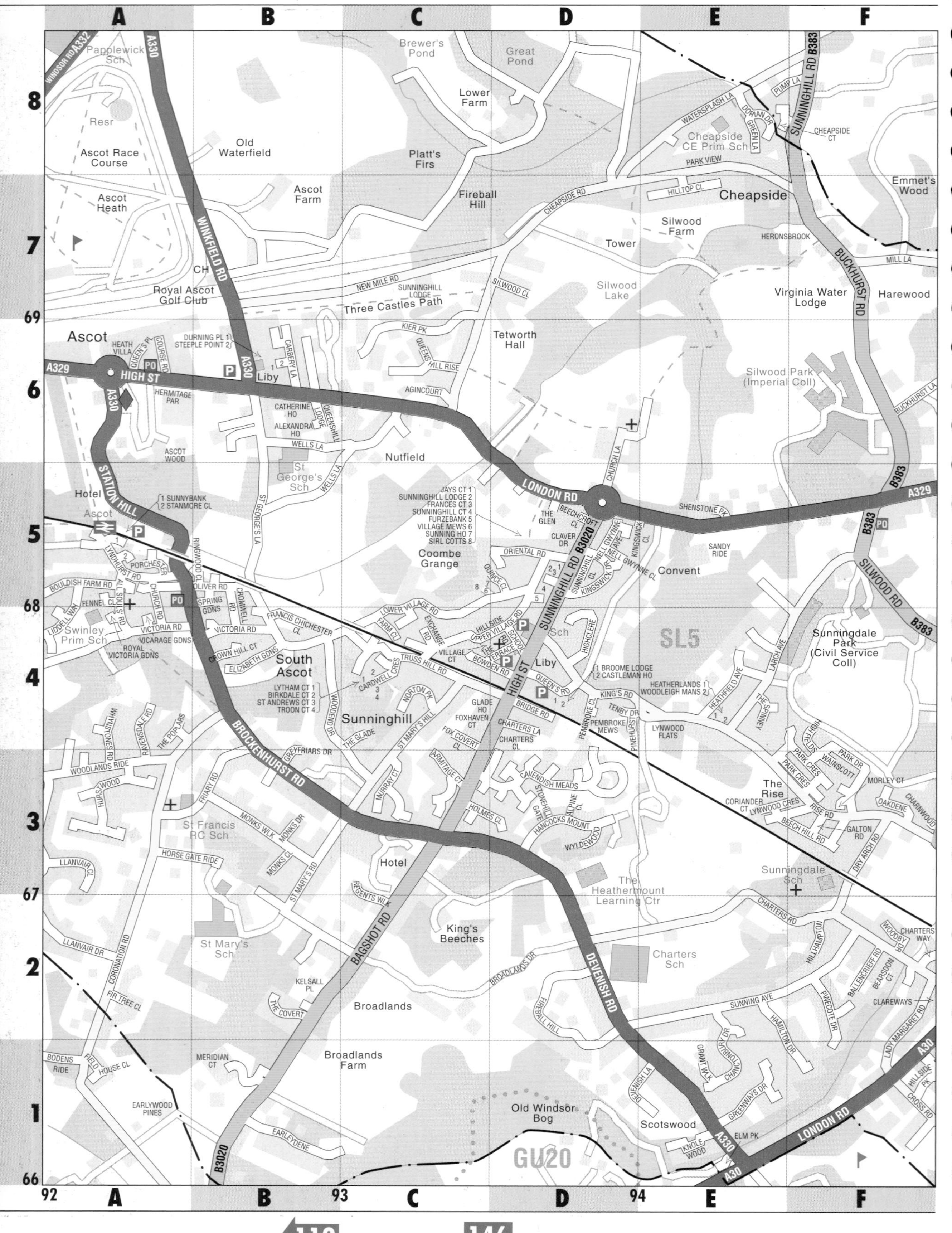
Ascot
Ascot Race Course
Ascot Heath
Royal Ascot Golf Club
Old Waterfield
Ascot Farm
Platt's Firs
Lower Farm
Brewer's Pond
Great Pond
Fireball Hill
Cheapside
Cheapside CE Prim Sch
Silwood Farm
Tower
Silwood Lake
Virginia Water Lodge
Harewood
Emmet's Wood
Three Castles Path
Tetworth Hall
Silwood Park (Imperial Coll)
Nutfield
St George's Sch
Coombe Grange
Convent
SL5
South Ascot
Sunninghill
Swinley Prim Sch
Sunningdale Park (Civil Service Coll)
The Rise
St Francis RC Sch
Hotel
The Heathermount Learning Ctr
Sunningdale Sch
King's Beeches
St Mary's Sch
Charters Sch
Broadlands
Broadlands Farm
Old Windsor Bog
Scotswood
GU20
HIGH ST
LONDON RD
WINKFIELD RD
STATION HILL
BROCKENHURST RD
BAGSHOT RD
DEVENISH RD
SUNNINGHILL RD
BUCKHURST RD
SILWOOD RD
A329
A330
A30
B3020
B383

94
122

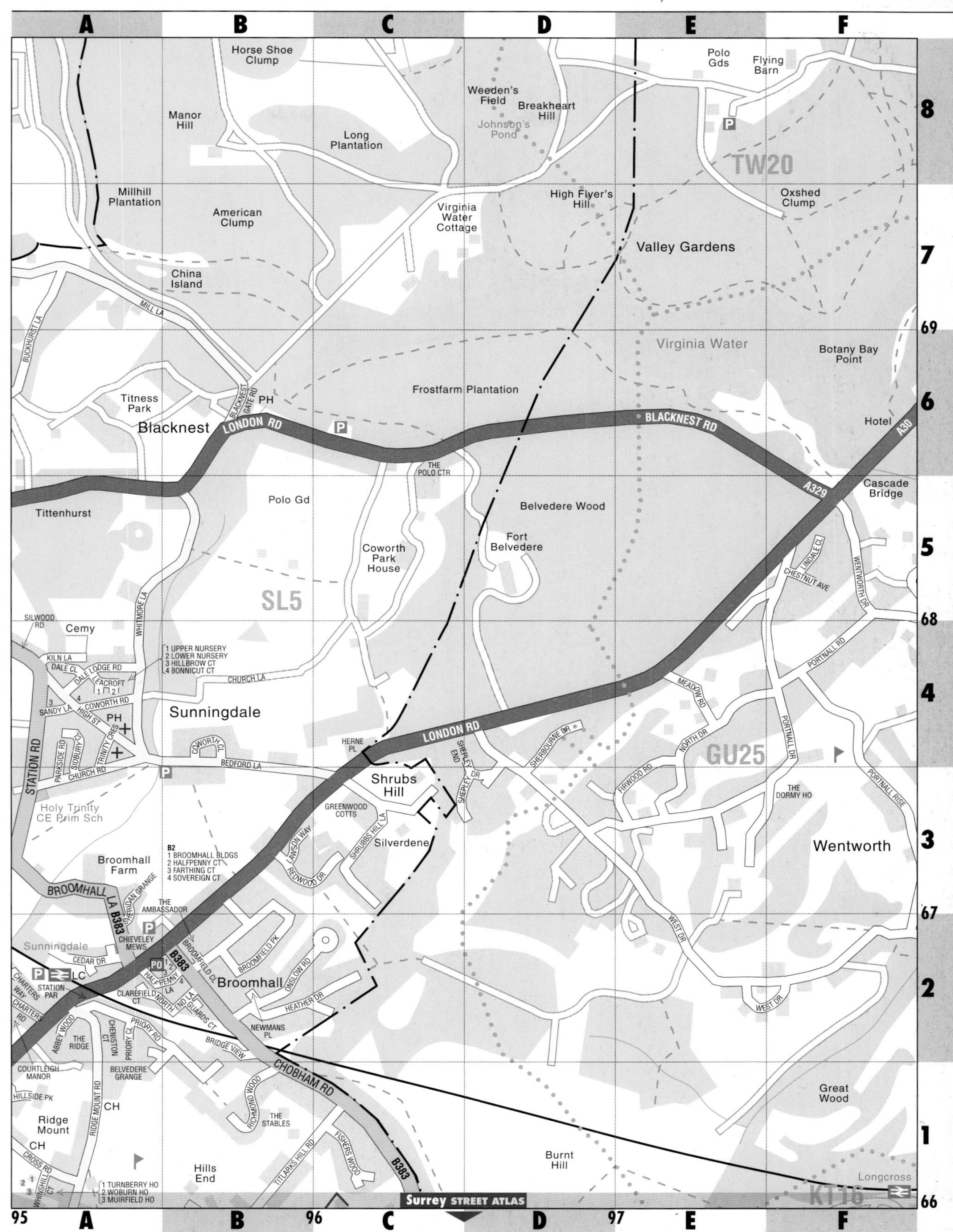
A
B
C
D
E
F
8
7
69
6
5
68
4
3
67
2
1
66
95
96
97
Horse Shoe Clump
Manor Hill
Long Plantation
Weeden's Field
Breakheart Hill
Johnson's Pond
Polo Gds
Flying Barn
TW20
Millhill Plantation
American Clump
Virginia Water Cottage
High Flyer's Hill
Oxshed Clump
Valley Gardens
China Island
MILL LA
BUCKHURST LA
Virginia Water
Botany Bay Point
Titness Park
BLACKNEST GATE RD
PH
Frostfarm Plantation
Blacknest
LONDON RD
BLACKNEST RD
Hotel
A30
THE POLO CTR
Tittenhurst
Polo Gd
A329
Cascade Bridge
Belvedere Wood
Fort Belvedere
Coworth Park House
SL5
LINDALE CL
WENTWORTH DR
CHESTNUT AVE
SILWOOD RD
Cemy
KILN LA
DALE CL
DALE LODGE RD
LEACROFT
1 UPPER NURSERY
2 LOWER NURSERY
3 HILLBROW CT
4 BONNICUT CT
WHITMORE LA
CHURCH LA
PORTNALL RD
MEADOW RD
COWORTH RD
SANDY LA
HIGH ST
Sunningdale
TRINITY CRES
PARKSIDE RD
SIDBURY CL
COWORTH CL
HERNE PL
SHERLEY END
SHERBOURNE DR
NORTH DR
PORTNALL DR
GU25
CHURCH RD
BEDFORD LA
STATION RD
Shrubs Hill
SHERLEY DR
FIRWOOD RD
THE DORMY HO
PORTNALL RISE
Holy Trinity CE Prim Sch
GREENWOOD COTTS
SHRUBBS HILL LA
Silverdene
LAWSON WAY
Wentworth
B2
1 BROOMHALL BLDGS
2 HALFPENNY CT
3 FARTHING CT
4 SOVEREIGN CT
Broomhall Farm
SHERIDAN GRANGE
REDWOOD DR
THE AMBASSADOR
BROOMHALL LA B383
CHIEVELEY MEWS
BROOMFIELD CL
BROOMFIELD PK
WEST DR
Sunningdale
CEDAR DR
PO
B383
ONSLOW RD
Broomhall
STATION PAR
LC
CHARTERS WAY
CHARTERS RD
CLAREFIELD CT
HALFPENNY LA
NORTH END LA
GUARDS CT
HEATHER DR
ABBEY WOOD
THE RIDGE
CHENISTON CT
PRIORY CL
PRIORY RD
NEWMANS PL
BRIDGE VIEW
CHOBHAM RD
COURTLEIGH MANOR
BELVEDERE GRANGE
HILLSIDE PK
RIDGE MOUNT RD
CH
Ridge Mount
RICHMOND WOOD
THE STABLES
Great Wood
CROSS RD
TITLARKS HILL RD
FISHERS WOOD
Burnt Hill
Hills End
WHINSHILL CT
1 TURNBERRY HO
2 WOBURN HO
3 MUIRFIELD HO
Longcross
KT16
Surrey STREET ATLAS

122

121
95

A
B
C
D
E
F
TW20
Egham Wick Plantations
Wick Pond
Totem Pole
Woodlee
LONDON RD
A30
American Com Sch
GLENWOOD
WOODLEE CL
CALLOW HILL
Callow Hill
Great Wood
Whitehall Farm
Stroude
Virginia Water Plantations
The Dell
Highmoor Farm
GLENRIDGE FARM CVN SITE
VIRGINIA BEECHES
HOLLOW LA
Stroude Farm
The Clockcase
Merlewood
Allot Gdns
Christ Church CE Inf Sch
CHRISTCHURCH COTTS
Virginia Water
B389
CHRISTCHURCH RD
SPRING WOODS
WAVERLEY DR
QUENTIN WAY
STUART WAY
WOODSIDE WAY
WATERFALL CL
PINEWOOD RD
General's Copse
STAYNE END
LAKE CL
LAKE RD
TROTSWORTH CT
TROTSWORTH AVE
PIPER'S END
HEATH CL
HEATH RISE
GORSE HILL RD
MORELLA CL
STATION APP
1 THE GRANGE
2 GILLESPIE HO
St Ann's Heath
Home Farm
PH
CHAPEL SQ
PINEL CL
CROSSLAND HO
CONNOLLY CT
UPPER WLK
LIMETREE WLK
ASPEN CT
SANDY LA
CYPRESS CT
LAMBLY HILL
THE LANE
EDGELL CL
STROUDE RD
WHITEHALL FARM LA
WHITEHALL LA
LUDDINGTON AVE
HURST LA
ABBOTS DR
BROCK WAY
VIRGINIA DR
FRIARS RD
MONKS RD
ABBEY RD
VIRGINIA CT
STATION PAR
Liby
BADGERS HILL
VIRGINIA AVE
NUNS WLK
OAKWOOD RD
KEEPERS WLK
THE CLOSE
IMPERIAL HO
Virginia Water
TRUMPS GREEN CL
IRVINE PL
SANDHILLS CT
WHITEHILL PL
THE ORCHARD
PALMERSTONE CT
RIDGE WAY
St Ann's Heath Jun Sch
SANDHILLS LA
THE DRIVE
Broom Hill
Wentworth Golf Club
CH
GU25
The Bourne
WENTWORTH DR
KEEPERS TERR
WELLINGTON AVE
HARPESFORD AVE
SUNDOON CRES
Waterloo Bridge
TRUMPS MILL LA
M3
BEECHMONT AVE
BOURNE RD
CABRERA AVE
Trumps Green Inf Sch
TRUMPS GREEN AVE
PO
CABRERA CL
HILLSIDE
HEATHERSIDE DR
EAST DR
WOODSHORE CL
PORTNALL RISE
Harpesford
CROWN RD
CROWN LA
HOME CL
FURNIVAL CL
1 FAIRVIEW COTTS
2 THE PARADE
THE PADDOCKS CVN SITE
BRIDGE LA
LYNE CL
HARROW BOTTOM RD
The Stag & Hounds (PH)
TITHE CL
TITHE
MOWS
TRUMPSGREEN RD
THE MOUNT
THE MOUNT CL
OAK TREE CL
LYNE RD
Trumps Green
BOURNESIDE
WEST DR
KNOWLE GROVE CL
KNOWLE GR
Knowle Hill
KNOWLE HILL
SOUTH DR
Beech Wood
Westwood
Knowle Hill
CORRIE GDNS
Knowle Grove
Trumps Farm
LYNE PLACE MANOR
LYNE CT
BEECHWOOD RD
Refuse Tip
Longcross Bridge
KITSMEAD LA
CHOBHAM LA
KT16
Hersham Copse
Works
Works
M3 Camberley
Surrey STREET ATLAS
8
7
69
6
5
68
4
3
67
2
1
66
98
99
00

121

96
124

A B C D E F

Milton Park
Great Fosters (Hotel)
STROUDE RD
BLACK LAKE CL
Nursery
HURST LA
Padd Farm
Longside Lake
HURST LA
Thorpe Green
GREEN RD
B389
SANDHILLS LA
GU 25
Redlands Farm
LYNE LA
Lyne Farm
FARM CL
LYNE CROSSING RD
Lyne Hill Nursery
The Brooks
The Rough
Merrywood Farm
Pantiles Farm
Royal Marine (PH)
Lyne
LYNE LA
ALMNERS RD
FANGROVE CVN PK
Fan Grove
Sewage Wks
M25
THORPE BY-PASS
B388
THORPE LEA RD
BOSCOMBE CL
WARWICK AVE
WARWICK VILLAS
LONGSIDE CL
CRABTREE CNR
Thorpe Ind Pk
BETA WAY
ALPHA WAY
DELTA WAY
OMEGA WAY
CRABTREE RD
EVERSLEY WAY
Thorpe Ind Est
Egham Bsns Village
Crabtree Office Village
TEN ACRE LA
Sky Bsns Pk
Cemy
TW20
MUCKHATCH LA
WESTERN AVE
VILLAGE RD
GILES TRAVERS CL
Thorpe CE Inf Sch
MIDWAY AVE
THE BENCE
ROSEMARY LA
PH
COLDHARBOUR CL
COLDHARBOUR LA
ANNERS CL
YEWTREES
THE GOWER
FLEETWAY
CHURCH APP
Thorpe
TASIS-The American Sch in England
COTTAGE FARM WAY
GREEN RD
The Moat
MILL LA
BOURNE MDW
MILL HOUSE LA
Green La
GREEN LA
CRAIGWELL CL
MOORFIELDS CL
A320
WEIR PL
AYMER CL
AYMER DR
PEKET CL
CLYVE WAY
ALTON CT
CHERTSEY LA
FISHING TEMPLE PARK HOMES
TEMPLE GDNS
TW18
RIVERSIDE CL
RIVERSIDE DR
River Thames
PENTON AVE
AVONDALE AVE
RIVER RD
THORPESIDE CL
BLACKETT CL
HOLLAND GDNS
PEDWOOD
NORLANDS LA
Sycamore Farm
Penton Hook Marina
STAINES RD
Works
Fleet Lake
Manor Lake
Thorpe Park
Miniature Rly
St Ann's Lake
Abbey Lake
The Bourne
2
THORPE RD
M3
St Ann's Hill
12
Ruxbury Farm
ST ANN'S HILL RD
KT16
Monk's Grove
Hamperstone Bridge (PH)
STAINES RD
STAINES LANE CL
DOWPER CL
ST ANN'S CL
B375 ST ANN'S RD B375
B388
A320
ST ANN'S RD
NORTH GR
SOUTH GR
MASONIC HALL RD
LONGBOURNE WAY
TWYNERSH AVE
GROVE RD
ALWYNS LA
HIGH MEADOW PL
GORDEROY PL
ERKENWALD CL
GOGMORE FARM CL
PH
ELM FARM CVN PK
RUXBURY RD
Hillside Farm
Pyrcroft Grange Prim Sch
Chilseygreen Farm
Freemantles Sch
CHILSEY GREEN RD
BROOKSIDE
PYRCROFT RD
FRITHWALD RD
1 LASSWADE CT
2 PYRCROFT CT
3 BELL CNR
ALMNERS RD
Almners Priory
Little Almners
WATERY LA
Caravan Site
DIANTHUS CL
RUTHERWYK RD
OLDBURY RD
VINCENT RD
VINCENT CL
LASSWADE RD
CEROTUS PL
BARKER RD
STYVENTON PL
COWLEY AVE
COWLEY LA
CURFEW BELL RD
ABBOTS WAY
PYRCROFT RD
A317
B375
RUSHMON CT
A320
BELL BRIDGE RD
CHARLES ST 4
FOX LA S 5
FLORAL HO 6
EASTWORTH RD 7
Chertsey
FOX LA N
GUILDFORD ST
STATION RD
LC
Sir William Perkin's Sch
Barrsbrook Farm
PANNELLS CL
A320 GUILDFORD RD
PRETORIA RD
KNOLL PARK RD
CROWN RISE
HANWORTH LA
CHERTSEY BVD
THE FORUM
Hanworth Trad Est
HANWORTH LA
RIVERSDELL CL
SANDGATES
HARDWICK LA
Great Cockcrow Rly
Cockcrow Hill
M25
A320 Woking M25 Leatherhead

8 7 69 6 5 68 4 3 67 2 1 66

01 A B 02 C D 03 E F

124

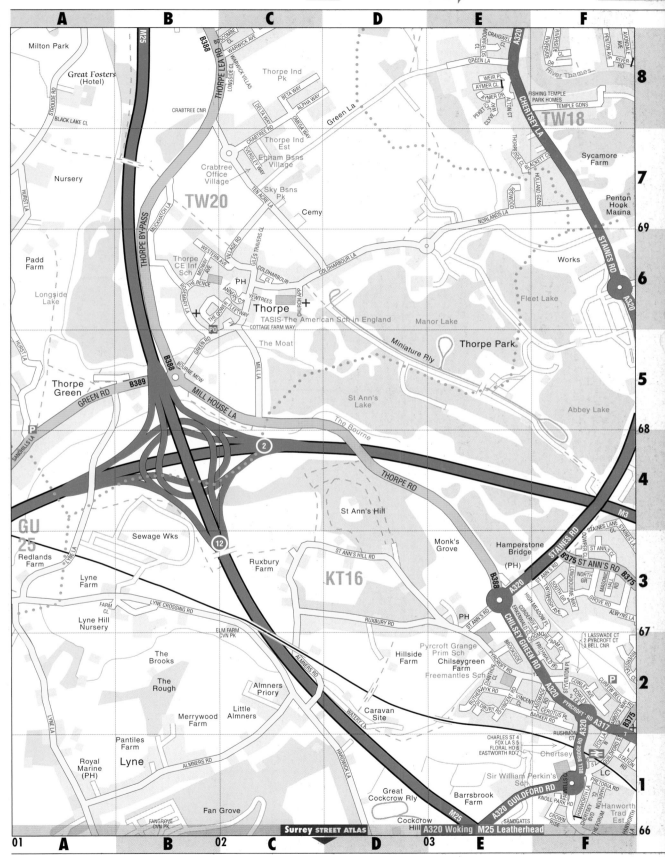

123
97

Laleham
CHERTSEY
Penton Hook
Penton Park
Laleham Burway
Abbey Mead
Abbey Chase
Abbey Chase Farm
Laleham Park
Greenfield Nurseries
Gravel Pit
Manor Farm
Laleham CE Prim Sch
Recn Gd
Queen Mary Resr
Shepperton Studios
Laleham Nurseries
Riverscroft
Abbeyfields
Caravan Site
Chertsey Bridge
Dumsey Eyot
Mead Farm
Dockett Eddy
Chertsey Meads
Marina
Stepgates Com Prim Sch
St Anne's RC Prim Sch
Salesian Sch
Hanworth Trad Est
Fordwater Trad Est
River Thames
Thames Path
STAINES RD
SHEPPERTON RD
LALEHAM RD
CHERTSEY BRIDGE RD
CHERTSEY RD
BRIDGE RD
LONDON ST
WINDSOR ST
EASTWORTH RD
WEIR RD
FORDWATER RD
ASHFORD RD
THE BROADWAY
LITTLETON LA
TW15
TW18
TW17
KT16
KT15
KT13
M3
A317 Weybridge
Surrey STREET ATLAS

123

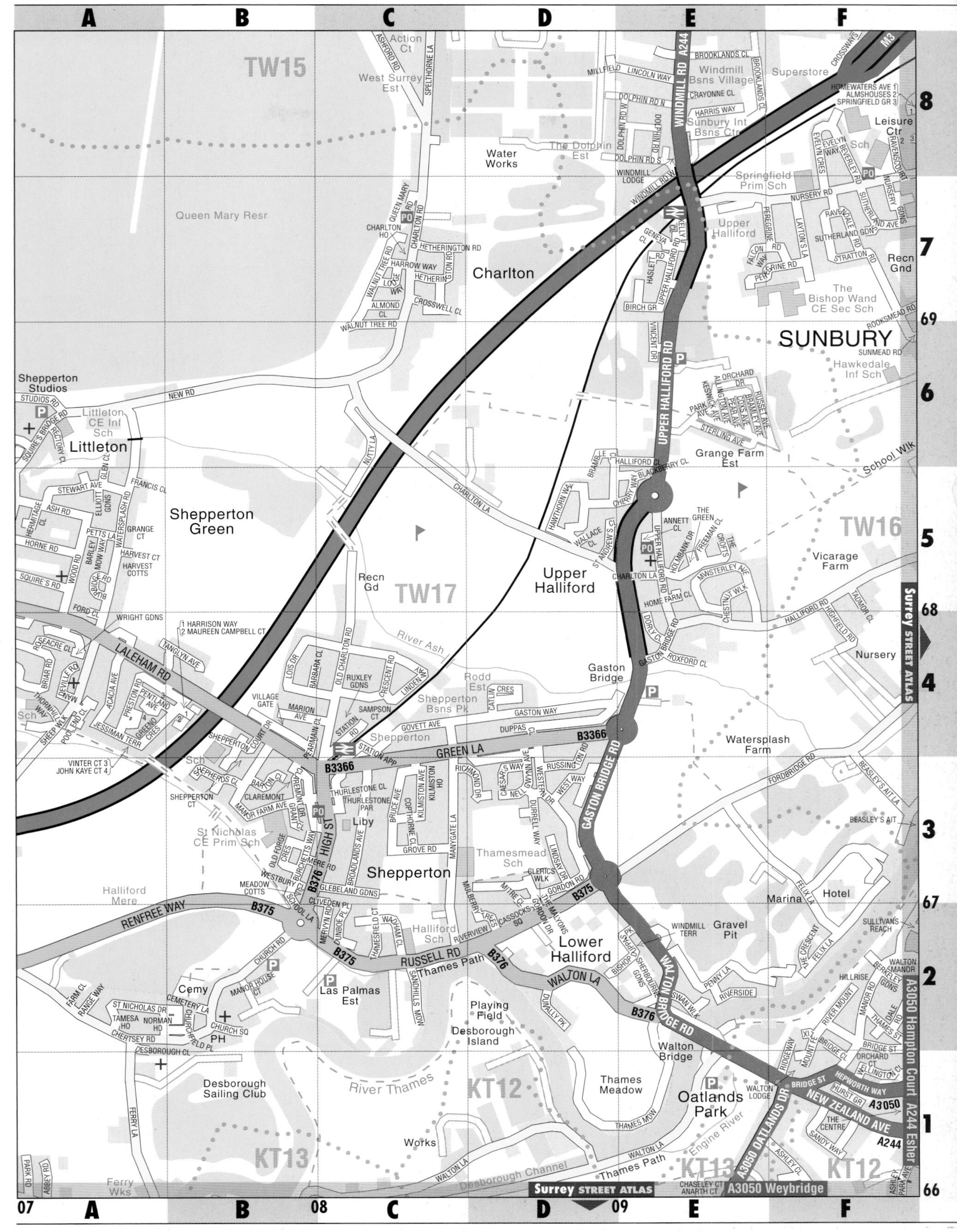

TW15

A B C D E F

Action Ct
West Surrey Est
SPELTHORNE LA
ASHFORD RD
MILLFIELD   LINCOLN WAY
DOLPHIN RD N
CRAYONNE CL
HARRIS WAY
DOLPHIN RD S
Windmill Bsns Village
Brooklands Cl
Brooklands Cl
Crosswater
Superstore
M3
Homewaters Ave 1
Almshouses 2
Springfield Gr 3
Sunbury Int Bsns Ctr
Leisure Ctr
Evelyn Way
WINDMILL RD A244
The Dolphin Est
Water Works
Windmill Lodge
Upper Halliford
Springfield Prim Sch
EVELYN WAY
Sch
PO
Queen Mary Resr
CHARLTON HO
CHARLTON HO RD
PO
HETHERINGTON RD
HARROW WAY
HETHERIN
Charlton
NURSERY RD
FALCON RD
PEREGRINE RD
RAVENDALE RD
SUTHERLAND GDNS
STRATTON
WINDMILL ROW
KELLY
HASLETT
GENEVA CL
BIRCH GR
VINCENT RD
Upper Halliford
Recn Gnd
WALNUT TREE RD
WALNUT TREE RD
LODGE
WY
ALMOND CL
CROSSWELL CL
CROSSWELL CL
The Bishop Wand CE Sec Sch
ROOKSMEAD RD
69
Shepperton Studios
STUDIOS RD
SQUIRE'S BRIDGE RD
P
NEW RD
NITTY LA
CHARLTON LA
Littleton CE Inf Sch
Littleton
UPPER HALLIFORD RD
SUNBURY
ORCHARD DR
RUSSELL AVE
BRADLEY AVE
KESWICK AVE
PARK AVE
ALLINGTON AVE
STERLING AVE
Grange Farm Est
Hawkedale Inf Sch
SUNMEAD CL
School Wlk
6
STEWART AVE
FRANCIS CL
ASH RD
GLEN CL
GRANGE CT
HERMITAGE CL
PETTS LA
BARLEY MOW WAY
WATERSPLASH RD
HARVEST CT
HARVEST COTTS
HORNE RD
WOOD RD
SQUIRE'S RD
BRIDGE RD
FORD CL
WRIGHT GDNS
Shepperton Green
BRAMBLE
HALLIFORD CL
BLACKBERRY CL
UPPER HALLIFORD RD
THE GREEN
THE CHILTS
CHILTS CL
MINSTERLEY AVE
FREEMAN RD
HOME FARM LA
ANNETT CL
HOLMBANK DR
CHESTNUT WLK
HALLIFORD RD
HIGHFIELD RD
NADMOR CL
Vicarage Farm
TW16
68
1 HARRISON WAY
2 MAUREEN CAMPBELL CT
OLD CHARLTON RD
LUIS DR
BARBARA CL
RUXLEY GDNS
CRESCENT RD
LINDEN AVE
River Ash
Recn Gd
TW17
Upper Halliford
CHARLTON LA
ST ANDREW'S CL
DORA CL
BRIDGE RD
ROXFORD CL
PO
Gaston Bridge
Nursery
Surrey STREET ATLAS
5
LALEHAM RD
TANGLYN AVE
ACACIA AVE
NEVILLE RD
MANOR
BRIAR RD
PRESTON RD
PENTLAND AVE
GRENO CRES
VILLAGE GATE
MARION AVE
SAMPSON CT
GOVETT AVE
CATLIN CRES
CUDWELL CRES
Shepperton Bsns Pk
Rodd Est
GREEN LA
GASTON WAY
DUPPAS
CAESAR'S WAY
RUSSING
WEST AVE
WEST AVE
GASTON BRIDGE RD
B3366
Watersplash Farm
FORDBRIDGE RD
BEASLEY'S AIT LA
Beasley's Ait
4
SEACRE CL
SHEEP WK
POOL END CL
JESSIMAN TERR
VINTER CT 3
JOHN KAYE CT 4
Sch
Shepperton Ct
SHEPHERDS CL
STATION
BARTON
CLAREMONT
MANOR FARM AVE
STATION APP
KILMISTON HO
KILMISTON AVE
DURRELL WAY
NEV
CASSOCKS SQ
LINDSAY RD
GORDON RD
B375
WINDMILL TERR
Gravel Pit
Marina
Hotel
AVE CRESCENT
SULLIVANS REACH
A3050 Hampton Court
67
RENFREE WAY
B375
St Nicholas CE Prim Sch
OLD FORGE
RUSSETTS WAY
HIGH ST
PO
THURLSTONE CL
THURLSTONE PAR
Liby
BRUCE AVE
THORNE RD
GROVE RD
MANYGATE LA
Shepperton
Thamesmead Sch
CLERICS WLK
THE MAYONS
Lower Halliford
WINDMILL TERR
FELIX LA
FELIX LA
KYE CRESCENT
PENNY LA
HILLRISE
RIVER MOUNT
WALTON MANOR
BERRYLANDS GDNS
BRIDGE ST
ORCHARD
ELLINGTON CL
2
FARM CL
RANGE WAY
St NICHOLAS DR
TAMESA HO
NORMAN HO
CHURCHFIELD PL
CHURCH RD
PH
CHURCH SQ
MANOR HOUSE CT
P
Cemy
CEMETERY LA
Las Palmas Est
P
MEADOW COTTS
WESTBURY RD
CLIVEDEN PL
THAMESFIELD CT
MELVYN RD
DUNBOE PL
MERYLN RD
B376
RUSSELL RD
Thames Path
B376
WALTON LA
B376
SWAN WLK
BISHOP
SHERBOURNE GDNS
Windmill Terr
Walton Bridge
WALTON BRIDGE RD
RIVERSIDE
DALE RD
BRIDGE ST
HEPWORTH WAY
NEW ZEALAND AVE
A3050
A244 Esher
THE CENTRE
A244
1
PARK RD
OLD
ABBEY RD
FERRY LA
FERRY RD
DESBOROUGH CL
CHERTSEY RD
Desborough Sailing Club
River Thames
KT12
Playing Field
Desborough Island
Thames Meadow
Works
WALTON LA
WALTON LA
Thames Path
Oatlands Park
P
OATLANDS DR
A3050
Walton Lodge
Engine River
A3050
Thames Path
CHASELEY CT
ANARTH CT
A3050 Weybridge
KT13
KT13
KT12
SANDY WAY
ASHLEY CL
MOUNT FELIX
KT12
66
07 A B 08 C D 09 E F

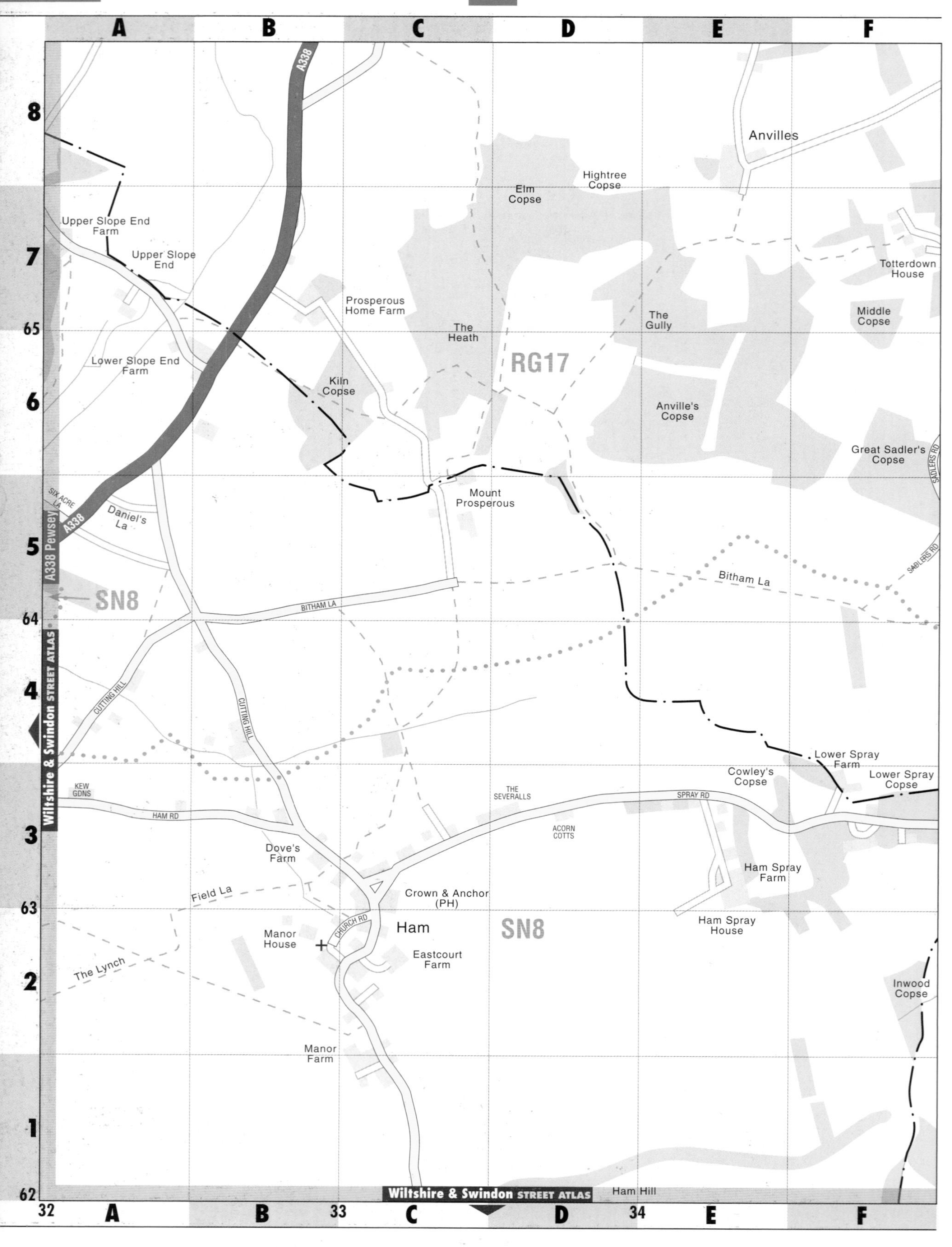

100

Anvilles

Hightree
Copse

Elm
Copse

Upper Slope End
Farm

Upper Slope
End

Prosperous
Home Farm

The Gully

Totterdown
House

Middle
Copse

65

The
Heath

RG17

Lower Slope End
Farm

Kiln
Copse

Anville's
Copse

Great Sadler's
Copse

6

SIX ACRE LA

A338 Pewsey

Daniel's
La

Mount
Prosperous

5

SN8

Bitham La

SADLERS RD

SADLERS RD

64

BITHAM LA

Wiltshire & Swindon STREET ATLAS

CUTTING HILL

CUTTING HILL

Lower Spray
Farm

Cowley's
Copse

Lower Spray
Copse

4

KEW
GDNS

THE
SEVERALLS

SPRAY RD

HAM RD

ACORN
COTTS

Ham Spray
Farm

3

Dove's
Farm

Field La

CHURCH RD

Crown & Anchor
(PH)

Ham

SN8

Ham Spray
House

63

Manor
House

Eastcourt
Farm

The Lynch

Inwood
Copse

2

Manor
Farm

1

62

Ham Hill

32   A   B   33   C   D   34   E   F

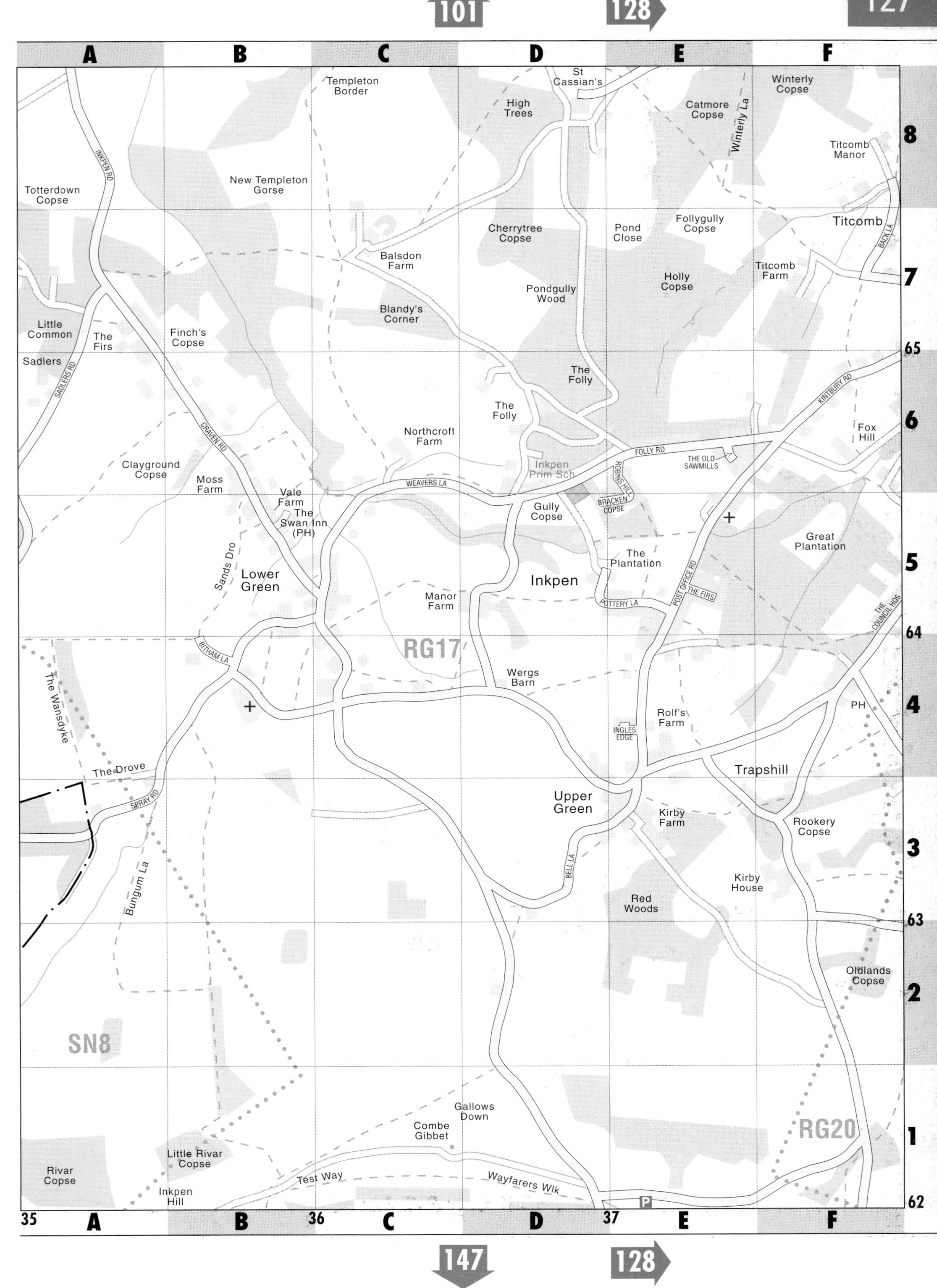
101
128
A
B
C
D
E
F
Templeton Border
St Cassian's
High Trees
Catmore Copse
Winterly La
Winterly Copse
Titcomb Manor
INKPEN RD
New Templeton Gorse
Totterdown Copse
Cherrytree Copse
Pond Close
Follygully Copse
Titcomb
BACK LA
Balsdon Farm
Titcomb Farm
Holly Copse
Pondgully Wood
Blandy's Corner
Little Common
The Firs
Finch's Copse
Sadlers
SADLERS RD
The Folly
The Folly
KINTBURY RD
Fox Hill
Northcroft Farm
CRAVEN RD
FOLLY RD
THE OLD SAWMILLS
Clayground Copse
Moss Farm
Inkpen Prim Sch
ROBINS HILL
WEAVERS LA
Vale Farm
The Swan Inn (PH)
Gully Copse
BRACKEN COPSE
Great Plantation
Sands Dro
The Plantation
Lower Green
Inkpen
POST OFFICE RD
THE FIRS
Manor Farm
POTTERY LA
THE COUNCIL HOS
RG17
BITHAM LA
Wergs Barn
The Wansdyke
Rolf's Farm
PH
INGLES EDGE
The Drove
Trapshill
SPRAY RD
Upper Green
Kirby Farm
Rookery Copse
BELL LA
Bungum La
Kirby House
Red Woods
Oldlands Copse
SN8
Gallows Down
RG20
Combe Gibbet
Little Rivar Copse
Rivar Copse
Test Way
Wayfarers Wlk
Inkpen Hill
P
8
7
65
6
5
64
4
3
63
2
1
62
35
36
37
147
128

127
102

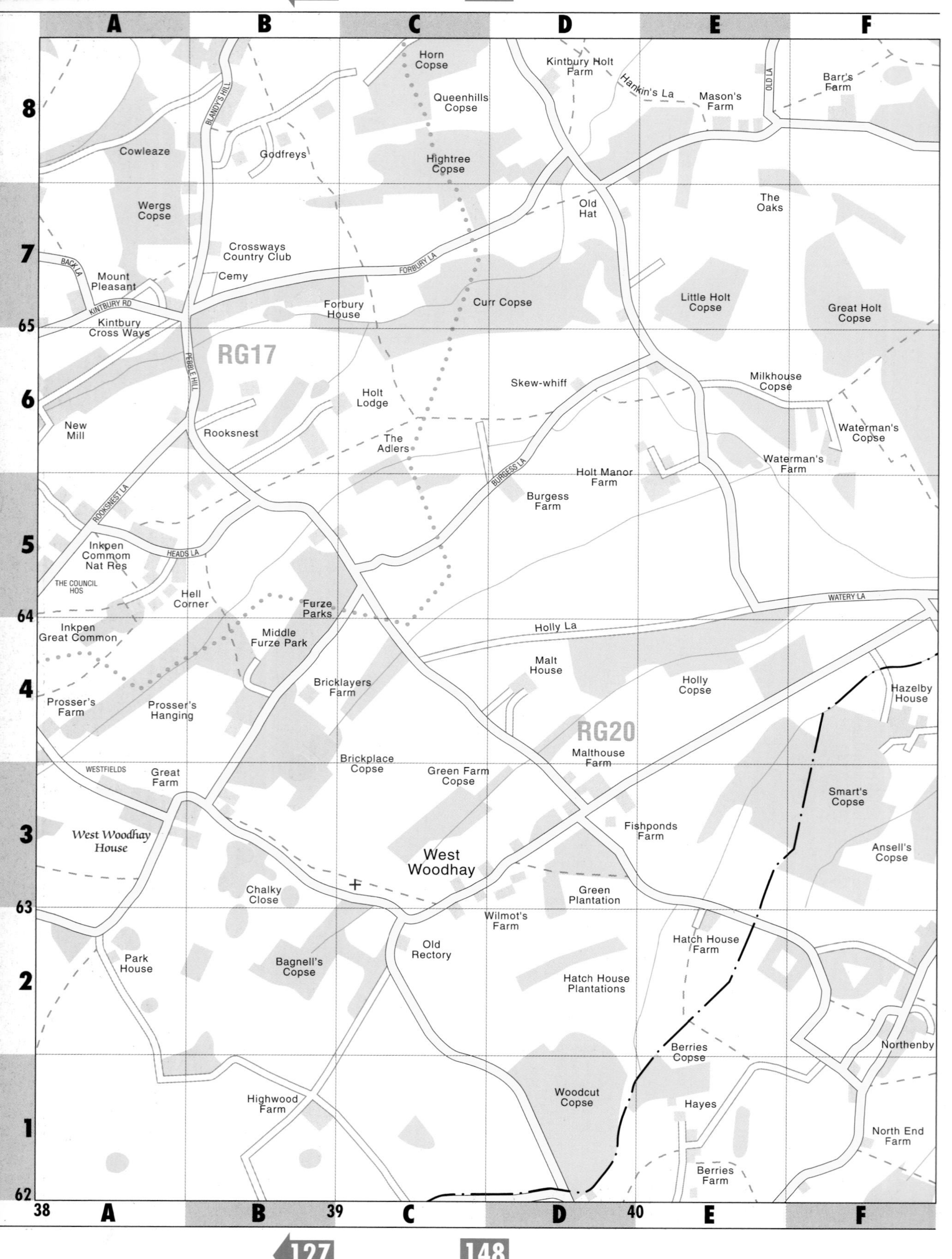
A
B
C
D
E
F
8
7
65
6
5
64
4
3
63
2
1
62
38
39
40
Horn Copse
Kintbury Holt Farm
Hankin's La
Mason's Farm
OLD LA
Barr's Farm
Queenhills Copse
BLANDY'S HILL
Cowleaze
Godfreys
Hightree Copse
Wergs Copse
Old Hat
The Oaks
Crossways Country Club
BACK LA
Mount Pleasant
Cemy
FORBURY LA
KINTBURY RD
Forbury House
Curr Copse
Little Holt Copse
Great Holt Copse
Kintbury Cross Ways
RG17
PEBBLE HILL
Holt Lodge
Skew-whiff
Milkhouse Copse
New Mill
Rooksnest
The Adlers
Waterman's Copse
Waterman's Farm
Holt Manor Farm
BURGESS LA
Burgess Farm
ROOKSNEST LA
Inkpen Commom Nat Res
HEADS LA
THE COUNCIL HOS
Hell Corner
Furze Parks
WATERY LA
Inkpen Great Common
Middle Furze Park
Holly La
Malt House
Bricklayers Farm
Holly Copse
Hazelby House
Prosser's Farm
Prosser's Hanging
RG20
Malthouse Farm
Brickplace Copse
WESTFIELDS
Great Farm
Green Farm Copse
Smart's Copse
West Woodhay House
Fishponds Farm
Ansell's Copse
West Woodhay
Chalky Close
Green Plantation
Wilmot's Farm
Hatch House Farm
Park House
Old Rectory
Bagnell's Copse
Hatch House Plantations
Berries Copse
Northenby
Woodcut Copse
Highwood Farm
Hayes
North End Farm
Berries Farm

127
148

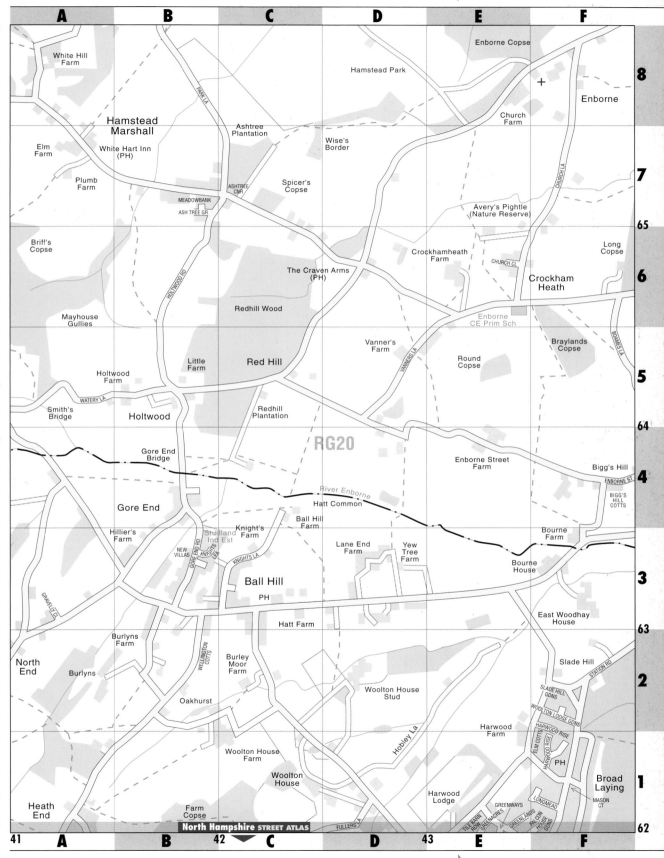

North Hampshire STREET ATLAS

A B C D E F
8 7 6 5 4 3 2 1
65 64 63 62
41 42 43
White Hill Farm
Hamstead Marshall
Elm Farm
White Hart Inn (PH)
Plumb Farm
Briff's Copse
Mayhouse Gullies
Holtwood Farm
Smith's Bridge
Holtwood
Gore End Bridge
Gore End
Hillier's Farm
Burlyns Farm
North End
Burlyns
Heath End
Ashtree Plantation
ASHTREE CNR
MEADOWBANK
ASH TREE GR
PARK LA
HOLTWOOD RD
WATERY LA
Little Farm
Red Hill
Redhill Wood
Redhill Plantation
The Craven Arms (PH)
Wise's Border
Spicer's Copse
Hamstead Park
RG20
River Enborne
Hatt Common
Ball Hill Farm
Knight's Farm
Studland Ind Est
NEW VILLAS
GORE END RD
KNIGHTS LEA
KNIGHTS LA
GRAVELLY CL
Ball Hill
PH
Hatt Farm
WELLINGTON COTTS
Burley Moor Farm
Oakhurst
Woolton House Farm
Woolton House
Farm Copse
Enborne Copse
Enborne
Church Farm
CHURCH LA
Avery's Pightle (Nature Reserve)
Crockhamheath Farm
CHURCH CL
Crockham Heath
Long Copse
Enborne CE Prim Sch
Vanner's Farm
VANNERS LA
Round Copse
Braylands Copse
BOAMES LA
Enborne Street Farm
Bigg's Hill
ENBORNE ST
BIGG'S HILL COTTS
Lane End Farm
Yew Tree Farm
Bourne Farm
Bourne House
East Woodhay House
Slade Hill
STATION RD
SLADE HILL GDNS
WOOLTON LODGE GDNS
HARWOOD RISE
ELM COTTS
PH
Woolton House Stud
Hobley La
Harwood Farm
Harwood Lodge
Broad Laying
MASON CT
LONGMEAD
GREENWAYS
GREENACRES
TILE BARN ROW
GREENLANDS
FALCON HOUSE GDNS
FULLERS LA

129
104

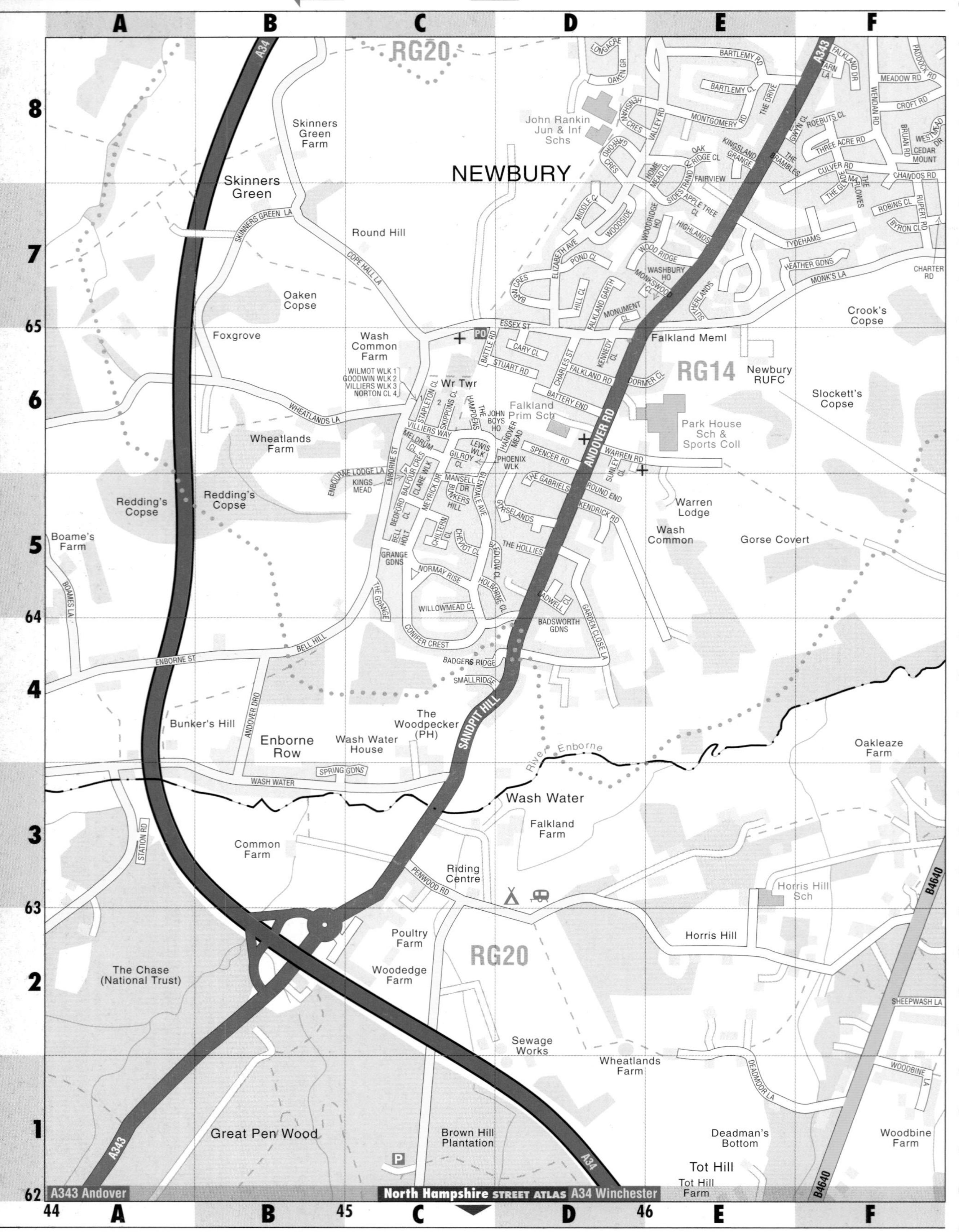
A
B
C
D
E
F
8
7
65
6
5
64
4
3
63
2
1
62
44
45
46
RG20
NEWBURY
Skinners Green Farm
Skinners Green
SKINNERS GREEN LA
Round Hill
COPE HALL LA
Oaken Copse
Foxgrove
Wash Common Farm
John Rankin Jun & Inf Schs
A34
A343
LONGACRE
OAKEN GR
BARTLEMY RD
BARTLEMY CL
MONTGOMERY RD
THE DRIVE
FALKLAND DR
PADDOCK RD
MEADOW RD
CROFT RD
WENDAN RD
ROEBUTS CL
GWYN CL
THREE ACRE RD
WESTMEAD DR
CEDAR MOUNT
BRIAN RD
CULVER RD
THE BRAMBLES
CHANDOS RD
THE GLADE
MARLOWES
ROBINS CL
RUPERT RD
BYRON CL
TYDEHAMS
HEATHER GDNS
MONK'S LA
CHARTER RD
KINGSLAND GRANGE
OAK RIDGE CL
FAIRVIEW
SIDESTRAND RD
APPLE TREE CL
HIGHLANDS
HOME MEAD CL
VALLEY RD
HENSHAW CRES
GAYFORD CRES
MIDDLE CL
WOODSIDE
WOODRIDGE HO
WOOD RIDGE
WASHBURY HO
MONKSWOOD CL
SUTHERLANDS
ELIZABETH AVE
POND CL
BARN CRES
HILL CL
FALKLAND GARTH
MONUMENT CL
ESSEX ST
PO
BATTLE RD
CARY CL
STUART RD
CHARLES ST
KENNEDY CL
FALKLAND RD
DORMER CL
BATTERY END
Falkland Meml
RG14
Newbury RUFC
Crook's Copse
Slockett's Copse
Park House Sch & Sports Coll
WILMOT WLK 1
GOODWIN WLK 2
VILLIERS WLK 3
NORTON CL 4
Wr Twr
STAPLETON CL
SKIPPONS CL
HAMPDENS
THE JOHN BOYS HO
Falkland Prim Sch
VILLIERS WAY
MELDRUM CL
LEWIS WLK
GILROY CL
HANOVER MEAD
PHOENIX WLK
SPENCER RD
ANDOVER RD
WARREN RD
SUNLEY CL
WHEATLANDS LA
Wheatlands Farm
ENBORNE LODGE LA
KINGS MEAD
ENBORNE ST
BALFOUR CRES
CLARE WLK
MEYRICK DR
MANSELL DR
BUNKERS HILL
GLENDALE AVE
THE GABRIELS
ROUND END
KENDRICK RD
BEDFORD CL
BELL HOLT
CHILTERN CL
CHEVIOT CL
GORSELANDS
THE HOLLIES
BIGLOW CL
GRANGE GDNS
NORMAY RISE
HOLBORNE CL
CADWELL CL
THE GRANGE
WILLOWMEAD CL
BADSWORTH GDNS
GARDEN CLOSE LA
CONIFER CREST
BADGERS RIDGE
SMALLRIDGE
Warren Lodge
Wash Common
Gorse Covert
Redding's Copse
Boame's Farm
BOAMES LA
BELL HILL
ENBORNE ST
Bunker's Hill
ANDOVER DRO
Enborne Row
Wash Water House
The Woodpecker (PH)
SANDPIT HILL
River Enborne
Oakleaze Farm
SPRING GDNS
WASH WATER
Wash Water
Falkland Farm
STATION RD
Common Farm
PENWOOD RD
Riding Centre
Horris Hill Sch
B4640
Poultry Farm
Horris Hill
RG20
Woodedge Farm
The Chase (National Trust)
SHEEPWASH LA
Sewage Works
Wheatlands Farm
DEADMOOR LA
WOODBINE LA
Great Pen Wood
Brown Hill Plantation
P
Deadman's Bottom
Woodbine Farm
Tot Hill
Tot Hill Farm
A343 Andover
North Hampshire STREET ATLAS
A34 Winchester

129

A
B
C
D
E
F
8
7
65
6
5
64
4
3
63
2
1
62
47
48
49
Greenham
West Wood
Greenham Court Prim Sch
Mill Hall Sch
Pigeon's Farm
Bury's Bank
CH
Visitor Ctr
Newbury Ret Pk
RG14
Newbury Coll
Hotel
RG19
Greenham Common
High Wood
Sandleford Farm
Brown's Pond
Drayton's Gully
St Gabriel's Sch
Sandleford Park
Sandleford Priory
New Greenham Pk
Brackenhurst
Aldernbridge Gully
Woodhouse Pond
Sandleford Place
Peckmoor Copse
Peaked Hill
The Swan Inn (PH)
River Enborne
Clarke's Gully
Aldern Bridge
Aldern Bridge Farm
Newtown House
Newtown
RG20
Newtown Farm
Arbuthnot Wood
Hill Farm
Aldern Bridge House
Adbury House
Sydmonton Common
Crambow Gully
Rosemore Copse
Newtown Grange
Newtown Common
Gold Copse
Sheepwash Farm
Burghclere Common
Adbury Farm
Short Bushes Copse
North Sydmonton
North Sydmonton Farm
Adbury Park
Durrel's Copse
Herbert Plantation
Ox Drove
North Sydmonton House
A339
NEWTOWN RD
B4640
MONKS LA
CHANDOS RD
THE OAKS
ROKEBY CL
PINCHINGTON LA
DEADMANS LA
PRIORY PL
SANDLEFORD LODGE PK
PECKMOOR DR
BURY'S BANK RD
GREENHAM RD
PIGEONS FARM RD
GREYBERRY COPSE RD
YOUNG CRES
WATER LA
DRAYTONS VIEW
SPA MEADOW CL
NEW RD
WORMERSLEY RD
1 MARCHANT CL
2 BLAGDON CL
3 PRITCHARD CL
1 LINGFIELD RD
2 WINDSOR RISE
SEDGEFIELD RD
1 SPRINGFIELD LA
2 BODIN GDNS
SEVENTH ST
MAIN ST
SIXTH ST
FIFTH ST
FOURTH ST
LINDENMUTH WAY
COMMUNICATIONS RD
WAREHOUSE RD
ALBURY WAY
JONATHAN HILL
SHEEPWASH
BROKEN WAY
PINEWOOD DR
YEOMANS LA
LINNET LA 1
GOLDFINCH LA 2
PHEASANT LA 3
LINDEN RD 4
ROBIN LA 5
SNIPE LA 6
WILLOW RD 7
ASH RD
PO
P

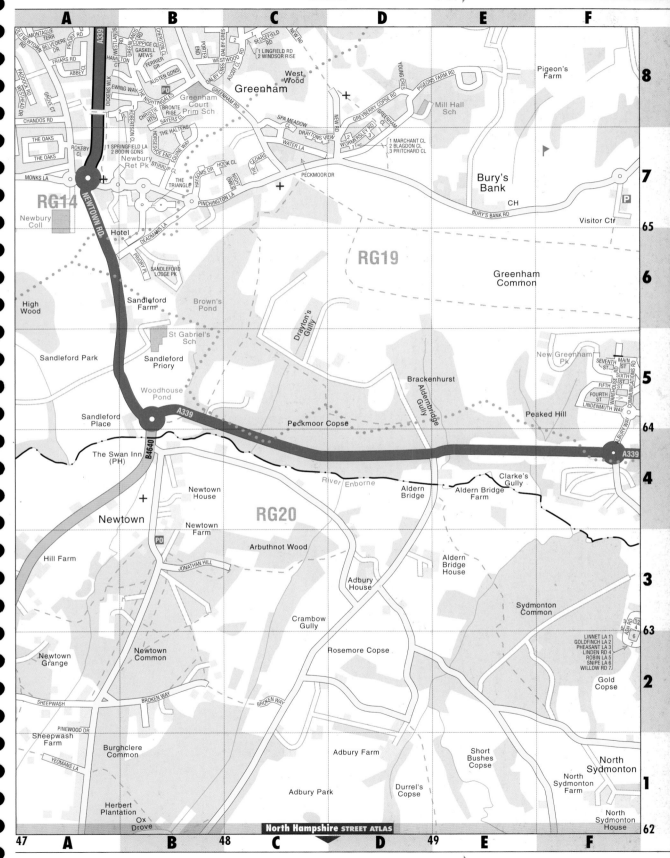

131
106

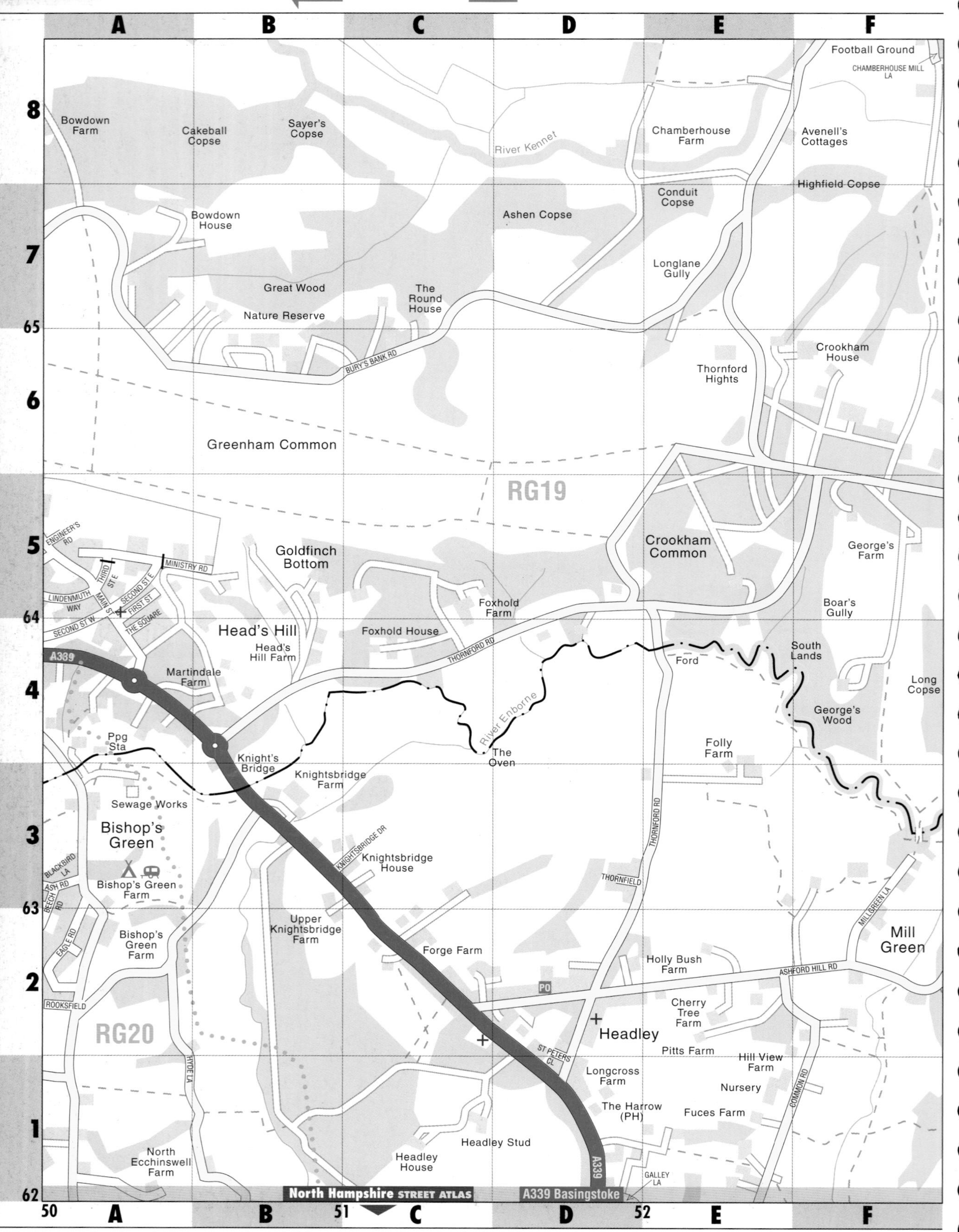
A B C D E F
8 7 65 6 5 64 4 3 63 2 1 62
50 51 52
Football Ground
CHAMBERHOUSE MILL LA
Bowdown Farm
Cakeball Copse
Sayer's Copse
River Kennet
Chamberhouse Farm
Avenell's Cottages
Highfield Copse
Conduit Copse
Bowdown House
Ashen Copse
Longlane Gully
Great Wood
Nature Reserve
The Round House
BURY'S BANK RD
Crookham House
Thornford Hights
Greenham Common
RG19
ENGINEER'S RD
MINISTRY RD
Goldfinch Bottom
Crookham Common
George's Farm
LINDENMUTH WAY
MAIN ST
SECOND ST E
FIRST ST
THIRD ST E
SECOND ST W
THE SQUARE
Foxhold Farm
Boar's Gully
Head's Hill
Foxhold House
Head's Hill Farm
THORNFORD RD
Ford
South Lands
A339
Martindale Farm
Long Copse
River Enborne
George's Wood
Ppg Sta
Knight's Bridge
The Oven
Folly Farm
Knightsbridge Farm
Sewage Works
Bishop's Green
KNIGHTSBRIDGE DR
Knightsbridge House
THORNFORD RD
BLACKBIRD LA
ASH RD
BEECH RD
Bishop's Green Farm
THORNFIELD
MILLGREEN LA
Mill Green
Upper Knightsbridge Farm
EAGLE RD
Bishop's Green Farm
Forge Farm
Holly Bush Farm
PO
ASHFORD HILL RD
ROOKSFIELD
Cherry Tree Farm
RG20
Headley
HYDE LA
ST PETERS CL
Pitts Farm
Hill View Farm
Longcross Farm
COMMON RD
Nursery
The Harrow (PH)
Fuces Farm
North Ecchinswell Farm
Headley Stud
Headley House
GALLEY LA
North Hampshire STREET ATLAS
A339 Basingstoke

131

107
134

A B C D E F

8 7 65 6 5 64 4 3 63 2 1 62

River Kennet
Crookham Manor
Prior's Moor Ditch
Brimpton Mill (disused)
King's Bridge
BRIMPTON RD
The Lynch
Waterside Copse
Hanging Lands Gully
Bonds Gully
Manor Farm
New Gully
East Field Copse
MANOR VIEW
Limberlost Farm
Highfield Farm
PO
Stone House
Burnell's Farm
CHURCH LA
PH
White Lodge
POPLAR CL
JUNIPER PL
LARCH DR
JASMIN WAY
MAGNOLIA CT
HOLLY CL
7 RHODODENDRON WLK
8 BIRCH AVE
9 FIR CL
10 OAKTREE AVE
11 LILAC WLK
12 CEDAR RISE
ENBORNE WAY 1
BANNISTER PL 2
Holdaway's Farm
Brimpton
Brimpton CE Prim Sch
MANOR LA
PH
Manor Farm
RG7
AZALEA RD 1
LAUREL AVE 2
LIME CL 3
ASH CRES 4
LABURNUM RISE 5
BEECH CL 6
Crookham
RG19
HYDE END LA
Upper Hyde End Farm
Arundell's Copse
Little Park House
Oak Cottage
Little Park Farm
Kenton's Wood
Park Copse
Hyde End Wood
Long Copse
Hyde End
Hyde End Farm
Park Gully Bridge
Flaggy Copse
River Enborne
Inwood Copse
Stonylands Copse
Park La
Oxford Bridge
Riddings Farm
WOODHOUSE LA
HOCKFORD LA
ASHFORD HILL RD
Goose Hill
HILLHOUSE LA
RIDDINGS LA
Stark House Farm
Woodhouse Farm
Broom Close Row
The Drove
Hillhouse La
Brook Farm
THE DROVE
Woodlands Farm
B3051
Huntsmoor Hill
HILLHOUSE LA
OLD LA
The Ship Inn (PH)
RAM ALLEY
CHAPEL LA
Ashford Hill
HOLLYCROFT
Kingsclere Woodlands
Old Farm
Chippings Gully
Ashford Hill Prim Sch
B3051

53 A B 54 C D 55 E F

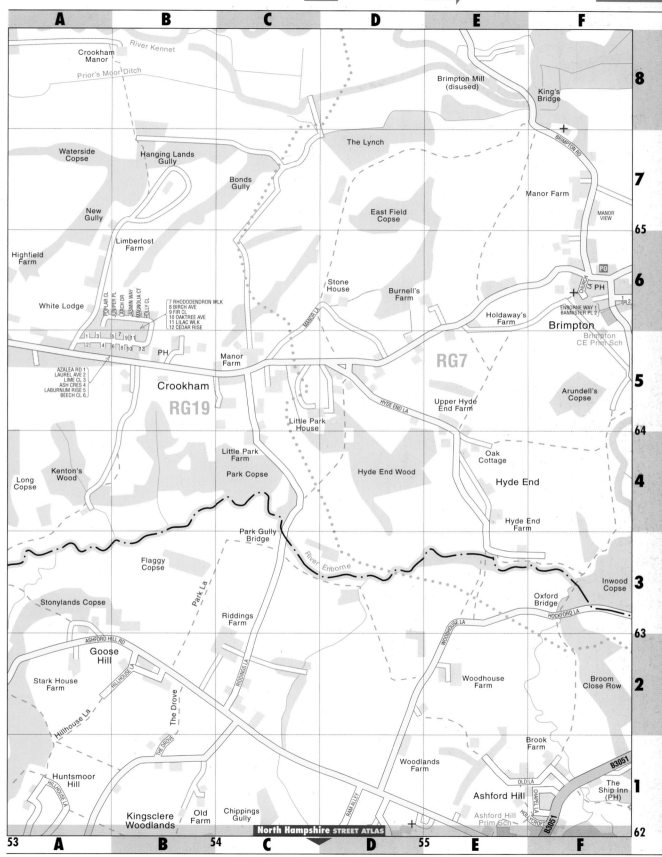

133
108

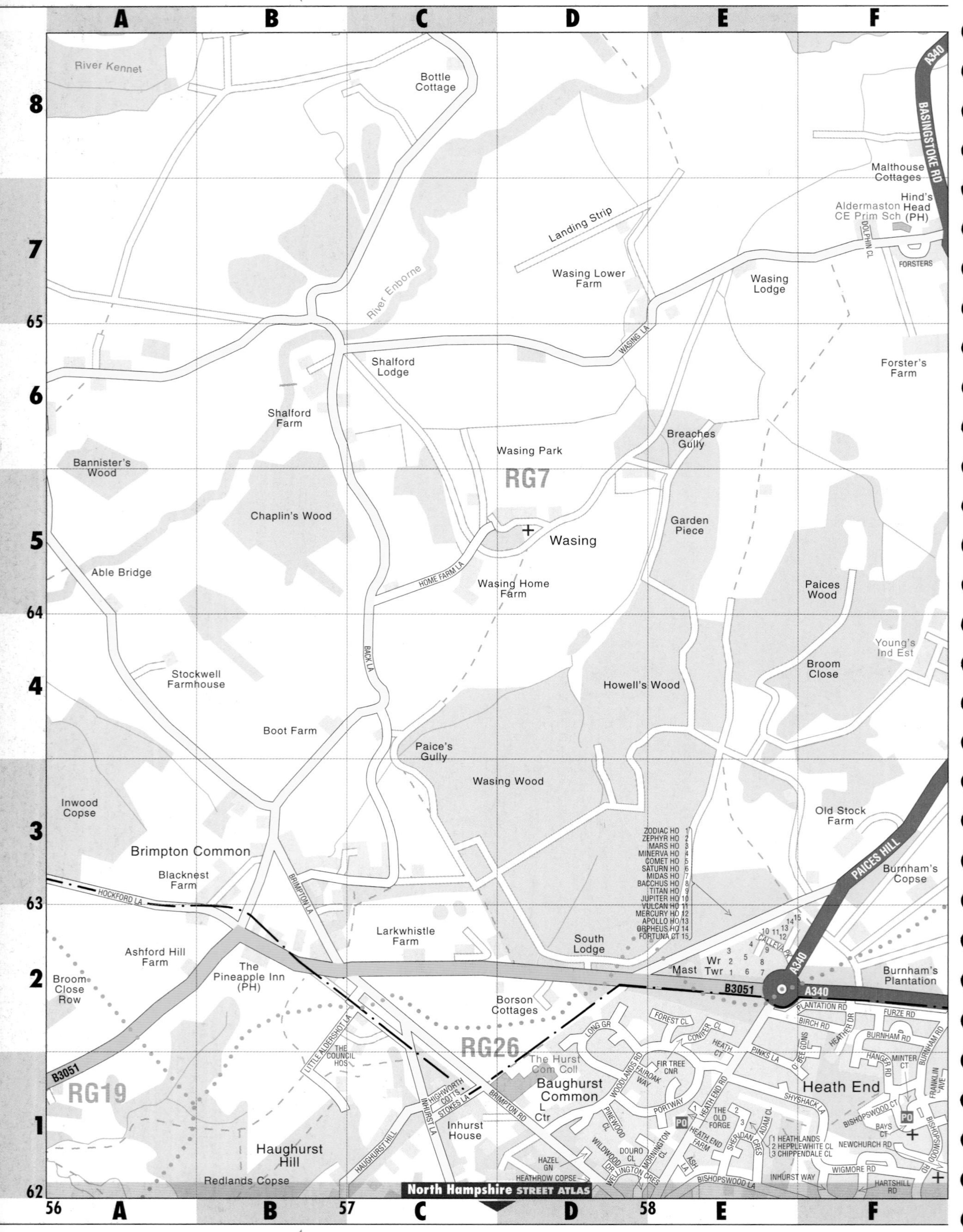
A
B
C
D
E
F
8
7
65
6
5
64
4
3
63
2
1
62
56
57
58
River Kennet
Bottle Cottage
A340
BASINGSTOKE RD
Malthouse Cottages
Hind's Head (PH)
Aldermaston CE Prim Sch
DOLPHIN CL
FORSTERS
Landing Strip
Wasing Lower Farm
Wasing Lodge
River Enborne
WASING LA
Shalford Lodge
Forster's Farm
Shalford Farm
Breaches Gully
Wasing Park
Bannister's Wood
RG7
Chaplin's Wood
Garden Piece
Wasing
Able Bridge
HOME FARM LA
Wasing Home Farm
Paices Wood
Young's Ind Est
BACK LA
Broom Close
Stockwell Farmhouse
Howell's Wood
Boot Farm
Paice's Gully
Wasing Wood
Inwood Copse
Old Stock Farm
ZODIAC HO 1
ZEPHYR HO 2
MARS HO 3
MINERVA HO 4
COMET HO 5
SATURN HO 6
MIDAS HO 7
BACCHUS HO 8
TITAN HO 9
JUPITER HO 10
VULCAN HO 11
MERCURY HO 12
APOLLO HO 13
ORPHEUS HO 14
FORTUNA CT 15
PAICES HILL
Brimpton Common
Burnham's Copse
Blacknest Farm
HOCKFORD LA
BRIMPTON LA
Larkwhistle Farm
South Lodge
CALLEVA PK
Ashford Hill Farm
The Pineapple Inn (PH)
Mast
Wr Twr
Burnham's Plantation
Broom Close Row
B3051
A340
Borson Cottages
PLANTATION RD
FURZE RD
FOREST CL
LONG GR
CONIFER CL
BIRCH RD
HEATHER DR
BURNHAM RD
LITTLE ALDERSHOT LA
THE COUNCIL HOS
RG26
The Hurst Com Coll
HEATH CT
PINKS LA
BEE GONS
HANGAR RD
MINTER CT
B3051
WOODLANDS RD
FIR TREE CNR
FAIROAK WAY
Heath End
RG19
HIGHWORTH COTTS
STOKES LA
BRIMPTON RD
Baughurst Common
L Ctr
SHYSHACK LA
FRANKLIN AVE
INHURST LA
PORTWAY
HEATH END RD
THE OLD FORGE
ADAM CL
BISHOPSWOOD CT
Inhurst House
PINEWOOD CL
PO
HEATH END FARM
SHERIDAN CRES
1 HEATHLANDS
2 HEPPLEWHITE CL
3 CHIPPENDALE CL
BAYS CT
NEWCHURCH RD
BISHOPSWOOD RD
Haughurst Hill
HAUGHURST HILL
WILDWOOD DR
DOURO CL
MORNINGTON CL
ASH LA
WIGMORE RD
HAZEL GN
WELLINGTON CRES
INHURST WAY
Redlands Copse
HEATHROW COPSE
BISHOPSWOOD LA
HARTSHILL RD

133

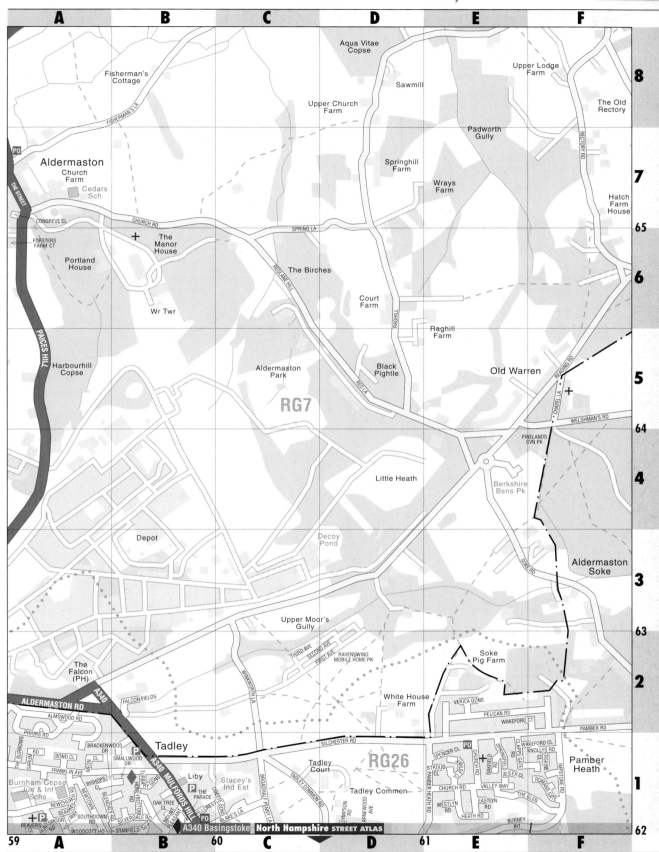

8

7

65

6

5

64

4

3

63

2

1

62

Fisherman's Cottage

Aqua Vitae Copse

Upper Lodge Farm

Upper Church Farm

Sawmill

The Old Rectory

RECTORY RD

PO

Aldermaston

Church Farm

Cedars Sch

Padworth Gully

Springhill Farm

THE STREET

Wrays Farm

Hatch Farm House

CONGREVE CL

CHURCH RD

SPRING LA

FORSTERS FARM CT

The Manor House

The Birches

Portland House

REDLANE HILL

Court Farm

RAGHILL

PAICES HILL

Wr Twr

Raghill Farm

Harbourhill Copse

RED LA

Aldermaston Park

Black Pightle

Old Warren

READING RD

RG7

CHAPEL LA

WELSHMAN'S RD

PINELANDS CVN PK

Little Heath

Berkshire Bsns Pk

64

Depot

SOKE RD

Aldermaston Soke

Decoy Pond

Upper Moor's Gully

63

THIRD AVE

SECOND AVE

FIRST AVE

RAVENSWING MOBILE HOME PK

Soke Pig Farm

The Falcon (PH)

WINKWORTH LA

White House Farm

VERICA GDNS

A340

FALCON FIELDS

PELICAN RD

WAKEFORD CT

PAMBER RD

ALDERMASTON RD

ALMSWOOD RD

SILCHESTER RD

WAKEFORD CL

KNOLLYS CL

PRIORS RD

BRACKENWOOD DR

P

Tadley

SPENCER CL

PO

CLAPPS GATE

HERSCHE

RG26

SMALLWOOD DR

STROUD CL

CHURCH RD

SPRINGFIELD RD

THE BURROWS

SARUM

BOND CL

CL

FRANKLIN AVE

Tadley Court

CHURCH RD

OXFORD RD

VALLEY WAY

ROMANS GATE

IMPSTONE RD

Pamber Heath

Liby

BISHOPS

P

Stacey's Ind Est

BROADHAL

FENNY LA

TADLEY COMMON RD

Tadley Common

WESTLYN RD

EASTLYN RD

HEATH RD

THE GLEN

BURNEY BIT

Burnham Copse Jun & Inf Schs

NEWTOWN

OAK TREE CL

MOUNT PLEASANT

ODELL CL

PO

SIMPSON RD

ARNEWOOD AVE

P

NEWCHURC

WY

SOUTHDOWN RD

SILVERDALE RD

BLAKE'S LA

A340 MULFORDS HILL

HONEYBOTTOM RD

TURF HILL

GLENDALE RD

BEAVERS

HUNTSMOOR

RD

SEARS

WOODCOTT HO

STANFIELD

CL

135
110

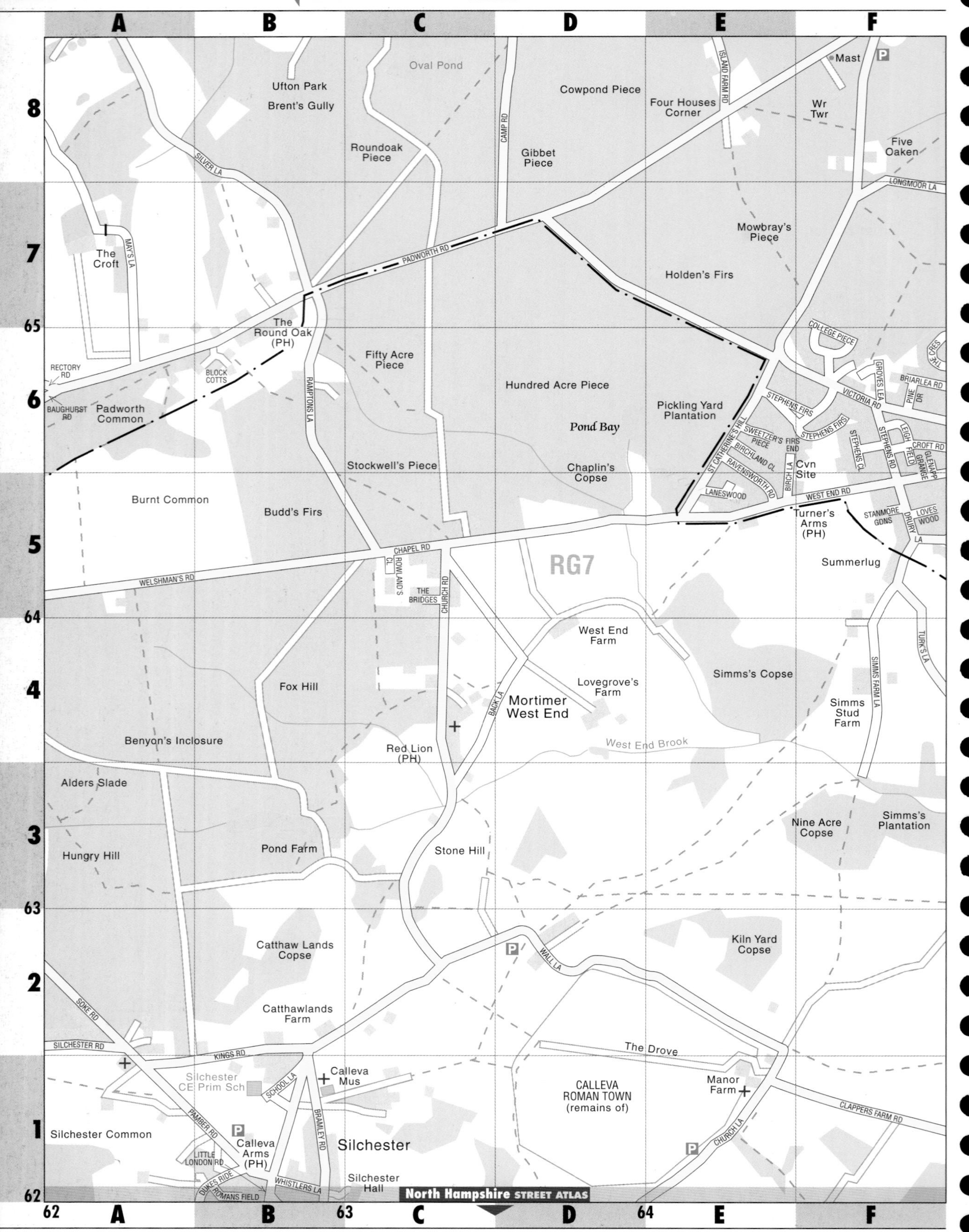
A
B
C
D
E
F
8
7
6
5
4
3
2
1
65
64
63
62
Oval Pond
Ufton Park
Brent's Gully
Roundoak Piece
Cowpond Piece
Four Houses Corner
Mast
Wr Twr
Five Oaken
Gibbet Piece
CAMP RD
ISLAND FARM RD
LONGMOOR LA
SILVER LA
MAY'S LA
The Croft
PADWORTH RD
Mowbray's Piece
Holden's Firs
The Round Oak (PH)
RECTORY RD
BLOCK COTTS
BAUGHURST RD
Padworth Common
Fifty Acre Piece
RAMPTONS LA
Hundred Acre Piece
Pickling Yard Plantation
Pond Bay
COLLEGE PIECE
GROVES LEA
BRIARLEA RD
PINE DR
THE CRES
VICTORIA RD
STEPHENS FIRS
ST CATHERINE'S HILL
SWEETZER'S PIECE
FIRS END
BIRCHLAND CL
RAVENSWORTH RD
BIRCH LA
LANESWOOD
STEPHENS CL
STEPHENS RD
LEIGH FIELD
CROFT RD
GLENAPP GRANGE
Cvn Site
WEST END RD
Stockwell's Piece
Chaplin's Copse
Burnt Common
Budd's Firs
Turner's Arms (PH)
STANMORE GDNS
DRURY LA
LOVES WOOD
CHAPEL RD
RG7
Summerlug
WELSHMAN'S RD
ROWLAND'S CL
THE BRIDGES
CHURCH RD
West End Farm
TURK'S LA
Fox Hill
Lovegrove's Farm
Simms's Copse
BACK LA
Mortimer West End
SIMMS FARM LA
Simms Stud Farm
Benyon's Inclosure
Red Lion (PH)
West End Brook
Alders Slade
Nine Acre Copse
Simms's Plantation
Hungry Hill
Pond Farm
Stone Hill
Catthaw Lands Copse
Kiln Yard Copse
WALL LA
SOKE RD
Catthawlands Farm
SILCHESTER RD
KINGS RD
The Drove
Silchester CE Prim Sch
SCHOOL LA
Calleva Mus
CALLEVA ROMAN TOWN (remains of)
Manor Farm
CLAPPERS FARM RD
PAMBER RD
BRAMLEY RD
Silchester Common
Calleva Arms (PH)
Silchester
CHURCH LA
LITTLE LONDON RD
DUKES RIDE
ROMANS FIELD
WHISTLERS LA
Silchester Hall

135

A B C D E F

8 7 65 6 5 64 4 3 63 2 1 62

Lockram Brook
Warenes Wood
LOCKRAM LA
NEW RD
Wokefield Park (Training Centre)
SAWYERS LEY
WOKEFIELD ROW
Starvale Woods
Headlands Farm
LONGMOOR LA
Bridge's Farm
Wokefield Park
Pond Wood
Lukin's Wood
BREWERY COMM
Mann's Farm
MORTIMER LA
Mortimer House
SPRING LA
WOODSIDE CL
WINDMILL CT
WINDMILL RD
NIGHTINGALE LA
1 THE CRESCENT
2 WINDMILL CNR
3 CARPENTERS CT
4 HEATHFIELD
BRIARLEA RD
THE BEVERS
KING ST
BADGERS CROFT
HAMMONDS HEATH
Liby
Wheat's Farm
VICTORIA RD
Mortimer Hill Farm
Sewage Works
CROFT RD
PO
P
PH
WEST END RD
GARTH RD
Monkton Copse
Mortimer St John's CE Sch
ST JOHN'S RD
ST MARY'S RD
ORCHARD RD
CAMPBELL'S GN
THE AVENUE
MONKTONS LA
Mortimer
THE STREET
The Railway Inn (PH)
Foudry Brook
KILN LA
GORDON PALMER CL
Mortimer St Mary's CE Jun Sch
CHURCH FARM BARNS
Tun Bridge
MORTIMER HALL
Stratfield Mortimer
RAILWAY TERR
Mortimer
STATION RD
DRURY LA
RG7
Admiral's Copse
Windabout Copse
THE FOREHEAD
TURK'S LA
PITFIELD LA
Furze Ground
Tanhouse Bridge
Home Wood
Brocas Lands Farm
Little Park Farm
Sheepgrove Farm
Silchester Brook
Ticklecorner La
Butlers Lands
Hogs Plat
Park La
The Devil's Highway
The Devil's Highway
PARK LA
Butlers Land Copse
Wigmore Farm
CLAPPERS FARM RD
MORTIMER LA
Garden Copse

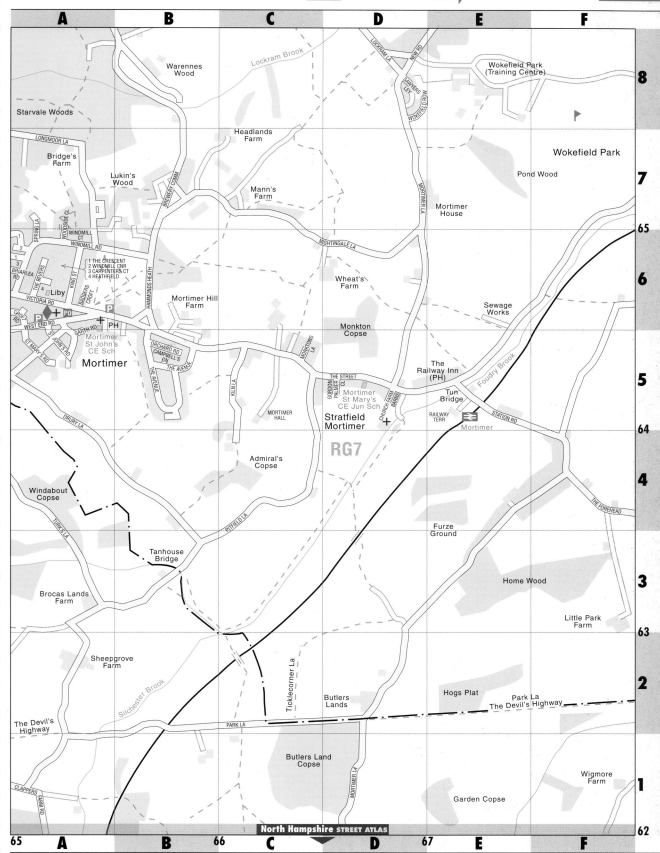

137
112

A
B
C
D
E
F
8
7
65
6
5
64
4
3
63
2
1
62
68
69
70
Bloomfield Hatch
GOODBOY'S LA
BLOOMFIELD HATCH LA
Clappers Farm
Foudry Brook
Brook Farm
Reid's Bridge
Caravan Site
WHITE HOUSE LA
White House Farm
May's Hill
A33
LODDON COURT FARM PARK HOMES
Great Park Copse
Missels Bridge
CROSS LA
Crosslane Farm
Woodcock La
Beech Hill Coverts
BEECH HILL RD
Wood La
Priory Copse
Little Copse
Home Farm
Great Park Farm
Trunkwell Farm
Beech Hill House
Priory Farm
Trunkwell House
WOOD LA
The Priory
PARK VIEW
VALE VIEW DR
Beech Hill
Broad Way
Old Elm Tree (PH)
RG7
Cannon Bridge
Perrins Farm
THE FOREHEAD
TROWE'S LA
BROAD WAY
BARGE LA
Stanford End Farm
River Loddon
Great Hills Farm
BULL LA
Stanford End
Chequers
CHEQUER LA
Stanfordend Bridge
PARK LA
WELSH LA
The Devil's Highway
FAIR CROSS
Fair Cross
Lake Pond
Home Farm
Stratfield Saye Park
Stone Bridge
RG27
Lower Tumbling Bay
Forelands
NEW ST

137

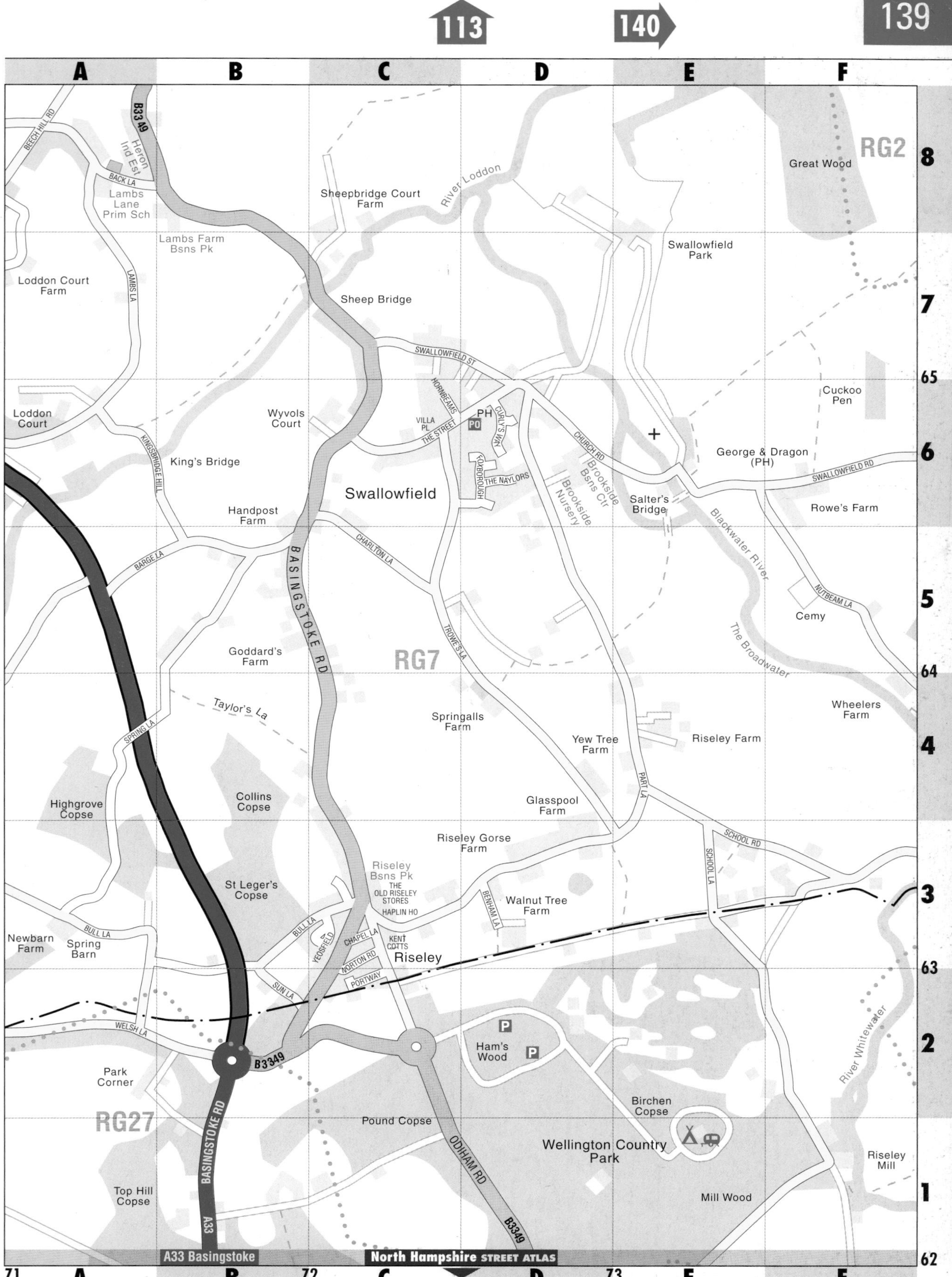
A B C D E F
8 7 6 5 4 3 2 1
65 64 63 62
71 72 73
RG2
Great Wood
B3349
Heron Ind Est
BEECH HILL RD
BACK LA
Lambs Lane Prim Sch
Lambs Farm Bsns Pk
Sheepbridge Court Farm
River Loddon
Swallowfield Park
Loddon Court Farm
LAMBS LA
Sheep Bridge
SWALLOWFIELD ST
Cuckoo Pen
Loddon Court
Wyvols Court
HORNBEAMS
VILLA PL
THE STREET
PH
PO
CURLY'S WAY
CHURCH RD
George & Dragon (PH)
KINGSBRIDGE HILL
King's Bridge
FOXBOROUGH
THE NAYLORS
Brookside Bsns Ctr
Brookside Nursery
Salter's Bridge
SWALLOWFIELD RD
Swallowfield
Handpost Farm
Rowe's Farm
Blackwater River
CHARLTON LA
BARGE LA
BASINGSTOKE RD
NUTBEAM LA
Cemy
Goddard's Farm
RG7
TROWE'S LA
The Broadwater
Taylor's La
Springalls Farm
Wheelers Farm
Yew Tree Farm
Riseley Farm
SPRING LA
PART LA
Collins Copse
Highgrove Copse
Glasspool Farm
Riseley Gorse Farm
SCHOOL RD
SCHOOL LA
Riseley Bsns Pk
THE OLD RISELEY STORES
HAPLIN HO
St Leger's Copse
BENHAM LA
Walnut Tree Farm
BULL LA
Newbarn Farm
Spring Barn
YEOSFIELD
CHAPEL LA
KENT COTTS
Riseley
NORTON RD
PORTWAY
SUN LA
WELSH LA
River Whitewater
P
Ham's Wood
B3349
Park Corner
Birchen Copse
RG27
BASINGSTOKE RD
Pound Copse
ODIHAM RD
Wellington Country Park
Riseley Mill
Top Hill Copse
Mill Wood
A33
B3349
A33 Basingstoke
North Hampshire STREET ATLAS

139
114

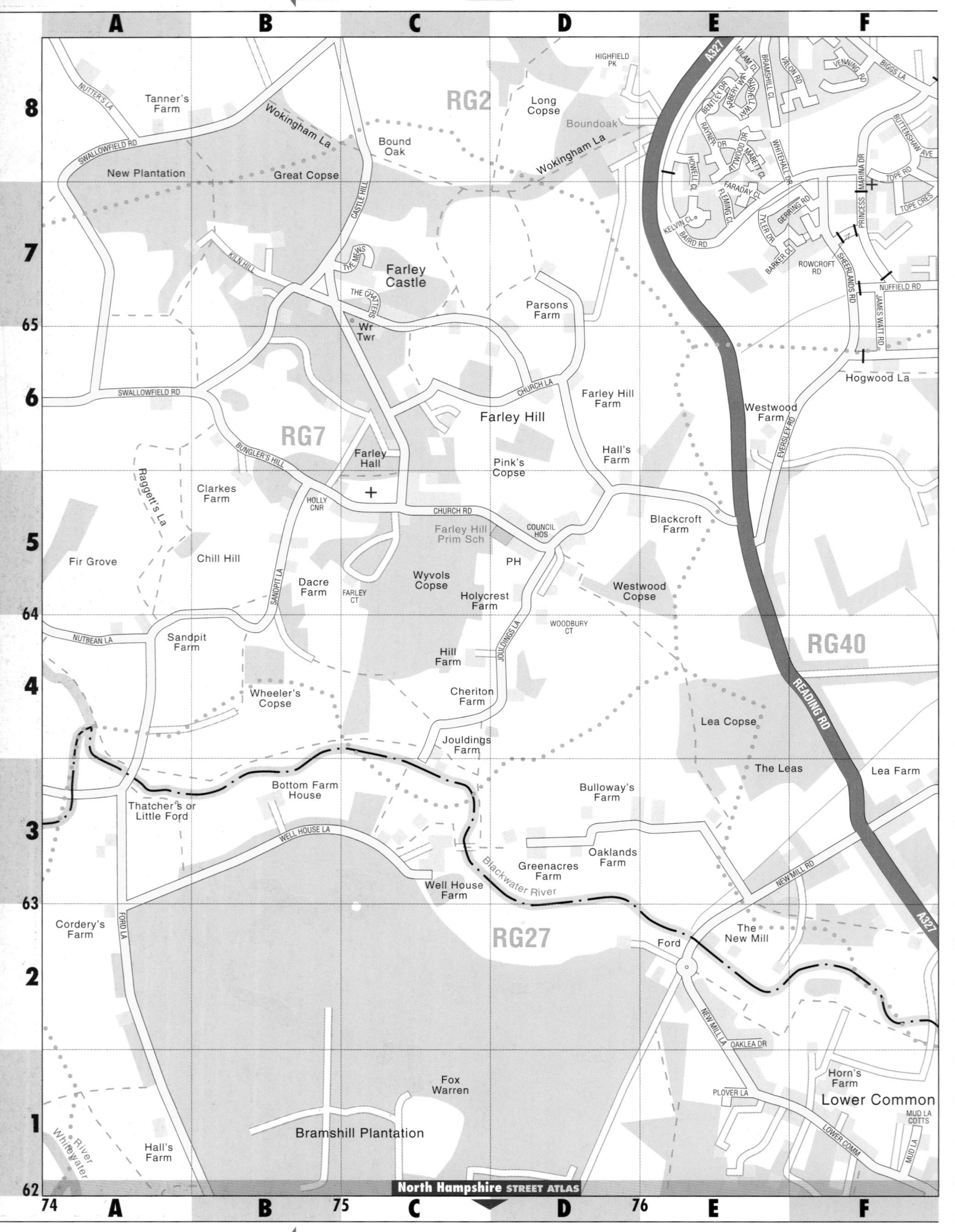
A
B
C
D
E
F
8
7
65
6
5
64
4
3
63
2
1
62
74
75
76
Tanner's Farm
NUTTER'S LA
SWALLOWFIELD RD
New Plantation
Wokingham La
Great Copse
Bound Oak
RG2
Long Copse
Boundoak
HIGHFIELD PK
Wokingham La
A327
CASTLE HILL
KILN HILL
THE MEWS
Farley Castle
THE CHATTERS
Wr Twr
Parsons Farm
SWALLOWFIELD RD
CHURCH LA
Farley Hill Farm
Farley Hill
RG7
BUNGLER'S HILL
Farley Hall
Pink's Copse
Hall's Farm
Raggett's La
Clarkes Farm
HOLLY CNR
CHURCH RD
Blackcroft Farm
Farley Hill Prim Sch
COUNCIL HOS
Fir Grove
Chill Hill
PH
Dacre Farm
Wyvols Copse
FARLEY CT
SANDPIT LA
Holycrest Farm
Westwood Copse
WOODBURY CT
NUTBEAN LA
Sandpit Farm
JOULDINGS LA
Hill Farm
RG40
Wheeler's Copse
Cheriton Farm
READING RD
Lea Copse
Jouldings Farm
The Leas
Lea Farm
Bottom Farm House
Bulloway's Farm
Thatcher's or Little Ford
WELL HOUSE LA
Oaklands Farm
Greenacres Farm
Blackwater River
Well House Farm
NEW MILL RD
Cordery's Farm
FORD LA
RG27
Ford
The New Mill
NEW MILL LA
OAKLEA DR
Fox Warren
PLOVER LA
Horn's Farm
Lower Common
MUD LA COTTS
Bramshill Plantation
LOWER COMM
MUD LA
Hall's Farm
River Whitewater
MILAM CL
BRAMSHILL CL
VALON RD
VENNING RD
BIGGS LA
BENTLEY DR
ARBERY WAY
BUSHELL WAY
BUTTENSHAW AVE
RAYNER DR
ATTWOOD DR
MABETT CL
WHITEHALL DR
MARINA DR
TOPE RD
TOPE CRES
HOWELL CL
FARADAY CL
FLEMING CL
KELVIN CL
BAIRD RD
GERRING RD
TYLER DR
PRINCESS
BARKER CL
ROWCROFT RD
SHEERLANDS RD
NUFFIELD RD
JAMES WATT RD
Hogwood La
Westwood Farm
EVERSLEY RD

139

115
142

Rifle Range
REME Mus of Technology
Arborfield Garrison
RG2
Model Farm
Rook's Nest Farm
Windmill Farm
California Country Park
Long Moor Bog
Longmoor Lake
Moor Farm
Long Moor
CALIFORNIA CVN PK
Gorse Ride Inf & Jun Schs
Longmoor Farm
Coleshill Farm
Falcon Bsns Pk
Hogwood Ind Est
Hogwood Farm
NINE MILE RIDE
Greenacres
Nine Mile Ride Ind
Nine Mile Ride Prim Sch
Wheatlands Farm
Furze Hill
Warren Lodge
Shepperlands Copse
RG40
Larchwood Farm
Church Farm
Ridge Farm
West Court
Manor House
North Court
Wheatlands Manor
Park Farm
Rectory Farm
East Court
Finchampstead CE Prim Sch
Manor Farm
THE VILLAGE
ROMAN MILESTONE
Banisters Farm
Agates Meadow
FLEET HILL
Fleet Copse
Finchampstead
READING RD
The Tally Ho (PH)
Eversley Bridge
Fleethill Farm
Eversley
Long Water
Blackwater River
RG27
Finchampstead Bridge
LONGWATER RD
A327 Farnborough (A30)

142

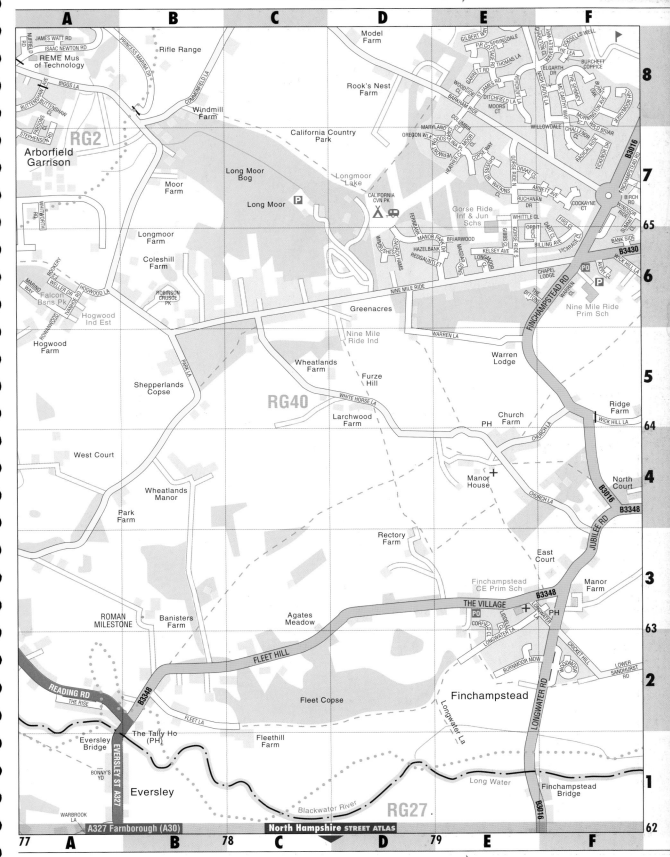

141
116

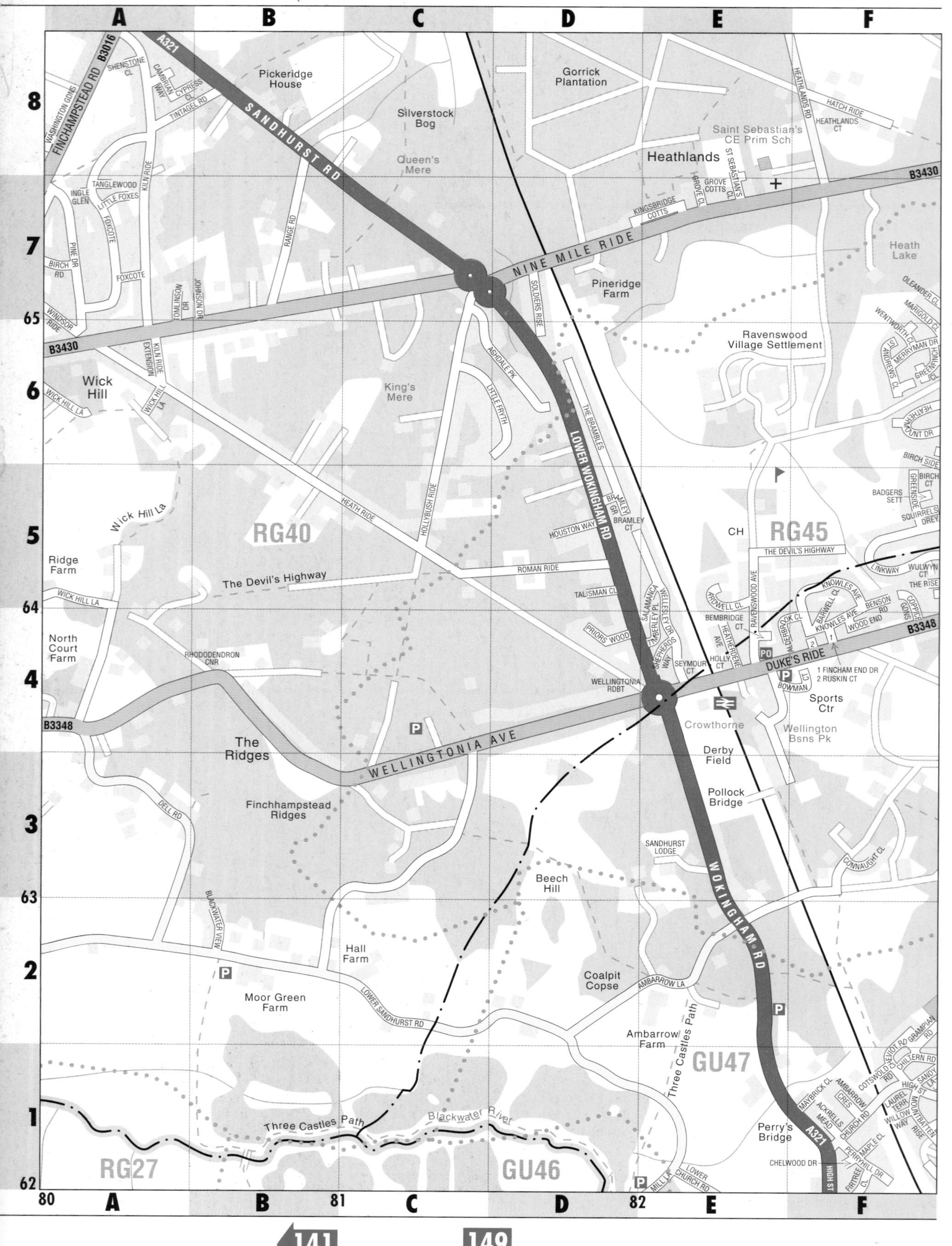
Pickeridge House
SANDHURST RD
A321
B3016
FINCHAMPSTEAD RD
Silverstock Bog
Queen's Mere
Gorrick Plantation
Heathlands
Saint Sebastian's CE Prim Sch
HEATHLANDS RD
HATCH RIDE
HEATHLANDS CT
B3430
NINE MILE RIDE
KINGSBRIDGE COTTS
GROVE CL
GROVE COTTS
ST SEBASTIAN'S CL
Heath Lake
Pineridge Farm
SOLDIERS RISE
Ravenswood Village Settlement
Wick Hill
King's Mere
ASHDALE PK
LITTLE FRYTH
THE BRAMBLES
LOWER WOKINGHAM RD
HEATH RIDE
HOLLYBUSH RIDE
RG40
RG45
CH
THE DEVIL'S HIGHWAY
The Devil's Highway
Wick Hill La
Ridge Farm
North Court Farm
ROMAN RIDE
HOUSTON WAY
BRAMLEY CT
TALISMAN CL
PRIORS WOOD
SALAMANCA
WELLESLEY DR
SHEPHERDS WAY
SEYMOUR CT
RHODODENDRON CNR
WELLINGTONIA RDBT
B3348
DUKE'S RIDE
Crowthorne
Sports Ctr
Wellington Bsns Pk
1 FINCHAM END DR
2 RUSKIN CT
BOWMAN CT
WELLINGTONIA AVE
The Ridges
Derby Field
Pollock Bridge
Finchhampstead Ridges
DELL RD
SANDHURST LODGE
WOKINGHAM RD
Beech Hill
CONNAUGHT CL
BLACKWATER VIEW
Hall Farm
Coalpit Copse
AMBARROW LA
Moor Green Farm
LOWER SANDHURST RD
Ambarrow Farm
Three Castles Path
GU47
Blackwater River
Perry's Bridge
RG27
GU46
LOWER CHURCH RD
MILL LA
CHELWOOD DR
HIGH ST
80
81
82
62
63
64
65

141
149

117
144

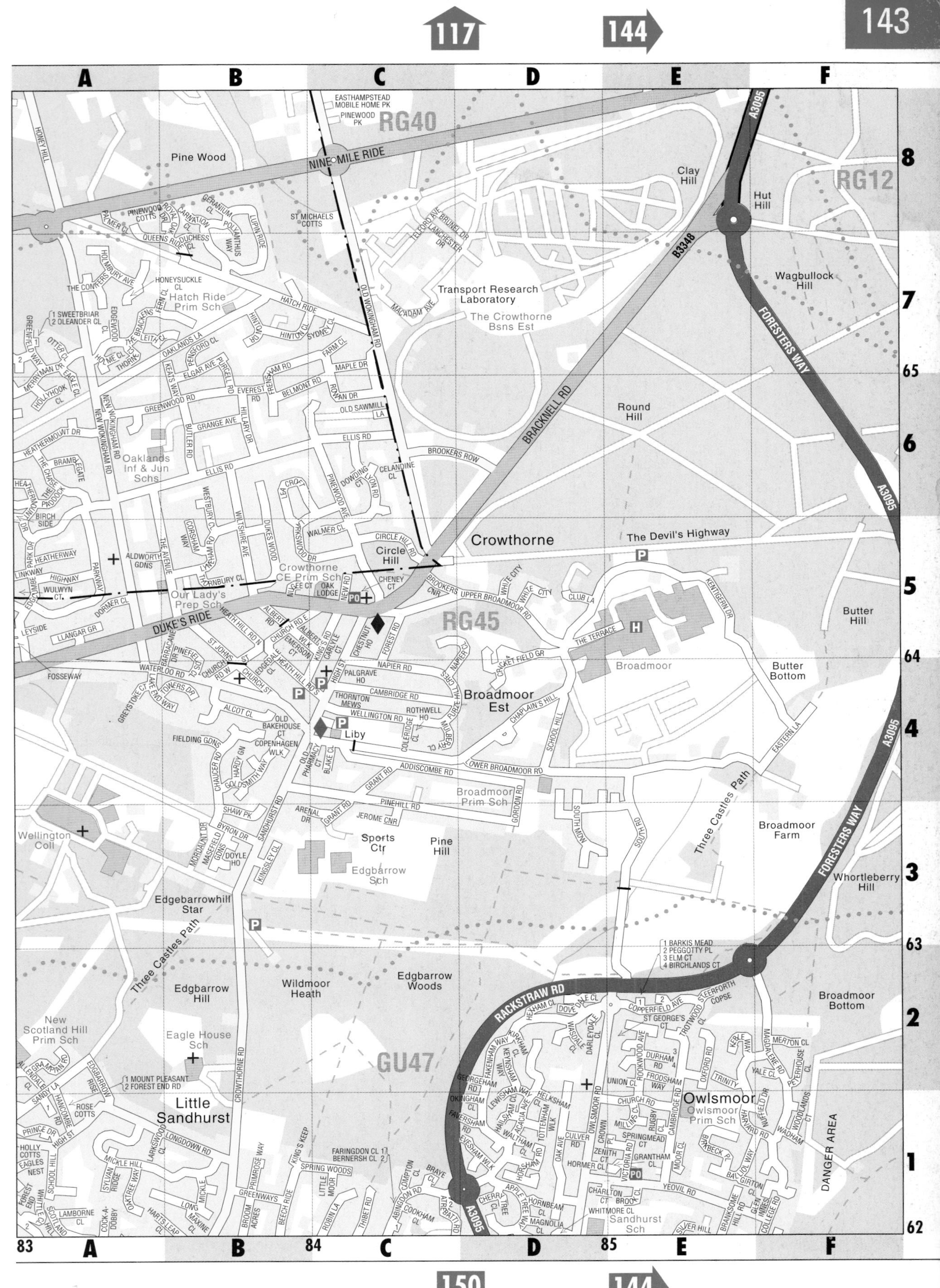
RG40
NINE MILE RIDE
Pine Wood
Clay Hill
Hut Hill
RG12
A3095
B3348
Transport Research Laboratory
The Crowthorne Bsns Est
Wagbullock Hill
FORESTERS WAY
Hatch Ride Prim Sch
HATCH RIDE
OLD WOKINGHAM RD
Round Hill
BRACKNELL RD
Oaklands Inf & Jun Schs
Crowthorne
The Devil's Highway
Circle Hill
Crowthorne CE Prim Sch
Our Lady's Prep Sch
DUKE'S RIDE
RG45
Butter Hill
Broadmoor
Butter Bottom
Broadmoor Est
Liby
Broadmoor Prim Sch
Sports Ctr
Pine Hill
Edgbarrow Sch
Three Castles Path
Broadmoor Farm
Wellington Coll
Whortleberry Hill
Edgebarrowhill Star
Edgbarrow Hill
Wildmoor Heath
Edgbarrow Woods
RACKSTRAW RD
Broadmoor Bottom
New Scotland Hill Prim Sch
Eagle House Sch
GU47
Little Sandhurst
Owlsmoor
Owlsmoor Prim Sch
DANGER AREA
Sandhurst Sch
CROWTHORNE RD
OWLSMOOR RD
1 BARKIS MEAD
2 PEGGOTTY PL
3 ELM CT
4 BIRCHLANDS CT
1 MOUNT PLEASANT
2 FOREST END RD
1 SWEETBRIAR
2 OLEANDER CL
FARINGDON CL 1
BERNERSH CL 2

150
144

143
118

A B C D E F
8
7
65
6
5
64
4
3
63
2
1
62
Gormoor Farm
Penny Hill
A322
Gravel Hill
Caesar's Camp
Pudding Hill
Three Castles Path
RG12
Mill Pond
New England Hill
Wickham Bushes
Roman Star or Upper Star Post
The Devil's Highway
DANGER AREA
Windsor Ride
FORESTERS WAY
A3095
DANGER AREA
GU19
Lower Star Post
RG45
DANGER AREA
Wishmoor Cross
Poppy Hills
Deer Rock Hill
DANGER AREA
GU15
Paschal Wood
GU47
Wishmoor Bottom
DANGER AREA
Olddean Common
Saddleback Hill
The Devil's Pound
WINDSOR RIDE
MATTHEWS RD
KING'S RIDE
QUEEN ELIZABETH RD
DUKE OF CORNWALL AVE
HIGHVIEW CRES
EDON RD
BRACKNELL CL
WIMBLEDON CL
BERKSHIRE RD
Sch
CAMBERLEY
86 A B 87 C D 88 E F

143
151

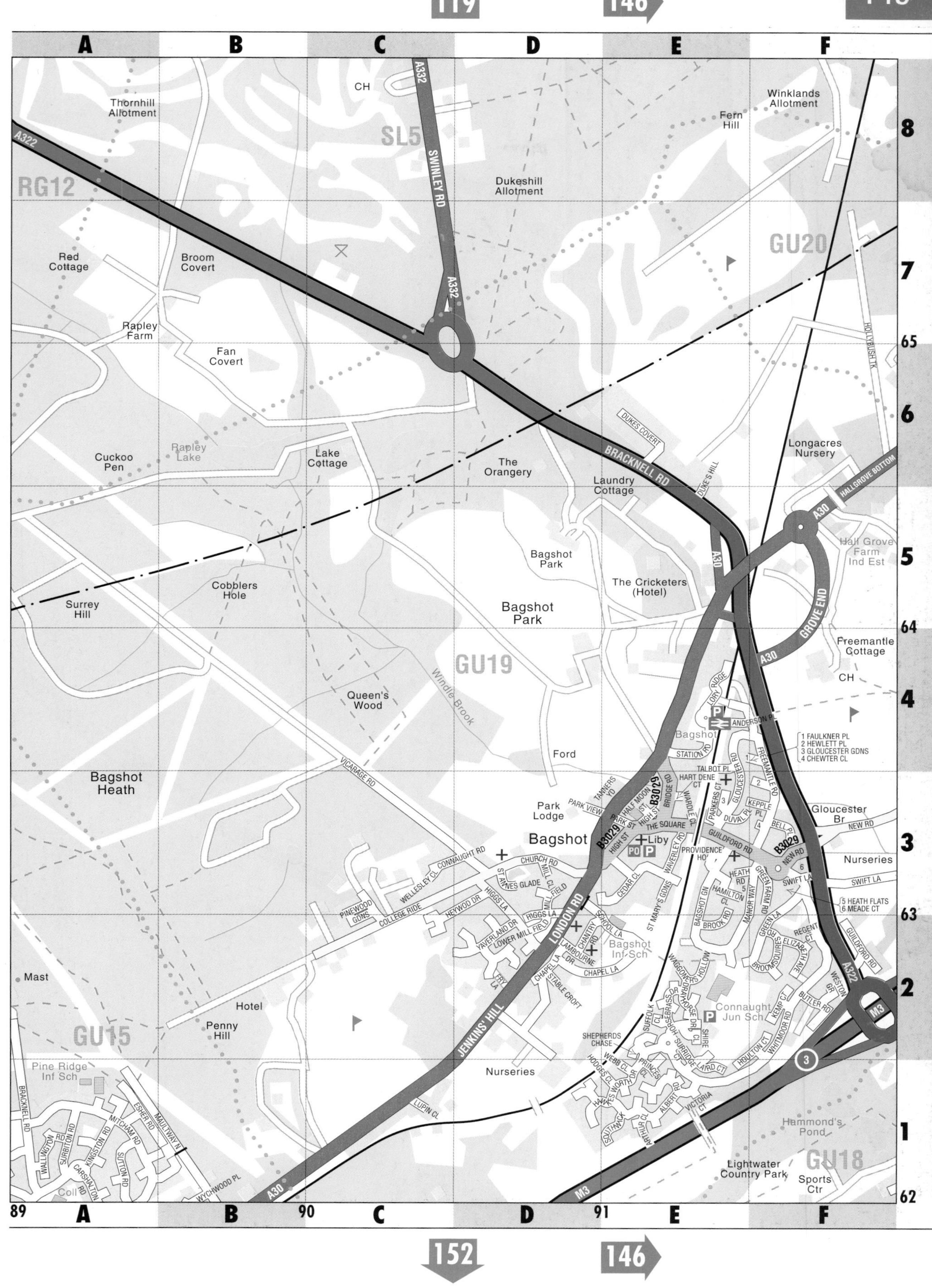
119
146
A
B
C
D
E
F
8
7
65
6
5
64
4
3
63
2
1
62
89
90
91
152
146
CH
Thornhill Allotment
A322
SL5
SWINLEY RD
A332
Winklands Allotment
Fern Hill
RG12
Dukeshill Allotment
GU20
Red Cottage
Broom Covert
Rapley Farm
Fan Covert
Cuckoo Pen
Rapley Lake
Lake Cottage
The Orangery
BRACKNELL RD
DUKES COVERT
DUKE'S HILL
Longacres Nursery
HALLGROVE BOTTOM
Laundry Cottage
Hall Grove Farm Ind Est
Bagshot Park
Cobblers Hole
Surrey Hill
The Cricketers (Hotel)
GROVE END
Freemantle Cottage
GU19
Windle Brook
Queen's Wood
Bagshot
ANDERSON PL
1 FAULKNER PL
2 HEWLETT PL
3 GLOUCESTER GDNS
4 CHEWTER CL
Ford
Bagshot Heath
VICARAGE RD
Park Lodge
Gloucester Br
NEW RD
Nurseries
SWIFT LA
5 HEATH FLATS
6 MEADE CT
CONNAUGHT RD
CHURCH RD
ST ANNES GLADE
WELLESLEY CL
PINEWOOD GDNS
COLLEGE RIDE
HEYWOOD DR
HIGGS LA
LONDON RD
Bagshot Inf Sch
Connaught Jun Sch
Mast
Hotel
Penny Hill
GU15
JENKINS' HILL
Nurseries
Pine Ridge Inf Sch
LUPIN CL
Hammond's Pond
Lightwater Country Park
Sports Ctr
GU18
M3
A30
WYCHWOOD PL
BRACKNELL RD
SURBITON RD
KINGSTON RD
MITCHAM RD
SUTTON RD
ESHER RD
CARSHALTON RD
WALLINGTON RD
MAULTWAY N
Coll

145
120

A
B
C
D
E
F
8
7
65
6
5
64
4
3
63
2
1
62
92
93
94
Earlywood
SL5
Windsor Manor
King's Hill
Sunning Ho
Windlesham Hall
Windlemere
Windlesham Hall Farm
Windlesham Moor
Merrywood
Lennoxwood
High Chimneys
Ribs Down
The Windmill (PH)
Erl Wood Manor
Nursery
Allerton Hill
Camus
Ribsden Hall
Wayside Cotts
PH
Hatton Hill
Windlesham Village Inf Sch
Woodcote House Sch
Hall Grove Sch
GU20
Mast
Recn Gd
Windlesham
Heathpark Wood
The Half Moon (PH)
Birch Hall
WC Lee's Resthouses
Oak Wood
Ashleigh Farm
Windlesham Park
GU19
Caravan Site
Twelve Oaks
South Farm
Windlesham Arboretum
Old House Farm
Windle Brook
Broadway Green Farm Ind Est
GU24
Halebourne Copse
Scutley La
Lee Lane Farm
Manor Farm Wood
Cemy
Sch
Rectory Farm
GU18
Liby
Sewage Works
The Willows
Hale Bourne
A30
London Rd
B3020
Sunninghill Rd
Bagshot Rd
Coronation Rd
Woodhall La
Westwood Rd
B386
School Rd
Kennel La
Updown Hill
Chertsey Rd
Church Rd
New Rd
Woodlands La
M3
A322
Guildford Rd
South Farm La
Hammond Way
Oldhouse La
Broadway Rd
Hook Mill La
Rye Gr
Burnt Pollard La
Surrey Street Atlas
M3 London (A316)

145
153

127
148

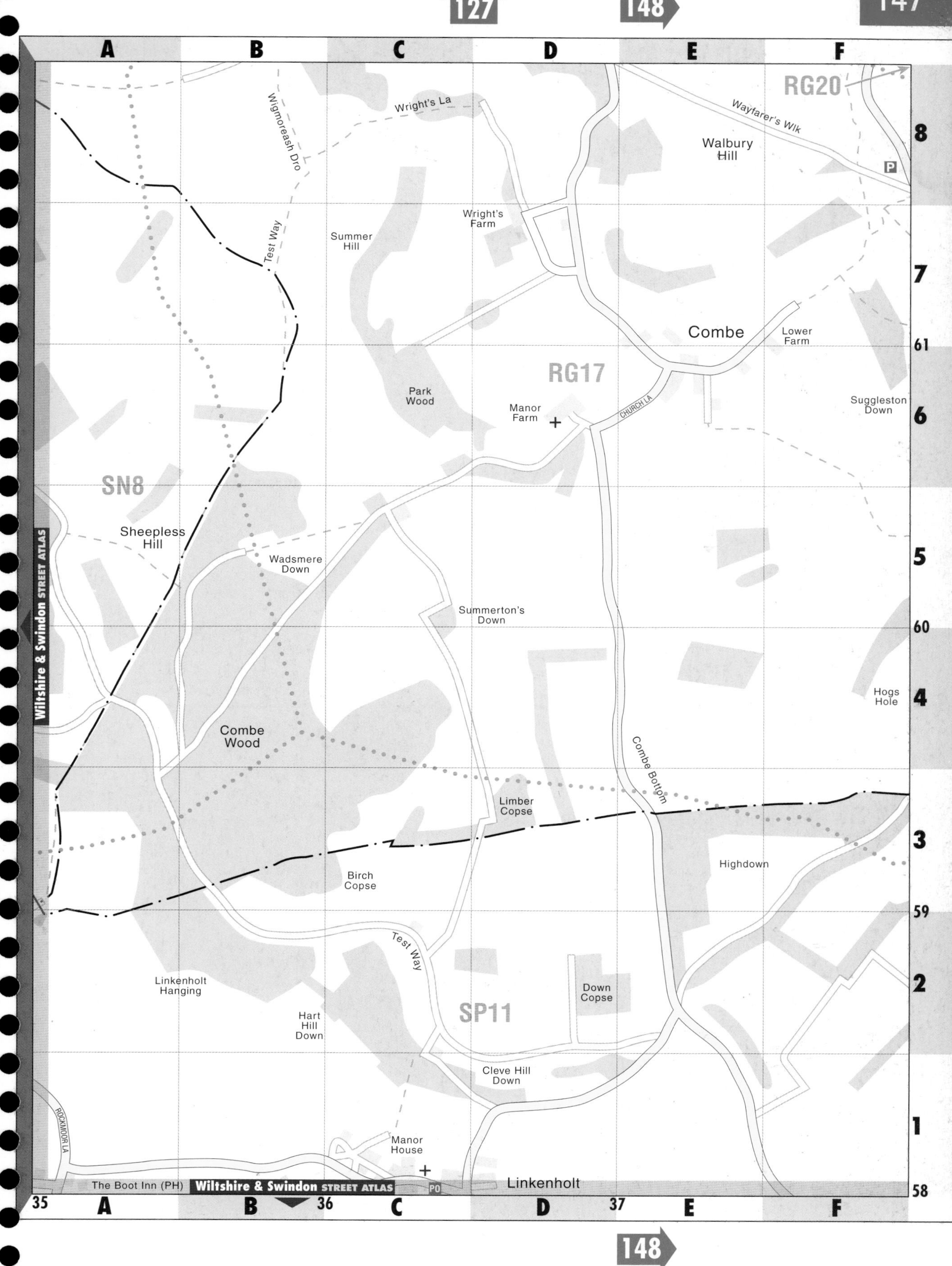
A
B
C
D
E
F
RG20
Wright's La
Wayfarer's Wlk
Wigmoreash Dro
Walbury Hill
8
Wright's Farm
Summer Hill
Test Way
7
Combe
Lower Farm
61
RG17
Park Wood
Manor Farm
CHURCH LA
Suggleston Down
6
SN8
Sheepless Hill
Wadsmere Down
5
Summerton's Down
60
Hogs Hole
4
Combe Wood
Combe Bottom
Limber Copse
3
Highdown
Birch Copse
59
Test Way
Linkenholt Hanging
2
Down Copse
Hart Hill Down
SP11
Cleve Hill Down
1
ROCKMOOR LA
Manor House
The Boot Inn (PH)
Wiltshire & Swindon STREET ATLAS
PO
Linkenholt
58
35
36
37
Wiltshire & Swindon STREET ATLAS

148

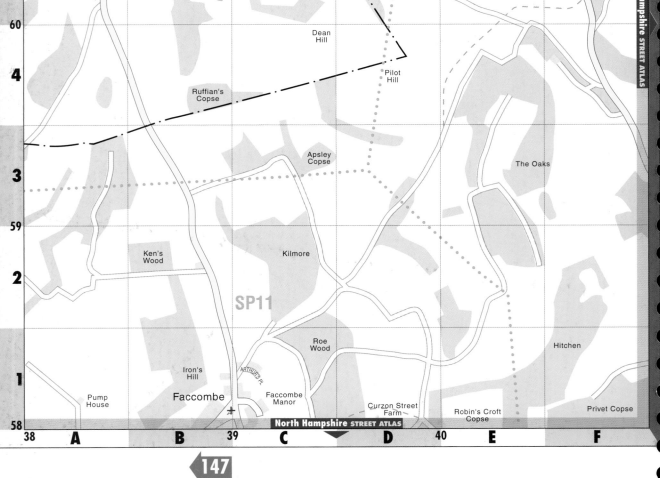

A   B   C   D   E   F

8

West Woodhay
Down

Park
Copse

Rectory
Farm

East
Woodhay

7

Sandpits
Down

Church
Farm

61

6

Combe
Hill

Rabbit Pit
Farm

RG20

RG17

Mast

Eastwick

Lower Eastwick
Copse

Upper Eastwick
Copse

Wayfarer's Wlk

5

60

Dean
Hill

4

Ruffian's
Copse

Pilot
Hill

The Oaks

Apsley
Copse

3

59

Ken's
Wood

Kilmore

2

SP11

Roe
Wood

Hitchen

Iron's
Hill

ARTHUR'S PL

1

Pump
House

Faccombe

Faccombe
Manor

Curzon Street
Farm

Robin's Croft
Copse

Privet Copse

58

38   A   B   39   C   D   40   E   F

North Hampshire STREET ATLAS

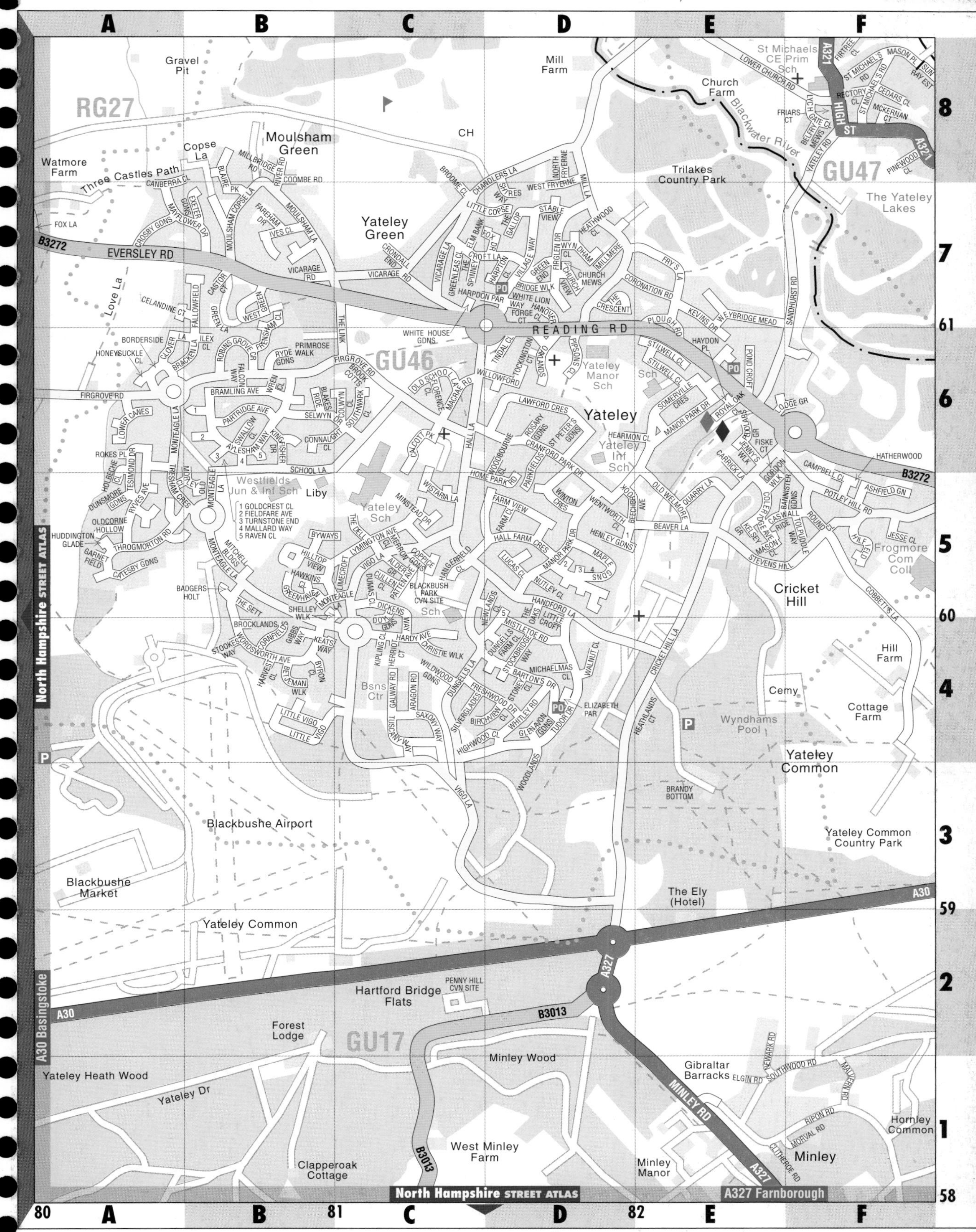

D5
1 DENHAM DR
2 LOWER MOOR
3 BARNFIELD
4 HOLLY ACRE
5 BROCKENHURST DR

D8
1 MULBERRY CL
2 MAY CL
3 SHRIVENHAM CL
4 CENTURION CL
5 CHAFFINCH CL
6 TARBAT CT
7 ROCKFIELD WAY
8 BALINTORE CT

Sandhurst Sch
College Town
Rifle Ranges
College Town Jun & Inf Schs
Richmond Academy
Royal Military Academy
Old College Sports Gd
GU15
Government House

Sandhurst
GU47
Uplands Prim Sch
Sewage Works
Darby Green
Frogmore
GU46
Clark's Farm
Potley Hill Prim Sch
Frogmore Com Coll
Heathcroft
Kingfisher Par
Frogmore Jun & Infs Schs
Blackwater
The Meadows (Superstores)
The Meadows Bsns Pk
White Hart Ind Est

Leafy Oak Farm
GU17
Hayward's Cottage
Yateley Common Country Park
Starve Acre

Hawley Garden Cotts
Henry Randell's Almshouses
Hawley Prim Sch
Hawley
Hawley Park
Cranberry Wlk
Kendall Ct Bsns Pk

Hornley Common
Hawley Hill
Hawley Common
Hawley Park Farm
Hawley Place Sch
Cypress Hill
FARNBOROUGH
GU14
Fernhill Prim Sch
Fernhill Sch

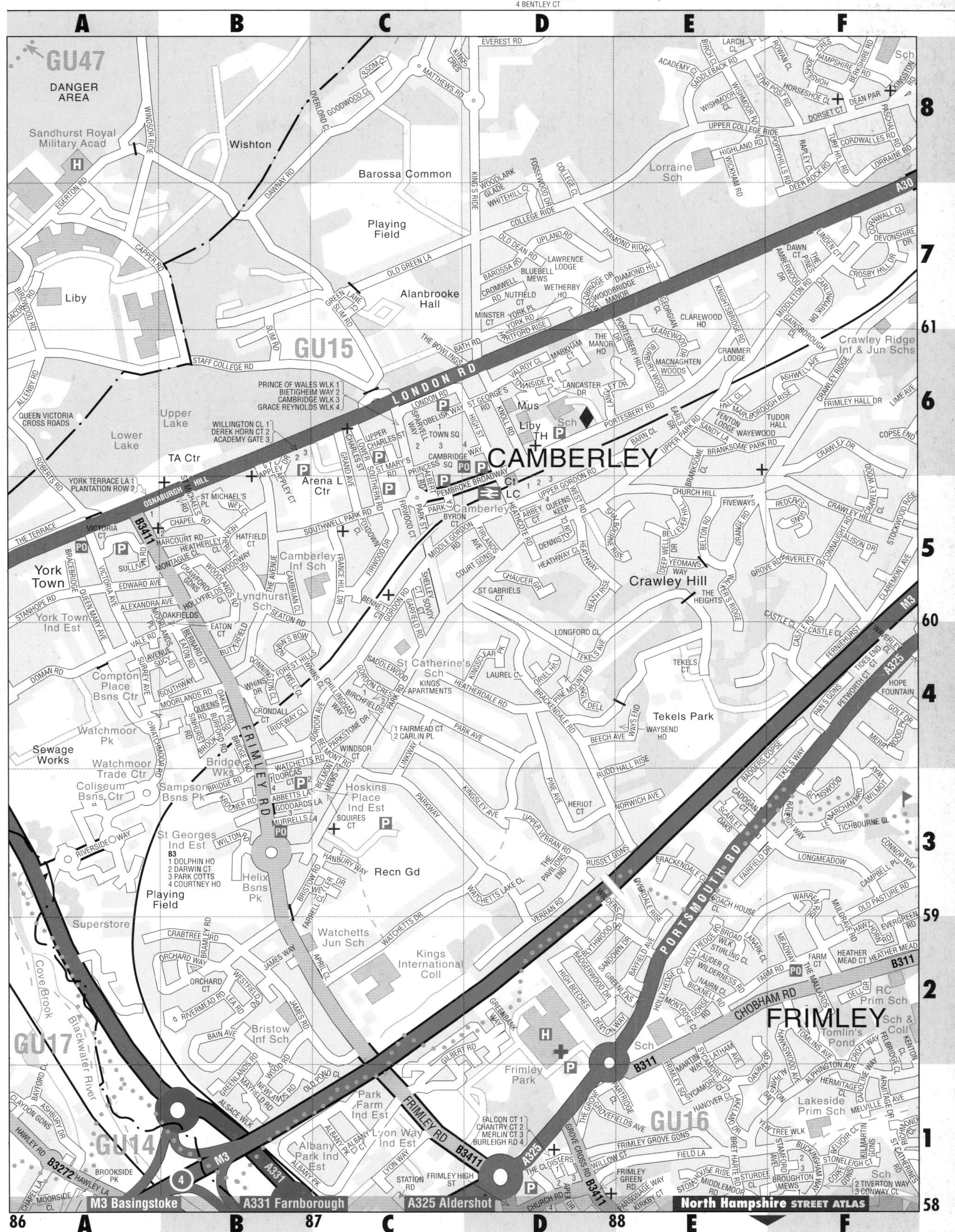

144

D5
1 CAMBERLEY TOWERS
2 KATHERINE CT
3 STRATHMORE CT
4 BENTLEY CT

152

F1
1 TINTAGEL DR

North Hampshire STREET ATLAS

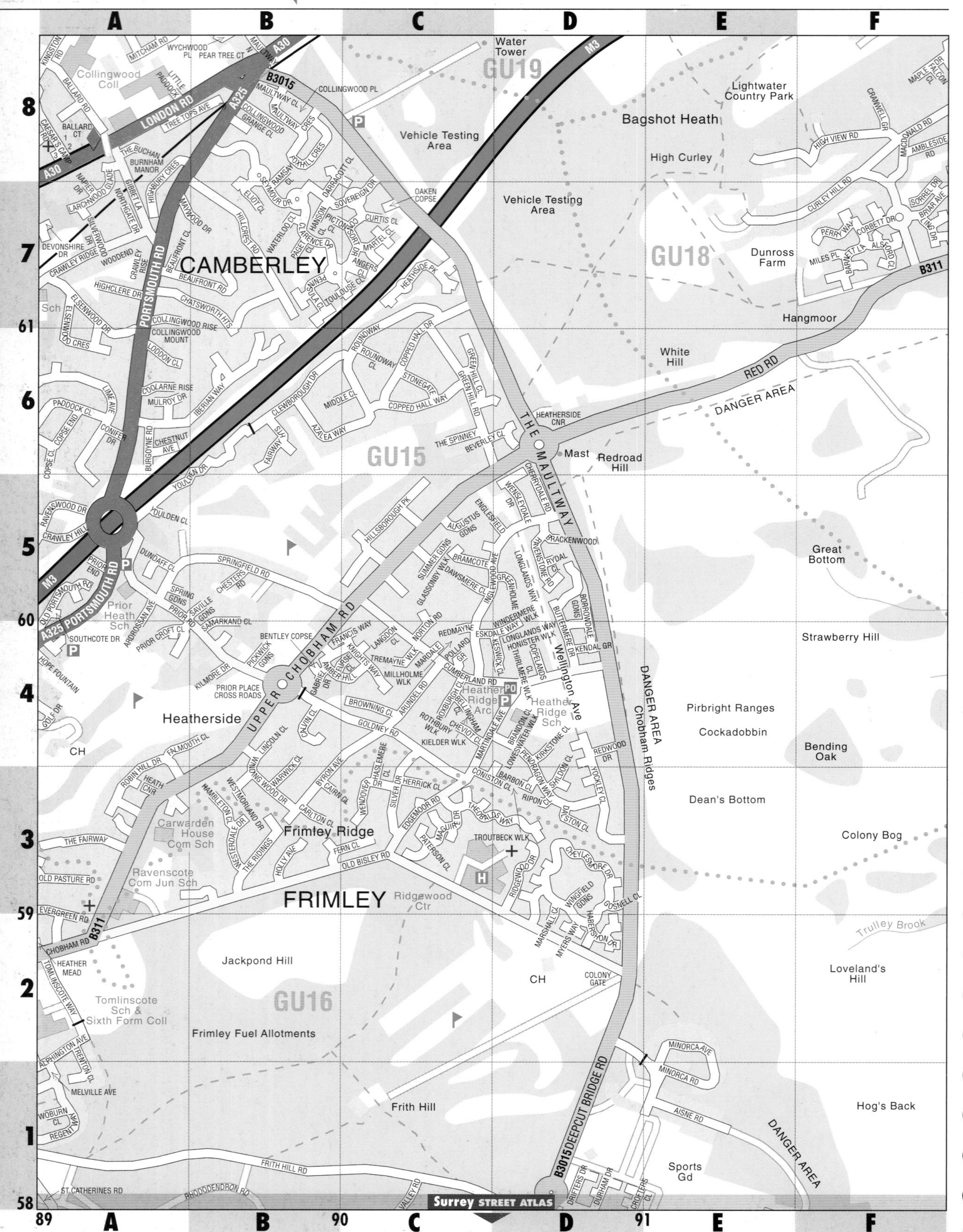
CAMBERLEY
FRIMLEY
Heatherside
Frimley Ridge
Bagshot Heath
Lightwater Country Park
High Curley
Vehicle Testing Area
Water Tower
GU19
GU18
GU15
GU16
Dunross Farm
Hangmoor
White Hill
Redroad Hill
Mast
Great Bottom
Strawberry Hill
Pirbright Ranges
Cockadobbin
Bending Oak
Dean's Bottom
Colony Bog
Loveland's Hill
Trulley Brook
Hog's Back
Sports Gd
Frith Hill
Frimley Fuel Allotments
Jackpond Hill
Tomlinscote Sch & Sixth Form Coll
Ravenscote Com Jun Sch
Carwarden House Com Sch
Ridgewood Ctr
Heather Ridge Arc
Heather Ridge Sch
Prior Heath Sch
Collingwood Coll
PORTSMOUTH RD
UPPER CHOBHAM RD
THE MAULTWAY
DEEPCUT BRIDGE RD
RED RD
LONDON RD
DANGER AREA
Chobham Ridges
Wellington Ave
Surrey STREET ATLAS

146

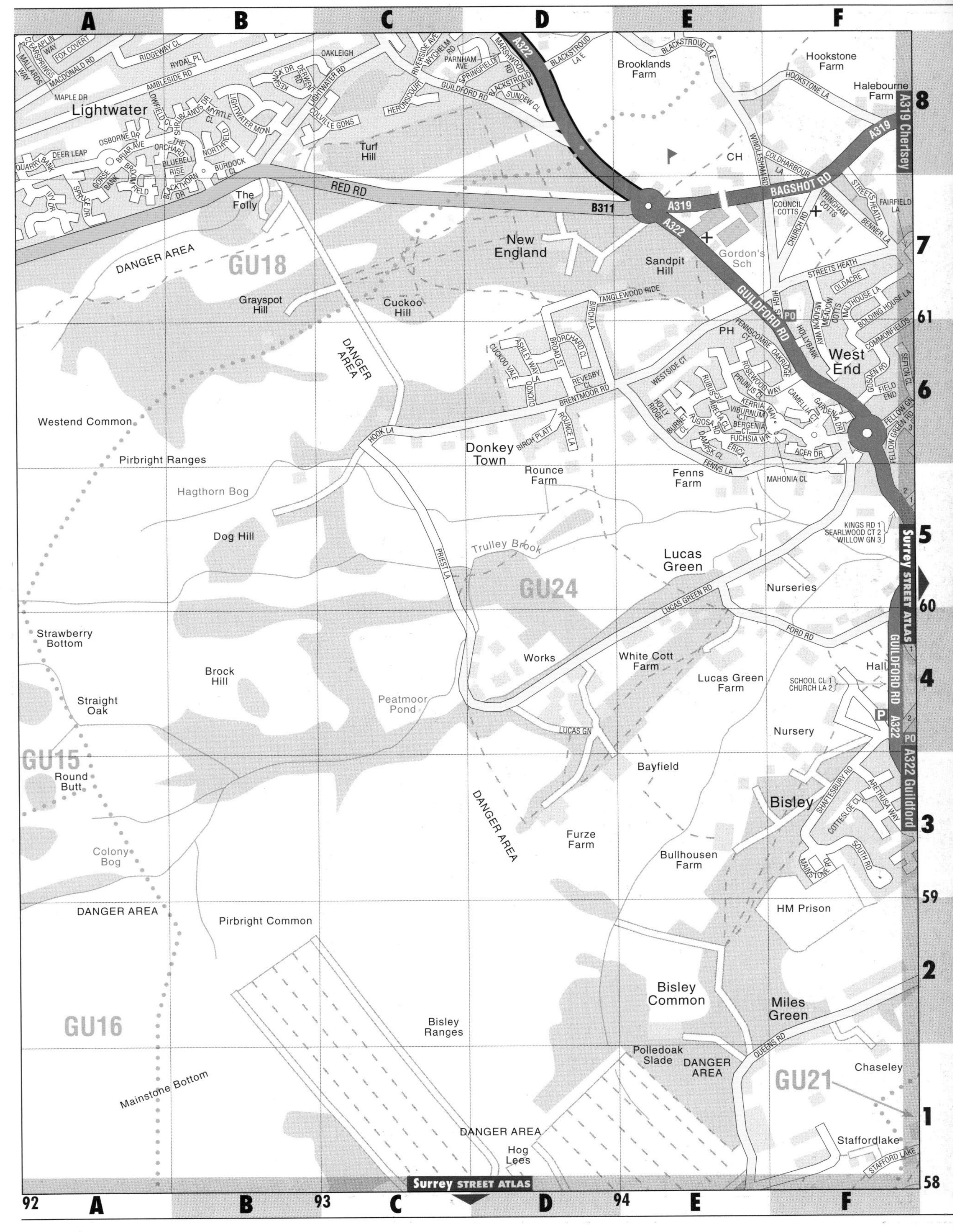
A
B
C
D
E
F
Lightwater
Turf Hill
Brooklands Farm
Hookstone Farm
Halebourne Farm
A319 Chertsey
A322
A319
RED RD
B311
BAGSHOT RD
The Folly
New England
Sandpit Hill
Gordon's Sch
DANGER AREA
GU18
Grayspot Hill
Cuckoo Hill
GUILDFORD RD
West End
DANGER AREA
Westend Common
Pirbright Ranges
Donkey Town
Rounce Farm
Fenns Farm
Hagthorn Bog
Dog Hill
Trulley Brook
Lucas Green
GU24
Nurseries
Surrey STREET ATLAS
Strawberry Bottom
Brock Hill
Works
White Cott Farm
Lucas Green Farm
Straight Oak
Peatmoor Pond
Nursery
GU15
Round Butt
Bayfield
Bisley
DANGER AREA
Furze Farm
Bullhousen Farm
Colony Bog
HM Prison
DANGER AREA
Pirbright Common
A322 Guildford
GU16
Bisley Common
Miles Green
Bisley Ranges
Polledoak Slade
DANGER AREA
Chaseley
GU21
Mainstone Bottom
DANGER AREA
Hog Lees
Staffordlake
8
7
61
6
5
60
4
3
59
2
1
58

Index

Church Rd 🔢 Beckenham BR2.........**53** C6

Place name	**Location number**	**Locality, town or village**	**Postcode district**	**Page and grid square**
May be abbreviated on the map	Present when a number indicates the place's position in a crowded area of mapping	Shown when more than one place has the same name	District for the indexed place	Page number and grid reference for the standard mapping

Public and commercial buildings are highlighted in magenta   **Places of interest** are highlighted in blue with a star★

Abbreviations used in the index

Acad	Academy	Comm	Common	Gd	Ground	L	Leisure	Prom	Promenade
App	Approach	Cott	Cottage	Gdn	Garden	La	Lane	Rd	Road
Arc	Arcade	Cres	Crescent	Gn	Green	Liby	Library	Recn	Recreation
Ave	Avenue	Cswy	Causeway	Gr	Grove	Mdw	Meadow	Ret	Retail
Bglw	Bungalow	Ct	Court	H	Hall	Meml	Memorial	Sh	Shopping
Bldg	Building	Ctr	Centre	Ho	House	Mkt	Market	Sq	Square
Bsns, Bus	Business	Ctry	Country	Hospl	Hospital	Mus	Museum	St	Street
Bvd	Boulevard	Cty	County	HQ	Headquarters	Orch	Orchard	Sta	Station
Cath	Cathedral	Dr	Drive	Hts	Heights	Pal	Palace	Terr	Terrace
Cir	Circus	Dro	Drove	Ind	Industrial	Par	Parade	TH	Town Hall
Cl	Close	Ed	Education	Inst	Institute	Pas	Passage	Univ	University
Cnr	Corner	Emb	Embankment	Int	International	Pk	Park	Wk, Wlk	Walk
Coll	College	Est	Estate	Intc	Interchange	Pl	Place	Wr	Water
Com	Community	Ex	Exhibition	Junc	Junction	Prec	Precinct	Yd	Yard

Index of localities, towns and villages

A

Abbotsbrook	.2	F3
Aldermaston	.135	A7
Aldermaston Wharf	.109	C3
Aldworth	.32	F3
Altmore	.38	E4
Arborfield	.114	C4
Arborfield Cross	.114	F2
Arborfield Garrison	.141	A7
Ascot	.120	A6
Ashampstead	.54	A6
Ashford	.97	F2
Ashford Common	.98	D2
Ashford Hill	.133	E1
Ashmore Green	.106	B8
Aston	.16	C5
Aston Tirrold	.12	E8
Avington	.101	E5

B

Bagnor	.104	C7
Bagshot	.145	D3
Ball Hill	.129	C3
Barkham	.115	C2
Beech Hill	.138	D5

Beedon	.51	D7
Beenham	.108	E6
Beenham Stocks	.109	A7
Binfield	.117	C8
Binfield	.90	D2
Birch Hill	.118	C2
Bisham	.18	E7
Bishopsgate	.94	F4
Bishops Green	.132	A3
Bisley	.153	F3
Blacknest	.121	A6
Blackwater	.150	D5
Blewbury	.12	B8
Borough Marsh	.61	A8
Bourne End	.3	B2
Boveney	.66	C8
Boxford	.104	C6
Boxford	.76	D3
Boyn Hill	.39	D6
Bracknell	.118	D6
Bradfield	.82	D5
Brands Hill	.69	A8
Bray	.40	D3
Bray Wick	.40	A4
Braywoodside	.64	C3
Brightwalton	.28	E3
Brightwalton Green	.28	D2
Brimpton	.133	F6
Broadmoor Estate	.143	D4
Brookside	.92	F2

Broomhall	.121	B2
Bucklebury	.80	E2
Bullbrook	.118	E7
Burchett's Green	.38	C8
Burghfield	.111	C6
Burghfield Common	.110	E2
Burnham	.21	C3
Burnt Hill	.54	B1
Burroughs Grove	.1	F7
Bury's Bank	.131	E7

C

Calcot	.84	B3
Calcot Row	.84	D5
Camberley	.151	D6
Catmore	.29	C5
Caversham	.59	D4
Caversham Heights	.58	F3
Caversham Park	.59	C5
Chaddleworth	.49	B8
Chalvey	.42	C3
Chapel Row	.108	C8
Charlton	.125	D7
Charvil	.61	A5
Chattern Hill	.98	B4
Chavey Down	.119	A8
Chazey Heath	.58	C7

Cheapside	.120	E7
Chertsey	.124	B2
Chieveley	.51	D1
Chilton	.10	E8
Chilton Foliat	.73	A2
Cholsey	.14	A8
Churchend	.84	F6
Cippenham	.41	F4
Cleeve	.34	D7
Clewer New Town	.67	A5
Clewer Village	.67	A7
Cockpole Green	.36	F8
Cold Ash	.106	D7
Cold Harbour	.38	A3
College Town	.150	E8
Colnbrook	.69	D7
Colthrop	.107	B2
Combe	.147	E7
Compton	.31	E4
Cookham	.20	B7
Cookham Dean	.19	B7
Cookham Rise	.19	E6
Cores End	.3	C4
Cox Green	.39	C3
Cranbourne	.93	B6
Crawley Hill	.151	E5
Crazies Hill	.36	F6
Cricket Hill	.149	F6
Crockham Heath	.129	F6
Crooked Soley	.72	E6

Crookham	.133	B5
Crown Wood	.118	D3
Crowthorne	.143	D5
Curridge	.78	D4

D

Darby Green	.150	B6
Datchet	.68	C6
Dedworth	.66	E6
Donkey Town	.153	D6
Donnington	.104	E7
Dorney	.41	C3
Dorney Reach	.40	F3
Dowlesgreen	.116	E8
Downend	.51	B3
Dunsden Green	.59	F7

E

Earley	.87	B5
East Bedfont	.98	E7
East Burnham	.22	A4
Eastbury	.46	F7
East Fields	.105	B2
East Garston	.47	D6

Easthampstead 118 B5
Eastheath 116 B3
East Ilsley 30 F6
Easton 76 C5
East Woodhay 148 B1
Eddington 100 E7
Egham 96 A4
Egham Hythe 96 E2
Egham Wick 95 A1
Egypt 22 B8
Egypt 50 A5
Elcot 102 D8
Eling 52 E3
Emmbrook 115 F8
Emmer Green 59 B6
Enborne Row 130 B4
Englefield 83 B5
Englefield Green 95 B1
Eton 67 C8
Eversley 141 B1

F

Faccombe 148 B1
Farley Castle 140 C7
Farley Hill 140 D6
Farnborough 150 E1
Farnborough 28 F8
Farnham Common 22 D6
Farnham Park 22 C4
Farnham Royal 22 C3
Fawley Berkshire 27 C7
Fawley Buckinghamshire . . .15 C8
Feltham 98 E6
Felthamhill 98 F3
Fern 2 E5
Fifield 65 D6
Finchampstead 141 E2
Fishery 40 B6
Flackwell Heath 3 A7
Forest Estate 95 A2
Forest Park 118 E3
Forty Green 1 A1
Frilsham 80 D6
Frimley 151 F2
Frimley Ridge 152 B3
Frogmore 150 C4
Froxfield 99 A5
Fulmer 23 C8
Furze Platt 19 C2

G

Gardeners Green 116 E2
George Green 43 E7
Goddard's Green 111 D2
Gore End 129 B7
Goring 34 D6
Grazeley 112 D2
Great Hollands 117 F3
Great Lea Common 113 A5
Great Shefford 48 B3
Greenham 131 C8

H

Ham 126 C2
Hambleden 16 D8
Ham Marsh 105 C3
Hampstead Norreys 52 F5
Hamstead Marshall 129 B7
Hanworth 118 A2
Hare Hatch 62 B8
Harlington 71 C8
Harmans Water 118 D5
Harmondsworth 70 E8
Harpesford 122 C3
Harpsden 35 D6
Hart's Hill 107 A5
Hatton 71 E7
Hatton Hill 146 C5
Hawley 150 E4
Headley 132 D2
Head's Hill 132 B4
Heath End 134 F1
Heatherside 152 B4
Heathlands 142 E8
Hedsor 3 F3
Henley-on-Thames 15 C1
Hermitage 79 B7
Highway 39 B7
Hillgreen 50 C5
Hoe Benham 102 F8
Hollingsworth 52 E5
Holloway 38 C5
Holly Cross 37 A6
Holme Green 116 F3
Holtwood 129 B5

Holyport 65 A7
Horncastle 84 E5
Horton 69 A4
Hungerford 100 E4
Hungerford Twyford 62 E2
Hungerford Newtown 74 A3
Hurley 17 F4
Hurst 88 F6
Hythe End 96 B6

I

Inkpen 127 D5
Iver 44 F7

K

Kiff Green 108 C6
Kiln Green 37 D1
Kintbury 102 A1
Knowle Green 97 A3
Knowle Hill 122 C2
Knowl Hill 37 E4

L

Lake End 41 B4
Laleham 124 C6
Lambourn 25 C2
Langley 44 A3
Larks Hill 91 C2
Leckhampstead 49 F5
Lent Rise 41 A8
Letcombe Bassett 6 E7
Lightwater 153 A8
Lilley 29 A4
Limmerhill 115 E5
Linkenholt 147 D1
Little Heath 84 A8
Little Hungerford 79 C8
Little Marlow 2 D5
Little Sandhurst 143 B1
Littlestead Green 59 E7
Littleton 125 A6
Littleton Common 98 D1
Littlewick Green 38 B4
Longford 70 C6
Longfordmoor 70 A6
Love Green 44 D8
Lower Assendon 15 A6
Lower Basildon 34 E2
Lower Caversham 59 D2
Lower Common 140 F1
Lower Earley 87 A1
Lower Feltham 98 E5
Lower Green 127 B5
Lower Halliford 125 D2
Lower Padworth 109 D5
Lower Shiplake 36 A4
Lucas Green 153 E5
Lyne 123 B1

M

Maidenhead 39 F4
Maidenhead Court 20 C4
Maiden's Green 92 B5
Malpas 83 E6
Mapledurham 57 E6
Marlow 1 B2
Marlow Bottom 1 C6
Marsh Benham 103 D4
Martin's Heron 118 F6
Matthewsgreen 116 A8
Mays Green 35 B4
Medmenham 17 A5
Merryhill Green 88 D3
Middle Green 43 E5
Midgham 107 E3
Mile End 25 C6
Mill End 16 D7
Minley 149 F6
Moneyrow Green 65 A7
Mortimer 137 A5
Mortimer West End 136 D4
Moss End 91 C6
Moulsford 13 F4
Moulsham Green 149 B8

N

Newbury 104 B3
Newell Green 92 A1
Newtown Henley-on-Thames 35 F8

Newtown Newbury 131 B4
New Town Pangbourne 55 D4
New Town Reading 86 F7
North Ascot 119 F8
North Street 83 D5
North Sydmonton 131 F1
North Town 19 F2
Nuptown 91 E7

O

Oakley Green 66 B5
Oare 79 B8
Oatlands Park 125 E1
Old Warren 135 E5
Old Windsor 95 A8
Orchardville 21 B1
Owlsmoor 143 E1

P

Padworth 109 F1
Paley Street 64 C5
Pamber Heath 135 F1
Pangbourne 56 D6
Parsonage Green 32 E4
Peasemore 50 C7
Pingewood 112 C7
Pinkneys Green 19 A1
Play Hatch 60 A5
Pooley Green 96 C2
Popeswood 117 D8
Poughley 73 F8
Poundgreen 112 C3
Poyle 69 E6
Priestwood 118 A8
Punt Hill 39 C6
Purley on Thames 57 B6
Purton 51 D8

Q

Quick's Green 54 D5

R

Reading 86 B4
Remenham 16 A5
Remenham Hill 16 C2
Ripley Springs 95 E2
Riseley 139 C3
Rotten Row 81 F3
Ruscombe 61 F6
Ryeish Green 113 C4

S

St Ann's Heath 122 E5
Sandford Park 88 B8
Sandhurst 150 C7
Sanham Green 100 D4
Schoolgreen 113 F4
Shaw 105 C5
Sheepridge 2 E7
Shefford Woodlands 74 D7
Shepperton 125 C3
Shepperton Green 125 B5
Shinfield 113 E4
Shiplake 35 F2
Shiplake Row 35 C2
Shreding Green 44 C7
Shrubs Hill 121 C3
Silchester 136 C1
Sindlesham 115 A8
Skinners Green 130 B8
Slough 42 D5
Sonning 60 E4
Sonning Eye 60 C5
South Ascot 120 B4
Southcote 85 C4
Southend 82 A2
South Fawley 27 C5
South Stoke 14 C4
Speen 104 C5
Spencers Wood 113 A1
Staines 96 B6
Stanford Dingley 81 C4
Stanford End 138 F3
Stanmore 30 B2
Stanwell 97 C7
Stanwell Moor 70 A1
Stanwell Place 70 C1
Stockcross 103 E6
Stoke Poges 22 F3

Straight Soley 73 A5
Stratfield Mortimer 137 D5
Streatley 34 A7
Stroude 122 F7
Stroud Green 105 B1
Stubbles 54 C6
Stud Green 64 E7
Sulham 56 E2
Sulhamstead 110 C6
Sulhamstead Abbots 110 F4
Sulhamstead Bannister
   Upper End 110 D5
Sunbury 125 F6
Sunbury Common 98 E1
Sunningdale 121 B4
Sunninghill 120 C4
Sunnymeads 68 E4
Sutton 44 C1
Swallowfield 139 C6

T

Tadley 135 B1
Taplow 20 E1
Temple 18 C5
Thatcham 106 E5
Theale 83 D4
The Holt 37 B1
The Mount 86 C5
The Village 94 A5
Thorpe 123 C6
Thorpe Green 123 A5
Thorpe Lea 96 B1
Three Mile Cross 113 B4
Tidmarsh 56 C2
Tilehurst 57 E1
Titcomb 127 F7
Tittle Row 39 A5
Tokers Green 58 D8
Touchen-end 64 D6
Trapshill 127 E4
Trash Green 111 B7
Trumps Green 122 D3
Twyford 61 C5

U

Ufton Green 110 B5
Ufton Nervet 110 D3
Upper Basildon 55 A5
Upper Bucklebury 107 C6
Upper Green 127 D3
Upper Halliford 125 D5
Upper Lambourn 24 F6
Upper Wargrove 36 F2
Upper Woolhampton 108 C4
Upton 43 B3
Upton Lea 43 C6

V

Virginia Water 122 C6

W

Waltham St Lawrence . . .62 F6
Warfield 91 E5
Wargrave 36 D1
Warren Row 37 C6
Wash Water 130 D3
Wasing 134 D5
Water Oakley 65 F8
Welford 76 A7
Well End 2 F5
Wellhouse 79 E6
Wentworth 121 F3
West Bedfont 97 F8
West End Chobham 153 F6
West End Twyford 62 E3
West Fields 104 E2
West Ilsley 10 B1
Weston 75 D8
Westridge Green 33 B4
West Woodhay 128 C3
Wexham Street 23 C4
Whistley Green 61 E1
Whitchurch-on-Thames . .56 C7
Whitegrove 91 E7
Whitehouse Green 110 F6
Whiteknights 86 E5
White Waltham 63 E7
Whitley 86 C1
Whitley Wood 113 C4
Wickham 75 C4
Wickham Heath 103 B8
Wick Hill Bracknell 118 C8

Wick Hill Wokingham . . .142 A6
Wildridings 118 A5
Windlesham 146 C4
Windsor 67 E6
Winkfield 92 D5
Winkfield Row 92 B2
Winnersh 88 B3
Winterbourne 77 C5
Wokingham 116 B5
Wooburn 3 D4
Wooburn Green 3 F7
Wooburn Moor 3 F8
Woodlands Park 38 E2
Woodlands St Mary 46 E2
Woodley 87 D7
Woodley Green 88 A7
Woodside 93 C4
Wooley Green 38 D5
Woolhampton 108 D2
Woose Hill 115 F6
World's End 51 D6
Wraysbury 68 E1

Y

Yateley 149 D6
Yateley Green 149 C7
Yattendon 53 F1
York Town 151 A5

A

Abattoirs Rd RG1 86 A8
Abberbury Cl RG14 104 E6
Abbetts La GU15 151 B3
Abbey Cl Bracknell RG12 118 D4
  Newbury RG14 131 A8
  Slough SL1 41 E6
  Wokingham RG40 116 C7
Abbey Cotts SL7 17 B4
Abbey Ct
  Camberley GU15 151 D5
  Chertsey KT16 124 B2
  Laleham TW18 124 C5
Abbey Dr TW18 124 C5
Abbey Gdns KT16 124 A3
Abbey Gn KT16 124 A3
Abbey Jun Sch RG1 86 C5
Abbey Lodge 6 TW18 96 F3
Abbey Mead SL8 2 F5
Abbey Mews TW18 124 C5
Abbey Pk RG7 110 F3
Abbey Rd Bourne End SL8 2 F5
  Chertsey KT16 124 B2
  Lower Halliford TW17 125 A1
  Virginia Water GU25 122 D5
Abbey River Cotts KT16 124 C3
Abbey Sq RG1 86 B7
Abbey St RG1 86 B7
Abbey Way SL7 18 D6
Abbey Wood SL5 121 A2
Abbeyfields Pk KT16 124 C2
Abbot Cl TW18 97 D1
Abbot's Wlk Reading RG1 86 B8
  Windsor SL4 66 E5
Abbots Dr GU25 122 C5
Abbots Mead OX10 14 A8
Abbots Rd
  Burghfield Common RG7 110 F2
  Newbury RG14 105 A1
Abbots Way KT16 123 F2
Abbotsbury RG12 117 F4
Abbotsbury Ct 3 RG30 85 B8
Abbotsbury Ho 4 RG2 113 C8
Abbotsmead Pl RG4 59 A2
Abbotts Way SL1 41 D6
Abelia Cl GU24 153 E6
Abell Gdns SL6 19 B1
Aberaman RG4 58 F6
Aberdeen Ave SL1 42 A6
Aberford Cl RG30 85 C7
Abex Rd RG14 105 C3
Abingdon Cl RG12 118 E4
Abingdon Dr RG4 59 C6
Abingdon Rd
  East Ilsley RG20 30 E7
  Sandhurst GU47 143 C1
Abingdon Wlk SL6 19 E3
Abington SL3 69 D7
Abney Court Dr SL8 3 A2
Abrahams Rd RG9 15 C3
Acacia RG9 15 D2
Acacia Ave
  Littleton TW17 125 A4
  Sandhurst GU47 143 D1
  Wraysbury TW19 68 E3
Acacia Ct RG12 118 B6
Acacia Mews UB7 70 D8
Acacia Rd Reading RG1 86 C6
  Staines TW18 97 B3
Academy Cl GU15 151 E8
Academy Gate GU15 151 B6
Academy Pl GU47 150 E7
Accommodation La UB7 70 C8
Acer Cl RG42 119 A8
Acer Dr GU24 153 F6
Ackrells Mead GU47 142 F1
Acorn Cotts SN8 126 D3
Acorn Dr Thatcham RG18 106 D5
  Wokingham RG40 116 C7
Acorn Gr UB3 71 F7
Acorn Rd GU17 150 B5
Acorn Wlk RG31 84 C5
Acre Bsns Pk RG2 113 B8
Acre Pas SL4 67 D6
Acre Rd RG2 113 A8
Acre The SL7 1 F2
Action Ct TW15 125 C8
Adam Cl Slough SL1 42 A5
  Tadley RG26 134 E1
Adam Ct RG9 15 E2
Adams Way RG6 86 F2
Addington Cl SL4 67 A4
Addington Rd RG1 86 D6
Addington Specl Sch
  RG5 87 F6
Addiscombe Chase RG31 57 B3
Addiscombe Rd RG45 143 C4
Addison Cl SL0 44 E6
Addison Ct SL6 20 B1
Addison Rd RG1 59 A1
Adelaide Cl SL1 42 A4
Adelaide Rd Reading RG6 87 A6
  Staines TW15 97 D3
  Windsor SL4 67 F6
Adelaide Sq SL4 67 D5
Adelphi Gdns SL1 42 E4
Adey's Cl RG14 105 B1
Adkins Rd RG10 62 E7
Admirals Ct RG2 86 A5
Admiralty Way GU15 150 F4
Admoor La RG7 82 C1
Adrians Wlk SL2 42 F5
Adwell Dr RG6 87 D1
Adwell Sq RG9 15 D2
Adwood Ct RG19 106 E3
Agar Cres RG42 91 B1
Agars Pl SL3 68 A8
Agate Cl RG41 115 E7
Aggisters La RG41 115 C3
Agincourt SL5 120 C6
Agincourt Cl RG41 115 E6
Agricola Way RG19 106 F2
Ainsdale Cres RG30 85 A4
Aintree RG17 25 B2
Aintree Cl Newbury RG14 105 C1
  Poyle SL3 69 E6
Air Forces Meml* TW20 95 D4
Airport Gate Bsns Ctr
  UB7 71 A7
Airport Way TW19 70 A3
Aisne Rd GU16 152 E1
Ajax Ave SL1 42 B6
Alan Pl RG30 85 A5
Alan Way SL3 43 E7
Alandale Cl RG2 113 D8
Albain Cres TW15 97 E6
Albany Ct GU16 151 C1
Albany Park Dr RG41 88 A3
Albany Park Ind Est
  GU15 151 C1
Albany Pk Frimley GU15 151 C1
  Poyle SL3 69 D7
Albany Pl TW20 96 B4
Albany Rd
  Old Windsor SL4 68 A2
  Reading RG30 85 D7
  Windsor SL4 67 D5
Alben Rd RG42 90 C3
Albert Ave KT16 124 A6
Albert Cl 3 SL1 42 F3
Albert Dr 1 TW18 97 A3
Albert Pl SL4 42 A1
Albert Rd Ashford TW15 97 F3
  Bagshot GU19 145 E1
  Bracknell RG42 118 B8
  Camberley GU15 151 C5
  Caversham RG4 58 F4
  Crowthorne RG45 143 B5
  Englefield Green TW20 95 D2
  Henley-On-T RG9 15 E1
  1 Newbury RG14 105 A3
  Windsor SL4 67 E3
  Wokingham RG40 116 B5
Albert St Maidenhead SL6 39 F7
  Slough SL1 42 F3
  Windsor SL4 67 B6
Albert Wlk RG45 143 B5
Albion SL3 44 B1
Albion Cl SL2 43 A5
Albion Cotts SL6 19 C7
Albion Pl 2 SL4 67 A5
Albion Rd GU47 150 B8
Albury Cl RG30 58 C1
Albury Ct TW15 98 D2
Albury Gdns RG31 84 E3
Albury Way RG19 131 F4
Alcot Cl RG45 143 B4
Aldborough Spur SL1 42 E7
Aldbourne Ave RG6 87 A4
Aldbourne Cl RG17 100 D5
Aldbourne Rd SL1 41 B8
Aldeburgh Cl RG4 59 C8
Aldebury Rd SL6 19 F2
Alden View SL4 66 D6
Aldenham Cl RG4 59 C6
Aldenham Terr RG12 118 C3
Alder Bridge Sch RG7 109 C3
Alder Cl
  Englefield Green TW20 95 E3
  Lower Earley RG6 87 D1
  Newbury RG14 105 D4
  Slough SL1 41 F5
Alder Ct RG12 118 B6
Alder Dr RG31 84 C6
Alder Field Cl RG7 83 F4
Alder Glade RG7 110 F3
Alder Gr GU46 149 C5
Alderbourne La SL3 23 E8
Alderbrook Cl RG45 142 E4
Alderbury Rd SL3 43 F4
Alderbury Rd W SL3 43 F4
Alderley Cl RG5 60 F1
Alderman Willey Cl
  RG41 116 B6
Aldermaston CE Prim Sch
  RG7 134 F7
Aldermaston Rd RG26 135 A2
Aldermaston Sta RG7 109 C3
Alderney Ct 13 RG1 86 D7
Alderney Gdns RG41 88 D2
Alders The RG18 106 D4
Alderside Wlk TW20 95 E3
Aldin Ave N SL1 43 A4
Aldin Ave S SL1 43 A4
Aldous Ho TW18 96 E4
Aldridge Pk RG42 92 B2
Aldridge Rd SL2 22 A1
Aldryington Prim Sch
  RG6 87 B4
Aldwick Dr SL6 39 D6
Aldworth Cl
  Bracknell RG12 118 A5
  Reading RG30 85 C5
Aldworth Gdns RG45 143 A5
Aldworth Rd
  Compton RG20 31 F4
  Upper Basildon RG8 55 A5
Aldwych Cotts RG14 104 F6
Aldwyn Ct TW20 95 B2
Alexander Ct 12 RG1 85 F7
Alexander Fst Sch SL4 66 C4
Alexander Rd
  Egham TW20 96 C3
  Thatcham RG19 106 E2
Alexander Wlk RG12 118 B4
Alexandra Ave GU15 151 A5
Alexandra Cl
  Ashford TW15 98 D1
  Staines TW18 97 D2
Alexandra Ct
  Ashford TW15 98 D2
  1 Windsor SL4 67 D5
  Wokingham RG40 116 C5
Alexandra Ho SL5 120 B6
Alexandra Rd
  Ashford TW15 98 E2
  Englefield Green TW20 95 C2
  Maidenhead SL6 39 D8
  Reading RG1 86 D6
  Slough SL1 42 D3
  Windsor SL4 67 D5
Alford Cl RG30 84 D8
Alfred Ct 3 SL8 3 B3
Alfred Davis Ct SL7 1 D3
Alfred Sutton Prim Sch
  RG1 86 F6
Alice Gough Meml Homes
  RG12 118 B6
Alice Ho TW18 97 A2
Alice La SL1 21 B1
Alison Cl RG7 110 F1
Alison Dr GU15 151 F5
All Hallows Rd RG4 59 D3
All Saints Ave SL6 39 D7
All Saints CE Inf Sch RG1 85 E7
All Saints CE Jun Sch
  SL6 39 C6
All Saints Cl RG40 116 C7
All Saints Cres GU14 150 E1
All Saints Ct RG1 85 E6
All Saints Rd GU18 146 C1
All Saints Rise RG42 91 E1
All Souls Cotts SL3 43 E8
All Souls' Rd SL5 120 A5
Allanson Rd SL7 1 F3
Allcot Cl TW14 98 F7
Allcroft Rd RG1 86 C5
Allenby Rd
  Maidenhead SL6 39 B7
  Sandhurst GU15 151 A6
Allendale Cl GU47 143 A2
Allendale Rd RG6 87 B3
Allerds Rd SL2 22 A4
Alleyns La SL6 19 D8
Allhusen Gdns SL3 23 E8
Alliance Ct TW15 98 C4
Allington Ave TW17 125 E6
Allington Ct SL2 42 F6
Allison Ct 2 RG1 85 F7
Allison Gdns RG8 57 C5
Allison Ho RG9 35 E8
Allkins Ct SL4 67 D5
Allnatt Ave RG41 88 C1
Allonby Cl RG6 87 D2
Allsmoor La RG12 118 F6
Allyn Cl TW18 96 F2
Alma Ct Burnham SL1 21 C2
  Eton SL4 41 F2
  Wokingham RG41 116 A5
Alma Rd Eton SL4 41 F2
  Windsor SL4 67 C5
Alma St RG30 85 C8
Almners Rd
  Chertsey KT16 123 C2
  Lyne KT16 123 B1
Almond Ave RG14 105 A5
Almond Cl
  Charlton TW17 125 C7
  Englefield Green TW20 95 B2
  Windsor SL4 67 B5
  Wokingham RG41 115 C4
Almond Dr Caversham RG4 59 F4
  Chieveley RG20 51 C5
  Thatcham RG18 106 D4
Almond Rd SL1 21 C2
Almons Way SL2 43 B8
Almshouses Eton SL4 67 D7
  Reading RG1 86 A7
  Sunbury TW16 125 F8
  Twyford RG10 61 D5
Almswood Rd RG26 135 A2
Alpha Ho 4 RG1 86 C6
Alpha St N 6 SL1 43 A4
Alpha St S SL1 42 F3
Alpha Way TW20 123 C8
Alphington Ave GU16 151 F1
Alphington Gn GU16 151 F1
Alphington Rd RG2 113 B8
Alpine Cl Ascot SL5 120 D3
  Maidenhead SL6 40 A6
Alpine St RG1 86 B6
Alsace Wlk GU15 151 B1
Alsford Cl GU18 152 F7
Alston Gdns SL6 39 E7
Alston Mews RG19 106 C2
Alston Wlk RG4 59 D2
Altmore SL6 38 E4
Alton Ct TW18 123 E8
Alton Ride GU17 150 C6
Altona Way SL1 42 B7
Altwood Bailey SL6 39 B5
Altwood Cl
  Maidenhead SL6 39 B5
  Slough SL1 41 E8
Altwood Dr SL6 39 B5
Altwood Rd SL6 39 B5
Altwood Sch SL6 39 B5
Alvista Ave SL6 41 B7
Alwyn Inf Sch SL6 39 C8
Alwyn Rd SL6 39 B8
Alwyns Cl KT16 124 A3
Alwyns La KT16 124 A3
Alyson Ct 2 SL6 19 F1
Amanda Ct Ashford TW15 97 F6
  Slough SL3 43 D3
Ambarrow Cres GU47 142 F1
Ambarrow La GU47 142 E2
Ambassador RG12 117 F4
Ambassador The SL5 121 B2
Amber Cl RG6 87 C4
Amber Ct 13 TW18 96 F3
Amber Hill GU15 152 B4
Amberley Cl RG14 104 F4
Amberley Ct SL6 20 C3
Amberley Dr RG10 61 D6
Amberley Pl 5 SL4 67 D6
Amberley Rd SL2 41 E8
Amberwood Dr GU15 151 F7
Amblecote Rd RG30 85 B7
Ambleside Cl RG5 87 E7
Ambleside Dr TW14 98 F7
Ambleside Rd GU18 153 B8
Ambleside Way TW20 96 B1
Ambrook Rd RG2 113 B8
Ambrose Pl RG1 85 F7
Ambury Rd RG8 32 E4
Amen Corner Bsns Pk
  RG12 117 D7
Amerden Cl SL6 40 D7
Amerden La SL6 40 D7
Amerden Priory Cvn Pk
  SL6 40 E4
Amerden Way SL1 42 A4
American Com Sch
  TW20 122 C7
American Magna Carta
  Meml* TW20 95 D6
Amersham Rd RG4 59 D2
Amethyst Cl RG41 115 D7
Amethyst La RG30 85 C6
Amherst Rd RG6 87 A6
Amhurst Mews RG6 87 A6
Amity Rd RG1 86 E7
Amity St RG1 86 E8
Ammanford RG4 58 F5
Amners Farm Rd RG30 112 A7
Ampere Rd RG14 105 B3
Anarth Ct KT13 125 E1
Ancaster Dr SL5 119 E8
Ancastle Gn RG9 15 D2
Anchor Ct SL6 19 F7
Anchorite Cl RG10 61 D5
Andermans SL4 66 D6
Anders Cnr RG42 117 F8
Anderson Ave RG6 87 A6
Anderson Cres RG2 114 E2
Anderson Dr TW15 98 C4
Anderson Pl GU19 145 E4
Andover Cl
  East Bedfont TW14 98 F7
  Reading RG31 57 D1
Andover Ct TW19 97 D8
Andover Dro RG20 130 B4
Andover Rd
  Blackwater GU17 150 C6
  Newbury RG14 130 D6
Andrew Cl RG40 116 E5
Andrews Cl RG7 83 E3
Andrews Rd RG6 87 B3
Andrews Reach SL8 3 A2
Andrews Way SL7 1 D8
Angel Ct RG14 104 F4
Angel Mead RG7 108 C2
Angel Pl RG42 90 C2
Angers Cl GU15 152 C7
Angle Field Rd RG4 59 C3
Anglers Way RG1 86 D7
Anglesey Cl TW15 98 A5
Angus Cl RG31 84 E4
Annadale RG18 79 C1
Anne Cl SL6 19 E2
Anneforde Pl RG42 91 A1
Anners Cl TW20 123 C6
Annesley Gdns RG41 88 C2
Annett Cl TW17 125 E5
Annie Brookes Cl TW18 96 D5
Ansculf Rd SL2 22 A2
Anslow Pl SL1 41 C8
Anson Cres RG2 113 D8
Anson Ct TW19 97 E8
Anson Wlk RG2 113 D8
Anstey Pl RG7 111 A3
Anstey Rd 16 RG1 85 F7
Anston Cl RG6 114 A8
Antares Cl RG41 115 F6
Anthian Cl RG5 88 B8
Anthony Wall RG42 118 F8
Anthony Way SL1 41 D6
Antrim Rd RG5 87 D6
Anvil Cl RG7 113 A1
Anvil Ct 4 Slough SL3 44 A2
  Thatcham RG18 106 D3
  Wokingham RG40 116 C5
Apex Dr GU16 151 D1
Aplin Way GU18 146 A1
Apollo Ho RG7 134 E2
Appelford Cl RG19 106 E2
Apple Cl Purley On T RG31 57 B4
  Wokingham RG41 115 F5
Apple Tree Cl RG14 130 E7
Apple Tree Way GU47 143 D1
Appleby End RG30 85 B7
Appleby Gdns TW14 98 F7
Applecroft SL6 39 C3
Appledore RG12 117 F3
Appleford Cl RG19 106 D2
Appleford Rd RG30 85 A5
Appleshaw Ct 1 RG31 84 D8
Appleton Ho 19 RG1 86 D7
Appletree La
  Shinfield RG7 113 B2
  Slough SL3 43 C3
Appletree Pl 4 RG42 118 A8
Appley Ct GU15 151 B6
Appley Dr GU15 151 B6
Approach Rd
  Ashford TW15 98 C2
  Taplow SL6 40 E7
April Cl GU15 151 C2
Apsey Ct RG42 90 E1
Apsley Cotts SL6 19 E7
Apsley Ho SL1 43 A4
Aquila Cl RG41 115 E6
Aragon Cl TW16 98 F1
Aragon Ct RG12 118 C5
Aragon Rd GU46 149 C4
Arbery Way RG2 140 E8
Arbor La RG41 88 B3
Arbor Mdws RG41 88 B3
Arborfield Cl SL1 42 E3
Arborfield Grange RG2 114 C4
Arborfield Rd RG2 113 F4
Arborfield, Newland &
  Barkham CE Jun Sch
  RG2 114 F2
Arbour Cl RG1 85 F5
Arbour Vale Sch SL2 43 A7
Arc The RG1 86 B7
Arcade Mews 10 RG14 105 A3
Arcade The Goring RG8 34 C6
  9 Newbury RG14 105 A3
Archangel Way RG18 106 F4
Archer Cl SL6 39 D8
Archway Rd RG4 59 A2
Arden Cl RG12 119 A7
Ardingly RG12 118 A4
Ardler Rd RG4 59 C2
Ardrossan Ave GU15 152 A5
Ardrossan Cl SL2 22 C1
Ardwell Cl RG45 142 E5
Arena The RG12 118 A7
Arenal Dr RG45 143 C3
Arethusa Way GU24 153 F3
Argent Cl TW20 96 C2
Argent Terr GU47 150 E8
Argonaut Pk SL3 69 F6
Argosy Gdns TW18 96 F2
Argosy La TW19 97 D8
Argyle Rd Newbury RG14 104 F2
  Reading RG1 85 E7
Argyle St RG1 85 E7
Argyll Ave SL1 42 A6
Aries Ho HP10 3 A8
Arkle Ave RG19 105 F3
Arkley Ct SL6 40 C1
Arkwright Dr RG42 117 D7
Arkwright Rd Poyle SL3 69 E5
  Reading RG2 86 B3
Arlington Bsns Pk
  Bracknell RG12 118 B7
  Theale RG7 83 F3
Arlington Cl
  Bracknell RG42 118 A8
  Maidenhead SL6 39 A8
Arlington Grange RG18 78 B3
Arlington La RG14 77 F3
Arlington Rd TW15 97 F3
Arlington Sq RG12 118 A7
Armadale Ct RG30 85 D6
Armitage Ct SL5 120 C3
Armitage Dr GU16 151 F1
Armour Hill RG31 57 D1
Armour Rd RG31 57 D1
Armour Wlk RG31 57 D1
Armstrong Rd TW20 95 C2
Armstrong Way RG5 88 A7
Arncliffe RG12 118 A4
Arndale Way TW20 96 A3
Arne Cl RG41 88 A3
Arnett Ave RG40 141 F7
Arnewood Ave RG26 135 D1
Arnhem Rd RG14 105 B3
Arnold Rd TW18 97 C1
Arnside Cl RG10 61 D7
Arnwood RG41 115 E8
Arrowhead Rd RG7 83 F2
Arrowsmith Way RG19 106 E1
Artemis Ho RG14 105 B4
Arthur Cl GU19 145 E1
Arthur Pl RG1 86 D7
Arthur Rd Newbury RG14 104 E2
  Slough SL1 42 D4
  Windsor SL4 67 C6
  Wokingham RG41 116 A6
Arthur's Pl SP11 148 C1
Arthurstone Birches
  RG42 90 D3
Artillery Dr RG19 106 E1
Artillery Mews RG30 85 D6
Arun Cl RG41 88 B1
Arun Ct RG30 85 C6
Arundel Cl SL6 39 A8
Arundel Ct SL3 43 D2
Arundel Rd Frimley GU15 152 C4
  Woodley RG5 87 E7
Ascot Cl RG14 131 C8
Ascot Heath CE Jun Sch
  SL5 92 E1
Ascot Heath Inf Sch SL5 92 E1
Ascot Ho 7 TW20 96 A3
Ascot Race Course SL5 119 F6
Ascot Rd
  East Bedfont TW14 98 B6
  Holyport SL6 65 A8

Ascot Rd *continued*
Newell Green RG42 ... 91 E8
Ascot Sta SL5 ... 120 A5
Ascot Twrs SL5 ... 119 F7
Ascot Wood SL5 ... 120 A6
Ascott Way RG14 ... 105 D4
Ash Cl Blackwater GU17 ... 150 C5
Brightwalton RG20 ... 28 D3
Slough SL3 ... 44 B3
Ash Copse RG4 ... 59 F7
Ash Cres RG19 ... 133 A5
Ash Ct Ashford TW15 ... 98 C3
Caversham RG4 ... 59 B3
11 Newbury RG14 ... 105 A4
Ash Gate RG18 ... 106 F4
Ash Gn RG2 ... 113 D8
Ash Gr Bradfield RG7 ... 82 B2
East Bedfont TW14 ... 98 E7
Staines TW18 ... 97 C2
Stoke Poges SL2 ... 22 F5
Ash La
Burghfield Common RG7 ... 111 A4
Tadley RG26 ... 134 E1
Windsor SL4 ... 66 D5
Ash Lodge 2 TW16 ... 98 F1
Ash Rd Littleton TW17 ... 125 A5
Reading RG30 ... 84 E7
Ash Terr RG18 ... 106 B8
Ash Tree Gr RG20 ... 129 B7
Ash Way RG41 ... 115 D3
Ashampstead Rd
Bradfield RG7 ... 82 B7
Reading RG30 ... 85 B4
Upper Basildon RG8 ... 55 A5
Ashbourne RG12 ... 117 F3
Ashbourne Ct RG30 ... 85 C7
Ashbourne Gr SL6 ... 39 C3
Ashbourne Ho 5 SL1 ... 42 E4
Ashbourne Way RG19 ... 106 B3
Ashbrook Mews OX11 ... 11 F8
Ashbrook Rd SL4 ... 95 B8
Ashburton Rd RG2 ... 86 C2
Ashbury Dr
Farnborough GU17 ... 151 A1
Reading RG31 ... 84 C7
Ashby Ct RG2 ... 113 B7
Ashby Way UB7 ... 71 A7
Ashcroft Cl RG4 ... 58 E5
Ashcroft Ct SL1 ... 21 B3
Ashcroft Rd SL6 ... 39 C8
Ashdale Pk RG40 ... 142 D6
Ashdene Cl TW15 ... 98 C1
Ashdene Ho TW20 ... 95 C2
Ashdown SL6 ... 20 B3
Ashdown Cl RG12 ... 119 A7
Ashdown Ho 11 RG1 ... 85 E5
Ashen Cross SL0 ... 44 B8
Ashenden Wlk SL2 ... 22 D8
Asher Dr SL5 ... 119 C8
Ashes The RG7 ... 113 B2
Ashfield Gn GU46 ... 149 F5
Ashford Ave TW15 ... 98 B2
Ashford CE Prim Sch
TW15 ... 98 B2
Ashford Cl TW15 ... 97 E4
Ashford Cres TW15 ... 97 E5
Ashford High Sch The
TW15 ... 97 E5
Ashford Hill Prim Sch
RG19 ... 133 E1
Ashford Hill Rd RG19 ... 132 F2
Ashford Hospl TW15 ... 97 E6
Ashford Ind Est TW15 ... 98 C4
Ashford La SL4 ... 41 B4
Ashford Park Prim Sch
TW15 ... 97 D4
Ashford Rd
Feltham TW13,TW15 ... 98 E4
Littleton TW15 ... 98 C1
Staines TW18 ... 124 D8
Ashford Sta TW15 ... 97 F4
Ashgrove Rd TW15 ... 98 D3
Ashlea Ho TW15 ... 97 F3
Ashleigh Ave TW20 ... 96 C1
Ashley HP10 ... 3 E7
Ashley Cl Earley RG6 ... 87 B2
Oatlands Park KT12,KT13 ... 125 F1
Ashley Ct SL6 ... 40 B7
Ashley Dr GU17 ... 150 C4
Ashley Hill Pl RG10 ... 36 F7
Ashley Park Ave KT12 ... 125 F1
Ashley Pk SL6 ... 20 B2
Ashley Rd RG1 ... 85 E5
Ashley Way GU24 ... 153 D6
Ashman Rd RG19 ... 107 A3
Ashmead Prim Sch RG2 ... 86 C1
Ashmere Cl RG31 ... 84 C4
Ashmere Terr RG30 ... 85 E8
Ashmore Green Rd
RG18 ... 106 B7
Ashmore Rd RG2 ... 86 C1
Ashridge Ct 4 RG14 ... 105 A2
Ashridge Gn 2 RG42 ... 118 B8
Ashridge Rd RG40 ... 116 D8
Ashton Cl RG31 ... 84 C8
Ashton Pl Kintbury RG17 ... 102 B2
Maidenhead SL6 ... 39 A6
Ashton Rd Newbury RG14 ... 105 B2
Wokingham RG41 ... 88 F1
Ashtree Cnr RG20 ... 129 C7
Ashtree Ct 3 TW15 ... 98 B3
Ashtrees Rd RG5 ... 87 F8
Ashurst Dr TW17 ... 124 E5
Ashview Cl TW15 ... 97 E3
Ashview Gdns TW15 ... 97 E3
Ashville Pk RG41 ... 116 B5
Ashville Way RG41 ... 116 A5
Ashwell Ave GU15 ... 151 F6
Ashwell Ct TW15 ... 97 E6
Ashwood RG5 ... 87 D4
Ashwood Cl RG31 ... 84 B6
Ashwood Dr RG14 ... 105 D4
Ashwood Rd TW20 ... 95 B2
Ashworth Dr RG19 ... 106 C2
Askew Dr RG7 ... 113 B3
Aspen Cl Slough SL2 ... 42 B8
Staines TW18 ... 96 F5
Aspen Ct GU25 ... 122 E5
Aspen Gdns TW15 ... 98 C3
Aspin Way GU17 ... 150 B5
Astleham Rd TW17 ... 124 E6
Astley Cl RG41 ... 115 F7
Aston Ave RG31 ... 84 B8
Aston Cl RG8 ... 56 D5
Aston Cotts SL4 ... 93 A4
Aston Ct RG30 ... 85 B5
Aston Ferry La RG9 ... 16 D5
Aston La RG9 ... 16 C3
Aston Mead SL4 ... 66 E6
Aston St OX11 ... 12 F8
Astonville SL2 ... 22 C8
Astor Cl Maidenhead SL6 ... 40 B6
Winnersh RG41 ... 88 D3
Astra Mead RG42 ... 92 B2
Atfield Gr GU20 ... 146 D4
Atherton Cl Reading RG30 ... 84 F8
Stanwell TW19 ... 70 D1
Atherton Cres RG17 ... 100 D5
Atherton Ct SL4 ... 67 D7
Atherton Pl RG17 ... 25 B3
Atherton Rd RG17 ... 100 D5
Athlone Cl SL6 ... 19 E1
Athlone Sq SL4 ... 67 C6
Atrebatti Rd GU47 ... 143 C1
Atte La RG42 ... 91 C2
Attebrouche Ct RG12 ... 118 D2
Attwood Dr RG2 ... 140 E8
Auburn Ct RG4 ... 59 A2
Auckland Cl SL6 ... 40 B8
Auckland Rd RG6 ... 87 A6
Auclum Cl RG7 ... 111 B2
Auclum La RG7 ... 111 B2
Audley Cl RG14 ... 105 D5
Audley Dr SL6 ... 39 B6
Audley St RG30 ... 85 E8
Audley Way SL5 ... 119 D6
Audrey Ct RG7 ... 109 C3
Augur Cl TW18 ... 96 F3
August End Reading RG30 ... 85 C8
Slough SL3 ... 43 E7
Augustine Cl SL3 ... 69 E4
Augustine Wlk RG42 ... 91 E1
Augustus Gdns GU15 ... 152 C5
Austen Gdns RG14 ... 131 B8
Austin Rd RG5 ... 87 F6
Austinsgate SL6 ... 38 F8
Australia Ave SL6 ... 39 F8
Australia Rd SL1 ... 43 B4
Auton Pl RG9 ... 35 D8
Autumn Cl Caversham RG4 ... 59 C7
Slough SL1 ... 41 F5
Autumn Wlk
Maidenhead SL6 ... 39 A5
Wargrave RG10 ... 36 D2
Avalon Rd Bourne End SL8 ... 3 B5
Earley RG6 ... 87 C3
Avebury Bracknell RG12 ... 118 A3
Slough SL1 ... 42 A6
Avebury Sq RG1 ... 86 D5
Aveley Wlk 2 RG1 ... 86 B5
Avenue Dr SL3 ... 23 F1
Avenue Ho RG4 ... 58 D3
Avenue Hts RG2 ... 86 C4
Avenue Rd Egham TW18 ... 96 D3
Feltham TW13 ... 98 F5
Maidenhead SL6 ... 40 B5
Avenue Sch The RG2 ... 86 C4
Avenue Sucy GU15 ... 151 B4
Avenue The Bourne End SL8 ... 2 F4
Camberley GU15 ... 151 B5
Crowthorne RG45 ... 143 B5
Datchet SL3 ... 68 B6
Egham TW20 ... 96 B4
Farnham Common SL2 ... 22 B8
Lightwater GU18 ... 146 A1
Maidenhead SL6 ... 20 C3
Mortimer RG7 ... 137 B5
North Ascot SL5 ... 92 F1
Old Windsor SL4 ... 68 B2
Staines TW18 ... 124 B8
Wraysbury TW19 ... 68 D4
Averil Ct SL6 ... 41 C7
Avery Cl RG40 ... 141 F6
Avington Cl RG31 ... 84 B8
Avocet Cres GU47 ... 150 E8
Avocet Ct 4 RG1 ... 86 A6
Avon Cl Reading RG31 ... 84 F5
Slough SL1 ... 41 E6
Avon Ct RG42 ... 90 C2
Avon Gr RG12 ... 91 C1
Avon Pl RG1 ... 86 D8
Avon Rd TW16 ... 98 F1
Avon Way RG7 ... 109 E6
Avondale SL6 ... 19 C1
Avondale Ave TW18 ... 96 F1
Avondale Rd TW15 ... 97 D5
Avonway RG14 ... 105 D4
Axbridge RG12 ... 118 E4
Axbridge Rd RG2 ... 86 C2
Ayebridges Ave TW20 ... 96 C1
Aylesbury Cres SL1 ... 42 D7
Aylesford Way RG19 ... 107 A2
Aylesham Way GU46 ... 149 B6
Aylesworth Ave SL2 ... 22 B2
Aylesworth Spur SL4 ... 95 B8
Aylsham Cl RG30 ... 84 E8
Aymer Cl TW18 ... 123 E8
Aymer Dr TW18 ... 123 E8
Ayrton Senna Rd RG31 ... 84 C7
Aysgarth RG12 ... 118 A3
Aysgarth Pk SL6 ... 40 B1
Azalea Cl RG41 ... 88 B2
Azalea Rd RG19 ... 133 A5
Azalea Way Frimley GU15 ... 152 B6
Slough SL3 ... 43 E7

B

Babbage Way RG12 ... 118 A3
Babbington Rd RG2 ... 113 D6
Bacchus Ho RG7 ... 134 E2
Bachelors Acre SL4 ... 67 D6
Back La Beenham RG7 ... 109 A7
Brimpton RG7 ... 134 C4
Kintbury RG17 ... 127 F7
Shinfield RG7 ... 139 A8
Silchester RG7 ... 136 D4
Stanford Dingley RG7 ... 81 E4
Back St RG17 ... 47 C6
Backsideans RG10 ... 36 D2
Bacon Cl GU47 ... 150 D6
Bad Godesberg Way SL6 ... 39 F7
Baden Cl TW18 ... 97 B1
Bader Gdns SL1 ... 42 A4
Bader Way The RG5 ... 88 A5
Badgebury Rise SL7 ... 1 C7
Badgemore La RG9 ... 15 D3
Badgemore Sch RG9 ... 15 D2
Badger Cl SL6 ... 39 D4
Badger Dr
Lightwater GU18 ... 146 A1
Twyford RG10 ... 61 D7
Badgers Cl TW15 ... 97 F3
Badgers Copse GU15 ... 151 E4
Badgers Croft RG7 ... 137 A6
Badgers Glade RG7 ... 111 A2
Badgers Hill GU25 ... 122 C4
Badgers Holt GU46 ... 149 B5
Badgers Ridge RG20 ... 130 D4
Badgers Rise RG4 ... 59 A5
Badgers Sett RG45 ... 142 F5
Badgers Way
Bracknell RG12 ... 118 F7
Marlow Bottom SL7 ... 1 D7
Badgers Wlk RG9 ... 36 A3
Badgers Wood SL2 ... 22 C7
Badgerwood Dr GU16 ... 151 D2
Badminton Rd SL6 ... 39 B6
Badsworth Gdns RG14 ... 130 D4
Bagnols Way RG14 ... 104 E2
Bagshot Gn GU19 ... 145 E3
Bagshot Inf Sch GU19 ... 145 E2
Bagshot Rd Ascot SL5 ... 120 C2
Bracknell RG12 ... 118 C4
Englefield Green TW20 ... 95 C2
Bagshot Sta GU19 ... 145 E4
Baigents La GU20 ... 146 D4
Bailey Cl Maidenhead SL6 ... 39 F7
Windsor SL4 ... 67 A5
Bailey Ho 9 SL8 ... 3 A4
Bailey's La RG10 ... 62 E3
Baileys Cl GU17 ... 150 C4
Baily Ave RG18 ... 106 B4
Bain Ave GU15 ... 151 B2
Bainbridge Rd RG31 ... 84 B4
Bainhurst Cotts SL6 ... 38 B5
Baird Cl SL1 ... 42 B4
Baird Rd Arborfield RG2 ... 140 E7
Arborfield Cross RG2 ... 114 E1
Bakeham La TW20 ... 95 D1
Bakehouse Ct SL5 ... 119 B8
Baker St
Aston Tirrold OX11 ... 12 F8
Reading RG1 ... 85 F7
Bakers Ct TW19 ... 70 D1
Bakers La SL6 ... 38 F8
Bakers Orch HP10 ... 3 E5
Bakers Row SL6 ... 38 F8
Baldwin Ct RG10 ... 61 E6
Baldwin Pl SL6 ... 39 C7
Baldwin Rd SL1 ... 21 C2
Baldwin's Shore SL4 ... 67 D8
Balfour Cres
Bracknell RG12 ... 118 B4
Newbury RG14 ... 130 C6
Balfour Dr RG31 ... 84 B4
Balfour Pl SL7 ... 1 C4
Balintore Ct 8 GU47 ... 150 D8
Ball Pit Rd RG20 ... 30 B5
Ballamoor Cl RG31 ... 84 B3
Ballard Ct GU15 ... 152 A8
Ballard Gn SL4 ... 66 E7
Ballard Rd GU15 ... 152 A8
Ballencrieff Rd SL5 ... 120 F2
Balliol Rd RG4 ... 58 D3
Balliol Way GU47 ... 143 E1
Balme Cl RG10 ... 61 B4
Balmoral SL6 ... 19 B1
Balmoral Cl SL1 ... 41 E7
Balmoral Gdns SL4 ... 67 D4
Balmoral Grange TW18 ... 124 B7
Balmore Dr RG4 ... 59 B4
Balmore Ho RG4 ... 59 B3
Balmore Pk RG4 ... 59 B3
Bamburgh Cl RG2 ... 86 C3
Bamford Pl RG31 ... 84 B4
Banbury RG12 ... 118 E2
Banbury Ave SL1 ... 41 F8
Banbury Cl RG41 ... 116 A6
Banbury Gdns RG4 ... 59 C3
Bancroft Cl TW15 ... 98 A3
Bancroft Pl RG31 ... 84 B3
Bangors Cl SL0 ... 44 F7
Bangors Rd S SL0 ... 44 E8
Bank Apartments SL7 ... 1 D3
Bank Side RG40 ... 141 F6
Banks Spur SL1 ... 42 B4
Bankside Cl RG2 ... 86 D2
Bannard Rd SL6 ... 39 A5
Bannister Cl SL3 ... 43 E4
Bannister Gdns GU46 ... 149 F5
Bannister Pl RG7 ... 133 F6
Bannister Rd RG7 ... 110 F2
Barbara Cl TW17 ... 125 B4
Barbara's Mdw RG31 ... 57 B2
Barbel Cl RG6 ... 87 B8
Barber Cl RG10 ... 88 E7
Barberry Way GU17 ... 150 F2
Barbon Cl GU15 ... 152 D3
Barbrook Cl RG31 ... 57 D3
Barchester Rd SL3 ... 43 F4
Barclay Rd RG31 ... 84 D4
Barclose Ave RG4 ... 59 C3
Bardney Cl SL6 ... 39 D3
Bardolph's Cl RG4 ... 58 D8
Bardown RG20 ... 51 B2
Barefoot Cl RG31 ... 57 B1
Barfield Rd RG18 ... 106 A4
Barge La RG7 ... 139 A5
Bargeman Rd SL6 ... 39 E5
Barholm Cl RG6 ... 87 E2
Barkby RG6 ... 87 C2
Barker Cl RG2 ... 140 E7
Barker Ct RG10 ... 88 F8
Barker Gn RG12 ... 118 B4
Barker Rd KT16 ... 123 F2
Barkers Mdw SL5 ... 119 D8
Barkham Manor RG41 ... 115 C3
Barkham Rd
Wokingham RG41 ... 115 D3
Wokingham RG41 ... 116 A5
Barkham Ride RG40 ... 141 E8
Barkham St RG40 ... 115 C2
Barkhart Dr RG40 ... 116 C7
Barkhart Gdns RG40 ... 116 C7
Barkis Mead GU47 ... 143 E2
Barkwith Cl RG6 ... 87 E2
Barley Cl RG19 ... 106 F2
Barley Ct TW19 ... 97 E7
Barley Fields HP10 ... 3 E8
Barley Mead
Bracknell RG42 ... 91 E1
Maidenhead SL6 ... 39 A5
Barley Mow Rd TW20 ... 95 C3
Barley Mow Way TW17 ... 125 A5
Barley Way 1 SL7 ... 1 D1
Barley Wlk RG31 ... 84 A5
Barn Cl Ashford TW15 ... 98 B3
Bracknell RG12 ... 118 D7
Camberley GU15 ... 151 E6
Farnham Common SL2 ... 22 B8
Kintbury RG17 ... 102 B2
Maidenhead SL6 ... 19 F2
Reading RG30 ... 85 D4
Barn Cotts RG17 ... 74 D7
Barn Cres RG14 ... 130 D7
Barn Dr SL6 ... 39 A4
Barn Farm SL7 ... 1 D3
Barn La RG9 ... 15 C4
Barn Owl Way RG7 ... 111 B3
Barn The RG18 ... 79 F5
Barnard Cl RG4 ... 59 C6
Barnard's Ct RG17 ... 100 D5
Barnards Hill SL7 ... 1 C2
Barnes Terr 12 RG14 ... 104 F2
Barnes Way SL0 ... 44 F6
Barnett Ct RG12 ... 118 C7
Barnett Gn RG12 ... 118 B3
Barnett La GU18 ... 152 F7
Barnfield Iver SL0 ... 44 E7
Slough SL1 ... 41 D5
3 Yateley GU46 ... 149 D5
Barnfield Cl SL6 ... 19 F5
Barnhill Cl SL7 ... 1 D4
Barnhill Gdns SL7 ... 1 D4
Barnhill Rd SL7 ... 1 D4
Barnsdale Rd RG2 ... 86 D3
Barnway TW20 ... 95 C3
Barnwood Cl RG30 ... 85 E8
Baroma Way RG9 ... 15 E2
Baron Ct RG30 ... 85 E7
Barons Way TW20 ... 96 D2
Baronsmead RG9 ... 15 D2
Barossa Rd GU15 ... 151 D7
Barr's Rd SL6 ... 41 B7
Barracane Dr RG45 ... 143 B5
Barrack La SL4 ... 67 D6
Barracks La RG7 ... 113 B1
Barrett Cres RG40 ... 116 E6
Barrett Ct RG1 ... 58 F1
Barrett's La RG2 ... 114 D6
Barrington Cl RG6 ... 87 B6
Barrington Ct TW18 ... 96 F2
Barrington Ho RG2 ... 113 B7
Barrington Way RG1 ... 85 E5
Barrow Lodge SL2 ... 22 C1
Barry Ave SL4 ... 67 C7
Barry Pl RG1 ... 86 A8
Barry Sq RG12 ... 118 D2
Barry Terr TW15 ... 97 F6
Barry View SL4 ... 66 C5
Bartelotts Rd SL2 ... 21 E1
Bartholomew Ct 9
RG14 ... 104 F2
Bartholomew Pl RG42 ... 91 E1
Bartlemy Cl RG14 ... 130 E8
Bartlemy Rd RG14 ... 130 E8
Bartletts La SL6 ... 65 A7
Barton Cl TW17 ... 125 B3
Barton Rd Reading RG31 ... 84 B7
Slough SL3 ... 43 F4
Barton's Dr GU46 ... 149 D4
Barwell Cl RG45 ... 142 F4
Basemoors RG12 ... 118 E7
Basford Way SL4 ... 66 D4
Basil Cl RG6 ... 86 F1
Basildon CE Prim Sch
RG8 ... 55 A6
Basildon Pk★ RG8 ... 34 D1
Basingstoke Rd
Aldermaston RG7 ... 109 B2
Reading RG2 ... 86 B3
Riseley RG7 ... 139 B1
Shinfield RG7 ... 113 B3
Swallowfield RG7 ... 139 B5
Three Mile Cross RG7 ... 113 A5
Baskerville La RG9 ... 36 A3
Baslow Rd RG41 ... 88 B2
Basmore La RG9 ... 36 B4
Bass Mead SL6 ... 19 F5
Bassett Cl RG6 ... 114 C8
Bassett Rd OX12 ... 6 F8
Bassett Way SL2 ... 21 E1
Batcombe Mead RG12 ... 118 E2
Bates Cl SL3 ... 43 E7
Bath Ct SL6 ... 39 C6
Bath Rd Camberley GU15 ... 151 D6
Colthrop RG7,RG19 ... 107 D2
Froxfield SN8,RG17 ... 99 C4
Harlington TW6,UB7,TW5 ... 71 D6
Harmondsworth TW6,UB7 ... 70 E6
Hungerford RG17 ... 100 F6
Knowl Hill RG10,SL6 ... 37 D2
Littlewick Green SL6 ... 38 C5
Maidenhead SL6 ... 39 C6
Maidenhead SL6 ... 40 E7
Newbury RG20 ... 104 D4
Padworth RG7 ... 109 D4
Poyle SL3,UB7,TW6 ... 69 E6
Reading RG30,RG31,RG1 ... 85 C5
Slough SL1 ... 42 C5
Slough,Cippenham SL1,SL6 ... 41 D6
Sonning RG4 ... 60 E2
Thatcham RG18 ... 105 F4
Thatcham RG18 ... 106 C4
Woolhampton RG7 ... 108 D2
Bath Road Cotts SL3 ... 69 E6
Bathurst Cl SL0 ... 44 F4
Bathurst Rd RG41 ... 88 B2
Bathurst Wlk SL0 ... 44 F4
Battalion Way RG19 ... 106 E1
Battery End RG14 ... 130 D6
Battle Cl RG14 ... 104 D4
Battle Hospl RG30 ... 85 C7
Battle Prim Sch RG30 ... 85 D7
Battle Rd Goring RG8 ... 34 F7
Newbury RG14 ... 130 D6
Battle St RG1 ... 85 F8
Battlemead Cl SL6 ... 20 C3
Batty's Barn Cl RG40 ... 116 D5
Baughurst Rd RG7 ... 136 A6
Baxendales The RG14 ... 105 C1
Baxter Cl SL1 ... 42 E3
Bay Cl RG6 ... 86 F1
Bay Dr RG12 ... 118 E7
Bay Rd RG12 ... 118 E8
Bay Tree Ct SL1 ... 21 C2
Bay Tree Rise RG31 ... 84 C5
Baydon Dr RG1 ... 85 E5
Baydon Ho 6 RG17 ... 25 B2
Baydon Rd Lambourn RG17 ... 24 E1
Shefford Woodlands RG17 ... 74 E7
Wickham RG20 ... 75 B4
Bayeux Ct RG30 ... 85 D7
Bayfield Ave GU16 ... 151 E2
Bayford Cl GU17 ... 151 A1
Bayford Dr RG31 ... 84 F4
Bayley Cres SL1 ... 41 A8
Bayley Ct RG41 ... 88 B1
Baylis Bsns Ctr SL1 ... 42 D6
Baylis Court Sch SL1,SL2 ... 42 D8
Baylis Par SL1 ... 42 E7
Baylis Rd SL1 ... 42 E6
Bayliss Rd RG10 ... 36 D1
Bays Ct RG26 ... 134 F1
Baysfarm Ct UB7 ... 70 C6
Beach's Ho 2 TW18 ... 97 A3
Beacon Ct Colnbrook SL3 ... 69 C7
3 Reading RG30 ... 85 D6
Beacon Rd TW6 ... 71 A1
Beacon Rdbt TW6 ... 71 A1
Beaconsfield Cotts SL8 ... 3 B2
Beaconsfield Rd SL2 ... 22 C6
Beaconsfield Way RG6 ... 87 A2
Beacontree Plaza RG2 ... 86 B2
Beal's La RG31 ... 84 A7
Beale Cl RG40 ... 116 B7
Beale Park Wildlife Pk★
RG8 ... 55 F8
Beales Farm Rd RG17 ... 25 B2
Bean Oak Rd RG40 ... 116 F6
Beancroft Rd RG19 ... 106 D2
Bear La Newbury RG14 ... 105 A3
Wargrave RG10 ... 37 B3
Bear Wharf RG1 ... 86 A6
Beard's Rd TW15 ... 98 E2
Bearfield La RG17 ... 73 B7
Bears Rail Pk SL4 ... 94 F8
Bearsdon Ct SL5 ... 120 F2
Bearwater RG17 ... 100 D6
Bearwood Coll RG41 ... 115 B7
Bearwood Park Mobile Home Pk RG41 ... 88 A2
Bearwood Path 5 RG41 ... 88 A3
Bearwood Prim Sch
RG41 ... 115 B8

Bearwood Rd RG41 115 C6
Beasley's Ait La TW16, TW17 125 F3
Beattie Cl TW14 98 F7
Beatty Dr RG30 84 E8
Beauchamp Ct SL1 42 E6
Beauchief Cl RG6 113 F8
Beaufield Cl RG5 87 D7
Beaufort Cl SL7 1 E2
Beaufort Gdns Marlow SL7 1 E2
North Ascot SL5 119 E8
Beaufort Lodge 5 TW15 98 B3
Beaufort Pl SL6 40 D4
Beauforts TW20 95 C3
Beaufront Cl GU15 152 A7
Beaufront Rd GU15 152 B7
Beaulieu Cl
Bracknell RG12 119 A6
Datchet SL3 68 B5
Beaulieu Ct GU17 150 B5
Beaulieu Gdns GU17 150 C5
Beaumaris Ct SL1 42 C8
Beaumont Cl SL6 39 A3
Beaumont Cotts SL4 67 C6
Beaumont Ct Ascot SL5 119 F5
Slough SL3 43 D7
Beaumont Dr TW15 98 D3
Beaumont Gdns RG12 118 E4
Beaumont Rd Slough SL2 42 D8
Windsor SL4 67 C5
Beaumont Rise SL7 1 E2
Beaver Cl RG41 116 B3
Beaver La GU46 149 E5
Beaver Way RG5 88 B7
Beavers Cl RG26 135 A1
Beck Ct RG1 86 C6
Becket Ho 4 RG14 104 F2
Beckett Cl RG40 116 E6
Beckford Ave RG12 118 B3
Beckford Cl RG41 88 F1
Beckford Ct RG19 106 D3
Beckfords RG8 55 A5
Beckings Way HP10 3 C7
Beckwell Rd SL1 42 C4
Bede Wlk RG2 86 C3
Bedfont Cl TW14 71 C1
Bedfont Ct TW19 70 B4
Bedfont Green Cl TW14 98 C7
Bedfont Ind Pk TW15 98 D5
Bedfont Ind Pk N TW15 98 C5
Bedfont Inf Sch TW14 71 E1
Bedfont Jun Sch TW14 71 E1
Bedfont La TW14 98 F8
Bedfont Lakes Ctry Pk* TW14 98 C6
Bedfont Rd
Feltham TW14,TW13 98 D6
Stanwell TW19 70 F1
Bedford Ave SL1 42 A7
Bedford Cl
Maidenhead SL6 39 A3
Newbury RG14 130 C5
Bedford Dr SL2 22 B6
Bedford Gdns RG41 115 F7
Bedford La SL5 121 B4
Bedford Rd RG1 85 F8
Bedfordshire Down RG42 91 F2
Bedfordshire Way RG41 115 E6
Bedwins La SL6 19 B6
Beech RG9 15 D2
Beech Ave GU15 151 D4
Beech Cl Ashford TW15 98 D3
Brimpton RG19 133 B5
Burghfield Common RG30 111 B4
Hampstead Norreys RG18 53 A5
Maidenhead SL6 39 B8
Stanwell TW19 97 D8
Beech Ct Caversham RG4 59 B3
1 Marlow SL7 1 E2
7 Newbury RG14 105 A4
Beech Dr GU17 150 D4
Beech Glen RG12 118 B5
Beech Hill Rd
Beech Hill RG7 138 E6
Spencers Wood RG7 113 A1
Sunningdale SL5 120 F3
Beech La Earley RG6 87 B2
South Stoke RG8 14 F1
Beech Lodge TW18 96 E3
Beech Rd
East Bedfont TW14 98 E8
Mapledurham RG4 58 D7
Newtown RG20 132 A3
Purley On T RG8 57 B5
Reading RG2 86 E2
Slough SL3 43 E4
Beech Ride GU47 143 B1
Beech Tree Ct TW18 124 B7
Beech Tree La TW18 124 B7
Beech Wlk RG19 106 E2
Beecham Rd RG30 85 C8
Beechbrook Ave GU46 149 D5
Beechcroft RG18 53 A5
Beechcroft Cl SL5 120 D5
Beechcroft Ct RG12 118 B6
Beeches Dr SL2 22 B7
Beeches Rd SL2 22 B7
Beeches The Goring RG8 34 B5
Reading RG31 57 D3
8 Staines TW18 97 A3
Beechfield RG18 80 D7
Beechfield Pl SL6 39 C4
Beechingstoke 4 SL7 1 F3
Beechmont Ave GU25 122 D4
Beechnut Cl RG41 115 F5
Beechnut Dr GU17 150 B6
Beechtree Ave
Englefield Green TW20 95 B2
Marlow Bottom SL7 1 D5
Beechwood Ave
Reading RG31 84 D8
Staines TW18 97 B2
Woodley RG5 87 D7
Beechwood Cl SL5 92 F1
Beechwood Dr
Maidenhead SL6 39 A6
Marlow SL7 18 B8
Beechwood Gdns SL1 42 E4
Beechwood Prim Sch RG5 87 E7
Beechwood Rd
Slough SL2 42 D8
Wentworth GU25 122 B1
Beechwood Sch SL2 22 B2
Beedon CE Prim Sch RG20 51 D8
Beedon Dr RG12 117 E3
Beehive La RG12 117 C7
Beehive Rd
Bracknell RG12,RG42 117 D7
Staines TW18 96 F3
Beenham Prim Sch RG7 108 F6
Beeston Way RG6 114 A8
Beggars Hill Rd RG10 61 B1
Beighton Cl RG6 113 F8
Belfast Ave SL1 42 D7
Belford Ct 13 RG1 86 A6
Belfry Mews GU47 149 F8
Belgrave Ct GU17 150 D3
Belgrave Par SL1 42 E6
Belgrave Rd SL1 42 F6
Belgravia Ct 21 RG30 85 D6
Bell Bridge Rd KT16 123 F1
Bell Bsns Ctr SL6 39 F6
Bell Cl SL2 43 B8
Bell Cnr KT16 123 F2
Bell Ct Caversham RG4 59 B6
Hurley SL6 17 F3
Twyford RG10 61 D5
Bell Foundry La RG40 116 C8
Bell Hill RG14,RG20 130 B4
Bell Holt RG14 130 C5
Bell House Gdns RG41 116 B6
Bell La Aldworth RG8 32 F4
Blackwater GU17 150 C5
Eton SL4 41 F2
Henley-On-T RG9 15 E3
Inkpen RG17 127 D3
Bell Pl GU19 145 F3
Bell St Henley-On-T RG9 15 E2
Maidenhead SL6 39 F6
Bell Street Mews RG9 15 E2
Bell View SL4 66 F5
Bell View Cl SL4 66 F5
Bell Weir Cl TW19 96 B6
Belle Ave RG6 87 A5
Belle Vue Cl TW18 124 A8
Belle Vue Rd
Henley-On-T RG9 35 D8
Reading RG1 85 F7
Belleisle RG8 57 B5
Bellever Hill GU15 151 E5
Bellevue Terr 5 RG1 85 E7
Bellingham Cl GU15 152 C4
Bellingham Wlk RG4 59 A5
Bellman Ct 2 RG1 86 A8
Bells Hill SL2 23 A4
Bells Hill Gn SL2 23 A5
Bells La SL3 69 B4
Bellsfield Ct SL4 41 F2
Bellswood La SL0 44 B8
Belmont SL2 42 A8
Belmont Cotts
Colnbrook SL3 69 C7
Speen RG20 104 C6
Belmont Cres SL6 39 D8
Belmont Dr SL6 39 D8
Belmont Mews GU15 151 C3
Belmont Park Ave SL6 39 D8
Belmont Park Rd SL6 39 D8
Belmont Rd
Camberley GU15 151 C4
Crowthorne RG45 143 B6
Maidenhead SL6 39 D8
Reading RG30 85 D7
Belmont Vale SL6 39 D8
Belsize Grange KT16 124 C2
Belton Rd GU15 151 E5
Belvedere Ct GU17 150 D3
Belvedere Dr RG14 131 A8
Belvedere Grange SL5 121 A1
Belvedere Mans SL1 42 D4
Belvedere Wlk 2 RG41 88 A3
Belvoir Cl GU16 151 F1
Bembridge Ct
Crowthorne RG45 142 E4
12 Slough SL1 42 F4
Bembridge Pl RG1 86 C7
Benbricke Gn RG42 91 A1
Bence The TW20 123 B6
Bencombe Rd SL7 1 E5
Benedict Dr TW14 98 D8
Benedict Gn RG42 91 E1
Benen-Stock Rd TW19 70 A2
Benetfeld Rd RG42 90 B2
Benett Cl RG14 104 F5
Benett Gdns RG14 104 F5
Benham Chase RG20 103 E5
Benham Hill
Newbury RG18 105 F4
Thatcham RG18 106 A4
Benham La RG7 139 D3
Benhams La RG9 15 E8
Benjamin Ct TW15 98 C1
Bennet Ct RG2 86 A1
Bennet Rd RG2 86 A1
Bennett Ct GU15 151 C5
Bennett's Hill RG7,RG30 111 C7
Bennetts Cl SL1 42 A5
Benning Cl SL4 66 D4
Benning Way RG40 116 D8
Bennings Cl RG42 91 A1
Bensington Ct TW14 71 D1
Benson Cl Reading RG2 86 D3
Slough SL2 43 A5
Benson Rd RG45 142 F5
Bensonholme RG7 109 C3
Bentley Copse GU15 152 B4
Bentley Ct 4 GU15 151 D5
Bentley Dr RG2 140 E8
Bentley Pk SL2 21 D3
Bentley Rd SL1 42 A5
Benyon Ct RG1 85 E6
Benyon Mews RG1 85 E6
Beomonds KT16 124 A2
Beomonds Row KT16 124 A2
Bere Court Rd RG8 56 B4
Bere Rd RG12 118 E3
Beresford Ave SL2 43 C6
Beresford Rd RG30 85 E8
Bergenia Ct GU24 153 E6
Berkeley Ave RG1 85 E6
Berkeley Cl TW19 96 D6
Berkeley Ct 1 RG1 85 F6
Berkeley Dr SL4 93 B7
Berkeley Gdns KT12 125 F2
Berkeley Mews Marlow SL7 1 F2
Slough SL1 41 E7
Berkeley Rd RG14 104 F2
Berkley Cl SL6 39 A8
Berkshire Ave SL1 42 B7
Berkshire Bsns Ctr RG19 107 A2
Berkshire Bsns Pk RG7 135 E4
Berkshire Coll of Agriculture SL6 18 A1
Berkshire Coll of Agriculture (Hall Place) SL6 38 A8
Berkshire Dr
Reading RG31 84 C7
Thatcham RG19 107 A2
Berkshire Ind Hospl RG1 85 E5
Berkshire Lodge 1 SL6 39 F6
Berkshire Rd
Camberley GU15 151 F8
Henley-On-T RG9 35 D8
Berkshire Way RG12 117 D6
Bernadine Cl RG42 91 E1
Bernard Ct GU15 151 B4
Berners Cl SL1 41 E6
Bernersh Cl GU47 143 C1
Berries Rd SL6 20 A8
Berry Field SL2 43 C7
Berry Hill SL6 40 D7
Berry Hill Ct SL6 40 D8
Berrybank GU47 150 E6
Berrycroft RG12 118 D8
Berrylands Rd RG4 59 B3
Berrys La RG30 85 A1
Berrys Rd RG7 107 C5
Berryscroft Ct TW18 97 C1
Berryscroft Rd TW18 97 C1
Berstead Cl 3 RG6 87 B1
Berwick Ave SL1 42 B6
Berwick Cl SL7 1 D3
Berwick La SL7 1 C3
Berwick Rd SL7 1 C3
Berwyn Ho RG2 113 C7
Beryl Cl RG41 115 E7
Bessel's Way OX11 12 B8
Bestobell Rd SL1 42 C7
Beswick Gdns RG12 118 F8
Beta Ho 6 RG30 85 D6
Beta Way TW20 123 C8
Betam Rd RG1 86 D7
Betchworth Ave RG6 87 A3
Bethany Waye TW14 98 E8
Bethesda Cl RG8 55 A6
Bethesda St RG8 55 A7
Betjeman Wlk GU46 149 B4
Betteridge Rd RG19 106 F2
Bettoney Vere SL6 40 C4
Betty Grove La RG41 114 F7
Bevan Gate RG42 118 A8
Beverley Cl
Frimley GU15 152 D6
Marlow SL7 1 B2
Thatcham RG18 106 C4
Beverley Ct SL1 43 B4
Beverley Gdns
Maidenhead SL6 19 B1
Wargrave RG10 36 E1
Beverley Rd Reading RG31 57 C1
Sunbury TW16 125 F8
Bevers The RG7 137 A6
Bewicks Reach RG14 104 F3
Bexley Ct RG30 85 D6
Bexley St SL4 67 C6
Bibury Cl RG5 87 D4
Bicknell Rd GU16 151 E2
Biddles Cl SL1 41 E5
Bideford Cl RG5 87 C5
Bideford Spur SL2 22 B2
Bietigheim Way GU15 151 C6
Big Barn Gr RG42 91 D1
Big La RG17 25 B3
Bigbury Gdns RG2 86 C3
Bigfrith La SL6 19 B6
Bigg's Hill Cotts RG20 129 F4
Biggs La
Arborfield Cross RG2 114 F1
Biggs La *continued*
Barkham RG2,RG40 141 A8
Billet La SL0,SL3 44 B7
Billet Rd TW18,TW19 97 A5
Billing Ave RG40 141 F6
Billingbear La RG42 90 B5
Billington Way RG18 106 C5
Bilton Ind Est RG12 117 E5
Binbrook Cl RG6 87 D2
Binbury Row TW18 96 E4
Binfield CE Prim Sch RG42 90 C2
Binfield Ho RG42 90 C3
Binfield Pk RG42 90 D4
Binfield Rd
Bracknell,Priestwood RG42 118 A8
Wokingham RG40 116 F7
Bingham Cotts RG42 91 B6
Bingham Dr TW18 97 D1
Bingham Rd SL1 41 A8
Binghams The SL6 40 B3
Bingley Gr RG5 60 F1
Binsted Dr GU17 150 D5
Birch Ave Brimpton RG19 133 B5
Reading RG30 85 A8
Birch Cl GU15 151 E8
Birch Copse Prim Sch RG31 84 C8
Birch Ct RG45 142 F6
Birch Dr GU17 150 D3
Birch Gn RG2 113 D8
Birch Gr Bracknell RG12 118 C5
Slough SL2 42 B8
Upper Halliford TW17 125 E7
Windsor SL4 66 D6
Birch Hill Prim Sch RG12 118 B1
Birch Hill Rd RG12 118 B2
Birch La Mortimer RG7 136 E5
West End GU24 153 D7
Winkfield RG12,SL5 119 B8
Birch Platt GU24 153 D6
Birch Rd
Burghfield Common RG7 111 A3
Tadley RG26 134 F2
Windlesham GU20 146 E4
Wokingham RG40 142 A7
Birch Side RG45 143 A6
Birch Tree View GU18 146 A1
Birches The
Blackwater GU17 150 B5
Goring RG8 34 B6
Birchetts Cl 1 RG42 118 B8
Birchfields GU15 151 C4
Birchington Rd SL4 67 A5
Birchland Cl RG7 136 E6
Birchlands Ct GU47 143 E2
Birchmead RG41 88 D2
Birchview Cl GU46 149 D4
Birchwood Cl RG4 59 C6
Birchwood Dr GU18 146 C1
Birchwood Rd RG14 105 D4
Birchwoods The RG31 84 B8
Bird Mews RG40 116 B6
Bird Mount Cotts SL4 67 C8
Birdhill Ave RG2 86 D2
Birds La RG7 107 E4
Birdwood Rd
Maidenhead SL6 39 B7
Sandhurst GU15 150 F6
Birkbeck Pl GU47 143 E1
Birkdale RG12 117 E2
Birkdale Ct SL5 120 C4
Birkhall Cl RG31 84 C5
Birley Rd SL1 42 D7
Biscuit Way RG2 112 F8
Bisham Abbey National Sports Ctr SL7 18 D7
Bisham CE Prim Sch SL7 18 D7
Bisham Ct Bisham SL7 18 E6
11 Slough SL1 42 F4
Bisham Gn SL7 18 E6
Bisham Rd SL7 18 E8
Bishop Ct SL6 39 D6
Bishop Ctr The SL6 40 F7
Bishop Duppas Pk TW17 125 E2
Bishop Wand CE Sec Sch The TW16 125 F7
Bishop's La SL4 92 B7
Bishop's Rd RG6 87 A6
Bishopdale RG12 118 A5
Bishops Cl RG26 135 A1
Bishops Ct
1 Ashford TW16 98 F1
North Ascot SL5 92 F2
Bishops Dr
East Bedfont TW14 71 D1
Wokingham RG40 116 C7
Bishops Farm Cl SL4 66 B6
Bishops Gr GU20 146 C4
Bishops Orch SL2 22 B2
Bishops Rd Slough SL1 43 A4
Stanford Dingley RG7 81 F3
Bishops Way TW20 96 D2
Bishops Wlk HP10 3 E5
Bishopsgate Rd TW20 95 B5
Bishopsgate Sch TW20 95 A5
Bishopswood Ct RG26 134 F1
Bishopswood La RG26 134 E1
Bishopswood Rd RG26 134 F1
Bispham Ct 2 RG1 86 C6
Bissley Dr SL6 39 A3
Bitham La Ham RG17 126 B5
Inkpen RG17 127 B4
Bitham Rd OX12 8 C7
Bittern Cl GU47 150 D8
Bitterne Ave RG31 84 B6
Bix Hill RG9 15 A6
Bix La SL6 38 F8
Black Boy La SL6 17 C3
Black Butt Cotts SL6 20 B7
Black Horse Cl SL4 66 D5
Black Lake Cl TW20 123 A8
Black Park Ctry Pk & Visitor Ctr* SL3 23 F3
Black Park Rd SL3 23 E4
Blackamoor La SL6 40 A8
Blackberry Cl TW17 125 E5
Blackbird Cl
Burghfield Common RG7 111 B3
Sandhurst GU47 150 D8
Blackbird La RG20 132 A3
Blackburn Trad Est TW19 70 F1
Blackbush Bsns Ctr GU46 149 C4
Blackbush Park Cvn Site GU46 149 C5
Blackcap Pl GU47 150 E8
Blackdown Way RG19 106 D2
Blackett Cl TW18 123 F7
Blacklands Rd RG7 107 C5
Blackley Cl RG6 87 E3
Blackmeadows RG12 118 C3
Blackmoor Cl SL5 119 D7
Blackmoor Wood SL5 119 D7
Blacknest Gate Rd SL5 121 B6
Blacknest Rd GU25,SL5 121 E6
Blackpond La SL2 22 B4
Blacksmith Row SL3 44 A2
Blacksmith's La TW18 124 C6
Blacksmiths La KT16 124 A2
Blackstroud La E GU18, GU24 153 E8
Blackstroud La W GU18 153 D8
Blackthorn Cl Earley RG6 87 A7
Purley On T RG31 57 B1
Blackthorn Dell SL3 43 C3
Blackthorn Dr
Lightwater GU18 153 B7
Thatcham RG18 106 D5
Blackthorne Cres SL3 69 E5
Blackthorne Rd SL3 69 E4
Blackwater Cl
Caversham RG4 59 E4
Shinfield RG7 113 B1
Blackwater Rise RG31 84 B4
Blackwater Sta GU17 150 E4
Blackwater View RG40 142 B2
Blaenant RG4 58 F5
Blaenavon RG4 58 F5
Blagdon Cl RG19 131 D7
Blagdon Rd RG2 86 D2
Blagrave Farm La RG4 58 D5
Blagrave La RG4 58 D4
Blagrave Rise RG31 84 C6
Blagrave St RG1 86 B8
Blagrove Dr RG41 115 F4
Blagrove La RG41 115 F3
Blair Rd SL1 42 E5
Blaire Pk GU46 149 B8
Blake Cl
Crowthorne RG45 143 C4
Wokingham RG40 116 E8
Blake's La RG26 135 C1
Blakeney Ct SL6 19 F1
Blakeney Fields RG17 48 B4
Blakes Cotts Reading RG1 86 C7
Wargrave RG10 37 B1
Blakes La RG10 37 B2
Blakes Rd RG10 36 F3
Blakes Ride GU46 149 B6
Blamire Dr RG42 90 F2
Blanchard Cl RG5 88 B8
Bland's Cl RG7 110 F2
Blandford Cl SL3 43 D3
Blandford Dr RG41 115 E4
Blandford Rd RG2 113 C8
Blandford Rd N SL3 43 D3
Blandford Rd S SL3 43 D3
Blands Ct RG7 111 A2
Blandy Rd RG9 35 D7
Blandy's La RG8 55 B6
Blandys Hill RG17 128 B8
Blane's La SL5 119 C3
Blatch's Cl RG7 83 D3
Blay's La TW20 95 B2
Blays Cl TW20 95 C2
Bledlow Cl RG14 130 D5
Blenheim Cl
Slough SL3 43 F5
Wokingham RG41 115 E6
Blenheim Cotts RG18 106 B8
Blenheim Ct 6 RG1 86 B6
Blenheim Gdns RG1 86 E6
Blenheim Rd
Caversham RG4 59 A3
Maidenhead SL6 39 B8
Newbury RG14 104 F2
Reading RG1 86 E6
Slough SL3 43 D2
Blenheim Terr 1 RG1 86 A6
Blessed Hugh Faringdon RC Sch RG30 85 C5
Bletchmore Cl UB3 71 D8
Blewburton Wlk RG12 118 E5
Blewbury Dr RG31 84 B7
Blewbury Hill OX11 12 B8
Blinco La SL3 43 E7
Blind La
Bourne End HP10,SL8 3 B6
Lambourn RG17 25 B2
Block Cotts RG7 136 B6
Blom Field Dale RG42 117 D7
Blondell Cl UB7 70 D8

Bloomfield Dr RG12 91 C1
Bloomfield Hatch La RG7 138 B8
Bloomfield Rd SL6 39 A5
Bloomsbury Way GU17 150 D3
Blossom Ave RG7 83 E4
Blossom La RG7 83 E4
Blossoms The RG20 51 C4
Blount Cres RG42 90 E1
Bloxworth Cl 10 RG12 118 F5
Blue Ball La TW20 95 F3
Blue Coat Wlk RG12 118 D4
Bluebell Dr RG7 110 F3
Bluebell Hill RG12 118 E8
Bluebell Mdw RG41 88 C3
Bluebell Mews GU15 151 D7
Bluebell Rise GU18 153 B8
Bluebell Way RG18 106 D5
Bluecoats RG18 106 D4
Bluethroat Cl GU47 150 E8
Blumfield Cres SL1 41 E8
Blumfield Ct SL1 21 D1
Blundell's Rd RG30 84 E8
Blunden Dr SL3 44 C2
Blunts Ave UB7 71 A7
Blyth Ave RG19 106 E2
Blyth Wlk 7 RG1 86 B5
Blythe Cl SL0 44 F7
Blythe Ho SL1 41 D5
Blythewood La SL5 119 E7
Blythwood Dr GU16 151 D2
Boadicea Cl SL1 41 E5
Boames La RG20 129 F5
Board La RG20 102 F5
Boarlands Cl SL1 41 F6
Boathouse Reach RG9 15 E1
Bobgreen Ct RG2 113 C6
Bobmore La SL7 1 F3
Bockhampton Rd RG17 25 C1
Bockmer La SL7 17 B7
Bodens Ride SL5 119 F1
Bodin Gdns RG14 131 B8
Bodmin Ave SL2 42 A8
Bodmin Cl RG19 106 C2
Bodmin Rd RG5 87 C5
Body Rd 1 RG1 86 A7
Bog La RG12 119 A5
Boham's Rd OX11 11 D6
Bold's Ct SL2 23 A5
Bolding House La GU24 153 F7
Boldrewood RG7 110 F2
Boleyn Cl TW18 96 E3
Bolingbroke Way RG19 106 F3
Bolney La RG9 36 A5
Bolney Rd RG9 36 B5
Bolney Trevor Dr RG9 36 A4
Bolton Ave SL4 67 D4
Bolton Cres SL4 67 C4
Bolton Rd SL4 67 C4
Bolton Row RG20 50 D7
Bolton's La TW6,UB7 71 B7
Boltons La RG42 90 F1
Bolwell Cl RG10 61 F4
Bomer Cl UB7 71 A7
Bomford Cl RG18 78 F6
Bond Cl RG26 135 A1
Bond St TW20 95 C3
Bond Way RG12 118 B8
Bone La RG14 105 C3
Bone Lane Ind Est RG14 105 C3
Bonemill La RG20 104 D2
Bones La RG9 35 A3
Bonhomie Ct RG10 89 A7
Bonnicut Ct SL5 121 A4
Bonny's Yd RG27 141 A1
Boole Hts RG12 118 A4
Boot End RG2 112 F8
Booth Dr Staines TW18 97 D2
 Wokingham RG40 115 E1
Borderside Slough SL2 43 A7
 Yateley GU46 149 A6
Borrowdale Cl TW20 96 B1
Borrowdale Gdns GU15 152 D4
Borrowdale Rd RG41 88 B4
Boscawen Way RG19 107 A3
Boscombe Cl TW20 123 C8
Bosham Cl RG6 114 B8
Boshers Gdns TW20 95 F2
Bosman Dr GU20 146 B6
Bossington Ct 9 TW18 96 F3
Bostock La RG7 83 A2
Boston Ave RG1 85 F6
Boston Dr SL8 3 B3
Boston Gr SL1 42 C7
Boston Rd RG9 35 E8
Bosworth Gdns RG5 87 E4
Botany Cl RG19 106 F3
Botham Dr SL1 42 E3
Bothy The RG10 36 D2
Botmoor Way RG20 48 F7
Bottisham Cl RG6 114 C8
Bottle La Knowl Hill SL6 38 A2
 Newell Green RG42 91 A6
Bottom La RG7 110 D8
Bottom Waltons Cvn Site SL2 21 F3
Bouldish Farm Rd SL5 120 A5
Boult St RG1 86 C7
Boulters Cl
 Maidenhead SL6 20 C1
 Slough SL1 42 A4
 Woodley RG5 87 F8
Boulters Ct SL6 20 C1
Boulters Gdns SL6 20 C1
Boulters Ho RG12 118 E5
Boulters La SL6 20 C1
Boulton Pl 5 RG14 105 A3
Boulton Rd RG2 86 A3
Boults Wlk RG2 86 B5
Boundary Cl RG31 84 C6
Boundary La RG4 58 E3
Boundary Pl HP10 3 D8
Boundary Rd
 Newbury RG14 105 B2
 Staines TW15 97 C3
 Taplow SL1,SL6 40 F8
 Wooburn Green HP10 3 D8
Boundoak RG2 140 D8
Bourn Cl RG6 87 C1
Bourne Arch RG18 106 B4
Bourne Ave
 Chertsey KT16 124 A6
 Reading RG2 86 B4
 Windsor SL4 67 C3
Bourne Cl Bourne End SL8 3 B5
 Reading RG31 84 B4
Bourne End Bsns Ctr 1 SL8 3 B3
Bourne End Rd SL6,SL8 20 E8
Bourne End Sta SL8 3 A3
Bourne Ho 4 TW15 98 A3
Bourne Mdw TW20 123 B5
Bourne Rd
 Pangbourne RG8 56 E5
 Slough SL1 42 D4
 Thatcham RG18,RG19 106 B4
 Wentworth GU25 122 D4
Bourne Vale RG17 100 C5
Bourne-Stevens Cl RG1 86 B7
Bourneside GU25 122 A2
Bourton Cl RG30 84 F7
Bouverie Way SL3 43 E2
Boveney Cl SL1 42 A4
Boveney Ho RG12 118 E5
Boveney New Rd SL4 41 E2
Boveney Rd SL4 41 C1
Bovingdon Hts SL7 1 B2
Bowden Cl TW14 98 E7
Bowden Rd SL5 120 D4
Bowdown Ct 10 RG14 104 F2
Bower Ct SL1 41 F6
Bower Way SL1 41 E6
Bowes Rd Egham TW18 96 E2
 Thatcham RG19 106 D2
Bowes-Lyon Cl 6 SL4 67 C6
Bowfell Cl RG31 57 C2
Bowland Dr RG12 118 E2
Bowling Ct RG9 15 D3
Bowling Green Farmhouse RG8 57 B5
Bowling Green La RG8 57 B5
Bowling Green Rd RG18 106 B6
Bowlings The GU15 151 C6
Bowman Ct RG45 142 F4
Bowmans Cl SL1 21 B3
Bowry Dr TW19 68 F1
Bowyer Cres RG40 116 C8
Bowyer Dr SL1 41 E6
Bowyer Wlk SL5 119 E8
Bowyer's La RG42 91 C6
Boxford Ridge RG12 118 B6
Boxshall Ct RG14 104 F2
Boyd Ct RG42 118 A8
Boyn Hill Ave SL6 39 D6
Boyn Hill Cl SL6 39 D6
Boyn Hill Rd SL6 39 D6
Boyn Valley Rd SL6 39 D5
Boyndon Rd SL6 39 D7
Boyne Hill CE Inf Sch SL6 39 D6
Bracebridge GU15 151 A5
Bracken Bank SL5 119 C8
Bracken Cl Ashford TW16 98 F2
 Farnham Common SL2 22 D8
 Purley On T RG31 57 C1
Bracken Copse RG17 127 E5
Bracken La GU46 149 B6
Bracken Rd SL6 39 C4
Bracken Way
 Burghfield Common RG7 111 A2
 Flackwell Heath HP10 3 B7
Brackendale Cl GU15 151 E3
Brackendale Rd GU15 151 D4
Brackendale Way RG6 87 A5
Brackenforde SL3 43 C4
Brackens The RG45 143 A7
Brackenwood GU15 152 D5
Brackenwood Dr RG26 135 A1
Brackley Ho 3 TW18 96 F3
Bracknell & Wokingham Coll RG40 116 C6
Bracknell Beeches RG12 118 B6
Bracknell Bsns Ctr The RG12 117 F7
Bracknell Cl GU15 144 F1
Bracknell Coll
 Bracknell RG12 118 C7
 Bracknell,Wick Hill RG12 118 C8
Bracknell Enterprise Ctr RG12 118 A7
Bracknell Rd
 Bagshot GU19 145 E6
 Camberley GU15 145 A1
 Crowthorne RG45 143 D6
 Winkfield RG42 92 A5
Bracknell Sta RG12 118 B6
Brackstone Cl RG4 59 C2
Bradbury Gdns SL3 23 D8
Bradcutts La SL6 19 E8
Bradenham La SL7 18 C5
Bradfield CE Prim Sch RG7 82 B2
Bradfield Coll RG7 82 C6
Bradfields RG12 118 D4
Bradford Rd SL1 42 A7
Brading Way RG8 57 D5
Bradley Cl RG17 102 B1
Bradley Dr RG40 116 A2
Bradley Rd SL1 42 E6
Bradley-Moore Sq RG18 106 E5
Bradmore Way RG6 114 A8
Bradshaw Cl SL4 66 E6
Bradwell Rd RG31 57 C3
Braemar SL6 63 D7
Braemar Ct 3 SL7 1 D2
Braemar Gdns SL1 42 A4
Braemore Cl RG19 106 D2
Braeside RG12 117 C7
Brakenhale Sch The RG12 118 B5
Brakes Rise GU47 150 E8
Bramber Ct SL1 42 A5
Bramber Mews RG4 59 E4
Bramble Cl TW17 125 D6
Bramble Cres RG30 84 E8
Bramble Ct 3 RG14 105 B2
Bramble Dr SL6 39 A4
Brambledown TW18 124 B8
Bramblegate RG45 143 A6
Brambles The
 Crowthorne RG45 142 D6
 Holyport SL6 65 B8
 Newbury RG14 130 E8
Bramblings RG4 58 E6
Bramcote GU15 152 C5
Bramley Ave TW17 125 E6
Bramley Chase SL6 39 C4
Bramley Cl
 Chertsey KT16 124 B1
 Earley RG6 87 B3
 Maidenhead SL6 39 C3
 Staines TW18 97 C2
Bramley Ct
 Crowthorne RG45 142 D5
 East Bedfont TW14 71 D1
Bramley Gr RG45 142 D5
Bramley La GU17 150 B5
Bramley Rd
 Camberley GU15 151 B2
 Silchester RG7 136 B1
Bramling Ave GU46 149 B6
Brammas Cl SL1 42 C3
Brampton Chase RG9 36 A4
Brampton Ct SL6 40 B8
Bramshaw Rd RG30 58 A1
Bramshill Cl RG2 140 E8
Bramwell Cl RG19 106 F2
Bran Cl RG30 84 E8
Brandon Ave RG5 88 A8
Brandon Cl GU15 152 D4
Brands Rd SL3 69 B8
Brandy Bottom GU46 149 E3
Branksome Cl GU15 151 E6
Branksome Ct 6 RG1 85 F7
Branksome Hill Rd GU47 150 E8
Branksome Park Rd GU15 151 E6
Brants Bridge RG12 118 E7
Brants Cl RG2 114 E2
Brattain Ct RG12 118 D6
Braunfels Wlk RG14 104 E2
Bravington Cl TW17 124 F4
Bray Cl SL6 40 C4
Bray Ct SL6 40 C2
Bray Rd Maidenhead SL6 40 B5
 Reading RG30 85 B4
Braybank SL6 40 C4
Braybrooke Dr RG10 88 F8
Braybrooke Gdns RG10 36 D1
Braybrooke Rd
 Bracknell RG42 91 B1
 Wargrave RG10 36 D1
Braye Cl GU47 143 C1
Brayfield Rd SL6 40 C4
Brayford Rd RG2 113 C8
Braywick Park & Nature Ctr SL6 40 B3
Braywick Rd SL6 40 A4
Braywood Ave TW20 96 A2
Braywood CE Fst Sch SL4 65 E5
Braywood Cotts SL4 66 A5
Braziers La RG42,SL4 92 D4
Breach Sq RG17 100 D4
Breadcroft La SL6 38 E3
Breadcroft Rd SL6 38 F3
Bream Cl SL7 18 C8
Brean Wlk RG6 87 A2
Brechin Ct 3 RG1 86 C6
Brecon Ct SL1 42 C4
Brecon Rd RG5 87 F8
Bredon Rd RG41 88 F1
Bredward Cl SL1 21 B2
Breech The GU47 150 E7
Breedons Hill RG8 56 C5
Bremer Rd TW18 97 A5
Brendon Cl
 Harlington UB7 71 C7
 Reading RG30 57 E1
Brent Cl RG19 106 D2
Brent Gdns RG2 86 B3
Brent Rd SL8 3 A4
Brentmoor Rd GU24 153 D6
Brerewood RG6 86 F2
Bret Harte Rd GU16 151 E1
Brew Twr 3 SL7 1 D1
Brewery Comm RG7 137 B7
Brewery Ct RG7 83 E3
Brewhouse Hill SN8 99 B4
Briant's Ave RG4 59 C2
Briants Piece RG18 79 B6
Briar Ave GU18 153 A8
Briar Cl Burnham SL6 41 B7
 Caversham RG4 59 A5
Briar Dene SL6 19 C1
Briar Glen SL6 19 E6
Briar Rd TW17 125 A4
Briar Way SL2 42 B8
Briarlea Rd RG7 136 F6
Briars Cl RG8 56 E5
Briars The SL3 43 F1
Briarwood RG40 141 E6
Briarwood Cl TW13 98 E5
Brickfield La Burnham SL1 21 B4
 Harlington UB3 71 D8
Brickfields Ind Pk RG12 118 A7
Bridge Ave
 Cookham Rise SL6 19 E6
 Maidenhead SL6 40 A7
Bridge Cl
 Lower Halliford KT12 125 F1
 Slough SL1 41 F6
 Staines TW18 96 E4
Bridge Ct Chertsey KT16 124 C2
 Taplow SL6 40 C7
Bridge End GU15 151 B4
Bridge Gdns TW15 98 C1
Bridge La GU25 122 F3
Bridge Rd Ascot SL5 120 D4
 Bagshot GU19 145 E3
 Camberley GU15 151 B3
 Chertsey KT16 124 B2
 Maidenhead SL6 40 B7
Bridge Ret Pk RG40 116 B5
Bridge St Caversham RG4 59 A2
 Colnbrook SL3 69 D7
 Hungerford RG17 100 D6
 Maidenhead SL6 40 A7
 Newbury RG14 105 A3
 Oatlands Park KT12 125 F2
 Reading RG1 86 A7
 Staines TW18 96 E4
Bridge View
 Maidenhead SL6 40 C7
 Sunningdale SL5 121 B2
Bridge Wlk GU46 149 D7
Bridge Works GU15 151 B3
Bridgeman Ct 5 SL4 67 A5
Bridgeman Dr SL4 67 A5
Bridges Cl RG41 115 F7
Bridges The RG7 136 C5
Bridgestone Dr SL8 3 C3
Bridgewater Cl RG30 58 C1
Bridgewater Ct SL3 44 A2
Bridgewater Terr SL4 67 D6
Bridgewater Way SL4 67 D6
Bridle Cl SL6 19 E1
Bridle Rd SL6 19 E1
Bridlepath Way TW14 98 E7
Bridlington Spur SL1 42 B4
Bridport Cl RG6 87 D2
Bridport Way SL2 22 B1
Brierley Pl RG31 57 C4
Briff La RG7 107 C7
Brigham Rd RG1 59 A1
Brighton Pl RG6 87 A6
Brighton Rd RG6 87 A6
Brighton Spur SL2 22 B1
Brightside Ave TW18 97 C1
Brightwalton CE Prim Sch RG20 28 D3
Brightwalton Gn RG20 28 D2
Brigidine Sch The SL4 67 D4
Brill Cl Caversham RG4 59 A4
 Maidenhead SL6 39 D3
 Marlow SL7 1 C2
Brimblecombe Cl RG41 89 A1
Brimpton CE Prim Sch RG7 133 F6
Brimpton La RG7 134 B3
Brimpton Rd
 Brimpton RG7 133 F7
 Reading RG30 85 B4
 Tadley RG26 134 D1
Brinkworth Pl SL4 95 B8
Brinn's La GU17 150 C5
Brinns Cotts GU17 150 C5
Briony Ho RG2 113 B7
Brisbane Rd RG30 85 B8
Bristol Cl TW19 70 E1
Bristol Ct 10 TW19 70 E1
Bristol Way SL1 42 F5
Bristow Ct Caversham RG4 59 B2
 Marlow SL7 2 A3
Bristow Inf Sch GU15 151 B2
Bristow Rd GU15 151 B3
Britannia Ind Est SL3 69 E5
Britannia Way TW19 97 D8
Brittain Ct GU47 150 C7
Britten Rd RG2 86 B5
Britwell Rd SL1 21 D2
Brixham Rd RG2 86 B2
Broad Hinton RG10 61 F3
Broad La Bracknell RG12 118 D6
 Bucklebury RG7 107 C6
 Wooburn Green HP10 3 F5
Broad Oak Ashford TW16 98 F2
 Slough SL2 22 C1
Broad Oak Ct SL2 22 C1
Broad Platts SL3 43 D3
Broad St East Ilsley RG20 30 E7
 Reading RG1 86 A7
 West End GU24 153 D6
 Wokingham RG40 116 C6
Broad St Wlk RG40 116 C6
Broad Street Mall RG1 86 A7
Broad Way RG7 138 D3
Broad Wlk GU16 151 E2
Broadacre TW18 97 A3
Broadcommon La RG10 89 C7
Broadcommon Rd RG10 89 B7
Broadhalfpenny La RG26 135 C1
Broadlands Ave TW17 125 C3
Broadlands Cl RG31 84 D5
Broadlands Ct RG42 117 E8
Broadlands Dr SL5 120 D2
Broadley Gn GU20 146 D4
Broadleys SL4 66 F7
Broadmark Rd SL2 43 B6
Broadmeadow End RG18 106 F4
Broadmoor Hospl RG45 143 E5
Broadmoor La RG4,RG10 60 E5
Broadmoor Prim Sch RG45 143 D4
Broadmoor Rd RG10, SL6 63 B6
Broadpool Cotts SL5 93 A1
Broadrick Heath RG42 91 E1
Broadview Est TW19 98 A8
Broadwater Cl TW19 95 E8
Broadwater La RG10 61 E1
Broadwater Pk SL6 40 E1
Broadwater Rd RG10 61 E2
Broadway Bracknell RG12 118 C7
 Maidenhead SL6 39 F7
 Staines TW18 97 B3
 Thatcham RG19 106 D3
 Winkfield SL4 93 B7
Broadway Ctyd RG19 106 D3
Broadway Green Farm Ind Est GU18 146 D2
Broadway Mall 6 SL6 39 F7
Broadway Rd GU18, GU20 146 C2
Broadway The
 Laleham TW18 124 C7
 Lambourn RG17 25 B3
 13 Newbury RG14 105 A4
 Sandhurst GU47 150 B8
Brocas Rd RG7 110 F1
Brocas St SL4 67 D7
Brocas Terr SL4 67 D7
Brock Gdns RG30 85 C8
Brock Hill Cotts RG42 92 A5
Brock La SL6 39 F7
Brock Lane Mall 7 SL6 39 F7
Brock Way GU25 122 C5
Brockbank Ho RG42 91 B1
Brockenhurst Dr 5 GU46 149 D5
Brockenhurst Rd
 Ascot SL5 120 B3
 Bracknell RG12 119 A6
Brockhurst (Marlston House) Sch RG18 79 F4
Brocklands GU46 149 B4
Brockley Cl RG30 85 A8
Brocks La RG7,RG18 80 B4
Brocks Way RG9 36 A4
Brocksett Cl RG30 85 D7
Brockton Ct SL6 39 F6
Brockway SL3 44 B1
Broken Furlong SL4 42 B1
Broken Way RG20 131 B2
Bromley Wlk RG30 84 F7
Brompton Cl 5 RG6 87 D1
Brompton Dr SL6 19 C2
Bromycroft Rd SL2 22 A2
Bronte Rise RG14 131 B8
Brook Cl Sandhurst GU47 143 E1
 Stanwell TW19 97 F8
 Wokingham RG41 116 A8
Brook Cotts GU46 149 C6
Brook Cres SL1 41 E7
Brook Dr Bracknell RG12 118 E5
 Reading RG30 112 E8
Brook Gn RG42 117 F8
Brook Ho Bradfield RG7 82 C7
 Newbury RG14 105 A3
 Slough SL1 42 D3
Brook La RG10 62 F3
Brook Lea RG4 59 C1
Brook Path SL1 41 F6
Brook Rd Bagshot GU19 145 E2
 Camberley GU15 151 B4
Brook St Twyford RG10 61 D4
 Windsor SL4 67 D5
Brook St W RG1 86 A6
Brookbank HP10 3 D3
Brookdene Cl SL6 19 F2
Brooke Furmston Pl SL7 1 E3
Brooke Pl RG42 90 D3
Brooker's Hill RG2 113 D6
Brookers Cnr RG45 143 C5
Brookers Row RG45 143 C6
Brookfield Ct GU18 146 C1
Brookfield Ho SL3 68 D6
Brookfield Rd HP10 3 D3
Brookfields Specl Sch RG31 57 C3
Brookhouse Dr SL8 3 C3
Brooklands Cl TW16 125 E8
Brooklyn Dr RG4 59 B6
Brookmill The RG1 85 F5
Brooks Rd RG18 106 E4
Brooksby Cl GU17 150 B5
Brooksby Rd RG31 57 D2
Brookside Chertsey KT16 123 E2
 Colnbrook SL3 69 C7
 Reading RG31 84 F4
 Sandhurst GU47 150 C8
 Slough SL3 43 E7
 Wokingham RG41 115 F7

Brookside Ave
Staines TW15 97 D3
Wraysbury TW19 68 E4
Brookside Bsns Ctr RG7 139 D6
Brookside Cl RG6 87 D2
Brookside Nursery RG7 139 D6
Brookside Pk GU14 151 A1
Brookside Wlk RG7 111 A4
Brookway RG14 105 E2
Brookway Trad Est RG14 105 E3
Broom Acres GU47 143 B1
Broom Cl RG31 84 C5
Broom Field GU18 153 A7
Broom Gr RG41 115 D4
Broom Hill
Cookham Rise SL6 19 E6
Stoke Poges SL2 23 A5
Broom Ho SL3 43 F2
Broom Way GU17 150 E4
Broome Cl GU46 149 C7
Broome Ct RG12 118 B6
Broome Lodge
Ascot SL5 120 D4
Staines TW18 97 B3
Broomfield TW18 97 A2
Broomfield Cl SL5 121 B2
Broomfield Gate SL2 22 B1
Broomfield Pk SL5 121 B2
Broomfield Rd RG30 84 F8
Broomhall Bldgs 1 SL5 121 B2
Broomhall La SL5 121 A3
Broomsquires Rd GU19 145 F2
Broughton Cl RG30 58 C1
Broughton Mews GU16 151 F1
Brownfield Gdns (Cvn Pk) SL6 39 E5
Browngraves Rd UB7 71 C7
Browning Cl
Frimley GU15 152 C4
Thatcham RG18 106 C4
Brownlow Dr RG42 91 C1
Brownlow Rd RG1 85 E7
Brownrigg Cres RG12 118 E8
Brownrigg Rd TW15 98 A4
Browns Ct SL1 41 E6
Brownsfield Rd RG18 106 C4
Bruan Rd RG14 130 F8
Bruce Ave TW17 125 C3
Bruce Cl SL1 42 A5
Bruce Rd RG5 87 D7
Bruce Wlk SL4 66 D5
Brucewood Par SL7 1 E5
Brudenell SL4 66 F3
Brummell Rd RG14 104 E5
Brunel Cl SL6 39 E5
Brunel Ctr SL6 39 D5
Brunel Dr
Crowthorne RG45 143 C8
Woodley RG5 60 F1
Brunel Rd Maidenhead SL6 39 D5
Reading RG30 85 B4
Theale RG7 83 F2
Brunel Ret Pk RG2 86 A3
Brunel Univ (Runnymede Campus) TW20 95 C5
Brunel Way SL1 42 F5
Brunswick RG12 118 A2
Brunswick Hill RG1 85 E7
Brunswick Lodge 3 RG1 85 E7
Brunswick St RG1 85 E6
Bruton Way RG12 118 E2
Bryant Ave SL2 42 E8
Bryant Pl RG8 57 B5
Bryants La RG18 53 E1
Brybur Cl RG2 113 D8
Bryer Pl SL4 66 D4
Bryony Ho RG42 117 E8
Bryony Way TW16 98 F2
Bsns Ctr The RG41 116 B4
Bsns Village The SL2 43 B5
Buccaneer Cl RG5 88 B8
Buccleuch Rd SL3 68 A7
Buchan The GU15 152 A8
Buchanan Dr RG40 141 E7
Buckden Cl RG5 88 A6
Buckfield Ct SL0 44 F4
Buckham Hill RG17,RG20 48 D6
Buckhurst Gr RG40 116 F5
Buckhurst Hill RG12 118 F5
Buckhurst La SL5 121 A6
Buckhurst Moors RG12 117 C6
Buckhurst Rd SL5 120 F7
Buckhurst Way RG6 87 A3
Buckingham Ave SL1 42 B7
Buckingham Ave E SL1 42 C7
Buckingham Ct
1 Staines TW18 97 A4
Wokingham RG40 116 C6
Buckingham Dr RG4 59 B5
Buckingham Gate SL7 17 D7
Buckingham Gdns 4 SL1 42 F4
Buckingham Ho 4 SL6 39 F6
Buckingham Rd RG14 104 F1
Buckingham Way GU16 151 F1
Buckland Ave SL3 43 B3
Buckland Cres SL4 66 F6
Buckland Gate SL3 23 B2
Buckland Jun & Inf Sch TW18 97 C1
Buckland Rd RG2 86 B3
Buckle La RG42 91 B6
Bucklebury RG12 118 A2
Bucklebury CE Prim Sch RG7 107 C5
Bucklebury Cl SL6 40 C1
Bucklebury Farm Pk* RG7 80 D1
Bucklebury Pl RG7 108 A5
Bucknell Ave RG8 56 E5
Bucknell Cl RG31 84 F4
Buckside RG4 59 A2
Buckthorn Cl RG40 116 E7
Buckthorns RG42 117 E8
Budebury Ct TW18 97 A3
Budebury Rd TW18 97 A3
Budge's Cotts RG40 116 E8
Budge's Gdns RG40 116 E7
Budge's Rd RG40 116 D7
Budham Way RG12 118 B3
Buffins SL6 20 E2
Builder's Cross SL6 65 E8
Bulkeley Ave SL4 67 B4
Bulkeley Cl TW20 95 C3
Bull La Bracknell RG42 118 B8
Riseley RG7 139 A3
Bull Mdw The RG8 33 F6
Bullbrook Dr RG12 118 F8
Bullbrook Row RG12 118 E7
Bullfinch Cl GU47 150 E8
Bulmershe Rd RG1 86 F6
Bulmershe Sch The RG5 87 C7
Bulpit La RG17 100 D4
Bulstrode Pl SL1 42 F3
Bunby Rd SL2 22 F5
Bunces Cl SL4 42 B1
Bunces La RG7 111 A2
Bundy's Way TW18 96 F2
Bungalow Dr RG31 84 D8
Bungler's Hill RG7 140 B6
Bunkers Hill RG14 130 C5
Bunten Meade SL1 42 B5
Bunyan Ct 12 RG1 86 A6
Burbage Gn RG12 118 F4
Burbidge Cl RG31 84 F3
Burbidge Rd TW17 125 A5
Burbury Woods GU15 151 E6
Burchell Rd RG14 104 E5
Burchett Coppice RG40 141 F8
Burchett's Green CE Inf Sch SL6 38 B7
Burchett's Green Rd SL6 38 B7
Burchetts Green La SL6 38 C6
Burchetts Way TW17 125 B3
Burcombe Way RG4 59 B4
Burcot Gdns SL6 19 E3
Burdens Heath RG7 107 A6
Burdett Ct RG2 86 D3
Burdock Cl
Burghfield Common RG7 111 B2
Lightwater GU18 153 B8
Burfield Rd SL4 95 B8
Burford Cl SL7 1 C5
Burford Ct 7 Reading RG1 85 F8
Wokingham RG40 116 E5
Burford Gdns SL1 41 C8
Burford Rd GU15 151 B4
Burford Sch SL7 1 C5
Burford's RG17 47 C6
Burges Way TW18 97 A3
Burgess Cl RG5 87 D4
Burgess La RG17,RG20 128 D6
Burgett Rd SL1 42 B3
Burghead Cl GU47 150 D7
Burghfield Bridge Cl RG30 84 F1
Burghfield Mill RG30 84 D2
Burghfield Rd RG30 85 A3
Burghfield St Mary's CE Prim Sch RG30 111 C6
Burgoyne Rd
Ashford TW16 98 F2
Camberley GU15 152 A6
Burleigh Gdns TW15 98 C3
Burleigh La SL5 119 E8
Burleigh Mews RG4 59 C6
Burleigh Rd
Frimley GU16 151 D1
North Ascot SL5 119 E7
Burley Orch KT16 124 A3
Burley Way GU17 150 C6
Burlingham Cl RG2 113 C6
Burlings The SL5 119 F7
Burlington Ave SL1 42 E4
Burlington Cl TW14 98 D8
Burlington Ct
Blackwater GU17 150 D3
1 Slough SL1 42 E4
Burlington Rd
Burnham SL1 21 B1
Reading RG30 84 D7
2 Slough SL1 42 E4
Burlsdon Way RG12 118 E8
Burn Moor Chase RG12 118 E2
Burn Wlk SL1 21 B2
Burne-Jones Dr GU47 150 D6
Burnet Cl GU24 153 E6
Burnetts Rd SL4 66 E6
Burney Bit RG26 135 E1
Burnham Beeches (Nature Reserve)* SL2 22 A7
Burnham Cl Bourne End SL8 3 A4
Windsor SL4 66 D5
Burnham Copse Inf Sch RG26 135 A1
Burnham Copse Jun Sch RG26 135 A1
Burnham Gr RG42 91 C1
Burnham Gram Sch SL1 21 D1
Burnham Hts SL1 41 C7
Burnham La SL1 41 E7
Burnham Manor GU15 152 A8
Burnham Rd RG26 134 F2
Burnham Rise RG4 59 C7
Burnham Sta SL1 41 D7
Burnham Upper Sch SL1 41 B8
Burniston Cl 5 RG6 87 E2
Burnmoor Mdw RG27 141 E2
Burns Cl RG5 87 E4
Burns Wlk RG18 106 C4
Burnt Oak
Cookham Rise SL6 19 F7
Wokingham RG40 141 F8
Burnt Pollard La GU24 146 E1
Burnthouse Gdns RG42 91 E1
Burnthouse La RG7, RG30 112 B6
Burrcroft Rd RG30 85 A5
Burrell Rd RG20 31 E4
Burrells The KT16 124 B1
Burroughs Cres SL8 3 A4
Burroway Rd SL3 44 B3
Burrows Hill La TW6, TW19 70 C3
Burrows The RG26 135 A1
Burton Cl Twyford RG10 61 E2
Windlesham GU20 146 D4
Burton Way SL4 66 E4
Burtons Hill RG17 102 B2
Burway Cres KT16 124 A5
Burwell Cl RG6 87 C1
Burwood Par KT16 124 A2
Bury La RG20 10 A2
Bury's Bank Rd RG19 132 C6
Bush Rd TW17 124 F4
Bush Wlk RG40 116 C6
Bushell Way RG2 140 E8
Butchers La SL6 63 D8
Butchers Row RG10 61 D4
Bute St RG30 85 B5
Butler Ct 5 SL7 1 F3
Butler Rd Bagshot GU19 145 F2
Crowthorne RG45 143 B6
Butlers Cl SL4 66 D6
Butson Cl RG14 104 E3
Buttenshaw Ave RG2 141 A8
Buttenshaw Cl RG2 141 A8
Butter Market RG1 86 B7
Buttercup Cl RG40 117 A6
Buttercup Pl RG18 106 D4
Buttercup Sq TW19 97 D7
Butterfield
Camberley GU15 151 B4
Wooburn HP10 3 D4
Buttermere Ave SL1 41 C8
Buttermere Cl TW14 98 F7
Buttermere Dr GU15 152 D4
Buttermere Gdns RG12 118 C6
Buttermere Way TW20 96 B1
Buttersteep Rise GU20, SL5 119 C1
Butts Furlong RG20 28 D3
Butts Hill Rd RG5 87 F8
Buxton Ave RG4 58 F4
Buxton Rd TW15 97 D3
Bybend Cl SL2 22 B4
Byefield Rd RG30 85 B4
Byeways Cl RG10 37 E3
Byland Dr SL6 40 B1
Byreton Cl RG6 87 B2
Byron SL3 44 B1
Byron Ave GU15 152 B3
Byron Cl 6 Marlow SL7 1 F3
Newbury RG14 130 F7
Twyford RG10 61 E4
Yateley GU46 149 B4
Byron Ct GU15 151 C5
Byron Dr RG45 143 B3
Byron Rd Earley RG6 87 A7
Twyford RG10 61 E4
Bythorn Cl RG6 87 E2
Byways Burnham SL1 41 A8
Yateley GU46 149 B5
Bywood RG12 118 A2
Byworth Cl RG2 113 B7

C

Cabbage Hill La RG42 90 E4
Cabin Moss RG12 118 E2
Cabrera Ave GU25 122 D3
Cabrera Cl GU25 122 D3
Cadbury Cl TW16 98 E1
Cadbury Rd TW16 98 E2
Caddy Cl 9 TW20 96 A3
Cadogan Cl Holyport SL6 65 A8
Reading RG30 84 E7
Cadogan Ct GU15 151 E3
Cadogan Pl RG4 59 B3
Cadwell Dr SL6 39 D3
Caesar's Camp Rd GU15 152 A8
Caesar's Cl 3 GU15 152 A8
Caesar's Way TW17 125 D3
Caesars Ct 2 GU15 152 A8
Caesars Gate RG42 91 E1
Cages Wood Dr SL2 22 B8
Cain Rd RG12 117 D7
Cain's La TW14 71 E2
Cairn Cl GU15 152 B3
Cairngorm Pl SL2 22 D1
Cairngorm Rd RG19 106 D2
Caistor Cl RG31 84 B4
Calard Dr RG18 106 A5
Calbourne Dr RG31 84 D4
Calbroke Rd SL2 21 F2
Calcot Ct RG31 84 E5
Calcot Inf Sch RG31 84 C4
Calcot Jun Sch RG31 84 C4
Calcot Place Dr RG31 84 F4
Calcott Pk GU46 149 C6
Caldbeck Dr RG5 87 F7
Calder Cl Maidenhead SL6 19 E1
Reading RG30 84 F8
Calder Ct Maidenhead SL6 19 D1
Slough SL3 43 F1
Calder Way SL3 69 E4
Caldicott Sch SL2 22 B5
Caldwell Rd GU20 146 D5
Caledonia Rd TW19 97 E7
Caleta Cl RG4 59 D2
Calfridus Way RG12 118 F6
California Ctry Pk* RG2 141 C7
California Cvn Pk RG40 141 D7
Calleva Mus* RG7 136 B1
Calleva Pk RG7 134 E2
Calleva Roman Town* RG7 136 D1
Callin's La RG10 63 B3
Callington Rd RG2 86 C1
Callis Farm Cl TW19 70 E1
Callow Hill GU25 122 C7
Calshot Pl RG31 84 D4
Calshot Rd TW6 71 B5
Calshot Way TW6 71 A5
Calvin Cl GU15 152 B4
Camberley Inf Sch GU15 151 C5
Camberley Rd TW6 71 A4
Camberley Sta GU15 151 D5
Camberley Twrs 1 GU15 151 D5
Camborne Cl Earley RG6 87 A1
Harmondsworth TW6 71 A4
Camborne Cres TW6 71 A4
Camborne Rd S TW6 71 A4
Camborne Way TW6 71 A4
Cambria Ct Slough SL3 43 C4
Staines TW18 96 E4
Cambria Gdns TW19 97 E8
Cambrian Cl GU15 151 B5
Cambrian Way
Reading RG31 84 D4
Wokingham RG40 142 A8
Cambridge Ave
Burnham SL1 21 B3
Slough SL1 42 A7
Cambridge Cl UB7 70 D8
Cambridge Ho 1 SL4 67 C6
Cambridge Rd
Crowthorne RG45 143 C4
Littleton TW15 98 C1
Marlow SL7 1 D2
Sandhurst GU47 143 E1
Cambridge Sq GU15 151 C6
Cambridge St 1 RG1 85 F8
Cambridge Wlk GU15 151 C6
Cambridgeshire Cl
Bracknell RG42 91 F1
Wokingham RG41 115 E6
Camden Pl Bourne End SL8 3 A3
Reading RG31 84 B4
Camden Rd SL6 19 D1
Camelford Cl RG2 86 B1
Camellia Ct GU24 153 F6
Camellia Way RG41 115 D7
Camilla Cl TW16 98 F2
Camley Gdns SL6 39 A8
Camley Park Dr SL6 38 F8
Camm Ave SL4 66 E4
Camp Rd RG7 110 D2
Campbell Cl GU46 149 F6
Campbell Pl GU16 151 F3
Campbell Rd RG5 87 D6
Campbell's Gn RG7 137 B5
Camperdown SL6 20 B1
Camperdown Ho 1 SL4 67 C5
Campion Cl GU17 150 F3
Campion Ho
Bracknell RG42 117 E8
6 Newbury RG14 104 F2
Campion Way RG40 116 E7
Canada Rd SL1 43 B4
Canal View Rd RG14 105 D3
Canal Way RG1 86 D7
Canal Wharf SL3 44 A4
Canal Wlk
Hungerford RG17 100 D6
Newbury RG14 105 A3
Canberra Cl GU46 149 A7
Canberra Rd TW6 71 A4
Candleford Cl RG12 91 C1
Candover Cl UB7 70 D7
Canford Ct RG30 85 D8
Canhurst La RG10 37 D3
Cannock Cl SL6 40 B6
Cannock Way RG6 87 C1
Cannon (West end of General Roy's base line)* TW6 71 B6
Cannon Cl GU47 150 F8
Cannon Court Rd SL6 19 D3
Cannon Gate SL2 43 C6
Cannon Hill RG12 118 C3
Cannon Hill Cl SL6 40 C2
Cannon La SL6 38 F3
Cannon Mews SL5 119 B8
Cannon St 1 RG1 85 E7
Cannondown Rd SL6 19 E5
Canon Hill Dr SL6 40 B3
Canon Hill Way SL6 40 B3
Canon's Cloisters SL4 67 D7
Canopus Way TW19 97 E8
Cansfield End RG14 104 F3
Canterbury Ave SL2 22 C1
Canterbury Ct TW15 97 F4
Canterbury Rd RG2 86 C3
Cantley Cres RG41 116 A8
Cape Villas SL0 44 E7
Capital Point 14 RG1 86 A6
Capper Rd GU15 151 A7
Capricorn Ho HP10 3 A8
Captains Gorse RG8 54 F6
Caraway Rd RG6 87 A1
Carbery La SL5 120 B6
Carbinswood La RG7 108 B5
Cardiff Mews RG4 58 F1
Cardiff Rd RG1 58 F1
Cardigan Cl SL1 41 F6
Cardigan Gdns RG1 86 E5
Cardigan Rd RG1 86 E6
Cardinal Cl RG4 59 B2
Cardinal's Wlk TW16 98 E2
Cardinals Wlk SL6 41 C7
Cardwell Cres SL5 120 C4
Carew Cl RG31 57 B4
Carew Rd TW15 98 C2
Carey Cl SL4 67 B4
Carey Rd RG40 116 C5
Carey St RG1 85 F7
Cariad Ct RG8 34 B7
Caribou Cl RG5 87 E8
Carisbrooke Cl
Caversham RG4 59 C6
Maidenhead SL6 39 C6
Carisbrooke Ct SL1 42 F6
Carland Cl RG6 87 A1
Carlesgill Pl RG9 35 E7
Carlile Gdns RG10 61 D6
Carlin Pl GU15 151 C4
Carlinwark Dr GU15 151 F7
Carlisle Rd Reading RG31 57 E3
Slough SL1 42 D6
Carlton Cl Frimley GU15 152 B3
Woodley RG5 87 E6
Carlton Ct TW18 97 A3
Carlton Ho TW14 71 F1
Carlton Rd Ashford TW16 98 F1
Caversham RG4 58 E5
Slough SL2 43 B6
Carlyle Ct RG45 143 C5
Carlyle Rd TW18 97 A1
Carmarthen Rd SL1 42 E6
Carmel Ct SL7 1 B1
Carmella Ct TW15 98 D1
Carnarvon Rd RG1 86 E6
Carnation Cl RG45 143 B8
Carnation Dr RG42 92 B2
Carnegie Rd RG14 105 A2
Carnoustie RG12 117 E2
Carnoustie Ct 10 RG1 86 D7
Carolina Pl RG40 141 E7
Caroline Ct TW15 98 B2
Caroline Dr RG41 116 A7
Caroline Pl UB3 71 E7
Caroline St 5 RG1 85 F8
Caroline Way GU16 151 F1
Carpenters Cl RG5 87 F5
Carpenters Ct RG7 137 A6
Carrick Gdns RG5 87 D7
Carrick La GU46 149 E6
Carrington Ave HP10 3 A8
Carrington Jun Sch HP10 3 A8
Carrington Rd SL1 42 E6
Carroll Cres SL5 119 F5
Carron Cl RG30 85 A7
Carsdale Cl RG1 85 F5
Carshalton Rd GU15 145 A1
Carshalton Way RG6 87 C1
Carston Gr RG31 84 F4
Carter Cl SL4 67 A5
Carter's Hill RG40,RG42 90 A4
Carters Rise RG31 84 F3
Cartmel Dr RG5 87 D6
Carwarden House Com Sch GU15 152 A3
Cary Cl RG14 130 D6
Casey Ct RG7 81 D3
Cassia Dr RG6 86 F1
Cassiobury Ave TW14 98 F8
Cassocks Sq TW17 125 D2
Castle Ave SL3 68 A8
Castle Cl
3 Charlton TW16 98 E1
Frimley GU15 151 F4
Castle Cres RG1 85 F6
Castle Ct SL6 39 D7
Castle Dr SL6 39 D7
Castle End RG10 62 B7
Castle End Rd RG10 62 A7
Castle Farm Cvn Site SL4 66 D5
Castle Gate 6 RG1 86 A7
Castle Gr RG14 104 F5
Castle Hill Maidenhead SL6 39 E7
Reading RG1 85 F6
Swallowfield RG2,RG7 140 C7
Windsor SL4 67 D6
Castle Hill Rd TW20 95 C5
Castle Hill Terr SL6 39 E7
Castle Ind Pk RG14 105 C5
Castle La RG14 104 E6
Castle Lodge SL6 39 F7
Castle Mews SL6 39 E7
Castle Rd GU15 151 F4
Castle St Reading RG1 86 A7
Slough SL1 42 F3
Castlecraig Ct GU47 150 D7
Castleman Ho SL5 120 D4
Castlemead Cotts SL4 67 C3
Castleton Ct SL7 1 E2
Castleview Ho 1 SL4 67 D6
Castleview Prim Sch SL3 43 D2
Castleview Rd SL3 43 C2
Castor Ct GU46 149 B7

Caswall Cl RG42 90 C2
Caswall Ride GU46 149 F5
Catalina Cl RG5 88 B7
Catalina Rd TW6 71 B5
Catcliffe Way RG6 113 F8
Catena Rise GU18 146 B1
Catesby Gdns GU46 149 A5
Catherine Dr TW16 98 F2
Catherine Ho SL5 120 B6
Catherine Rd RG14 105 A2
Catherine St RG30 85 E8
Catlin Cres TW17 125 D4
Catmore Rd RG20 29 C7
Caunter Rd RG14 104 D4
Causeway Est TW20 96 C4
Causeway The
Caversham RG4 59 D1
Egham TW18,TW20 96 D4
Maidenhead SL6 40 C4
Marlow SL7 1 E1
Causmans Way RG31 57 C2
Cavalier Cl
Newbury RG14 105 C5
Theale RG7 83 D2
Cavalier Ct TW15 98 D1
Cavalry Cres SL4 67 C4
Cavendish Cl
Ashford TW16 98 F2
Burnham SL6 41 A7
Cavendish Ct
Ashford TW16 98 F2
Blackwater GU17 150 D3
Newbury RG14 105 E5
Poyle SL3 69 E6
Cavendish Gdns 1 RG41 88 A3
Cavendish Meads SL5 120 D3
Cavendish Pk GU47 150 E6
Cavendish Rd
Ashford TW16 98 F2
Caversham RG4 59 C6
Caversham Hill RG4 59 B4
Caversham Park Dr RG4 59 C5
Caversham Park Prim Sch
RG4 59 D6
Caversham Park Rd RG4 59 E6
Caversham Prim Sch
RG4 59 A3
Caversham Rd RG1 59 A1
Caversham Wharf RG1 59 A1
Caves Farm Cl GU47 150 A8
Cawcott Dr SL4 66 E6
Cawsam Gdns RG4 59 D4
Caxton Cl RG30 58 C1
Caxton Ct RG9 15 E1
Cecil Aldin Dr RG31 57 C5
Cecil Cl TW15 98 C1
Cecil Rd Ashford TW15 98 C2
Iver SL0 44 E7
Cecil Way SL2 21 F1
Cedar RG9 15 D2
Cedar Ave GU17 150 D5
Cedar Chase SL6 20 D1
Cedar Cl Bagshot GU19 145 E3
Laleham TW18 124 C6
Wokingham RG40 116 C6
Cedar Ct Egham TW20 96 A4
Maidenhead SL6 39 D7
Marlow SL7 1 E2
6 Windsor SL4 67 A5
Cedar Dr Bracknell RG42 91 C1
Cookham SL6 20 A7
Marlow Bottom SL7 1 C7
Pangbourne RG8 56 C4
Sunningdale SL5 121 A2
Cedar Gr RG19 106 C3
Cedar Ho TW16 98 F1
Cedar Mount RG14 130 F8
Cedar Pl RG5 87 F6
Cedar Rd
East Bedfont TW14 98 D7
Reading RG2 86 E1
Cedar Rise RG19 133 B5
Cedar Way Charlton TW16 98 E1
Slough SL3 43 E2
Cedar Wood Cres RG4 59 B4
Cedars Cl GU47 149 F8
Cedars Ho SL6 40 A7
Cedars Rd SL6 40 A7
Cedars Sch RG7 135 A7
Cedars The
2 Bracknell RG12 118 F5
Greenham RG19 131 C7
Reading RG31 57 D2
Slough SL2 21 F2
Celandine Cl RG45 143 C6
Celandine Ct GU46 149 B7
Celandine Gr RG18 106 F3
Celia Cres TW15 97 D2
Cell Farm SL4 68 B2
Cell Farm Ave SL4 68 B2
Celsea Pl OX10 14 A8
Cemetery La TW17 125 B2
Centenary Bsns Pk RG9 15 E1
Central Dr SL1 41 F6
Central Est SL6 39 E8
Central La SL4 93 B7
Central Way SL4 93 B7
Central Wlk RG40 116 C6
Centre The
Farnham Common SL2 22 C6
Oatlands Park KT12 125 F1
Centurion Cl Reading RG1 86 B6
4 Sandhurst GU47 150 D8
Century Cl RG10 37 E4
Century Dr RG7 113 C1
Century Rd TW18,TW20 96 C3
Cerotus Pl KT16 123 F2
Chackfield Dr RG41 115 D8
Chaddleworth St Andrews CE Prim Sch RG20 49 B7
Chaffinch Cl
Reading RG31 84 B7
5 Sandhurst GU47 150 D8
Wokingham RG41 115 E5
Chagford Rd RG2 86 B1
Chain St RG1 86 A7
Chainhill Rd Ox12 8 A7
Chalcott SL1 42 E3
Chalcraft Cl RG9 35 C8
Chalfont Cl RG6 87 A1
Chalfont Ct RG6 87 A1
Chalfont Way RG6 87 A1
Chalford Flats HP10 3 F6
Chalford Rd RG14 104 E2
Chalgrove Cl SL6 40 B6
Chalgrove Way RG4 59 B6
Chalk Hill
Aston Tirrold OX11 12 F8
Shiplake RG9 35 C6
Windsor SL4 67 F6
Chalk Pit La SL1 21 B4
Chalkhousegreen La
RG4 59 C8
Chalklands SL8 3 A4
Chalkpit Cotts RG7 83 C6
Chalkpit La SL7 1 B2
Chalkpits The HP10 3 E6
Chalkstream Way HP10 3 E7
Challenge Rd TW15 98 D5
Challenor Cl RG40 141 F7
Challis Pl RG42 117 E8
Challow Ct SL6 19 D1
Chalmers Rd TW15 98 B3
Chalmers Rd E TW15 98 C3
Chalvey Gdns SL1 42 E4
Chalvey Gr SL1 42 B4
Chalvey Pk SL1 42 E4
Chalvey Rd E SL1 42 E4
Chalvey Rd W SL1 42 D4
Chamberhouse Mill La
RG19 106 F1
Chamberlain's Gdns
RG2 114 E2
Chambers Bsns Pk UB7 71 A8
Chambers The 10 RG1 86 B7
Champion Rd RG4 59 C1
Champney Cl SL3 69 A4
Chancel Mans RG42 91 C2
Chancellor's Way The
RG2,RG6 86 E4
Chancery Mews 13 RG1 85 F7
Chancery Pl SL4 67 D7
Chanctonbury Dr SL5 120 E1
Chandlers Cl TW14 98 F8
Chandlers La GU46 149 D8
Chandlers Quay SL6 40 C8
Chandos Mall 8 SL1 42 F4
Chandos Rd Egham TW18 96 D3
Newbury RG14 131 A8
Chantry Cl SL4 67 A6
Chantry Ct GU16 151 D1
Chantry Mead RG17 100 C5
Chantry Rd
Bagshot GU19 145 D2
Chertsey KT16 124 C2
Chapel Arches SL6 40 A7
Chapel Cl Bracknell RG12 118 D6
South Stoke RG8 14 C3
Chapel Cotts SL2 23 B5
Chapel Ct
Hungerford RG17 100 D6
Maidenhead SL6 39 D4
8 Reading RG1 86 B7
Thatcham RG18 106 E3
Chapel Hill Reading RG31 84 C8
Windsor SL4 67 D6
Chapel La
Ashampstead RG8 54 B7
Bagshot GU19 145 D2
Binfield RG42 90 C1
Blewbury OX11 12 A8
Curridge RG18 78 E4
Farnborough GU14 151 A1
Headley RG19 133 F1
Hermitage RG18 79 C8
Lambourn RG17 25 B3
Riseley RG7 139 C3
Shinfield RG7 113 B2
Silchester RG7 135 F5
Stoke Poges SL2 23 B5
Yattendon RG18 53 E1
Chapel Lodge RG40 141 F6
Chapel Rd
Camberley GU15 151 B5
Flackwell Heath HP10 3 A8
Silchester RG7 136 C5
Stockcross RG20 103 E6
Chapel Sq
Sandhurst GU15 150 F6
Thorpe GU25 122 E5
Chapel St Marlow SL7 1 E2
Slough SL1 42 F4
Thatcham RG18,RG19 106 D3
Chapel Terr RG42 90 C1
Chapels Cl SL1 41 E5
Chaplain's Hill RG45 143 D4
Chaplin Cres TW16 98 E2
Chapman La HP10,SL8 3 A6
Chapman Wlk RG18 106 B4
Chapter Mews SL4 67 D7
Chard Cl RG5 87 E6
Charfield Ct RG1 86 E7
Charlbury Cl 8 RG12 118 F5
Charlecombe Ct TW18 97 B3
Charlecombe Ho RG40 116 C6
Charles Ct TW15 98 C4
Charles Evans Way RG4 59 D2
Charles Gdns SL2 43 A7
Charles Ho
Henley-On-T RG9 15 E3
8 Windsor SL4 67 C6
Charles Pl 12 RG1 86 D7
Charles Rd Cholsey OX10 14 A8
Staines TW18 97 D2
Charles Sq RG12 118 C7
Charles St Chertsey KT16 123 F1
Newbury RG14 130 D6
Reading RG1 85 F8
Windsor SL4 67 C6
Charlock Cl RG18 106 E5
Charlott's Pl 16 SL4 67 D6
Charlotte Ave SL2 42 F6
Charlotte Cl RG18 79 A6
Charlotte Way 9 SL7 1 E2
Charlton SL4 66 C5
Charlton Cl Slough SL1 42 B4
Wokingham RG40 141 F8
Charlton Ct GU47 143 D1
Charlton Ho TW17 125 C7
Charlton La
Swallowfield RG7 139 C5
Upper Halliford TW17 125 D5
Charlton Pl
Newbury RG14 105 A4
2 Windsor SL4 66 C5
Charlton Rd TW17 125 C7
Charlton Row 5 SL4 66 C5
Charlton Sq 4 SL4 66 C5
Charlton Way SL4 66 C5
Charlton Wlk 3 SL4 66 C5
Charlville Dr RG31 84 B4
Charmile Ct 1 TW16 98 E1
Charmwood Cl RG14 104 F5
Charndon Cl RG2 86 B5
Charnham Ct RG17 100 E6
Charnham La RG17 100 D6
Charnham Pk RG17 100 D7
Charnham St RG17 100 D6
Charnwood SL5 120 F3
Charnwood Ct RG2 86 B2
Charnwood Ho 9 RG1 85 E5
Charrington Rd RG31 84 C4
Charta Rd W TW20 96 C2
Charter Cl SL1 42 F3
Charter Pl TW18 97 A2
Charter Rd
Newbury RG14 130 F7
Slough SL1 41 E6
Charterhouse Cl RG12 118 E4
Charters Cl SL5 120 D4
Charters La SL5 120 D4
Charters Rd SL5 120 E2
Charters Sch SL5 120 D2
Charters Way SL5 120 F2
Charvil House Rd RG10 61 A5
Charvil La RG4 60 F4
Charvil Meadow Rd RG10 61 B5
Charwood Rd RG40 116 F7
Chase Gdns RG42 90 C3
Chase The Ascot SL5 93 A1
Crowthorne RG45 143 A6
Maidenhead SL6 19 C3
Marlow SL7 2 A3
Newbury RG14 104 F7
Reading RG31 84 D4
Chaseley Ct KT13 125 E1
Chaseside Ave RG10 61 D7
Chaseside Gdns KT16 124 B2
Chatfield SL2 42 A8
Chatham Ct
Bracknell RG12 118 B3
3 Slough SL1 43 A3
Chatham St RG1 85 F8
Chatham The 1 RG1 86 A8
Chatsworth Ave RG41 88 B2
Chatsworth Cl
Caversham RG4 59 C6
Maidenhead SL6 39 C5
Chatsworth Hts GU15 152 B7
Chatteris Way RG6 114 C8
Chattern Ct TW15 98 B4
Chattern Hill TW15 98 B4
Chattern Rd TW15 98 C4
Chatters The RG7 140 C7
Chatton Cl RG6 114 A8
Chaucer Cl
Caversham RG4 59 A5
Windsor SL4 67 D4
Wokingham RG40 116 F6
Chaucer Cres RG14 104 E5
Chaucer Gr GU15 151 D5
Chaucer Rd Ashford TW15 97 F4
Crowthorne RG45 143 B4
Chaucer Way Slough SL1 42 F5
Wokingham RG41 115 E5
Chauntry Cl SL6 40 C6
Chauntry Rd SL6 40 B6
Chavey Down Rd RG42 92 B2
Chawridge La SL4 92 C7
Chazey Cl RG4 58 C8
Chazey Rd RG4 58 D3
Cheam Cl RG12 118 D4
Cheap St Compton RG20 31 E5
Newbury RG14 105 A2
Cheapside RG1 86 A7
Cheapside CE Prim Sch
SL5 120 E8
Cheapside Ct SL5 120 E8
Cheapside Rd SL5 120 D7
Cheddar Rd TW6 71 B5
Cheddington Cl RG30 84 F6
Cheeseman Cl RG40 116 D7
Cheffrey Ct TW15 98 B2
Chelford Way RG4 58 F4
Chelmsford Ct 4 SL4 67 C5
Chelsea Cl RG30 84 F8
Chelwood Dr GU47 142 F1
Chelwood Rd RG6 87 B2
Cheney Cl RG42 90 D2
Cheney Ct RG45 143 C5
Cheniston Ct SL5 121 A2
Cheniston Gr SL6 38 F7
Chepstow Rd RG31 57 D2
Chequer La RG7 138 E2
Chequers Bridge Cotts
SL0 44 C4
Chequers Orch SL0 44 F7
Chequers Way RG5 87 C7
Cherbury Cl RG12 118 E5
Cherington Gate SL6 19 B1
Cherington Way SL5 119 E7
Cheriton Ave RG10 61 D6
Cheriton Cl RG14 131 B8
Cheriton Ct 2 RG1 86 A6
Cheriton Way GU17 150 D5
Cherries The SL2 43 B7
Cherry Ave SL3 43 D4
Cherry Cl Caversham RG4 59 C8
Flackwell Heath HP10 3 B7
Newbury RG14 104 F4
Cherry Cnr HP10 3 B8
Cherry Garden La
Littlewick Green SL6 38 E4
White Waltham SL6 63 E8
Cherry Gr
Hungerford RG17 100 C5
Reading RG2 86 E2
Cherry Orch
Great Shefford RG17 48 B4
Staines TW18 97 A3
Stoke Poges SL2 23 A5
Cherry Rise HP10 3 B7
Cherry Tree Ave TW18 97 B2
Cherry Tree Cl
Chieveley RG20 51 C4
Sandhurst GU47 143 D1
Cherry Tree Dr RG12 118 D6
Cherry Tree Gr RG41 115 D4
Cherry Tree La SL3 23 F6
Cherry Tree Rd SL2 22 C5
Cherry Way Horton SL3 69 C4
Upper Halliford TW17 125 E5
Cherrydale Rd GU15 152 D5
Cherrywood Ave TW20 95 B1
Cherrywood Gdns HP10 3 B8
Chertsey Bridge Rd
KT16,TW18 124 D2
Chertsey Bvd KT16 123 F1
Chertsey La TW18 96 F2
Chertsey Mus★ KT15 124 A3
Chertsey Rd
Ashford TW15,TW16 98 D2
Feltham TW13,TW16 98 E4
Lower Halliford TW17 125 A2
Shepperton TW17 124 F2
Windlesham GU20 146 E5
Chertsey Sta KT16 123 F1
Chertsey Wlk KT16 124 A2
Chervil Way RG7 111 B2
Cherwell Cl
Brands Hill SL3 69 B8
Maidenhead SL6 40 A8
Cherwell Cres 3 RG1 85 F7
Cherwell Rd
Bourne End SL8 3 B4
Caversham RG4 59 A6
Cheseridge Rd RG20 31 C4
Cheshire Ct SL1 43 B4
Cheshire Pk RG42 91 E2
Chessholme Ct TW16 98 E1
Chessholme Rd TW15 98 C2
Chester Cl Ashford TW15 98 D3
Newbury RG14 105 C1
Chester Rd
Harlington TW6 71 A4
Slough SL1 42 D7
Chester St Caversham RG4 59 A2
Reading RG30 85 D8
Chesterblade La RG12 118 E2
Chesterfield Ct TW15 97 E4
Chesterfield Mews TW15 97 E4
Chesterfield Rd
Ashford TW15 97 E3
Newbury RG14 105 A1
Chesterman St RG1 86 B6
Chesterment Way RG6 87 D1
Chesters Rd GU15 152 B5
Chesterton Dr TW19 97 F7
Chesterton Rd RG18 106 C5
Chestnut Ave
Camberley GU15 152 A6
Caversham RG4 59 E4
Slough SL3 43 E4
Wentworth GU25 121 F5
Wokingham RG41 115 E7
Chestnut Chase RG42 92 A1
Chestnut Cl
Ashford,Chattern Hill TW15 98 B4
Ashford,Felthamhill TW16 98 F2
Blackwater GU17 150 E4
Englefield Green TW20 95 C2
Fawley OX12 27 C7
Harlington UB7 71 B7
Maidenhead SL6 20 B1
Medmenham SL7 17 D7
Theale RG7 83 E4
Chestnut Cotts RG8 34 A6
Chestnut Cres
Newbury RG14 105 A4
Shinfield RG2 113 F4
Chestnut Ct 10 RG14 105 A4
Chestnut Dr
Burghfield Common RG30 111 B4
Englefield Green TW20 95 D2
Windsor SL4 66 F3
Chestnut Gr
Purley On T RG8 57 D5
Staines TW18 97 C2
Chestnut Ho RG45 143 C5
Chestnut La RG17 25 E4
Chestnut Manor Cl TW18 97 B3
Chestnut Pk SL6 40 E3
Chestnut Rd TW15 98 B4
Chestnut Wlk
Hungerford RG17 100 D4
Upper Halliford TW17 125 E5
Chestnuts The RG9 36 A3
Chetwode Cl RG40 116 E6
Cheveley Gdns SL1 21 C3
Cheviot Cl Frimley GU15 152 C4
Harlington UB3 71 D7
Maidenhead SL6 40 B6
Newbury RG14 130 C5
Cheviot Dr RG10 61 B4
Cheviot Rd
Sandhurst GU47 142 F2
Slough SL3 44 A1
Chewter Cl GU19 145 F3
Chewter La GU20 146 B6
Cheylesmore Dr GU16 152 D3
Cheyne Rd TW15 98 D2
Chichester Ct Slough SL1 43 B4
Stanwell TW19 97 E7
Chichester Rd RG30 84 E8
Chicory Cl RG6 86 F1
Chieveley Cl RG31 84 C8
Chieveley Mews SL5 121 A2
Chieveley Prim Sch
RG20 78 A8
Chilbolton TW20 95 E3
Chilcombe Way RG6 87 D2
Child Cl RG40 116 D8
Child St RG17 25 A3
Childrey Way RG31 84 B8
Chillingham Way GU15 151 C4
Chilsey Green Rd KT16 123 E2
Chiltern Cl
Henley-On-T RG9 35 B8
Newbury RG14 130 C5
Staines TW18 97 A3
Chiltern Coll The RG4 59 B3
Chiltern Court Mews SL4 67 B6
Chiltern Cres RG6 87 A8
Chiltern Ct
Caversham RG4 59 B6
Windsor SL4 67 B6
Chiltern Dr RG10 61 B4
Chiltern End Cl RG9 35 C8
Chiltern Gn HP10 3 A8
Chiltern Hts RG4 59 C4
Chiltern Manor RG10 36 D2
Chiltern Rd Burnham SL1 41 B8
Caversham RG4 59 C4
Maidenhead SL6 40 B6
Marlow SL7 1 C2
Sandhurst GU47 142 F1
Chiltern View RG8 57 D5
Chiltern Wlk RG8 56 D5
Chilterns Cl HP10 3 B7
Chilterns Pk SL8 3 B5
Chilton Ct SL6 41 C7
Chilton Cty Prim Sch
OX11 10 C8
Chilton Ent Ctr RG7 83 E3
Chilton Foliat CE Prim Sch
RG17 73 A2
Chilton Way RG17 100 C5
Chilwick Rd SL2 21 F1
Chimney La HP10 3 E8
Chippendale Cl
Blackwater GU17 150 E4
Tadley RG26 134 E1
Chippenham Cl RG6 113 F8
Chisbury Cl RG12 118 E3
Chiswick Lodge 4 SL7 1 D2
Chitterfield Gate UB7 71 A7
Chittering Cl RG6 87 C1
Chive Rd RG6 87 A1
Chivers Dr RG40 141 E7
Chives Pl RG42 91 D1
Chobham Rd GU16 152 A2
Choke La SL6 19 B4
Cholmeley Pl RG1 86 E7
Cholmeley Rd RG1 86 E8
Cholmeley Terr RG1 86 E7
Cholsey Rd RG19 106 E3
Choseley Cl RG10 37 E4
Choseley Rd RG10 37 E4
Chrislaine Cl TW19 70 D1
Christ Church CE Inf Sch
GU25 122 B6
Christ The King RC Fst Sch
TW19 70 E1
Christ the King RC Prim Sch
RG2 113 C8
Christchurch Cotts
GU25 122 B6
Christchurch Ct 4 RG1 86 C5
Christchurch Dr GU47 150 D6
Christchurch Gdns RG2 86 C5
Christchurch Rd
Harlington TW6 71 A4
Reading RG2 86 C5
Virginia Water GU25 122 C5
Christian Sq 3 SL4 67 C6
Christie Cl GU18 146 C1

Christie Hts RG14 ....131 B8
Christie Wlk GU46 ......149 C4
Christopher Ct
  Ashford TW15 ....97 E3
  Newbury RG14 ....105 B2
Christopher Ho SL2 ......22 C7
Chudleigh Gdns RG2 .....86 C2
Chuff Cnr RG42 ....91 D2
Church App TW20 ....123 C6
Church Ave RG9 ....15 E2
Church Cl Eton SL4 ....67 D8
  Hamstead Marshall RG20 .129 C6
  Laleham TW18 ....124 C6
  Lambourn RG17 ....25 B2
  Maidenhead SL6 ....39 D6
  Winnersh RG41 ....88 C2
Church Cotts SL6 ....20 E2
Church Croft RG17 ......100 D6
Church Dr SL6 ....40 C4
Church End La RG30 ......84 F7
Church Farm Barns
  RG7 ....137 D5
Church Farm Cotts RG10 .62 F7
Church Gate RG19 ....106 D3
Church Gr SL3 ....43 C8
Church Hams RG40 ......141 D6
Church Hill Binfield RG42 .90 C5
  Camberley GU15 ....151 E5
  Chilton OX11 ....10 D8
  East Ilsley RG20 ....30 E6
  Hurst RG10 ....88 E6
  Wickham RG20 ....75 C3
  Woolhampton RG7 ......107 E3
Church La Arborfield RG2 .114 D4
  Ascot SL5 ....120 C5
  Ashampstead RG8 ....54 A6
  Barkham RG40 ....115 C1
  Binfield RG42 ....90 E4
  Bisley GU24 ....153 F4
  Brimpton RG7 ....133 F6
  Burghfield Common RG30 .111 E6
  Caversham RG4 ....59 E7
  Chieveley RG20 ....51 B1
  Combe RG17 ....147 E6
  Finchampstead RG40 ....141 E4
  Hamstead Marshall RG20 .129 F7
  Hungerford RG17 ....100 D6
  Maidenhead SL6 ....40 C4
  Newbury RG14 ....104 D4
  Newell Green RG42 ......91 D5
  Shinfield RG2 ....113 C5
  Shiplake RG9 ....35 F1
  Silchester RG7 ....136 E1
  Slough SL2,SL3 ....43 C8
  Stoke Poges SL2 ....22 F2
  Sunningdale SL5 ....121 B4
  Swallowfield RG7 ......140 D6
  Thatcham RG19 ....106 D3
  Twyford RG10 ....61 F5
  Ufton Nervet RG7 ......110 C4
  🄰 Windsor SL4 ....67 D6
  Yattendon RG18 ....53 E1
Church Mews
  Purley On T RG8 ....57 D5
  Woodley RG5 ....87 F8
  Yateley GU46 ....149 D7
Church Par TW15 ....97 F4
Church Path SL6 ....40 C4
Church Rd
  Aldermaston RG7 ......135 B7
  Arborfield RG7 ....140 C5
  Ascot SL5 ....120 A5
  Ashford TW15 ....97 F4
  Bagshot GU19 ....145 D3
  Blewbury OX11 ....12 A8
  Bracknell RG12 ....118 C7
  Caversham RG4 ....59 A2
  Cookham Dean SL6 ......19 B6
  Egham TW20 ....96 A3
  Farnham Royal SL2 ......22 C2
  Frimley GU16 ....151 D1
  Froxfield SN8 ....99 B5
  Ham SN8 ....126 C2
  Little Marlow SL7 ....2 C5
  Lower Halliford TW17 ...125 B2
  Maidenhead SL6 ....40 B5
  Newbury RG14 ....105 B5
  Old Windsor SL4 ....68 B2
  🄱 Pangbourne RG8 .....56 C6
  Sandhurst GU15 ....150 F7
  Sandhurst, Little Sandhurst
    GU47 ....142 F1
  Sandhurst,Owlsmoor
    GU47 ....143 E1
  Silchester RG7 ....136 C5
  Silchester,Pamber Heath
    RG26 ....135 E4
  Stockcross RG20 ....103 E5
  Sunningdale SL5 ....121 A3
  Swallowfield RG7 ......139 D6
  West End GU24 ....153 F7
  Windlesham GU20 .....146 C4
  Winkfield SL4 ....92 C5
  Winkfield,Chavey Down
    SL5 ....119 B8
Church Rd E RG45 ....143 B5
Church Rd W RG45 ......143 B4
Church Row SL3 ....23 D8
Church Side RG20 ....30 E6
Church Sq TW17 ....125 B2
Church St Burnham SL1 ..21 C1
  Caversham RG4 ....59 A2
  Crowthorne RG45 ....143 B4
  Froxfield SN8 ....99 A1
  Great Shefford RG17 ....48 A3

Church St continued
  Hampstead Norreys RG18 .52 F5
  Henley-On-T RG9 ....15 D1
  Hungerford RG17 ......100 D6
  Kintbury RG17 ....102 A2
  Reading RG1 ....86 B6
  Slough SL1 ....42 D4
  Slough, Upton Park SL1 ..42 F4
  Staines TW18 ....96 E4
  Theale RG7 ....83 D3
  Twyford RG10 ....61 D4
  Wargrave RG10 ....36 C2
  🄷 Windsor SL4 ....67 D6
Church Terr
  🄸 Reading RG1 ....86 A6
  Windsor SL4 ....66 E5
Church View
  Beenham RG7 ....109 A6
  🄸 Slough SL1 ....43 A3
  White Waltham SL6 ......63 E8
  Yateley GU46 ....149 D7
Church Views SL6 ....39 F8
Church Way RG17 ......100 D5
Church Wlk KT16 ....124 A3
Churchend Prim Sch
  RG30 ....84 F6
Churchfield Mews SL2 ...43 B7
Churchfield Pl TW17 ....125 B2
Churchill Cl
  East Bedfont TW14 ......98 C4
  Flackwell Heath HP10 .....3 B7
  Reading RG2 ....86 B2
Churchill Ct TW18 ....97 C2
Churchill Dr Marlow SL7 ...1 F4
  Winnersh RG41 ....88 B1
Churchill Rd
  North Ascot SL5 ....119 F7
  Slough SL3 ....43 C8
Churchmead CE Sch SL3 .68 B7
Churchward Wlk RG31 ..84 F4
Churchway RG20 ....10 B1
Churn Rd RG20 ....31 D5
Cinnamon Cl Earley RG6 .86 F1
  Windsor SL4 ....66 F6
Cintra Ave RG2 ....86 C5
Cintra Cl RG1 ....86 D5
Cippenham Inf & Jun Schs
  SL1 ....41 D6
Cippenham La SL1 ....42 B5
Circle Hill Rd RG45 ....143 C5
Circuit La RG30 ....85 C5
City Rd RG31 ....84 B7
Clacy Gn RG42 ....91 A1
Claires Court Sch
  Maidenhead SL6 ....20 B1
  Maidenhead SL6 ....39 E7
Clairmore Gdns RG31 ...57 C4
Clandon Ave TW20 ......96 C1
Clanfield Cres RG31 .....57 C2
Clanfield Ride GU17 ...150 D5
Clappers Farm Rd RG7 .136 F1
Clappers Mdw SL6 ......20 C1
Clapps Gate Rd RG26 ..135 E1
Clapton App HP10 ....3 D8
Clare Ave RG40 ....116 C7
Clare Ct RG40 ....116 C7
Clare Dr SL2 ....22 B8
Clare Gdns TW20 ....96 A3
Clare Rd Maidenhead SL6 .39 D6
  Slough SL1 ....41 C7
  Stanwell TW19 ....97 E8
Clare Wlk RG14 ....130 C5
Clarefield Cl SL6 ....19 B1
Clarefield Ct SL5 ......121 A2
Clarefield Dr SL6 ....19 A1
Clarefield Rd SL6 ....19 B1
Claremont Poyle SL3 .....69 D6
  Shepperton TW17 ......125 B3
Claremont Ave GU15 ...151 F5
Claremont Cres RG14 ...105 D4
Claremont Dr TW17 ....125 B3
Claremont Gdns SL7 .....1 E2
Claremont Rd
  Egham TW20 ....96 D3
  Marlow SL7 ....1 E2
  Windsor SL4 ....67 C5
Clarence Cres SL4 ....67 C6
Clarence Ct Egham TW20 .95 F2
  Maidenhead SL6 ....39 E8
  Windsor SL4 ....67 B6
Clarence Dr
  Camberley GU15 ....152 B7
  Englefield Green TW20 ...95 C4
Clarence Lodge TW20 ...95 C4
Clarence Rd
  Henley-On-T RG9 ....15 D2
  Windsor SL4 ....67 B6
Clarence St Egham TW20 .95 F2
  Staines TW18 ....96 E4
Clarence Way RG31 .....84 B4
Clarendon Cl RG41 ......88 C2
Clarendon Copse SL6 ....39 D6
Clarendon Ct
  Blackwater GU17 ......150 D3
  Slough SL2 ....43 B6
  Windsor SL4 ....67 B6
Clarendon Gdns RG14 ..105 A4
Clarendon Prim Sch
  TW15 ....97 F4
Clarendon Rd
  Ashford TW15 ....97 F4
  Reading RG6 ....87 A6
Clares Green Rd RG7 ..113 B3
Clareways SL5 ....120 F2
Clarewood Dr GU15 ....151 E6
Clarewood Ho GU15 ....151 E6
Clark's Gdns RG17 .....100 D5

Clarke Cres GU15 ......150 E7
Classics The RG17 ....25 B1
Claver Dr SL5 ....120 D5
Claverdon RG12 ....118 A2
Clay Cl Flackwell Heath HP10 .3 B8
  Purley On T RG31 ....57 B1
Clay Cnr KT15 ....124 B1
Clay Hill Cres RG14 ....105 D5
Clay La Beenham RG7 ...108 F6
  Wokingham RG40 ......116 F5
Claycots Sch SL2 ....22 A1
Claydon Ct
  🄱 Caversham RG4 ......59 A2
  🄴 Staines TW18 ....97 A4
Claydon Gdns GU17 ...151 A1
Clayhall La SL4 ....67 F2
Clayhill Cl RG12 ....119 A6
Clayhill Rd RG7,RG30 ..111 B4
Clayton Ct SL3 ....44 A3
Clayton Gr RG12 ......118 E8
Clayton Rd GU14 ......150 E1
Clayton Wlk RG2 ....86 C4
Claytons Comb Sch SL8 ..3 A5
Claytons Mdw SL8 ....3 B3
Cleares Pasture SL1 .....21 B2
Clearsprings GU18 .....153 A8
Cleeve Ct TW14 ....98 E7
Cleeve Down RG8 ....34 D7
Cleeve Ho RG12 ....118 E5
Cleeve Park Cotts RG8 ..34 D8
Cleeve Rd RG8 ....34 B7
Clements Cl Slough SL1 ..43 B4
  Spencers Wood RG7 ....113 A1
Clements Mead RG31 ....57 B1
Clements Rd RG9 ....15 C3
Clent Rd RG2 ....86 B4
Cleopatra Pl RG42 ......91 E1
Clerewater Pl RG19 ....105 F3
Clerics Wlk TW17 .....125 D3
Cleve Ct SL4 ....34 B7
Clevedon Dr RG6 ....87 A2
Clevedon Rd RG31 ......57 E3
Clevehurst Cl SL2 ....23 A6
Cleveland Cl
  Maidenhead SL6 ....40 B6
  Wooburn Green HP10 .....3 B8
Cleveland Dr TW18 ....124 B8
Cleveland Gr RG14 .....104 F3
Cleveland Pk TW19 ......70 E1
Clevemede RG8 ....34 C7
Cleves Ct RG8 ....66 F4
Cleves Way TW16 ....98 F2
Clewborough Dr GU15 .152 B6
Clewborough House Sch
  GU16 ....151 F1
Clewer Ave SL4 ....67 B5
Clewer Court Rd SL4 ....67 B7
Clewer Fields SL4 ....67 C6
Clewer Green CE Fst Sch
  SL4 ....67 A4
Clewer Hill Rd SL4 ......66 F4
Clewer New Town SL4 ...67 A5
Clewer Pk SL4 ....67 A7
Clifford Gr RG5 ....98 A4
Cliffords Way SL8 ....3 B5
Clifton Cl 🄸 TW19 ......70 E1
Clifton Lodge Eton SL4 ..42 A1
  🄱 Slough SL1 ....43 A4
Clifton Park Rd RG4 .....59 A2
Clifton Rd Harlington TW6 .71 B4
  Newbury RG14 ....104 E2
  Slough SL1 ....43 B4
  Wokingham RG41 ......116 A8
Clifton Rise
  Wargrave RG10 ....36 C1
  Windsor SL4 ....66 D6
Clifton St RG1 ....85 F7
Clintons Gn RG42 ......118 A8
Clitheroe Rd GU17 ....149 E1
Clive Ct SL1 ....42 D4
Clive Gn RG12 ....118 B4
Clivedale Rd RG5 ....87 C4
Cliveden* SL6 ....20 E7
Cliveden Mead SL6 .....20 C2
Cliveden Pl TW17 ......125 C3
Cliveden Rd SL6 ....20 E4
Clivemont Rd SL6 ......39 F8
Clockhouse La
  Ashford TW14,TW15 ....98 B5
  East Bedfont TW14,TW15 .98 B5
Clockhouse La E TW20 ..96 B1
Clockhouse La W TW20 ..96 A1
Cloister Mews RG7 .....83 E3
Cloisters The
  Caversham RG4 ....59 A3
  Frimley GU16 ....151 D1
  Slough SL1 ....42 D4
Clonmel Cl RG4 ....59 D2
Clonmel Way SL1 ....21 B2
Close End RG17 ....25 B2
Close The
  Aston Tirrold OX11 ......12 F8
  Bourne End SL8 ....3 A6
  Bracknell RG12 ....118 C5
  Burghfield Common RG7 .111 A3
  Burnham SL1 ....41 D6
  Great Shefford RG17 ....48 A3
  Hampstead Norreys RG18 .52 F5
  Henley-On-T RG9 ....35 D2
  Lightwater GU18 ......146 A1
  North Ascot SL5 ......119 D7
  Sandhurst GU47 ......150 E8
  Thatcham RG18 ....106 B4
  Virginia Water GU25 ...122 D4
  Woodley RG5 ....87 C5
Clough Dr RG18 ....78 F6

Clove Cl RG6 ....86 F1
Clover Cl RG40 ....116 E7
Clover La GU46 ....149 A6
Club La RG45 ....143 D5
Clumps The TW15 ....98 D4
Clyde Rd TW19 ....97 E7
Clyve Way TW19 ......123 E8
Coach Ho The HP10 ......3 E6
Coach House Ct GU16 ..151 E3
Coach House Ct RG8 ....56 E5
Coach Rd SL5 ....92 E1
Coach Ride SL7 ....1 C4
Coachman's Ct RG14 ...105 A3
Coachman's Lodge 🄱
  SL4 ....67 D5
Coachmans Dr GU47 ...150 B7
Coalmans Way SL1,SL6 ..41 A8
Coalport Way RG30 .....57 C1
Coaters La HP10 ....3 E7
Cobb Cl SL3 ....68 D6
Cobbett's La GU46 ....149 F5
Cobblers Cl SL2 ....22 B3
Cobb's La SL1 ....41 F5
Cobham Ho RG2 ....113 E4
Cobham Rd RG5 ....87 F7
Cochrane Cl RG19 .....106 C3
Cochrane Pl GU20 .....146 D5
Cock La RG7 ....82 A2
Cock's La RG42 ....92 A6
Cock-A-Dobby GU47 ...143 A1
Cockayne Ct RG40 .....141 F7
Cockett Rd SL3 ....43 E3
Cockney Hill RG30 ......84 F6
Cody Rd GU15 ....88 B8
Coe Spur SL1 ....42 B3
Coftards SL2 ....43 C7
Cokers Ct 🄱 SL8 ....3 A4
Cold Ash Hill RG18 ....106 C7
Cold Ash St Mark's CE Prim
  Sch RG18 ....79 C1
Cold Grove Cotts SL6 ...20 E2
Coldharbour Cl
  Henley-On-T RG9 ....35 C8
  Thorpe TW20 ....123 C6
Coldharbour La
  Thorpe TW20 ....123 D6
  West End GU24 ....153 F8
Coldharbour Rd
  Chilton OX12 ....9 A7
  Hungerford RG17 ......100 D4
Coldicutt St RG4 ....59 C1
Coldmoorholme La SL8 ...2 E4
Colemans Moor La RG5 ..87 F5
Colemans Moor Rd RG5 ..88 A6
Colenorton Cres SL4 ....41 E2
Coleridge Ave GU46 ...149 E5
Coleridge Cl
  Crowthorne RG45 ......143 C4
  Twyford RG10 ....61 F3
Coleridge Cres SL3 .....69 E6
Coleridge Rd TW15 .....97 F4
Coley Ave RG1 ....85 F6
Coley Hill RG1 ....85 F6
Coley Park Prim Sch
  RG1 ....85 E5
Coley Park Rd RG1 ......85 E6
Coley Pl RG1 ....86 A6
Coley Prim Sch RG1 .....86 A6
Colin Way SL1 ....42 B3
Coliseum Bsns Ctr
  GU15 ....151 A3
College Ave Egham TW20 .96 B2
  Maidenhead SL6 ....39 E7
  Slough SL1 ....42 E3
College Cl GU15 ....151 D7
College Cres
  Sandhurst GU47 ......150 E8
  Windsor SL4 ....67 C5
College Glen SL6 ....39 D7
College Ho 🄱 RG17 .....25 B2
College Piece RG7 .....136 F6
College Rd
  Bracknell RG12 ....118 D5
  Maidenhead SL6 ....39 E7
  Reading RG6 ....86 F6
  Sandhurst GU47 ......150 E8
  Slough SL1 ....41 F5
College Ride
  Bagshot GU19 ....145 C2
  Camberley GU15 ......151 D7
College Rise SL6 ....39 D7
College Town Inf Sch
  GU47 ....150 E8
College Town Jun Sch
  GU47 ....150 E8
College Way
  Ashford TW15 ....97 F4
  East Garston RG17 ......47 D6
Colleton Dr RG10 ....61 E3
Colleton Prim Sch The
  RG10 ....61 E3
Collier Cl SL6 ....19 F1
Colliers Way RG30 ......85 B7
Collingwood Coll GU15 .152 A8
Collingwood Ct KT16 ..124 A1
Collingwood Grange Cl
  GU15 ....152 B8
Collingwood Mount
  GU15 ....152 A7
Collingwood Pl GU15 ..152 B8
Collingwood Rise GU15 .152 A7
Collingwood Wlk RG31 ..84 B7
Collins Cl RG14 ....105 C4
Collins Dr RG6 ....78 F6
Collis St RG2 ....86 B5
Colliston Wlk RG31 ....84 F3

Collum Green Rd SL2 ...23 A8
Colmworth Cl RG6 ....114 A8
Coln Cl SL6 ....39 F8
Coln Trad Est SL3 ......69 F6
Colnbrook By-Pass
  Colnbrook SL3,UB7 .....69 D3
  Harmondsworth UB7 .....70 C7
Colnbrook CE Prim Sch
  SL3 ....69 D7
Colnbrook Ct SL3 ....69 E6
Colndale Rd SL3 ....69 E5
Colne Bank SL3,TW19 ...69 D5
Colne Orch SL0 ....44 F6
Colne Reach TW19 ......69 F2
Colne Way TW19 ....96 B6
Colnebridge Cl TW18 ...96 F4
Colonel's La KT16 .....124 A3
Colonial Rd
  East Bedfont TW14 ......98 E8
  Slough SL1 ....43 A4
Colonnade SL6 ....40 A7
Colony Gate GU16 .....152 D2
Colston Cl RG31 ....84 D4
Colthrop Bsns Pk RG19 .107 A1
Colthrop Cotts RG19 ...107 B1
Colthrop La RG19 .....107 B2
Colthrop Way RG19 ....107 B2
Coltsfoot Cl RG7 ......111 B3
Columbia Ct RG40 ....141 E8
Colville Gdns GU18 ...153 C8
Colwyn Cl GU46 ......149 C6
Colyer Cl RG18 ....79 C8
Colyton Way RG8 ....57 D5
Combe Rd RG30 ....84 F7
Combe View RG17 .....100 D4
Combermere Cl SL4 ....67 B5
Comet Ho RG12 ....134 E2
Comet Rd TW19 ....97 D8
Comet Way RG5 ....88 B7
Comfrey Cl RG40 .....116 E8
Commerce Pk RG7 .....83 E3
Commercial Rd
  Reading RG2 ....86 A1
  Staines TW18 ....97 A2
Common Hill RG7 ....82 F4
Common La
  Brightwalton RG20 ......28 C5
  Eton SL4 ....42 D1
Common Rd Dorney SL4 ..41 D2
  Eton SL4 ....42 A2
  Flackwell Heath HP10 ....3 B8
  Headley RG19 ....132 F1
  Slough SL3 ....44 A1
Common The HP10 ....3 B8
Common Wood SL2 .....22 C8
Commonfield La RG40 .141 B8
Commonfields GU24 ...153 F6
Commons Rd RG41 ......88 F1
Communications Rd
  RG19 ....131 F5
Compass Cl TW15 ....98 C1
Compass Ho 🄸🄱 RG1 ...86 B7
Compton Ave RG31 .....84 B7
Compton CE Prim Sch
  RG20 ....31 E4
Compton Cl
  Bracknell RG12 ....117 C5
  Earley RG6 ....87 C4
  Sandhurst GU47 ......143 C1
Compton Ct SL1 ....41 E7
Compton Dr SL6 ....39 A8
Compton Manor RG20 ..31 D4
Compton Place Bsns Ctr
  GU15 ....151 A4
Comsaye Wlk RG12 ....118 C4
Concorde Rd SL6 ....39 D4
Concorde Way Slough SL1 .42 C4
  Woodley RG5 ....88 A7
Condor Cl RG31 ....57 C3
Condor Rd TW18 ......124 C6
Conduit La SL3 ....43 D7
Conegar Ct SL1 ....42 E5
Coney Grange RG42 ....91 B2
Congreve Cl RG7 ......135 A7
Conifer Cl RG26 ....134 E2
Conifer Crest RG14 ...130 C4
Conifer Dr
  Camberley GU15 ......152 A6
  Purley On T RG31 ......57 B2
Conifer La TW20 ....96 C3
Conifers The
  Crowthorne RG45 ......143 A7
  Maidenhead SL6 ....39 A8
Coningham Rd RG2 ....113 C6
Coningsby RG12 ....118 C5
Coningsby Cl SL6 ....39 D3
Coningsby La SL6 ....65 C6
Conisboro Ave RG4 .....58 E5
Conisboro Way RG4 ....58 E5
Coniston Cl
  Frimley GU15 ....152 C3
  Thatcham RG19 ....106 A3
  Woodley RG5 ....87 F5
Coniston Ct Ashford TW15 .97 D5
  Lightwater GU18 ......146 B1
  🄸 Newbury RG14 ......105 A4
Coniston Dr RG30 ......57 F2
Coniston Way TW20 ....96 B1
Conkers SL6 ....40 B8
Connaught Ave TW15 ...97 E4
Connaught Cl
  Crowthorne RG45 ......142 F3
  Maidenhead SL6 ....19 E1
  Reading RG30 ....85 D7
  Yateley GU46 ....149 B6
Connaught Jun Sch
  GU19 ....145 E2

Connaught Rd
Bagshot GU19 145 C3
Camberley GU15 151 F5
Newbury RG14 105 B3
Reading RG30 85 D7
Slough SL1 43 B4
Connection The RG14 105 A6
Conniston Cl SL7 1 B2
Connolly Ct GU25 122 E5
Connop Way GU16 151 F3
Conought Ho RG9 15 E3
Conquest Ct 16 RG1 86 C7
Consort Dr GU15 152 C7
Constable Cl RG5 88 B8
Constable Way GU47 150 E6
Constitution Rd RG30 85 B8
Consul Cl RG5 88 A6
Control Tower Rd TW6 71 B4
Convent Lodge TW15 98 B3
Convent Rd Ashford TW15 98 B3
Windsor SL4 67 A5
Conway Cl GU16 151 F1
Conway Dr Ashford TW15 98 C2
Thatcham RG18 106 B5
Conway Rd Burnham SL6 41 B7
Harlington TW6 71 B4
Reading RG31 84 C5
Conygree Cl RG6 87 B1
Cooke Rise RG42 91 B2
Cookham Cl GU47 143 C1
Cookham Dean Bottom
SL6 19 C8
Cookham Dean CE Prim Sch
SL6 19 B7
Cookham Lodge 15 SL6 39 F6
Cookham Montessori Sch
SL6 19 F7
Cookham Rd
Bracknell RG12 117 E7
Maidenhead SL6 19 F1
Cookham Rise Prim Sch
SL6 19 E6
Cookham Sta SL6 19 F7
Coolarne Rise GU15 152 A6
Coolgardie Rd TW15 98 C3
Coombe Cotts RG8 33 F6
Coombe Ct RG19 106 E3
Coombe Hill OX12 28 B7
Coombe Hill Ct SL4 66 D4
Coombe Pine RG12 118 D3
Coombe Rd Compton RG20 31 F2
Yateley GU46 149 B7
Coombe Sq RG19 106 E3
Coombe The RG8 33 F6
Coombes Inf Sch RG2 114 E3
Coombes La RG41 115 C4
Coombesbury La RG20 76 D1
Cooper Cl RG2 113 C7
Cooper Rd
Henley-On-T RG9 15 D3
Windlesham GU20 146 D4
Cooper Way SL1 42 B3
Cooper's Hill La TW20 95 D4
Coopers Cl TW18 96 E3
Coopers Cres RG18 106 C4
Cope Ct SL6 39 C7
Cope Hall La RG14 130 C7
Copelands Cl GU15 152 D4
Copenhagen Cl RG2 113 C7
Copenhagen Wlk RG45 143 B4
Copped Hall Dr GU15 152 C6
Copped Hall Way GU15 152 C6
Copper Beech RG42 119 A8
Copper Beech Cl SL4 66 D6
Copperage Rd OX12 9 A2
Copperdale Cl RG6 86 F3
Copperfield Ave GU47 143 E2
Copperfield Terr SL2 43 B6
Copperfields RG4 58 F3
Coppermill Rd TW19 69 B2
Coppice Dr TW19 95 D8
Coppice Gdns
Crowthorne RG45 142 F5
Yateley GU46 149 C5
Coppice Gn RG42 90 F1
Coppice Rd RG5 87 E4
Coppice The TW15 98 B2
Coppins La SL0 44 F8
Copse Ave RG4 59 E3
Copse Cl
Camberley GU15 152 A6
Marlow SL7 1 C2
Purley On T RG31 57 D3
Slough SL1 41 F5
Copse Dr RG41 116 A7
Copse End GU15 152 A6
Copse Mead RG5 60 F2
Copse The RG10 36 E3
Copse View Cotts SL6 64 C4
Copse Way RG40 141 E7
Copthall Ho SL6 40 A7
Copthorn Cl SL6 39 A4
Copthorne Chase TW15 97 F4
Copthorne Cl TW17 125 C3
Copthorne Dr GU18 146 B1
Corbett Dr GU18 152 F7
Corbett Gdns RG5 87 F7
Corbridge Rd RG2 86 C4
Corby Cl
Englefield Green TW20 95 C2
Woodley RG5 61 A1
Corby Dr TW20 95 C2
Cordelia Croft RG42 118 E8
Cordelia Gdns TW19 97 E8
Cordelia Rd TW19 97 E8
Corderoy Cl RG19 106 F2
Corderoy Pl KT16 123 F3
Cordwalles Jun Sch
GU15 151 F8
Cordwalles Rd GU15 151 F8
Cordwallis Est 1 SL6 39 F8
Cordwallis Pk SL6 39 E8
Cordwallis Rd SL6 39 F8
Cordwallis St SL6 39 E8
Cores End Rd SL8 3 B3
Corfe Gdns Frimley GU16 151 F1
Slough SL1 42 A6
Corfe Mews RG4 59 E4
Corfe Pl SL6 39 C7
Corfield Cl RG40 141 E3
Corfield Gn RG41 115 F8
Coriander Ct SL5 120 E3
Coriander Way RG6 86 F1
Corinne Cl RG2 86 B1
Cormorant Pl GU47 150 E7
Corn Croft RG42 91 D1
Cornbunting Cl GU47 150 D8
Cornel Ho 1 SL4 67 D4
Cornerside TW15 98 C1
Cornerstones RG30 84 E8
Cornfield Rd RG5 88 A8
Cornfields GU46 149 B4
Cornflower Cl RG41 115 D7
Cornwall Ave SL2 22 C1
Cornwall Cl
Bracknell RG42 91 F2
Camberley GU15 151 F7
Eton SL4 41 E1
Maidenhead SL6 19 E2
Purley On T RG31 57 B4
Wokingham RG41 115 E6
Cornwall Lodge 11 SL6 39 F6
Cornwall Way TW18 96 E2
Cornwell Rd SL4 68 A1
Cornwood Gdns RG2 86 C3
Coronation Ave
Slough SL3 43 E7
Windsor SL4 67 F5
Coronation Cotts RG10 88 D4
Coronation Rd
Ascot SL5 120 A2
Littlewick Green SL6 38 B5
Yateley GU46 149 E7
Coronation Sq
Reading RG30 85 B4
Wokingham RG40 116 D7
Corporation Cotts 1
RG14 105 A4
Corrie Gdns GU25 122 C2
Corsair Cl TW19 97 E8
Corsair Rd TW19 97 E8
Corsham Rd RG31 84 F3
Corsham Way RG45 143 B5
Corwen Rd RG30 84 E7
Coster Cl RG14 104 D5
Costers Cotts SL8 3 B2
Cotswold Cl
Maidenhead SL6 40 B6
Slough SL1 42 B3
Staines TW18 97 A3
Cotswold Rd GU47 142 F1
Cotswold Way RG31 57 C2
Cottage Farm Way
TW20 123 C6
Cottage La RG30 85 C2
Cotterell Cl RG42 91 B1
Cotterell Gdns RG10 61 F3
Cottesbrooke Cl SL3 69 D6
Cottesloe Cl GU24 153 F3
Cottesmore RG12 118 A2
Cottesmore Rd RG5 87 D6
Cottrell Cl RG17 100 E6
Coulson Way SL1 41 B7
Council Cotts GU24 153 F7
Council Hos
Barkham RG41 115 B2
Farley Hill RG7 140 D5
Shiplake RG9 35 B2
Sindlesham RG41 115 A7
Winterbourne RG20 77 C5
Council Hos The
Inkpen RG17 127 F5
Tadley RG26 134 B1
Country Life Ho SL3 68 B7
County La RG42 91 E2
County Lane Rdbt RG42 91 E2
Courage Ct RG30 85 B5
Course Rd SL5 120 A6
Court Cl SL6 40 C2
Court Cres SL1 42 D7
Court Dr SL6 20 C3
Court Farm Ho SL1 42 B5
Court Farm Ind Est TW19 70 F1
Court Gdns
Camberley GU15 151 D5
Goring RG8 34 C7
Court Hill Rd OX12 7 C7
Court La Burnham SL1 21 D2
Dorney SL4 41 B3
Court One TW15 98 C5
Court Rd SL6 20 C3
Court The RG18 106 D4
Court Three TW15 98 C5
Court Two TW15 98 C5
Courtenay Dr RG4 59 B7
Courtfield Dr SL6 39 C6
Courtfield Rd TW15 98 B2
Courthouse Jun Sch SL6 39 B8
Courthouse Rd SL6 39 C8
Courtlands 14 SL6 39 F6
Courtlands Ave SL3 43 D2
Courtlands Hill RG8 56 C4
Courtlands Rd RG14 105 B1
Courtleigh Manor SL5 121 A2
Courtney Ho 4 GU15 151 B3
Courtney Pl RG42 90 C2
Courtney Rd TW6 71 A4
Courtney Way TW6 71 A5
Courts Rd RG6 87 B4
Courtyard The
12 Bourne End SL8 3 B3
7 Marlow SL7 1 D2
Marlow SL7 1 E2
Theale RG7 83 E3
Coventry Rd RG1 86 E8
Coverdale Way SL2 21 E1
Covert La RG12 118 C5
Covert The SL5 120 B2
Coves Farm Wood
RG42 117 D7
Cow La East Ilsley RG20 30 F7
Moulsford OX10 13 F3
Reading RG1,RG30 85 E8
Cowley Ave KT16 123 F2
Cowley La KT16 123 F2
Coworth Cl SL5 121 B4
Coworth Rd SL5 121 A4
Cowper Cl KT16 123 F3
Cowper Rd SL2 22 A1
Cowper Way RG30 85 D4
Cowslade RG14 104 D5
Cowslip Cl RG31 84 A6
Cowslip Cres RG18 106 E5
Cox Green La SL6 39 C3
Cox Green Rd SL6 39 D3
Cox Green Sch SL6 39 A4
Cox's La RG7 107 D3
Coxborrow Cl SL6 19 E7
Coxeter Rd RG14 104 E4
Coxgreen GU47 150 D6
Coxs Ave TW17 125 E6
Crabtree Cl
Chilton Foliat RG17 72 E2
Hermitage RG18 78 F6
Crabtree Cnr TW20 123 B8
Crabtree La RG18 78 F6
Crabtree Office Village
TW20 123 C7
Crabtree Rd
Camberley GU15 151 B2
Thorpe TW20 123 C7
Cradock Rd RG2 86 B4
Crafnant Ct TW15 97 F3
Crafts End OX11 10 E8
Craig Ave RG30 85 B8
Craigwell Cl TW18 123 E8
Crail Cl RG41 116 A3
Crake Pl GU47 150 D8
Cramond Ct TW14 98 E7
Cranberry Wlk GU17 150 F3
Cranbourne Ave
Reading RG31 84 C4
Windsor SL4 66 F5
Cranbourne Cl SL1 42 C5
Cranbourne Cotts SL4 93 B5
Cranbourne Gdns RG30 58 A2
Cranbourne Hall Cvn Site
SL4 93 B7
Cranbourne Prim Sch
SL5 93 A4
Cranbourne Rd SL1 42 C5
Cranbrook Dr SL6 19 C1
Cranbury Rd RG30 85 D7
Crane Ct GU47 150 D8
Crane Rd TW6,TW19 71 A1
Crane Wharf 4 RG1 86 B7
Craneswater UB3 71 F7
Cranford Ave TW19 97 F8
Cranford Cl TW19 97 E8
Cranford Dr RG10 88 F8
Cranford House Sch
OX10 13 F5
Cranford La
Harlington TW6 71 F6
Harlington UB3 71 E7
Hatton TW6 71 F5
Hatton TW6 71 F4
Cranford Mews 10 RG1 86 A6
Cranford Park Dr GU46 149 D6
Cranleigh Rd TW13 98 F4
Cranmer Cl RG31 57 B3
Cranmer Lodge GU15 151 E6
Cranwell Gr
Lightwater GU18 152 F8
Littleton TW17 124 F5
Cranwell Rd TW6 71 B5
Craufurd Ct SL6 39 E8
Craufurd Rise SL6 39 E8
Craven Cl RG17 102 B1
Craven Ct GU15 150 F4
Craven Dene RG14 105 B4
Craven Farm Cotts RG17 72 F2
Craven Rd Inkpen RG17 127 B6
Newbury RG14 104 F2
Reading RG1 86 D6
Craven Way RG17 102 B2
Crawford Cl RG6 87 B3
Crawford Gdns GU15 151 B5
Crawford Pl RG14 104 F3
Crawley Chase RG42 92 B2
Crawley Dr GU15 151 F6
Crawley Hill GU15 151 F5
Crawley Ridge GU15 151 F6
Crawley Ridge Inf Sch
GU15 151 F6
Crawley Ridge Jun Sch
GU15 151 F7
Crawley Rise GU15 152 A7
Crawley Wood Cl GU15 151 F5
Crawshay Dr RG4 59 B7
Crawshays SL6 40 C8
Crayle St SL2 22 B2
Crayonne Cl TW16 125 E8
Crazies Hill CE Prim Sch
RG10 36 F6
Crecy Cl RG41 115 E6
Creden Cl SL6 19 D1
Crediton Cl RG5 88 A6
Cree's Mdw GU20 146 D3
Creighton Ct RG2 86 D4
Cremyll Rd RG1 58 F1
Crendon Ct RG4 59 A2
Crescent Ct 5 TW18 96 F3
Crescent Dale SL6 39 F6
Crescent Dr SL6 39 E7
Crescent Rd
Reading,Tilehurst RG31 57 D1
Reading,Whiteknights RG1 86 F6
Shepperton TW17 125 C4
Wokingham RG40 116 C5
Crescent The
Ashford TW15 97 F3
Bracknell RG12 118 C5
Chertsey KT16 124 A6
Earley RG6 87 C4
Egham TW20 95 F2
Harlington UB7 71 D7
Kintbury RG17 102 A1
Knowl Hill RG10 37 A6
Lower Halliford TW17 125 F2
Maidenhead SL6 39 E7
Mortimer RG7 137 A6
Padworth RG7 109 C4
Shiplake RG9 36 B4
Slough SL1 42 E4
Theale RG7 83 E4
Yateley GU46 149 D7
Crescent Villas 4 SL4 67 C6
Cress Rd SL1 42 B4
Cressex Cl RG42 90 C2
Cressida Chase RG42 91 E1
Cressingham Rd RG2 86 D2
Cressington Ct 2 SL8 3 A4
Cressington Pl SL8 3 A4
Cresswell Rd RG14 105 D4
Cresswells Mead SL6 40 C1
Crest Cl RG10 61 E6
Crest The RG4 59 C5
Creswell Cl RG2 113 C6
Creswell Row SL7 1 D2
Cricket Field Gr RG45 143 D4
Cricket Hill RG40 141 F2
Cricket Hill La GU17,
GU46 149 E4
Cricketers RG20 103 E6
Cricketers La
Englefield Green TW20 95 C4
Windlesham GU20 146 D4
Winkfield RG42 92 A3
Crimp Hill SL4,TW20 95 A6
Crisp Gdns RG42 90 E1
Crisp Rd RG9 15 C3
Crispin Cl RG4 58 D5
Crispin Way SL2 22 D8
Crocker Cl SL5 119 F8
Crockford Pl RG42 90 F1
Crockhamwell Rd RG5 87 E6
Crocus Mead RG18 106 E4
Crocus Way RG41 115 D7
Croft Cl Harlington UB7 71 C7
Wokingham RG41 116 A2
Croft Cnr SL4 68 A2
Croft La Newbury RG14 104 E4
Yateley GU46 149 D7
Croft Rd Goring RG8 34 C5
Hungerford RG17 100 D6
Mortimer RG7 136 F6
Newbury RG14 130 F8
Shinfield RG7 113 C2
Wokingham RG40 116 A1
Croft The Bracknell RG42 91 B1
Kintbury RG17 102 A2
Maidenhead SL6 39 C5
Marlow SL7 2 A3
Wokingham RG40 116 D5
Croft Way GU16 151 F2
Crofter's Cl GU47 150 A8
Crofters SL4 68 A1
Crofters Cl Frimley GU16 152 D1
Stanwell TW19 70 D1
Crofthill Rd SL2 22 B1
Crofton Cl RG12 118 E4
Crofts The TW17 125 E5
Cromer Cl RG31 57 C1
Cromer Ct SL1 42 E7
Cromer Rd TW6 71 A5
Cromwell Cl RG9 35 E8
Cromwell Dr SL1 42 E8
Cromwell Gdns SL7 1 E2
Cromwell Lodge TW13 98 F5
Cromwell Pl 3 RG14 105 A3
Cromwell Rd Ascot SL5 120 B4
Camberley GU15 151 D7
Caversham RG4 59 B2
Henley-On-T RG9 35 E8
Maidenhead SL6 39 D7
Marlow SL7 1 E2
Newbury RG14 105 C5
Cromwell Terr RG14 104 D5
Crondall Ct GU15 151 B4
Crondall End GU46 149 C7
Cropper Cl RG19 107 A3
Crosby Gdns GU46 149 A7
Crosby Hill Dr GU15 151 F7
Crosfields Cl 113 E8
Crosfields Sch RG2 113 E8
Cross Fell RG12 118 A5
Cross Gates Cl RG12 118 F6
Cross Keys Rd RG8 14 C4
Cross La RG7 138 C7
Cross Oak SL4 67 A5
Cross Rd SL5 121 A1
Cross St Reading RG1 86 B8
Wokingham RG40 116 C6
Crossland Ho GU25 122 E5
Crossland Rd RG1 86 B7
Crossway RG12 118 C7
Crossways Ashford TW16 98 F1
Egham TW20 96 D2
Woodley RG5 87 E5
Crossways Ct 8 SL4 67 C5
Crosswell Cl TW17 125 C7
Crosthwaite Way SL1 41 D8
Crouch La SL4 92 F7
Crow Piece La SL2 21 F4
Crowfield Dr RG19 106 C3
Crowle Rd RG17 25 A2
Crown Acre Cl RG19 106 C3
Crown Cl SL3 69 C7
Crown Colonnade 3
RG1 86 E7
Crown Cotts
Bracknell SL5 119 C4
Englefield Green TW20 95 A1
Windsor SL4 67 D3
Crown Ct RG19 106 C3
Crown Hill Ct SL5 120 B4
Crown La Burnham SL2 22 A4
Maidenhead SL6 40 A7
Marlow SL7 1 D2
Theale RG7 83 E3
Wentworth GU25 122 D3
Crown Mdw SL3 69 B7
Crown Mead RG18,RG19 106 C3
Crown Mews RG17 100 D5
Crown Pl Reading RG1 86 C6
Sandhurst GU47 143 E1
Crown Rd Marlow SL7 1 D2
Wentworth GU25 122 C3
Crown Rise KT16 123 F1
Crown Row RG12 118 D3
Crown St Egham TW20 96 A4
Reading RG1 86 B6
Crown Wood Prim Sch
RG12 118 E3
Crowsley Rd RG9 36 A3
Crowthorne Bsns Est The
RG45 143 D7
Crowthorne CE Prim Sch
RG45 143 C5
Crowthorne Lodge
RG12 118 B5
Crowthorne Rd
Bracknell RG40,RG12 117 F2
Bracknell,Easthampstead
RG12 118 A5
Sandhurst GU47 143 B2
Crowthorne Rd N RG12 118 B6
Crowthorne Sta RG45 142 E4
Croxley Rise SL6 39 D6
Croydon Rd TW6 71 B4
Cruikshank Lea GU47 150 E6
Crummock Cl SL1 41 C7
Crutchley Rd RG40 116 D7
Cuba Cotts SL6 20 B3
Cuckoo La GU24 153 D6
Cuckoo Vale GU24 153 D6
Culford Cl RG6 87 D2
Culham Ct RG30 85 A4
Culham Dr SL6 19 E2
Culham Ho RG12 118 E5
Cullen Cl GU46 149 C5
Cullern's Pass SL6 39 F6
Culley Way SL6 39 A4
Culloden Way RG41 115 E6
Culver Croft RG42 90 E1
Culver La RG6 87 A7
Culver Rd Newbury RG14 130 F8
Reading RG6 86 F6
Sandhurst GU47 143 D1
Cumberland Ave SL2 22 C1
Cumberland Ct TW15 97 D5
Cumberland Dr RG12 118 E8
Cumberland Lodge SL4 94 D4
Cumberland Rd
Ashford TW15 97 D5
Frimley GU15 152 C4
Reading RG1 86 E7
Cumberland St TW18 96 D3
Cumberland Way RG41 115 D6
Cumbernauld Gdns TW16 98 F3
Cumbrae Cl SL2 43 A5
Cumbria Cl SL6 39 C4
Cumnor Way RG41 118 E5
Cunworth Ct RG12 117 F3
Curfew Bell Rd KT16 123 F2
Curl Way RG41 116 A5
Curlew Cl RG19 106 C3
Curlew Dr RG31 84 C6
Curley Hill Rd GU18 152 F7
Curling Way RG14 105 C4
Curls La SL6 39 E4
Curls Rd SL6 39 D4
Curly's Way RG7 139 D6
Curnock Ct RG14 104 E1
Curridge Gn RG18 78 E4
Curridge Piece RG18 78 F5
Curridge Prim Sch RG18 78 D4
Curridge Rd RG18 78 D4
Curriers La SL1 21 D7
Curtis Cl GU15 152 C7
Curtis Rd RG31 84 C4
Curzon Mall 7 SL1 42 F4
Curzon St RG30 85 E8
Cutbush Cl RG6 114 B8
Cutbush La Earley RG6 87 C1

Cutbush La *continued*
Lower Earley RG6 ....114 B8
Shinfield RG2 ....113 F6
Cutting Hill SN8,RG17 ..126 A4
Cuttings The RG18 ......52 F5
Cwmcarn RG4 ....58 F6
Cygnet Cl RG19 ....106 B3
Cygnet Way RG17 ......100 D7
Cygnets The 14 TW18 ....96 F3
Cypress Cl RG40 ....142 A8
Cypress Ct GU25 ....122 F5
Cypress Hill Ct GU14 ...150 F1
Cypress Ho
3 Newbury RG14 ....104 F2
Slough SL3 ....44 B1
Cypress Rd RG5 ....88 A6
Cypress Way GU17 .....150 B5
Cypress Wlk TW20 ......95 B2
Cyril Vokins Rd RG14 ...105 E2

D

Daceberry Ct RG9 ....16 C2
Dacre Ave RG4 ....59 E4
Dagmar Rd SL4 ....67 D5
Dair House Sch SL2 .....22 C4
Dairy Ct SL6 ....65 A7
Dairy La RG9 ....16 B8
Daisy Mdw TW20 ....96 A3
Dalby Cl RG10 ....88 F8
Dalby Cres RG14 ....131 B8
Dalcross RG12 ....118 E3
Dale Cl SL5 ....121 A4
Dale Ct SL1 ....42 C4
Dale Gdns GU47 ....150 A8
Dale Lodge Rd SL5 .....121 A4
Dale Rd Ashford TW16 ....98 F1
Oatlands Park KT12 .....125 F2
Reading RG2 ....86 B5
Daleham Ave TW20 ......96 A2
Dalley Ct GU47 ....150 D7
Dalston Cl GU15 ....152 D3
Dalton Cl RG30 ....84 E8
Damask Cl GU24 ....153 E6
Damer Gdns RG9 ....35 E8
Damson Gr SL1 ....42 C4
Dandridge Cl SL3 ....43 D2
Dandridge Dr SL8 ....3 C3
Dane Rd TW15 ....98 D2
Danehill RG6 ....114 B8
Danehurst Cl TW20 ......95 E2
Danes Ct SL6 ....39 D7
Danes Gdns SL6 ....19 F6
Danesfield RG40 ....116 D6
Danesfield Sch SL7 .....17 E7
Danvers Cl RG19 ......106 D2
Danywern Dr RG41 ......88 C2
Darby Green La GU17 ..150 B6
Darby Green Rd GU17 ..150 B5
Darby La RG8 ....55 B5
Darby Vale RG42 ....91 B2
Darell Rd RG4 ....58 F3
Dark La Bradfield RG7 ....82 C7
Purley On T RG31 ....57 B2
Wargrave RG10 ....36 D2
Wickham RG17 ....101 A7
Darleydale Cl GU47 ...143 D2
Darling's La SL6 ....18 E1
Darracott Cl GU15 .....152 B8
Darrell Cl SL3 ....43 F2
Dart Cl Brands Hill SL3 ....69 B8
Thatcham RG18 ....106 B8
Wokingham RG40 ......141 F6
Dartington Ave RG5 .....87 D4
Dartington Cl RG30 .....84 F8
Dartmouth Cl RG12 ....118 E6
Dartmouth Ct 2 SL1 ....42 F3
Dartmouth Terr 1 RG1 ...86 C6
Darvill's La SL1 ....42 D4
Darvills La RG10 ....62 F1
Darwall Dr SL5 ....119 D7
Darwin Cl RG2 ....86 A1
Darwin Ct 2 GU15 .....151 B3
Darwin Rd SL3 ....43 F4
Dashwood Cl
Bracknell RG12 ....118 D8
Slough SL3 ....43 C2
Datchet Pl SL3 ....68 B6
Datchet Rd Horton SL3 ...68 F4
Old Windsor SL4 ....68 A3
Slough SL3 ....42 F2
Windsor SL4 ....67 D7
Datchet St Mary's CE Prim Sch SL3 ....68 B6
Datchet Sta SL3 ....68 B6
Dauntless Rd RG7 .....111 B3
Davenport Rd RG12 ...118 E8
Daventry Cl SL3 ....69 F6
Daventry Ct RG42 .....118 B8
David Cl UB3 ....71 E7
David Ct 3 TW18 ....97 A4
David Rd SL3 ....69 F5
David Smith Ct RG31 ....84 F5
Davis Cl SL7 ....1 E1
Davis Gdns GU47 ......150 E7
Davis St RG10 ....88 D5
Davis Way RG10 ....88 D4
Davy Cl RG40 ....116 C5
Dawes East Rd SL1 .....21 C2
Dawes Moor Cl SL2 .....43 C7
Dawley Ride SL3 ....69 E6
Dawlish Rd RG2 ....86 C2
Dawn Ct GU15 ....151 F7
Dawn Redwood Cl SL3 ...69 A4
Dawnay Cl SL5 ....119 F8
Dawnay Rd GU15 ......151 B7
Daws Ct SL0 ....44 F7
Dawsmere Cl GU15 ....152 C5
Dawson Cl SL4 ....67 A5
Daytona Dr RG19 ......107 B2
Dayworth Mews 2 RG30 85 C7
De Beauvoir Rd RG1 ....86 E6
De Bohun Rd RG1 ......86 B8
De Havilland Way TW19 .70 E1
De Montfort Gr RG17 ..100 D4
De Montfort Rd
Newbury RG14 ....104 E5
Reading RG1 ....59 A1
De Ros Pl TW20 ....96 A2
De-Vitre Gn RG40 .....116 F7
Deacon Cl RG40 ......116 C8
Deacon Ct SL4 ....66 D5
Deacon Way RG30 ......58 A2
Deaconfield RG8 ....14 C3
Deacons La RG18 ....79 C7
Deadman's La RG7 ......83 D3
Deadmans La RG14, RG19 ....131 B6
Deadmoor La RG20 ....130 E1
Deal Ave SL1 ....41 F7
Dean Cl SL4 ....66 D4
Dean Ct KT16 ....124 A3
Dean Gr RG40 ....116 C7
Dean La SL6 ....19 C8
Dean Par GU15 ....151 F8
Dean St SL7 ....1 D2
Dean View SL6 ....19 E6
Dean's Cloisters SL4 ....67 D7
Deanfield Ave RG9 .....15 D1
Deanfield Cl SL7 ....1 D3
Deanfield Rd RG9 ......15 D1
Deans Cl SL2 ....23 B4
Deans Ct GU20 ....146 D4
Deans Farm RG4 ....59 D1
Deansfield Cl SL6 .....19 D2
Deansgate RG12 ......118 B2
Deansgate Rd RG1 ......86 B6
Deanwood Ho RG20 ....104 B5
Decies Way SL2 ....23 A4
Dedmere Ct SL7 ....1 F2
Dedmere Rd SL7 ....1 F2
Dedmere Rise SL7 ....1 E2
Dedworth Dr SL4 ....66 F6
Dedworth Green Fst Sch SL4 ....66 E5
Dedworth Manor SL4 ....66 F6
Dedworth Mid Sch SL4 ..66 E6
Dedworth Rd SL4 ......66 D5
Dee Rd RG30 ....85 A7
Deena Cl SL1 ....41 E6
Deep Field SL3 ....68 B7
Deep Well Dr GU15 ....151 E5
Deepdale RG12 ....118 A5
Deepdene Cl RG1 ......85 E7
Deepfield Rd RG12 ....118 D7
Deer Leap GU18 ......153 A8
Deer Rock Hill RG12 ...118 C3
Deer Rock Rd GU15 ...151 F8
Deerhurst Ave RG41 ....88 C2
Deerhurst Cl RG31 .....84 E4
Deerswood SL6 ....20 A1
Defford Cl RG41 ....88 F1
Delafield Dr RG31 ......84 C4
Delaford Cl SL0 ....44 F7
Delamere Ho 5 RG1 ....85 E5
Delamere Rd RG6 ......87 B8
Delane Dr RG41 ....88 B1
Delaney Cl RG30 ....84 F8
Delft Cl RG30 ....84 F8
Dell Cl SL2 ....22 C7
Dell Gr GU16 ....151 F2
Dell Rd
Finchampstead RG40 ...142 A3
Purley On T RG31 ......57 C2
Dell The
Englefield Green TW20 ...95 A5
Maidenhead SL6 ....38 F2
10 Reading RG1 ....86 C7
Yateley GU46 ....149 C5
Deller St RG42 ....90 F1
Dellwood Com Hospl RG30 ....85 C6
Dellwood Pk RG4 ....58 F4
Delph The RG6 ....87 D2
Delta Way TW20 ......123 C8
Dempsey Ho RG30 ......84 F7
Denbeigh Pl RG1 ....58 F1
Denbury Gdns 1 RG2 ..113 C8
Denby Way RG30 ....57 F1
Dencliffe 2 TW15 ......98 A3
Dene Cl RG6 ....87 A3
Dene Hollow OX11 ......10 E8
Dene Way RG14 ......105 A5
Denefield Sch RG31 ....57 B3
Denford La RG17 .....101 C8
Denham Cl SL6 ....39 C6
Denham Dr 1 GU46 ....149 D5
Denham Gr RG12 ......118 C3
Denham Rd TW20 ....96 A4
Denison Rd TW13 ......98 F4
Denly Way GU18 ......146 C1
Denman Dr TW15 ......98 B2
Denmark Ave RG5 ......61 A1
Denmark Rd
Newbury RG14 ....105 A3
Reading RG1 ....86 D6
Denmark St
Maidenhead SL6 ....39 E8
Wokingham RG40 .....116 C5
Denmead Ct RG12 ....118 E3
Dennis Cl TW15 ....98 D1
Dennis Way SL1 ....41 D6
Dennisford Rd RG20 ....31 A6
Dennistoun Cl GU15 ...151 D5
Dennose Cl RG6 ....87 A1
Denny Rd SL3 ....43 F2
Denton Cl RG19 ......106 C2
Denton Ct SL7 ....1 F3
Denton Mews RG40 ....116 C6
Denton Rd RG40 ......116 C6
Denton Way GU16 .....151 D2
Denvale Trade Pk RG14 .105 D2
Depot Rd SL6 ....40 A6
Derby Cl RG17 ....25 A2
Derby Rd Caversham RG4 .59 B3
Newbury RG14 ....104 F1
Derby St RG1 ....85 F8
Derbyshire Gn RG42 ....91 F1
Derek Horn Ct GU15 ...151 B6
Derek Rd SL6 ....40 C8
Deridene Cl 2 TW19 ....70 E1
Derrick Cl RG31 ....84 C4
Derwent Ave RG30 .....57 E2
Derwent Cl
East Bedfont TW14 ......98 F7
Wokingham RG41 ......115 E6
Derwent Dr Burnham SL1 .41 C8
Maidenhead SL6 ....39 D8
Derwent Rd
Lightwater GU18 ......153 B8
Thatcham RG19 ....106 A3
Thorpe Lea TW20 ....96 B1
Desborough Cl TW17 ..125 A2
Desborough Cres SL6 ...39 C5
Desborough Sch SL6 ...39 E5
Deseronto Wharf Ind Est SL3 ....43 E4
Desford Way TW15 .....97 F6
Devenish La GU20,SL5 ..120 D1
Devenish Rd GU20,SL5 ..120 D2
Devereux Rd SL4 ......67 D5
Deverills Way SL3 ......44 C2
Deveron Dr RG30 ......85 A8
Devil's Highway The RG45 ....142 F5
Devils La TW20 ....96 C2
Devitt Cl RG2 ....86 F1
Devon Ave SL1 ....42 C7
Devon Chase RG42 .....91 E2
Devon Cl Sandhurst GU47 150 D7
Wokingham RG41 .....115 E6
Devon Dr RG4 ....59 E4
Devonshire Cl SL2 ......22 B3
Devonshire Dr GU15 ...151 F7
Devonshire Gdns RG31 ..57 B3
Devonshire Gn SL2 .....22 B3
Devonshire Lodge 10 SL6 39 F6
Devonshire Pk RG2 .....86 E2
Dewberry Down RG18 ..106 F4
Dewe La RG30 ....84 E2
Dhoon Rise SL6 ....39 F6
Diamedes Ave TW19 .....97 D7
Diamond Cotts RG10 ....37 C6
Diamond Hill GU15 ....151 E7
Diamond Rd SL1 ....43 B4
Diamond Ridge GU15 ..151 E7
Diamond Way RG41 ....115 E7
Diana Cl Slough SL3 ....43 E7
Spencers Wood RG7 ...113 A1
Dianthus Cl KT16 .....123 E2
Dianthus Pl RG42 ......92 B2
Dibleys OX11 ....12 A8
Dick Turpin Way TW14 ...71 F3
Dickens Cl RG4 ....59 D2
Dickens Pl SL3 ....69 E6
Dickens Way GU46 ....149 C5
Dickens Wlk RG14 ....131 A8
Dickson Glade RG19 ...106 E2
Diddenham Cotts RG7 .112 D2
Dido Rd OX11 ....9 F8
Dieppe Cl RG41 ....115 E6
Digby Rd RG14 ....104 E4
Digital Acad RG41 .....116 B4
Dines Way RG18 ....79 C7
Dingle Rd TW15 ....98 B3
Dinton Pastures Ctry Pk* RG10 ....88 C5
Discovery Ct 6 RG14 ..105 A2
Disraeli Ct SL3 ....69 B8
Ditchfield La RG40 ....141 E8
Ditchling RG12 ....118 A2
Dittany Gdns RG18 ....106 D5
Ditton Park Rd SL3 ....68 E8
Ditton Pk Cvn Site SL3 ..43 F1
Ditton Rd Datchet SL3 ...68 D7
Slough SL3 ....68 F8
Dittons The RG40 .....141 F6
Dobson's La RG9 ......15 C8
Dockett Eddy La TW17 .124 F1
Dockett Moorings KT16 .124 F1
Doctors La RG18 ......79 A6
Doddington Cl RG6 ....87 C1
Doddsfield Rd SL2 .....22 A2
Dodsells Well RG40 ...141 F8
Dog La RG8 ....54 A6
Doghurst Ave UB7 .....71 B7
Doghurst Dr UB7 ......71 B7
Dogkennel La OX12 ....27 C4
Doles Hill RG41 ....115 D4
Doles La RG41 ....115 E3
Dolman Rd RG14 ......105 A4
Dolphin Cl Brimpton RG7 134 F7
Winnersh RG41 ....88 C1
Dolphin Ct
Bracknell RG12 ....118 C5
Slough SL1 ....43 B4
Stanwell TW19 ....97 A5
Dolphin Ct N TW19 .....97 A5
Dolphin Est The TW16 ..125 D8
Dolphin Ho
1 Camberley GU15 .....151 B3
Wokingham RG40 ......116 B6
Dolphin Rd
Charlton TW16 ....125 E8
Slough SL1 ....43 B4
Dolphin Rd N TW16 ....125 E8
Dolphin Rd S TW16 ....125 E8
Dolphin Rd W TW16 ....125 E8
Dolphin Sch RG10 ......62 A2
Dolton Mews RG14 .....104 F3
Doman Rd GU15 ......151 A4
Domoney Cl RG19 .....106 E3
Don Cl RG30 ....85 A8
Donaldson Way RG5 ....88 B8
Doncastle Rd RG12 ...117 E6
Donegal Cl RG4 ....59 C3
Donkey La SL8 ....3 A3
Donkin Hill RG4 ....59 C3
Donnington Castle* RG14 ....104 E7
Donnington Cl
Bucklebury RG7 ......108 C8
Camberley GU15 ......151 B4
Donnington Gdns
Maidenhead SL6 ....19 F1
Reading RG1 ....86 E6
Donnington Hosp RG14 .104 F6
Donnington Lodge RG14 ....104 F7
Donnington Pk RG14 ...104 F6
Donnington Pl RG41 ....88 D2
Donnington Rd RG1 ....86 D6
Donnington Sq RG14 ...104 F5
Donnybrook RG12 ....118 A2
Dorcas Ct GU15 ......151 B3
Dorchester Cl SL6 .....19 B1
Dorchester Ct
Reading RG30 ....85 C6
8 Staines TW18 ....97 A4
Dorchester Dr TW14 ....71 E1
Dorian Dr SL5 ....120 E8
Doris Rd TW15 ....98 D2
Dorking Way RG31 .....84 B4
Dorly Cl TW17 ....125 E4
Dormer Cl
Crowthorne RG45 .....143 A5
Newbury RG14 ....130 E6
Dormy Ho The GU25 ...121 F3
Dorndon Ho RG10 ......88 F8
Dornels SL2 ....43 C7
Dorney Ct* SL4 ....41 B3
Dorney Lake Pk* SL4 ...66 B8
Dorney Lake Rowing Ctr* SL4 ....41 B1
Dorney Reach Rd SL6 ...40 F3
Dorney Sch SL6 ....40 F3
Dorney Wood Rd SL1 ...21 D6
Dorneywood Way RG14 105 D4
Dorothy Ct RG14 .....105 D4
Dorothy St 7 RG1 .....86 B6
Dorset Ct GU15 ......151 F8
Dorset Lodge 9 SL6 ...39 F6
Dorset Rd Ashford TW15 ..97 D5
Windsor SL4 ....67 C6
Dorset St RG30 ....85 C8
Dorset Vale RG42 ......91 E2
Dorset Way RG41 .....115 E5
Dorton Villas UB7 .....71 A6
Doublet Cl RG19 .....106 A3
Douglas Ct Earley RG6 ..87 A3
Marlow SL7 ....2 A3
Douglas Grange RG10 ...88 D4
Douglas La TW19 ......68 F1
Douglas Rd
Caversham RG4 ....59 D2
Slough SL2 ....42 D8
Stanwell TW19 ....70 D1
Doultons The TW18 ....97 A2
Douro Cl RG26 ....134 D1
Dove Cl RG6 ....113 F8
Dove Ct TW19 ....97 E8
Dove House Cres SL2 ...21 E2
Dovecote Rd RG2 .....113 B7
Dovedale Cl
Caversham RG4 ....58 F3
Sandhurst GU47 ......143 D2
Dover Rd SL1 ....41 F7
Dover St RG1 ....86 A6
Doveton Way RG14 ....105 B4
Dowding Cl RG5 ....88 A7
Dowding Ct RG45 .....143 C6
Dower Pk SL4 ....66 E3
Down Pl SL4 ....66 A8
Down View RG17 ......100 E5
Downe House Sch RG18 .79 A3
Downend La RG20 .....51 B2
Downfield La SL6 .....63 C5
Downfield Rd RG10 ....63 A4
Downham Ct RG2 ......86 E1
Downing Rd RG31 .....84 D8
Downlands RG17 ......47 C6
Downmill Rd RG12 ....117 F7
Downs Cl RG17 ....46 F7
Downs Rd Aldworth RG20 .32 A4
Slough SL3 ....43 D4
Downs Sch The RG20 ....31 D4
Downs View OX11 ......12 F8
Downs Way Chilton OX11 ..9 F8
Purley On T RG31 ......57 C2
Downshire Cl RG17 ....48 B4
Downshire Sq RG1 ....85 E6
Downshire Way
Bracknell RG12 ......118 B6
Bracknell RG12,RG42 ...118 A7
Downside OX11 ....10 C8
Downsway Prim Sch RG31 ....57 C3
Doyle Gdns GU46 .....149 C4
Doyle Ho RG45 ....143 B3
Drain Hill RG17 ....25 A4
Drake Ave Slough SL3 ...43 D2
Staines TW18 ....96 F3
Drake Cl Bracknell RG12 .118 B4
Wokingham RG40 .....141 E7
Draper Cl RG19 ......106 D2
Draycott RG12 ......118 E4
Drayhorse Dr GU19 ....145 E2
Draymans La 4 SL7 ......1 D1
Drayton Cl RG12 ......118 D7
Drayton Rd RG30 ......85 B8
Draytons View RG19 ...131 C7
Dresden Way RG30 .....57 F1
Drew Mdw SL2 ....22 C8
Drewett Cl RG2 ......113 C6
Drey Ho RG41 ....115 F7
Drift Rd SL4,SL6 ......65 D3
Drift Way SL3 ....69 C7
Drifters Dr GU16 .....152 D1
Driftway Cl 4 RG6 .....87 C1
Drill Hall Rd KT16 ....124 A2
Drive The Ashford TW15 ..98 D1
Bourne End SL8 ....2 F4
Datchet SL3 ....68 B6
Earley RG6 ....87 A7
Newbury RG14 ....130 E8
Slough SL3 ....43 E4
Thorpe GU25 ....122 F4
Wraysbury TW19 ....68 D2
Droitwich Cl RG12 ....118 E6
Drome Path RG41 ......88 A3
Dropmore Rd SL1 ......21 C5
Drove La RG18 ....79 C2
Drove The RG19 ......133 B1
Drovers Way
Bracknell RG12 ......118 F6
Woodley RG5 ....87 E5
Druce Way RG19 .....106 D3
Druce Wood SL5 .....119 E8
Drummond Cl RG12 ....118 F8
Drummond Ho 4 SL4 ....67 D4
Drury La RG7 ....137 A5
Dry Arch Rd SL5 ......120 F3
Dryden RG12 ....118 A2
Dryden Cl RG18 ......106 D5
Dryland Ho RG30 ......84 F7
Du Pre Wlk HP10 ....3 D4
Duchess Cl RG45 .....143 B7
Duchess St SL1 ....41 E5
Dudley Cl RG31 ....57 E1
Dudley Ct SL1 ....43 A3
Dudley Ho RG12 ......118 C7
Dudley Mews RG31 .....57 E1
Dudley Rd Ashford TW15 ..97 F4
East Bedfont TW14 .....98 D7
Duffield La SL2 ....22 F6
Duffield Pk SL2 ....23 A2
Duffield Rd RG5 ....60 F1
Dugdale Ho TW20 ......96 C3
Duke Of Cornwall Ave GU15 ....144 D1
Duke St Eton SL4 ......67 C7
Henley-On-T RG9 ......15 E2
Reading RG1 ....86 B7
Duke's Hill GU19 .....145 E5
Duke's La
Old Windsor SL4,SL5 ....94 B3
Winkfield SL5 ....93 F1
Duke's Ride RG45 ....143 B5
Dukes Cl TW15 ....98 C4
Dukes Covert GU19 ...145 E6
Dukes Dr SL1,SL2 .....22 A8
Dukes Pl Marlow SL7 .....1 D2
Slough SL1 ....42 F6
Dukes Ride RG7 .....136 B1
Dukes Wood RG45 ....143 B5
Dukeshill Rd RG42 ....118 B8
Dulnan Cl RG30 ....85 A8
Dulverton Gdns RG2 ....86 C2
Dumas Cl GU46 ......149 C5
Dumbarton Way RG4 ....59 E5
Dunally Pk TW17 .....125 D2
Dunaways Cl RG6 ......87 D3
Dunbar Cl SL2 ....43 A6
Dunbar Dr RG5 ....88 A6
Dunboe Pl TW17 ......125 C2
Duncan Dr RG40 ......116 E5
Duncan Gdns
Purley On T RG8 ......57 C4
Staines TW18 ....97 A2
Duncan Rd RG5 ....87 E6
Duncannon Cres SL4 ...66 D4
Duncombe Ct TW18 .....96 F1
Duncroft SL4 ....66 F4
Duncroft Manor TW18 ...96 E4
Dundaff Cl GU15 .....152 A5
Dundas Cl RG12 ......118 B5
Dundee Rd SL1 ....42 A8
Dundela Cl RG5 ....87 E6
Dunford Pl RG42 ......90 E1
Dungells Farm Cl GU46 149 D4
Dungells La GU46 ....149 C4
Dungrovehill La SL6 ....18 D3
Dunholme Cl RG6 ......87 E2
Dunholme End SL6 .....39 D3
Dunkirk Cl RG41 ......115 E6
Dunleary Ct 13 RG30 ....85 D6
Dunluce Gdns RG8 ......56 E5
Dunn Cres RG17 ......102 B1
Dunnock Way RG10 .....36 E3
Dunoon Cl RG31 ....84 E4
Dunsfold Rd RG30 ......84 F7
Dunsmore Gdns GU46 ..149 A5
Dunstable Ho 3 SL7 .....1 E1
Dunstall Cl RG31 ....84 D8
Dunstan Ct TW18 ......97 A4

Dunstan Park Inf Sch
RG18 106 D4
Dunstan Rd RG18 106 E4
Dunstans Dr RG41 88 B2
Dunster Cl RG4 59 C6
Dunster Gdns SL1 42 A6
Dunt Ave RG10 88 F4
Dunt La RG10 88 E4
Dunwood Ct SL6 39 C5
Duppas Cl TW17 125 D4
Dupre Cl SL1 41 E4
Durand Rd RG6 87 A1
Durant Way RG31 57 D3
Durham Ave SL1 42 A7
Durham Cl Reading RG2 113 C8
Wokingham RG41 115 E6
Durham Dr GU16 152 D1
Durham Rd GU47 143 E2
Durley Mead RG12 118 F4
Durning Pl SL5 120 B6
Durrell Way TW17 125 D3
Dutch Barn Cl TW19 70 D1
Dutton Way SL0 44 E7
Duval Pl GU19 145 E3
Dwyer Rd RG30 85 A4
Dyer Rd RG40 116 E7
Dyer Straits OX12 9 F8
Dyers Ct RG5 87 D7
Dyson Cl SL4 67 B4
Dysons Cl RG14 104 E3
Dysonswood La RG4 58 E8

E

Eagle Cl
Crowthorne RG45 143 A7
Wokingham RG41 115 F5
Eagle House Sch GU47 143 B2
Eagle Rd Hatton TW6 71 F4
Newtown RG20 132 A2
Eaglehurst Cotts RG42 90 C3
Eagles Nest GU47 143 A1
Earle Croft RG42 91 C1
Earley Hill Rd RG6 87 A5
Earley Pl RG1 86 B7
Earley Sta RG6 87 C4
Earleydene SL5 120 B1
Earls Gr GU15 151 E6
Earls La SL1 41 F5
Earlsfield SL6 40 C2
Earlsfield Cl RG4 59 E4
Earlswood RG12 118 B2
Earlywood Pines SL5 120 A1
Easby Way RG6 87 D1
Easington Dr RG6 87 E2
East Berkshire Coll
Maidenhead SL6 39 D6
Slough SL3 44 A3
Windsor SL4 67 C5
East Burnham Cotts SL2 22 A4
East Burnham La SL2 22 A4
East Cres SL4 66 F6
East Dr Reading RG31 84 E5
Stoke Poges SL2 22 E2
Wentworth GU25 122 B3
East Gn GU17 150 C4
East La RG20 51 B1
East Paddock SL6 18 F6
East Park Farm Dr RG10 61 B4
East Ramp TW6 71 B6
East Rd East Bedfont TW14 98 D8
Maidenhead SL6 39 E7
East Ridge SL8 3 B4
East St RG1 86 B7
East Stratton Cl RG12 118 F4
East Terr SL4 67 E6
East View Cl RG10 36 E2
East View Rd RG10 36 E2
Eastbourne Rd SL1 42 A7
Eastbridge SL2 43 B5
Eastbury Ave RG31 84 B8
Eastbury Ct RG42 90 F1
Eastbury Pk RG41 88 D2
Eastbury Shute RG17 46 E2
Eastchurch Rd TW6 71 E4
Eastchurch Rd Rdbt TW6 71 E5
Eastcourt Ave RG6 87 A6
Eastcroft SL2 22 B1
Eastern Ave
Chertsey KT16 124 A6
Reading RG1 86 E6
Eastern Bsns Pk TW6 71 F5
Eastern Dr SL8 3 C4
Eastern Ind Area RG12 118 D7
Eastern La RG45 143 F4
Eastern Perimeter Rd
TW14,TW6 71 F5
Eastern Rd RG12 118 D7
Eastfield OX11 12 A8
Eastfield Cl [4] SL1 43 A3
Eastfield La RG8 56 D7
Eastfield Rd SL1 41 A8
Easthampstead Mobile Home
Pk RG40 143 C8
Easthampstead Park Sch
RG12 117 D3
Easthampstead Rd
Bracknell RG12 118 A7
Wokingham RG40 116 E4
Eastheath Ave RG41 116 A4
Eastheath Gdns RG41 116 B3
Eastleigh Rd TW6 71 F4
Eastlyn Rd RG26 135 E1
Easton Hill RG20 76 A4
Eastwood Ct [1] SL7 1 F3
Eastwood Rd RG5 87 E4
Eastworth Rd KT15,KT16 124 A1

Eaton Ct GU15 151 B4
Eaton Pl RG1 85 F7
Eaton Rd GU15 151 B4
Ebborn Sq RG6 114 C8
Ebsworth Cl SL6 20 C3
Eccles Cl RG4 59 C2
Echelford Prim Sch The
TW15 98 B3
Echelforde Dr TW15 98 A4
Eddington Hill RG17 100 F7
Eddington Rd RG12 117 E3
Eddystone Wlk TW19 97 E8
Eden Cl SL3 44 A1
Eden Way RG41 88 B1
Edenhall Cl RG31 57 D3
Edenham Cl RG6 87 E2
Edenham Cres RG1 85 E5
Edgar Milward Cl RG30 58 A1
Edgar Wallace Pl SL8 3 B5
Edgbarrow Rise GU47 143 A2
Edgbarrow Sch RG45 143 C3
Edgcumbe Park Dr
RG45 143 A5
Edgecombe La RG14 105 C5
Edgedale Cl RG45 143 B4
Edgehill St RG1 86 B5
Edgell Cl GU25 122 F6
Edgell Rd TW18 96 F3
Edgemoor Rd GU16 152 C3
Edgewood Cl RG45 143 A7
Edinburgh Ave SL1 42 B7
Edinburgh Dr TW18 97 D2
Edinburgh Gdns SL4 67 D5
Edinburgh Rd
Maidenhead SL6 19 E2
Marlow SL7 1 E3
Reading RG30 85 E7
Edith Rd SL6 39 A7
Edmonds Ct RG12 118 C8
Edmunds Way SL2 43 B7
Edneys Hill RG41 115 D2
Edward Ave GU15 151 A5
Edward Ct TW18 97 C2
Edward Pauling Ho
TW14 98 F8
Edward Pauling Prim Sch
TW13 98 E6
Edward Pl [11] RG1 86 D7
Edward Rd Hatton TW14 71 E2
Twyford RG10 61 B5
Windlesham GU20 146 D4
Edward Way TW15 97 F6
Edwards Ct SL1 42 E4
Edwards Hill RG17 25 B2
Edwin Cl RG19 106 F3
Eeklo Pl RG14 105 A1
Egerton Rd Reading RG2 86 E1
Sandhurst GU15 150 F7
Sandhurst GU15 151 A7
Slough SL2 21 E1
Egham Bsns Village
TW20 123 C7
Egham By-Pass TW20 96 A4
Egham Hill TW20 95 D2
Egham Hill Rdbt TW20 95 F3
Egham Mus★ TW20 96 A3
Egham Sta TW20 96 A3
Eghams Ct [4] SL8 3 B3
Egremont Dr RG6 87 D3
Egremont Gdns SL1 42 A5
Egypt La SL2 22 B8
Eight Acres SL1 21 B1
Eight Bells [8] RG14 104 F2
Eighth Ave RG31 84 B6
Eisenhower Ave RG20 49 A4
Elan Cl RG30 84 F7
Elbow Mdw SL3 69 F6
Eldart Cl RG30 85 B7
Elder Cl RG31 57 C1
Elderberry Way RG6 87 D1
Elderfield Cres OX11 10 D8
Elderfield Rd SL2 22 F6
Eldon Pl RG1 86 C7
Eldon Rd RG1 86 C7
Eldon Sq RG1 86 D7
Eldon St RG1 86 D7
Eldon Terr RG1 86 D7
Eldrick Ct TW14 98 D7
Electra Ave TW6 71 F4
Elford Cl RG6 87 C1
Elgar Ave RG45 143 B7
Elgar Rd RG2 86 A5
Elgar Rd S RG2 86 B4
Elgarth Dr RG40 141 F8
Elgin Ave TW15 98 C2
Elgin Cres TW6 71 E5
Elgin Gate [5] RG1 85 F7
Elgin Ho SL3 69 E6
Elgin Rd GU17 149 E1
Eliot Cl Camberley GU15 152 B7
Caversham RG4 59 A4
Thatcham RG18 106 C5
Eliot Dr SL7 1 F4
Elizabeth Ave
Bagshot GU19 145 F2
Newbury RG14 130 D7
Staines TW18 97 C2
Elizabeth Cl
Bracknell RG12 118 C5
Cookham Rise SL6 19 F7
Henley-On-T RG9 35 B8
Elizabeth Ct
[2] Reading RG31 84 D8
[1] Slough SL1 43 A4
Theale RG7 83 F3
Wargrave RG10 36 E2
[6] Windsor SL4 67 C5

Elizabeth Gdns
Ascot SL5 120 B4
Kintbury RG17 102 B2
Elizabeth Ho TW15 97 F4
Elizabeth Mews [5] RG1 86 B6
Elizabeth Par GU46 149 D4
Elizabeth Rd
Henley-On-T RG9 35 B8
Marlow SL7 1 E3
Wokingham RG40 116 D6
Elizabeth Rout Cl RG7 113 C2
Elizabeth Way SL2 22 F4
Elizabeth Wlk [4] RG1 86 B5
Elizabethan Cl TW19 97 D8
Elizabethan Way TW19 97 D8
Ellenborough Cl RG12 118 D8
Ellerton Cl RG7 83 E4
Ellesfield Ave RG12 117 E5
Ellesmere Cl RG4 59 B3
Ellies Mews TW15 97 E6
Elliman Ave SL2 42 F6
Ellington Ct SL6 40 C7
Ellington Gdns SL6 40 C7
Ellington Pk SL6 19 E1
Ellington Prim Sch SL6 19 F1
Ellington Rd
Feltham TW13 98 F4
Taplow SL6 40 C7
Elliots Way RG4 59 B2
Elliott Gdns TW17 125 A5
Elliott Rise SL5 119 D7
Ellis Ave SL1 42 E4
Ellis Rd RG45 143 B6
Ellis's Hill RG2 114 F4
Ellison Cl SL4 66 F4
Ellison Ho [17] SL4 67 D6
Ellison Way RG40 116 B6
Elm Bank GU46 149 C7
Elm Cl
Farnham Common SL2 22 C6
Stanwell TW19 97 D7
Elm Cotts Ball Hill RG20 129 F1
Holyport SL6 65 A8
Elm Croft SL3 68 C6
Elm Ct [5] Ashford TW16 98 F1
Henley-On-T RG9 35 D7
Sandhurst GU47 143 E2
Elm Dr
Burghfield Common RG30 111 B5
Winkfield SL4 93 B7
Elm Farm Cvn Pk KT16 123 C3
Elm Gr Maidenhead SL6 39 E7
Thatcham RG18 106 B5
Elm La Bourne End SL8 2 F5
Earley RG6 86 F2
Elm Lodge Ave RG30 85 D8
Elm Park Ct [5] RG30 85 E7
Elm Park Rd RG30 85 D7
Elm Pk Reading RG30 85 C7
Sunningdale SL5 120 E1
Elm Rd Earley RG2,RG6 86 F2
East Bedfont TW14 98 D8
Mapledurham RG4 58 D7
Windsor SL4 67 B4
Elm Tree Cl TW15 98 B3
Elmar Gn SL2 22 A2
Elmbank Ave TW20 95 B2
Elmcroft RG8 34 C5
Elmcroft Cl TW14 71 F1
Elmcroft Dr TW15 98 A3
Elmdon Rd TW6 71 F4
Elmfield Gdns RG14 104 E4
Elmhurst Ct SL3 44 A3
Elmhurst Rd Goring RG8 34 C7
Reading RG1 86 D5
Slough SL3 44 A3
Thatcham RG18 106 A5
Elmleigh Ct RG4 59 C3
Elmley Cl RG41 88 F1
Elms Ave RG19 106 E3
Elms Dr SL8 3 C3
Elms Rd RG40 116 B5
Elms The
[5] Ashford TW15 98 A3
Blackwater GU17 150 D4
Newell Green RG42 92 A1
Elmshott La SL1 41 E6
Elmsleigh Ctr The TW18 96 F4
Elmsleigh Rd TW18 96 F3
Elmslie Ct SL6 39 E7
Elmstone Dr RG31 57 C1
Elmsway TW15 98 A3
Elmwood SL6 20 B4
Elmwood Cl RG5 87 D8
Elmwood Rd SL2 43 B6
Elsenwood Cres GU15 152 A6
Elsenwood Dr GU15 152 A7
Elsinore Ave TW19 97 E8
Elsley Rd RG31 57 E3
Elstow Ave RG4 59 C6
Elstree Cl RG31 57 D2
Elstree Sch RG7 108 D4
Elsworth Cl TW14 98 E7
Eltham Ave
Caversham RG4 59 E5
Slough SL1 41 E4
Elton Dr SL6 39 D8
Elvaston Way RG30 85 A7
Elveden Cl RG6 87 E2
Elvedon Rd TW13 98 F5
Elvendon Rd RG8 34 D7
Elwell Cl TW20 96 A2
Ely Ave SL1 42 C8
Ely Rd Hatton TW6 71 F5
Theale RG7 83 F3
Elyham RG8 57 B5
Embankment The TW19 95 C7
Ember Rd SL3 44 B3

Emblen Cres RG2 114 E2
Embrook Way RG31 84 A4
Emerald Cl RG41 115 E7
Emerald Ct SL1 42 E4
Emerson Ct
Crowthorne RG45 143 B5
Wooburn Green HP10 3 E6
Emery Acres RG8 55 A6
Emery Down Cl RG12 119 A6
Emilia Cl SL6 19 F1
Emlyns Bldgs SL4 67 D7
Emm Cl RG41 115 F8
Emma La RG10 36 E2
Emmbrook Ct RG2 86 E2
Emmbrook Gate RG41 115 F8
Emmbrook Inf Sch RG41 88 F1
Emmbrook Jun Sch RG41 88 F1
Emmbrook Rd RG41 115 F8
Emmbrook Sch The
RG41 116 A8
Emmbrook Vale RG41 89 A1
Emmer Green Ct RG4 59 C5
Emmer Green Prim Sch
RG4 59 B6
Emmets Nest RG42 90 C2
Emmets Pk RG42 90 D2
Emmview Cl RG41 115 F7
Empress Rd RG31 84 C5
Empstead Ct RG9 15 D2
Enborne CE Prim Sch
RG20 129 E6
Enborne Cl RG31 84 C8
Enborne Gate RG14 104 D1
Enborne Gdns RG12 91 D1
Enborne Gr RG14 104 E2
Enborne Lodge La
RG14 130 C6
Enborne Pl RG14 104 E2
Enborne Rd RG14 104 D1
Enborne St RG14 130 C6
Enborne Way RG7 133 F6
Enfield Rd TW6 71 E5
Enfield Road Rdbt TW6 71 E5
Engineer's Rd RG19 132 A5
Englefield CE Prim Sch
RG7 83 B4
Englefield Cl TW20 95 C2
Englefield Green Inf Sch
TW20 95 C3
Englefield Rd RG7 83 D4
Englehurst TW20 95 C2
Englemere Pk SL5 119 D5
Englemere Pond Nature
Trail★ SL5 119 C6
Englemere Rd RG42 90 F1
Englesfield GU15 152 D5
English Gdns TW19 68 D2
English Martyrs RC Prim Sch
RG30 85 A7
Enid Wood Ho RG12 118 C7
Ennerdale RG12 118 A5
Ennerdale Cl TW14 98 F7
Ennerdale Cres SL1 41 C8
Ennerdale Rd RG2 86 D3
Ennerdale Way RG19 106 A3
Ensign Cl TW19 97 D7
Ensign Way TW19 97 D7
Enstone Rd RG5 88 A8
Enterprise Ct RG12 117 F7
Enterprise Way RG19 107 A2
EP Collier Prim Sch RG1 59 A1
Epping Cl RG1 85 F7
Epping Ho [3] RG1 85 E5
Epping Way RG12 118 F5
Epsom Cl GU15 151 C8
Epsom Cres RG14 105 B1
Epsom Ct RG1 85 F6
Epsom Sq TW6 71 F5
Equine Way RG14 131 B7
Eric Ave RG4 59 A6
Erica Cl Slough SL1 41 E6
West End GU24 153 E6
Erica Dr RG40 116 D5
Eriswell Cl RG6 87 E2
Erkenwald Cl KT16 123 E3
Erleigh Court Dr RG6 87 B7
Erleigh Court Gdns RG6 87 A7
Erleigh Dene RG14 104 F1
Erleigh Rd RG1 86 D6
Ermin St Lambourn RG17 46 D2
Stockcross RG20 103 D7
Ermin Wlk RG19 106 B3
Errington Dr SL4 67 A6
Erskine Cl RG26 135 F1
Escot Rd TW16 98 E1
Esher Cres TW6 71 F5
Esher Rd GU15 145 A1
Eskdale Gdns SL6 40 B2
Eskdale Rd RG41 88 B4
Eskdale Way GU15 152 D4
Eskin Cl RG30 85 A7
Essame Cl RG40 116 D6
Essex Ave SL2 42 C8
Essex Cotts RG7 111 B3
Essex Pl RG17 25 B3
Essex Rise RG42 91 F1
Essex St Newbury RG14 130 D7
Reading RG2 86 B5
Ethel Rd TW15 97 E3
Eton Cl SL3 68 A8
Eton Coll SL4 67 C8
Eton Coll Mus★ SL4 67 C8
Eton Ct Eton SL4 67 D7
Staines TW18 96 F3
Eton End PNEU Sch SL3 68 A8
Eton Ho [6] TW20 96 A3
Eton Pl SL7 1 D2

Eton Porny CE Fst Sch
SL4 67 D8
Eton Rd Datchet SL3 68 A8
Harlington UB3 71 F7
Eton Riverside SL4 67 D7
Eton Sq SL4 67 D7
Eton Wick CE Fst Sch
SL4 42 A1
Eton Wick Rd SL4 42 B1
Eton Wlk [1] SL1 42 E3
European Weather Ctr
RG2 113 D7
Eustace Cres RG40 116 D8
Evedon RG12 118 B2
Evelyn Cres TW16 125 F8
Evelyn Ct RG5 87 F5
Evelyn Way TW16 125 F8
Evendon's Cl RG41 116 A3
Evendon's La RG41 115 E2
Evenlode Rd SL8 3 B4
Evenlode Way GU47 150 D8
Everard Ave SL1 42 E4
Everest Rd
Camberley GU15 151 D8
Crowthorne RG45 143 B6
Stanwell TW19 97 E8
Evergreen Ct TW19 97 D8
Evergreen Dr RG31 84 F4
Evergreen Oak Ave SL4 68 A4
Evergreen Rd GU16 152 A3
Evergreen Way
Stanwell TW19 97 D8
Wokingham RG41 115 F5
Everington La RG18 53 C1
Everland Rd RG17 100 D6
Eversley Rd
Arborfield Cross RG2 114 E2
Barkham RG40 140 E6
Yateley GU46 149 A7
Eversley St RG27 141 A1
Eversley Way TW20 123 C7
Evesham Rd RG4 59 B5
Evesham Wlk GU47 143 D1
Evreham Rd SL0 44 E7
Evreux Cl RG19 106 F2
Ewing Way RG14 131 B8
Exbourne Rd RG2 113 C8
Exchange Rd SL5 120 C4
Exeforde Ave TW15 98 A4
Exeter Ct RG2 113 B8
Exeter Gdns GU46 149 B7
Exeter Rd TW6 71 E4
Exeter Way
Harlington TW6 71 E5
Theale RG7 83 F3
Exmoor Rd RG19 106 C3
Explorer Ave TW19 97 E7
Express Way RG14 105 E2
Exwick Sq RG2 113 D8
Eynsford Cl RG4 59 E5
Eynsham Cl RG5 87 E8
Eyre Ct RG40 116 B4
Eyre Gn SL2 22 A2

F

Faculty The [16] RG1 86 B6
Fagg's Rd TW14 71 F3
Fair Close Ho [1] RG14 105 A2
Fair Cross RG7 138 D2
Fair Lawn Gn RG2 86 F1
Fair Mile RG9 15 C4
Fair Mile Hospl OX10 14 B8
Fair View Cotts SL6 19 E7
Fairacre SL6 39 C6
Fairacres Ind Est SL4 66 D5
Faircroft SL2 22 B1
Faircross Bracknell RG12 118 B6
Hermitage RG18 78 F6
Faircross Rd RG30 85 C5
Fairfax RG42 118 A8
Fairfax Cl RG4 59 B3
Fairfax Pl RG14 105 E5
Fairfield RG20 31 D4
Fairfield App TW19 68 D1
Fairfield Ave Datchet SL3 68 D7
Staines TW18 96 F4
Fairfield Cl Bourne End SL8 3 A4
Datchet SL3 68 D7
Fairfield Dr GU16 151 E3
Fairfield La
Farnham Royal SL2 22 B3
West End GU24 153 F7
Fairfield Rd Burnham SL1 21 C2
Goring RG8 34 D7
Wraysbury TW19 68 D1
Fairfields Chertsey KT15 124 B1
Hungerford RG17 100 D5
Fairford Rd
Maidenhead SL6 39 F8
Purley On T RG31 57 C2
Fairhaven TW20 95 F3
Fairhaven Ct [1] TW20 95 F3
Fairholme TW14 98 E8
Fairholme Rd TW15 97 F3
Fairholme Sch TW14 98 D7
Fairlawn Pk SL4 66 E3
Fairlawns Cl TW18 97 B2
Fairlea SL6 39 B3
Fairlie Rd SL1 42 A8
Fairlight Ave SL4 67 D5
Fairlop Cl RG31 84 D4
Fairmead Cl GU47 150 E7
Fairmead Ct GU15 151 C4

Fairmead Rd RG2 113 E5
Fairmile Ct RG9 15 D3
Fairoak Way RG26 134 D1
Fairsted Cl RG30 85 A8
Fairview RG14 130 E8
Fairview Ave RG6 87 B6
Fairview Cotts GU25 122 D3
Fairview Ct Ashford TW15 98 A3
Staines TW18 97 A2
Fairview Dr TW17 124 F4
Fairview Est RG9 35 F8
Fairview Rd Burnham SL6 41 A7
Hungerford RG17 100 D5
Slough SL2 21 F1
Wokingham RG40 116 C5
Fairwater Dr RG5 87 D6
Fairway KT16 124 B1
Fairway Ave RG30 84 D6
Fairway Ct RG42 91 A1
Fairway Dr RG10 61 A5
Fairway Hts GU15 152 B6
Fairway The Burnham SL1 21 C3
Flackwell Heath HP10 3 C7
Frimley GU15 152 A3
Maidenhead SL6 39 B3
Fairways TW15 98 B2
Faithfull Cl RG42 91 B2
Fakenham Cl RG6 114 A8
Fakenham Way GU47 143 D2
Falaise TW20 95 F3
Falcon Ave RG2 86 F1
Falcon Bsns Pk RG40 141 A6
Falcon Cl GU18 152 F8
Falcon Ct GU16 151 D1
Falcon Dr TW19 70 E1
Falcon Fields RG26 135 B2
Falcon House Gdns
RG20 129 F1
Falcon Way
Sunbury TW16 125 E7
Wokingham RG41 115 F6
Yateley GU46 149 B6
Falcons Croft HP10 3 E8
Falconwood TW20 95 E3
Falkland Dr RG14 130 F8
Falkland Garth RG14 130 D7
Falkland Ho SL6 39 F8
Falkland Prim Sch
RG14 130 D6
Falkland Rd
Caversham RG4 59 B2
Newbury RG14 130 D6
Fallowfield GU46 149 B7
Fallowfield Cl RG4 59 B4
Fallows The SL6 20 A1
Falmouth Cl GU15 152 A4
Falmouth Rd
Reading RG2 113 C7
Slough SL1 42 A7
Falmouth Way RG19 106 F3
Falstaff Ave RG6 86 F2
Fane Way SL6 39 D5
Fanes Cl RG42 117 F8
Fangrove Cvn Pk KT16 123 B1
Fannys La RG7 80 C1
Faraday Cl
Arborfield RG2 140 E7
Slough SL2 42 B8
Faraday Rd
Newbury RG14 105 B3
Slough SL2 42 B8
Farcrosse Cl GU47 150 C8
Fareham Dr GU46 149 B7
Faringdon Cl GU47 143 C1
Faringdon Dr RG12 118 D4
Faringdon Wlk RG30 85 B4
Farleigh Mews RG4 59 E5
Farley Copse RG42 117 E8
Farley Ct RG7 140 C5
Farley Hill Prim Sch
RG7 140 D5
Farley Moor RG42 117 D8
Farm Cl Ascot SL5 120 C4
Bracknell RG42 117 F8
Crowthorne RG45 143 C7
Egham TW18 96 E3
Holyport SL6 40 C1
Lower Halliford TW17 125 A2
Lyne KT16 123 A3
Maidenhead SL6 39 A7
Purley On T RG8 57 C5
Yateley GU46 149 D5
Farm Cotts RG17 100 A1
Farm Cres SL2 43 C8
Farm Ct GU16 151 F2
Farm Dr Old Windsor SL4 68 B1
Reading RG31 84 B6
Farm Lea HP10 3 F7
Farm Rd Bourne End SL8 2 F4
Burnham SL6 41 A6
Frimley GU16 151 F2
Goring RG8 34 C6
Henley-On-T RG9 35 F8
Maidenhead SL6 39 A7
Staines TW18 97 B2
Farm View GU46 149 D5
Farm Way TW19 69 F1
Farm Yd SL4 67 D7
Farman Cl RG5 88 B8
Farmer's Rd TW18 96 E3
Farmers Cl
Maidenhead SL6 39 A4
Reading RG2 113 C6
Farmers End RG10 61 B4
Farmers Gate RG18 106 D5
Farmers Way SL6 39 A4
Farmiloe Cl RG8 57 C4
Farnburn Ave SL1 42 B8
Farnell Rd TW18 97 A5
Farnesdown Dr RG41 115 F8
Farnham Cl RG12 118 D7
Farnham Common Inf Sch
SL2 22 B8
Farnham Common Jun Sch
SL2 22 C8
Farnham Dr RG4 59 E4
Farnham La SL2 21 E2
Farnham Park La SL2 22 C4
Farnham Rd SL1, SL2 42 C7
Farnham Royal CE Comb Sch
SL2 22 C2
Farningham RG12 118 E3
Farnsfield Cl RG6 114 A8
Farrell Cl GU15 151 C3
Farrer Theatre SL4 42 D1
Farrier Ct 6 SL8 3 B3
Farrier Pl GU47 150 B7
Farriers Cl RG5 87 E7
Farriers La RG20 30 E7
Farringdon Ct RG1 86 E6
Farrowdene Rd RG2 113 C8
Farthing Ct 3 SL5 121 B2
Farthing Green La SL2 23 B4
Farthingales The SL6 40 B7
Fatherson Rd RG1 86 D7
Faulkner Pl GU19 145 F4
Faversham Rd GU47 143 D1
Fawcett Cres RG5 87 D6
Fawcett Rd SL4 67 B6
Fawler Mead RG12 118 F5
Fawley Bottom La RG9 15 A8
Fawley Cl SL6 19 D2
Fawley Court House & Mus*
RG9 15 F5
Fawley Mews 2 RG1 85 F6
Fawley Rd RG30 85 C5
Fawns Manor Cl TW14 98 C7
Fawns Manor Rd TW14 98 D7
Fawsley Cl SL3 69 E7
Faygate Way RG6 87 B1
Feathers La TW19 96 A6
Felbridge Cl GU16 151 F1
Felbridge Ct UB3 71 D8
Felix La TW17 125 F3
Felixstowe Cl RG6 87 D2
Fellow Gn GU24 153 F6
Fellow Green Rd GU24 153 F6
Fellowes Ct UB3 71 D8
Fells The RG31 84 A6
Fellstead Ct SL6 39 C6
Felstead Cl RG6 86 F3
Feltham Hill Inf Sch
TW13 98 F5
Feltham Hill Jun Sch
TW13 98 F5
Feltham Hill Rd TW15 98 C2
Feltham Rd TW15 98 C4
Felthorpe Cl RG6 114 A8
Felton Way RG31 84 C8
Fenchurch Mews 3
RG41 88 A3
Fencote RG12 118 D3
Fennel Cl Ascot SL5 120 A5
Earley RG6 86 F1
Newbury RG14 105 D5
Fennel Ct RG18 106 D4
Fenns La GU24 153 E5
Fennscombe Ct GU24 153 F6
Fenton Ave TW18 97 C3
Fenton Lodge GU15 151 E6
Fern Cl Crowthorne RG45 143 A7
Frimley GU16 152 C3
Reading RG31 84 C5
Fern Cotts SL7 2 E5
Fern Dr SL6 41 B7
Fern Glen RG31 57 C1
Fern La SL7 2 E5
Fern Wlk Ashford TW15 97 D3
Reading RG31 84 C5
Fernbank RG40 141 D6
Fernbank Cres SL5 119 D8
Fernbank Pl SL5 119 D7
Fernbank Rd SL5 119 D8
Fernbrook Rd RG4 58 E5
Ferndale Ave RG30 85 A4
Ferndale Cl RG31 57 E3
Ferndale Ct RG19 106 D3
Ferndale Pk Cvn Pk SL6 65 E8
Ferndale Rd TW15 97 E3
Ferne Cl RG8 34 C7
Fernery The TW18 96 E3
Fernhill Cl Bracknell RG42 90 F1
Farnborough GU17 150 F1
Fernhill La GU17 150 F1
Fernhill Prim Sch GU14 150 F1
Fernhill Rd GU14,GU17 150 E2
Fernhill Sch GU14 150 F1
Fernhill Wlk GU17 150 F1
Fernhurst Rd
Ashford TW15 98 C4
Reading RG31 84 C4
Ferniehurst GU15 151 F4
Fernley Ct SL6 19 D1
Ferrard Cl SL5 119 D8
Ferrers Cl SL1 41 E5
Ferriby Ct RG12 118 C7
Ferrier Gr RG14 131 B8
Ferry Ave TW18 96 E1
Ferry End SL6 40 C4
Ferry La Bourne End SL8 3 B1
Chertsey KT16 124 A3
Cookham SL6 20 B7
Goring RG8 34 B6
Ferry La continued
Hambleden RG9 16 D6
Laleham TW18 124 C6
Lower Halliford TW17 125 A1
Medmenham SL7 17 B5
Moulsford OX10,RG8 14 B4
South Stoke RG8 14 A4
Wargrave RG10 36 C2
Wraysbury TW19 96 B5
Ferry Rd Maidenhead SL6 40 C4
South Stoke RG8 14 C4
Ferry Wks TW17 125 A1
Festival Cotts SL3 69 C7
Fettiplace RG17 48 B3
Fetty Pl SL6 39 D4
Fidler's La RG20 30 E7
Fidlers Wlk RG10 36 E2
Field Cl
Burghfield Common RG7 111 B2
Harlington UB7 71 C7
Field End Wargrave RG10 36 F2
West End GU24 153 F6
Field House Cl SL5 120 A1
Field Hurst SL3 43 F1
Field La GU16 151 E1
Field Path GU14 150 F1
Field Pk RG12 118 D8
Field Rd
Farnborough GU14 150 F1
Peasemore RG20 50 D8
Reading RG1 86 A6
Field View Caversham RG4 59 B3
Egham TW20 96 C3
Feltham TW13 98 D4
Fielden Pl RG12 118 D7
Fieldfare Ave GU46 149 B6
Fieldhead Gdns SL8 3 A3
Fieldhouse Ind Est SL7 1 F2
Fieldhouse La SL7 1 F2
Fieldhouse Way SL7 1 F2
Fielding Gdns
Crowthorne RG45 143 B4
Slough SL3 43 C4
Fielding Rd
Maidenhead SL6 39 B8
Sandhurst GU47 150 E6
Fieldings The SL6 65 A7
Fieldridge RG14 105 D5
Fields The SL1 42 D4
Fieldview Ct TW18 97 A2
Fieldway RG41 88 D2
Fifehead Cl TW15 97 E2
Fifield Cotts SL6 65 D5
Fifield La SL4,SL6 65 D4
Fifield Rd SL6 65 D7
Fifield Way Cotts SL6 65 D6
Fifth Ave RG31 84 B6
Fifth Rd RG14 104 E1
Fifth St RG19 131 F5
Filbert Dr RG31 84 C8
Filey Rd RG1 86 E7
Filey Spur SL1 42 B4
Filley Alley OX12 6 E7
Filmer Rd SL4 66 D5
Finbeck Way RG6 113 F8
Finch Ct SL6 39 D5
Finch Rd RG6 87 C4
Finch Way RG7 111 B3
Fincham End Dr RG45 142 F4
Finchampstead CE Prim Sch
RG40 141 E3
Finchampstead Rd
Wokingham RG40 141 F6
Wokingham RG41,RG40 116 B3
Findhorn Cl GU47 150 D7
Finlay Ho RG9 15 E3
Finmere RG12 118 C2
Finney Dr GU20 146 D4
Finstock Cl RG6 87 D1
Finstock Gn RG12 118 F5
Fir Cl RG19 133 B5
Fir Cottage Rd RG40 141 E8
Fir Dr GU17 150 D3
Fir Tree Ave SL2 22 F1
Fir Tree Cl SL5 120 A2
Fir Tree Cnr RG26 134 E2
Fir Tree Cotts RG20 10 B2
Fir Tree La RG14 105 E4
Fir Tree Paddock RG20 10 A2
Fir Tree Pl 1 TW15 98 A3
Fir Tree Prim Sch RG14 105 E4
Fir's End RG7 111 A2
Firbank Pl TW20 95 B2
Fircroft Cl Reading RG31 57 C1
Stoke Poges SL2 23 A6
Fircroft Ct SL2 23 A6
Fireball Hill SL5 120 D2
Firfield SL6 40 B1
Firglen Dr GU46 149 D7
Firgrove Rd RG27,GU46 149 C6
Firlands Bracknell RG12 118 C4
North Ascot SL5 119 D6
Firlands Ave GU15 151 D5
Firmstone Cl RG6 87 C1
Firs Ave SL4 66 F4
Firs Cl RG40 141 F7
Firs Dr SL3 43 F5
Firs End RG7 136 E6
Firs La Maidenhead SL6 38 F4
Reading RG30 85 D5
Firs Rd RG31 84 C6
Firs The
5 Bracknell RG12 118 F5
Inkpen RG17 127 E5
Maidenhead SL6 39 E7
Reading RG1 85 F6
Thatcham RG18 106 B4
First Ave Marlow SL7 2 A2
First Ave continued
Reading RG31 84 B6
Tadley RG7 135 D2
First Cres SL1 42 C8
First St RG19 132 A5
Firtree Cl GU47 142 F1
Firview Cl SL7 1 F1
Firwood Ct GU15 151 C5
Firwood Dr GU15 151 C5
Firwood Rd GU25 121 E3
Fisher Gn RG42 90 B2
Fisher Ho 5 RG14 104 F2
Fisher's La RG18 79 A1
Fisherman's La RG7 135 B8
Fisherman's Way SL8 3 B4
Fishermans Retreat SL7 1 E1
Fishers Cotts RG4 59 C6
Fishers Ct RG4 59 C6
Fishers Wood SL5 121 C1
Fishery Rd SL6 40 C5
Fishguard Spur SL1 43 B4
Fishing Temple Park Homes
TW18 123 F8
Fishponds Cl RG41 116 A4
Fishponds Est RG41 116 A4
Fishponds Rd RG41 116 A4
Fiske Ct GU46 149 E6
Fitzgerald Ct RG14 104 F3
Fitzrobert Pl TW20 96 A2
Fitzroy Cl RG12 118 A3
Fitzroy Cres RG5 88 A6
Five Acre RG31 57 B1
Five Acres HP10 3 F7
Fiveways GU15 151 E5
Flagstaff Sq RG19 106 E2
Flambards RG4 59 C2
Flamborough Cl RG6 87 E2
Flamborough Path 4
RG6 87 E2
Flamborough Spur SL1 42 A4
Flamingo Cl RG41 115 E5
Flanders Ct TW20 96 C3
Flats The GU17 150 C4
Flaxman Cl RG6 86 F2
Flecker Cl RG18 106 C5
Fleet Cl RG41 115 E6
Fleet Hill RG40 141 C2
Fleet La RG40 141 B2
Fleetbrook Ho SL3 68 D6
Fleetham Gdns RG6 87 C1
Fleetway TW20 123 C6
Fleetwood Cl RG14 105 D5
Fleetwood Ct 7 TW19 70 E1
Fleetwood Rd SL2 42 F6
Fleming Cl RG2 140 E7
Fleming Rd RG14 105 B3
Flemish Fields KT16 124 A2
Flemish Pl RG42 91 D1
Fletcher Gdns RG42 117 D8
Flexford Gn RG12 117 E3
Flintgrove RG12 118 D8
Flintjack Pl RG17 25 A2
Flintlock Cl TW19 70 A3
Flodden Dr RG31 84 D4
Floral Ct RG10 62 A8
Floral Ho KT16 123 F1
Floral Way RG18 106 E5
Floreat Gdns RG14 104 E1
Florence Ave SL6 40 A8
Florence Cl GU46 149 C6
Florence Cotts SL4 92 C7
Florence Ct 19 RG30 85 D6
Florence Gdns
Staines TW18 97 B1
Thatcham RG18 106 A5
Florence Rd GU47 150 E7
Florence Villas GU18 146 B1
Florence Wlk RG1 86 D7
Florian Gdns RG30 85 B5
Florida Ct Reading RG1 85 E6
Staines TW18 97 A3
Flower's Hill RG8 56 C4
Flowers Piece RG8 54 B6
Fobney St RG1 86 A7
Fokerham Rd RG19 106 F2
Folder's La RG42 91 C1
Foliejohn Way SL6 38 F1
Folkestone Ct SL3 44 A1
Follet Cl SL4 68 B1
Folly La RG7,RG30 110 F5
Folly Rd Inkpen RG17 127 E6
Lambourn RG17 25 A3
Folly The RG14 105 B1
Fontmell Cl TW15 98 A3
Fontmell Pk TW15 98 A3
Fontwell Cl SL6 39 A8
Fontwell Dr RG30 84 F5
Fontwell Rd RG14 105 B1
Forbes Chase GU47 150 D7
Forbury Ho 3 RG30 85 B7
Forbury La RG17,RG20 128 C7
Forbury Rd RG1 86 C8
Forbury Ret Pk RG1 86 C8
Forbury The RG1 86 B8
Ford Cl Ashford TW15 97 E2
Littleton TW17 125 A4
Ford La RG7 140 A2
Ford Rd Ashford TW15 97 F4
Bisley GU24 153 F4
Chertsey KT16 124 B1
Fordbridge Cl KT16 124 B1
Fordbridge Ct TW15 97 E2
Fordbridge Rd
Ashford TW15 97 F3
Upper Halliford TW16,
TW17 125 F3
Fordham Way RG6 87 C1
Fordwater Rd KT15,KT16 124 B1
Fordwater Trad Est
KT16 124 C1
Fordwells Dr RG12 118 F5
Forehead The RG7 137 F4
Forest Cl Bracknell SL5 119 C6
Tadley RG26 134 E2
Forest Ct RG41 116 A4
Forest Dean RG2 113 C7
Forest Dr TW16 98 F1
Forest End GU47 143 A1
Forest End Rd GU47 150 A8
Forest Gn Bracknell RG12 118 D7
Holyport SL6 65 A6
Forest Green Rd SL6 65 C5
Forest Hill RG30 57 F2
Forest Hills GU15 151 B4
Forest Rd Binfield RG42 90 D3
Crowthorne RG45 143 C5
Windsor SL4 93 E7
Windsor, Dedworth SL4 66 E5
Winkfield RG42,SL5 92 D2
Forest Sch The RG41 88 C2
Forest View Cotts SL6 65 C6
Forest Way RG42 92 A2
Foresters Sq RG12 118 E6
Foresters Way RG45 143 F1
Forge Cl Caversham RG4 59 C2
Kintbury RG17 102 A2
Forge Cotts SN8 99 B5
Forge Ct GU46 149 D7
Forge Dr SL2 22 C6
Forge Hill RG18 53 A5
Forge The Harlington UB3 71 D8
Hungerford RG17 100 D6
Forlease Cl SL6 40 A6
Forlease Dr SL6 40 A6
Forlease Rd SL6 40 A6
Formby Cl Earley RG6 87 E3
Slough SL3 44 C2
Forndon Cl RG6 87 E2
Forsters RG7 134 F7
Forsters Farm Ct RG7 135 A6
Forsythia Gdns SL3 43 E3
Fort Narrien GU15 150 F7
Fortrose Cl GU47 150 D7
Fortrose Wlk RG31 84 E4
Fortuna Ct RG7 134 E2
Forty Green Dr SL7 1 B2
Forum The KT16 123 F1
Fosseway RG45 143 A5
Fossewood Dr GU15 151 D7
Foster Ave SL4 66 E4
Fosters Gr GU20 146 B6
Fosters La RG5 87 E6
Fosters Path SL2 21 F1
Fotherby Ct SL6 40 A6
Fotheringay Gdns SL1 42 A6
Foundation Pk SL6 38 F4
Foundry Ct KT16 124 A2
Foundry Ho RG17 100 E7
Foundry La SL3 69 B4
Foundry Mews KT16 124 A2
Foundry Pl 20 RG1 86 A6
Fountain Gdns SL4 67 D4
Fountains Garth RG12 118 A6
Fourth Ave Marlow SL7 2 A2
Reading RG31 84 B6
Fourth St RG19 131 F5
Fowler Cl RG6 87 A3
Fowlers La RG42 118 B8
Fox Cl RG7 111 A3
Fox Covert GU18 153 A8
Fox Covert Cl SL5 120 C4
Fox Ct GU47 150 C8
Fox Dr GU46 149 D7
Fox Hill Prim Sch RG12 118 B4
Fox La RG27 149 A7
Fox La N KT16 123 F1
Fox La S KT16 123 F1
Fox Rd Bracknell RG12 118 C5
Slough SL3 43 D2
Foxborough RG7 139 D6
Foxborough Cl SL3 44 A1
Foxborough Ct SL6 39 E4
Foxborough Prim Sch
SL3 44 A1
Foxbury RG17 25 B2
Foxcombe Dr RG31 84 C7
Foxcote RG40 142 A7
Foxdown Cl GU15 151 C5
Foxes Piece SL7 1 E2
Foxes Piece Sch SL7 1 E3
Foxes Wlk RG10 61 A3
Foxglove Cl
Stanwell TW19 97 D7
Winkfield RG42 92 A2
Wokingham RG41 115 D7
Foxglove Gdns 2 RG1 85 E7
Foxglove Way RG18 106 D5
Foxhaven Ct SL5 120 C4
Foxhays Rd RG2 113 D8
Foxheath RG12 118 E4
Foxherne SL3 43 C4
Foxhill Cl RG4 60 A5
Foxhill Cres GU15 152 B8
Foxhill La RG4 59 D7
Foxhill Rd RG1 86 E6
Foxhollow Dr SL2 22 C7
Foxhunt Gr RG31 84 F4
Foxhunter Way RG19 105 F3
Foxleigh Ct TW18 96 C3
Foxley Cl GU17 150 C5
Foxley La RG42 90 C1
Framewood Manor SL2 23 C6
Framewood Rd SL2,SL3 23 C6
Framlingham Dr RG4 59 E5
Frampton Bridge Rdbt
RG42 90 F2

Frampton Cl RG5 ....60 E1
France Hill Dr GU15 ...151 C5
Frances Ave SL6 ....20 C1
Frances Ct GU15 ....120 D5
Frances Rd SL4 ....67 D5
Frances The RG18 .....106 D4
Francis Baily Prim Sch RG19 ....106 F3
Francis Chichester Cl SL5 ....120 B4
Francis Cl TW17 ....125 A5
Francis Gdns RG42 ......91 D1
Francis St RG1 ....86 B6
Francis Way Burnham SL1 41 D6
Frimley GU15 ....152 C4
Francomes Field RG17 ..25 C1
Frank Lunnon Cl SL8 .....3 C3
Frank Sutton Way SL1 ...42 D6
Franklin Ave Slough SL2 ..42 B8
Tadley RG26 ....135 A1
Franklin Ct 8 RG1 ....85 F7
Franklin St RG1 ....85 F7
Franklyn Cres SL4 ....66 D4
Frantons The SL6 ....39 A7
Frascati Way SL6 ....39 F7
Fraser Ave RG4 ....59 C6
Fraser Mead GU47 ......150 E6
Fraser Rd RG42 ....118 B8
Fraunchies Ct SL1 ....42 E6
Frederick Ho TW15 ......97 E4
Frederick Pl RG41 ......116 A6
Free Prae Rd KT16 .....124 A1
Freeborn Way RG12 ....118 E7
Freeman Cl TW17 ....125 E5
Freeman Ct RG14 ....104 F3
Freemans Cl
Hungerford RG17 ....100 C5
Stoke Poges SL2 ....23 A6
Freemantle Rd GU19 ...145 F4
Freemantles Sch KT16 .123 E2
Freesia Cl RG41 ....115 D7
French Gdns GU17 ......150 D4
Frenchum Gdns SL1 ......41 E6
Frensham RG12 ....118 D3
Frensham Cl GU46 .....149 B6
Frensham Gn RG2 ....86 F1
Frensham Rd RG45 .....143 B7
Frensham Wlk SL2 ....22 C7
Freshfield Cl RG6 ....87 E3
Freshfields La RG20 .....51 B2
Freshwater Rd RG1 ......86 E8
Freshwood Dr GU46 ...149 D4
Friar St RG1 ....86 A8
Friars Ct GU47 ....149 F8
Friars Keep RG12 ....118 B5
Friars Rd Newbury RG14 .131 A8
Virginia Water GU25 ....122 D5
Friars Way KT16 ....124 A3
Friars Wlk 4 RG1 ....86 A8
Friary Island TW19 ......95 C8
Friary Rd Ascot SL5 ....120 B3
Wraysbury TW19 ....68 C1
Friary The SL4 ....68 C1
Friday St RG9 ....15 E2
Friends Wlk 1 TW18 .....96 F3
Friendship Ho 4 TW18 ...97 A3
Friendship Way RG12 ..118 B6
Frieth Cl RG6 ....87 A1
Frieth Rd SL7 ....1 A3
Frilsham Rd RG30 ....85 B4
Frimley Cl RG5 ....87 D8
Frimley Green Rd GU16 151 D1
Frimley Grove Gdns GU16 ....151 E1
Frimley Hall Dr GU15 ...151 F6
Frimley High St GU16 ..151 D1
Frimley Park Hospl GU16 ....151 D2
Frimley Rd GU15,GU16 ..151 B3
Frimley Sq GU16 ....151 E1
Fringford Cl RG6 ....87 C1
Frith Hill Rd GU16 .....152 B1
Frithe The SL2 ....43 B7
Frithwald Rd KT16 .....123 F2
Frobisher RG12 ....118 C2
Frobisher Cres TW19 ....97 E8
Frobisher Gdns TW19 ...97 E8
Frodsham Way GU47 ..143 E2
Frog Hall RG40 ....116 F5
Frog Hall Dr RG40 .....116 E5
Frog La RG12 ....118 A6
Frogmill SL6 ....17 C3
Frogmill Ct SL6 ....17 C3
Frogmore Cl SL1 ....42 A4
Frogmore Com Coll GU46 ....149 F5
Frogmore Ct
Blackwater GU17 ....150 C4
11 Maidenhead SL6 ....39 F7
Frogmore Dr SL4 ....67 F5
Frogmore Flats SL4 .....67 F5
Frogmore Gr GU17 .....150 C4
Frogmore Inf Sch GU17 150 B5
Frogmore Jun Sch GU17 ....150 B5
Frogmore Park Dr GU17 ....150 D4
Frogmore Rd GU17 ....150 C5
Frogmore Way RG30 ....85 B5
Fromer Rd HP10 ....3 D4
Fromont Dr RG19 ......106 D3
Fromow Gdns GU20 ....146 D4
Fronds Pk RG7 ....109 A2
Front St RG17 ....47 D6
Frouds Bridge Marina RG7 ....108 F1
Frouds La RG7 ....109 A1
Froxfield Ave RG1 ....85 F5
Froxfield Down 6 RG12 118 F4
Fruen Rd TW14 ....98 F8
Fry Ct RG4 ....59 B3
Fry La GU19 ....145 D2
Fry's La GU46 ....149 E7
Frymley View SL4 ....66 D6
Fuchsia Cl RG31 ....84 C5
Fuchsia Way GU24 .....153 E6
Fullbrook Cl
Maidenhead SL6 ....40 A8
Wokingham RG41 ....89 A1
Fullbrook Cres RG31 ....57 D3
Fuller Cl RG19 ....106 F2
Fuller's La RG7 ....112 B4
Fullers La RG20 ....129 D1
Fullers Yd SL6 ....20 B2
Fulmead Rd RG30 ....85 C8
Fulmer Chase SL3 ....23 C8
Fulmer Cl RG6 ....87 A2
Fulmer Common Rd SL3 .23 E6
Fulmer Inf Sch SL3 ......23 E8
Fulmer Rd SL3 ....23 E8
Fulwood Ct TW19 ....70 F1
Furlong Cl SL8 ....3 B3
Furlong Rd SL8 ....3 B3
Furness SL4 ....66 C5
Furness Pl 8 SL4 ....66 C5
Furness Row 9 SL4 .....66 C5
Furness Sq 6 SL4 ....66 C5
Furness Way SL4 ....66 C5
Furness Wlk 7 SL4 ......66 C5
Furnival Ave SL2 ....42 B8
Furnival Cl GU25 ....122 D3
Furrow Way SL6 ....39 A4
Furse Cl GU15 ....152 C4
Furze Hill Cres RG45 ..143 C4
Furze Platt Halt SL6 .....19 E1
Furze Platt Inf Sch SL6 .19 C1
Furze Platt Jun Sch SL6 .19 C1
Furze Platt Rd SL6 ......19 B1
Furze Platt Senior Sch SL6 ....19 C2
Furze Rd Maidenhead SL6 .19 D1
Tadley RG26 ....134 F2
Furzebank SL5 ....120 D5
Furzecroft 3 TW15 ......98 A3
Furzedown Cl TW20 .....95 E2
Furzemoors RG12 ......118 B4
Furzen Cl SL2 ....22 A2
Fuzzens Wlk SL4 ....66 E5
Fydlers Cl SL4 ....93 B2
Fyfield Cl GU17 ....150 D5
Fyfield Rd RG19 ....106 D2
Fylingdales RG19 ......106 C2

G

Gables Ave TW15 ....97 F3
Gables Cl Datchet SL3 ...68 A6
Maidenhead SL6 ....40 B8
Gables Way RG19 ......107 C2
Gabriel Dr GU15 ....152 B4
Gabriels The RG14 .....130 D5
Gadd Cl RG40 ....116 F7
Gage Cl SL6 ....39 E4
Gainsborough
Bracknell RG12 ....118 C3
Cookham Rise SL6 ....19 F5
Gainsborough Ave RG17 ....102 B2
Gainsborough Cl
Camberley GU15 ....151 F7
Woodley RG5 ....88 A6
Gainsborough Cres RG9 .35 C8
Gainsborough Dr
Maidenhead SL6 ....39 D3
North Ascot SL5 ....119 D7
Gainsborough Hill RG9 ..35 D8
Gainsborough Rd
Henley-On-T RG9 ....35 D8
Reading RG30 ....85 B5
Gairn Cl RG30 ....85 A7
Galahad Cl SL1 ....42 A4
Gale Dr GU18 ....146 A1
Galileo Ct RG12 ....118 E7
Galley La RG19 ....132 D1
Galleymead Rd SL3 .....69 F6
Gallop The GU46 ....149 D7
Gallops The RG20 ....30 E6
Galloway Chase SL2 ....43 A6
Galloway Ctr The RG14 .105 E2
Galloway Ho 4 RG1 .....85 E5
Gallys Rd SL4 ....66 D6
Galsworthy Dr RG4 ......59 E5
Galsworthy Rd KT16 ...124 A2
Galton Rd SL5 ....120 F3
Galvin Rd SL1 ....42 C6
Galway Rd GU46 ....149 C4
Garde Rd RG4 ....60 E3
Garden Cl Ashford TW15 ..98 C2
Maidenhead SL6 ....39 A5
Garden Close La RG14 .130 D4
Garden Cotts SL3 ....69 D7
Garden Mews
8 Reading RG30 ....85 D6
Slough SL1 ....42 F5
Gardeners La RG8 ....55 C4
Gardeners Rd RG42 .....92 A2
Gardenia Dr GU24 ......153 F6
Gardens The Hatton TW14 71 D1
South Stoke RG8 ....14 C3
Gardner Ho SL6 ....19 E1
Gardner Rd SL6 ....19 D2
Garfield Pl 2 SL4 ....67 C5
Garfield Rd GU15 ....151 C5
Garford Cres RG14 ....130 D8
Garland Ho RG14 ......104 F2
Garland Jun Sch RG7 ..111 A3
Garlands Cl RG7 ....111 A2
Garnet Cl SL1 ....42 A4
Garnet Ct SL7 ....1 C1
Garnet Field GU46 .....149 A5
Garnet Hill 7 RG1 ....86 A6
Garnet St RG1 ....86 A6
Garrard Rd SL2 ....21 F1
Garrard St RG1 ....86 A8
Garrett Rd RG40 ....141 E8
Garrick Cl TW18 ....97 A1
Garson La TW19 ....95 D8
Garson's La SL4 ....92 A7
Garston Cl RG30 ....85 A4
Garston Cres RG31 .....84 B5
Garston Gr RG40 ....115 F1
Garston Park Home Village RG31 ....84 B6
Garswood RG12 ....118 D3
Garth Cl RG41 ....88 C2
Garth Hill Coll RG12 ..118 C8
Garth Rd RG7 ....137 A5
Garth Sq RG42 ....91 B1
Garthlands SL6 ....19 D2
Gas House Hill RG17 ...25 C3
Gas La Maidenhead SL6 ..40 B3
Twyford RG10 ....61 D4
Gas Works Rd RG1 ......86 C7
Gascon's Gr SL2 ....22 A1
Gaskell Mews RG14 ....131 B8
Gaskells End RG4 ....58 D8
Gaston Bridge Rd
Shepperton TW17 ....125 D3
Upper Halliford TW17 ...125 E4
Gaston Way TW17 .....125 D4
Gatcombe Cl RG31 .....84 C4
Gatehampton Rd RG8 ...34 C5
Gatehouse Cl SL4 ....67 B4
Gatewick Cl SL1 ....42 E5
Gatward Ave SL6 ....39 A3
Gaveston Rd SL2 ....21 F2
Gayhurst Cl RG4 ....59 D6
Gays La SL6 ....65 B8
Gaywood Dr RG14 .....105 D4
Gazelle Cl RG41 ....88 A3
Geffers Ride SL5 ......119 E7
Gelder Cl RG6 ....87 D1
Genesis Cl TW19 ....97 F7
Geneva Cl TW17 ....125 E7
Geoffrey Ct TW18 ....97 A1
Geoffrey Field Jun & Inf Schs RG2 ....113 C8
Geoffreyson Rd RG4 .....58 E5
George Cl SL7 ....1 F4
George Green Dr SL3 ....43 F8
George Green Rd SL3 ...43 E7
George Palmer Prim Sch RG2 ....86 C4
George St Caversham RG4 .59 B1
Reading RG1 ....85 F8
Staines TW18 ....96 F4
George V Pl SL4 ....67 D7
Georgeham Rd GU47 ..143 D2
Georges Dr HP10 ....3 C7
Georgian Cl
Camberley GU15 ....151 E7
Staines TW18 ....97 B4
Georgian Hts SL8 ....3 B5
Geranium Cl RG45 .....143 B8
Gerrards Cross Rd SL2 ..23 A7
Gerring Rd RG2 ....140 F7
Gervaise Cl SL1 ....41 F5
Gibbet La GU15 ....152 A7
Gibbins La RG42 ....91 D3
Gibbons Cl GU47 ......150 C8
Gibbs Cl RG40 ....141 E6
Gibbs Way GU46 ....149 B4
Gibraltar La SL6 ....2 C1
Gibson Ct SL3 ....43 F1
Gibson Pl TW19 ....70 C1
Gidley La RG20 ....50 E2
Gifford Cl RG4 ....59 E5
Gifford Ho 2 RG4 ....59 C1
Gilbert Ct RG18 ....106 D3
Gilbert Rd GU15 ....151 C2
Gilbert Way RG40 .....115 E1
Gilbey Wlk HP10 ....3 D4
Gilchrist Way SL6 ......38 B5
Giles Ct RG14 ....104 F2
Giles Travers Cl TW20 .123 C6
Gill Rise RG42 ....91 C2
Gillespie Ho GU25 .....122 E5
Gillette Way RG2 ....86 B2
Gilliat Rd SL1 ....42 E6
Gilliatt Cl SL0 ....44 E7
Gillott Ct SL6 ....39 F8
Gillott's Hill RG9 ....35 C7
Gillott's La RG9 ....35 B7
Gillotts Cl RG9 ....35 B8
Gillotts Sch RG9 ....35 B7
Gilman Cres SL4 ....66 D4
Gilmore Cl SL3 ....43 C4
Gilmore Cres TW15 .....98 A2
Gilpin Way UB3 ....71 D7
Gilroy Cl RG14 ....130 C6
Gilson Ct SL4 ....95 C8
Gingells Farm Rd RG10 ..61 B5
Gipsy La Bracknell RG12 .118 D7
Earley RG6 ....87 D1
Hungerford RG17 ......100 E8
Lower Earley RG6 ....87 D3
Reading RG30 ....57 E1
Sindlesham RG41 ......114 F7
Wokingham RG40 .....116 C4
Girton Cl GU47 ....143 E1
Glade Ho Ascot SL5 ....120 C4
3 Marlow SL7 ....1 E2
Glade Rd SL7 ....1 E2
Glade The Ascot SL5 ...120 C4
Newbury RG14 ....130 F7
Purley On T RG8 ....57 C4
Staines TW18 ....97 B2
Gladridge Cl RG6 ....87 C4
Gladstone Cl RG17 ....102 B2
Gladstone Ind Est SL6 ...39 E8
Gladstone La RG18 ....106 C8
Gladstone Way SL1 .....42 A5
Glaisdale RG19 ....106 C2
Glamis Way RG31 ....84 B4
Glanmor Rd SL2 ....43 B6
Glanty The TW20 ....96 B4
Glassonby Wlk GU15 ..152 C5
Glebe Cl Dorney SL6 ....40 F4
Lightwater GU18 ....146 C1
Moulsford OX10 ....13 F5
Glebe Cotts RG8 ....14 C3
Glebe Fields RG20 ......49 A7
Glebe Gdns RG4 ....60 E3
Glebe La Sonning RG4 ...60 E3
Stockcross RG20 ....103 E5
Glebe Pl RG17 ....73 A2
Glebe Rd Egham TW20 ...96 C2
Maidenhead SL6 ....40 B5
Old Windsor SL4 ....68 B2
Purley On T RG8 ....57 B5
Reading RG2 ....86 C5
Staines TW18 ....97 B3
Glebe Ride RG8 ....34 B6
Glebe The Aldworth RG8 ..32 F3
Blackwater GU17 ......150 E4
Glebefields RG14 ......105 B5
Glebeland Gdns TW17 ..125 C3
Glebeland Rd GU15 ....150 F4
Glebelands RG19 ......106 C3
Glebelands Rd RG40 ...116 C7
Glebewood RG12 ......118 C4
Glen Ave TW15 ....98 A4
Glen Cl TW17 ....125 A5
Glen Ct TW18 ....96 F1
Glen Innes GU47 ......143 E1
Glen The Ascot SL5 ....120 D5
Silchester RG26 ....135 E1
Slough SL3 ....43 C2
Glenalmond Ho TW15 ...97 E5
Glenapp Grange RG7 ...136 F6
Glenavon Gdns
Slough SL3 ....43 C3
Yateley GU46 ....149 D4
Glenbeigh Terr RG1 .....85 E6
Glendale Ave RG14 ....130 C5
Glendale Cl RG41 ......116 A3
Glendale Rd RG26 .....135 A1
Glendevon Rd RG5 ......87 F8
Gleneagles Cl TW19 .....70 D1
Gleneagles Ct 17 RG1 ...86 D7
Gleneagles Ho RG12 ...117 E3
Glenfield Cl SL2 ....22 F4
Glenfield Ho RG12 .....118 C5
Glenfield Rd TW15 ......98 C2
Glenhurst GU20 ....146 A6
Glenhurst Cl GU17 .....150 E4
Glenmore Cl RG19 .....106 D2
Glenn Miller Cl RG20 ...49 A5
Glennon Cl RG30 ....85 C4
Glenore SL6 ....20 A8
Glenrhondda RG4 ....58 F6
Glenridge Farm Cvn Site GU25 ....122 B6
Glenrosa Rd RG30 ......85 A8
Glentworth Pl SL1 ......42 C5
Glenwood
Bracknell RG12 ....118 D5
Virginia Water GU25 ...122 C8
Glenwood Dr RG31 .....84 C7
Globe Farm La GU17 ..150 B5
Globeside Bsns Pk SL7 ...1 F2
Glory Cl HP10 ....3 F7
Glory Hill La HP9 ....3 F8
Glory Mill La HP10 ....3 E7
Gloucester Ave SL1 .....42 C8
Gloucester Cres TW18 ...97 D2
Gloucester Ct RG30 .....85 D7
Gloucester Dr TW18 ....96 D5
Gloucester Gdns GU19 .145 E3
Gloucester Pl
Bracknell RG42 ....91 F1
Windsor SL4 ....67 D5
Gloucester Rd
Bagshot GU19 ....145 E3
Maidenhead SL6 ....19 E2
Newbury RG14 ....104 E2
Reading RG30 ....85 D7
Gloucestershire Lea RG42 ....91 F1
Glyme Wlk RG31 ....84 F3
Glyncastle RG4 ....58 F5
Glynswood GU15 ....151 F3
Glynwood Ho SL6 ....40 A7
Goaters Rd SL5 ....119 C7
Goddard Cl
Littleton TW17 ....124 F6
Shinfield RG2 ....113 E5
Goddard Ct RG41 ....88 B1
Goddard Dr RG7 ....107 F3
Goddard Way RG42 .....91 D2
Goddards La GU15 ....151 B3
Goddinton Rd SL8 ....3 A5
Godfrey Cl GU47 ......150 D7
Godolphin Inf Sch SL1 ..42 C7
Godolphin Jun Sch SL1 .42 D7
Godolphin Rd SL1 ......42 D6
Godstow Cl RG5 ....87 E8
Goffs Rd TW15 ....98 D2
Gogmore Farm Cl KT16 .123 F2
Gogmore La KT16 .....124 A2
Gold Cup La SL5 ......119 D8
Goldcrest Cl GU46 .....149 B6
Goldcrest Way RG31 .....84 B6
Golden Ball La SL6 ......19 A3
Golden Oak Cl SL2 ......22 C6
Golden Orb Wood RG42 117 D8
Goldfinch La RG20 .....131 F3
Golding Cl RG19 ....106 F3
Goldney Rd GU15 ......152 C4
Goldsmid Rd RG1 ....85 F7
Goldsmith Cl
Thatcham RG18 ....106 C5
Wokingham RG40 ......115 E1
Goldsmith Way RG45 ..143 B4
Goldsworthy Way SL1 ...41 C7
Goldthorpe Gdns RG6 ..113 F8
Goldwell Dr RG14 ......104 F4
Golf Dr GU15 ....151 F4
Gooch Cl RG10 ....61 F3
Goodall Cl RG9 ....15 D1
Goodboy's La RG7 .....112 A1
Goodchild Rd RG40 ...116 D6
Goodings Gn RG40 .....116 F6
Goodings La RG17 ......47 B3
Goodliffe Gdns RG31 ...57 C4
Goodman Pk SL2 ....43 C5
Goodman Pl TW18 ......96 F4
Goodrich Cl RG4 ....59 E5
Goodways Dr RG12 ....118 D7
Goodwin Cl RG31 ....84 E4
Goodwin Mdws HP10 .....3 E6
Goodwin Rd SL2 ....21 F2
Goodwin Wlk RG14 ....130 C6
Goodwind Villas SL1 ....41 F5
Goodwood Cl
Burghfield Common RG7 ..111 A2
Camberley GU15 ....151 C8
Goodwood Rise SL7 ......1 C7
Goodwood Way RG14 ..105 C1
Goose Cnr RG42 ....91 F3
Goose Gn
Farnham Royal SL2 ......22 B3
Lambourn RG17 ....25 B3
Goose Green Way RG19 106 D3
Goose La RG20 ....49 E5
Goosecroft La RG8 ......57 B5
Gordon Ave GU15 .....151 C4
Gordon Cl TW18 ....97 B2
Gordon Cres
Camberley GU15 ....151 C4
Compton RG20 ....31 D4
Gordon Ct 1 RG14 .....105 B2
Gordon Dr TW17 ....125 D2
Gordon Palmer Cl RG7 .137 D5
Gordon Palmer Ct RG30 .85 C8
Gordon Pl RG30 ....85 C8
Gordon Rd Ashford TW15 .97 E5
Camberley GU15 ....151 C5
Crowthorne RG45 ......143 D3
Egham TW18 ....96 C4
Maidenhead SL6 ....39 D7
Newbury RG14 ....105 B2
Shepperton TW17 ......125 D3
Thatcham RG18 ....106 A5
Windsor SL4 ....66 F5
Gordon Wlk GU46 .....149 F5
Gordon's Sch GU24 ...153 E7
Gore End Rd RG20 .....129 B3
Gore Rd SL1 ....21 B2
Gore The SL1 ....21 A2
Goring & Streatley Sta RG8 ....34 C6
Goring CE Prim Sch RG8 34 C7
Goring La RG7 ....111 A1
Goring Pl TW18 ....96 D3
Goring Rd TW18 ....96 E3
Goring's Sq TW18 ....96 E4
Gorrick Sq RG41 ....116 B3
Gorse Bank GU18 ......153 A8
Gorse Cottage Dr RG18 ..79 C1
Gorse Dr RG5 ....88 A8
Gorse Hill La GU25 ....122 D5
Gorse Hill Rd GU25 ....122 D5
Gorse Meade SL1 ....42 B5
Gorse Pl RG42 ....92 B1
Gorse Rd
Cookham Rise SL6 ....19 E6
Frimley GU16 ....151 E2
Gorse Ride Inf Sch RG40 ....141 E7
Gorse Ride Jun Sch RG40 ....141 E7
Gorse Ride N RG40 ....141 E7
Gorse Ride S RG40 .....141 E6
Gorselands
Caversham RG4 ....59 B6
Newbury RG14 ....130 D5
Gosbrook Ho 1 RG4 ....59 C1
Gosbrook Rd RG4 ....59 B2
Gosden Rd GU24 ......153 F6
Gosforth Cl RG6 ....87 D2
Goslar Way SL4 ....67 B5
Gosling Gn SL3 ....43 E3
Gosling Rd SL3 ....43 E3
Gosnell Cl GU16 ....152 D3
Gossmore Cl SL7 ....1 F1
Gossmore La SL7 ....1 F1
Gossmore Wlk SL7 ....1 F1
Goswell Hill SL4 ....67 D6
Goswell Rd SL4 ....67 D6
Gothic Ct Harlington UB3 .71 D8
Sandhurst GU47 ....150 B7
Gough's Barn La RG42 ..91 A8
Gough's La RG12 ....91 D1
Gough's Mdw GU47 ...150 B7
Gould Cl RG14 ....105 B3

Gould Rd TW14 98 E8
Goulders Cotts RG10 36 F7
Governor's Rd GU15 150 F6
Govett Ave TW17 125 C4
Govett Gr GU20 146 D5
Gower Pk GU47 150 D7
Gower St RG1 85 E8
Gower The TW20 123 C6
Gowings Gn SL1 41 E4
Grace Ct SL1 42 C5
Grace Reynolds Wlk GU15 151 C6
Graces La RG20 78 B8
Graffham Cl RG6 114 B8
Grafton Cl Maidenhead SL6 19 E2
Slough SL3 43 E7
Grafton Ct TW14 98 D7
Grafton Rd RG30 84 D7
Graham Cl Blewbury OX11 12 A8
Maidenhead SL6 39 C5
Reading RG31 84 E4
Graham Rd
Cookham Rise SL6 19 E6
Windlesham GU20 146 C4
Grahame Ave RG8 56 D5
Grainford Ct RG40 116 C5
Gramp's Hill OX12 6 E5
Grampian Cl UB3 71 D7
Grampian Rd GU47 143 A2
Grampian Way SL3 44 A1
Granby Ct RG1 86 E7
Granby End RG7 111 B3
Granby Gdns RG1 86 E7
Grand Ave GU15 151 C6
Grand Regency Hts SL5 119 E6
Grandison Ho RG9 15 E3
Grange Ave
Crowthorne RG45 143 B6
Reading RG6 87 A6
Grange Cl Goring RG8 34 B6
Wraysbury TW19 68 E1
Grange Ct Earley RG6 87 B8
Egham TW20 95 F3
Littleton TW17 125 A5
Newbury RG14 105 B2
7 Staines TW18 97 A3
Grange Dr HP10 3 D3
Grange Gdns
Farnham Common SL2 22 D7
Newbury RG14 130 C5
Grange La SL6 19 F8
Grange Pl TW18 124 C7
Grange Rd
Bracknell RG12 118 C8
Camberley GU15 151 E5
Cookham Rise SL6 19 F7
Egham TW20 95 F3
Henley-On-T RG9 15 E1
Grange The Burnham SL1 21 C2
Caversham RG4 58 D6
Newbury RG14 130 C5
Old Windsor SL4 68 B2
Thorpe GU25 122 E5
Grange Way SL0 44 F7
Grangely Cl RG31 84 D4
Grangewood SL3 43 C8
Grant Ave SL1 42 E7
Grant Cl TW17 125 B3
Grant Ho 6 SL8 3 A4
Grant Rd RG45 143 C3
Grant Wlk SL5 120 E1
Grantham Cl GU47 143 E1
Grantham Ho 5 TW16 98 E1
Grantham Rd RG30 84 F4
Granthams The RG17 25 B3
Grantley Hts 3 RG1 86 C7
Granville Ave SL2 42 D8
Granville Rd RG30 85 B5
Grasholm Way SL3 44 C2
Grasmere SL4 66 E7
Grasmere Ave
Reading RG30 57 F2
Slough SL2 43 A6
Grasmere Cl
East Bedfont TW14 98 F7
Thorpe Lea TW20 96 B1
Winnersh RG41 88 B1
Grasmere Par SL2 43 B6
Grasmere Rd GU18 146 B1
Grass Hill RG4 58 E3
Grassington Pl RG19 106 D3
Grassmead RG19 106 F2
Grassy La SL6 39 E7
Grattan Ct SL7 2 A3
Gratton Dr SL4 66 E3
Gratton Rd RG2 113 C8
Gratwicke Rd RG30 84 E8
Gravel Hill Caversham RG4 59 A6
Henley-On-T RG9 15 D2
Stockcross RG20 103 E5
Gravel Rd RG9 35 A1
Gravelly Cl RG20 129 A3
Graveney Dr RG4 58 E3
Gravett Cl RG9 35 C8
Gray Pl RG42 117 E8
Gray's Mon* SL2 22 F2
Grayling Cl SL7 18 C8
Grayling Ct 3 RG1 59 A1
Grays Cres RG5 87 C7
Grays La TW15 98 B4
Grays Park Rd SL2 23 A2
Grays Pl SL2 42 F5
Grays Rd SL1 42 F5
Grayshot Dr GU17 150 C5
Grazeley Parochial CE Prim Sch RG7 112 E2
Grazeley Rd RG7 113 A4
Great Auclum Pl RG7 111 B2
Great Barn Ct RG19 106 C3
Great Hill Cres SL6 39 C6
Great Hollands Prim Sch RG12 117 F4
Great Hollands Rd RG12 117 F3
Great Hollands Sq RG12 117 F3
Great Knollys St RG1 85 F8
Great Lea RG7 113 A5
Great Marlow Sch SL7 1 F4
Great Severals RG17 102 A2
Great South-West Rd TW14,TW6,TW4,TW5 71 D2
Grebe Ct TW18 97 B4
Green Acre Mount RG30 84 D8
Green Bsns Ctr The TW18 96 C4
Green Cl Burnham SL6 41 A7
Maidenhead SL6 19 F1
Green Cres HP10 3 C7
Green Croft RG40 116 E8
Green Ct TW16 98 F2
Green Dr RG40 116 E4
Green Dragon La HP10 3 B7
Green End GU46 149 D7
Green End Cl RG7 113 B2
Green Farm Rd GU19 145 F3
Green Farm Rise SN8 99 B5
Green Hill Cl GU15 152 C6
Green Hill Rd GU15 152 C6
Green La Ascot SL5 120 E8
Ashford TW16 98 F2
Bagshot GU19 145 F2
Binfield RG40 90 A3
Blackwater GU17 150 B4
Blackwater,Hawley GU17 150 E4
Burghfield Common RG30 85 A2
Burnham SL1 21 D4
Caversham RG9 35 A1
Chieveley RG20 78 B7
Datchet SL3 68 B6
Egham TW20 96 B3
Farnham Common SL2 22 B6
Henley-On-T RG9 35 D8
Holyport SL6 64 A5
Hurst RG10 88 E3
Littlewick Green SL6 38 B5
Maidenhead SL6 40 A6
Newbury RG14 104 E2
Pangbourne RG8 56 C5
Sandhurst GU47 150 C7
Shepperton TW17 125 C4
Staines TW18 123 E8
Stanford Dingley RG7 81 F3
Thatcham RG19 106 C3
Ufton Nervet RG7 110 C2
Windsor SL4 67 B5
Wokingham RG41 88 D1
Yateley GU46 149 B7
Green Lane Cl GU15 151 C7
Green Lane Ct SL1 21 C2
Green Leas TW16 98 F2
Green Leas Cl TW16 98 F2
Green Leys SL6 19 F2
Green Pk TW18 96 E5
Green Rd Reading RG6 87 A5
Virginia Water TW20 123 A5
Green The Ashford TW18 97 D3
Blackwater GU17 150 C5
Bracknell RG12 118 B5
Burnham SL1 21 B1
Chieveley RG20 51 B2
Chilton OX11 10 E8
Datchet SL3 68 B7
Kintbury RG17 102 B1
Slough SL1 42 D3
Theale RG7 83 C2
Upper Halliford TW17 125 E5
Wokingham RG41 115 E7
Wooburn Green HP10 3 E5
Wraysbury TW19 68 E1
Green Verges SL7 1 E3
Greenacre SL4 66 E5
Greenacre Ct TW20 95 C2
Greenacres RG20 129 E1
Greenacres Ave RG41 88 A3
Greenacres La RG41 88 A3
Greenaway Terr TW19 97 E7
Greenbank Way GU15 151 D2
Greencroft Gdns RG30 84 F4
Greendale Mews SL2 43 A6
Greene Fielde End TW18 97 D1
Greenfern Ave SL1 41 C7
Greenfield Way RG45 143 A7
Greenfields SL6 40 A5
Greenfields Rd RG2 113 B8
Greenfinch Cl
Crowthorne RG45 142 F6
Reading RG31 84 B6
Sandhurst GU47 150 D8
Greengates 1 RG30 85 C7
Greenham Cl
Greenham RG19 131 D8
Woodley RG5 88 A6
Greenham Court Prim Sch RG14 131 B8
Greenham Mill RG14 105 B3
Greenham Rd RG14 105 B1
Greenham Road Ret Pk RG14 105 A2
Greenham Wood RG12 118 C3
Greenhaven GU46 149 B5
Greenholme GU15 152 D5
Greenhow RG12 118 A6
Greenidge Cl 2 RG1 85 E5
Greenlake Terr TW18 97 A1
Greenlands
Ball Hill RG20 129 E1
Flackwell Heath HP10 3 B8
Greenlands Ct
Maidenhead SL6 39 B8
7 Staines TW18 97 A4
Greenlands Rd
Camberley GU15 151 B1
Newbury RG14 105 B1
Staines TW18 97 A4
Greenleaf Ct SL3 68 A8
Greenleas GU16 151 E2
Greenleas Ave RG4 59 B7
Greenleas Cl GU46 149 C7
Greeno Cres TW17 125 A4
Greenock Rd SL1 42 A7
Greenside Bourne End SL8 3 A5
Crowthorne RG45 142 F5
Slough SL2 42 A8
Greensward La RG2 114 C2
Greenview Ct TW15 97 F4
Greenway SL1 21 B3
Greenway Dr TW18 124 D8
Greenway The
Fawley OX12 27 C7
Slough SL1 41 D5
Greenways Ball Hill RG20 129 E1
Egham TW20 95 E3
Lambourn RG17 25 B1
Pangbourne RG8 56 D5
Sandhurst GU47 143 B1
Greenways Dr
Maidenhead SL6 39 A8
Sunningdale SL5 120 E1
Greenways Ho RG14 104 E2
Greenwood
4 Bracknell RG12 118 F5
North Ascot SL5 119 C8
Greenwood Cotts SL5 121 C3
Greenwood Gr RG41 88 D3
Greenwood Rd
Crowthorne RG45 143 B6
Reading RG30 84 F5
Gregory Cl RG6 114 C8
Gregory Dr SL4 68 B1
Grenfell Ave SL6 39 F6
Grenfell Pl SL6 39 F6
Grenfell Rd SL6 39 E6
Grenville Cl SL1 21 B3
Grenville Pl RG12 118 C7
Gresham Ct 3 TW18 97 A3
Gresham Rd Slough SL1 42 A7
Staines TW18 97 A3
Gresham Way RG30 58 A2
Greyberry Copse Rd RG19 131 D8
Greycoat Ct RG4 59 B3
Greyfriars Dr SL5 120 B3
Greyfriars Rd RG1 86 A8
Greys Ct 7 RG1 86 C7
Greys Hill RG9 15 D1
Greys Rd RG9 35 C8
Greystock Rd RG42 91 D2
Greystoke Ct RG45 143 A4
Greystoke Ho 6 RG1 85 E5
Greystoke Rd
Caversham RG4 59 C4
Slough SL2 41 F8
Griffin Cl Maidenhead SL6 39 E5
Slough SL1 42 C4
Griffiths Cl RG19 106 F2
Grindle Cl RG18 106 C5
Gringer Hill SL6 39 E8
Groombridge Pl RG14 104 E6
Grosvenor Ct
Blackwater GU17 150 D3
Slough SL1 42 E7
Grosvenor Dr SL6 40 C8
Grosvenor Ho 2 RG1 85 F8
Grosvenor Lawn RG14 104 E2
Grosvenor Rd
Caversham RG4 59 C4
Staines TW18 97 A1
Grove Cl Old Windsor SL4 95 B8
2 Slough SL1 43 A3
Wokingham RG40 142 E7
Grove Cotts
Caversham RG4 59 A5
Wokingham RG40 142 E7
Grove Cross Rd GU16 151 D1
Grove Ct Egham TW20 96 A3
Maidenhead SL6 39 D7
Newbury RG14 131 A8
Grove End GU19 145 F5
Grove Hill RG4 59 A4
Grove Ho SL4 95 C8
Grove La RG42 92 B4
Grove Pk SL6 63 E8
Grove Prim Sch The GU16 151 E2
Grove Rd Burnham SL1 21 E4
Camberley GU15 151 F5
Chertsey KT16 123 F3
Emmer Green RG4 59 B6
Henley-On-T RG9 15 E1
Maidenhead SL6 39 F7
Newbury RG14 104 E5
Shepperton TW17 125 C3
South Stoke RG8 14 E2
Windsor SL4 67 D5
Grove The Egham TW20 96 A3
Frimley GU16 151 D1
Medmenham SL7 17 E6
North Ascot SL5 119 C8
Reading RG1 86 C7
Slough SL1 43 A4
Thatcham RG18 106 D4
Grove The *continued*
Twyford RG10 61 D5
Grovebarns TW18 97 A2
Grovefields Ave GU16 151 D1
Groveland Avenue Workshops RG41 88 D3
Groveland Pl RG30 85 B8
Groveland Rd RG14 104 E5
Grovelands Ave RG41 88 D2
Grovelands Cl RG41 88 D3
Grovelands Rd
Reading RG30 85 B8
Shinfield RG7 113 C2
Groveley Rd TW16 98 F3
Groves Cl SL8 3 C3
Groves Lea RG7 136 F6
Groves The RG17 73 A2
Groves Way SL6 19 E6
Grovestile Waye TW14 98 D8
Grubwood La SL6 19 A7
Guards Club Rd SL6 40 C7
Guards Ct SL5 121 B2
Guards Rd SL4 66 C5
Guards Wlk 1 SL4 66 C5
Guerdon Pl RG12 118 D2
Guildford Ave TW13 98 F6
Guildford Rd
Bagshot GU19 145 E3
Bagshot GU19 145 F2
Bisley GU24 153 F4
Chertsey KT16 123 F1
Lightwater GU18,GU19 146 B1
West End GU24 153 F7
Guildford St
Chertsey KT16 124 A2
Staines TW18 97 A2
Gull Cl RG41 115 E4
Gullane Ct 16 RG1 86 D7
Gun St RG1 86 A7
Gunthorpe Rd SL7 2 A3
Gurney Cl RG4 58 D5
Gurney Dr RG4 58 D5
Gwendale SL6 19 C1
Gwendolen Ho TW19 97 E7
Gwendoline Ct TW15 97 E4
Gweneth Ct SL7 1 D3
Gwent Cl SL6 39 B4
Gwyn Cl RG14 130 E8
Gwynne Cl
Purley On T RG31 57 D3
Windsor SL4 66 E6
Gwyns Piece RG17 25 B3
Gypsy La Marlow SL7 1 E4
Stoke Poges SL2 22 E8

H

Habershon Dr GU16 152 D2
Hackney Bottom RG18 53 A8
Haddenhurst Ct RG42 90 C2
Haddon Dr RG5 87 E8
Haddon Rd SL6 39 C5
Hadfield Rd TW19 70 D1
Hadleigh Rise RG4 59 E5
Hadley Ct SL3 69 E6
Hadlow Ct SL1 42 C5
Hadrian Cl TW19 97 E8
Hadrian Way TW19 97 D8
Hadrian Wlk E RG2 86 C4
Hadrian Wlk W RG2 86 C3
Hafod RG4 58 F6
Hag Hill La SL6 41 A7
Hag Hill Rise SL6 41 A7
Hagley Rd RG2 86 B4
Haig Dr SL1 42 B4
Haig Rd GU15 150 F6
Hailey La RG20 29 F1
Haileybury Ct SL4 67 A4
Hailsham Cl GU47 143 D1
Halcyon Ct TW18 124 B7
Halcyon Terr RG30 84 E8
Haldane Rd RG4 58 F5
Hale SL4 66 F6
Hale End RG12 118 F5
Hale St TW18 96 E4
Halewood RG12 117 F3
Half Mile Rd RG17 46 A1
Half Moon St GU19 145 E3
Halfacre Cl RG7 113 B3
Halfpenny Ct 2 SL5 121 B2
Halfpenny La
Cholsey OX10 13 D5
Sunningdale SL5 121 A2
Halfway Farm Cotts RG20 102 E5
Halfway Hos SL6 19 E4
Halifax Cl SL6 39 A8
Halifax Pl RG18 106 C4
Halifax Rd SL6 39 B8
Halifax Way SL6 39 A8
Halkingcroft SL3 43 C4
Hall Cl GU15 151 E6
Hall Ct SL3 68 B7
Hall Farm Cres GU46 149 D5
Hall Grove Farm Ind Est GU19 145 F5
Hall Grove Sch GU19 146 A5
Hall La Harlington UB3 71 D7
Yateley GU46 149 C6
Hall Mdw SL1 21 C3
Hall Place La SL6 38 B7
Hallbrooke Gdns RG42 90 E1
Halldore Hill SL6 19 E7
Halley Dr SL5 119 D7
Hallgrove Bottom GU19 145 F5
Halliford Cl TW17 125 E6
Halliford Rd TW16,TW17 125 F5
Halliford Sch TW17 125 C2
Hallmark Cl GU47 150 E8
Halls La Earley RG2 86 E1
Waltham St Lawrence RG10 63 A7
Halls Rd RG30 84 D6
Hallsmead Ct 2 RG1 59 A1
Halpin Cl RG31 84 C4
Halse Dr SL1,SL2 21 F7
Halstead Cl RG5 87 E7
Halters The RG14 131 B7
Ham Island SL4 68 C3
Ham La
Englefield Green TW20 95 B4
Old Windsor SL4 68 C3
Ham Rd SN8 126 A3
Hamble Ave GU17 150 D5
Hamble Ct 3 RG1 86 B6
Hambleberry Ct RG31 84 C8
Hambleden Ct RG12 118 E5
Hambleden Mill RG9 16 C7
Hambleden Pl RG9 16 D6
Hambleden Rise RG9 16 D8
Hambleden Wlk SL6 19 E2
Hambledon Cl RG6 87 E1
Hambleton Cl GU16 152 B3
Hamblin Mdw RG17 100 E7
Hambridge La RG14 105 E2
Hambridge Rd RG14 105 D2
Hamfield Cotts SL6 19 E7
Hamilton Ave RG9 15 E1
Hamilton Cl Ashford TW13 98 F3
Bagshot GU19 145 E3
Chertsey KT16 123 F1
Hamilton Ct
Farnborough GU17 150 E1
Newbury RG14 131 B8
Hamilton Dr SL5 120 E2
Hamilton Gdns SL1 21 B2
Hamilton Pk SL6 39 A6
Hamilton Rd
Feltham TW13 98 F4
Reading RG1 86 E6
Slough SL1 42 A7
Wargrave RG10 36 E2
Hamlet St RG42 118 E8
Hammond Cl RG19 106 F2
Hammond Com Jun Sch GU18 146 A1
Hammond Ct RG42 91 A1
Hammond End SL2 22 B8
Hammond Way GU18 146 B1
Hammonds Heath RG7 137 B6
Hampden Cl SL2 23 A2
Hampden Rd
Caversham RG4 59 B2
Maidenhead SL6 39 B8
Slough SL3 43 F3
Hampdens The RG14 130 C6
Hampshire Ave SL1 42 C8
Hampshire Lodge 8 SL6 39 F6
Hampshire Rd GU15 151 F8
Hampshire Rise RG42 91 F2
Hampshire Way RG41 115 D6
Hampshire Wlk RG31 84 A7
Hampstead Ct RG30 85 B7
Hampstead Hill RG9 60 C8
Hampstead Norreys CE Prim Sch RG18 52 F5
Hampstead Norreys Rd RG18 79 C8
Hampton Ho SL3 69 D7
Hampton Rd RG14 104 F1
Hampton Twrs 4 RG30 85 D6
Hamstead Mill RG20 103 C2
Hanbury Cl SL1 41 A8
Hanbury Dr RG31 84 D4
Hanbury Way GU15 151 C3
Hanbury Wlk RG19 106 D2
Hancocks Mount SL5 120 D3
Hancombe Rd GU47 143 A1
Handford La GU46 149 D5
Handpost Cnr RG40 116 A1
Hanger Rd RG26 134 F1
Hangerfield Cl GU46 149 C5
Hangman's Stone La RG20 49 A5
Hanley Cl SL4 66 D6
Hannibal Rd TW19 97 E8
Hanningtons Way RG7 111 C3
Hanover Cl
Englefield Green TW20 95 B2
Frimley GU16 151 E1
Slough SL1 43 A3
Windsor SL4 66 F6
Yateley GU46 149 D7
Hanover Ct
Caversham RG4 59 C6
Reading RG30 84 F6
Hanover Gate SL1 42 A5
Hanover Gdns
Bracknell RG12 117 F2
Wargrave RG10 36 F3
Hanover Gn RG20 103 E6
Hanover Mead
Maidenhead SL6 40 C3
Newbury RG14 130 D6
Hanover Way SL4 66 F6
Hanson Cl GU15 152 B7
Hanwood Cl RG5 87 C8
Hanworth Cl RG12 118 C3
Hanworth La KT16 123 F1
Hanworth Rd RG12 118 A2
Hanworth Trad Est KT16 123 F1
Haplin Ho RG7 139 C3
Harborough Cl SL1 41 D5
Harbury Ct RG14 105 B2
Harcourt TW19 68 E1

Harcourt Cl Dorney SL6 ...40 F3
Egham TW20 ...96 C2
Henley-On-T RG9 ...15 C1
Harcourt Dr RG6 ...86 F3
Harcourt Rd
Bracknell RG12 ...118 B4
Camberley GU15 ...151 B5
Dorney SL6 ...40 F3
Windsor SL4 ...66 F6
Hardell Cl TW20 ...96 A3
Harding Rd RG5 ...87 C8
Hardwell Way RG12 ...118 E5
Hardwick Cl SL6 ...39 A8
Hardwick La KT16 ...123 D1
Hardwick Rd
Reading RG30 ...84 F7
Whitchurch-on-T RG8 ...56 D7
Hardy Ave GU46 ...149 C4
Hardy Cl Caversham RG4 ...59 C2
Slough SL1 ...42 A5
Thatcham RG18 ...106 C5
Hardy Gn RG45 ...143 B4
Hare Shoots SL6 ...39 E5
Harebell Dr RG18 ...106 E4
Harefield Cl RG41 ...88 C2
Harefield Rd SL6 ...39 A7
Harewood Dr RG18 ...106 C8
Harewood Pl SL1 ...43 A3
Hargrave Rd SL6 ...39 D8
Hargreaves Way RG31 ...84 F4
Harkness Rd SL1 ...41 B8
Harlech Ave RG4 ...59 D6
Harlech Rd GU17 ...150 D4
Harley Ct SL1 ...42 C4
Harley Rd RG4 ...59 B2
Harleyford La SL7 ...18 B7
Harlington Cl UB7 ...71 C7
Harlington Cnr UB3 ...71 D6
Harlton Cl RG6 ...114 C8
Harman Ct RG41 ...88 B2
Harmans Water Prim Sch RG12 ...118 E4
Harmans Water Rd RG12 ...118 D4
Harmar Cl RG40 ...116 E6
Harmondsworth La UB7 ...70 E8
Harmondsworth Moor Ctry Pk UB7 ...70 B7
Harmondsworth Prim Sch UB7 ...70 D8
Harness Cl RG2 ...113 B6
Harold Rd RG17 ...102 B2
Harpdon Par GU46 ...149 D7
Harpesford Ave GU25 ...122 C4
Harpsden Rd RG9 ...35 E8
Harpsden Way RG9 ...35 E7
Harpton Cl GU46 ...149 D7
Harrier Cl RG5 ...88 A6
Harrington Cl Earley RG6 ...87 C2
Newbury RG14 ...105 E5
Windsor SL4 ...66 F3
Harris Arc 5 RG1 ...86 B8
Harris Cl Lambourn RG17 ...25 B3
Woodley RG5 ...88 B8
Harris Gdns SL1 ...42 C4
Harris Way TW16 ...125 E8
Harrison Cl RG10 ...61 F3
Harrison Way
Burnham SL1 ...41 D5
Shepperton TW17 ...125 B4
Harrogate Ct SL3 ...44 A1
Harrogate Rd RG4 ...58 E4
Harrow Bottom Rd GU25 ...122 F3
Harrow Cl SL6 ...19 E1
Harrow Ct RG1 ...85 F6
Harrow La SL6 ...19 E1
Harrow Mkt The SL3 ...44 A3
Harrow Rd Ashford TW15 ...98 A6
Slough SL3 ...43 F3
Harrow Way
Charlton TW17 ...125 C7
Sindlesham RG41 ...115 A8
Harry Tee Ct 12 RG1 ...86 C7
Hart Dene Ct GU19 ...145 E3
Hart Dyke Cl RG41 ...116 B2
Hart St Henley-On-T RG9 ...15 E2
Reading RG1 ...85 E8
Hart's La RG7 ...110 C5
Hartford Rise GU15 ...151 D6
Hartigan Pl RG5 ...88 A8
Hartland Cl SL1 ...42 D5
Hartland Rd RG2 ...86 C1
Hartley Cl
Blackwater GU17 ...150 B5
Stoke Poges SL3 ...23 C4
Hartley Copse SL4 ...68 A1
Hartley Court Rd RG7 ...112 F6
Hartley Way RG18 ...106 E4
Hartmead Rd RG19 ...106 E3
Harts Cl RG2 ...114 E2
Harts Hill Rd RG18 ...106 F4
Harts Leap Cl GU47 ...143 B1
Harts Leap Rd GU47 ...150 A8
Hartsbourne Rd RG6 ...87 A3
Hartshill Rd RG26 ...134 F1
Hartslock Bridleway RG8 56 B8
Hartslock Ct RG8 ...56 C6
Hartslock View RG8 ...34 E2
Hartslock Way RG31 ...57 C2
Hartvale Ct 1 GU15 ...152 A8
Harvard Cl RG5 ...88 B8
Harvard Rd GU47 ...143 E1
Harvaston Par RG30 ...84 F7
Harvest Cl Reading RG31 ...84 B6
Yateley GU46 ...149 B4
Harvest Cotts TW17 ...125 A5
Harvest Ct TW17 ...125 A5
Harvest Dr RG41 ...115 B7
Harvest Gn RG14 ...104 E1
Harvest Hill SL8 ...3 D2
Harvest Hill Rd SL6 ...39 F3
Harvest Rd TW20 ...95 D2
Harvest Ride
Bracknell RG42 ...91 C2
Winkfield RG12,RG42,SL5 ...119 A8
Harvey Ho 11 RG30 ...85 D6
Harvey Rd
Oatlands Park KT12 ...125 F2
Slough SL3 ...44 B4
Harveys Nurseries Pk Cvn Site RG4 ...59 C4
Harwell Int Bsns Ctr OX11 9 F8
Harwell International Bsns Ctr OX11 ...10 C8
Harwich Cl 4 RG6 ...87 D1
Harwich Rd SL1 ...42 A7
Harwood Gdns SL4 ...95 B8
Harwood Rd SL7 ...1 C1
Harwood Rise RG20 ...129 F2
Haslemere Cl GU16 ...152 C3
Haslemere Rd SL4 ...67 A6
Haslett Rd TW17 ...125 E7
Hasting Cl SL6 ...40 C2
Hastings Cl RG30 ...85 A4
Hastings Mdw SL2 ...23 A4
Hatch Cl RG7 ...108 C7
Hatch End GU20 ...146 C4
Hatch Gate Ct RG10 ...88 E6
Hatch Gate La RG10 ...37 A6
Hatch La Bucklebury RG7 108 C7
Burghfield Common RG30 ...111 D6
Harmondsworth UB7 ...70 D7
Windsor SL4 ...67 A5
Hatch Ride
Crowthorne RG45 ...143 B7
Wokingham RG40 ...142 F8
Hatch Ride Prim Sch RG45 ...143 B7
Hatch The SL4 ...66 C7
Hatchet La SL4,SL5 ...93 B5
Hatchets La RG18 ...80 C7
Hatchett Rd TW14 ...98 C7
Hatchgate Cl RG18 ...106 C7
Hatchgate Copse RG12 ...117 E3
Hatchgate Gdns SL1 ...21 D1
Hatchley RG2 ...113 C7
Hatfield Cl SL6 ...39 C6
Hatfield Ct
Camberley GU15 ...151 B5
Reading RG31 ...84 B4
Hatfield Rd SL1 ...43 A4
Hatford Rd RG30 ...85 B4
Hatherley Rd RG1 ...86 E6
Hatherwood GU46 ...149 F5
Hatt Cl RG20 ...50 D7
Hatton Ave SL2 ...22 D1
Hatton Cross Rdbt TW6 ...71 F4
Hatton Cross Sta TW6 ...71 F3
Hatton Ct SL4 ...67 C5
Hatton Hill
Ashampstead RG8 ...54 B7
Windlesham GU20 ...146 C5
Hatton Rd
East Bedfont TW14 ...98 D8
Hatton TW14,TW6 ...71 E2
Hatton Rd N TW6 ...71 D6
Haughurst Hill RG26 ...134 C1
Havelock Bsns Pk SL6 ...39 C7
Havelock Cres SL6 ...39 B7
Havelock Rd
Maidenhead SL6 ...39 B7
Wokingham RG41 ...116 A6
Havelock St RG41 ...116 A6
Haven Ct 8 RG1 ...86 D7
Haven Of Rest SL6 ...40 B7
Haven Rd TW15 ...98 B5
Haven The RG17 ...102 A1
Haversham Dr RG12 ...118 B3
Haw La RG8,RG18 ...53 E7
Hawk La RG12 ...118 D5
Hawkchurch Rd RG2 ...113 D8
Hawkedale Inf Sch TW16 ...125 F6
Hawkedon Prim Sch RG6 87 E2
Hawkedon Way RG6 ...87 E2
Hawker Ct SL3 ...44 A3
Hawker Way RG5 ...88 A7
Hawkes Cl RG41 ...116 A7
Hawkes Leap GU20 ...146 B6
Hawkes Worth Dr GU19 145 E1
Hawkesbury Dr RG31 ...84 E3
Hawkins Cl
Bracknell RG12 ...119 A7
Yateley GU46 ...149 B5
Hawkins Way RG40 ...116 E6
Hawkridge Ct RG12 ...118 E6
Hawks Hill SL8 ...3 C2
Hawkshill Rd SL2 ...22 A2
Hawksway TW18 ...96 F5
Hawkswood Ave GU16 ...151 F2
Hawkswood Gr SL3 ...23 F6
Hawkswood Ho RG42 ...117 E8
Hawkswood La SL9 ...23 F8
Hawksworth Rd RG7 ...111 B3
Hawley Cl RG31 ...84 C4
Hawley Garden Cotts GU17 ...150 D4
Hawley Gn GU17 ...150 E3
Hawley Gr GU17 ...150 E2
Hawley Lodge GU17 ...150 F2
Hawley Place Sch GU17 150 E1
Hawley Prim Sch GU17 ...150 E3
Hawley Rd GU14,GU17 ...150 E3
Hawley Way TW15 ...98 B3
Hawthorn Cl RG42 ...118 A8
Hawthorn Cotts RG7 ...112 C3
Hawthorn Gdns
Maidenhead SL6 ...39 E5
Reading RG2 ...86 E2
Hawthorn La Burnham SL2 22 A5
Newell Green SL4 ...92 A7
Newell Green,Hawthorn Hill RG42 ...91 E8
Hawthorn Rd
Frimley GU16 ...151 F2
Newbury RG14 ...105 A4
Hawthorn Way
Sonning RG4 ...60 E3
Upper Halliford TW17 ...125 D5
Hawthorne Ave SL4 ...93 B6
Hawthorne Cl Marlow SL7 ...1 E4
Thatcham RG18 ...106 D4
Hawthorne Cres
Blackwater GU17 ...150 E4
Slough SL1 ...42 F7
Hawthorne Ct TW19 ...97 D8
Hawthorne Dr SL4 ...93 B7
Hawthorne Rd
Caversham RG4 ...59 E4
Egham TW18 ...96 C4
Hawthorne Way
Great Shefford RG17 ...48 B4
Stanwell TW19 ...97 D8
Winkfield SL4 ...93 B7
Hawthornes RG31 ...57 B3
Hawthornes The HP10 ...3 E6
Hawthorns Prim Sch The RG41 ...115 E7
Hawthorns The
Charvil RG10 ...61 A3
Flackwell Heath HP10 ...3 B8
Poyle SL3 ...69 F6
Wooburn Green HP10 ...3 E6
Hawtrey Cl SL1 ...43 B4
Hawtrey Rd SL4 ...67 C5
Hay La SL3 ...23 D8
Hay Rd RG1 ...85 F5
Haydon Ct
Maidenhead SL6 ...39 E6
Twyford RG10 ...61 E4
Haydon La RG20 ...30 E7
Haydon Pl GU46 ...149 E6
Hayes La RG41 ...115 C4
Hayes Pl SL7 ...1 D1
Hayfield Cl RG31 ...84 C8
Hayfield Ct RG17 ...46 F6
Hayley Gn RG42 ...91 F3
Haymill Rd SL1,SL2 ...21 D1
Haynes Cl SL3 ...43 F1
Hayse Hill SL4 ...66 D6
Haysoms Dr RG19 ...131 B7
Hayward Pl SL8 ...3 C2
Haywards Cl RG9 ...15 C1
Haywards Mead SL4 ...41 F1
Haywards The RG18 ...106 D4
Haywood RG12 ...118 C2
Haywood Ct RG1 ...86 F7
Haywood Way RG30 ...84 F5
Hazel Cl
Burghfield Common RG30 ...111 B5
Englefield Green TW20 ...95 B2
Marlow Bottom SL7 ...1 C6
Wokingham RG41 ...115 F5
Hazel Cres RG2 ...86 E2
Hazel Dr RG5 ...87 C5
Hazel Gn RG26 ...134 D1
Hazel Gr Staines TW18 ...97 C2
Thatcham RG18 ...106 D5
Hazel Rd RG8 ...57 C4
Hazelbank RG40 ...141 E6
Hazelbank Ct KT16 ...124 C1
Hazelbank Rd KT16 ...124 C2
Hazeldene RG20 ...51 B1
Hazelhurst Rd SL1 ...21 D3
Hazell Hill RG12 ...118 C6
Hazell Way SL2 ...22 F6
Hazelmere Cl TW14 ...71 E1
Hazels Paddock RG18 ...106 C8
Hazelwood Cl RG31 ...57 C1
Hazelwood La RG42 ...90 F4
Hazlemere Rd SL2 ...43 B5
Heacham Cl RG6 ...114 A8
Headington Cl
Maidenhead SL6 ...39 A7
Wokingham RG40 ...116 D8
Headington Dr RG40 ...116 D8
Headington Rd SL6 ...39 A7
Headlands Ct RG7 ...110 F1
Headley Cl RG5 ...88 A8
Headley Park Ind Est RG5 ...87 F7
Headley Rd RG5 ...87 E7
Headley Rd E RG5 ...88 A7
Heads La RG17 ...128 A5
Heardman Cl RG19 ...106 F2
Hearmon Cl GU46 ...149 E6
Hearn Rd RG5 ...87 E5
Hearn Wlk RG12 ...118 E8
Hearne Dr SL6 ...40 A1
Hearsey Gdns GU17 ...150 C6
Heath Cl Harlington UB3 ...71 D7
Stanwell TW19 ...70 C1
Virginia Water GU25 ...122 D5
Wokingham RG41 ...116 B4
Heath Cnr GU15 ...152 A3
Heath Ct RG26 ...134 E2
Heath Dr RG9 ...35 A1
Heath End Farm RG26 ...134 E1
Heath End Rd RG26 ...134 E1
Heath Flats GU19 ...145 E3
Heath Gr TW16 ...98 F1
Heath Hill Rd N RG45 ...143 B5
Heath Hill Rd S RG45 ...143 B4
Heath La RG18 ...106 C5
Heath Rd Bagshot GU19 ...145 E3
Bradfield RG7 ...82 A2
Reading RG6 ...87 A5
Silchester RG26 ...135 E1
Wooburn Moor HP9 ...3 F8
Heath Ride RG40,RG45 ...142 C5
Heath Rise
Camberley GU15 ...151 D5
Virginia Water GU25 ...122 D5
Heath Villa SL5 ...120 A6
Heathacre SL3 ...69 E6
Heathcote SL6 ...40 B2
Heathcote Ct 2 SL4 ...67 D4
Heathcote Rd GU15 ...151 D5
Heathcroft Ave TW16 ...98 F1
Heather Cl RG40 ...141 E7
Heather Dr
Sunningdale SL5 ...121 B2
Tadley RG26 ...134 F2
Thatcham RG18 ...106 D5
Heather Gdns RG14 ...130 F7
Heather Mead GU16 ...151 F2
Heather Mead Ct GU16 ...151 F2
Heather Ridge Arc GU15 ...152 C4
Heather Ridge Inf Sch GU15 ...152 D4
Heatherdale Rd GU15 ...151 D4
Heatherden Cl RG2 ...113 C7
Heatherdene Ave RG45 ...142 E4
Heatherlands SL5 ...120 E4
Heatherley Cl GU15 ...151 B5
Heatherley Rd GU15 ...151 B5
Heathermount RG12 ...118 E5
Heathermount Dr RG45 143 A6
Heathermount Learning Ctr The SL5 ...120 D3
Heathers The TW19 ...97 F8
Heatherside Cnr GU15 ...152 D6
Heatherside Dr GU25 ...122 A3
Heatherway RG45 ...143 A5
Heatherwood Hospl SL5 ...119 E6
Heathfield RG7 ...137 A6
Heathfield Ave
Ascot SL5 ...120 E4
Reading RG30 ...84 D6
Shiplake RG9 ...35 B2
Heathfield Cl RG9 ...35 B2
Heathfield Ct TW15 ...97 E5
Heathfield Rd SL1 ...3 F1
Heathfield Sch SL5 ...119 B7
Heathfields RG20 ...78 A8
Heathlands RG26 ...134 E1
Heathlands Ct
Wokingham RG40 ...142 F8
Yateley GU46 ...149 E4
Heathlands Dr SL6 ...39 A6
Heathlands Rd RG40 ...116 E2
Heathlea Ho RG31 ...84 B7
Heathmoors RG12 ...118 C4
Heathpark Dr GU20 ...146 E4
Heathrow Airport London TW6 ...71 A5
Heathrow Airport Visitor Ctr★ TW6 ...71 C6
Heathrow Bvd UB7 ...70 F7
Heathrow Cl TW6 ...70 B6
Heathrow Copse RG26 ...134 D1
Heathrow Prim Sch UB7 ...70 F8
Heathrow Terminal 4 Sta TW6 ...71 C1
Heathrow Terminals 1, 2, 3 TW6 ...71 B4
Heathside Pk GU15 ...152 C7
Heathway
Camberley GU15 ...151 D5
North Ascot SL5 ...119 E8
Reading RG31 ...84 C8
Heathway Cl GU15 ...151 D5
Heathwood Cl GU46 ...149 D7
Heavens Lea SL8 ...3 C2
Hebbecastle Down RG42 91 C2
Hebden Cl RG19 ...106 C2
Hedge Lea HP10 ...3 D8
Hedgeway RG14 ...105 C4
Hedingham Mews SL6 ...39 D7
Hedley Rd HP10 ...3 B8
Hedsor Hill SL8 ...3 C1
Hedsor La HP10,SL1 ...3 F2
Hedsor Rd SL8 ...3 B2
Hedsor View Cotts SL6 ...19 F7
Heelas Rd RG41 ...116 A5
Heights The
Camberley GU15 ...151 E5
Marlow SL7 ...18 B8
Helen Cotts SL4 ...66 D5
Helena Rd SL4 ...67 D5
Helgiford Gdns TW16 ...98 E1
Helix Bsns Pk GU15 ...151 B3
Helksham Cl GU47 ...143 D1
Hellyer Way SL8 ...3 C3
Helmsdale RG12 ...118 E4
Helmsdale Cl RG30 ...85 B8
Helston Gdns RG2 ...86 B1
Helston La SL4 ...67 B6
Helvellyn Cl TW20 ...96 C1
Hemdean Hill RG4 ...59 A3
Hemdean House Sch RG4 ...59 A3
Hemdean Rd RG4 ...59 A3
Hemdean Rise RG4 ...59 A3
Hemming Way SL2 ...22 B2
Hemmyng Cnr RG42 ...91 C2
Hempson Ave SL3 ...43 C3
Hemsdale SL6 ...19 B1
Hemwood Rd SL4 ...66 D4
Hencroft St N SL1 ...42 F4
Hencroft St S SL1 ...42 F3
Hendon Terr TW15 ...98 D2
Hendon Way TW19 ...70 D1
Hendons Way SL6 ...40 B1
Hengrave Cl RG6 ...87 E2
Hengrove Cres TW15 ...97 D5
Henley Coll The (Deanfield Bldgs) RG9 ...15 D1
Henley Coll The (Rotherfield Bldgs) RG9 ...15 C1
Henley Gdns GU46 ...149 D5
Henley Lodge 12 SL6 ...39 F6
Henley Rd Caversham RG9 59 D3
Hurley SL6 ...17 D3
Maidenhead SL6 ...38 E7
Marlow SL7 ...18 B8
Shiplake RG9 ...60 C8
Slough SL1 ...41 F7
Henley Wood Rd RG6 ...87 D4
Henley-on-Thames Sta RG9 ...15 E1
Henry Ct 15 RG1 ...86 C7
Henry Randell's Almshouses GU17 ...150 E3
Henry Rd SL1 ...42 D4
Henry St RG1 ...86 B6
Henrys The RG18 ...106 D4
Henshaw Cres RG14 ...130 D8
Hensworth Rd TW15 ...97 D3
Henwick Cl RG18 ...106 B6
Henwick La RG18 ...106 A4
Henwood Copse RG8 ...55 A6
Hepplewhite Cl RG26 ...134 E1
Hepworth Croft GU47 ...150 E6
Hepworth Way KT12 ...125 F1
Herald Way RG5 ...88 A6
Herbert Cl RG12 ...118 B4
Hereford Cl TW18 ...124 B8
Herewood Cl RG14 ...104 F4
Heriot Ct GU15 ...151 D3
Heriot Rd KT16 ...124 A2
Heritage Ct
8 Egham TW20 ...96 A3
15 Reading RG1 ...85 F7
Hermes Cl RG41 ...115 B7
Hermitage Cl
Frimley GU16 ...151 F1
Littleton TW17 ...125 A5
Slough SL3 ...43 C3
Hermitage Ct TW18 ...96 F3
Hermitage Cvn Pk The RG42 ...91 D3
Hermitage Dr
North Ascot SL5 ...119 E7
Twyford RG10 ...61 D5
Hermitage La SL4 ...67 A4
Hermitage Par SL5 ...120 A6
Hermitage Prim Sch RG18 ...79 B8
Hermitage Rd RG18 ...79 B2
Hermitage The
Feltham TW13 ...98 F5
Lambourn RG17 ...46 E7
Hermits Cl RG7 ...111 B3
Hermits Hill RG7,RG30 ...111 D4
Herndon Cl TW20 ...96 A4
Herne Pl SL5 ...121 C4
Hernes Cl TW18 ...124 B8
Heroes Wlk RG2 ...113 B7
Heron Cl SL5 ...119 D8
Heron Ct Staines TW18 ...97 B4
Stanwell TW19 ...97 E7
Heron Dr Slough SL3 ...44 B2
Twyford RG10 ...61 E6
Heron Ho RG14 ...105 D3
Heron Ind Est RG7 ...139 A8
Heron Island RG4 ...59 C1
Heron Rd RG41 ...115 E6
Heron Shaw RG8 ...34 C7
Heron Way
Padworth RG7 ...109 B3
Reading RG1 ...85 E4
Thatcham RG19 ...106 B3
Heron's Way RG40 ...116 E7
Herondale RG12 ...118 C2
Heronfield TW20 ...95 C2
Herongate RG17 ...100 D7
Herons Pl Maidenhead SL6 20 C3
Marlow SL7 ...1 E3
Heronsbrook SL5 ...120 F7
Heronscourt GU18 ...153 C8
Herrick Cl GU16 ...152 C3
Herries Sch SL6 ...19 B8
Herrings La
Chertsey KT16 ...124 A3
Windlesham GU20 ...146 D4
Herriot Ct GU46 ...149 C4
Herschel Gram Sch SL1 ...42 C7
Herschel Grange RG42 ...91 D3
Herschel Park Dr SL1 ...42 F4
Herschel St SL1 ...42 F4
Hertford Cl
Caversham RG4 ...59 D6
Wokingham RG41 ...115 E5
Hetherington Cl SL2 ...21 F2
Hetherington Rd TW17 ...125 C7
Hever Cl SL6 ...39 C6
Hewett Ave RG4 ...58 D4
Hewett Cl RG4 ...58 D4
Hewgate Ct RG9 ...15 E1
Hewlett Pl GU19 ...145 F3
Hexham Cl GU47 ...143 D2
Hexham Rd RG2 ...86 C3
Heynes Gn SL6 ...39 B3

Heywod Dr GU19 145 D3
Heywood Ave SL6 39 A1
Heywood Court Cl SL6 39 A2
Heywood Gardens Cvn Site SL6 39 A1
Hibbert Rd SL6 40 B4
Hibbert's Alley 15 SL4 67 D6
Hickox Ct HP10 3 F7
Hicks La GU17 150 B5
Higgs La GU19 145 D3
High Beech RG12 118 F5
High Beeches GU16 151 D2
High Beeches Cl SL7 1 C6
High Chys GU20 146 E7
High Close Sch RG40 116 C7
High Fields SL5 120 F4
High Heavens Wood SL7 1 C8
High Mdw RG4 58 D3
High Meadow Pl KT16 123 F3
High Pines The RG42 92 B5
High Rd SL6 19 E6
High St Ascot SL5 120 A6
  Ascot,Sunninghill SL5 120 D4
  Bagshot GU19 145 E3
  Boxford RG20 76 B2
  Bracknell RG12 118 B7
  Bray SL6 40 C4
  Burnham SL1 21 C2
  Camberley GU15 151 D6
  Chalvey SL1 42 D3
  Chieveley RG20 51 B1
  Colnbrook SL3 69 C7
  Compton RG20 31 D4
  Cookham SL6 20 B7
  Crowthorne RG45 143 C4
  Datchet SL3 68 B6
  East Ilsley RG20 30 E7
  Egham TW20 96 A3
  Eton SL4 67 D8
  Goring RG8 34 C6
  Harlington UB3 71 D8
  Harmondsworth UB7 70 D8
  Hungerford RG17 100 D5
  Iver SL0 44 F7
  Kintbury RG17 102 A2
  Lambourn RG17 25 B2
  Lambourn, Upper Lambourn RG17 24 E6
  Maidenhead SL6 39 F7
  Marlow SL7 1 E1
  4 Pangbourne RG8 56 C6
  Reading RG1 86 B7
  Sandhurst GU47 149 F8
  Sandhurst,Little Sandhurst GU47 143 A1
  Shepperton TW17 125 C3
  Slough, Upton SL1 42 F4
  Slough,Langley SL3 44 A2
  Sonning RG4 60 D4
  Staines TW18 96 F4
  Stanwell TW19 70 D1
  Streatley RG8 34 A6
  Sunningdale SL5 121 A4
  Taplow SL6 20 E1
  Thatcham RG19 106 D3
  Theale RG7 83 E3
  Twyford RG10 61 D5
  Wargrave RG10 36 D2
  West End GU24 153 F7
  Whitchurch-on-T RG8 56 C7
  Windsor SL4 67 D6
  Wraysbury TW19 68 F1
  Feltham,Lower Feltham TW13 98 F5
High St Mall 11 SL6 39 F7
High Street Harlington TW6 71 D7
High Town Rd SL6 39 F7
High Tree Dr RG6 87 B6
High View Cl SL7 1 D8
High View Rd GU18 152 F8
Highbridge Cl RG4 59 E5
Highbridge Wharf 3 RG1 86 B7
Highbury Cres GU15 152 A8
Highbury Rd RG31 84 B7
Highclere SL5 120 D4
Highclere Cl RG12 118 E7
Highclere Dr GU15 152 A7
Highcliffe Cl RG5 60 F1
Highdown Ave RG4 59 A6
Highdown Hill Rd RG4 59 A6
Highdown Sch RG4 59 A5
Higher Alham RG12 118 E2
Highfield Bracknell RG12 117 F3
  Earley RG6 87 B6
Highfield Ave RG14 105 A2
Highfield Cl
  Englefield Green TW20 95 C2
  Wokingham RG40 116 B6
Highfield Ct
  Burghfield Common RG7 111 B3
  Burnham SL2 22 B4
  Englefield Green TW20 95 D2
  Twyford RG10 61 E4
Highfield La SL6 39 A4
Highfield Pk
  Arborfield RG2 140 D8
  Marlow SL7 1 B1
  Wargrave RG10 36 F3
Highfield Rd
  Bourne End SL8 3 B4
  Chertsey KT16 124 A1
  Flackwell Heath HP10 3 A8
  Maidenhead SL6 39 B8
Highfield Rd *continued*
  Newbury RG14 104 F1
  Purley On T RG31 57 B4
  Upper Halliford TW16 125 F4
  Windsor SL4 66 F4
Highfields Sch SL6 39 E7
Highgate Rd RG5 87 D5
Highgrove RG41 88 C1
Highgrove Pk SL6 39 E8
Highgrove Pl RG10 61 E5
Highgrove St RG1 86 C5
Highgrove Terr RG1 86 B6
Highland Pk TW13 98 F4
Highland Rd GU15 151 E8
Highlands
  Flackwell Heath HP10 3 B7
  Newbury RG14 130 E7
Highlands Ave RG41 115 C5
Highlands La RG9 35 A8
Highlands Sch The RG31 57 D1
Highlands The SL2 22 C7
Highlea Ave HP10 3 A8
Highmead Cl RG2 86 E2
Highmoor Rd RG4 58 F3
Highview RG31 84 B5
Highview Cres GU15 144 F1
Highway RG45 143 A5
Highway Ave SL6 39 A6
Highway Rd SL6 39 B6
Highwayman's Ridge GU20 146 B6
Highwood Cl
  Newbury RG14 105 B6
  Yateley GU46 149 D4
Highwood Prim Sch RG5 87 C6
Highwoods Cl SL7 1 C7
Highwoods Dr SL7 1 C7
Highworth Cotts RG26 134 C1
Highworth Way RG31 57 B2
Hilary Cl RG2 113 D7
Hilary Ho 2 RG14 105 A1
Hilborn Way RG2 115 A1
Hilbury Rd RG6 87 A3
Hilcot Rd RG30 85 D8
Hildens Dr RG31 84 C7
Hildesley Ct RG20 30 E7
Hilfield GU46 149 F5
Hilgrove Ho SL6 19 D1
Hill Cl Newbury RG14 130 D7
  Wooburn Green HP10 3 F7
Hill Copse View RG12 118 E8
Hill Cres RG7 108 C3
Hill Farm App HP10 3 F7
Hill Farm Rd
  Marlow Bottom SL7 1 E6
  Taplow SL6 20 E2
Hill Gdns RG8 34 A6
Hill Lands RG10 36 D2
Hill Piece OX11 10 E7
Hill Pl SL2 22 B5
Hill Prim Sch The RG4 59 C5
Hill Rd
  Arborfield Cross RG2 114 F1
  Newbury RG14 104 E4
Hill Side RG1 86 C5
Hill St RG1 86 B6
Hill Top Dr SL7 1 B2
Hill View RG7 113 A1
Hill View Mews RG30 84 E8
Hill View Rd TW19 68 D1
Hillary Ct TW19 97 E7
Hillary Dr RG45 143 B6
Hillary Rd SL3 43 E4
Hillberry RG12 118 C2
Hillbrow RG2 86 E1
Hillbrow Ct SL5 121 A4
Hillcrest
  Hampstead Norreys RG18 52 F6
  Tadley RG26 135 B1
Hillcrest Ave SL6 19 E6
Hillcrest Cotts RG14 104 F7
Hillcrest Rd GU15 152 B7
Hilldrop La RG17 46 A3
Hillersdon SL2 43 B8
Hillfoot RG7 81 A1
Hillgreen La RG20 50 C7
Hillhampton SL5 120 F2
Hillhouse La RG19 133 A1
Hillingdon Ave TW19 97 E7
Hillmead Ct SL6 40 F8
Hillrise Brands Hill SL3 69 A8
  Oatlands Park KT12 125 F2
Hills La SL6 19 D7
Hillsborough Pk GU15 152 C5
Hillside Ascot SL5 120 C4
  Burghfield Common RG7 111 C3
  East Garston RG17 47 C6
  Maidenhead SL6 39 D5
  Sandhurst GU15 150 F7
  Slough SL1 42 E4
  Wentworth GU25 122 C3
  Whitchurch-on-T RG8 56 D8
Hillside Dr RG42 90 C2
Hillside Pk Earley RG2 86 F1
  Sunningdale SL5 120 F1
Hillside Rd Earley RG6 87 D3
  Hungerford RG17 100 D4
  Marlow SL7 1 E4
Hilltop Cl SL5 120 E7
Hilltop Fst Sch SL4 66 E4
Hilltop Rd Caversham RG4 58 D5
  Earley RG6 87 B8
  Twyford RG10 61 E7
Hilltop View GU46 149 B5
Hillview Cl RG31 57 B2
Hilmanton RG6 113 F8
Hilperton Rd 3 SL1 42 E4
Hind's Head 7 RG17 25 B2
Hindhay La SL6 19 C3
Hindhead Rd RG6 87 A3
Hinksey Cl SL3 44 B3
Hinton Cl RG45 143 B7
Hinton Dr RG45 143 B7
Hinton Rd Hurst RG10 62 A1
  Slough SL1 41 E6
Hintonhatch Cnr RG10 62 B2
Hirstwood RG30 57 E1
Hirtes Ave RG2 113 E5
Hitcham Ho SL1 21 A1
Hitcham La SL1,SL6 20 F2
Hitcham Rd SL1,SL6 41 A8
Hitchcock Cl TW17 124 F6
Hitherhooks Hill RG42 90 E1
Hithermoor Rd TW19 70 A2
Hobart Ct SL7 2 A3
Hobbis Dr SL6 39 A6
Hobbs End RG9 35 B8
Hockett La SL6 19 A6
Hockford La RG7 134 A3
Hockham Rd RG20 31 E5
Hockley La SL2 23 B5
Hodcott Bglws RG20 30 B8
Hodge La SL5 93 A3
Hodgedale La RG10 37 D6
Hodges Cl GU19 145 E1
Hodsoll Rd RG1 85 F8
Hoe Benham La RG20 102 F7
Hoffman Cl RG42 91 D2
Hogarth Ave
  Ashford TW15 98 C2
  Reading RG30 84 F5
Hogarth Cl
  Sandhurst GU47 150 E6
  Slough SL1 41 E6
Hogfair La SL1 21 C1
Hogmoor La RG10 61 F1
Hogoak La SL4 92 A8
Hogwood Ind Est RG40 141 A6
Hogwood La RG40 141 A6
Holbeche Cl GU46 149 A6
Holbeck RG12 117 F3
Holberton Rd RG2 113 D8
Holborn Hill OX12 6 D7
Holborne Cl RG14 130 D5
Holbrook Ct TW20 96 C3
Holbrook Mdw TW20 96 C2
Holder Cl RG2 113 D5
Holford Cl RG31 84 C8
Holkam Cl RG30 84 F8
Holland Gdns TW20 123 F7
Holland Pines RG12 117 F2
Holland Rd Marlow SL7 1 F3
  Reading RG30 84 D7
Hollands The RG19 106 E3
Hollerith Rise RG12 118 B3
Hollicombe Cl RG30 84 E7
Hollies The RG14 130 D5
Hollington Pl RG19 106 C3
Hollins Wlk RG30 85 D6
Hollow Hill La SL0 44 C5
Hollow La Shinfield RG2 113 E5
  Virginia Water GU25 122 C6
Holloway Dr GU25 122 E5
Holloway La UB7 70 E8
Holly Acre 4 GU46 149 D5
Holly Ave GU16 152 B3
Holly Cl Brimpton RG19 133 B6
  Englefield Green TW20 95 B2
  Farnham Common SL2 22 C8
Holly Cnr RG7 140 B7
Holly Cotts GU47 143 A1
Holly Cres SL4 66 D5
Holly Ct RG45 142 E4
Holly Dr Maidenhead SL6 39 F8
  Windsor SL4 67 E2
Holly Hedge Cl GU16 151 E2
Holly Hedge Rd GU16 151 E2
Holly Ho RG12 118 B3
Holly La Ashampstead RG8 54 B6
  Bucklebury RG18 80 B3
Holly Orch RG41 115 F5
Holly Rd RG5 88 A6
Holly Ridge GU24 153 E6
Holly Spring Inf Sch RG12 118 E7
Holly Spring Jun Sch RG12 118 E7
Holly Spring La RG12 118 D8
Holly Way GU17 150 D4
Holly Wlk SL4 93 E4
Hollybank GU24 153 F6
Hollybush Hill SL2 23 B5
Hollybush La
  Burghfield Common RG7 110 E3
  Cookham Dean SL6 19 B6
  Iver SL0 44 B7
Hollybush Ride RG40, RG45 142 C6
Hollybush Tk GU19,GU20 145 F6
Hollycombe TW20 95 D4
Hollycroft RG19 133 F1
Hollycroft Cl UB7 71 A8
Hollycroft Gdns UB7 71 A8
Hollydale Cl RG2 86 E1
Hollyfields Cl GU15 151 B5
Hollyhook Cl RG45 143 A6
Hollym Cl RG6 87 E2
Holmanleaze SL6 40 A8
Holmbank Dr TW17 125 E5
Holmbury Ave RG45 143 A7
Holmdale SL2 43 C6
Holmdene RG7 111 B3
Holme Cl RG45 143 A7
Holme Grange Sch RG40 116 F3
Holme Park Farm La RG4 60 C2
Holmemoor Dr RG4 60 E2
Holmes Cl Ascot SL5 120 C3
  Wokingham RG41 116 A4
Holmes Cres RG41 116 A4
Holmes Rd RG6 87 A5
Holmewood Cl RG41 116 A2
Holmlea Rd Datchet SL3 68 D6
  Goring RG8 34 C5
Holmlea Wlk SL3 68 C6
Holmsdale Cl SL0 44 F7
Holmwood Ave RG30 84 F4
Holmwood Cl SL6 39 B5
Holsworthy Cl RG6 87 E3
Holt La Brightwalton RG20 49 F8
  Wokingham RG41 116 B7
Holt Rd RG17 102 B2
Holt Sch The RG41 116 B7
Holt The RG8 57 D4
Holton Heath 9 RG12 118 F5
Holtspur Ave HP10 3 F7
Holtspur La HP10 3 F6
Holtwood Rd RG20 129 B6
Holy Brook Sch The RG30 85 A4
Holy Family RC Sch SL3 43 F1
Holy Trinity CE Prim Sch
  Cookham SL6 20 B7
  Sunningdale SL5 121 A3
Holy Trinity CE Sch SL7 1 D3
Holybrook Cres RG30 85 A4
Holybrook Rd RG1 85 F5
Holyport CE Prim Sch SL6 65 B8
Holyport Manor Sch SL6 64 E6
Holyport Rd SL6 40 B1
Holyport St SL6 65 A8
Holyrood Cl RG4 59 D6
Holywell Cl TW19 97 E7
Holywell Ct RG19 106 D3
Holywell Way TW19 97 E7
Hombrook Dr RG42 117 E8
Hombrook Ho RG42 117 E8
Home Cl GU25 122 D3
Home Croft RG31 57 B1
Home Farm RG20 75 F6
Home Farm Cl
  Reading RG2 86 C4
  Upper Halliford TW17 125 E5
Home Farm Cotts RG41 115 B7
Home Farm La RG7 134 C5
Home Farm Way SL3 23 C4
Home Mdw SL2 22 C3
Home Mead Cl RG14 130 E8
Home Meadow Dr HP10 3 B7
Home Park Rd GU46 149 D6
Home Wood SL7 17 F6
Homefield Way RG17 100 C5
Homelands Way RG9 15 D1
Homer Fst Sch SL4 66 D6
Homers Rd SL4 66 D6
Homeside Cl SL6 19 E2
Homestead Rd
  Maidenhead SL6 39 D4
  Staines TW18 97 B2
Homestead The RG9 35 B1
Homewaters Ave TW16 125 F8
Homewood SL3 43 D7
Hone Hill GU47 150 B8
Honesty Bottom RG20 28 D2
Honey End La RG30 85 A6
Honey Hill Lambourn RG17 25 B3
  Wokingham RG40 117 A1
Honey La SL6 17 E2
Honey Meadow Cl RG4 59 E2
Honeybottom Rd RG26 135 B1
Honeyfields RG17 100 D5
Honeyhill Rd RG42 118 A8
Honeysuckle Cl
  Crowthorne RG45 143 A7
  Iver SL0 44 C7
  Yateley GU46 149 A6
Honeysuckle Ct SL3 69 C7
Honister Wlk GU15 152 D4
Honiton Rd RG2 86 C2
Honnor Rd TW18 97 D1
Hook Cl RG19 131 B7
Hook End La RG8 34 B2
Hook La GU24 153 C6
Hook Mill La GU18 146 D2
Hookstone La GU24 153 F8
Hoops Way RG2 112 F8
Hop Gdns RG9 15 D2
Hope Ave RG12 118 E2
Hope Cotts RG42 92 A5
Hope Fountain GU15 151 F4
Hopeman Cl GU47 150 D7
Hopper Vale RG12 118 A3
Hopwood Cl RG14 105 D4
Horatio Ave RG42 118 E8
Horewood Rd RG12 118 B3
Horizon West Ind Est RG14 105 D3
Hormer Cl GU47 143 D1
Horn St RG20 31 E5
Hornbeam Cl
  Purley On T RG8 57 C5
  Sandhurst GU47 143 D1
  Wokingham RG41 115 D3
Hornbeam Copse RG42 119 A8
Hornbeam Dr RG6 87 D1
Hornbeam Gdns 7 SL1 43 A3
Hornbeam Pightle RG7 111 B3
Hornbeams RG7 139 C6
Hornby Ave RG12 118 D2
Horncastle Dr RG30 84 F5
Horndean Rd RG12 118 F3
Horne Rd Littleton TW17 125 A5
  Thatcham RG19 106 E2
Hornsea Cl RG30 57 E1
Horris Hill Sch RG20 130 E3
Horse Cl The RG4 59 C4
Horse Gate Ride SL5 120 A3
Horsebrass Dr GU19 145 E2
Horseguards Dr SL6 40 B7
Horsell Ct KT16 124 B2
Horsemoor Cl SL3 44 A2
Horseshoe Cl GU15 151 F8
Horseshoe Cloisters 2 SL4 67 D6
Horseshoe Cres
  Burghfield Common RG7 111 B3
  Camberley GU15 151 F8
Horseshoe End RG14 131 B7
Horseshoe Hill SL1 21 C8
Horseshoe Pk RG8 56 D5
Horseshoe Rd RG8 56 D5
Horsham Rd
  East Bedfont TW14 71 C1
  Sandhurst GU47 143 D1
Horsham Reach SL6 20 C2
Horsnape Gdns RG42 90 B2
Horsneile La RG42 118 B8
Horton Cl SL6 20 C1
Horton Depot SL3 69 C4
Horton Gdns SL3 68 F4
Horton Grange SL6 20 C1
Horton Rd Datchet SL3 68 D6
  Horton SL3 69 A6
  Poyle SL3,TW19 69 E4
  Stanwell TW19 70 A2
Horton Trad Est SL3 69 C4
Hose Hill RG7,RG30 111 A7
Hosier St RG1 86 A7
Hoskins Place Ind Est GU15 151 B3
Houlton Ct GU19 145 F2
Houston Ct 5 SL4 67 C5
Houston Way RG45 142 D5
Howard Ave SL2 42 E8
Howard Cl TW16 98 F2
Howard Ct SL8 3 A3
Howard Mews SL3 69 B8
Howard Rd
  Newbury RG14 105 A1
  Wokingham RG40 116 C5
Howard St 17 RG1 85 F7
Howards Gate SL2 22 C2
Howarth Rd SL6 40 A6
Howe La RG42 63 F2
Howell Cl Arborfield RG2 140 E8
  Bracknell RG42 91 C2
Howgate Dr RG8 34 C7
Howorth Ct RG12 118 E5
Howth Dr RG5 87 D7
Hoylake Cl SL1 41 E4
Hubbard Cl RG10 61 F2
Hubberholme RG12 118 A6
Hubert Rd SL3 43 D3
Huckleberry Cl RG8 57 C4
Huddington Glade GU46 149 A5
Hudson Rd Harlington UB7 71 D8
  Woodley RG5 87 F6
Hugh Fraser Dr RG31 84 C6
Hughenden Cl SL6 39 C6
Hughenden Rd SL1 42 D7
Hughes Rd Ashford TW15 98 C2
  Wokingham RG40 116 E7
Hull Cl SL1 42 C4
Humber Cl
  Thatcham RG18 106 B5
  Wokingham RG41 115 E7
Humber Way
  Sandhurst GU47 150 D8
  Slough SL3 44 A2
Hummer Rd TW20 96 A4
Humphrey's La RG17 47 C6
Humphries Yd RG12 118 C5
Hungerford Ave SL2 42 E8
Hungerford Cl GU47 150 C8
Hungerford Dr
  Maidenhead SL6 19 E3
  Reading RG1 85 E5
Hungerford Hill
  East Garston RG17 47 F1
  Lambourn RG17 25 A2
Hungerford La
  Kintbury RG17 101 E3
  Stanford Dingley RG7 81 F1
  Waltham St Lawrence RG10 62 E2
Hungerford Newtown RG17 74 A3
Hungerford Prim Sch RG17 100 D5
Hungerford Sta RG17 100 E5
Hungerford Trad Est RG17 100 C5
Hunsford Lodge SL4 67 A4
Hunstanton Cl SL3 69 C7
Hunt's La SL6 20 E3
Hunter Ct SL1 41 C8
Hunter's Ct RG5 87 E6
Hunter's Hill RG7 110 F3
Huntercombe Cl SL6 41 C7
Huntercombe La N SL6 41 C7
Huntercombe La S SL6 41 C6
Huntercombe Manor Hospl SL6 41 C6
Huntercombe Spur SL1 41 C6
Hunters Chase RG4 58 F5
Hunters Mdw RG17 48 A3
Hunters Mews SL4 67 C6
Hunters Way
  Shinfield RG7 113 B1

Hunters Way continued
Slough SL1 41 E4
Hunters Wharf 19 RG1 86 A6
Huntingdon Cl RG6 87 E2
Huntingdonshire Cl RG41 115 D6
Huntingfield Way TW20 96 D2
Huntington Pl SL3 44 B3
Huntley Ct RG1 86 E6
Huntley The RG30 85 D6
Hunts Cotts RG14 104 E6
Huntsgreen Ct RG12 118 C7
Huntsmans Mdw SL5 119 F8
Huntsmoor Rd RG26 135 A1
Huntswood La SL1,SL6 20 F4
Hurford Dr RG19 106 F3
Hurley Ct RG12 118 E5
Hurley High St SL6 17 F4
Hurley La SL6 18 B3
Hurricane Way
Slough SL3 44 B1
Woodley RG5 88 B8
Hursley Cl RG30 84 E7
Hurst Com Coll The RG26 134 D1
Hurst Gr KT12 125 F1
Hurst La TW20 123 A7
Hurst Park Rd RG10 61 E2
Hurst Rd Slough SL1 41 D8
Twyford RG10 61 E3
Hurst Way RG2 112 F8
Hurstdene Ave TW18 97 B2
Hurstfield Dr SL6 41 B7
Hurstwood SL5 120 A3
Hurworth Ave SL3 43 C3
Huscarle Way RG31 57 C4
Huson Rd RG42 91 C2
Hutsons Cl RG40 116 D8
Hutton Cl Earley RG6 87 A2
Newbury RG14 105 B4
Windlesham GU20 146 D3
Hyde Cl TW15 98 E2
Hyde End La
Brimpton RG7 133 D5
Shinfield RG7 113 C3
Hyde End Rd RG7 113 D2
Hyde Gn SL7 1 F1
Hyde La RG20 132 A1
Hyde Terr TW15 98 E2
Hydes The RG31 57 C4
Hyland Ho 5 SL8 3 B3
Hylle Cl SL4 66 E6
Hyperion Way RG2 86 B3
Hythe Cl RG12 118 E4
Hythe End Rd TW19 96 A5
Hythe Field Ave TW20 96 D2
Hythe Park Rd TW20 96 D2
Hythe Prim Sch TW18 96 D3
Hythe Rd TW18 96 D3
Hythe The TW18 96 E3

I

Ian Mikardo Way RG4 59 D2
Iberian Way GU15 152 B6
Ibotson Ct SL3 69 E6
Ibstock Cl RG30 85 B7
Ibstone Ave RG4 59 E5
Icarus Ct 5 RG1 86 D7
Icknield Cotts RG8 34 A6
Icknield Pl RG8 34 D8
Icknield Rd RG8 34 D8
Iden Ct RG14 105 B4
Iffley Ct 11 TW18 96 F3
Ilbury Cl RG2 113 E5
Ilchester Cl SL6 39 C5
Ilchester Ct 7 RG14 105 A2
Ilchester Mews RG4 59 E6
Ilex Cl
Englefield Green TW20 95 B1
Silchester RG26 135 E1
Yateley GU46 149 B6
Ilfracombe Way RG6 87 E3
Ilkley Rd RG4 58 E3
Ilkley Way RG19 106 C2
Illingworth SL4 66 E4
Illingworth Ave RG4 59 E6
Illingworth Gr RG12 118 F8
Ilsley Rd RG20 31 D4
Ilsleys' Prim Sch The RG20 30 E6
Imperial Ct
Henley-On-T RG9 15 E1
7 Newbury RG14 104 F2
Windsor SL4 67 A4
Imperial Ho GU25 122 E4
Imperial Rd
East Bedfont TW14 98 E8
Windsor SL4 67 A4
Imperial Way RG2 113 A7
Impstone Rd RG26 135 F1
In The Ray SL6 40 B8
Inchwood RG12 118 C1
India Rd SL1 43 B4
Ingle Dell GU15 151 D4
Ingle Glen RG40 142 A7
Ingleglen SL2 22 B7
Ingles Edge RG17 127 E4
Ingleside SL3 69 F6
Ingleton RG12 118 A6
Inglewood Ave GU15 152 D5
Inglewood Ct RG30 85 C6
Inglewood Rd RG17 101 E2
Ingoldsby Copse RG14 105 D5
Inhurst La RG26 134 C1
Inhurst Way RG26 134 F1
Inkerman Rd SL4 41 F2
Inkpen Cl RG30 85 A4
Inkpen Common Nature Reserve* RG17 128 A5
Inkpen Prim Sch RG17 127 D6
Inkpen Rd
Hungerford RG17 100 F3
Kintbury RG17 102 A1
Inner Ring E TW6 71 B4
Inner Ring W TW6 71 A4
Innings La
White Waltham SL6 63 D7
Winkfield RG12 118 E8
Inniscrown Ho SL3 68 B7
Institute Rd Marlow SL7 1 E1
Taplow SL6 40 F7
Instow Rd RG6 87 B2
Invergordon Cl RG31 84 E4
Inverness Way GU47 150 D7
Invicta Cl TW14 98 F7
Inwood Cl SL6 19 B6
Iona Cres SL1 41 E7
Ipswich Rd SL1 42 A7
Iris Ct RG30 84 E7
Irish Hill Rd RG17 102 B2
Irvine Ho SL4 66 E5
Irvine Pl GU25 122 E4
Irvine Way RG6 114 C8
Isaac Newton Rd RG2 115 A1
Isis Cl RG41 88 B1
Isis Ct 1 RG1 59 A1
Isis Way Bourne End SL8 3 B4
Sandhurst GU47 150 D8
Island Cl TW18 96 E4
Island Farm Rd RG7 110 D2
Island Rd RG2 85 F2
Island The TW19 96 A5
Islandstone La RG10 89 A6
Islet Park Dr SL6 20 C3
Islet Park Ho SL6 20 C3
Islet Pk SL6 20 C3
Islet Rd SL6 20 C3
Ivanhoe Rd RG40 141 A6
Iveagh Ct RG12 118 C4
Iver La SL0 44 F7
Iver Lodge SL0 44 F8
Iver Sta SL0 44 F4
Iver Village Inf Sch SL0 44 F7
Iver Village Jun Sch The SL0 44 E7
Iverdale Cl SL0 44 C6
Iverna Gdns TW14 71 D2
Ives Cl GU46 149 B7
Ives Rd SL3 44 A3
Ivy Cl SL6 65 A7
Ivy Cres SL1 41 F6
Ivy Dr GU18 153 A7
Ivybank RG31 57 C1
Ivydene Rd RG30 58 C1

J

Jack Price Ct 1 RG1 86 B5
Jack St RG14 105 A3
Jackson Cl RG12 118 B4
Jackson Ind Est SL8 3 B2
Jacksons La RG4 58 C5
Jacob Cl Bracknell RG42 117 D7
Windsor SL4 66 E6
Jacob Rd GU15 151 A7
Jakes Ho SL6 40 A8
James Butcher Dr RG7 83 F3
James Cl SL7 1 F4
James Ct RG30 85 D5
James Elliman Sch SL2 42 E6
James Rd GU15 151 B2
James St Reading RG1 85 F7
Windsor SL4 67 D6
James Watt Rd
Arborfield RG2 140 F7
Barkham RG2 141 A8
James Way GU15 151 B2
James's La RG7,RG30 111 E4
Jameston RG12 118 C1
Jamnagar Cl TW18 96 F2
Janson Ct RG1 85 F6
Japonica Cl RG41 115 D4
Jaques's La RG7 111 A6
Jardine Cotts SL2 23 A8
Jarratt Ho SL4 67 B4
Jarry Ct SL7 1 F3
Jarvis Dr RG10 61 D6
Jasmin Way RG19 133 B6
Jasmine Cl RG41 115 D7
Jay Cl RG6 87 B1
Jays Ct SL5 120 D5
Jays Nest Cl GU17 150 D4
Jayworth Ho RG1 86 E8
Jealott's Hill RG42 91 B7
Jedburgh Cl RG19 106 F3
Jefferson Cl
Caversham RG4 59 C7
Slough SL3 44 A2
Jeffries Ct SL8 3 B2
Jellicoe Cl SL1 42 B4
Jenkins Cl RG30 85 C6
Jenkins' Hill London Rd GU19 145 D2
Jenner Wlk RG31 84 A7
Jennery La SL1 21 C2
Jennetts Cl RG7 81 E3
Jennings Field HP10 3 C7
Jennings Wharf SL4 67 D7
Jenny's Wlk GU46 149 E6
Jerome Cl SL7 1 F4
Jerome Cnr RG45 143 C3
Jerome Rd RG5 87 E6
Jerrymoor Hill RG40 141 F8
Jesmond Dene RG14 104 F4
Jesse Cl GU46 149 F5
Jesse Terr RG1 85 F7
Jessiman Terr TW17 125 A4
Jesus Hospl SL6 40 C3
Jevington RG12 118 C1
Jig's La N RG42 91 E2
Jig's La S Bracknell RG42 91 E1
Winkfield RG42 118 E8
Job's La SL6 19 B8
Jock's La RG42 90 F1
Joel Cl RG6 87 A3
Johannes Ct 5 RG30 85 D6
John Balliol Ct 14 RG1 86 D7
John Boys Ho RG14 130 C6
John Childs Cl RG14 105 A1
John F Kennedy Meml* TW20 95 D6
John Hunt Cl RG19 106 E2
John Kaye Ct TW17 125 A4
John Kimber's Almshouses 1 RG14 104 F2
John Nike Way RG12 117 C7
John Norgate Ho RG14 105 E3
John O'Gaunt Com Tech Coll RG17 100 D3
John Rankin Inf Sch RG14 130 D8
John Rankin Jun Sch RG14 130 D8
John Taylor Ct SL1 42 C5
Johns Cl TW15 98 C4
Johnson Dr RG40 142 B7
Johnsons La RG18 106 C8
Jonathan Ct SL6 39 E7
Jonathan Hill RG20 131 B3
Jones Cnr SL5 119 E7
Jordan Cl Caversham RG4 59 E5
Shinfield RG7 113 D1
Jordan's La RG7 110 F2
Jordans Cl TW19 97 C8
Joseph Ct RG42 91 E2
Josephine Ct RG30 85 E6
Jouldings La RG7 140 D4
Jourdelay's Pas SL4 67 D8
Journeys End SL2 42 E8
Joviel Ho TW18 97 A1
Jubilee Ave
North Ascot SL5 119 E8
Wokingham RG41 116 B7
Jubilee Cl
North Ascot SL5 119 E8
Silchester RG26 135 E1
Stanwell TW19 97 C8
Woodley RG5 87 E6
Jubilee Ct
Bracknell RG12 118 C6
9 Staines TW18 97 A4
Thatcham RG19 106 A3
Jubilee Rd
Finchampstead RG40 141 F3
Littlewick Green SL6 38 B5
Newbury RG14 105 B2
Reading RG6 87 A6
Jubilee Sq RG1 86 B6
Jubilee Way Datchet SL3 68 C7
East Bedfont TW14 98 F7
Juliet Gdns RG42 118 F8
Julius Hill RG42 118 F8
Julkes La RG2 114 E7
Junction Rd
Ashford TW15 98 D3
Lightwater GU18 146 B1
Reading RG1 86 E6
Junction Terr RG14 105 C2
Juniper RG12 118 C1
Juniper Ct SL1 43 A4
Juniper Dr SL6 40 B8
Juniper Gdns TW16 98 F2
Juniper Hill Sch HP10 3 B7
Juniper La HP10 3 D7
Juniper Pl RG19 133 B6
Juniper Rd SL7 1 D5
Juniper Way RG31 57 D2
Junipers The RG41 115 D4
Jupiter Ho RG7 134 E2
Jupiter Way RG41 115 F6
Justice Cl RG19 106 F2
Jutland Cl RG41 115 E6
Jutland Ho SL4 66 F5
Jutland Pl TW20 96 C3

K

Katesgrove La RG1 86 A6
Katesgrove Prim Sch RG1 86 A6
Katherine Ct 2 GU15 151 D5
Kathleen Sanders Ct RG7 83 E4
Kaynes Pk SL5 119 E8
Kaywood Cl SL3 43 C3
Keane Cl RG5 87 E8
Kearsley Rd RG30 85 C6
Keates Gn RG42 118 B8
Keats Cl RG5 87 E4
Keats La SL4 67 C8
Keats Rd RG5 87 E4
Keats Way
Crowthorne RG45 143 B6
Yateley GU46 149 B4
Keble Rd SL6 39 E8
Keble Way GU47 143 E2
Keeble Ho RG41 116 A6
Keel Dr SL1 42 C4
Keeler Cl SL4 66 E4
Keep Hatch Prim Sch RG40 116 D7
Keepers Combe RG12 118 D3
Keepers Farm Cl SL4 66 E5
Keepers Terr GU25 122 B4
Keepers Wlk GU25 122 D4
Keephatch Ho RG40 116 F7
Keephatch Rd RG40 116 E7
Keighley Cl RG19 106 C2
Kelburne Cl RG41 88 C3
Keldholme RG12 118 A6
Kelly Cl TW17 125 E7
Kelmscott Cl RG4 58 F3
Kelpatrick Rd SL1 41 D7
Kelsall Pl SL5 120 B2
Kelsey Ave RG40 141 E6
Kelsey Cl SL6 39 D3
Kelsey Gr GU46 149 E5
Kelso Mews RG4 59 E6
Kelton Cl RG6 87 E2
Kelvedon Way RG4 58 E5
Kelvin Cl RG2 140 E7
Kelvin Rd RG14 105 B4
Kemble Ct RG31 84 D4
Kemerton Cl RG31 84 D4
Kemp Ct GU19 145 F2
Kempe Cl SL3 44 C2
Kempton Cl RG14 105 C1
Kemsley Chase SL2 22 C4
Kenavon Dr RG1 86 C8
Kendal Ave
Caversham RG4 59 E5
Shinfield RG2 113 E6
Kendal Cl
East Bedfont TW14 98 F7
Slough SL2 43 A6
Thatcham RG18 106 C4
Kendal Dr SL2 43 A6
Kendal Gr GU15 152 D4
Kendall Ct Bsns Pk GU15 150 F4
Kendrick Cl RG40 116 C5
Kendrick Ct 5 RG1 86 C6
Kendrick Girls' Gram Sch RG1 86 C7
Kendrick Rd
Newbury RG14 130 D5
Reading RG1 86 C6
Slough SL3 43 B3
Kenilworth Ave
Bracknell RG12 118 D8
Reading RG30 85 D5
Kenilworth Cl SL1 42 F3
Kenilworth Gdns TW18 97 C3
Kenilworth Rd TW15 97 D5
Kenneally SL4 66 C5
Kenneally Cl 11 SL4 66 C5
Kenneally Pl 12 SL4 66 C5
Kenneally Row 13 SL4 66 C5
Kenneally Wlk 10 SL4 66 C5
Kennedy Cl
Farnham Common SL2 22 C6
Maidenhead SL6 39 C6
Marlow SL7 1 E3
Newbury RG14 130 D6
Kennedy Ct TW15 98 C3
Kennedy Dr RG8 56 E5
Kennedy Gdns RG6 87 B3
Kennedy Ho SL1 41 D5
Kennedy Mdw RG17 100 C4
Kennel Ave SL5 119 F8
Kennel Cl SL5 92 F2
Kennel Gn SL5 119 E8
Kennel La Bracknell RG42 91 B1
Cookham Dean SL6 19 C7
Windlesham GU20 146 C5
Kennel Lane Sch RG42 91 B2
Kennel Ride SL5 92 F1
Kennel Wood SL5 119 F8
Kennet & Avon Canal Visitor Ctr* RG7 109 C3
Kennet Cl RG19 106 E3
Kennet Cotts RG30 85 A1
Kennet Ct
Hungerford RG17 100 E7
1 Newbury RG14 105 A1
Wokingham RG41 115 F6
Kennet Ctr The RG14 105 A2
Kennet Ent Ctr RG17 100 D7
Kennet Pl
Burghfield Common RG7 111 B3
Chilton Foliat RG17 73 A1
10 Newbury RG14 105 B4
Kennet Rd Bourne End SL8 3 B4
Kintbury RG17 102 B2
Maidenhead SL6 39 F8
Newbury RG14 104 F2
Kennet Sch RG19 106 E3
Kennet Side
Newbury RG14 105 C3
13 Reading RG1 86 C7
Kennet St RG1 86 C7
Kennet Valley Prim Sch RG31 84 F4
Kennet Way RG17 100 D7
Kennet Weir Bsns Pk RG7 83 F2
Kennet Wlk RG1 86 D8
Kennett Rd SL3 44 B3
Kensington Cl RG6 87 B1
Kensington Rd RG30 85 D7
Kent Ave SL1 42 C8
Kent Cl Staines TW18 97 D2
Wokingham RG41 115 D5
Kent Cotts RG7 139 C3
Kent Folly RG42 91 F2
Kent Lodge 6 SL6 39 F6
Kent Rd Reading RG30 85 D7
Windlesham GU20 146 D5
Kent Way SL6 19 E1
Kentigern Dr RG45 143 E5
Kenton Cl
Bracknell RG12 118 D7
Frimley GU16 151 F1
Marlow SL7 1 E2
Kenton Rd RG6 87 C4
Kenton's La RG10 36 D7
Kentons La SL4 66 F5
Kentwood Cl RG30 57 E1
Kentwood Farm RG40 116 D8
Kentwood Hill RG31 57 E1
Kenwood Cl
Harmondsworth UB7 71 A8
Maidenhead SL6 39 A7
Kenworth Gr GU18 146 A1
Keppel Spur SL4 95 B8
Keppel St SL4 67 D5
Kepple Pl GU19 145 F3
Kernham Dr RG31 57 C4
Kerria Way GU24 153 F6
Kerris Way RG6 87 B1
Kersey Cres RG14 104 E5
Kesteven Way RG41 115 E6
Keston Cl RG4 59 C2
Kestrel Ave TW18 96 F5
Kestrel Cl RG19 106 B3
Kestrel Path SL2 21 E1
Kestrel Way
Burghfield Common RG7 111 B3
Reading RG30 85 A4
Wokingham RG41 115 F5
Keswick Ave TW17 125 E6
Keswick Cl Frimley GU15 152 D4
Reading RG30 84 D7
Keswick Ct SL2 42 F6
Keswick Dr GU18 153 B8
Keswick Gdns RG5 87 E5
Keswick Rd TW20 96 B1
Ketcher Gn RG42 90 C4
Kettering Cl RG31 84 E4
Kevins Dr GU46 149 E7
Kew Cotts RG14 104 E1
Kew Gdns SN8 126 A3
Keynsham Way GU47 143 D2
Keys Pl SL6 39 F6
Kibble Gn RG12 118 C3
Kibblewhite Cres RG10 61 D6
Kidderminster Rd SL2 22 A2
Kidmore End Rd RG4 59 B7
Kidmore Rd RG4 58 F5
Kidwells Cl SL6 39 F8
Kidwells Park Dr SL6 39 F7
Kielder Wlk GU15 152 C4
Kier Pk SL5 120 C6
Kilburn Cl RG31 84 D4
Kildare Gdns RG4 59 C3
Killarney Dr SL6 39 E7
Killigrew Ho 4 TW16 98 E1
Kilmartin Gdns GU16 151 F1
Kilmington Cl RG12 118 E2
Kilmiston Ave TW17 125 C3
Kilmiston Ho TW17 125 C3
Kilmore Dr GU15 152 B4
Kilmuir Cl GU47 150 D7
Kiln Cl Harlington UB3 71 D8
Hermitage RG18 79 C7
Kiln Croft Cl SL7 2 A3
Kiln Dr RG18 78 E5
Kiln Hill RG7 140 B7
Kiln La Bracknell RG12 118 A7
Mortimer RG7 137 C5
Reading RG31 84 B8
Shiplake RG9 35 C2
Sunningdale SL5 121 A4
Winkfield SL4 93 B2
Wooburn SL8,HP10 3 D3
Kiln Pl SL6 19 A3
Kiln Rd Caversham RG4 59 D8
Newbury RG14 105 C5
Kiln Ride
Upper Basildon RG8 54 F5
Wokingham RG40 142 A8
Kiln Ride Extension RG40 142 A6
Kiln Terr RG18 78 E5
Kiln View Rd RG2 86 D2
Kilnsea Dr RG6 87 D1
Kilnside RG12 91 D1
Kilowna Cl RG10 61 A4
Kilross Rd TW14 98 E7
Kimber Cl SL4 67 A4
Kimber's Cl RG14 104 F3
Kimber's La SL6 39 E3
Kimberley RG12 118 C1
Kimberley Cl
1 Reading RG1 85 E5
Slough SL3 43 F2
Kimbers Dr Burnham SL1 21 D2
Newbury RG14 104 C5
Kimmeridge RG12 118 E3
Kimpton Cl RG6 113 E8
Kinburn Dr TW20 95 E3
King Acre Ct TW18 96 E5
King Edward Ct 4 SL4 67 D6
King Edward St SL1 42 D4
King Edward VII Ave SL4, SL3 67 E8
King Edward VII Hospl SL4 67 C4
King Edwards Cl SL5 119 E8
King Edwards Rd SL5 119 E8
King Edwards Rise SL5 119 E8
King George Cl TW16 98 E3
King James Way RG9 35 C8
King John's Cl TW19 68 C1

King John's Pal SL3 69 D6
King St Chertsey KT16 124 A1
Maidenhead SL6 39 F6
Mortimer RG7 137 A6
Reading RG1 86 B7
King Stable St SL4 67 D7
King Street La RG41 88 C1
King's Ave TW16 98 F2
King's Cl TW18 97 D1
King's Court Fst Sch SL4 95 B8
King's Keep GU47 143 B1
King's Meadow Rd RG1 86 B8
King's Oak Ct 5 RG1 86 C7
King's Rd Ascot SL5 120 D4
Caversham RG4 59 C2
Crowthorne RG45 143 C5
Egham TW20 96 A4
Henley-On-T RG9 15 D2
Reading RG1 86 D7
Slough SL1 42 E3
King's Ride Bracknell SL5 119 D5
Camberley GU15 151 D7
King's Ride Ho SL5 119 E5
King's Road Ho 2 SL4 67 D5
King's Terr SL3 69 B8
King's Wlk GU15 150 F6
King's Yd SL5 119 E5
Kingfisher Cl RG7 109 B3
Kingfisher Court Ind Est RG14 105 D3
Kingfisher Ct Slough SL2 22 B1
Twyford RG10 61 E3
Kingfisher Dr
Staines TW18 96 F4
Woodley RG5 87 C6
Yateley GU46 149 B6
Kingfisher Gr RG7 113 A3
Kingfisher Ho SL7 1 F2
Kingfisher Par GU17 150 B5
Kingfisher Pl RG1 86 B8
Kinghorn La SL6 19 D3
Kinghorn Pk SL6 19 D3
Kings Apartments GU15 151 C4
Kings Cl RG9 15 D2
Kings Common Cl RG9 35 B1
Kings Cres GU15 151 C8
Kings Gr SL6 39 E6
Kings Grove Ind Est SL6 39 E6
Kings International Coll for Bsns & Fine Arts GU15 151 C2
Kings La
Cookham Dean SL6 19 B8
Englefield Green TW20 95 A2
Windlesham GU20 146 E5
Kings Mead RG14 130 C5
Kings Rd Newbury RG14 105 B2
Silchester RG7 136 B2
West End GU24 153 F5
Windsor SL4 67 D5
Kings Rd W RG14 105 A2
Kings Reach Ct 7 RG1 86 B7
Kings Ride Pk SL5 119 C4
Kings Wlk
Henley-On-T RG9 15 D2
4 Maidenhead SL6 39 F7
Reading RG1 86 B7
Kings Wood SL7 17 D7
Kingsbridge Cotts RG40 142 E7
Kingsbridge Hill RG7 139 A6
Kingsbridge Rd
Newbury RG14 104 E1
Reading RG2 86 C2
Kingsbury Cres TW18 96 D4
Kingsbury Dr SL4 95 A8
Kingsclear Pk GU15 151 D4
Kingscroft Jun Sch TW18 97 A2
Kingscroft La RG42 92 A6
Kingsdown Cl RG6 87 B2
Kingsfield SL4 66 D6
Kingsford Cl RG5 88 A5
Kingsgate Pl 7 RG1 86 D7
Kingsgate St RG1 86 D7
Kingsland Ctr RG19 106 D3
Kingsland Grange RG14 130 E8
Kingsley Ave
Camberley GU15 151 D3
Englefield Green TW20 95 B2
Kingsley Cl Charvil RG10 61 A5
Crowthorne RG45 143 B3
Newbury RG14 105 B5
Reading RG2 113 B7
Kingsley Dr SL7 1 C6
Kingsley Path SL2 21 D1
Kingsmead Ho SL1 42 C5
Kingsmere Rd RG42 117 F8
Kingston Ave TW14 71 F1
Kingston Cres TW15 97 D2
Kingston Gdns RG2 86 C2
Kingston La RG7 110 D6
Kingston Rd Ashford TW15 97 F2
Camberley GU15 145 A1
Staines TW15,TW18 97 B2
Kingsway
Blackwater GU17 150 E5
Caversham RG4 59 E6
Farnham Common SL2 22 C6
Stanwell TW19 97 E7
Kingswick Cl SL5 120 D5
Kingswick Dr SL5 120 D5
Kingswood Cl TW20 95 D4
Kingswood Creek TW19 68 D2
Kingswood Ct
Maidenhead SL6 39 F5
Kingswood Ct continued
17 Reading RG30 85 D6
Kingswood Hall of Residence TW20 95 D4
Kingswood Ho SL1 42 C8
Kingswood Par SL7 1 D5
Kingswood Rise TW20 95 D4
Kinnaird Cl SL1 41 C7
Kinross Ave SL5 119 F4
Kinross Cl TW16 98 F3
Kinross Ct SL5 119 F4
Kinross Dr TW16 98 F3
Kinson Rd RG30 58 A1
Kintbury Mill RG17 102 B3
Kintbury Rd RG17 127 F6
Kintbury Sq RG17 102 A2
Kintbury Sta RG17 102 B3
Kinver Wlk 6 RG1 86 B5
Kipling Cl
Thatcham RG18 106 C5
Woodley RG5 87 E4
Yateley GU46 149 C4
Kipling Ct SL4 67 B5
Kirkby Ct GU16 151 E1
Kirkfell Cl RG31 57 C2
Kirkham Cl
Caversham RG4 59 E6
Sandhurst GU47 143 D2
Kirkstall Ct RG31 84 D4
Kirkstone Cl GU15 152 D4
Kirkwall Spur SL1 42 E8
Kirkwood Cres RG7 110 F3
Kirton Cl RG30 85 B7
Kirtons Farm Rd RG30 85 C1
Kittiwake Cl RG5 88 B7
Kitwood Dr RG6 87 E1
Klondyke SL7 1 D2
Knapp Rd TW15 97 F4
Knapp The RG6 87 B4
Knappe Cl RG9 35 C8
Knight's Pl 9 SL4 67 C5
Knighton Cl RG4 59 A3
Knights Cl Egham TW20 96 D2
Windsor SL4 66 D6
Knights La RG20 129 C3
Knights Lea RG20 129 B3
Knights Way
Caversham RG4 59 B5
Frimley GU15 152 C4
Knightsbridge Cres TW18 97 B2
Knightsbridge Ct 7 SL3 44 A2
Knightsbridge Dr RG19 132 B3
Knightsbridge Rd GU15 151 E7
Knightswood RG12 118 B1
Knock The GU47 150 D7
Knole Wood SL5 120 E1
Knoll Cl OX12 6 E7
Knoll Park Rd KT16 123 F1
Knoll Rd GU15 151 D6
Knoll The RG31 57 B2
Knollmead RG31 84 D4
Knollys Rd RG26 135 F1
Knolton Way SL2 43 C7
Knossington Cl RG6 87 C2
Knott La RG7 109 B4
Knowl Hill CE Prim Sch RG10 37 F4
Knowl Hill Comm RG10 37 E3
Knowl Hill Terr RG10 37 E4
Knowle Cl RG4 58 D4
Knowle Gn TW18 97 A3
Knowle Gr GU25 122 C2
Knowle Grove Cl GU25 122 C2
Knowle Hill GU25 122 C2
Knowle Park Ave TW18 97 B3
Knowle Park Inf Sch TW18 97 A3
Knowle Rd RG5 87 E4
Knowles Ave RG45 142 F5
Knowsley Cl SL6 19 A1
Knowsley Rd RG31 57 C3
Knox Gn RG42 90 C3
Kola Ho SL2 43 B6
Korda Cl TW17 124 F6
Krooner Rd GU15 151 B3
Kybes La RG7 112 D5
Kyftle Court Flat 11 RG14 104 F2
Kyle Cl RG12 118 B6

L

La Roche Cl SL3 43 C3
Laburnham Rd SL6 39 E6
Laburnum Cl SL7 1 E4
Laburnum Ct KT16 124 A1
Laburnum Gdns RG2 86 E1
Laburnum Gr
Brands Hill SL3 69 B8
Newbury RG14 105 A4
Laburnum Pl TW20 95 B2
Laburnum Rd
Chertsey KT16 124 A1
Winnersh RG41 88 C1
Laburnum Rise RG19 133 B5
Laburnum Way TW19 97 F7
Laburnums The GU17 150 B5
Lacewood Gdns RG2 86 E1
Lacey Cl TW20 96 D1
Ladbroke Cl RG5 87 F6
Ladbrooke Rd SL1 42 D3
Ladwell Cl RG14 130 D5
Lady Jane Ct RG4 59 C3
Lady Margaret Rd SL5 120 F2
Ladybank RG12 118 B1
Ladyday Pl SL1 42 C5
Ladymask Cl RG31 84 F4
Laffords The RG7 82 A2
Laggan Rd SL6 19 F1
Laggan Sq SL6 19 F1
Laird Ct GU19 145 E1
Lake Ave SL1 42 D6
Lake End Ct SL6 41 A7
Lake End Rd SL4,SL6 41 B5
Lake End Way RG45 143 A4
Lake Rd GU25 122 B5
Lake Side The GU17 150 D4
Lake View SL6 20 A1
Lakeland Dr GU16 151 E1
Lakes The SL7 18 A6
Lakeside Earley RG6 87 B3
Maidenhead SL6 20 B1
Lakeside Bsns Pk GU47 150 A7
Lakeside Dr SL2 22 F4
Lakeside Est SL3 70 A8
Lakeside Pk KT16 124 C1
Lakeside Prim Sch GU16 151 F1
Lakeside Rd SL3 69 F7
Lakeview SL5 119 D6
Lalande Cl RG41 115 E6
Laleham Abbey TW18 124 C5
Laleham CE Prim Sch TW18 124 C7
Laleham Ho TW18 124 C5
Laleham Rd
Littleton TW17 125 A4
Staines TW18 96 F2
Laleham Reach KT16 124 A6
Lamb Cl RG18 106 C5
Lambdens Hill RG7 109 D7
Lambert Ave SL3 43 E3
Lambert Cres GU17 150 C4
Lambeth Ct RG30 84 F7
Lambfields RG7 83 D3
Lambly Hill GU25 122 E6
Lamborne Cl GU47 143 A1
Lambourn CE Prim Sch RG17 25 B1
Lambourn Ct RG14 105 B4
Lambourn Pl RG17 25 B3
Lambourn Rd RG20 104 C6
Lambourne Cl RG31 84 D8
Lambourne Ct SL6 40 C7
Lambourne Ct Cvn Site RG17 25 B2
Lambourne Dr
Bagshot GU19 145 D2
Maidenhead SL6 39 C3
Lambourne Gdns RG6 87 D4
Lambourne Gr RG12 118 E7
Lambridge La RG9 15 C3
Lambridge Wood Rd RG9 15 B4
Lambrook Haileybury Sch RG42 92 A3
Lambs Farm Bsns Pk RG7 139 B8
Lambs La RG7 139 A7
Lambs Lane Prim Sch RG7 139 A8
Lambswood Ind Est RG7 112 C1
Lambton Ho SL4 67 A4
Lambwood Hill RG7 112 D1
Lamden Way RG7 111 B3
Lamerton Rd RG2 86 C1
Lamesley Ho SL6 39 E6
Lammas Ave 4 SL4 67 D5
Lammas Cl TW18 96 E5
Lammas Ct Staines TW19 96 D5
Windsor SL4 67 C5
Lammas Dr TW18 96 D4
Lammas Mead RG42 90 E1
Lammas Rd SL1 41 D8
Lamorna Cres RG31 57 C1
Lamp Acres RG14 105 B5
Lamplighters Wlk RG31 84 F4
Lanark Cl Frimley GU16 151 E2
Woodley RG5 88 A6
Lancashire Hill RG42 91 F2
Lancaster Ave SL2 22 C1
Lancaster Cl
Ashford TW15 97 E4
Englefield Green TW20 95 D3
Hungerford RG17 100 C4
2 Reading RG1 86 C5
Stanwell TW19 70 E1
Thatcham RG18 106 C4
Lancaster Ct Reading RG2 86 E1
Stanwell TW19 97 E7
Lancaster Dr GU15 151 D6
Lancaster Gdns RG6 87 B3
Lancaster Ho RG12 118 B4
Lancaster Rd SL6 39 B8
Lancaster Sq RG17 100 D4
Lancastria Mews SL6 39 D7
Lancelot Cl SL1 42 A4
Lanchester Dr RG45 143 C7
Lancing Cl RG30 85 D7
Lancing Rd TW13 98 F6
Landen Ct RG40 116 B4
Landon Way TW15 98 B2
Landrake Cres RG2 86 C1
Landseer Cl GU47 150 E6
Landsend La RG10 61 B2
Lane End Cl RG2 113 E6
Lane The Chertsey KT16 124 A6
Chilton OX11 10 E8
Thorpe GU25 122 E6
Laneswood RG7 136 E5
Lang Ho TW15 97 E7
Langborough Rd RG40 116 C5
Langdale Cl SL6 40 A6
Langdale Dr SL5 119 E7
Langdale Gdns RG6 86 F2
Langdon Cl GU15 152 C4
Langford Cl RG4 59 C5
Langham Pl TW20 95 F3
Langhams Way RG10 36 E2
Langley Broom SL3 43 F1
Langley Bsns Ct RG20 51 C5
Langley Bsns Ctr SL3 44 A4
Langley Bsns Pk SL3 44 A4
Langley Cnr SL3 23 F6
Langley Common Rd RG2,RG40 114 F1
Langley Cres UB3 71 F7
Langley Dr GU15 151 D6
Langley Farm Cotts RG20 51 E6
Langley Gram Sch SL3 43 F2
Langley Hill RG31 84 C5
Langley Hill Cl RG31 84 C6
Langley Manor Sch SL3 43 E5
Langley Park Rd SL0 44 C6
Langley Rd Slough SL3 43 E3
Staines TW18 96 F2
Langley Sta SL3 44 A4
Langley Way SL7 1 C2
Langleywood Sch SL3 43 E3
Langton Cl SL1 41 D5
Langton Way TW20 96 C2
Langton's Mdw SL2 22 C6
Langworthy End SL6 65 B8
Langworthy La SL6 65 A8
Laniver Cl RG6 87 B1
Lansdowne Ave SL1 42 E5
Lansdowne Ct SL1 42 E5
Lansdowne Gdns RG7 113 C1
Lansdowne Rd
Reading RG30 84 C7
Staines TW18 97 B1
Lanterns Wlk SL6 40 B7
Lapwing Cl RG31 84 C6
Larbert Cotts SL6 38 B5
Larch Ave Ascot SL5 120 E4
Wokingham RG41 116 A7
Larch Cl
Burghfield Common RG30 111 B4
Camberley GU15 151 E8
Newbury RG14 104 D5
Slough SL2 42 B8
Larch Ct RG4 59 B3
Larch Dr Brimpton RG19 133 B6
Woodley RG5 87 E5
Larches The RG42 92 A1
Larches Way GU17 150 B5
Larchfield Prim Sch SL6 39 E4
Larchfield Rd SL6 39 E5
Larchmoor Pk SL2 23 A7
Larchside Cl RG7 113 B2
Larchwood 6 RG12 118 F5
Larchwood Dr TW20 95 B2
Larchwood Glade GU15 152 A7
Lardon Cotts RG8 34 A6
Larges Bridge Dr RG12 118 D6
Larges La RG12 118 C7
Larissa Cl RG31 57 E1
Lark Ave TW18 96 F5
Larkes-Meade RG6 87 A1
Larkfield SL6 40 B1
Larkham Cl TW13 98 E5
Larkings La SL2 23 B4
Larksfield TW20 95 C1
Larkspur Cl RG41 115 D7
Larkspur Gdns RG18 106 F4
Larkswood Cl
Reading RG31 57 D3
Sandhurst GU47 143 A1
Larkswood Dr RG45 143 B5
Lascelles Ho 3 SL1 43 A4
Lascelles Rd SL3 43 B3
Lashbrook Mead RG9 36 B3
Lashbrook Rd RG9 36 B4
Lassell Gdns SL6 40 B7
Lasswade Ct KT16 123 F2
Lasswade Rd KT16 123 F2
Lastingham Ct TW18 97 A2
Latham Ave GU16 151 E2
Latimer RG12 118 B1
Latimer Dr RG31 84 C4
Latimer Rd RG41 116 B5
Latton Cl OX11 10 E8
Laud Cl Newbury RG14 105 D5
Reading RG2 86 A6
Laud Way RG40 116 E6
Laud's Cl RG9 15 C1
Lauder Cl GU16 151 E2
Lauderdale Ho 12 TW18 96 F3
Launceston Ave RG4 59 E6
Launcestone Cl RG6 87 B2
Laundry Ct 4 RG14 105 B2
Laundry La GU47 150 E5
Lauradale RG12 118 A5
Laurel Ave
Brimpton RG19 133 A5
Englefield Green TW20 95 B3
Slough SL3 43 E4
Laurel Cl
Camberley GU15 151 D4
Poyle SL3 69 E7
Wokingham RG41 115 F5
Laurel Ct 7 RG12 118 F5
Laurel Dr RG31 84 B8
Laurel Terr GU47 142 F1
Laurels The
Hungerford RG17 100 E7
Pangbourne RG8 56 D5
Laurence Allison Mews RG4 58 E2
Laurence Ct 1 SL7 1 D2
Lauser Rd TW19 97 C8
Lautree Gdns SL6 19 E7
Lavender Pk SL5 119 C6
Lavender Row SL5 92 E1
Lavenham Dr RG5 87 F8
Lawford Cres GU46 149 D6
Lawkland SL2 22 C2
Lawn Cl SL3 68 C7
Lawn The SL3 68 C6
Lawns The
North Ascot SL5 119 D6
Reading RG2 86 D3
Lawrence Cl RG40 116 D6
Lawrence Cres GU20 146 D4
Lawrence Ct SL4 67 C5
Lawrence Ctr RG41 116 A4
Lawrence Gr RG42 117 D8
Lawrence Lodge GU15 151 D7
Lawrence Mead RG17 102 B2
Lawrence Pl RG14 105 C5
Lawrence Rd RG30 85 A8
Lawrence Way
Camberley GU15 150 F4
Slough SL1 41 D8
Lawrences La RG18 106 D6
Lawrences Way RG18 106 D5
Lawson Dr RG4 58 E5
Lawson La OX11 10 E8
Lawson Rd RG9 35 F7
Lawson Way SL5 121 B3
Laxton Gn SL6 39 C3
Layburn Cres SL3 69 B8
Layland's Gn RG17 102 B1
Laylands Gn RG17 102 B1
Layleys Gn RG18 78 F4
Laytom Rise RG31 57 C3
Layton's La TW16 125 F7
Lazare Ct 7 TW18 96 F3
Le Marchant Rd GU15, GU16 151 F3
Lea Cl Marlow Bottom SL7 1 D6
Reading RG30 85 A3
Lea Croft RG45 143 B6
Lea Inf Sch SL2 43 B6
Lea Jun Sch SL2 43 B6
Lea Rd GU15 151 B2
Lea The Thorpe Lea TW20 96 C1
Wokingham RG40 141 F8
Leacroft Staines TW18 97 B4
Sunningdale SL5 121 A4
Leacroft Cl TW18 97 B4
Leacroft Rd SL0 44 E7
Leafield Copse RG12 118 F5
Leaholme Gdns SL1 41 D8
Leander Pl RG31 84 D4
Leas Dr SL0 44 E7
Leaver Rd RG9 15 C1
Leaves Gn RG12 118 D3
Ledbury Cl RG30 58 C1
Ledbury Dr RG31 84 D4
Ledger La SL6 65 D5
Ledger's Rd SL1 42 D4
Ledran Cl Earley RG6 87 C1
Lower Earley RG6 114 C8
Lee Ct RG5 87 E7
Lee La SL6 18 E2
Leeds Rd SL1 42 E6
Lees Cl SL6 39 B5
Lees Gdns SL6 39 B5
Lees Wlk SL7 1 C2
Leeson Gdns SL4 41 E2
Legoland Windsor* SL4 66 D2
Leicester RG12 118 E2
Leicester Cl RG9 15 D3
Leigh Field RG7 136 F6
Leigh Pk SL3 68 B7
Leigh Rd SL1 42 B6
Leigh Sq SL4 66 D5
Leighton Ct RG2 86 E3
Leighton Gdns SL6 20 B1
Leighton Ho 5 SL7 1 E2
Leighton Park Sch RG2 86 E4
Leiston Cl 3 RG6 87 D1
Leiston Spur SL1 42 E7
Leith Cl Crowthorne RG45 143 A7
Slough SL1 43 A5
Lemart Cl RG30 84 E8
Lemington Gr RG12 118 B3
Leney Cl RG40 116 D8
Lenham Cl RG41 88 E1
Lennox Cl RG31 84 B4
Lennox Rd RG6 87 A5
Lent Gn SL1 21 B1
Lent Green La SL1 21 B1
Lent Rise Comb Sch SL1 41 B8
Lent Rise Rd SL1 21 B1
Leonard Ct RG7 83 E3
Leonardslee Cres RG14 105 D4
Leopold Mall 6 SL1 42 F4
Leopold Wlk RG1 86 D7
Leppington RG12 118 B2
Lerwick Dr SL1 42 E8
Lesford Rd RG1 85 E5
Lesley Ct 16 RG30 85 D6
Leslie Southern Ct RG14 105 B4
Lesters Rd SL6 19 D6
Letchworth Ave TW14 98 F8
Letcombe Ct 4 RG1 86 B6
Letcombe Sq RG12 118 F5
Letcombe St RG1 86 B7
Leverkusen Rd RG12 118 B6
Leverton La RG17 73 B1
Lewendon Rd RG14 104 E5
Lewes Ct SL1 42 C4
Lewington Mews RG17 100 D4
Lewins Farm Ct SL1 41 F6
Lewins Way SL1 41 F6
Lewis Wlk RG14 130 C6
Lewisham Way GU47 143 D2

Lexington Ave SL6 . . . . . .39 D5
Lexington Gr RG2 . . . . . .113 C6
Leyburn Cl RG5 . . . . .88 A8
Leycester Cl GU20 . . . . .146 B6
Leyland Gdns RG2 . . . . .113 E6
Leylands La TW19 . . . . . . .70 A2
Leys Gdns RG14 . . . . .104 F4
Leyside RG45 . . . . .143 A5
Libra Ho HP10 . . . . .3 A8
Library Par RG5 . . . . .87 E7
Licensed Victuallers Sch SL5 . . . . .119 C7
Lichfield Cl 1 RG6 . . . . . .87 C1
Lichfields RG12 . . . . .118 E7
Liddel Way SL5 . . . . .119 F5
Liddell SL4 . . . . .66 C4
Liddell Cl RG40 . . . . .141 E3
Liddell Pl SL4 . . . . .66 C4
Liddell Sq 14 SL4 . . . . . . .66 C5
Liddell Way SL4 . . . . .66 C4
Lido Rd OX11 . . . . .9 F8
Lidstone Cl RG6 . . . . . . .114 D8
Liebenrood Rd RG30 . . . .85 C6
Lightlands La SL6 . . . . . . .19 F5
Lightwater Ctry Pk GU18 . . . . .145 F1
Lightwater Mdw GU18 . .153 B8
Lightwater Rd GU18 . . . .153 C8
Lightwater Village Sch GU18 . . . . .146 A1
Lightwood RG12 . . . . . . .118 D3
Liguel Cl RG17 . . . . .100 D4
Lilac Cl RG8 . . . . .57 C5
Lilac Ct SL2 . . . . .21 F2
Lilac Wlk Brimpton RG19 .133 B5
Reading RG31 . . . . .84 C5
Lilacs The RG41 . . . . . . .115 C4
Lilley Way SL1 . . . . .41 E5
Lillibrooke Cres SL6 . . . . .39 A3
Lily Ct RG41 . . . . .116 A6
Lily Hill Dr RG12 . . . . . . .118 E7
Lily Hill Rd RG12 . . . . . . .118 F7
Lima Ct RG1 . . . . .85 F6
Lime Ave
Camberley GU15 . . . . .152 A6
Windsor SL4 . . . . .67 F7
Winkfield SL4 . . . . .93 F5
Lime Cl Brimpton RG19 . .133 A5
Newbury RG14 . . . . .105 D4
Wokingham RG41 . . . . . . .115 F5
Lime Lodge 3 TW16 . . . . . .98 F1
Lime Mews TW20 . . . . .95 F3
Lime Tree Copse RG42 . . .92 A1
Lime Tree Ct SL4 . . . . .95 C8
Lime Tree Rd RG8 . . . . . . .34 B6
Lime Wlk Bracknell RG12 118 C5
Maidenhead SL6 . . . . .39 A8
Limecroft GU46 . . . . .149 C5
Limefield Cl RG6 . . . . .87 E3
Limerick Cl RG42 . . . . . .118 A8
Limes Cl TW15 . . . . .98 A3
Limes Rd TW20 . . . . .95 F3
Limes The SL4 . . . . .66 C6
Limetree Wlk GU25 . . . . .122 E5
Limmer Cl RG41 . . . . .115 C4
Limmerhill Rd RG41 . . . .115 E5
Linchfield Rd SL3 . . . . . . .68 C6
Lincoln Cl Frimley GU15 .152 B4
Winnersh RG41 . . . . .88 A3
Lincoln Ct Newbury RG14 104 F2
3 Slough SL1 . . . . .42 E3
Lincoln Gdns RG10 . . . . . .61 D5
Lincoln Hatch La SL1 . . . . .21 C1
Lincoln Ho HP10 . . . . .3 D3
Lincoln Rd
Maidenhead SL6 . . . . .39 B8
Reading RG2 . . . . .86 C4
Lincoln Way
Charlton TW16 . . . . .125 E8
Slough SL1 . . . . .41 D6
Lincolnshire Gdns RG42 . .91 E1
Lind Cl RG6 . . . . .87 B2
Lindale Cl GU25 . . . . .121 F5
Lindberg Way RG5 . . . . . . .61 B1
Linden 3 Bracknell RG12 118 F4
Slough SL3 . . . . .44 B1
Linden Ave SL6 . . . . .19 D1
Linden Cl Newbury RG14 .104 F4
Wokingham RG41 . . . . . . .115 F4
Linden Ct
Camberley GU15 . . . . .151 F7
Englefield Green TW20 . . . .95 B2
North Ascot SL5 . . . . .119 E6
Linden Dr SL2 . . . . .22 C4
Linden Hill La RG10 . . . . . .37 C2
Linden Pl TW18 . . . . .97 A4
Linden Rd Reading RG2 . . .86 E2
Woodley RG5 . . . . .87 D4
Linden Way TW17 . . . . . . .125 C4
Lindenhill Rd RG42 . . . . .117 F8
Lindenmuth Way RG19 . .131 F5
Lindores Ho SL6 . . . . .65 B8
Lindores Rd SL6 . . . . .65 B8
Lindsay Cl TW19 . . . . .70 D2
Lindsay Dr TW17 . . . . . . .125 D3
Lindsey Cl RG41 . . . . .115 E6
Lindsey Gdns TW14 . . . . . .98 D8
Lines Rd RG10 . . . . .88 F5
Ling Dr GU18 . . . . .152 F7
Lingholm Cl
Maidenhead SL6 . . . . .39 C6
Reading RG30 . . . . .84 F5
Lingwood RG12 . . . . .118 C3
Link Ho 2 RG14 . . . . .105 A2
Link Rd Datchet SL3 . . . . . .68 C6
East Bedfont TW14 . . . . . . .98 F8
Newbury RG14 . . . . .105 A2
Link The Slough SL2 . . . . . .43 B7
Link The *continued*
Yateley GU46 . . . . .149 C7
Link View RG14 . . . . .104 F7
Link Way
Arborfield Cross RG2 . . . .114 E2
Staines TW18 . . . . .97 B2
Thatcham RG18 . . . . .106 B4
Links App HP10 . . . . .3 B8
Links Dr RG30 . . . . .85 A8
Links Rd Ashford TW15 . . .97 E3
Flackwell Heath HP10 . . . . . .3 C8
Links The SL5 . . . . .119 E7
Links Way HP10 . . . . .3 B8
Linkscroft Ave TW15 . . . . .98 B2
Linkswood Rd SL1 . . . . . . .21 C3
Linkway Camberley GU15 151 C4
Crowthorne RG45 . . . . . . .142 F5
Linnet Cl RG31 . . . . .84 B6
Linnet La RG20 . . . . .131 F3
Linnet Wlk RG41 . . . . . . .115 F6
Lintott Ct TW19 . . . . .70 D1
Lion Cl TW17 . . . . .124 E6
Lion Mews 3 RG17 . . . . . .25 B2
Lionel Ct RG10 . . . . .61 D5
Lip La Wickham RG20 . . . . .75 E2
Wickham,Elcot RG20 . . . .102 D8
Lippincote Ct RG31 . . . . . .57 E3
Lipscomb Cl RG18 . . . . . . .79 B6
Lipscombe Cl RG14 . . . . .104 E2
Liscombe RG12 . . . . .118 B2
Liscombe Ho RG12 . . . . .118 B2
Lisle Cl RG14 . . . . .104 F5
Lismore Cl RG5 . . . . .87 E4
Lismore Ct TW18 . . . . .97 B3
Lismore Pk SL2 . . . . .42 F7
Lisset Rd SL6 . . . . .40 A6
Lister Cl RG8 . . . . .57 C5
Liston Ct 5 SL7 . . . . .1 D2
Liston Rd SL7 . . . . .1 D2
Litcham Spur SL1 . . . . . . .42 D7
Lithgow's Rd TW14,TW6 . .71 F3
Littington Cl RG6 . . . . . .114 C8
Little Aldershot La RG26 . . . . .134 B2
Little Boltons 7 SL7 . . . . . .1 E2
Little Bowden La RG8 . . . .55 F4
Little Buntings SL4 . . . . . .66 F4
Little Cl HP10 . . . . .3 B6
Little Copse GU46 . . . . . .149 D7
Little Croft GU46 . . . . . . .149 D4
Little Croft Rd RG8 . . . . . .34 C5
Little Elms UB3 . . . . .71 D7
Little Foxes RG40 . . . . . .142 A7
Little Fryth RG40 . . . . . .142 D6
Little Glebe RG4 . . . . .60 E3
Little Heath Rd RG31 . . . .84 A7
Little Heath Sch RG31 . . .84 B7
Little Hill Rd RG10 . . . . . .88 D4
Little John's La RG30 . . . .85 C8
Little La RG7 . . . . .107 C6
Little London Rd RG7 . . .136 B1
Little Marlow CE Fst Sch SL7 . . . . .2 C5
Little Marlow Rd SL7 . . . . .1 E3
Little Moor GU47 . . . . . . .143 C1
Little Oak Cl TW17 . . . . . .124 F5
Little Oaks Dr RG31 . . . . .84 C8
Little Paddock GU15 . . . .152 A8
Little Ringdale RG12 . . . .118 E5
Little Saffron RG18 . . . . . .79 B6
Little St RG1 . . . . .85 E8
Little Sutton La SL3 . . . . . .44 C1
Little Vigo GU46 . . . . . . .149 B4
Little Woodlands SL4 . . . .66 F4
Littlebrook Ave SL2 . . . . . .41 E8
Littlecote Dr RG1 . . . . . . .85 E6
Littlecote Rd SN8 . . . . . . .99 B5
Littlecroft Rd 2 TW20 . . . .95 F3
Littledale Cl RG12 . . . . . .118 E6
Littledown Cotts SL1 . . . .42 F5
Littledown Rd SL1 . . . . . . .42 F5
Littledown Sch SL1 . . . . . .42 F6
Littlefield Ct UB7 . . . . . . .70 D7
Littlefield Gn SL6 . . . . . . .63 F6
Littlejohn's La RG30 . . . . .58 C1
Littleport Spur SL1 . . . . . .42 E7
Littlestead Cl RG4 . . . . . . .59 E5
Littleton CE Inf Sch TW17 . . . . .125 A6
Littleton La TW17,TW18 .124 E4
Littleton Rd TW15 . . . . . . .98 C1
Littlewick Green Montessori Sch SL6 . . . . .38 C4
Litton Rd RG2 . . . . .86 D2
Liverpool Rd Reading RG1 86 E8
Slough SL1 . . . . .42 B7
Livery Cl RG1 . . . . .86 B7
Living Rainforest The★ RG18 . . . . .53 C5
Livingstone Ct TW19 . . . .97 E7
Livingstone Gdns RG5 . . .87 E5
Livingstone Rd RG14 . . .105 B2
Llangar Gr RG45 . . . . . . .143 A5
Llanvair Cl SL5 . . . . .120 A3
Llanvair Dr SL5 . . . . .119 F3
Llewellyn Pk RG10 . . . . . .61 D6
Lochinvar Cl SL1 . . . . . . .42 B4
Lochinver RG12 . . . . .118 B2
Lock Ave SL6 . . . . .20 C2
Lock Bridge Rd SL8 . . . . . . .3 A3
Lock La SL6 . . . . .39 C4
Lock Mead SL6 . . . . .20 C2
Lock Path SL4 . . . . .66 D8
Lock Pl RG1 . . . . .86 D7
Lock Rd SL7 . . . . .1 F1
Lockbridge Ct SL6 . . . . . . .40 C8
Locke Gdns SL3 . . . . .43 C4
Lockets Cl SL4 . . . . .66 D6
Lockram La RG7 . . . . . . .111 C1
Locks Ride SL5 . . . . .92 C2
Lockside Ct RG7 . . . . . . .109 C3
Locksley Ct 4 SL1 . . . . . . .42 E3
Lockstile Mead RG8 . . . . .34 C7
Lockstile Way RG8 . . . . . .34 C6
Lockton Chase SL5 . . . .119 D6
Lockton Ho RG40 . . . . . .116 C6
Lockyer Cl RG41 . . . . .88 A2
Lodden View RG10 . . . . . .61 E3
Loddon Bridge Rd RG5 . .87 F6
Loddon Cl GU15 . . . . . . .152 A6
Loddon Court Farm Park Homes RG7 . . . . .138 F7
Loddon Dr Charvil RG10 . .61 A8
Maidenhead SL6 . . . . .39 D8
Loddon Hall Rd RG10 . . . .61 E5
Loddon Inf Sch The RG6 .87 D3
Loddon Jun Sch RG6 . . . .87 D3
Loddon Rd SL8 . . . . .3 A4
Loddon Spur SL1 . . . . . . .42 E7
Loddon Vale Ctr RG5 . . . .88 A7
Lodge Cl
Englefield Green TW20 . . . .95 D3
Marlow SL7 . . . . .1 E1
Slough SL1 . . . . .42 C4
Lodge Gr GU46 . . . . .149 F6
Lodge Rd RG10 . . . . .88 E7
Lodge The
Newbury RG14 . . . . .105 A4
Slough SL2 . . . . .43 B8
Lodge Way
Charlton TW17 . . . . .125 C7
Stanwell TW15 . . . . .97 E6
Windsor SL4 . . . . .66 E4
Lodgings of the Military Knights 3 SL4 . . . . .67 D6
Logan Cl RG30 . . . . .84 F7
Lois Dr TW17 . . . . .125 B4
Lomond Ave RG4 . . . . .59 E5
London Ct RG14 . . . . . . .105 C3
London Rd Ascot SL5 . . . .120 D5
Ashford TW15,TW18,TW19 .97 D5
Bagshot GU15,GU19 . . . . .145 D2
Blackwater GU15,GU17 . . .150 E4
Blewbury OX11 . . . . .11 E8
Bracknell RG12,SL5 . . . . .119 C6
Brands Hill SL3 . . . . .69 B8
Camberley GU15 . . . . .151 C6
Datchet SL3 . . . . .68 C7
Egham TW18 . . . . .96 F4
Englefield Green TW20 . . . .95 C1
Newbury RG14 . . . . .105 C3
Reading RG1 . . . . .86 D7
Slough SL3 . . . . .43 D2
Sunningdale,Blacknest SL5 121 B6
Sunningdale,Shrubs Hill SL5,GU25 . . . . .121 C4
Thatcham RG18,RG19 . . . .106 F3
Twyford RG10 . . . . .61 E6
Virginia Water GU25, TW20 . . . . .122 B7
Windlesham GU19,GU20, SL5 . . . . .146 C7
Wokingham RG40 . . . . . . .116 E6
Woodley RG6 . . . . .87 B8
London Road Bsns Pk RG14 . . . . .105 C4
London Road Ind Est RG14 . . . . .105 B3
London St Chertsey KT16 124 A2
Reading RG1 . . . . .86 B7
Loneacre GU20 . . . . .146 E4
Long Barn La RG2 . . . . . .86 C3
Long Cl
Farnham Common SL2 . . . . .22 B5
Kintbury RG17 . . . . .102 B2
Long Close Sch SL3 . . . . .43 A3
Long Dr SL1 . . . . .21 C2
Long Furlong Dr SL2 . . . .21 E1
Long Gr Tadley RG26 . . . .134 D2
Upper Bucklebury RG7 . . .107 C5
Long Half Acre SL6 . . . . .38 B4
Long Hedge RG17 . . . . . . .25 D2
Long Hill Rd RG12,SL5 . . .119 A7
Long La Brightwalton RG20 28 E3
Cookham Rise SL6 . . . . . . .19 D5
Hermitage RG14,RG18 . . . .78 F2
Holyport,Braywoodside SL6 64 D4
Holyport,Touchen-end SL6 . .64 E6
Newbury RG18 . . . . .105 D7
Purley On T RG31 . . . . .57 B4
Stanwell TW19 . . . . .97 F7
Long Lane Prim Sch RG31 . . . . .57 B4
Long Mdw RG8 . . . . .34 B5
Long Mickle GU47 . . . . . .143 B1
Long Readings La SL2 . . .22 B2
Long Row RG20 . . . . .49 A7
Long Wlk The
Old Windsor SL4 . . . . .94 D7
★ Windsor SL4 . . . . .67 D4
Long's Way RG40 . . . . . .116 E7
Longacre RG14 . . . . .130 D8
Longbourn SL4 . . . . .67 A4
Longbourne Way KT16 . .123 F3
Longbridge Rd RG19 . . . .106 F2
Longcroft Rd RG19 . . . . .106 E2
Longcross Sta KT16 . . . . .121 F1
Longdon Rd RG41 . . . . . . .88 C1
Longdown Lodge GU47 .150 B8
Longdown Rd GU47 . . . . .143 B1
Longfield Rd RG10 . . . . . .61 D6
Longford Ave
Feltham TW14 . . . . .71 F1
Stanwell TW19 . . . . .97 E7
Longford Cl GU15 . . . . . .151 D4
Longford Com Sch TW14 98 F8
Longford Rdbt UB7 . . . . . .70 B6
Longford Way TW19 . . . . .97 E7
Longhurst Cl RG4 . . . . . . .59 C3
Longlands Way GU15 . . .152 D5
Longleat Dr RG31 . . . . . . .57 B3
Longleat Gdns SL6 . . . . . .39 D6
Longleat Way TW14 . . . . .98 D8
Longmead Ball Hill RG20 .129 F1
Windsor SL4 . . . . .66 E6
Longmead La SL1 . . . . . . .21 D5
Longmeadow GU15, GU16 . . . . .151 F3
Longmoor Cl RG40 . . . . .141 E6
Longmoor La RG7 . . . . . .137 A7
Longmoors RG42 . . . . . . .117 E8
Longmore Rd RG2 . . . . . .113 D6
Longridge Cl RG30 . . . . . .85 B7
Longshot Ind Est RG12 . .117 E7
Longshot La RG12 . . . . . .117 E7
Longside Cl TW20 . . . . . .123 C8
Longview HP9 . . . . .3 F8
Longwater Ave RG2, RG30 . . . . .112 D8
Longwater La RG40 . . . .141 E2
Longwater Rd
Bracknell RG12 . . . . .118 C3
Finchampstead RG40 . . . .141 E2
Longworth Ave RG31 . . . .84 B7
Longworth Dr SL6 . . . . . . .20 C1
Lonsdale Cl SL6 . . . . .20 A1
Lonsdale Way SL6 . . . . . .40 C1
Look Ahead SL1 . . . . .42 E4
Look Out Discovery Ctr The★ RG12 . . . . .118 D1
Loosen Dr SL6 . . . . .39 A3
Lord Knyvett Cl TW19 . . . .70 D1
Lord Knyvetts Ct 12 TW19 . . . . .70 E1
Lord Mayors Dr SL2 . . . . .22 A7
Lord Raglan Ho SL4 . . . . .67 C4
Loring Rd SL4 . . . . .66 F6
Lorne Cl SL1 . . . . .42 B3
Lorne Pl 4 RG1 . . . . .85 E7
Lorne St RG1 . . . . .85 E7
Lorraine Rd GU15 . . . . . .151 F8
Lorraine Sch GU15 . . . . .151 E8
Lory Ridge GU19 . . . . . . .145 E4
Losfield Rd SL4 . . . . .66 E6
Lossie Dr SL0 . . . . .44 B6
Loughborough RG12 . . . .118 E3
Loundyes Cl RG18 . . . . . .106 B4
Lovatt Cl RG31 . . . . .84 B7
Love Green La SL0 . . . . . .44 E8
Love Hill La SL3 . . . . .44 A6
Love La Iver SL0 . . . . .44 D7
Newbury RG14 . . . . .105 A6
Love's Cl RG7 . . . . .111 A3
Lovedean Ct RG12 . . . . .118 E3
Lovegrove Dr SL2 . . . . . . .21 F1
Lovejoy La SL4 . . . . .66 D5
Lovel La SL4 . . . . .93 B3
Lovel Rd SL4 . . . . .93 A4
Lovelace Cl SL6 . . . . .17 F4
Lovelace Rd RG12 . . . . . .117 E5
Lovell Cl RG9 . . . . .35 C8
Lovells Cl GU18 . . . . .146 B1
Loverock Rd RG30 . . . . . . .58 D1
Loves Wood RG7 . . . . . . .136 F5
Lovett Gdns SL6 . . . . .20 C3
Lovett Rd TW18 . . . . .96 C4
Lowbrook Dr SL6 . . . . .39 A3
Lowbrook Prim Sch SL6 .39 A3
Lowbury RG12 . . . . .118 E5
Lower Armour Rd RG31 . .57 D1
Lower Boyndon Rd SL6 . .39 E6
Lower Britwell Rd SL2 . . .21 D1
Lower Broadmoor Rd RG45 . . . . .143 D4
Lower Brook St 18 RG1 . .86 A6
Lower Canes GU46 . . . . .149 A6
Lower Charles St GU15 .151 C6
Lower Church Rd GU47 .149 E8
Lower Cippenham La SL1 . . . . .41 F6
Lower Comm RG27 . . . . .140 F1
Lower Cookham Rd SL6 .20 C2
Lower Earley Way RG6 .114 C8
Lower Earley Way (W) RG6 . . . . .113 F7
Lower Earley Way N RG6 87 F2
Lower Earley Way W RG6 . . . . .114 A8
Lower Elmstone Dr RG31 57 C1
Lower Farm Ct RG19 . . .105 F1
Lower Field Rd RG1 . . . . .86 A6
Lower Henley Rd RG4 . . .59 D3
Lower Lees Rd SL2 . . . . . .22 B2
Lower Meadow Rd RG2 . .86 D2
Lower Mill Field GU19 . .145 D2
Lower Moor 2 GU46 . . . .149 D5
Lower Mount RG1 . . . . . .86 D5
Lower Nursery SL5 . . . . .121 A4
Lower Pound La SL7 . . . . .18 D8
Lower Raymond Almshouses 13 RG14 . . . . .104 F2
Lower Rd Chilton OX11 . . .10 D8
Cookham Rise SL6 . . . . . . .19 E7
Lower Ridge SL8 . . . . .3 B4
Lower Sandhurst Rd RG40,GU47 . . . . .142 C2
Lower Ventnor Cotts SL6 19 C8
Lower Village Rd SL5 . . .120 C4
Lower Way RG19 . . . . . .106 B3
Lower Wokingham Rd RG40,RG45 . . . . .142 D5
Lowes Cl RG9 . . . . .36 B4
Lowestoft Cl RG6 . . . . . . .87 D2
Lowestoft Dr SL1 . . . . . . .41 D7
Loweswater Wlk GU15 .152 D4
Lowfield Cl GU18 . . . . . .153 A8
Lowfield Ct RG4 . . . . .59 C5
Lowfield Gn RG4 . . . . .59 E4
Lowfield Rd RG4 . . . . .59 D5
Lowlands Dr TW19 . . . . . .70 D2
Lowlands Rd GU17 . . . . .150 C4
Lowry Cl GU47 . . . . .150 D6
Lowther Cl RG41 . . . . . . .115 F8
Lowther Rd RG41 . . . . . .115 F8
Loxwood RG6 . . . . .87 C2
Loxwood Cl
East Bedfont TW14 . . . . . . .98 D7
Three Mile Cross RG7 . . . .113 A4
Lucan Dr TW18 . . . . .97 D1
Lucas Cl GU46 . . . . .149 D5
Lucas Gn GU24 . . . . .153 D4
Lucas Green Rd GU24 . .153 E5
Lucey Cl RG31 . . . . .57 B3
Lucie Ave TW15 . . . . .98 B2
Luckley Path RG40 . . . . .116 C6
Luckley Rd RG41 . . . . . . .116 B3
Luckley Wood RG41 . . . .116 B3
Luckley-Oakfield Sch RG40 . . . . .116 B3
Luckmore Dr RG6 . . . . . . .87 A3
Lud Lodge TW15 . . . . .97 E6
Luddington Ave GU25 . .122 F7
Ludgrove Sch RG40 . . . .116 D3
Ludlow RG12 . . . . .118 B2
Ludlow Cl RG14 . . . . .105 E4
Ludlow Ho SL6 . . . . .39 E6
Ludlow Rd Feltham TW13 . .98 F5
Maidenhead SL6 . . . . .39 E6
Luff Cl SL4 . . . . .66 E4
Luker Ave RG9 . . . . .15 D3
Lulworth Rd RG2 . . . . . .113 C8
Lunds Farm Rd RG5 . . . . .88 A8
Lundy Ct SL1 . . . . .41 E6
Lundy La RG30 . . . . .85 C7
Lupin Ct GU19 . . . . .145 C1
Lupin Ride RG45 . . . . . . .143 B7
Luscombe Cl RG4 . . . . . . .59 D2
Lutman La SL6 . . . . .19 F2
Lutman's Haven RG10 . . . .37 E5
Lutter Worth Cl RG42 . . . .91 C1
Lutton Cl RG6 . . . . .113 F8
Lych Gate Cl GU47 . . . . .149 F8
Lycroft Cl RG8 . . . . .34 C7
Lydbury RG12 . . . . .118 F6
Lydford Ave SL2 . . . . .42 D8
Lydford Rd RG1 . . . . .86 E6
Lydiaville Mobile Home Pk RG41 . . . . .88 A2
Lydney RG12 . . . . .118 B2
Lydsey Cl SL2 . . . . .22 A2
Lyefield Ct RG4 . . . . .59 B6
Lyell Place E SL4 . . . . . . .66 C4
Lyell Place W SL4 . . . . . . .66 C4
Lyell Rd SL4 . . . . .66 C4
Lyell Walk E SL4 . . . . .66 C4
Lyell Walk W SL4 . . . . . . .66 C4
Lyme Gr RG31 . . . . .57 D1
Lymington Ave GU46 . . .149 C5
Lymington Gate RG4 . . . . .58 E5
Lynch Hill La SL1 . . . . . . .21 E2
Lynch Hill Prim Sch SL2 .21 F2
Lynch La RG17 . . . . .25 B3
Lynchets View RG17 . . . . .24 E5
Lynden Cl SL6 . . . . .65 B8
Lynden Mews RG2 . . . . . . .86 B5
Lyndhurst Ave
Blackwater GU17 . . . . . . .150 C6
Cookham Rise SL6 . . . . . . .19 E6
Lyndhurst Cl RG12 . . . . .119 A6
Lyndhurst Rd Ascot SL5 .120 A5
Goring RG8 . . . . .34 C7
Reading RG30 . . . . .58 A1
Lyndhurst Sch GU15 . . . .151 B5
Lyndwood Dr SL4 . . . . . . .68 A1
Lyndwood Par SL4 . . . . . .68 A1
Lyne Cl GU25 . . . . .122 F3
Lyne Crossing Rd KT16, GU25 . . . . .123 B3
Lyne Ct KT16 . . . . .122 F2
Lyne La Lyne KT16 . . . . . .123 A2
Virginia Water KT16,TW20, GU25 . . . . .123 A3
Lyne Place Manor GU25 122 F2
Lyne Rd GU25 . . . . .122 E3
Lynegrove Ave TW15 . . . .98 C3
Lyneham Gdns SL6 . . . . . .19 B1
Lyneham Rd RG45 . . . . . .143 B5
Lyngfield Pk SL6 . . . . .65 D8
Lynmouth Ct RG1 . . . . . . .59 B1
Lynmouth Rd RG1 . . . . . . .59 A1
Lynn Cl TW15 . . . . .98 D3
Lynton Cl RG5 . . . . .87 C5
Lynton Ct
4 Newbury RG14 . . . . . . .105 A4
4 Reading RG1 . . . . .59 A1
Lynton Gn SL6 . . . . .39 E7
Lynwood Ave
Egham TW20 . . . . .95 E2
Slough SL3 . . . . .43 D3
Lynwood Cres SL5 . . . . .120 E3
Lynwood Ct TW15 . . . . . . .97 F3
Lynwood Flats SL5 . . . . .120 E4
Lyon Cl RG19 . . . . .106 F2
Lyon Oaks RG42 . . . . .91 B2
Lyon Rd RG45 . . . . .143 C6
Lyon Sq RG30 . . . . .85 A8
Lyon Way GU16 . . . . .151 C1
Lyon Way Ind Est GU16 .151 C1
Lysander Cl RG5 . . . . .88 A8

Lysander Mead SL6 40 C8
Lytchet Minster Cl 4
RG12 118 F4
Lytham RG12 117 E3
Lytham Cl RG30 85 C4
Lytham Ct SL5 120 C4
Lytham End RG31 57 B3
Lytham Rd RG5 87 E7

M

Mabett Cl RG2 140 E8
Mabley Ct RG12 118 A3
Macadam Ave RG45 143 C7
Macbeth Ct RG42 118 E8
Macdonald Rd GU18 153 A8
Mace Cl RG6 87 A1
Mackay Cl RG31 84 E3
Mackenzie Mall 3 SL1 42 F4
Mackenzie St 2 SL1 42 F4
Macklin Cl RG17 100 D5
Maclaren Dr RG42 119 A8
Macnaghten Woods
GU15 151 E6
Macphail Cl RG40 116 E8
Macrae Rd GU46 149 C6
Maddle Rd RG17 24 D7
Madeira Pl 8 RG14 105 A2
Madejski Stad (Reading FC)
RG2 112 F8
Madingley RG12 118 B1
Madox Brown End
GU47 150 E6
Mafeking Rd TW19 96 B6
Magdalene Rd
Littleton TW17 124 F6
Sandhurst GU47 143 F2
Magill Cl RG7 113 B2
Magna Carta La TW19 95 E7
Magna Carta Sch The
TW18 96 D2
Magna Rd TW20 95 B2
Magnolia Cl
Sandhurst GU47 143 D1
Winkfield RG42 119 A8
Magnolia Ct
Brimpton RG19 133 B6
Woodley RG5 88 A7
Magnolia Gdns SL3 43 C3
Magnolia Way
Wokingham RG41 115 F5
Wooburn Green HP10 3 E7
Magpie Cl RG19 106 B3
Magpie Way
Reading RG31 84 B6
Slough SL2 21 F1
Maguire Dr GU16 152 C3
Mahonia Cl GU24 153 F6
Maiden Erlegh Dr RG6 87 B4
Maiden Erlegh Sch RG6 87 B4
Maiden Lane Ctr 1 RG6 87 D1
Maiden Pl RG6 87 D2
Maiden's Gn SL4 92 B6
Maidenhead Bsns Campus
The SL6 38 E3
Maidenhead Court Pk
SL6 20 B3
Maidenhead Office Pk
SL6 38 E2
Maidenhead Rd
Binfield RG40 89 E3
Cookham Rise SL6 19 F6
Newell Green RG42 91 B6
Windsor SL4 66 E7
Maidenhead Sta SL6 39 F6
Maidensfield RG41 88 D2
Main Ave RG31 84 B6
Main Dr Bracknell RG42 91 F1
Iver SL0 44 E3
Winkfield RG42,SL5 119 B8
Winkfield,Newell Green
RG42 92 A1
Main Gate Lodges SL4 94 F5
Main St
Chaddleworth RG20 49 A7
Chilton OX11 10 D8
Greenham RG19 131 F5
Newtown RG19 132 A5
Mainprize Rd RG12 118 E7
Mainstone Rd GU24 153 F3
Maise Webster Cl TW19 97 D8
Maisonettes The RG8 34 D8
Maitland Rd RG1 85 E7
Maiwand Gdns RG30 84 D7
Maize La RG42 91 E2
Majendie Cl RG14 104 D5
Major's Farm Rd SL3 68 D7
Makepiece Rd RG42 91 B1
Maker Cl RG30 85 B5
Makins Rd RG9 35 B7
Malders La SL6 19 C3
Maldon Cl RG30 85 D6
Malet Cl TW20 96 D2
Malham Fell RG12 118 A5
Malham Rd RG19 106 C3
Mallard Cl Earley RG6 87 A3
Twyford RG10 61 E3
Mallard Ct RG14 104 F3
Mallard Dr SL1 41 F6
Mallard Row RG1 86 A7
Mallard Way
Padworth RG7 109 B3
Yateley GU46 149 B6
Mallards The
Frimley GU16 151 F2
Great Shefford RG17 48 A3
Laleham TW18 124 B7
Mallards Way GU18 153 A8
Mallory Ave RG4 59 D6
Mallow Gdns RG18 106 D5
Mallow Pk SL6 19 C1
Mallowdale Rd RG12 118 E2
Malone Rd RG5 87 D6
Malpas Rd SL2 43 B6
Malt Hill Egham TW20 95 E3
Newell Green RG42 91 E5
Malt Ho SL4 95 B8
Malt House Cl SL4 95 B8
Malt Shovel La RG17 24 F4
Maltby Way RG6 113 F8
Malthouse Cl RG19 106 F2
Malthouse Flats RG9 16 D6
Malthouse La
4 Reading RG1 85 F8
West End GU24 153 F7
Malthouse Way 2 SL7 1 D1
Maltings Pl 3 RG1 86 A7
Maltings The
Staines TW18 96 E4
Thatcham RG19 106 F2
West Ilsley RG20 10 B1
Malton Ave SL1 42 B6
Malvern Cl RG5 87 F6
Malvern Ct Brands Hill SL3 69 A8
Newbury RG14 104 F1
Reading RG1 86 D6
Malvern Rd
Harlington UB3 71 E7
Maidenhead SL6 19 D1
Yateley GU17 149 F1
Malvern Way RG10 61 D7
Malyons The TW17 125 D3
Man's Hill RG7 111 C2
Managua Cl RG4 59 E2
Manchester Rd RG1 86 E7
Mandarin Ct RG14 105 C2
Mandela Ct 2 RG1 86 D7
Mandeville Cl RG30 84 F6
Mandeville Ct TW20 96 A4
Mandeville Rd TW17 125 A4
Manea Cl RG6 114 C8
Manfield Cl SL2 22 A2
Manners Rd RG5 87 D7
Mannock Way RG5 88 B8
Manor Bglws RG20 31 D4
Manor Cl RG42 91 A1
Manor Cres RG20 31 D4
Manor Ct Marlow SL7 1 C3
Slough, Cippenham SL1 41 F5
4 Slough, Upton Park SL1 42 F3
Manor Farm Ave TW17 125 B3
Manor Farm Cl SL4 66 F4
Manor Farm Cotts SL4 68 A2
Manor Farm Ct TW20 96 A3
Manor Farm Ho SL4 66 F4
Manor Farm La
Egham TW20 96 A3
Tidmarsh RG8 56 C2
Manor Farm Rd RG2 86 B2
Manor Gdns HP10 3 E5
Manor Gr SL6 65 D6
Manor Ho The GU15 151 D6
Manor House Ct
Lower Halliford TW17 125 B2
Reading RG6 87 A5
Manor House Dr SL5 93 A1
Manor House La SL3 68 B6
Manor La Brimpton RG7 133 C6
Chieveley RG20 51 B1
Harlington UB3 71 D8
Hermitage RG18 79 B8
Leckhampstead RG20 49 F4
Maidenhead SL6 39 E4
Newbury RG14 105 E5
Manor Leaze TW20 96 B3
Manor Mead Sch TW17 125 B4
Manor Park Cl RG30 84 C6
Manor Park Dr
Wokingham RG40 141 E6
Yateley GU46 149 E6
Manor Pk Froxfield SN8 99 B4
Staines TW18 96 D5
Manor Pl Newbury RG14 104 D5
Staines TW18 97 B3
Manor Prim Sch RG30 85 A4
Manor Rd Ashford TW15 98 A3
Goring RG8 34 B5
Henley-On-T RG9 35 D8
Letcombe Bassett OX12 7 C5
Maidenhead SL6 39 E4
Oatlands Park KT12 125 F2
Whitchurch-on-T RG8 56 C7
Windsor SL4 66 E5
Wokingham RG41 116 A2
Manor The RG2 113 E5
Manor Way
Bagshot GU19 145 F3
Egham TW20 95 F2
Holyport SL6 65 A8
Manor Wood Gate RG9 36 A4
Manorcroft Prim Sch
TW20 96 A2
Manorcrofts Rd TW20 96 A2
Manse Cl UB3 71 D8
Mansel Cl SL2 43 B8
Mansell Cl SL4 66 E5
Mansell Ct RG2 86 E2
Mansell Dr RG14 130 C5
Mansfield Cl SL5 119 D7
Mansfield Cres RG12 118 B3
Mansfield Ho 4 TW18 96 F3
Mansfield Pl SL5 119 D8
Mansfield Rd Reading RG1 85 F6
Wokingham RG41 116 A5
Mansion House St 7
RG14 105 A3
Mansion La SL0 44 C6
Manston Dr RG12 118 C3
Mant Cl RG20 75 D5
Manygate La TW17 125 C3
Maple Bank RG10 61 E6
Maple Cl
Blackwater GU17 150 C5
Maidenhead SL6 39 C5
Sandhurst GU47 142 F1
Winnersh RG41 88 D3
Maple Cres
Newbury RG14 105 A4
Slough SL2 43 B6
Maple Ct Ashford TW15 98 D1
3 Bracknell RG12 118 F5
Englefield Green TW20 95 B2
Goring RG8 34 B6
Marlow SL7 1 E3
Windsor SL4 67 C4
Maple Dr
Crowthorne RG45 143 C7
Lightwater GU18 152 F8
Reading RG30 84 D6
Maple Gdns Reading RG2 86 E2
Stanwell TW19 97 E6
Yateley GU46 149 D5
Maple Gr RG4 60 E1
Maple La RG8 55 B5
Maple Rise SL7 1 E3
Mapledene RG4 58 E3
Mapledurham Dr RG8 57 C5
Mapledurham Ho★ RG31 57 E6
Mapledurham View
RG31 57 D2
Mapledurham Watermill★
RG31 57 D6
Mapledurham Wlk SL6 19 E3
Maples The 10 SL8 3 B3
Maplin Pk SL3 44 B4
Marathon Cl RG5 88 B8
Marbeck Cl SL4 66 D6
Marbull Way RG42 91 B2
Marchant Cl RG19 131 D7
Marchant Ct SL7 2 A3
Marcheria Cl RG12 118 B3
Marchwood Ave RG4 59 C7
Marcia Ct SL1 41 F5
Marconi Rd RG14 105 B4
Marcus Cl RG30 85 B7
Mardale GU15 152 C4
Mardy RG4 58 E5
Mare La RG10 63 E3
Marefield RG6 87 C2
Marefield Rd SL7 1 D2
Marescroft Rd SL2 21 E1
Mareshall Ave RG42 91 B2
Marfleet Cl 1 RG6 87 E2
Margaret Cl
Reading RG2 113 C7
Staines TW18 97 D2
Maria Ct 15 RG30 85 D6
Marie Davis Ct 11 RG1 86 B7
Marigold Cl RG45 142 F6
Marina Cl KT16 124 C1
Marina Way Burnham SL1 41 D6
Iver SL0 44 F6
Mariners La RG7 82 B3
Marino Way RG40 141 A6
Marion Ave TW17 125 B4
Marish Ct SL3 44 A3
Marish Inf Sch SL3 44 A3
Marish Jun Sch SL3 44 A3
Marish Wharf Ind Est
SL3 43 E4
Marjory Kinnon Sch
TW14 71 E2
Markby Way RG6 87 E2
Market La SL3 44 C3
Market Pl Bracknell RG12 118 B7
Colnbrook SL3 69 C7
Henley-On-T RG9 15 D2
Lambourn RG17 25 B2
8 Newbury RG14 105 A3
Reading RG1 86 B7
Wargrave RG10 36 E1
Wokingham RG40 116 C5
Market Place Mews RG9 15 D2
Market Sq 8 Marlow SL7 1 D2
Staines TW18 96 E4
Market St Bracknell RG12 118 B7
Maidenhead SL6 39 F7
Newbury RG14 105 A2
6 Windsor SL4 67 D6
Market Way 5 RG1 86 B7
Markham Centre Trad Est
The RG7 83 F2
Markham Ct GU15 151 D6
Markham Mews RG40 116 C6
Marks Rd RG41 116 A8
Marlborough Ave RG1 86 D5
Marlborough Cl SL6 39 A6
Marlborough Cres UB3 71 D7
Marlborough Ct
Hungerford RG17 100 D5
Reading RG1 85 F6
Slough SL1 41 E7
Wokingham RG40 116 D7
Marlborough Ho
5 Maidenhead SL6 39 F6
Reading RG1 86 D5
Marlborough Rd
Ashford TW15 97 E3
Maidenhead SL6 39 A6
Marlborough Rd *continued*
Slough SL3 43 D2
Marlborough Rise GU15 151 E6
Marlborough Way RG31 84 B4
Marley Croft TW18 96 E5
Marlin Cl TW16 98 E2
Marlin Ct SL7 1 D1
Marling Cl RG31 57 C2
Marlow Bridge La SL7 18 E8
Marlow CE Inf Sch SL7 1 D3
Marlow Com Hospl SL7 1 E2
Marlow Lodge 13 SL6 39 F6
Marlow Mill SL7 1 E1
Marlow Rd Bisham SL6 18 E4
Bisham SL7 18 E7
Henley-On-T RG9 15 E3
Little Marlow SL7,SL8 2 D5
Maidenhead SL6 39 F7
Marlow Bottom SL7 1 B7
Marlow Sta SL7 1 F2
Marlowes The RG14 130 F8
Marlston Cotts RG18 79 F5
Marlston Rd RG18 79 D5
Marmion Rd RG9 35 E8
Marquis Ct TW19 97 E7
Marquis Pl 4 RG1 86 E7
Marriott Cl TW14 71 D1
Mars Cl RG41 115 F6
Mars Ho RG7 134 E2
Marsack St RG4 59 C2
Marsh Ct RG30 85 D8
Marsh La Curridge RG18 78 D4
Hungerford RG17 100 B5
Newbury RG14 105 A3
Taplow SL6 40 E5
Marsh Mills RG9 36 A8
Marsh Rd RG18 106 E4
Marshall Cl
Frimley GU16 152 D2
Purley On T RG8 57 D4
Marshall Ho 1 RG30 85 B7
Marshall Rd GU47 150 D6
Marshalls Ct RG14 104 D5
Marsham Ho RG42 91 B1
Marshaw Ct RG2 86 C3
Marshfield SL3 68 C6
Marshgate Trad Est SL6 41 A7
Marshland Sq RG4 59 B5
Marshwood Rd GU18 153 D8
Marston Dr RG14 105 D5
Marston Way SL5 119 E7
Martel Cl GU15 152 C7
Marten Pl RG31 57 B3
Martin Cl Windsor SL4 66 D6
Woodley RG5 87 E6
Martin Rd Maidenhead SL6 39 F8
Slough SL1 42 E3
Martin Way GU16 151 E2
Martin's Heron Sta
RG12 118 F5
Martin's Plain SL2 22 F3
Martindale Ave GU15 152 C4
Martineau La RG10 88 E7
Martins Cl GU17 150 D4
Martins Dr RG41 116 B7
Martins La RG12 118 E6
Martins The RG19 106 F2
Marunden Gn SL2 21 F2
Marvyn Cotts RG7 110 C3
Mary Drew Almshouses The
TW20 95 D2
Mary Hare Gram Sch
RG14 77 F3
Mary Lyne Almshouses
RG30 84 F5
Mary Mead RG42 91 D2
Mary Morgan Ct SL2 42 D8
Maryland RG40 141 E8
Maryside SL3 43 E4
Mascoll Path SL2 21 F2
Masdar Gdns RG40 141 E6
Masefield Gdns RG45 143 B3
Masefield Rd RG18 106 D4
Masefield Way TW19 97 F7
Mason Cl GU46 149 E5
Mason Ct Ball Hill RG20 129 F1
3 Reading RG1 85 F8
Mason Pl GU47 149 F8
Mason St RG1 85 E8
Mason's Ct SL1 41 E6
Masonic Hall Rd KT16 123 F3
Masons Rd SL1 41 E6
Master Cl RG5 88 B8
Mathisen Way SL3 69 E6
Matlock Rd RG4 58 E4
Matson Dr RG9 15 F2
Matthew Arnold Cl TW18 97 C2
Matthew Arnold Sch The
TW18 97 C2
Matthew Ct TW15 97 E5
Matthews Chase RG42 90 F1
Matthews Cl RG19 106 B4
Matthews La TW18 96 F4
Matthews Rd GU15 151 C8
Matthewsgreen Rd
RG41 116 A8
Maudsley Ho SL6 40 B7
Maultway Cl GU15 152 B8
Maultway Cres GU15 152 B8
Maultway N GU15 145 B1
Maultway The GU15,
GU16 152 D6
Maureen Campbell Ct
TW17 125 B4
Mawbray Cl RG6 87 C2
Maxdata Ctr The RG12 118 A7
Maxine Cl GU47 143 B1
Maxwell Cl RG5 87 E8
Maxwell Ct SL1 21 C1
Maxwell Rd TW15 98 C2
May Cl 2 GU47 150 D8
May Fields
Sindlesham RG41 115 A8
Winnersh RG41 88 A1
May Pk RG31 84 E4
May Tree Cl SL7 1 C6
May's La RG7 136 A7
Maybrick Cl GU47 142 F1
Maybury Cl SL1 41 D7
Mayfair RG30 84 D7
Mayfair Dr RG14 104 E1
Mayfield Ave RG31 84 B4
Mayfield Cl TW15 98 B2
Mayfield Cotts RG20 31 C4
Mayfield Dr
Caversham RG4 59 D3
Windsor SL4 67 A4
Mayfield Gdns TW18 96 F2
Mayfield Light Ind Est
SL4 93 B5
Mayfield Rd
Camberley GU15 151 B1
Wooburn Green HP10 3 E6
Mayflower Ct 6 RG1 86 B7
Mayflower Dr GU46 149 B7
Mayflower Way SL2 22 C8
Maying The RG2 113 B6
Maynard Cl RG18 106 D5
Maynard Ct
6 Staines TW18 97 A4
Windsor SL4 67 A6
Mayo Rd KT12 125 F2
Mayors La RG14 105 A2
Mayow Cl RG19 106 F2
Maypole Rd SL6 41 A8
Mays Cl RG6 87 B5
Mays La RG6 87 B5
Mays Rd RG40 116 E6
Maywood Dr GU15 152 A7
Mc Carthy Way RG40 141 F8
McAuliffe Dr SL1,SL2 21 F8
McCrae's Wlk RG10 36 D2
McKay Trad Est SL3 69 E5
McKernan Ct GU47 149 F8
McNair Cl RG6 87 A1
Meachen Ct RG40 116 C6
Mead Ave SL3 44 B4
Mead Cl Egham TW20 96 B2
7 Marlow SL7 1 F3
Reading RG31 84 B6
Slough SL3 44 B4
Mead Ct TW20 96 C2
Mead Haze SL6 20 C2
Mead La Chertsey KT16 124 C1
Upper Basildon RG8 55 D6
Mead The RG17 48 B3
Mead Way SL1 41 D8
Mead Wlk SL3 44 B4
Meade Ct GU19 145 F3
Meadfield Ave SL3 44 A3
Meadfield Rd SL3 44 B3
Meadhurst Pk TW16 98 E2
Meadhurst Rd KT16 124 B1
Meadow Bank 11 SL8 3 B3
Meadow Cl
Blackwater GU17 150 D4
Compton RG20 31 E5
Goring RG8 34 C6
Marlow SL7 1 F1
Moulsford OX10 13 F4
Old Windsor SL4 68 B2
Thatcham RG19 106 C3
Meadow Cotts
Shepperton TW17 125 B3
West End GU24 153 F7
Meadow Croft RG17 73 A1
Meadow Ct TW18 96 E5
Meadow Gdns TW18 96 D3
Meadow La Eton SL4 67 C7
Pangbourne RG8 56 D5
Meadow Rd Ashford TW15 98 D3
Earley RG6 87 D3
Henley-On-T RG9 15 E1
Newbury RG14 130 F8
Reading RG1 58 F1
Slough SL3 43 E3
Wentworth GU25 121 E4
Wokingham RG41 116 A5
Meadow Vale Prim Sch
RG42 117 F8
Meadow View
Chertsey KT16 124 C1
Marlow Bottom SL7 1 E6
Winnersh RG41 88 D3
Meadow View Ct RG1 58 E1
Meadow View La SL6 64 E8
Meadow Way
Blackwater GU17 150 C5
Bracknell RG42 91 A1
Dorney SL6 40 F4
Fifield SL6 65 D6
Old Windsor SL4 68 B1
Theale RG7 83 D3
West End GU24 153 F6
Wokingham RG41 116 A5
Meadow Wlk
Bourne End SL8 3 A5
Wokingham RG41 116 A6
Meadowbank RG20 129 B7
Meadowbank Rd GU18 146 C1
Meadowbrook Cl SL3 69 F6
Meadowbrook Montessori
Sch RG42 91 F4
Meadowcroft Rd RG2 113 C8
Meadowlea Cl UB7 70 D8

Meadows (Superstores) The GU47 150 E5
Meadows Bsns Pk The GU17 150 E4
Meadows Sch The HP10 3 E7
Meadows The HP10 3 B8
Meadowside RG31 57 B1
Meadowside Rd RG8 56 D5
Meadowsweet Cl RG18 106 E4
Meadowview TW19 69 F2
Meads Cl RG20 50 D7
Meads The
Stoke Poges SL2 23 A2
4 Windsor SL4 67 A5
Meadway Ashford TW15 98 A4
Frimley GU16 151 F2
Staines TW18 97 A1
Meadway Cl TW18 97 A1
Meadway Prec RG30 85 A6
Meadway The RG30 84 E7
Meare Est HP10 3 E8
Mearings The RG30 111 F5
Measham Way RG6 87 C2
Meashill Way OX11 9 F8
Meavy Gdns RG2 86 B2
Medallion Pl SL6 40 B7
Mede Cl TW19 95 D7
Mede Ct TW18 96 E5
Medina Cl RG41 115 E7
Medlake Rd TW20 96 C2
Medlar Dr GU17 150 F3
Medway Cl
Thatcham RG18 106 B5
Wokingham RG41 115 F7
Medway Ct RG30 85 D6
Melbourne Ave
Slough SL1 42 C7
Winnersh RG41 88 C1
Melbury Cl KT16 124 A2
Meldreth Way Earley RG6 87 C1
Shinfield RG6 114 D8
Meldrum Cl RG14 130 C6
Melford Gn RG4 59 E6
Melksham Cl RG6 113 E8
Melling Cl RG6 87 E3
Mellor Wlk
3 Reading RG1 86 B5
12 Windsor SL4 67 D6
Melody Cl RG41 88 C3
Melrose RG12 118 B1
Melrose Ave RG6 87 A5
Melrose Gdns RG2 114 E2
Melton Ct SL6 39 F6
Melville Ave GU16 151 F1
Membury Wlk RG12 118 F5
Memorial Ave RG9 35 E2
Mendip Cl Charvil RG10 61 B4
Harlington UB3 71 D7
Slough SL3 44 A1
Mendip Dr RG31 84 A6
Mendip Rd RG12 118 E4
Menpes Rd RG31 57 C4
Mentone Cotts RG10 62 F5
Meon Cl RG26 135 A1
Merchants Pl 5 RG1 86 A8
Mercia Rd SL6 39 C4
Mercian Way SL1 41 D5
Mercury Ave RG41 115 E6
Mercury Ho RG7 134 E2
Mere Cl SL7 1 F2
Mere Rd
Shepperton TW17 125 B3
Slough SL1 42 F3
Mereoak La
Grazeley RG7 112 F4
Three Mile Cross RG7 113 A5
Mereoak Orch RG7 113 A5
Mereoak Pk RG7 113 A5
Mereside Pk TW15 98 C4
Meridian Ct SL5 120 B1
Merlewood RG12 118 D4
Merlin Cl SL3 69 B8
Merlin Clove RG42 92 B2
Merlin Ct Frimley GU16 151 D1
Maidenhead SL6 39 B8
Mermaid Cl RG41 88 B2
Merrifield Cl RG6 114 D8
Merrivale Gdns RG2 86 B1
Merron Cl GU46 149 C5
Merryhill Green La RG41 88 D3
Merryhill Rd RG42 118 B8
Merryman Dr RG45 143 A7
Merryweather Cl RG40 115 F1
Merrywood Pk GU15 151 F4
Mersey Way RG18 106 B5
Merthyr Vale RG4 59 A6
Merton Cl Maidenhead SL6 39 C3
Sandhurst GU47 143 F2
Merton Rd SL1 43 A3
Merton Rd N RG2 86 B1
Merton Rd S RG2 86 B1
Mertonford RG40 116 D5
Mervyn Rd TW17 125 C2
Merwin Way SL4 66 D4
Meryton Ho SL4 67 A4
Metcalf Rd TW15 98 B3
Meteor Cl RG5 88 A7
Metro Ctr The RG41 89 A2
Mews The Newbury RG14 104 E2
Reading RG1 86 E6
Sonning RG4 60 D4
Swallowfield RG7 140 C7
Mey Cl RG31 84 C5
Meyrick Dr RG14 130 C5
Mezel Hill Cotts SL4 94 C3
Michael Cl SL6 39 C5
Michaelmas Cl GU46 149 D4
Micheldever Way RG12 118 F4
Michelet Cl GU18 146 B1
Micklands Prim Sch RG4 59 D4
Micklands Rd RG4 59 E3
Mickle Hill GU47 143 A1
Micro Ctr The RG2 86 B2
Midas Ho RG7 134 E2
Midcroft SL2 22 B1
Middle Cl Frimley GU15 152 C6
Newbury RG14 130 D7
Middle Farm Cl RG20 51 B2
Middle Gn Slough SL3 43 E6
Staines TW18 97 D1
Middle Gordon Rd
GU15 151 D5
Middle Hill TW20 95 D3
Middle Springs RG8 34 C8
Middle Wlk SL1 21 C2
Middlefields RG10 61 E6
Middlefields Ct RG10 61 E6
Middlegreen Rd SL3 43 D5
Middlegreen Trad Est
SL3 43 D4
Middleton Ct RG14 105 E5
Middleton Rd GU15 151 F7
Middletons Cl RG17 100 E7
Midgham Halt RG7 108 C2
Midsummer Mdw RG4 58 F6
Midway Ave
Chertsey KT16 124 A6
Thorpe TW20 123 B6
Midway Cl TW19 97 B5
Midwinter Cl RG30 84 E8
Milam Cl RG2 140 E8
Milbanke Ct RG12 117 F7
Milbanke Way RG12 117 F7
Mildenhall Cl RG6 87 D2
Mildenhall Rd SL1 42 E7
Mile Elm SL7 2 A3
Miles Pl GU18 152 F7
Miles Way RG5 88 A7
Milestone Ave RG10 61 A5
Milestone Cres RG10 61 A4
Milestone View Ct RG4 59 E4
Milestone Way RG4 59 D6
Milford Ct SL1 43 A4
Milkhouse Rd RG20 103 D4
Mill Bank RG17 102 A3
Mill Cl Bagshot GU19 145 D3
Wokingham RG41 115 F7
Mill Cotts HP10 3 D5
Mill Ct SL3 69 C4
Mill Farm Ave TW16 98 E1
Mill Field GU19 145 D3
Mill Gn Bracknell RG42 90 E1
Caversham RG4 59 C1
Mill Hall Sch RG20 131 D8
Mill House La KT16 123 B5
Mill La Ascot SL5 121 A7
Bracknell RG12 117 F5
Colthrop RG19 107 B2
Cookham SL6 20 C7
Earley RG6 87 E3
Henley-On-T RG9 35 F8
Horton SL3 69 C4
Hurley SL6 17 F4
Lambourn RG17 25 C2
Newbury RG14 105 B3
Padworth RG7 109 C2
Reading RG1 86 B7
Reading,Horncastle RG31 84 E4
Shiplake RG9 36 A2
Sindlesham RG41 115 A8
Taplow SL6 40 C8
Thorpe TW20 123 C5
Windsor SL4 67 A7
Winnersh RG41 87 F1
Yateley GU46 149 D8
Mill Mead TW18 96 F4
Mill Pl SL3 68 D5
Mill Place Cvn Pk SL3 68 C5
Mill Pond Rd GU20 146 B6
Mill Rd
Burghfield Common RG30 84 F2
Caversham RG4 59 C1
Goring RG8 34 C8
Marlow SL7 1 E1
Shiplake RG9 36 B3
Mill Reef Cl RG19 105 F3
Mill Ride SL5 119 D8
Mill St Colnbrook SL3 69 D7
Slough SL2 42 F5
Mill W SL2 42 F5
Millars Bsns Ctr RG41 116 A4
Millbank SL7 1 F1
Millbank Cres RG5 87 F6
Millboard Rd SL8 3 B3
Millbridge Rd GU46 149 B8
Millbrook Way SL3 69 E5
Milldown Ave RG8 34 C7
Milldown Rd RG8 34 C7
Millennium Ct RG2 86 C4
Millennium Way RG12 118 C8
Miller Dr RG41 88 A2
Miller's Ct TW20 96 D2
Miller's Field RG17 48 B3
Miller's La SL4 68 A1
Millers Cl Goring RG8 34 B7
Staines TW18 97 B3
Millers Ct RG4 59 D1
Millers Gr RG31 84 E4
Milley La RG10 62 B8
Milley Rd RG10 62 E6
Millfield Charlton TW16 125 D8
Lambourn RG17 25 B2
Millford Rd RG1 58 F1
Millgreen La RG19 132 F3
Millholme Wlk GU15 152 C4
Millington Cl RG2 86 D3
Millins Cl GU47 143 E1
Millmead RG41 116 A7
Millmere GU46 149 D7
Mills Spur SL4 95 B8
Millside SL8 3 C3
Millstream Ho RG14 105 D3
Millstream La SL1 41 E5
Millstream Way HP10 3 E8
Millworth La RG2 113 E4
Milman Cl RG12 119 A7
Milman Rd RG2 86 B5
Milner Rd SL1 41 A8
Milsom Cl RG2 113 E5
Milton Cl Bracknell RG12 118 B3
Henley-On-T RG9 15 D2
Horton SL3 69 A4
Milton Ct RG40 116 B7
Milton Dr Littleton TW17 124 E5
Wokingham RG40 116 B7
Milton Gdns
Stanwell TW19 97 F7
Wokingham RG40 116 B6
Milton Rd Earley RG6 87 A7
Egham TW20 95 F3
Slough SL2 22 D1
Wokingham RG40,RG41 116 B6
Milton Way RG10 61 F5
Milverton Cl SL6 39 B3
Milward Gdns RG12 117 C7
Mina Ave SL3 43 D4
Minchin Gn RG42 90 C3
Minden Cl RG41 115 E6
Minerva Cl TW19 70 A2
Minerva Ho RG7 134 E2
Ministry Rd RG19 132 A5
Minley Rd GU17 149 E1
Minniecroft Rd SL1 21 B2
Minorca Ave GU16 152 E2
Minorca Rd GU16 152 E1
Minoru Pl RG42 90 D3
Minstead Cl RG12 118 F6
Minstead Dr GU46 149 C5
Minster Ct
Camberley GU15 151 D7
Camberley,York Town
GU15 150 F4
Minster St RG1 86 B7
Minster Way SL3 43 F4
Minsterley Ave TW16,
TW17 125 E5
Mint Cl RG6 86 F1
Minter Ct RG26 134 F1
Minton Cl RG30 84 F8
Minton Rise SL6 41 B7
Mirador Cres SL2 43 B6
Mire La RG10 62 D4
Misbourne Ct SL3 44 A2
Missenden Cl TW14 98 F7
Missenden Gdns SL1 41 B7
Mistletoe Rd GU46 149 D4
Mitcham Cl RG2 86 B5
Mitcham Rd GU15 145 A1
Mitchell Bldgs GU46 149 B5
Mitchell Cl SL1 42 A4
Mitchell Way RG5 88 B7
Mitford Cl RG2 113 D8
Mitre Cl TW17 125 D3
Mitre Pl RG42 91 B2
Mixnams La KT16 124 A6
Moat Dr SL2 43 C8
Modbury Gdns RG2 86 C2
Moffatts Cl GU47 150 A8
Moffy Hill SL6 19 E2
Mohawk Way RG5 88 B7
Mole Rd RG2,RG41 114 F5
Moles Cl RG40 116 D5
Mollison Cl RG5 88 B8
Molly Millar Bridge
RG41 116 B4
Molly Millar's La RG41 116 A4
Molyneux Rd GU20 146 D4
Molyns Ho RG9 15 E3
Molyns Mews SL1 41 E5
Monarch Cl TW14 98 E8
Monastry The 22 RG30 85 D6
Monck Ct 7 RG30 85 D6
Mondial Way UB7 71 C7
Moneyrow Gn SL6 65 A7
Monkey Island Ct SL6 65 E8
Monkey Island La SL6 40 E2
Monkley Ct 5 RG4 59 C1
Monks Cl SL5 120 B3
Monks Dr SL5 120 B3
Monks Hollow SL7 1 E5
Monks La RG14 130 F7
Monks Rd
Virginia Water GU25 122 D5
Windsor SL4 66 D5
Monks Way
Harmondsworth UB7 70 E8
Reading RG30 85 D5
Staines TW18 97 D1
Monks Wlk SL5 120 B3
Monksbarn RG2 86 D2
Monksfield Way SL2 22 A2
Monkshood Cl RG40 116 E7
Monkswood Cl RG14 130 E7
Monkswood Ct 6 SL7 1 E2
Monktons La RG7 137 C5
Monmouth Ct 5 RG1 59 A1
Mons Cl RG41 115 E6
Mons Wlk TW20 96 C3
Monsell Gdns TW18 96 E3
Montacute Dr RG19 106 F2
Montagu Rd SL3 68 B6
Montague Cl
Camberley GU15 151 B5
Lightwater GU18 146 A1
Montague Cl *continued*
Wokingham RG40 116 E7
Montague Rd SL1 42 F6
Montague St
Caversham RG4 59 C2
Reading RG1 86 D7
Monteagle La
Yateley GU46 149 A6
Yateley GU46 149 B5
Montem La SL1 42 D4
Montem Prim Sch SL1 42 B4
Montgomery Cl GU47 150 B8
Montgomery Dr RG7 113 B2
Montgomery Pl SL2 43 C7
Montgomery Rd RG14 130 E8
Montpelier Dr RG4 59 D5
Montpellier Ct SL4 67 C5
Montreal Terr RG10 61 E4
Montrose Ave Datchet SL3 68 C7
Slough SL1 42 B7
Montrose Cl
Ashford TW15 98 C3
Frimley GU16 151 E2
Montrose Dr SL6 39 A6
Montrose Ho 3 RG1 86 A8
Montrose Rd TW14 71 D1
Montrose Way SL3 68 D7
Montrose Wlk RG31 84 E4
Monument Cl RG14 130 D7
Monycrower Dr SL6 39 E7
Moor Cl Sandhurst GU47 143 E1
Wokingham RG40 141 E7
Moor Copse Cl RG6 87 B3
Moor End SL6 40 C1
Moor Furlong SL1 41 E5
Moor La Bracknell RG12 117 C6
Harmondsworth UB7 70 C8
Maidenhead SL6 19 F1
Newbury RG14 104 E3
Staines TW19 96 D6
Moor Park Ho RG12 117 E3
Moor Pl GU20 146 B5
Moor The SL7 2 D4
Moorbridge Rd SL6 40 A7
Moordale Ave RG42 90 F1
Moore Cl SL1 42 B4
Moore Grove Cres TW20 95 F1
Moore's Pl RG17 100 C5
Moores Gn RG40 116 E8
Moores La SL4 41 F2
Moorfield Terr SL6 40 A8
Moorfields Cl TW18 123 E8
Moorhayes Dr TW18 124 C6
Moorhen Dr RG6 87 B1
Moorings The
Old Windsor SL4 95 C8
Windsor SL4 67 A7
Moorland Rd UB7 70 C8
Moorlands Dr SL6 38 F8
Moorlands Pl GU15 151 B5
Moorlands Prim Sch
RG30 84 F7
Moorlands Rd GU15 151 B4
Moormede Cres TW18 96 F4
Moors Ct RG40 141 E8
Moors The
Pangbourne RG8 56 D5
Thatcham RG19 106 D2
Moorside HP10 3 E8
Moorside Cl
Farnborough GU14 151 A1
Maidenhead SL6 19 F1
Moorstown Ct 7 SL1 42 E4
Moray Ave GU47 150 D7
Moray Dr SL2 43 A7
Mordaunt Dr RG45 143 B3
Morden Cl RG12 118 F5
Moreau Wlk SL3 43 E7
Morecambe Ave RG4 58 E5
Moreland Ave SL3 69 C7
Moreland Cl SL3 69 C7
Moreleigh Cl RG2 113 B8
Morella Cl GU25 122 D5
Morello Dr SL3 43 F5
Moretaine Rd TW15 97 D5
Moreton Ct RG1 86 C5
Moreton Way SL1 41 D5
Morgan Ct 2 TW15 98 B3
Morgan Rd RG1 86 C6
Moriston Cl RG30 85 B8
Morlais RG4 59 A5
Morlands Ave RG30 85 A5
Morley Cl Slough SL3 43 F4
Yateley GU46 149 B5
Morley Ct SL5 120 F3
Morley Pl RG17 100 D5
Mornington Ave RG40 141 F8
Mornington Cl RG26 134 E1
Mornington Rd TW15 98 C3
Morpeth Cl RG2 86 C4
Morrell Ct TW18 97 B3
Morrice Cl 3 SL3 44 A2
Morris Ct SL4 66 E6
Morriss Ct 14 RG1 86 C7
Mortimer Cl RG2 113 C7
Mortimer Hall RG7 137 C5
Mortimer La
Mortimer RG7 137 D7
Silchester RG7 137 D1
Mortimer Rd
Grazeley RG7 112 D2
Slough SL3 43 D3
Mortimer St John's CE Sch
RG7 137 A5
Mortimer St Mary's CE Jun
Sch RG7 137 D5
Mortimer Sta RG7 137 E5
Morton Dr SL1 21 F8
Morton Pl RG7 83 E4
Morval Rd GU17 149 F1
Moss Cl RG4 59 C3
Mossy Vale SL6 19 D1
Mostyn Ho RG42 91 B1
Moulsford Prep Sch
OX10 14 A5
Moulsham Copse La
GU46 149 B7
Moulsham La GU46 149 B7
Moundsfield Way SL1 41 E4
Mount Cl
Farnham Common SL2 22 C8
Newbury RG14 105 A1
Mount Cl The GU25 122 D3
Mount Felix KT12 125 F2
Mount La Bracknell RG12 118 C7
Chaddleworth RG20 49 A8
Mount Lee TW20 95 F3
Mount Pleasant
Beenham RG7 108 F6
Bracknell RG12 118 C6
Reading RG1 86 B6
Sandhurst GU47 143 A1
Tadley RG26 135 B1
Wokingham RG41 116 A6
Mount Pleasant Cl
GU18 146 A1
Mount Pleasant Cotts
7 Bourne End SL8 3 B3
Englefield Green TW20 95 D2
Mount Pleasant Gr RG1 86 B6
Mount Rd RG18 106 E4
Mount St RG2 86 B5
Mount The Caversham RG4 58 F3
Reading RG1 86 D5
Wentworth GU25 122 D3
Mount View RG9 15 D2
Mount View Ct RG9 15 D2
Mountain Ash SL7 1 D6
Mountbatten Cl
Newbury RG14 105 C5
6 Slough SL1 43 A3
Mountbatten Rise GU47 142 F1
Mountbatten Sq 7 SL4 67 C6
Mountfield RG8 34 C7
Mounts Hill SL4 93 C3
Mountsfield Cl TW19 70 A2
Mowbray Cres TW20 96 A3
Mowbray Dr RG30 85 A8
Mower Cl RG40 116 F7
Moyleen Rise SL7 1 C1
Mrs Bland's Inf Sch
RG7 110 F2
Muckhatch La TW20 123 B7
Mud La
Finchampstead RG27 140 F1
Peasemore RG20 50 D6
Mud La Cotts RG27 140 F1
Muirfield Cl RG1 86 D7
Muirfield Ho
Bracknell RG12 117 E3
Sunningdale SL5 121 A1
Mulberry Ave
Stanwell TW19 97 E7
Windsor SL4 67 F5
Mulberry Bsns Pk RG41 116 A4
Mulberry Cl
Crowthorne RG45 143 C4
1 Sandhurst GU47 150 D8
Woodley RG5 87 E6
Mulberry Ct
1 Bracknell RG12 118 F4
2 Newbury RG14 104 F2
Wokingham RG40 116 C6
Mulberry Dr SL3 43 E1
Mulberry Ho RG42 91 B1
Mulberry Trees TW17 125 D2
Mulberry Way RG7 83 E3
Mulberry Wlk SL6 39 C8
Mulfords Hill RG26 135 B1
Mulgrave Rd GU16 151 F2
Mullens Rd TW20 96 C3
Mullens Terr RG4 58 D8
Mullion Ct 10 RG1 85 F7
Mulroy Dr GU15 152 A6
Mumbery Hill RG10 36 E1
Muncaster Cl TW15 98 A4
Muncaster Rd TW15 98 B3
Munces Rd SL7 1 D6
Munday Ct RG42 90 E1
Mundaydean La SL7 1 B4
Mundesley Spur SL1 42 F7
Mundesley St RG1 86 B6
Munkle Marsh RG19 107 A3
Munnings Dr GU47 150 E6
Munro Ave RG5 87 F4
Murdoch Cl TW18 97 A3
Murdoch Ct RG40 116 D5
Murdoch Rd RG40 116 D5
Murray Ct SL5 120 C3
Murray Ho RG41 116 A6
Murray Rd RG41 116 A6
Murrellhill La
Binfield RG42 90 C1
Bracknell RG42 117 C8
Murrells La GU15 151 B3
Murrin Rd SL6 39 C8
Mus of Berkshire Aviation
The★ RG5 88 B6
Mus of English Rural Life★
RG2 86 E4
Mus of Reading★ RG1 86 B8
Mushroom Castle RG42 92 B2
Mustard La RG4 60 E2

Mustard Mill Rd TW18 96 F4
Muswell Cl RG7 83 E3
Mutton Oaks RG12 117 D8
Myers Way GU16 152 D2
Mylne Sq RG40 116 D6
Mylum Cl RG2 113 C6
Myrke The SL3 42 F2
Myrtle Ave TW14 71 E2
Myrtle Cl
Burghfield Common RG7 111 B3
Lightwater GU18 153 B8
Poyle SL3 69 E6
Purley On T RG31 57 C3
Myrtle Cres SL2 42 F6
Myrtle Dr GU17 150 D5
Myton Wlk RG7 83 E3

N

Nabbs Hill Cl RG31 84 C5
Nairn Cl GU16 151 E2
Nalderhill Rd RG20 103 B6
Napier Cl RG45 143 D5
Napier Dr GU15 152 A8
Napier Lodge TW15 98 D2
Napier Rd Ashford TW15 98 D1
Crowthorne RG45 143 C4
Harmondsworth TW6 70 D6
Maidenhead SL6 39 B6
Reading RG1 86 C8
Napier Wlk TW15 98 D1
Napper Cl SL5 119 D7
Narromine Dr RG31 84 F4
Naseby RG12 118 B1
Naseby Rise RG14 105 D5
Nash Cl RG6 87 A3
Nash Gdns SL5 119 E7
Nash Grove La RG40 115 E1
Nash Pk RG42 90 B2
Nash Rd SL3 44 A2
Nashdom SL1 20 F5
Nashdom La SL1 21 A6
Natalie Cl TW14 98 D8
Nathan Ct 7 RG1 85 F7
Naylors The RG7 139 D6
Neath Gdns RG30 84 F7
Needham Cl SL4 66 E6
Neil Cl TW15 98 C3
Nell Gwynn Ave TW17 125 D3
Nell Gwynne Ave SL5 120 D5
Nell Gwynne Cl SL5 120 D5
Nelson Cl Bracknell RG12 118 E7
East Bedfont TW14 98 F7
Slough SL3 43 D2
Nelson Ct KT16 124 A1
Nelson Rd Ashford TW15 97 E3
Caversham RG4 59 C2
Harmondsworth TW6 70 F6
Windsor SL4 66 F4
Nelson Terr 9 RG1 86 B6
Nelson Way GU15 150 F4
Nelson's La RG10 89 B6
Nene Rd TW6,UB7 71 B6
Nene Rd Rdbt TW6 71 B6
Neptune Cl RG41 115 E6
Neptune Rd TW6 71 C6
Neptune Way SL1 41 E4
Netherton RG12 118 A5
Netley Cl RG4 59 E6
Netley Rd (W) TW6 71 D6
Nettlecombe RG12 118 D3
Nettleton Rd TW6 71 B6
Neuman Cres RG12 118 A3
Neve Ho SL6 39 F8
Nevelle Cl RG42 117 D8
Neville Cl Stoke Poges SL2 22 F6
Waltham St Lawrence RG10 62 F6
Neville Ct SL1 21 C2
Neville Dr RG19 106 E3
Nevis Rd RG31 57 D3
New Bath Rd RG10 61 C6
New Bldgs RG7 81 D4
New Bright St 6 RG1 86 A6
New Christ Church CE Prim Sch RG1 86 B5
New Cl RG9 16 A8
New Ct SL7 1 D2
New Forest Ride RG12 118 F4
New Greenham Pk RG19 131 F5
New Hill RG8 57 C5
New Hope Terr RG1 59 A1
New Lane Hill RG30 84 E6
New Mdw SL5 119 D8
New Mile Rd SL5 120 C7
New Mill La RG27 140 E2
New Mill Rd RG40 140 E3
New Par TW15 97 F4
New Park Rd TW15 98 C3
New Rd Bagshot GU19 145 F3
Blackwater GU17 150 E4
Bourne End SL8 3 B4
Bracknell RG12 118 D7
Burghfield Common RG7 111 E1
Cookham Rise SL6 19 E7
Crowthorne RG45 143 C5
Datchet SL3 68 D6
East Bedfont TW14 71 D1
Egham TW18 96 C4
Harlington TW6,UB7 71 C7
Holyport SL6 65 B8
Hurley SL6 17 F3
Littleton TW17 125 B6
Marlow Bottom SL7 1 D6
New Rd *continued*
Newbury RG14 105 C1
North Ascot SL5 92 F1
Reading RG1 86 D5
Sandhurst GU47 150 A8
Shiplake RG9 36 A3
Sindlesham RG41 115 B8
Slough SL3 44 A3
Twyford RG10 61 D7
Twyford,Ruscombe RG10 61 F6
Windlesham GU19,GU20 146 A4
New Road Hill RG7 108 B3
New Scotland Hill Prim Sch GU47 143 A2
New Sq East Bedfont TW14 98 C7
Slough SL1 42 F4
New St Beech Hill RG7 138 B1
Henley-On-T RG9 15 E2
Staines TW18 97 A4
New Town Prim Sch RG1 86 D8
New Villas RG20 129 B3
New Way RG7 82 A2
New Wickham La TW20 96 B1
New Wokingham Rd RG45 143 A6
New Zealand Ave KT12 125 F1
Newall Rd TW6 71 C6
Newalls Rise RG10 36 E2
Newark Rd
Windlesham GU20 146 B6
Yateley GU17 149 E2
Newark St RG1 86 B6
Newberry Cres SL4 66 D5
Newbery Cl RG31 57 D1
Newbery Way SL1 42 D4
Newbold Coll RG42 90 D1
Newbold Rd RG14 104 D5
Newbold Sch RG42 90 D1
Newbolt Cl RG18 106 C5
Newbury Cl RG10 61 B4
Newbury Coll RG14 131 A7
Newbury Dr SL6 40 B6
Newbury Hill RG18 52 F5
Newbury La RG20 31 D4
Newbury Racecourse Sta RG14 105 C2
Newbury Rd
Great Shefford RG17 48 B2
Harmondsworth TW6 70 F6
Hermitage RG18 79 B6
Lambourn RG17 25 C1
Newbury Ret Pk RG14 131 B7
Newbury St
Kintbury RG17 102 B2
Lambourn RG17 25 B2
Newbury Sta RG14 105 A2
Newcastle Rd RG2 86 C4
Newchurch Rd Slough SL2 41 F8
Tadley RG26 135 A1
Newell Gn RG42 91 C3
Newell Hall RG42 91 C3
Newfield Gdns SL7 1 F3
Newfield Rd SL7 1 F3
Newfield Way SL7 1 F2
Newhaven Cres TW15 98 D3
Newhaven Spur SL2 22 B1
Newhurst Gdns RG42 91 D3
Newlands Ave RG4 59 B3
Newlands Cl GU46 149 D5
Newlands Cotts RG41 114 F7
Newlands Dr
Maidenhead SL6 39 A7
Poyle SL3 69 E4
Newlands Girls' Sch SL6 39 A7
Newlands Prim Sch GU46 149 C5
Newlands Rd GU15 151 B1
Newlyn Gdns RG2 86 B1
Newmans Pl SL5 121 B2
Newmarket Cl RG6 87 D2
Newport Cl 11 RG14 105 B4
Newport Dr RG42 91 B2
Newport Rd
Harmondsworth TW6 71 A6
Newbury RG14 105 B4
Reading RG1 59 A1
Slough SL2 21 E1
Newquay Dr RG6 87 B1
Newstead Rise RG2 86 E1
Newton Ave RG4 59 D5
Newton Cl SL3 43 F4
Newton Ct SL4 68 A1
Newton La SL4 68 B1
Newton Mews RG17 100 D6
Newton Side Orch SL4 68 A1
Newtonside SL4 68 A1
Newtown RG26 135 A1
Newtown Gdns RG9 35 E8
Newtown Rd
Henley-On-T RG9 35 F8
Marlow SL7 1 F3
Newbury RG14,RG19, RG20 131 A7
Sandhurst GU47 150 B8
Niagara Rd RG9 35 E8
Nicholas Ct 11 RG1 85 F7
Nicholas Gdns SL1 41 E5
Nicholas Rd RG9 35 B8
Nicholls SL4 66 C4
Nicholls Wlk SL4 66 C4
Nicholson Wlk 2 TW20 96 A3
Nicholsons Ctr 5 SL6 39 F7
Nicholsons La SL6 39 F7
Nideggan Cl RG19 106 D3
Night Owls RG19 131 C7
Nightingale Cres RG12 118 D4
Nightingale Ct Slough SL1 43 A3
9 Slough SL1 43 A3
Nightingale Gdns GU47 150 B8
Nightingale Ho 1 RG1 85 F5
Nightingale La
Maidenhead SL6 19 D3
Mortimer RG7 137 D6
Nightingale Pk SL2 21 F5
Nightingale Pl SL6 19 F7
Nightingale Rd RG5 87 D4
Nightingale Shott TW20 95 F2
Nightingale Wlk SL4 67 C4
Nightingales The
Newbury RG14 131 B8
Stanwell TW19 97 F7
Nimrod Cl RG5 88 B7
Nimrod Way RG2 86 B5
Nine Acres SL1 41 F5
Nine Elms Cl TW14 98 F7
Nine Mile Ride
Bracknell RG12,RG40 118 C1
Crowthorne RG40 142 D7
Wokingham RG40 141 D6
Nine Mile Ride Ind RG40 141 D5
Nine Mile Ride Prim Sch RG40 141 F6
Ninth Ave RG31 84 B6
Niplands Cotts HP10 3 D2
Nire Rd RG4 59 E2
Nixey Cl SL1 43 A4
No 4 RG30 85 C6
Noakes Hill RG8 54 B7
Nobel Dr TW6 71 E7
Noble Ct SL2 42 F5
Noble Rd RG9 35 F7
Nobles Way TW20 95 E2
Nodmore RG20 49 B7
Norcot Rd RG30 84 F8
Norden Cl SL6 39 C4
Norden Mdws SL6 39 C5
Norden Rd SL6 39 C5
Norelands Dr SL1 21 C3
Nores Rd RG2 113 D7
Norfolk Ave SL1 42 C8
Norfolk Chase RG42 91 F1
Norfolk Cl RG41 115 E6
Norfolk Park Cotts SL6 39 F8
Norfolk Rd
Maidenhead SL6 39 F8
Reading RG30 85 D7
Norland Dr HP10 3 C8
Norland Nursery Training Coll RG17 101 C7
Norlands RG18 106 C5
Norlands La TW18,TW20 123 E7
Norman Ave RG9 15 E1
Norman Ct 4 TW18 97 A4
Norman Ho TW17 125 A2
Norman Keep RG42 118 F8
Norman Pl RG1 59 B1
Norman Rd Ashford TW15 98 D2
Caversham RG4 59 C4
Normandy Wlk TW20 96 C3
Normanhurst TW15 98 A3
Normans The SL2 43 B7
Normanstead Rd RG31 84 C8
Normay Rise RG14 130 C5
Normoor Rd RG7 110 F1
Norreys Ave RG40 116 D7
Norreys Dr SL6 39 D4
Norris Field RG20 49 B8
Norris Gn RG5 61 A1
Norris Ho SL6 39 E7
Norris La RG20 49 B8
Norris Rd Reading RG6 87 A6
Staines TW18 96 F4
North Burnham Cl SL1 21 B3
North Cl
East Bedfont TW14 71 D1
Medmenham SL7 17 D7
Windsor SL4 66 F6
North Cotts SL2 22 C2
North Dr
Sulhamstead RG7 110 D7
Wentworth GU25 121 E4
North End La SL5 121 B2
North Farm Cl RG17 25 C3
North Fryerne GU46 149 D8
North Gn Bracknell RG12 118 D8
3 Maidenhead SL6 19 F1
Slough SL1 42 E6
North Gr KT16 123 F3
North Links Rd HP10 3 B8
North Lodge Dr SL5 119 C7
North Lodge Mews RG30 85 D5
North Pk SL0 44 D3
North Rd
East Bedfont TW14 71 D1
Maidenhead SL6 39 E7
Moulsford OX10 13 F4
Winkfield SL5 119 B8
North Row SL3 23 E8
North St Caversham RG4 59 B2
Egham TW20 95 F2
Reading RG1 85 F8
Winkfield SL4 93 A6
North Standen Rd RG17 100 A4
North Star La SL6 39 C6
North Terr SL4 67 E7
North Town Cl 1 SL6 19 F1
North Town Mead 4 SL6 19 F1
North Town Moor SL6 19 F1
North Town Rd SL6 19 F1
North View RG12 117 C6
North View Gdns 8 RG14 105 B4
North Wlk RG7 83 E4
Northam Cl RG6 87 E3
Northampton Ave SL1 42 C7
Northampton Cl RG12 118 E6
Northborough Rd SL2 22 B1
Northbourne Cl RG6 87 B2
Northbrook Copse RG12 118 F3
Northbrook Pl RG14 105 A3
Northbrook Rd RG4 59 D6
Northbrook St RG14 105 A3
Northbury Ave RG10 61 E5
Northbury La RG10 61 E6
Northcott RG12 118 A1
Northcourt Ave RG2 86 D4
Northcroft Slough SL2 22 B1
Wooburn Green HP10 3 F6
Northcroft Cl TW20 95 B3
Northcroft Gdns TW20 95 B3
Northcroft La RG14 104 F3
Northcroft Rd TW20 95 B3
Northcroft Terr RG14 104 F3
Northcroft Villas TW20 95 B3
Northdean 5 SL6 19 F1
Northend Cl HP10 3 C7
Northern Ave RG14 105 A6
Northern Hts SL8 3 B5
Northern Perimeter Rd TW6 71 E6
Northern Perimeter Road (W) TW6 70 D6
Northern Rd SL2 22 D1
Northern Way RG2 85 F1
Northern Woods HP10 3 C7
Northfield GU18 153 B8
Northfield Ave RG9 36 A4
Northfield Ct
Henley-On-T RG9 15 D3
Staines TW18 124 B8
Northfield End RG9 15 D3
Northfield Rd Eton SL4 41 F2
Maidenhead SL6 19 F1
Reading RG1 59 A1
Shiplake RG9 36 B4
Staines TW18 124 B8
Thatcham RG18 106 B4
Northfields
Chieveley RG20 51 B4
Lambourn RG17 25 B3
Northfields Terr RG17 25 C3
Northgate Dr GU15 152 A7
Northington Cl RG12 118 F3
Northmead Rd SL2 41 F8
Northolt Rd TW6 70 E6
Northrop Rd TW6 71 E6
Northumberland Ave RG2 86 C3
Northumberland Cl
Bracknell RG42 91 F1
Stanwell TW19 70 E1
Northumberland Cres TW14 71 E1
Northumbria Rd SL6 39 B4
Northview RG17 100 D5
Northview Hts RG17 100 D5
Northway Newbury RG14 105 B2
Thatcham RG18 106 C5
Wokingham RG41 115 E7
Northwood Dr RG14 105 C4
Northwood Rd TW6 70 D6
Norton Cl RG14 130 C6
Norton Pk SL5 120 C4
Norton Rd Frimley GU15 152 C4
Reading RG1 86 E7
Riseley RG7 139 C3
Wokingham RG40 116 C5
Woodley RG5 87 F5
Norway Dr SL2 43 B8
Norwich Ave GU15 151 E3
Norwich Dr RG5 87 C8
Norwich Ho SL6 39 E8
Norwood Cres TW6 71 C6
Norwood Rd RG1 86 E7
Notley End TW20 95 C1
Notton Way RG6 113 F8
Nuffield Dr GU47 143 F1
Nuffield Rd
Barkham, Arborfield Garrison RG2 140 F7
Barkham,Langley Common RG2 141 A8
Nugee Ct RG45 143 B5
Nugent Ct SL7 1 F3
Nun's Acre RG8 34 B7
Nuneaton RG12 118 E3
Nunhide La RG8,RG31 83 F6
Nuns Wlk GU25 122 D4
Nuptown La
Newell Green SL4 92 A8
Winkfield RG42 91 F7
Nursery Cl Hurst RG10 88 E7
Shiplake RG9 36 A4
Nursery Gdns
Purley On T RG8 57 B5
Staines TW18 97 B1
Sunbury TW16 125 F7
Nursery La
North Ascot SL5 119 E8
Slough SL3 43 D5
Nursery Pl SL4 68 B1
Nursery Rd Burnham SL6 41 B7
Sunbury TW16 125 F7
Nursery Way TW19 68 D1
Nursery Wlk SL7 1 B1
Nut La RG10 62 E6
Nutbean La RG7 139 F5
Nutbourne Ct TW18 96 F1
Nutfield Ct GU15 151 D7
Nuthatch Cl TW19 97 F7
Nuthatch Dr RG6 87 B4
Nuthurst RG12 118 E4
Nutley RG12 118 A1
Nutley Cl GU46 149 D5
Nutmeg Cl RG6 86 F1
Nutter's La RG2 140 A8
Nuttingtons RG20 49 F6
Nutty La TW17 125 C6

O

O'Bee Gdns RG26 134 F1
Oak Ave Egham TW20 96 D1
Sandhurst GU47 143 D1
Oak Dr
Burghfield Common RG7 110 F2
Newbury RG14 104 F2
Woodley RG5 88 A6
Oak End Way RG7 109 C4
Oak Farm Cl GU17 150 C5
Oak Gn RG2 113 D8
Oak Grove Cres GU15 150 F6
Oak Hill SN8 99 C3
Oak La
Englefield Green TW20 95 C5
Windsor SL4 67 A6
Oak Leaf Ct SL5 119 D8
Oak Lodge
4 Ashford TW16 98 F1
Crowthorne RG45 143 C5
Oak Ridge Cl RG14 130 E8
Oak Stubbs La SL6 40 F4
Oak The OX10 14 C6
Oak Tree Ave SL7 1 D3
Oak Tree Cl Tadley RG26 135 B1
Wentworth GU25 122 D3
Oak Tree Copse RG31 57 E3
Oak Tree Dr TW20 95 C3
Oak Tree Rd Marlow SL7 1 D4
Reading RG31 57 E2
Thatcham RG19 106 E2
Oak Tree Wlk RG8 57 D5
Oak View RG31 84 C8
Oak Way
East Bedfont TW14 98 E7
Woodley RG5 87 D4
Oakdale RG12 118 D3
Oakdale Cl RG31 84 C8
Oakdale Wlk RG5 88 A8
Oakdene
Burghfield Common RG7 111 A2
Sunningdale SL5 120 F3
Oaken Copse GU15 152 C7
Oaken Gr Maidenhead SL6 19 C1
Newbury RG14 130 D8
Oakengates RG12 118 A1
Oakes Ct RG17 100 D5
Oakey Dr RG40 116 B5
Oakfield RG1 86 D5
Oakfield Ave SL1 42 B5
Oakfield Ct RG41 116 A5
Oakfield Fst Sch SL4 67 B5
Oakfield Rd Ashford TW15 98 B3
Blackwater GU17 150 F3
Bourne End SL8 3 A3
Silchester RG26 135 E1
Oakfields GU15 151 B5
Oakhall Ct TW16 98 F3
Oakhall Dr TW16 98 F3
Oakham Cl RG31 57 D2
Oakhurst SL6 20 B4
Oaklands Curridge RG18 78 C3
Reading RG1 86 F6
Yateley GU46 149 D6
Oaklands Bsns Ctr RG41 116 A4
Oaklands Cl SL5 92 F1
Oaklands Cvn Pk RG41 114 F1
Oaklands Dr
North Ascot SL5 92 F1
Wokingham RG41 116 A5
Oaklands Inf & Jun Schs RG45 143 A6
Oaklands La RG45 143 B7
Oaklands Pk RG41 116 A4
Oaklea Dr RG27 140 E2
Oakleigh GU18 153 C8
Oakley HP10 3 F7
Oakley Cres SL1 42 E6
Oakley Green Rd
Fifield SL4 65 E5
Oakley Green SL4 66 B5
Oakley Green SL4 66 B7
Oakley Rd
Camberley GU15 151 B4
Caversham RG4 58 F4
Newbury RG14 105 D4
Oakmede Pl RG42 90 C2
Oakridge GU24 153 F6
Oakridge Pl SL2 22 C8
Oaks Rd Shiplake RG9 36 A4
Stanwell TW19 70 D1
Oaks The
Blackwater GU17 150 E3
Bracknell RG12 118 D7
Newbury RG14 131 A7
Staines TW18 96 F4
Yateley GU46 149 D5
Oakside Way RG2 113 E8
Oaktree Ave RG19 133 B5
Oaktree Cl SL7 1 D3
Oaktree Way GU47 143 A1
Oakview RG40 116 B4
Oakway Dr GU16 151 E1
Oakwood Rd
Bracknell RG12 118 E7
Virginia Water GU25 122 C4
Windlesham GU20 146 E4
Oareborough RG12 118 E4

Oareborough La RG18 . . .52 A1
Oast Ct TW18 . . . . .96 F4
Oast House Cl TW19 . . . .95 E8
Oatlands Dr SL1 . . . . .42 D7
Oatlands Rd RG2 . . . . . . .113 F5
Oban Ct SL1 . . . . .42 D4
Oban Gdns RG5 . . . . .87 E4
Obelisk Way GU15 . . . . .151 C6
Oberon Way TW17 . . . . .124 E6
Observatory The [6] RG30 85 E7
Ockwells Rd SL6 . . . . . . .39 C2
Octavia RG12 . . . . .118 A1
Octavia Way TW18 . . . . . .97 A2
Oddfellows Rd RG14 . . .104 F2
Odell Cl RG6 . . . . .114 B8
Odencroft Rd SL2 . . . . . .22 A2
Odette Gdns RG26 . . . . .135 C1
Odiham Ave RG4 . . . . .59 E5
Odiham Rd RG7 . . . . . . .139 D1
Odney La SL6 . . . . .20 B7
Ogden Pk RG12 . . . . .118 E6
Ogmore Cl RG30 . . . . .84 E7
Okingham Cl GU47 . . . . .143 D1
Old Acre La RG10 . . . . . . .61 B5
Old Apple Yd The RG41 . .88 A3
Old Bakehouse Ct RG45 143 B4
Old Bakery Ct SL0 . . . . . .44 F7
Old Barn Cl RG4 . . . . .59 A6
Old Bath Rd Charvil RG10 .61 B5
Newbury RG14 . . . . .104 F4
Sonning RG4 . . . . .60 D1
Old Bisley Rd GU16 . . . .152 C3
Old Bix Rd RG9 . . . . .15 A6
Old Bothampstead Rd
RG20 . . . . .51 D6
Old Bracknell Cl RG12 . .118 B6
Old Bracknell La E
RG12 . . . . .118 B6
Old Bracknell La W
RG12 . . . . .118 B6
Old Chapel Cotts RG18 . . .53 E1
Old Chapel The RG7 . . . .113 A2
Old Charlton Rd TW17 . .125 C4
Old Coalyard The TW20 . . .95 F2
Old College Rd RG14 . . .104 F4
Old Court Cl SL6 . . . . .39 B3
Old Dean Rd GU15 . . . . .151 D7
Old Elm Dr RG30 . . . . . . .84 D7
Old Farm Cres RG31 . . . . .57 C2
Old Farm Dr RG12 . . . . . .91 C1
Old Ferry Dr TW19 . . . . . .68 D1
Old Fives Ct SL1 . . . . .21 B2
Old Forest Rd RG41 . . . . .88 F1
Old Forge Cl SL6 . . . . . . .40 A3
Old Forge Cres TW17 . . .125 B3
Old Forge End GU47 . . .150 B7
Old Forge The
Streatley RG8 . . . . .34 A6
Tadley RG26 . . . . .134 E1
Old Green La GU15 . . . . .151 C7
Old Hayward La RG17 . . .73 D2
Old House Ct SL3 . . . . . .43 D7
Old Kennels Ct RG30 . . . .85 A5
Old Kiln Ind Est SL6 . . . . .19 A3
Old Kiln Rd HP10 . . . . .3 A8
Old La
Hamstead Marshall RG20 .102 E1
Headley RG19 . . . . .133 F1
Old La The RG1 . . . . .85 F5
Old Lands Hill RG12 . . . .118 D8
Old Marsh La SL6 . . . . . . .40 F4
Old Mill Ct RG10 . . . . .61 D5
Old Mill La SL6 . . . . .40 D4
Old Mill Pl TW19 . . . . . . .69 B1
Old Mill The RG8 . . . . . . .56 D6
Old Monteagle La GU46 149 B5
Old Moor La HP10 . . . . . . .3 E8
Old Newtown Rd RG14 . .104 F1
Old Nursery Pl TW15 . . . .98 B3
Old Orch The RG31 . . . . . .84 E4
Old Palace Ct SL3 . . . . . .69 D6
Old Papermill Cl HP10 . . . .3 E8
Old Pasture Rd GU16,
GU15 . . . . .151 F3
Old Pharmacy Ct RG45 .143 C4
Old Pond Cl GU15 . . . . .151 C1
Old Portsmouth Rd
GU15 . . . . .152 A5
Old Post Office La [10] SL6 39 F7
Old Priory La RG42 . . . . .91 D2
Old Riseley Stores The
RG7 . . . . .139 C3
Old Row Ct RG40 . . . . . .116 C6
Old Sawmill La RG45 . . .143 C6
Old Sawmills The RG17 .127 E6
Old School Ct TW19 . . . . .95 E8
Old School La GU46 . . . .149 C6
Old School Mews TW20 .96 D3
Old School The
Hampstead Norreys RG18 . .52 F5
Wooburn HP10 . . . . .3 D4
Old School Yd The [4]
RG17 . . . . .25 B2
Old Silk Mill The RG10 . .61 D5
Old Slade La SL0 . . . . . . .44 F2
Old St Chieveley RG18 . . . . .51 F1
Chieveley,Beedon Common
RG20 . . . . .51 C5
Hermitage RG18 . . . . .78 F8
Old Stanmore Rd RG20 . .30 E6
Old Station Bsns Pk
RG20 . . . . .31 E4
Old Station Way HP10 . . . .3 E5
Old Station Yd The RG17 .25 B2
Old Stocks Ct RG8 . . . . . .54 F5
Old Vicarage Way HP10 . . .3 D4
Old Watery La HP10 . . . . . .3 E8
Old Welmore GU46 . . . .149 E5
Old Whitley Wood La
RG2 . . . . .113 C6
Old Wokingham Rd
RG45 . . . . .143 C7
Old Woosehill La RG41 .115 F7
Oldacre GU24 . . . . .153 F7
Oldacres SL6 . . . . .40 B7
Oldbury RG12 . . . . .117 F6
Oldbury Rd KT16 . . . . . .123 E2
Oldcorne Hollow GU46 .149 A5
Olde Farm Dr GU17 . . . .150 B5
Oldean Cl RG31 . . . . .57 C1
Oldershaw Mews SL6 . . .39 B8
Oldfield Cl RG6 . . . . .87 B7
Oldfield Prim Sch SL6 . . .40 B6
Oldfield Rd SL6 . . . . .40 B7
Oldfield Rd Ind Est SL6 . .40 B7
Oldhouse La GU18 . . . . .146 C2
Oldstead RG12 . . . . .118 D4
Oldway La SL1 . . . . .41 D5
Oleander Cl RG45 . . . . . .143 A7
Oliver Dr RG31 . . . . .84 C5
Oliver Rd SL5 . . . . .120 B5
Oliver's Paddock SL7 . . . . .1 D5
Ollerton RG12 . . . . .118 A1
Omega Way TW20 . . . . . .123 C8
Omer's Rise RG7 . . . . . .110 F3
One Pin La SL2 . . . . .22 C8
Onslow Dr SL5 . . . . .93 A1
Onslow Gdns RG4 . . . . . . .59 C3
Onslow Lodge TW18 . . . . .96 F1
Onslow Mews KT16 . . . .124 A3
Onslow Rd SL5 . . . . .121 B2
Onyz The RG12 . . . . .118 E6
Opal Ct SL3 . . . . .23 C1
Opal Way RG41 . . . . .115 E7
Opendale Rd SL1 . . . . . . .41 B8
Opladen Way RG12 . . . .118 E4
Oracle Ctr The RG1 . . . . .86 B7
Oracle Parkway RG6 . . . . .60 A1
Oram Ct [2] SL7 . . . . .1 D2
Orbit Cl RG40 . . . . .141 E6
Orchard Ave
Ashford TW15 . . . . .98 C2
Hatton TW14 . . . . .71 D2
Slough SL1 . . . . .41 D8
Windsor SL4 . . . . .67 A6
Orchard Bglws Mobile Home
Pk SL2 . . . . .21 F5
Orchard Chase RG10 . . . .88 F7
Orchard Cl Ashford TW15 .98 C2
Egham TW20 . . . . .96 B3
Farnborough GU17 . . . . .150 E1
Henley-On-T RG9 . . . . .15 E1
Hermitage RG18 . . . . .79 C8
Maidenhead SL6 . . . . .40 A3
Newbury RG14 . . . . .105 C5
Purley On T RG31 . . . . . . .57 B4
Shinfield RG7 . . . . .113 B2
Shiplake RG9 . . . . .35 E2
West End GU24 . . . . .153 D6
Wokingham RG40 . . . . . .116 D6
Woolhampton RG7 . . . . .108 C2
Orchard Cotts RG10 . . . . .62 F6
Orchard Ct
Bracknell RG12 . . . . .118 C7
Camberley GU15 . . . . . . .151 B2
Harmondsworth UB7 . . . . .70 C7
Oatlands Park KT12 . . . . .125 F1
Reading RG2 . . . . .113 C7
Thatcham RG19 . . . . .106 E3
Orchard Dene Dr RG7 . .109 C2
Orchard Dr
Sunbury TW17 . . . . .125 E6
Wooburn HP10 . . . . .3 D4
Orchard Est RG10 . . . . . .61 E5
Orchard Gate
Farnham Common SL2 . . . .22 C7
Sandhurst GU47 . . . . . . .150 B8
Orchard Gdns SL6 . . . . . .20 B7
Orchard Gn RG17 . . . . . . .73 A1
Orchard Gr
Caversham RG4 . . . . .59 E4
Flackwell Heath HP10 . . . . .3 B7
Maidenhead SL6 . . . . .39 C7
Orchard Hill GU20 . . . . .146 D3
Orchard Ho [8] SL8 . . . . . .3 A4
Orchard Lea RG20 . . . . . .30 E7
Orchard Lodge SL1 . . . . .41 E5
Orchard Mill SL8 . . . . .3 B1
Orchard Park Cl RG17 . .100 D4
Orchard Pl RG40 . . . . . .116 C6
Orchard Rd Hurst RG10 . . .88 F7
Mortimer RG7 . . . . .137 B5
Old Windsor SL4 . . . . .68 B1
Orchard St RG1 . . . . .86 B6
Orchard The
Flackwell Heath HP10 . . . . .3 B7
Lightwater GU18 . . . . . . .153 B8
Marlow SL7 . . . . .1 E3
Theale RG7 . . . . .83 E4
Thorpe GU25 . . . . .122 E4
Orchard Way
Ashford TW15 . . . . .97 F6
Camberley GU15 . . . . . . .151 B2
Slough SL3 . . . . .43 E5
Orchardene RG14 . . . . . .105 B4
Orchardville SL1 . . . . . . .21 B1
Orchardwood SL5 . . . . . .119 E7
Orchids The OX11 . . . . . . .10 D7
Oregon Ave RG31 . . . . . . .57 D3
Oregon Wlk RG40 . . . . . .141 E7
Oriel Hill GU15 . . . . .151 D4
Oriental Rd SL5 . . . . . . .120 D5
Orion RG12 . . . . .118 A1
Orkney Cl RG31 . . . . .84 E4
Orkney Ct SL6 . . . . .20 E5
Ormathwaites Cnr RG42 .91 E1
Ormonde Rd RG41 . . . . .116 A5
Ormsby St RG1 . . . . .85 E7
Orpheus Ho RG7 . . . . . . .134 E2
Orpington Cl RG10 . . . . . .61 E4
Orrin Cl RG30 . . . . .85 A8
Orts Rd Newbury RG14 . .105 B2
Reading RG1 . . . . .86 D7
Orville Cl RG5 . . . . .88 A7
Orwell Cl Caversham RG4 .58 F4
Windsor SL4 . . . . .67 D4
Osborne Ave TW19 . . . . . .97 F7
Osborne Ct SL4 . . . . .67 C5
Osborne Dr GU18 . . . . . .153 A8
Osborne La RG42 . . . . . . .91 C4
Osborne Mews SL4 . . . . . .67 C5
Osborne Rd Egham TW20 .95 F2
Reading RG30 . . . . .85 B8
Windsor SL4 . . . . .67 D4
Wokingham RG40 . . . . . .116 C6
Osborne St SL1 . . . . .42 F4
Osier Pl TW20 . . . . .96 C2
Osman's Cl RG42 . . . . . . .92 B1
Osnaburgh Hill GU15 . . .151 B5
Osney Rd SL6 . . . . .19 E2
Osprey Ct [4] RG1 . . . . . . .86 C7
Osterley Cl RG40 . . . . . .116 F5
Osterley Dr RG4 . . . . .59 E6
Ostler Gate SL6 . . . . .19 C1
Ostlers Dr TW15 . . . . .98 C3
Oswald Cl RG42 . . . . .91 D2
Othello Gr RG42 . . . . . . .118 E8
Otter Cl RG45 . . . . .143 A7
Otter Ct RG2 . . . . .113 C7
Our Lady of Peace RC Inf Sch
SL1 . . . . .41 C8
Our Lady of Peace RC Jun
Sch SL1 . . . . .41 C8
Our Lady of the Rosary RC
Sch TW18 . . . . .97 A2
Our Lady's Prep Sch
RG45 . . . . .143 B5
Our Ladys RC First Sch
KT16 . . . . .124 A1
Ouseley Lodge SL4 . . . . . .95 C8
Ouseley Rd TW19 . . . . . . .95 D8
Overbecks RG14 . . . . . . .105 D4
Overbridge Sq RG14 . . . .105 E3
Overbury Ave RG41 . . . . . .88 F1
Overdale Rise GU16 . . . .151 E3
Overdown Rd RG31 . . . . . .57 D3
Overlanders End RG31 . . . .57 E3
Overlord Cl GU15 . . . . . .151 C8
Owen Cl SL3 . . . . .43 F1
Owen Rd Newbury RG14 .105 B6
Windlesham GU20 . . . . . .146 D5
Owl Cl RG41 . . . . .115 E5
Owletts Gr RG14 . . . . . . .105 D4
Owlsmoor Prim Sch
GU47 . . . . .143 E1
Owlsmoor Rd GU47 . . . .143 D1
Owston RG6 . . . . .87 C2
Oxenhope RG12 . . . . . . .118 A5
Oxford Ave Burnham SL1 . .21 B3
Harlington TW6 . . . . .71 F7
Slough SL1 . . . . .41 F8
Oxford Cl TW15 . . . . .98 C1
Oxford Ho RG41 . . . . . . .116 A6
Oxford Rd Chieveley RG20 .51 C1
Marlow SL7 . . . . .1 D2
Newbury RG14 . . . . .104 F5
Reading RG30,RG1 . . . . . .85 D8
Reading,Purley on T RG8,
RG30 . . . . .57 D4
Sandhurst GU47 . . . . . . .143 E2
Windsor SL4 . . . . .67 C6
Wokingham RG41 . . . . . .116 A6
Oxford Rd E SL4 . . . . . . .67 C6
Oxford Road Com Sch
RG1 . . . . .85 F7
Oxford St Caversham RG4 .59 A2
Hungerford RG17 . . . . . . .100 E7
Lambourn RG17 . . . . .25 B3
Newbury RG14 . . . . .104 F4
Oxfordshire Pl RG42 . . . . .91 F1

P

Pacific Cl TW14 . . . . .98 F7
Pack & Prime La RG9 . . . .15 C2
Packman Dr RG10 . . . . . .61 D6
Padbury Cl TW14 . . . . . . .98 D7
Padbury Oaks UB7 . . . . . .70 B6
Paddick Cl RG4 . . . . .60 E3
Paddick Dr Earley RG6 . . .87 D1
Lower Earley RG6 . . . . . .114 D8
Paddison Ct RG19 . . . . .106 E2
Paddock Cl
Camberley GU15 . . . . . . .152 A6
Maidenhead SL6 . . . . .39 A2
Paddock Cotts SL6 . . . . . .39 A2
Paddock Hts RG10 . . . . . .61 E4
Paddock Rd RG4 . . . . .59 D1
Paddock The
Bracknell RG12 . . . . .118 C6
Chilton OX11 . . . . .10 D8
Crowthorne RG45 . . . . . .143 A6
Datchet SL3 . . . . .68 B6
Maidenhead SL6 . . . . .19 C2
Newbury RG14 . . . . .105 C2
Paddocks Cvn Site The
GU25 . . . . .122 E3
Paddocks The HP10 . . . . . .3 B8
Paddocks Way KT16 . . . .124 B1
Padley Ct [8] RG1 . . . . . . .86 C7
Padstow Cl SL3 . . . . .43 E3
Padstow Gdns RG2 . . . . . .86 B1
Padstow Wlk TW14 . . . . . .98 F7
Padworth Coll RG7 . . . . .109 E1
Padworth La RG7 . . . . . .109 E3
Padworth Rd RG7 . . . . . .136 C7
Page Rd TW14 . . . . .71 D1
Page's Croft RG40 . . . . .116 D5
Pages Wharf SL6 . . . . . . .40 C8
Paget Cl Camberley GU15 152 B7
Marlow SL7 . . . . .1 F4
Paget Dr SL6 . . . . .39 A4
Paget Rd SL3 . . . . .43 F2
Pagoda The SL6 . . . . .20 B1
Paice Gn RG40 . . . . .116 D7
Paices Hill RG7 . . . . . . .135 A5
Pakenham Rd RG12 . . . .118 D2
Palace Cl SL1 . . . . .41 F5
Paley St SL6 . . . . .64 B6
Palgrave Ho RG45 . . . . .143 C4
Palmer CE Jun Sch The
RG40 . . . . .116 D7
Palmer Cl
Crowthorne RG40 . . . . . .143 A8
Peasemore RG20 . . . . .50 D7
Palmer Park Ave RG6 . . . .87 A6
Palmer School Rd RG40 116 C6
Palmer The [23] RG30 . . . . .85 D6
Palmer's Hill RG8 . . . . . . .54 C5
Palmer's La
Burghfield Common RG7 . .111 A2
Burghfield Common,Poundgreen
RG7 . . . . .112 A3
Palmera Ave RG31 . . . . . .84 C4
Palmers Cl SL6 . . . . .39 A3
Palmerston Ave SL3 . . . . .43 B3
Palmerstone Ct GU25 . . .122 E4
Palmerstone Rd RG6 . . . .87 B6
Pamber Heath Rd RG26 135 E1
Pamber Rd RG7 . . . . . . .136 B1
Pamela Row SL6 . . . . .65 A8
Pan's Gdns GU15 . . . . . .151 F4
Pangbourne Coll RG8 . . . .56 A4
Pangbourne Hill RG8 . . . .56 C5
Pangbourne Mews RG8 . .56 D6
Pangbourne Pl RG8 . . . . .56 D6
Pangbourne Prim Sch
RG8 . . . . .56 E5
Pangbourne Rd RG8 . . . . .55 C4
Pangbourne St [2] RG30 . . .85 B8
Pangbourne Sta RG8 . . . .56 C6
Pankhurst Dr RG12 . . . .118 D4
Pannells Cl KT16 . . . . . . .123 F1
Pantile Row SL3 . . . . .44 A2
Papist Way OX10 . . . . . . .14 A8
Papplewick Sch SL5 . . .120 A8
Paprika Cl RG6 . . . . .86 F1
Parade Ct [7] SL8 . . . . .3 A4
Parade The Ashford TW16 .98 F1
Bourne End SL8 . . . . .3 A3
Earley RG6 . . . . .87 B3
Egham TW18 . . . . .96 D3
Farnham Common SL2 . . . .22 C6
Reading RG30 . . . . .85 D5
Tadley RG26 . . . . .135 B1
Wentworth GU25 . . . . . . .122 D3
Windsor SL4 . . . . .66 D6
Woodley RG5 . . . . .87 E4
Woodley RG5 . . . . .87 F8
Paradise La RG7 . . . . . . .108 C7
Paradise Mews RG9 . . . . .15 D2
Paradise Rd RG9 . . . . . . .15 D1
Paradise Way RG7 . . . . .108 C7
Park Ave
Camberley GU15 . . . . . . .151 D4
Staines TW18 . . . . .97 A2
Thatcham RG18 . . . . .106 D4
Thorpe Lea TW20 . . . . . . .96 C1
Upper Halliford TW17 . . . .125 E6
Wokingham RG40 . . . . . .116 B6
Wraysbury TW19 . . . . .68 D3
Park Cl SL4 . . . . .67 D5
Park Close Cotts TW20 . .94 F3
Park Cnr SL4 . . . . .66 E4
Park Cotts
[3] Camberley GU15 . . . . .151 B3
Kintbury RG17 . . . . .101 B3
Park Cres Reading RG30 . .85 B6
Sunningdale SL5 . . . . . . .120 F3
Park Dr SL5 . . . . .120 F3
Park End RG14 . . . . .105 A4
Park Farm Ind Est GU15 151 C1
Park Gr RG30 . . . . .85 B6
Park Ho
Englefield Green TW20 . . . .95 C2
Maidenhead SL6 . . . . .39 E6
Park House Sch & Sports Coll
RG14 . . . . .130 E6
Park La Barkham RG40 . . .141 B5
Beech Hill RG7 . . . . .138 C2
Bracknell RG42 . . . . .90 E1
Burnham SL1 . . . . .21 E7
Camberley GU15 . . . . . . .151 C5
Charvil RG10 . . . . .61 B3
Horton SL3 . . . . .69 A4
Newbury RG14 . . . . .105 A4
Reading RG31 . . . . .84 C7
Silchester RG7 . . . . .137 C2
Slough SL3 . . . . .43 B3
Stockcross RG20 . . . . . . .103 B2
Thatcham RG18 . . . . .106 D4
Winkfield SL4 . . . . .93 B7
Park Lane Prim Sch
RG31 . . . . .84 D8
Park Lane Prim Sch Annexe
RG31 . . . . .84 D8
Park Lawn SL2 . . . . .22 C2
Park Mews TW19 . . . . . . .97 F8
Park Pl GU17 . . . . .150 F3
Park Rd Ashford TW15 . . . .98 B3
Bracknell RG12 . . . . .118 D8
Park Rd *continued*
Camberley GU15 . . . . . . .151 C4
Egham TW20 . . . . .96 A4
Henley-On-T RG9 . . . . .15 E1
Lower Halliford TW17 . . . .125 A1
Sandhurst GU47 . . . . . . .150 C8
Stanwell TW19 . . . . .70 C1
Stoke Poges SL2 . . . . .22 E3
Wokingham RG40 . . . . . .116 B6
Park St Bagshot GU19 . . .145 E3
Camberley GU15 . . . . . . .151 C5
Hungerford RG17 . . . . . . .100 D5
Maidenhead SL6 . . . . .39 F7
Newbury RG14 . . . . .105 A4
Poyle SL3 . . . . .69 D6
Slough SL1 . . . . .42 F4
Windsor SL4 . . . . .67 D6
Park Terr RG14 . . . . .105 A3
Park The RG17 . . . . .25 A3
Park View Ascot SL5 . . . .120 E8
Bagshot GU19 . . . . .145 D3
Burghfield Common RG7 . .111 A2
Reading RG1 . . . . .86 A5
Beech Hill RG7 . . . . .138 D5
Park View Dr N RG10 . . . .61 A5
Park View Dr S RG10 . . . .61 A4
Park Wall La RG8 . . . . . . .34 C1
Park Way
Hungerford RG17 . . . . . . .100 E4
Newbury RG14 . . . . .105 A3
Park Wlk RG8 . . . . .57 D5
Parkcorner La RG2,RG41 114 F6
Parker's Cnr RG7 . . . . . . .83 A3
Parker's La RG42 . . . . . . .92 B5
Parkers Ct GU19 . . . . . . .145 E3
Parkfields GU46 . . . . . . .149 D6
Parkgate SL1 . . . . .21 C1
Parkhill Cl GU17 . . . . . . .150 D4
Parkhill Dr RG31 . . . . .57 D2
Parkhill Rd GU17 . . . . . .150 D4
Parkhouse Ct [9] RG30 . . . .85 D6
Parkhouse La RG30 . . . . .85 D6
Parkhurst [20] RG30 . . . . . .85 D6
Parkland Ave SL3 . . . . . . .43 D2
Parkland Dr RG12 . . . . . .118 E8
Parkland Gr TW15 . . . . . .98 A4
Parkland Rd TW15 . . . . . .98 A4
Parkside Henley-On-T RG9 .15 C2
Maidenhead SL6 . . . . .19 D1
Woolhampton RG7 . . . . . .108 D4
Parkside Lo [11] SL3 . . . . .43 A3
Parkside Pl TW18 . . . . . . .97 A2
Parkside Rd Reading RG30 85 D6
Sunningdale SL5 . . . . . . .121 A4
Thatcham RG18 . . . . .106 D5
Parkside Wlk SL1 . . . . . . .43 A3
Parkstone Dr GU15 . . . . .151 C4
Parkview
Flackwell Heath HP10 . . . . .3 B7
Maidenhead SL6 . . . . .39 F7
Parkview Chase SL1 . . . . .41 E7
Parkway Camberley GU15 151 C3
Crowthorne RG45 . . . . . .143 A5
Marlow SL7 . . . . .2 A3
Parkway Dr RG4 . . . . .60 E3
Parlaunt Park Prim Sch
SL3 . . . . .44 B3
Parlaunt Rd SL3 . . . . .44 B2
Parliament La SL1,SL6 . . .20 F5
Parnham Ave GU18 . . . . .153 D8
Parry Gn N SL3 . . . . .43 F2
Parry Green S SL3 . . . . . .44 A2
Parsley Cl RG6 . . . . .86 F1
Parson's Wood La SL2 . . .22 D5
Parsonage Gdns SL7 . . . . .1 E1
Parsonage La
Farnham Common SL2 . . . .22 D4
Hungerford RG17 . . . . . . .100 D6
Lambourn RG17 . . . . .25 A3
Windsor SL4 . . . . .67 A6
Parsonage Pl RG17 . . . . . .25 A3
Parsonage Rd TW20 . . . . .95 D3
Parsonage Way GU16 . . .151 E1
Parsons Cl Barkham RG2 141 A8
Newbury RG14 . . . . .104 E2
Parsons Down Jun & Inf Schs
RG19 . . . . .106 A3
Parsons Field GU47 . . . .150 B8
Parsons Rd SL3 . . . . .43 F1
Part La RG7 . . . . .139 E4
Parthia Cl RG1 . . . . .86 A6
Partridge Ave GU46 . . . .149 B6
Partridge Cl GU16 . . . . . .151 E1
Partridge Dr RG31 . . . . . . .84 C6
Partridge Mead SL6 . . . . .19 F2
Paschal Rd GU15 . . . . . .151 F8
Pasture Cl RG6 . . . . .114 B8
Patches Field SL7 . . . . .1 E5
Paterson Cl GU16 . . . . . .152 C3
Pates Manor Dr TW14 . . . .98 D8
Pathway The RG42 . . . . . .90 C3
Patricia Cl SL1 . . . . .41 E6
Patrick Gdns RG42 . . . . . .91 E1
Patrick Rd RG4 . . . . .59 B2
Patriot Pl RG1 . . . . .86 C7
Patten Ash Dr RG40 . . . .116 E7
Patten Ave GU46 . . . . . . .149 C5
Patterson Ct HP10 . . . . . . .3 E7
Pattinson Rd RG2 . . . . . .113 D6
Pavenham Cl RG6 . . . . . .114 B8
Pavilion Gdns TW18 . . . . .97 B1
Pavilions End The GU15 151 D3
Pavy Cl RG19 . . . . .106 F2
Paxton Ave SL1 . . . . .42 C3
Payley Dr RG40 . . . . .116 E8

Paynesdown Rd RG19 ...106 B4
Peace La SL6 ....19 F6
Peach St RG40 ....116 C6
Peachey Dr RG19 .....106 F2
Peacock Ave TW14 ....98 D7
Peacock Cotts RG40 ..117 C5
Peacock La RG12 .....117 D6
Peacock Rd SL7 ....2 A3
Peacock Wlk RG41 ....115 E5
Pear Ave TW17 ....125 E6
Pear Tree Ct GU15 ...152 B8
Pear Tree La RG14 ...105 C6
Pear Tree Rd TW15 ....98 C3
Pearce Cl SL6 ....19 F5
Pearce Dr SL6 ....19 F7
Pearce Rd SL6 ....19 F5
Pearce's Orch RG9 ....15 D3
Pearl Gdns SL1 ....42 B5
Pearmain Cl TW17 ....125 B4
Pearmans Glade RG2 ..113 E8
Pearson Rd RG4 ....60 D3
Pearson Way RG5 ......87 E5
Peartree Cl SL1 ....41 F5
Peascod Pl **11** SL4 ....67 D6
Peascod St SL4 ....67 D6
Pease Hill RG7 ....107 F7
Peasemore Hill RG20 ..50 B8
Pebble Hill RG17 .....128 B6
Peckmoor Dr RG19 ...131 C7
Peddlars Gr GU46 ....149 E6
Peel Cl Caversham RG4 ..59 D2
  Windsor SL4 ....67 B4
  Woodley RG5 ....88 B8
Peel Ct SL1 ....42 B8
Peel Ctr The RG12 ...118 B7
Peel Ho TW20 ....95 F2
Peg's Green Cl RG30 ..85 B6
Pegasus Cl RG19 .....106 A4
Pegasus Ct
  2 Lambourn RG17 ....25 B2
  Reading RG31 ....84 C7
Peggotty Pl GU47 ....143 E2
Peket Cl TW18 ....123 E8
Pelham Ct
  Maidenhead SL6 ......39 E7
  12 Reading RG30 ...85 D6
  Staines TW18 ....97 B3
Pelican La RG14 .....105 A4
Pelican Rd RG26 .....135 E2
Pell St RG1 ....86 B6
Pelling Hill SL4 ....95 B7
Pemberley Lodge SL4 ..67 A4
Pemberton Gdns RG1 ..84 D4
Pemberton Rd SL2 ....21 E1
Pembroke RG12 ....118 A1
Pembroke Broadway
  GU15 ....151 C5
Pembroke Cl Ascot SL5 ..120 D4
  Burghfield Common RG7 ..111 C3
Pembroke Ho **3** RG4 ..59 C1
Pembroke Mews SL5 ..120 D4
Pembroke Pl RG4 ......59 C3
Pembroke Rd **4** RG14 ..105 A3
Pembury Ct UB3 ....71 D8
Pendals Cl RG18 ......52 F5
Pendeen Ct SL1 ....42 A5
Pendell Ave UB3 ....71 F7
Pendennis Ave RG4 ....59 E6
Pendine Pl RG12 .....118 B4
Pendlebury RG12 ....118 A2
Pendragon Ct RG30 ...85 D5
Pendragon Way GU15 ..152 B3
Pendred Rd RG2 .....113 D6
Penfurzen La RG42 ....91 D8
Peninsula Cl GU15 ...152 B7
Peninsular Cl TW14 ...71 E1
Penling Cl SL6 ....19 E6
Penn Cl RG4 ....59 A6
Penn Ct **8** SL7 ....1 E2
Penn Mdw SL2 ....22 F4
Penn Rd Datchet SL3 ..68 D6
  Newbury RG14 ....104 D5
  Slough SL2 ....22 D1
Pennfields RG10 ......61 E6
Pennine Rd RG31 .....84 B6
Pennine Rd SL2 ....22 F4
Pennine Way Charvil RG10 ..61 B4
  Harlington UB7 ....71 D7
Penny Hill Cvn Site
  GU17 ....149 C2
Penny La TW17 ....125 E2
Pennylets Gn SL2 .....23 A5
Pennypiece RG8 ....34 C7
Pennyroyal Ct RG1 ....86 A6
Penroath Ave RG30 ...85 C6
Penrose Ave RG5 ......87 E6
Penrose Cl RG14 .....104 F5
Penrose Ct TW20 ......95 C2
Pensford Cl RG45 ....143 B7
Penshurst Rd SL6 .....39 D5
Pentangle The **12** RG14 ..105 A4
Pentland Ave TW17 ...125 A4
Pentland Cl RG30 .....84 F5
Pentland Pl RG19 ....106 C2
Pentland Rd SL2 ....42 A8
Pentlands The RG17 ..102 C2
Penton Ave TW18 ....123 F8
Penton Ct TW18 ....96 F2
Penton Hall TW18 ....124 A8
Penton Hall Dr TW18 ..124 A8
Penton Hook Marina
  KT16 ....124 A6
Penton Hook Rd TW18 ..124 A8
Penton Rd TW18 ....96 F1
Pentridge Ho **2** RG2 ..113 C8

Penwood Ct SL6 ....39 B7
Penwood Gdns RG12 ..117 D3
Penwood La SL7 ....1 C1
Penwood Rd RG20 ...130 C3
Penyston Rd SL6 ......39 C7
Penzance Spur SL2 ...22 B1
Pepler Way SL1 ....21 B2
Peppard Cl RG2 ....86 E3
Peppard La RG9 ....35 E7
Peppard Rd
  Caversham RG4 ......59 B3
  Emmer Green RG4 ....59 C6
Pepper La RG2 ....86 E3
Pepys Cl SL3 ....69 B8
Perch Cl SL7 ....18 C8
Percival Rd TW13 .....98 F4
Percy Ave TW15 ....98 A3
Percy Bryant Rd TW16 ..98 E1
Percy Pl SL3 ....68 B6
Peregrine Cl
  Bracknell RG12 .....118 A4
  Wokingham RG41 ....115 F5
Peregrine Rd TW16 ..125 F7
Periam Cl RG9 ....35 C8
Perkins Ct TW15 ......97 F3
Perkins Way RG41 ...116 A5
Perpetual Park Dr RG9 ..35 F8
Perrin Cl TW15 ....97 F3
Perrin Ct TW15 ....98 A1
Perry Ho SL1 ....21 B1
Perry Oaks RG12 .....118 E7
Perry Oaks Dr TW6,UB7 ..70 C5
Perry Way
  Bracknell RG12 .....118 E7
  Lightwater GU18 ....152 F7
Perrycroft SL4 ....66 F4
Perryfields Way SL1 ..21 B1
Perryhill Dr GU47 ...142 F1
Perryman Way SL2 ...21 F2
Perseverance Hill RG9 ..35 A5
Perth Ave SL1 ....42 B7
Perth Cl RG5 ....61 A1
Perth Trad Est SL1 ...42 B8
Peterhead Mews SL3 ..44 A1
Peterhouse Cl GU47 ..143 F1
Petersfield Ave
  Slough SL2 ....43 A5
  Staines TW15,TW18 ..97 C2
Petersfield Rd TW18 ..97 C3
Petrel Cl RG41 ......115 E5
Petts La TW17 ....125 A5
Petty Cl SL1 ....41 E7
Petty Cross SL1 ....41 E7
Petworth Ave RG30 ...84 F3
Petworth Ct
  Frimley GU15 ....151 F4
  Reading RG1 ....85 E6
  Windsor SL4 ....67 A6
Pevensey Ave RG4 ....59 E5
Pevensey Ct RG2 .....86 E1
Pevensey Rd SL2 .....42 A8
Pewsey Vale RG12 ...118 F4
Pheasant Cl RG41 ....88 C2
Pheasant La RG20 ...131 F3
Pheasants Croft SL6 ..39 A4
Pheasants Ridge SL7 ..1 A5
Philbye Mews SL1 ....41 F4
Philip Cotts SL8 ....3 C3
Philip Dr HP10 ....3 C7
Philip Rd TW18 ....97 D2
Phillimore Rd RG4 ....59 C8
Phillip Copse RG12 ..118 D2
Phillips Cl RG5 ....61 B1
Phipps Cl SL6 ....39 A2
Phipps Rd SL1 ....41 E8
Phoebe Ct RG1 ....86 A6
Phoenix Bsns Pk RG12 ..117 C7
Phoenix Cl RG41 .....115 E6
Phoenix Ct SL6 ....39 D4
Phoenix Pl **5** TW18 ..97 A3
Phoenix Wlk RG14 ..130 C3
Phyllis Court Dr RG9 ..15 E3
Pickering RG12 ....118 A5
Picket Post Cl RG12 ..118 E6
Picketts La RG8 ....55 E4
Pickford Dr SL3 ....43 F5
Pickfords Gdns SL1 ...42 E5
Pickins Piece SL3 .....69 A5
Pickwell Cl RG6 ....87 C1
Pickwick Gdns GU15 ..152 B4
Pickwick Terr SL2 ....43 B6
Picton Cl GU15 ....152 B7
Picton Way RG4 ....59 B4
Pierce's Hill RG31 ....57 C1
Piercefield RG31 ......84 C4
Pierson Rd SL4 ....66 D6
Pigeonhouse La SL5 ..92 A4
Pigeons Farm Rd RG19 ..131 D8
Piggott's Rd **4** RG4 ..59 C1
Pightle The RG7 .....111 F3
Pigott Rd RG40 .....116 D6
Pigott Rd RG40 .....116 E8
Pike Cl SL7 ....18 C8
Pike St RG14 ....105 B4
Pikeshaw Way RG31 ..57 C2
Pimento Dr RG6 ....86 F1
Pimpernel Pl RG18 ..106 F4
Pincents Kiln Ind Est
  RG31 ....84 A4
Pincents La RG31 .....84 A4
Pinchcut RG7 ....111 A3
Pinchington La RG14,
  RG19 ....131 B7
Pindar Pl RG14 .....105 E5
Pine Ave GU15 ....151 D3
Pine Cl Maidenhead SL6 ..39 B7
  Sandhurst GU15 .....150 E7

Pine Croft Rd RG41 ..116 A2
Pine Ct RG12 ....118 E5
Pine Dr Blackwater GU17 ..150 B4
  Mortimer RG7 ......136 F6
Pine Gr Twyford RG10 ..61 D5
  Windlesham SL20 ...146 D4
Pine Mount Rd GU15 ..151 D4
Pine Ridge RG14 ....105 C5
Pine Ridge Inf Sch
  GU15 ....145 A1
Pine Ridge Rd RG7 ..111 A3
Pine Trees Bsns Pk
  TW18 ....96 E3
Pine Way TW20 ....95 B2
Pinecote Dr SL5 .....120 F2
Pinecroft SL7 ....1 D4
Pinefields Cl RG45 ..143 B4
Pinehill Rd RG45 ....143 C3
Pinehill Rise GU47 ..150 C8
Pinehurst SL5 ....120 D4
Pinel Cl GU25 ....122 E5
Pinelands Cvn Pk RG7 ..135 F4
Piner Cotts SL4 ....66 E4
Pineridge Dr **10** RG30 ..85 D6
Pines Inf Sch The RG12 ..118 A2
Pines Jun Sch The
  RG12 ....118 A2
Pines The
  Camberley GU15 ....151 F7
  Twyford RG10 ....61 E7
Pinetree Ct RG4 ......59 A5
Pinewood Ave
  Sandhurst GU47 ....149 F8
  Tadley RG26 ....134 D1
Pinewood Cotts RG45 ..143 A8
Pinewood Dr
  Caversham RG4 ......58 E5
  Newtown RG20 ......131 A2
  Staines TW18 ....97 A3
Pinewood Gdns GU19 ..145 C3
Pinewood Mews TW19 ..70 D1
Pinewood Pk RG40 ..143 C8
Pinewood Rd GU25 ...122 A5
Pingewood Cl RG30 ...85 A2
Pingewood Rd N RG30 ..85 A1
Pingewood Rd S RG7,
  RG30 ....112 C7
Pinglestone Cl UB7 ...70 E7
Pink La SL1 ....21 B3
Pinkneys Dr SL6 ......38 F8
Pinkneys Rd SL6 ......39 A8
Pinks La RG26 ....134 E1
Pinnacle The RG1 .....86 B7
Piper's End GU25 ....122 D6
Pipers Cl SL1 ....21 C5
Pipers Ct Burnham SL1 ..21 C1
  Thatcham RG18 .....107 A2
Pipers La RG41 ......106 F1
Pipers Way RG19 ....106 F2
Pipit Cl RG19 ....106 B3
Pippins Ct TW15 ......98 B2
Pippins Sch SL3 ....69 F6
Pippins The SL3 ......43 F5
Pipsons Cl GU46 ....149 D6
Pitch Pl RG42 ....90 D3
Pitcroft Ave RG6 ......87 A6
Pitfield La RG7 .....137 C4
Pitford Rd RG5 ....88 B3
Pitt's La RG6 ....87 B8
Pitts Cl RG42 ....90 C2
Pitts Rd SL1 ....42 C5
Plackett Way SL1 .....41 D5
Plaines Cl SL1 ....41 F5
Planes The TW16 ....124 C2
Plantagenet Pk RG42 ..118 F8
Plantation Cl RG18 ...78 F5
Plantation Rd Chilton OX12 ..9 F8
  Tadley RG26 ....134 F2
Plantation Row GU15 ..151 B5
Plantinum Apartments **14**
  RG1 ....86 B6
Plateau The RG42 .....92 A1
Platt Ct RG17 ....100 E3
Platt La RG17 ....45 C6
Play Platt RG7 ....83 D4
Players Gn RG5 ....87 E5
Playhatch Rd RG4 ....60 B5
Plough La Shiplake RG9 ..35 E1
  Stoke Poges SL2 ....23 B4
  Wokingham RG40 ...116 F6
Plough Rd GU46 ....149 D6
Ploughlands RG42 ..117 F8
Ploughlees La SL1 ....42 E6
Plover Cl Staines TW18 ..96 F5
  Wokingham RG41 ...115 F5
Plover La RG27 .....140 E1
Plowden Way RG9 ....35 E1
Plummery The **1** RG1 ..86 C7
Plumpton Rd RG14 ..105 C1
Plumtrees RG6 ....87 B2
Pluto Cl SL1 ....41 E4
Pluto Rd OX11 ....9 F8
Plymouth Ave RG5 ...87 C5
Plymouth Rd SL1 .....41 E8
Plympton Cl RG5 ......87 E3
Pocket Cl Bracknell RG42 ..117 D7
  Earley RG6 ....87 B4
Pocketts Yd SL6 ....20 B7
Pococks La SL4 ....42 E1
Poffley Pl RG19 .....107 A3
Point Royal RG12 ...118 B3
Pointers Cl RG20 ......51 B2
Points The SL6 ....39 B3
Polehampton CE Inf Sch
  RG10 ....61 D5
Polehampton Cl RG10 ..61 D4

Polehampton Ct RG10 ..61 D4
Polehampton Jun Sch
  RG10 ....61 E6
Pollard Cl SL4 ....68 B2
Pollard Ct SL5 ......152 C4
Pollardrow Ave RG42 ..117 F8
Pollards Way RG41 ...84 D4
Polo Ctr The SL5 ....121 C6
Polsted Rd RG31 .....57 D7
Polyanthus Way RG45 ..143 B8
Polygon Bsns Ctr SL3 ..69 F5
Pond Cl
  Farnborough (Berks) OX12 ..12 A1
  Newbury RG14 ......130 D7
Pond Croft GU46 ....149 E6
Pond Head La RG6 ....87 D4
Pond Ho KT16 ....124 B2
Pond La Hermitage RG18 ..79 F7
  Mapledurham RG4 ....58 A6
Pond Rd TW16 ....96 C2
Pondmoor Rd RG12 ..118 B4
Pondside Cl UB3 ......71 D7
Pool End Cl TW17 ...125 A4
Pool La Slough SL1 ...42 E6
  Waltham St Lawrence RG10 ..63 A5
Poole Cl RG30 ....85 A7
Pooley Ave TW20 .....96 C3
Pooley Green Cl TW20 ..96 C3
Pooley Green Rd TW20 ..96 C3
Poolmans Rd SL4 .....66 D4
Pope Cl TW14 ....98 F7
Popel's Cotts RG42 ...92 D5
Popes Cl SL3 ....69 C7
Popes La SL5 ....121 D6
Popeswood Rd RG42 ..117 D8
Popeswood Rdbt RG42 ..117 D7
Popham Cl RG12 .....118 E4
Poplar Ave Reading RG30 ..84 F5
  Windlesham GU20 ..146 B6
Poplar Cl Bracknell RG12 ..118 B8
  Brimpton RG19 .....133 A6
  Poyle SL3 ....69 E6
Poplar Gdns RG2 .....86 E1
Poplar Ho SL3 ....43 F1
Poplar La Hurst RG10 ..62 A2
  Winnersh RG41 ......88 D3
Poplar Pl RG14 .....105 A1
Poplar Rd Ashford TW15 ..98 C3
  Wooburn Green HP10 ..3 E2
Poplars Gr SL6 ....20 B2
Poplars The SL5 .....120 A4
Poppy Dr RG18 .....106 F4
Poppy Pl RG40 .....116 B6
Poppy Way GU15 .....84 C5
Poppyhills Rd GU15 ..151 F8
Porchester SL5 .....120 A5
Porchester Rd RG14 ..105 A1
Porchfield Cl RG6 ....87 A1
Porlock Cl RG19 .....106 D2
Porlock Pl RG31 ......84 C4
Port Down RG17 ....100 E5
Porter Cl RG6 ....114 C8
Porter End RG14 ....131 B8
Portesbery Hill Dr GU15 ..151 E6
Portesbery Rd GU15 ..151 E6
Portesbery Sch GU15 ..151 D6
Portia Gr RG42 .....118 E8
Portland Bsns Ctr SL3 ..68 B6
Portland Cl SL2 ....21 D1
Portland Cres TW13 ..98 D4
Portland Gdns Marlow SL7 ..1 D1
  Reading RG30 ....84 D7
Portland Rd TW15 ....97 E5
Portlock Rd SL6 ......39 C7
Portman Cl **5** RG42 ..118 A8
Portman Ctr The RG30 ..58 D1
Portman Rd RG30 ....58 C1
Portmeirion Gdns RG30 ..57 F1
Portnall Dr GU25 ...121 F4
Portnall Rd GU25 ...121 F4
Portnall Rise GU25 ..121 F3
Portrush Cl RG5 ......87 D6
Portsmouth Cl SL1 ...42 E6
Portsmouth Rd GU15 ..152 A7
Portway Riseley RG7 ..139 C2
  Tadley RG26 ....134 E1
Portway Cl RG1 ....85 E6
Post Horn Pl RG31 ...84 F4
Post Office Cotts SL2 ..23 A5
Post Office La
  Burghfield Common RG30 ..111 D5
  Slough SL3 ....43 D7
Post Office Rd RG17 ..127 C5
Posting House Mews
  RG14 ....104 E4
Potbury Cl SL3 ....93 B2
Potley Hill Prim Sch
  GU46 ....150 A5
Potley Hill Rd GU46 ..149 F5
Pottery La RG17 ....127 C5
Pottery Rd RG30 .....57 F1
Potts Pl **6** SL7 ......1 D2
Poulcott TW19 ....68 E1
Pound Cotts RG8 .....34 A6
Pound Cres SL7 ....1 C1
Pound La Hurst RG10 ..89 B5
  Little Marlow SL7 .....2 C4
  Marlow SL7 ....1 D1
  Newbury RG20 ......104 D4
  Sonning RG4 ....60 E2
  Thatcham RG18,RG19 ..106 A3
  Windlesham GU20 ..146 C4
Pound Piece RG17 ..100 C5
Pound Rd KT16 ....124 B2
Pound St RG14 ....104 F2
Pound Terr SL1 ....21 C1
Poundfield La SL6 ....19 F7
Poundfield Way RG10 ..61 F3

Powis Cl SL6 ....39 B4
Powney Rd SL6 ....39 C7
Poyle 14 Trad Est SL3 ..69 E4
Poyle Gdns RG12 ...118 D8
Poyle La SL1 ....21 B3
Poyle New Cotts SL3 ..69 F5
Poyle Rd SL3 ....69 E5
Poyle Tech Ctr The SL3 ..69 E5
Poynings The SL0 .....44 F2
Prancing Horse Cl
  RG19 ....106 A3
Precinct The TW20 ....96 A3
Precincts The SL1 ....21 C1
Prescott RG12 ....117 F2
Prescott Rd SL3 ......69 E5
Presentation Coll RG30 ..85 D5
Preston Pl
  Littleton TW17 .....125 A4
  Reading RG2 ....86 B5
  Slough SL2 ....43 C6
Prestwick Ct **21** RG1 ..86 D7
Prestwood SL2 ....43 B7
Pretoria Rd KT16 ...123 F1
Price Gdns RG42 .....91 B2
Prides Crossing SL5 ..93 A1
Priest Ave RG40 ....116 F5
Priest Hill Caversham RG4 ..59 A3
  Englefield Green SL4,TW20 ..95 C6
Priest La GU24 .....153 C5
Priestwood Ave RG42 ..117 F8
Priestwood Court Rd
  RG42 ....117 F8
Priestwood Sq **1** RG42 ..118 A8
Primrose Cl RG8 ......57 C5
Primrose La RG41 ....88 C3
Primrose Way GU47 ..143 B1
Primrose Wlk
  Bracknell RG12 .....118 C4
  Yateley GU46 ....149 B6
Prince Albert Ct **6** TW16 ..98 E1
Prince Albert Dr SL5 ..119 D4
Prince Albert's Wlk SL3,
  SL4 ....68 B6
Prince Andrew Cl SL6 ..20 B1
Prince Andrew Rd SL6 ..20 B1
Prince Andrew Way
  SL5 ....119 D7
Prince Consort Cotts
  SL4 ....67 D5
Prince Consort Dr SL5 ..119 D5
Prince Consort's Dr
  Old Windsor SL4 .....94 A6
  Windsor SL4 ....67 A1
Prince Dr GU47 .....143 A1
Prince Hold Rd RG14 ..106 A2
Prince Of Wales Ave
  RG30 ....85 D7
Prince of Wales Wlk
  GU15 ....151 C6
Prince William Ct TW15 ..97 F3
Prince William Dr RG31 ..57 C1
Prince's La RG20 .....50 D6
Prince's St RG1 ....86 C7
Princes Cl Bagshot GU19 ..145 E1
  Eton SL4 ....41 F1
Princes Ct Bourne End SL8 ..3 C4
  Englefield Green TW20 ..95 C3
Princes Rd Ashford TW15 ..97 F3
  Bourne End SL8 ....3 C3
  Egham TW20 ....95 F2
  Feltham TW13 ....98 C3
Princes St SL1 ....43 B4
Princes Terr SL8 ....3 C3
Princess Ave SL4 .....67 B4
Princess Christians Hospl
  SL4 ....67 C6
Princess Margaret Hospl The
  SL4 ....67 D5
Princess Marina Dr
  Barkham, Arborfield Garrison
    RG2 ....140 F7
  Barkham,Langley Common
    RG2 ....115 A1
Princess Sq RG12 ...118 B7
Princess St SL6 ....39 F6
Princess Way GU15 ..151 C5
Prior Croft Cl GU15 ..152 A4
Prior End GU15 ......152 A5
Prior Heath Com Inf Sch
  GU15 ....152 A5
Prior Place Cross Roads
  GU15 ....152 B4
Prior Rd GU15 ......152 A5
Prior's La GU17 .....150 A5
Priors Cl Maidenhead SL6 ..40 B2
  5 Slough SL1 ......43 A3
Priors Court Cotts
  Chieveley RG18 ......78 A4
  Hermitage RG18 .....78 F7
Priors Court Rd RG18 ..78 E7
Priors Court Sch RG18 ..78 D8
Priors Ct **8** RG1 ....86 B6
Priors Rd Tadley RG26 ..135 A1
  Windsor SL4 ....66 D4
Priors Way SL6 ....40 B2
Priors Way Ind Est SL6 ..40 B2
Priors Wood RG45 ..142 D4
Priory Ave Caversham RG4 ..59 A2
  Hungerford RG17 ...100 D4
Priory Cl
  Hungerford RG17 ...100 D4
  Sunningdale SL5 ...121 A2
Priory Ct
  Camberley GU15 ....150 F5
  Caversham RG4 ......59 A2
  Egham TW20 ....96 C2
  Winnersh RG41 ......88 C3

Priory Gdns TW15 98 D3
Priory Gn TW18 97 B3
Priory La RG42 91 C2
Priory Mews TW18 97 B3
Priory Pl
  Hungerford RG17 100 D4
  Newbury RG19 131 B6
Priory Rd Burnham SL1 41 C8
  Hungerford RG17 100 D4
  Newbury RG14 105 A1
  Sunningdale SL5 121 A2
  Winkfield SL5 119 B7
Priory Sch SL1 41 D8
Priory The RG41 88 C3
Priory Way Datchet SL3 68 B7
  Harmondsworth UB7 70 E8
Priory Wlk RG12 118 F5
Priscilla Ho 8 TW16 98 F1
Pritchard Cl RG19 131 D7
Privet Cl RG6 87 B1
Proctors Rd RG40 116 F6
Progress Bsns Ctr SL1 41 D7
Promenade SL4 67 C7
Promenade Rd RG4 59 A2
Prospect Coll RG30 85 A5
Prospect Cotts RG42 117 D8
Prospect La TW20 95 A3
Prospect Mews 4 RG1 85 F7
Prospect Park Hospl
  RG30 85 B6
Prospect Pl Hurley SL6 17 F3
  Newbury RG14 105 A1
  Staines TW18 96 F3
  3 Windsor SL4 67 D4
Prospect Rd
  Hungerford RG17 100 D5
  Marlow SL7 1 D2
Prospect St
  Caversham RG4 59 B2
  Reading RG1 85 F7
Providence Ho GU19 145 E3
Providence La UB3 71 D7
Providence Pl SL6 39 F7
Prudential Bldgs 1 SL1 42 F4
Prune Hill TW20 95 E1
Prunus Cl GU24 153 E6
Pudding Hill RG10 37 D6
Pudding La RG20 28 E1
Pudseys Cl SL6 19 B6
Puffers Way RG14 104 E2
Pullmans Pl 6 TW18 97 A3
Pump La Ascot SL5 120 E8
  Grazeley RG7 112 C2
Pump La N SL7 1 F6
Pump La S SL7 2 A4
Pumpkin Hill SL1 21 E6
Pundles La SL6 63 C6
Purbeck Ho 3 RG2 113 C8
Purbrook Ct RG12 118 E3
Purcell Rd RG45 143 B7
Purfield Dr RG10 36 E2
Purley CE Inf Sch RG8 57 C5
Purley La RG8 57 C5
Purley Rise RG8 57 A5
Purley Village RG8 57 C5
Purley Way RG8 56 E5
Pursers Ct SL2 42 E6
Pursers Farm RG7 113 B3
Purslane RG40 116 D5
Pursell Cl SL6 39 A3
Purton Ct SL2 22 C5
Purton La SL2 22 C5
Putman Pl RG9 15 E1
Pyegrove Chase RG12 118 E2
Pyke Cl RG40 116 D6
Pykes Hill RG8 54 D4
Pyle Hill RG14 105 B1
Pyrcroft Ct KT16 123 F2
Pyrcroft Grange Prim Sch
  KT16 123 E3
Pyrcroft Rd KT16 123 E2

Q

Quadrant Ct
  Bracknell RG12 118 E6
  12 Reading RG1 86 B6
Quadrant The SL6 40 A6
Qualitas RG12 117 F1
Quantock Ave RG4 59 D5
Quantock Cl Charvil RG10 61 B4
  Harlington UB3 71 D7
  Slough SL3 44 A1
Quantocks The RG19 106 D2
Quarrington Cl RG19 106 E2
Quarry Bank GU18 153 A8
Quarry La Shiplake RG9 36 A4
  Yateley GU46 149 E5
Quarry Wood Rd SL6,SL7 19 A8
Quarrydale Dr SL7 1 F2
Quartz Cl RG41 115 D7
Quaves Rd SL3 43 C3
Quebec Gdns GU17 150 D4
Quebec Rd RG9 35 E8
Queen Anne Royal Free CE
  Fst Sch The SL4 67 D4
Queen Anne's Cl SL4 94 B5
Queen Anne's Ct 9 SL4 67 C6
Queen Anne's Rd SL4 67 C3
Queen Anne's Sch RG4 59 B3
Queen Annes Gate RG4 59 C3
Queen Charlotte St 8
  SL4 67 D6
Queen Cl RG9 15 E1
Queen Elizabeth Rd
  GU15 144 D1
Queen Elizabeth's Wlk
  SL4 67 F5
Queen Mary Ave GU15 151 A5
Queen Mary Ct TW19 97 E7
Queen Mary Rd TW17 125 C7
Queen St Caversham RG4 59 A3
  Chertsey KT16 124 A1
  Henley-On-T RG9 15 E1
  Maidenhead SL6 39 F7
Queen Victoria Cross Roads
  GU15 151 A6
Queen Victoria Ho
  RG40 116 D6
Queen Victoria St RG1 86 B8
Queen Victoria's Wlk SL4 67 F6
Queen's Cl
  North Ascot SL5 119 E8
  Old Windsor SL4 68 A2
Queen's Cotts
  Reading RG1 86 B7
  Wargrave RG10 36 D2
Queen's Ct TW18 97 D2
Queen's Dr SL3 23 F4
Queen's Dr The RG2,RG6 86 E4
Queen's La 8 SL6 39 F7
Queen's Pl SL5 120 A6
Queen's Rd Ascot SL5 120 D4
  Caversham RG4 59 C1
  Datchet SL3 68 B7
  Egham TW20 95 F2
  Marlow SL7 1 D2
  Newbury RG14 105 B2
  Reading RG1 86 C7
Queen's Terr 5 SL4 67 D4
Queen's Wharf RG1 86 C7
Queens Acre SL4 67 D3
Queens Acre Ho 6 SL4 67 D4
Queens Ct
  3 Newbury RG14 105 A1
  Slough SL1 42 F6
Queens Gate SL4 67 D3
Queens Hill Rise SL5 120 C6
Queens Keep GU15 151 D5
Queens Lawns RG1 86 D6
Queens Park Gdns TW13 98 F5
Queens Pine RG12 118 E3
Queens Rd Bisley GU24 153 F1
  Camberley GU15 151 B4
  Eton SL4 41 F1
  Slough SL1 42 F6
  Windsor SL4 67 C5
Queens Ride RG45 143 B7
Queens Way RG17 102 C1
Queens Wlk TW15 97 D4
Queens Wlk Mall 3 SL6 39 F7
Queensborough Dr RG4 58 E5
Queensbury Pl GU17 150 C3
Queenshill Lodge SL5 120 B6
Queensmead
  Ashford TW15 97 F3
  Datchet SL3 68 B6
Queensmere Rd 5 SL1 43 A4
Queensmere Sh Ctr SL1 42 F4
Queensway
  Caversham RG4 59 D6
  Maidenhead SL6 19 E2
Quelm Park Rdbt RG42 91 B2
Quentin Rd RG5 87 D6
Quentin Way GU25 122 B5
Quinbrookes SL2 43 C7
Quince Cl SL5 120 D5
Quincy Rd TW20 96 A3
Quinn Ct 4 RG30 85 C7
Quintilis RG12 117 F1
Quoiting Sq SL7 1 D2
Quoitings Dr SL7 1 C2
Quoitings Gdns SL7 1 C2

R

Race Course Rd RG14 105 B1
Raceview Bsns Ctr
  RG14 105 B2
Rachaels Lake View
  RG42 91 E1
Rackstraw Rd GU47 143 D2
Radbourne Rd RG31 84 D4
Radcliffe Way RG42 117 E8
Radcot Ave SL3 44 B3
Radcot Cl Maidenhead SL6 19 E3
  Woodley RG5 60 E1
Radical Ride RG40 141 F7
Radius Pk TW14 71 F3
Radley Bottom
  Hungerford RG17 101 E7
  Hungerford Newtown RG17 74 B3
Radley Cl TW14 98 F7
Radnor Cl RG9 15 E2
Radnor Ho 10 RG1 85 E5
Radnor Rd
  Bracknell RG12 118 F6
  Earley RG6 87 C3
Radnor Way SL3 43 E2
Radstock La RG6 87 A2
Radstock Prim Sch RG6 87 B2
Radstock Rd RG1 86 E7
Raeburn Way GU47 150 D6
RAF Staff Coll RG12 118 D5
Ragdale RG7 111 A3
Raggleswood Cl RG6 87 C3
Raghill RG7 135 D6
Raglan Ct RG2 86 D2
Raglan Gdns RG4 59 C4
Ragley Mews RG4 59 D6
Ragmans Cl SL7 1 D8
Ragstone Rd SL1 42 E3
Railside RG7 108 F2
Railton Cl RG2 113 D7
Railway App KT16 123 F1
Railway Cotts RG8 34 C6
Railway Rd RG14 105 E3
Railway Terr Egham TW18 96 D3
  Mortimer RG7 137 E5
  Slough SL2 42 F5
Rainbow Pk RG41 88 B2
Rainsborough Chase SL6 39 B3
Rainworth Cl RG6 114 A8
Raleigh Cl Slough SL1 42 A5
  Woodley RG5 87 E5
Raleigh Ct TW18 97 A4
Raleigh Rd TW13 98 F6
Raleigh Way GU16 151 F3
Ralphs Ride RG12 118 E6
Ralston Ct 19 SL4 67 D6
Ram Alley RG19 133 D1
Rambler Cl SL6 41 B7
Rambler La SL3 43 C3
Ramptons La RG7 136 B6
Ramsay Cl GU15 152 B8
Ramsay Rd GU20 146 E5
Ramsbury Cl RG12 117 E3
Ramsbury Dr Earley RG6 87 B4
  Hungerford RG17 100 E5
Ramsbury Terr RG17 100 E5
Ramsey Cl RG6 87 E2
Ramsey Ct SL2 21 D1
Ramslade Cotts RG12 118 C6
Ramslade Rd RG12 118 D5
Rances La RG40 116 E5
Randall Cl SL3 43 F1
Randall Ct SL4 68 A1
Randall Mead RG42 90 B2
Randell Cl GU17 150 E1
Randolph Rd Reading RG1 59 A1
  Slough SL3 43 E3
Ranelagh CE Sch RG12 118 C6
Ranelagh Cres SL5 119 D8
Ranelagh Dr RG12 118 C6
Range Rd RG40 142 B7
Range Ride GU15 150 F7
Range View GU47 150 E8
Range Villas TW17 124 E2
Range Way TW17 125 A2
Rangewood Ave RG30 84 F3
Ranikhet Prim Sch RG30 85 A8
Rapley Cl GU15 151 F8
Rapley Gn RG12 118 C3
Ratby Cl RG6 87 C2
Raven Cl GU46 149 B6
Ravendale Rd TW16 125 F7
Ravenglass Cl RG6 87 C3
Ravens Field SL3 43 D4
Ravensbourne Ave TW19 97 E7
Ravensbourne Dr RG5 87 E8
Ravenscote Com Jun Sch
  GU16 152 A3
Ravenscourt Marlow SL7 2 A3
  Sunbury TW16 125 F8
Ravenscroft Rd RG9 15 D2
Ravensdale Mews TW18 97 B2
Ravensdale Rd SL5 120 A4
Ravensfield TW20 95 C2
Ravenshoe Cl SL8 3 A3
Ravenstone Rd GU15 152 D5
Ravenswing Mobile Home Pk
  RG7 135 D2
Ravenswood Ave RG45 142 E5
Ravenswood Dr GU15 152 A5
Ravenswood Village
  Settlement RG45 142 E6
Ravensworth Rd
  Mortimer RG7 136 E5
  Slough SL2 22 A2
Rawcliffe Ho SL6 40 A6
Rawlinson Rd GU15 150 F6
Ray Dr SL6 40 B7
Ray Ho 5 SL8 3 A4
Ray Lea Cl SL6 40 B8
Ray Lea Rd SL6 40 B8
Ray Lodge SL6 40 B7
Ray Lodge Mews SL6 40 B7
Ray Mdw SL6 20 A1
Ray Mead Ct SL6 20 C1
Ray Mead Rd SL6 40 C8
Ray Mill Rd E SL6 20 B1
Ray Mill Rd W SL6 40 A8
Ray Park Ave SL6 40 B8
Ray Park La SL6 40 B7
Ray Park Rd SL6 40 B8
Ray St SL6 40 B7
Rayfield SL6 40 B8
Raymond Cl SL3 69 E6
Raymond Rd
  Maidenhead SL6 39 D7
  Slough SL3 44 A3
Rayner Dr RG2 140 E8
Rayners Cl SL3 69 C7
Rays Ave SL4 66 F7
Raywood Cl UB7 71 C7
Reade Ct SL2 22 C6
Reading Alternative Sch
  RG1 86 C5
Reading Blue Coat Sch
  RG4 60 C3
Reading Bridge RG1 86 B8
Reading Coll & School of
  Arts & Design
  Reading RG1 86 D7
  Reading RG1 86 F6
Reading Gate Ret Pk
  RG2 85 F1
Reading Girls Sch RG2 86 C3
Reading International Bsns
  Pk RG2 113 A6
Reading Link Ret Pk RG2 86 A5
Reading Rd
  Aldermaston RG7 135 F5
  Aldworth RG8 33 A2
  Arborfield RG2 114 C3
  Blackwater GU17 150 B4
  Burghfield Common RG7 111 B2
  Finchampstead RG27 140 F4
  Goring RG8 34 E6
  Henley-On-T RG9 15 E1
  Moulsford OX10 14 A7
  Pangbourne RG8 56 D5
  Streatley RG8 34 A6
  Winnersh RG41 88 C2
  Wokingham RG41 115 E8
  Woodley RG5 87 D8
  Yateley GU46 149 D6
Reading Sch RG1 86 D6
Reading Sta RG1 86 A8
Reading Stadium (Speedway)
  RG2 85 F1
Reading West Sta RG30 85 E7
Recreation Cl GU14 150 F1
Recreation La RG7 113 B2
Recreation Rd
  Bourne End SL8 3 B3
  Burghfield Common RG7 111 A2
  Reading RG30 84 E8
  Wargrave RG10 36 E2
Rectory Cl
  Bracknell RG12 118 C5
  Farnham Royal SL2 22 C2
  Littleton TW17 125 A6
  Newbury RG14 104 F1
  Sandhurst GU47 149 F8
  Windsor SL4 67 A6
  Wokingham RG40 116 C6
Rectory La
  Aston Tirrold OX11 12 F8
  Bracknell RG12 118 B5
  Letcombe Bassett OX12 6 E7
  Windlesham GU20 146 C4
Rectory Rd
  Caversham RG4 59 A2
  Padworth RG7 135 F7
  Streatley RG8 33 C7
  Taplow SL6 20 E1
  Wokingham RG40 116 C6
Rectory Row RG12 118 B5
Rectory Terr SL2 22 C3
Red Cottage Dr RG31 84 C4
Red Cottage Mews SL3 43 C3
Red Cross Rd RG8 34 C6
Red Ct SL1 42 E5
Red Hill RG9 35 A5
Red House Cl RG6 114 B8
Red La RG7 135 D5
Red Leaf Cl SL3 43 F5
Red Lion Cotts SL2 23 B1
Red Lion Way HP10 3 E6
Red Rd GU18,GU24,GU15 153 C7
Red Rose RG42 90 C3
Red Shute Hill RG18 79 A4
Red Shute Ind Est RG18 79 A4
Redberry Cl RG4 59 D5
Redcrest Gdns GU15 151 F5
Reddington Dr SL3 43 E2
Redditch RG12 118 D2
Redfield Ct RG14 105 D4
Redford Cl TW13 98 F6
Redford Rd SL4 66 D6
Redgauntlet RG40 141 D6
Redgrave Pl SL7 1 F3
Redhatch Dr RG6 87 A2
Redlake La RG40 116 F2
Redlands Pl RG40 115 F2
Redlands Prim Sch RG1 86 E5
Redlands Rd RG1 86 D6
Redlane Ct RG1 86 D5
Redlane Hill RG7 135 C6
Redlane Rd RG20 30 A3
Redleaves Ave TW15 98 B2
Redmayne GU15 152 C4
Redpitch Pk HP10 3 F6
Redriff Cl SL6 39 D6
Redruth Gdns RG2 86 B1
Redshank Ct RG19 106 A3
Redshots Cl SL7 1 E4
Redvers Rd RG12 118 B4
Redwood Burnham SL1 21 B3
  Staines TW20 123 E7
Redwood Ave RG5 88 A6
Redwood Dr
  Frimley GU15 152 D4
  Sunningdale SL5 121 B3
Redwood Gdns SL1 42 D6
Redwood Mews TW15 98 D1
Redwood Way RG31 57 D3
Redwoods The SL4 67 D4
Reed Cl SL0 44 E7
Reed Wlk RG14 105 C4
Reed's Hill RG12 118 B4
Reeds Ave
  Lower Earley RG6 87 A3
  Reading RG6 86 F3
Reedsfield Cl TW15 98 B5
Reedsfield Rd TW15 98 B4
Reeve Rd SL6 65 B8
Reeves Way RG41 116 A4
Reform Rd SL6 40 B7
Regal Ct SL6 40 B2
Regatta Ho 8 TW18 96 F3
Regency Hts RG4 58 E4
Regent Cl Earley RG6 87 C1
  Hungerford RG17 100 C5
Regent Ct Bagshot GU19 145 F2
  9 Maidenhead SL6 39 F7
  Reading RG1 86 A8
  Slough SL1 42 E7
Regent Ct *continued*
  Windsor SL4 67 D5
Regent St RG1 86 E7
Regent Way GU16 152 A1
Regents Ct
  Newbury RG14 104 F3
  Staines TW18 97 B2
Regents Ho 3 TW20 96 A3
Regents Pl GU47 150 C8
Regents Riverside RG1 59 A1
Regents Wlk SL5 120 C2
Regis Cl RG2 113 D7
Regis Ct TW14 71 D1
Regnum Dr RG14 105 B5
Reid Ave SL6 39 E5
Rembrandt Cl RG41 115 D6
Rembrandt Way RG1 85 E5
REME Mus of Technology*
  RG2 141 A8
Remembrance Rd RG14 104 E2
Remenham Church La
  RG9 16 A4
Remenham La RG9 15 F3
Remenham Row RG9 15 F2
Remenham Terr RG9 16 C2
Renault Rd RG5 88 A6
Renfree Way TW17 125 A2
Rennie Cl TW15 97 D5
Rennie Ct RG14 104 F4
Repton Cl SL6 39 C3
Repton Rd RG6 87 C3
Restwold Cl RG30 85 C4
Retford Cl RG5 60 F1
Retreat The
  Englefield Green TW20 95 E3
  Fifield SL6 65 D7
Revel Rd HP10 3 D8
Revesby Cl
  Maidenhead SL6 39 D3
  West End GU24 153 D6
Rex Ave TW15 98 A3
Reynards Cl RG41 88 C2
Reynolds Ct RG18 106 D3
Reynolds Gn GU47 150 D6
Rhema Ct 9 RG1 85 F7
Rhigos RG4 58 F6
Rhine Cl RG4 59 D2
Rhodes Cl Earley RG6 87 E3
  Egham TW20 96 B3
Rhodes Ct TW20 96 C3
Rhododendron Cl SL5 92 E1
Rhododendron Cnr
  RG40 142 B4
Rhododendron Rd
  GU16 152 B1
Rhododendron Ride SL4,
  TW20 94 F3
Rhododendron Wlk
  Brimpton RG19 133 B5
  North Ascot SL5 92 E1
Ribbleton Cl RG6 87 E3
Ribstone Rd SL6 39 B3
Ricardo Rd SL4 68 B1
Richard Ct TW15 97 F3
Richard Nevill Ct 1 RG4 59 C2
Richards Cl UB3 71 D8
Richards Way SL1 42 A5
Richardson's Lawn Cotts
  SL4 94 B5
Richborough Cl RG6 87 B2
Richfield Ave RG1 58 F1
Richings Way SL0 44 F3
Richmond Ave
  Feltham TW14 71 E1
  Thatcham RG19 106 A3
Richmond Cl GU16 151 F1
Richmond Cres
  Slough SL1 43 A5
  Staines TW18 96 F3
Richmond Dr TW17 125 D3
Richmond Ho GU47 150 E7
Richmond Rd
  Caversham RG4 58 E4
  Reading RG30 85 D8
  Sandhurst GU47 150 E8
  Staines TW18 96 F3
Richmond Rise RG41 115 E7
Richmond Wood SL5 121 B1
Rickman Cl
  Arborfield Cross RG2 114 E1
  Bracknell RG12 118 C3
  Woodley RG5 87 D5
Rickman's La SL2 22 E6
Riddings La RG19 133 C2
Rider's La RG7 112 A4
Rideway Cl GU15 151 B4
Ridge Ct SL4 67 C4
Ridge Hall Cl RG4 58 E3
Ridge Mount Rd SL5 121 A1
Ridge The Cold Ash RG18 106 D8
  Sunningdale SL5 121 A2
  Upper Basildon RG8 55 F8
Ridge Way Iver SL0 44 F6
  Thorpe GU25 122 E4
Ridgebank SL1 41 F6
Ridgemead Rd TW20 95 B5
Ridgemount Cl RG31 57 B2
Ridgeway
  Oatlands Park KT12 125 F1
  Wargrave RG10 36 E2
Ridgeway Cl
  Hermitage RG18 79 B7
  Lightwater GU18 153 A8
  Marlow SL7 1 E4

Ridgeway Prim Sch The RG2 86 D1
Ridgeway Sch SL6 38 E5
Ridgeway The
Bracknell RG12 118 C6
Caversham RG4 59 B3
Letcombe Bassett OX12 7 D5
Lightwater GU18 146 B1
Marlow SL7 1 E4
Woodley RG5 87 F5
Ridgeway Trad Est The SL0 44 E6
Ridgewood Ctr (Hospl) GU16 152 C3
Ridgewood Dr GU16 152 D3
Riding Court Rd SL3 68 D7
Riding Ct SL3 68 C8
Riding Way RG41 115 E6
Ridings The
Caversham RG4 59 C8
Frimley GU16 152 B3
Iver SL0 44 F2
Maidenhead SL6 39 A7
Ridlington Cl RG6 87 E2
Rigby Lodge SL1 42 E7
Righton Cl RG10 61 B3
Riley Rd Marlow SL7 1 D2
Reading RG30 84 F8
Ring The RG12 118 C7
Ringmead
Bracknell, Great Hollands RG12 117 E4
Bracknell,Hanworth RG12 118 B2
Ringwood RG12 117 F2
Ringwood Cl SL5 120 B5
Ringwood Rd
Blackwater GU17 150 C6
Reading RG30 58 A1
Ripley Ave TW20 95 E2
Ripley Cl SL3 43 E2
Ripley Rd RG30 58 A1
Ripon Cl GU15 152 D3
Ripon Rd GU17 149 F1
Ripplesmere RG12 118 D5
Ripplesmere Cl GU47 150 B8
Ripston Rd TW15 98 D3
Risborough Rd SL6 39 E8
Rise Rd SL5 120 F3
Rise The Caversham RG4 59 B4
Cold Ash RG18 106 C7
Crowthorne RG45 142 F5
Finchampstead RG40 141 A2
Winkfield RG42 119 A8
Wokingham RG41 116 A7
Riseley Bsns Pk RG7 139 C3
Riseley Rd SL6 39 D7
Rissington Cl RG31 57 E3
River & Rowing Mus★ RG9 15 F1
River Ct Taplow SL6 40 C7
Twyford RG10 61 B5
River Gdns
Maidenhead SL6 40 D4
Purley On T RG8 57 D5
River Mount KT12 125 F2
River Park Ave TW18 96 D4
River Rd Caversham RG4 58 D3
Maidenhead SL6 40 C6
15 Reading RG1 86 A6
Staines TW18 123 F8
Yateley GU46 149 B8
River Side Cotts HP10 3 E8
River St SL4 67 D7
River View
Flackwell Heath HP10 3 B7
Froxfield SN8 99 C5
River Wlk RG14 105 C4
Riverbank TW18 96 F2
Riverbank The SL4 67 B7
Riverdale Ct RG14 105 C3
Riverdene Dr 4 RG41 88 A3
Riverfield Rd TW18 96 F2
Rivermead Ct SL7 18 E8
Rivermead Ind Est RG19 106 F1
Rivermead Prim Sch RG5 87 F6
Rivermead Rd
Camberley GU15 151 B2
Woodley RG5 87 F5
Riverpark Dr SL7 1 F1
Riverpark Ind Est RG14 105 B3
Riversdale SL8 3 B1
Riversdale Cotts SL8 3 B1
Riversdale Ct
Bourne End SL8 3 B1
Reading RG1 86 E8
Riversdell Cl KT16 123 F2
Riverside Bradfield RG7 82 C6
Chilton Foliat RG17 72 F1
Egham TW20 96 A5
Marlow SL7 1 E1
Oatlands Park TW17 125 E2
Wraysbury TW19 95 C8
Riverside Ave GU18 153 C8
Riverside Cl TW18 123 F8
Riverside Ct 1 RG4 59 A2
Riverside Dr Egham TW18 96 E3
Staines TW18 123 F8
Riverside Ho RG1 86 A7
Riverside Mus★ RG1 86 C8
Riverside Pk SL3 69 E5
Riverside Pl TW19 70 D1
Riverside Rd Staines TW18 96 F1
Stanwell TW19 70 E1
Riverside Way GU15 151 A3
Riverside Wlk SL4 67 D7
Riverview TW17 125 D2
Riverview Rd RG8 56 C5
Riverway
Great Shefford RG17 48 A3
Staines TW18 124 B8
Riverwood Ave SL7 2 A1
Riverwoods Dr SL7 2 A1
Rixman Cl SL6 39 D5
Rixon Cl SL3 43 E7
Robert Palmer Cotts The RG4 60 D3
Robert Piggott CE Inf Sch RG10 36 E1
Robert Piggott CE Jun Sch RG10 36 D1
Robert Sandilands Prim Sch RG14 104 E4
Roberts Cl TW19 70 C1
Roberts Gr RG41 115 F4
Roberts Rd GU15 151 A6
Roberts Way TW20 95 C1
Robertsfield RG19 105 F3
Robertson Cl RG14 131 B8
Robin Cl RG7 111 B3
Robin Hill Dr GU15 152 A3
Robin Hood Cl SL1 41 F5
Robin Hood Way RG41 88 C3
Robin La
Bishops Green RG20 131 F3
Sandhurst GU47 143 C1
Robin Par SL2 22 C7
Robin Way Reading RG31 84 B6
Staines TW18 96 F5
Robin Willis Way SL4 68 A1
Robin's Bow GU15 151 B4
Robina Ho RG42 117 F8
Robindale Ave RG6 87 D3
Robinhood La RG41 88 C3
Robins Cl RG14 130 F7
Robins Grove Cres GU46 149 B6
Robins Hill RG17 127 E6
Robinson Cl OX11 12 A8
Robinson Crusoe Pk RG40 141 B6
Robinson Ct RG6 87 A1
Roby Dr RG12 118 D2
Rochester Ave
Feltham TW13 98 F6
Woodley RG5 60 E1
Rochester Rd TW20 96 D2
Rochford Way SL6 41 A7
Rochfords Gdns SL2 43 C5
Rockall Ct SL3 44 B3
Rockbourne Gdns RG30 58 A1
Rockfel Rd RG17 25 A2
Rockfield Way 7 GU47 150 D8
Rockingham Rd RG14 104 F2
Rockley Ct RG7 83 D2
Rockmoor La SP11 147 A1
Rodd Est TW17 125 D4
Rodney Ct 11 RG1 86 A6
Rodney Way SL3 69 E6
Rodway Rd RG30 57 F1
Roebuck Est RG42 90 C1
Roebuck Gn SL1 41 E5
Roebuck Rise RG31 57 D3
Roebuts Cl RG14 130 F8
Rogers La SL2 22 F4
Rogers's La RG17 47 C6
Rokeby Cl
Bracknell RG12 118 D8
Newbury RG14 131 A7
Rokeby Dr RG4 58 D8
Rokes Pl GU46 149 A6
Rokesby Rd SL2 21 F2
Roland's Copse RG7 108 C2
Rolls La SL6 64 E8
Roman Lea SL6 19 F7
Roman Pl SL6 39 C6
Roman Ride RG45 142 D5
Roman Way Bourne End SL8 3 B4
Earley RG6 87 D3
Thatcham RG18 106 B4
Winkfield RG42 118 F8
Romana Ct TW18 97 A4
Romano Ct 2 RG14 105 B2
Romans Field RG7 136 B1
Romans Gate RG26 135 F1
Romany Cl RG30 58 A1
Romany La RG30 58 A1
Romeo Hill RG42 118 F8
Romney Cl TW15 98 C3
Romney Ct 11 SL7 1 F3
Romney Ho RG12 118 E5
Romney Lock Rd SL4 67 D7
Romsey Cl
Blackwater GU17 150 C6
Slough SL3 43 F3
Romsey Rd RG30 58 A1
Rona Ct RG30 85 B8
Ronaldsay Spur SL1 42 E8
Ronita Ct RG1 86 F6
Rood Hill RG20 76 B4
Rook Cl RG41 115 E5
Rook Rd HP10 3 D4
Rookery Ct
Barkham RG40 141 A6
Marlow SL7 1 D2
Rookery Rd TW18 97 B3
Rookery The RG20 50 D7
Rooksfield RG20 132 A2
Rooksmead Rd TW16 125 F7
Rooksnest La RG17 128 A5
Rookswood
Bracknell RG42 91 B1
Stockcross RG20 103 F6
Rookwood Ave GU47 143 E2
Rope Wlk RG19 106 C3
Rosa Ave TW15 98 A4
Rosary Gdns
Ashford TW15 98 B4
Yateley GU46 149 D6
Rose Bsns Est SL7 1 D5
Rose Cl RG5 88 B7
Rose Cotts
Maidenhead SL6 39 C3
Sandhurst GU47 143 A1
Rose Ct RG40 116 C6
Rose Gdns Stanwell TW19 97 D8
Wokingham RG40 116 C6
Rose Hill Binfield RG42 90 C3
Burnham SL1 21 A5
Rose Kiln La RG1,RG2 86 A4
Rose La RG10,RG9 37 A8
Rose St RG40 116 C6
Rose Wlk Reading RG1 86 A7
Slough SL2 42 B8
Roseacre Cl TW17 125 A4
Rosebank Cl SL6 19 E7
Rosebay RG40 116 E8
Rosebery Rd RG4 58 D7
Rosecroft Way RG2 113 E5
Rosedale RG42 90 C3
Rosedale Cres RG6 87 A8
Rosedale Gdns
Bracknell RG12 118 A4
Thatcham RG19 106 C2
Rosedene La GU47 150 D7
Rosefield Rd TW18 97 A4
Rosehill Ct SL1 43 A3
Rosehill Ho RG4 59 C7
Rosehill Pk RG4 59 C7
Roselawn Park Cvn Site RG30 111 D5
Roseleigh Cl SL6 39 A7
Rosemary Ave RG6 86 F1
Rosemary Gdns GU17 150 D5
Rosemary La
Blackwater GU17 150 D5
Thorpe TW20 123 B6
Rosemary Terr RG14 104 E2
Rosemead KT16 124 B2
Rosemead Ave
Feltham TW13 98 F6
Purley On T RG31 57 B3
Rosemoor Gdns RG14 105 D4
Rosen Ct RG19 106 E3
Rosery The SL8 3 A3
Roses La SL4 66 D5
Rosewood RG5 87 D4
Rosewood Dr TW17 124 F4
Rosewood Way
Farnham Common SL2 22 C7
West End GU24 153 E6
Rosier Cl RG19 106 F2
Rosken Gr SL2 22 B3
Roslyn Rd RG5 87 D6
Ross Ho 2 RG30 85 D6
Ross Rd Maidenhead SL6 39 E4
Reading RG1 59 A1
Rossendale Rd RG4 59 D3
Rosset Cl RG12 118 B5
Rossington Pl 5 RG2 113 C8
Rossiter Cl SL3 43 E2
Rosslea GU20 146 A6
Rosslyn Cl TW16 98 E2
Rothbury Wlk GU15 152 C4
Rother Cl GU47 150 C8
Rother Field Cl RG7 83 F4
Rotherfield Ave RG41 116 A7
Rotherfield Rd RG9 35 E7
Rotherfield Way RG4 59 B4
Rothwell Gdns RG5 61 A1
Rothwell Ho RG45 143 C4
Rothwell Wlk RG4 59 D2
Rotten Row Hill RG7 81 F3
Roughgrove Copse RG42 90 B2
Rounce La GU24 153 D6
Round Cl GU46 149 F5
Round End RG14 130 D5
Roundabout La RG41 115 D8
Roundfield RG7 107 B6
Roundhead Rd RG7 83 D3
Roundway Egham TW20 96 C3
Frimley GU15 152 C6
Roundway Cl GU15 152 C6
Routh Ct TW14 98 D7
Routh La RG30 84 E6
Row La RG4 59 E7
Rowallan Cl RG4 59 D6
Rowan 2 RG12 118 F4
Rowan Ave TW20 96 C3
Rowan Cl
Camberley GU15 151 F8
Wokingham RG41 115 F5
Rowan Ct RG6 87 B1
Rowan Dr
Crowthorne RG45 143 C6
Newbury RG14 105 A5
Woodley RG5 87 F8
Rowan Ho
1 Bourne End SL8 3 A4
East Bedfont TW14 71 D1
Rowan Way
Burghfield Common RG30 111 B5
Slough SL2 42 B8
Rowanhurst Dr SL2 22 C7
Rowans Cl GU14 150 E1
Rowans The TW16 98 F3
Rowanwood RG40 141 A6
Rowcroft Rd RG2 140 F7
Rowdell Dr RG2 86 D1
Rowdown RG17 24 E5
Rowe Ct RG30 85 B8
Rowland Cl SL4 66 D4
Rowland Hill Almshouses 7 TW15 98 A3
Rowland Way Earley RG6 86 F2
Littleton TW15 98 D1
Rowland's Cl RG7 136 C5
Rowles Paddock RG20 10 A2
Rowley Cl RG12 118 E6
Rowley La SL3 23 D4
Rowley Rd RG2 86 B4
Roxborough Way SL6 38 F4
Roxburgh Cl GU15 152 C4
Roxeth Ct 6 TW15 98 A3
Roxford Cl TW17 125 E4
Roxwell Cl SL1 41 E5
Roy Cl RG18 78 F6
Royal Ave RG31 84 C5
Royal Berkshire Hospl The RG1 86 C6
Royal Cotts SL6 19 C7
Royal Ct 11 RG1 86 C7
Royal Free Ct 13 SL4 67 D6
Royal Fst Sch The SL4 94 C4
Royal Holloway Univ of London TW20 95 D2
Royal Hunt Ho SL5 119 D8
Royal Mans RG9 15 E1
Royal Military Acad GU15 150 F6
Royal Oak Cl GU46 149 E6
Royal Oak Dr RG45 143 B8
Royal Station Ct RG10 61 D4
Royal Victoria Gdns SL5 120 A4
Royal Way RG2 112 F8
Roycroft La RG40 141 E8
Roydon Ct TW20 96 D2
Royston Cl RG30 84 F7
Royston Way SL1 41 D8
Rubus Cl GU24 153 E6
Ruby Cl Slough SL1 42 A4
Wokingham RG41 115 E7
Rudd Hall Rise GU15 151 E4
Ruddlesway SL4 66 D6
Rudland Cl RG19 106 D2
Rudsworth Cl SL3 69 D7
Rufus Isaacs Rd RG4 59 B2
Rugby Cl GU47 143 E1
Ruggles-Brise Rd TW15 97 D3
Rugosa Rd GU24 153 E6
Rumsey's La OX11 12 A8
Runnemede Rd TW20 96 A4
Runnymede★ TW20 95 F5
Runnymede Cotts TW19 96 D7
Runnymede Ct TW20 96 A4
Runnymede Rdbt TW20 96 B4
Rupert Cl RG9 15 E3
Rupert House Sch RG9 15 E2
Rupert Rd RG14 130 F7
Rupert Sq 6 RG1 86 D7
Rupert St RG1 86 D7
Rupert Wlk 4 RG1 86 D7
Rupert's La RG9 15 E3
Ruscombe Bsns Pk RG10 61 E5
Ruscombe Gdns SL3 68 A7
Ruscombe La RG10 61 E5
Ruscombe Pk RG10 61 E5
Ruscombe Rd RG10 61 E5
Ruscombe Turn RG10 61 F4
Ruscombe Way TW14 98 F8
Rushall Cl RG6 113 E7
Rusham Park Ave TW20 96 A2
Rusham Rd TW20 95 F2
Rushbrook Rd RG5 87 C7
Rushburn HP10 3 F6
Rushden Dr RG2 86 E1
Rushes The
Maidenhead SL6 40 C6
Marlow SL7 18 C8
Rushey Ho RG12 118 E5
Rushey Way Earley RG6 87 C2
Lower Earley RG6 114 A8
Rushington Ave SL6 39 F5
Rushmere Cotts RG5 88 A5
Rushmere Pl TW20 95 E3
Rushmon Ct KT16 123 F2
Rushmoor Gdns RG31 84 B4
Ruskin Ave TW14 71 F1
Ruskin Ct RG45 142 F4
Ruskin Rd TW18 96 F2
Ruskin Way RG41 115 D6
Russel Cl RG12 118 D2
Russell Ct
Blackwater GU17 150 D5
Maidenhead SL6 39 F7
Russell Dr TW19 70 D1
Russell Gdns UB7 71 A8
Russell Ho 4 SL8 3 A4
Russell Rd
Lower Halliford TW17 125 C2
Mapledurham RG4 58 D7
Newbury RG14 104 E2
Russell St Reading RG1 85 F7
Windsor SL4 67 D6
Russell Way RG41 88 B1
Russet Ave TW17 125 E6
Russet Cl TW19 69 F1
Russet Gdns GU15 151 D3
Russet Glade
Burghfield Common RG7 111 B2
Caversham RG4 59 C7
Russet Rd SL6 39 C3
Russet Way RG20 51 C5
Russett Gdns RG10 61 E6
Russington Rd TW17 125 D3
Russley Gn RG40 116 A1
Rustington Cl 1 RG6 87 B1
Ruston Way SL5 119 E7
Rutherford Cl SL4 66 F6
Rutherford Wlk RG31 84 A7
Rutherwyk Rd KT16 123 E2
Rutland Ave SL1 42 C8
Rutland Gate SL6 39 C6
Rutland Pl SL6 39 C6
Rutland Rd
Maidenhead SL6 39 D6
Reading RG30 85 D7
Ruxbury Ct TW15 97 E5
Ruxbury Rd KT16 123 D3
Ruxley Gdns TW17 125 C4
Ryan Mount GU47 150 A8
Ryans Mount SL7 1 C2
Rycroft SL4 66 F4
Rydal Ave RG30 57 F2
Rydal Cl GU15 152 D5
Rydal Dr RG19 106 A3
Rydal Pl GU18 153 B8
Rydal Way TW20 96 B1
Ryde Gdns GU46 149 B6
Ryde The TW18 124 B8
Rydings SL4 66 F4
Rye Cl Bracknell RG12 91 D1
Maidenhead SL6 39 A4
Winkfield RG12 118 D8
Rye Ct 1 SL1 43 A3
Rye Gr GU20,GU18 146 F2
Ryecroft Cl
Wargrave RG10 36 E2
Woodley RG5 60 E1
Ryecroft Gdns GU17 150 E4
Ryefield Terr SL3 69 D7
Ryehurst La RG42 90 F5
Ryeish Green Sch RG7 113 C4
Ryeish La RG7 113 C3
Ryemead La SL4 92 C5
Ryhill Way RG6 113 F8
Ryland Cl TW13 98 F4
Rylstone Cl SL6 39 C3
Rylstone Rd RG30 85 D8
Ryvers End SL3 43 F3
Ryvers Prim Sch SL3 43 D3
Ryvers Rd SL3 43 F3
Ryves Ave GU46 149 A5

S

Sabah Ct TW15 98 A4
Sabin Gates RG12 118 B6
Sackville St RG1 86 A8
Sacred Heart RC Prim Sch The RG9 15 D1
Saddleback Rd GU15 151 E8
Saddlebrook Pk TW16 98 E1
Saddler Cnr GU47 150 B7
Saddlewood GU15 151 C4
Sadlers Ct RG41 88 D1
Sadlers End RG41 115 C7
Sadlers La RG41 115 D8
Sadlers Mews SL6 40 B7
Sadlers Rd RG17 127 A6
Sadlers The RG31 57 B1
Saffron Cl Datchet SL3 68 B6
Earley RG6 87 C4
Newbury RG14 104 F3
Saffron Ct TW14 98 C8
Saffron Rd RG12 118 B5
Sage Cl RG6 87 A1
Sage Ct SL4 95 A8
Sage Rd RG31 57 C3
Sage Wlk RG42 91 D1
Sagecroft Rd RG18 106 C5
Sailing Club Rd SL8 3 A3
Sainsbury Ctr The KT16 124 A2
Saint Sebastian's CE Prim Sch RG40 142 E8
Saint-Cloud Way SL6 40 A7
St Adrian's Cl SL6 39 B4
St Agnes Mews RG2 86 C2
St Agnes Terr RG17 25 B2
St Alban's St SL4 67 D6
St Albans Cl 10 SL4 67 D6
St Andrew's Ave SL4 66 F5
St Andrew's Cl
Old Windsor SL4 68 A1
Upper Halliford TW17 125 D5
Wraysbury TW19 68 E1
St Andrew's Cres SL4 66 F5
St Andrew's Rd
Caversham RG4 58 F4
Henley-On-T RG9 35 D8
St Andrew's Sch RG8 55 C1
St Andrew's Way SL1 41 D6
St Andrews RG12 117 E3
St Andrews Cl
Bradfield RG7 82 C6
Crowthorne RG45 142 F6
St Andrews Cotts 1 SL4 67 A5
St Andrews Ct Ascot SL5 120 C4
Colnbrook SL3 69 D7
20 Reading RG1 86 D7
2 Slough SL1 42 E3
St Ann's Cl KT16 123 F3
St Ann's Heath Jun Sch GU25 122 E4
St Ann's Hill Rd KT16 123 D3
St Ann's Rd KT16 123 F3
St Anne's Ave TW19 97 D8
St Anne's Cl RG9 15 D1
St Anne's Prim Sch TW19 97 E8
St Anne's RC Prim Sch
Caversham RG4 59 B2
Chertsey KT16 124 A1
St Anne's Rd RG4 59 A2
St Annes Dr RG40 117 A6
St Annes Glade GU19 145 D3

St Anthony's RC Prim Sch
SL2 ....22 C1
St Anthony's Way TW14 ..71 F3
St Anthonys CI RG42 ...118 A8
St Augustine's RC Prim Sch
GU16 ....151 F2
St Barnabas Rd
Caversham RG4 ....59 A6
Earley RG2 ....86 F1
St Bartholomew's Sch
RG14 ....104 E1
St Bartholomews Rd RG1 86 F7
St Bernard's Convent Sch
SL3 ....43 C4
St Bernard's Prep Sch
SL1 ....43 B4
St Bernards Rd SL3 ....43 C3
St Birinus Rd RG31 ....84 C5
St Catherine's CI RG41 ..88 B1
St Catherine's Hill RG7 .136 E6
St Catherine's Ct
GU15 ....151 C4
St Catherines Ct
2 Staines TW18 ....97 A4
3 Windsor SL4 ....67 A5
St Catherines PI 1
TW20 ....96 A3
St Cecelia Ct RG2 ......86 C2
St Chad's Rd SL6 ......39 B4
St Christophers Gdns
SL5 ....119 D8
St Clements CI RG6 .....87 C1
St Columba's CI SL6 ....39 B4
St Crispin's Sch RG40 ..116 E6
St Cuthbert's CI TW20 ..95 D2
St Cuthbert's RC Prim Sch
TW20 ....95 C1
St David's CI
Caversham RG4 ....58 F5
Maidenhead SL6 ....39 A4
St David's Rd RG14 ....104 E1
St David's Sch TW15 ....97 F5
St Davids Dr TW20 .....95 C1
St Dominic Savio RC Prim
Sch RG5 ....87 D8
St Donats PI RG14 .....105 A2
St Dunstan's Rd TW13 ..98 F1
St Edmund Campion RC Prim
Sch SL4 ....39 B6
St Edward's RC Fst Sch
SL4 ....67 A6
St Edward's Rd RG6 ....87 A6
St Edward's Royal Free
Ecumenical Mid Sch
Reading RG30 ....85 D7
Windsor SL4 ....67 A6
St Edward's Sch RG30 ..85 D7
St Elizabeth CI RG2 ...113 B7
St Elmo CI SL2 ....22 D1
St Elmo Cres SL2 ......22 D1
St Ethelbert's RC Prim Sch
SL2 ....43 A7
St Finian's RC Prim Sch
RG18 ....106 D8
St Francis RC Sch SL5 ..120 A3
St Gabriel's Sch RG20 ..131 B5
St Gabriels Ct GU15 ...151 D5
St George's Ave RG14 ..104 E2
St George's CI SL4 .....66 C6
St George's Cres SL1 ...41 D6
St George's Ct GU47 ...143 E2
St George's La SL5 ....120 B5
St George's Rd
Camberley GU15 ......151 D6
Reading RG30 ....85 C8
St George's Sch
Ascot SL5 ....120 B6
Windsor SL4 ....67 D7
St George's Terr RG30 ..85 B8
St Georges Ind Est
GU15 ....151 B3
St Giles Ct RG1 ....86 B6
St Giles Ct 1 RG1 ....86 B6
St Helens Cres GU47 ..150 B8
St Helier CI RG41 .....116 B3
St Hilda's Ave TW15 ...97 E3
St Ives CI RG7 ....83 D2
St Ives Rd SL6 ....40 A7
St James CI
Pangbourne RG8 ......56 C6
Twyford RG10 ....61 E5
St James Ctyd 4 SL7 ...1 E2
St James PI SL1 ....41 C7
St James Rd RG40 ....141 E8
St James Wlk SL0 .....44 E4
St John the Evangelist CE
Sch RG14 ....104 F1
St John's Beaumont Sch
TW19 ....95 B6
St John's CE Prim Sch
RG1 ....86 D7
St John's Gdns RG14 ..104 F1
St John's Hill RG1 .....86 C7
St John's Rd
Caversham RG4 ....59 C2
Mortimer RG7 ....137 A5
Newbury RG14 ....105 A1
North Ascot SL5 ....92 H1
Reading RG1 ....86 C7
Sandhurst GU47 ......150 C7
Thatcham RG19 ......106 C3
St John's St RG1 ......86 C7
St Johns CI RG5 ....87 F8
St Johns Ct TW20 .....96 A3
St Johns Dr SL4 ....67 A5
St Johns Rd Slough SL2 .43 A6
Windsor SL4 ....67 A5
St Johns St RG45 .....143 B4

St Johns Way KT16 ....124 A1
St Joseph's Convent Sch
RG1 ....86 E5
St Joseph's RC High Sch
SL2 ....43 A7
St Joseph's RC Prim Sch
Bracknell RG12 ....118 D7
Newbury RG14 ....105 B4
St Josephs Ct 7 RG14 .105 B4
St Jude's CE Sch TW20 .95 C2
St Jude's CI SL6 ....95 C3
St Jude's Cotts TW20 ...95 C3
St Jude's Rd TW20 .....95 C3
St Katherine's Rd RG9 ..35 D7
St Laurence Way SL1 ...43 A3
St Lawrence Sq RG17 .100 C6
St Leger Ct RG14 .....104 E4
St Leonard's Ave SL4 ..67 C5
St Leonard's Rd
Windsor SL4 ....67 C4
Windsor,Clewer Green SL4 .66 D1
St Leonards Hill SL4 ...66 A4
St Leonards Wlk SL0 ...44 F3
St Luke's CE Prim Sch
SL6 ....39 F8
St Luke's Rd
Maidenhead SL6 ......39 F8
Old Windsor SL4 ......68 A1
St Lukes Ct RG4 ......59 B4
St Lukes Way RG4 .....59 B5
St Margaret Clitherow RC
Prim Sch RG12 ....117 D2
St Margaret's Rd SL6 ..39 A7
St Margarets Ave TW15 .98 B3
St Mark's CI RG7 ......83 B5
St Mark's Cres SL6 ....39 B7
St Mark's Hospl SL6 ...39 C7
St Mark's PI SL4 ......67 C5
St Mark's Rd
Bracknell RG42 ....117 C8
Henley-On-T RG9 .....35 C8
Maidenhead SL6 ......39 D7
Windsor SL4 ....67 C5
St Marks CI RG19 .....106 C3
St Marks Ct TW15 .....97 C3
St Martin's RC Prim Sch
RG4 ....59 A6
St Martins CI 3 RG6 ..87 C1
St Mary's All Saints CE Prim
Sch RG1 ....85 B5
St Mary's Ave
Purley On T RG8 ......57 D5
Stanwell TW19 ....97 D8
St Mary's Butts RG1 ...86 A7
St Mary's CE Jun Sch
Stanwell TW19 ....97 E8
Thatcham RG18 ......106 D4
St Mary's CE Prim Sch
Kintbury RG17 ....102 B2
Slough SL1 ....43 A3
St Mary's CI
Henley-On-T RG9 .....35 A8
Maidenhead SL6 ......40 A7
Stanwell TW19 ....97 D8
St Mary's Cres TW19 ...97 D8
St Mary's Ct 6 RG14 ..105 A4
St Mary's Dr TW14 ....98 C8
St Mary's Gdns GU19 .145 E2
St Mary's Gr RG1 .....86 A7
St Mary's Hill SL5 ....120 C4
St Mary's Ho RG18 ....79 C1
St Mary's PI 8 RG14 .105 A4
St Mary's RC Prim Sch
SL6 ....19 F2
St Mary's Rd Ascot SL5 .120 B3
Camberley GU15 ......151 C6
Mortimer RG7 ....137 A5
Newbury RG14 ....105 A4
Sindlesham RG41 .....115 B8
Slough SL3 ....43 E4
Winnersh RG41 ....88 B1
St Mary's Sch SL5 ....120 B2
St Mary's Way RG7 ...111 B3
St Marys CI GU47 ....150 C8
St Marys La SL4 ......92 D5
St Matthew's Ct 8
TW15 ....98 A3
St Michael Prim Sch
RG30 ....85 A4
St Michael's Ct SL2 ....21 D1
St Michael's Easthampstead
CE Prim Sch RG12 ...118 A4
St Michael's PI GU15 .151 B3
St Michael's RC Prim Sch
TW15 ....98 A3
St Michael's Rd
Newbury RG14 ....104 F2
Reading RG30 ....84 D7
Sandhurst GU47 ......149 F8
St Michaels CE Prim Sch
GU47 ....149 F8
St Michaels CI RG17 ...25 A2
St Michaels Cotts RG40 143 C8
St Michaels Ct RG10 ...61 C6
St Michaels La RG7 ...110 D5
St Michaels Rd
Ashford TW15 ....98 A3
Camberley GU15 .....151 B5
St Micheal's CE Prim Sch
SL5 ....120 D4
St Nazaire CI SL4 .....67 C6
St Nicholas CE Comb Sch
SL6 ....20 E1
St Nicholas CE Prim Sch
Hurst RG10 ....88 F7
Shepperton TW17 ...125 B3
St Nicholas Dr TW17 .125 A2

St Nicholas' Rd RG14 ..104 F2
St Nicolas CE Jun Sch
RG14 ....105 A2
St Olave's CI TW18 ....96 F1
St Patrick's Ave RG10 ..61 A5
St Patrick's CI SL6 ....39 B4
St Paul's CE Comb Sch,
Wooburn HP10 ....3 D4
St Paul's CE Jun Sch
RG41 ....116 A6
St Paul's CI TW15 .....98 C3
St Paul's Ct
Maidenhead SL6 ......39 F6
Reading RG1 ....86 A6
St Paul's Gate RG41 ..116 A6
St Paul's Mews RG2 ..113 B7
St Paul's RC Prim Sch
RG31 ....84 C7
St Paul's Rd TW18 ....96 D2
St Pauls Ave SL2 ......43 A5
St Peter St SL7 ....1 A1
St Peter's Ave RG4 ....58 E3
St Peter's CE Comb Sch
SL1 ....21 B2
St Peter's CE Jun Sch
GU46 ....149 E6
St Peter's CE Mid Sch
SL4 ....67 F1
St Peter's CE Prim Sch
RG6 ....87 B5
St Peter's Cl Burnham SL1 21 B1
Old Windsor SL4 ......68 A2
Staines TW18 ....96 F2
St Peter's Gdns GU46 .149 D6
St Peter's Hill RG4 ....58 F3
St Peter's RC Prim Sch
SL7 ....1 D3
St Peter's Rd
Maidenhead SL6 ......19 D2
Reading RG6 ....87 A5
St Peters CI RG19 ....132 D2
St Peters Rd RG6 .....87 A5
St Peters Way UB3 ....71 D8
St Pinnock Ave TW18 .124 A8
St Pirans St SL6 ....19 E1
St Richards Rd RG14 ..105 A4
St Ronans Rd RG30 ....85 B8
St Saviour's Rd RG1 ...85 F5
St Saviour's Terr 9 RG1 .86 A6
St Sebastian's CE RG40 .142 E7
St Stephens CI RG4 ...59 A2
St Swithins CI RG20 ...75 D4
St Swithuns Ct RG10 ..61 C1
St Teresa's RC Prim Sch
RG40 ....116 D5
St Theresa's Rd TW14 ..71 F3
St Thomas Ct RG18 ..106 E3
St Thomas Wlk SL3 ...69 D7
Salamanca RG45 .....142 E5
Salcombe Dr RG6 .....87 B4
Salcombe Rd
Ashford TW15 ....97 E5
Newbury RG14 ....104 E1
Reading RG2 ....86 D3
Sale Garden Cotts RG40 116 C5
Saleby CI RG6 ....87 E2
Salesian Sch KT16 ....124 A1
Salford RG2 ....113 C7
Salisbury Ave SL2 .....42 C8
Salisbury CI RG41 ....116 A2
Salisbury Ct SL6 ......39 C6
Salisbury Mews SL2 ..22 C1
Salisbury Rd
Blackwater GU17 ....150 C5
Harlington TW6 ....71 C1
Hungerford RG17 ...100 C3
Reading RG30 ....85 E8
Salisbury Row RG17 .100 C3
Salmon CI RG7 ......113 B2
Salmond Rd RG2 .....113 C6
Salt Hill Ave SL1 ......42 C5
Salt Hill Dr SL1 ....42 C5
Salt Hill Mans SL1 ....42 C5
Salt Hill Way SL1 .....42 D5
Salters CI SL6 ....40 A7
Salters Rd SL6 ....40 A7
Saltersgate CI RG6 ....87 D2
Saltire Gdns 2 RG42 .118 A8
Salwey CI RG12 ......118 B3
Salwey CI RG12 ......118 B3
Samarkand CI GU15 ..152 B4
Samian PI RG42 ....90 C1
Sampage CI RG2 ......113 C6
Sampson Bsns Pk GU15 151 B3
Sampson CI TW17 ....125 C4
Sampson Pk RG42 ...117 D8
Sampsons Gn SL2 .....21 F2
Sanctuary CI RG30 ....84 F8
Sanctuary Rd TW19,TW6 .71 A1
Sandbrooke Wlk RG7 .111 A3
Sandcroft Rd RG4 .....58 E6
Sandells Ave TW15 ....98 C4
Sanden CI RG10 ......100 C5
Sandford CI RG41 .....88 C1
Sandford Down RG12 .118 F4
Sandford Dr RG5 ......60 F1
Sandford La RG5,RG10 .88 C6
Sandgate Ave RG30 ...57 F2
Sandgates KT16 ......123 E1
Sandhills RG10 ....37 D3
Sandhills Ct GU25 ....122 E4
Sandhills La GU25 ....122 E4
Sandhills Mdw TW17 .125 C2
Sandhills Way RG31 ...84 F4
Sandhurst La GU17 ...150 B6
Sandhurst Lodge RG45 142 E3
Sandhurst Rd
Crowthorne RG45 ....143 B3

Sandhurst Rd continued
Wokingham RG40 .....142 B8
Yateley GU46 ....149 F7
Sandhurst Royal Military
Acad Hospl GU15 ....151 A8
Sandhurst Sta GU47 ..150 B8
Sandhurst Sta GU47 ..150 A7
Sandisplatt Rd SL6 ....39 A6
Sandleford CI RG2 ....113 C6
Sandleford Lodge Pk
RG19 ....131 B6
Sandlers End SL2 .....22 B1
Sandown Ave RG31 ....84 B4
Sandown CI GU17 ....150 D5
Sandown Dr GU16 ....151 E2
Sandown Rd SL2 ......41 F8
Sandown Way RG14 ..105 C5
Sandpit Hill RG14,RG20 .130 C4
Sandpit La Caversham SL4 59 F8
Swallowfield RG7 .....140 B5
Sandringham Ct SL1 ...41 D7
Sandringham Dr TW15 .97 D4
Sandringham Rd
Maidenhead SL6 ......19 E2
Stanwell TW6 ....70 E2
Sandringham Way RG31 .84 B4
Sands Farm Dr SL1 ....21 C1
Sandstone CI RG41 ....88 C1
Sandy CI RG18 ....79 A4
Sandy Dr TW14 ....98 E2
Sandy La Bracknell RG12 .118 C8
Camberley GU15 .....151 E6
Hermitage RG18 ....78 F4
North Ascot SL5 .....119 C8
Sandhurst GU47 .....143 A2
Sunningdale SL5 ....121 A4
Thorpe GU25 ....122 A5
Wokingham RG40 ...115 D4
Sandy Lane Prim Sch
RG2 ....91 C1
Sandy Mead SL6 ......40 C1
Sandy Ride SL5 ....120 E5
Sandy Way KT12 .....125 F1
Sandygate CI SL7 ......1 D3
Sandygate Rd SL7 ......1 D3
Sapphire CI RG41 ....115 E7
Sargood CI RG19 .....106 E2
Sarsby Dr TW19 ......96 A6
Sarum RG12 ....117 F1
Sarum Cres RG40 ....116 D7
Sarum Ct 1 RG30 ....85 D6
Sarum Rd RG26 ......135 A1
Sarum Way RG17 ....100 D4
Satis Ho SL3 ....68 C7
Saturn CI RG41 ......115 E6
Saturn Croft RG42 ....92 B2
Saturn Rd RG7 ....134 E2
Saunders CI RG10 ....61 F3
Saunders Ct RG8 .....57 B5
Saunton Ave UB3 .....71 F7
Savernake CI RG30 ...84 F7
Savernake Way RG12 .118 F4
Savill Gardens The *
TW20 ....94 E2
Savill Mews TW20 ....95 D2
Savill Way SL7 ....1 F2
Saville Cres TW15 .....98 D2
Saville Gdns GU15 ...152 B5
Saville Ho 5 TW20 ...95 D2
Savory Wlk RG42 .....90 C2
Savoy CI SL6 ....19 F1
Savoy Gr GU17 ......150 D3
Sawmill Cotts SL3 ....23 F2
Sawmill Rd RG18 .....79 A4
Sawpit Rd RG10 ......88 E7
Sawtry CI RG6 ....87 E2
Sawyer's CI SL4 ......66 E7
Sawyers CI SL6 ....39 A2
Sawyers Cres SL6 ....39 A2
Sawyers Ley RG7 ....137 D8
Saxby CI RG7 ....111 B3
Saxham Lodge RG40 .116 C5
Saxon CI SL3 ....41 F8
Saxon Ct 9 Reading RG1 .86 D7
Stanwell TW19 ....70 A2
Thatcham RG19 .....106 A3
Saxon Dr RG42 ......118 F8
Saxon Gdns SL6 ......20 D1
Saxon Lodge SL1 .....41 D7
Saxon Prim Sch TW17 .125 A4
Saxon Rd TW15 ......98 D2
Saxon Way
Harmondsworth UB7 .70 C8
Old Windsor SL4 .....68 B1
Saxons Acre RG20 ....28 D3
Saxony Way GU46 ...149 C4
Sayers CI RG14 ......131 B8
Scafell CI RG31 ....57 B2
Scafell Rd SL2 ....41 F8
Scania Wlk RG42 .....92 B2
Scarborough Rd TW6 ..71 C1
Scarborough Way SL1 ..42 B4
Scarlet Oaks GU15 ..151 A3
Scarletts La RG10 .....37 C1
Sch of Electronic
Engineering RG2 ....114 F1
Scholars CI
Caversham RG4 ....58 F3
Great Shefford RG17 ..48 A3
Scholars Wlk SL3 .....44 A4
School CI GU24 ....153 F4
School Gn RG2 ....113 C6
School Hill
Crowthorne RG45 ...143 D4
Sandhurst GU47 .....143 A1
Wargrave RG10 ......36 D1
Woolhampton RG7 ..107 F3
School Ho TW19 ......70 C1

School La Bagshot GU19 .145 E2
Boxford RG20 ....76 E4
Burghfield Common RG7 .110 C3
Caversham RG4 ....59 A2
Cookham SL6 ....20 B7
Cookham Dean SL6 ..19 B7
East Garston RG17 ...47 D6
Egham TW20 ....96 A3
Emmer Green RG4 ...59 B6
Froxfield SN8 ....99 A1
Little Marlow SL7 ....2 C5
Littlewick Green SL6 .38 B5
Lower Halliford TW17 .125 B2
Maidenhead SL6 ......19 E1
Medmenham SL7 .....17 B6
North Ascot SL5 ....119 D8
Riseley RG7 ....139 E3
Silchester RG7 ......136 B1
Slough SL2 ....42 F6
Stoke Poges SL2 .....23 B5
Wargrave RG10 ......36 D2
Windlesham GU20 ..146 D4
Yateley GU46 ....149 B6
School of Military Survey
RG18 ....78 F7
School Rd
Arborfield Cross RG2,
RG41 ....114 F2
Ascot SL5 ....120 D4
Ashford TW15 ....98 B2
Burghfield Common RG30 .110 C6
Chieveley RG20 ......77 F8
Compton RG20 ....31 E4
Harmondsworth UB7 .70 D8
Hurst RG10 ....88 F8
Padworth RG7 ......109 F1
Reading RG31 ....84 D8
Riseley RG7 ....139 E3
Waltham St Lawrence RG10 62 F3
Windlesham GU20 ...146 B5
Wokingham RG40 ...116 D6
Wooburn Green HP10 ...3 E6
School Terr RG1 ......86 B5
Schroder Ct TW20 ....95 B3
Scobell CI RG2 ......113 D5
Scotland Hill GU47 ..150 A8
Scotlands Dr SL2 ....22 B6
Scots CI TW19 ....97 D7
Scots Dr RG41 ......115 E7
Scott CI Caversham RG4 .59 A5
Farnham Common SL2 .22 C7
Woodley RG5 ....88 A7
Scott Terr RG12 .....118 E8
Scott's Ave TW16 .....98 E1
Scott's Way TW16 ....98 E1
Scottalls La RG18 .....52 F5
Scotts Mews SL5 ....119 B8
Scours La RG30 ......58 B1
Scratchface La RG7 ...81 E7
Scrivens Mead RG19 .106 F3
Scylla Cres TW6,TW14 .98 B8
Scylla Rd TW14,TW6 ..71 B1
Seacourt Rd SL3 ......44 B2
Seafield Ct 14 RG41 ...85 F7
Seaford Gdns RG5 ....87 E6
Seaford Rd Stanwell TW6 .70 D2
Wokingham RG40 ...116 D6
Sealand Rd TW6 ......71 A1
Searing Way RG26 ..135 A1
Searles Farm La RG30 .85 B1
Searlwood Ct GU24 ..153 F5
Seaton Dr TW15 ......97 E6
Seaton Gdns RG2 .....86 C2
Seaton Rd GU15 .....151 B5
Second Ave Reading RG31 84 B6
Tadley RG26 ....135 C2
Second Cres SL1 .....42 C8
Second St E RG19 ...132 A5
Seddon Hill RG42 .....91 B2
Sedge Gr RG18 ......106 E4
Sedgefield Rd RG14 .131 C8
Sedgmoor CI HP10 .....3 A7
Sedgmoor Gdns HP10 ..3 A8
Sedgmoor La HP10 .....3 B7
Sedgmoor Rd HP10 ....3 A8
Seebys Oak GU47 ...150 E6
Sefton CI Stoke Poges SL2 .22 F4
West End GU24 .....153 F6
Sefton Paddock SL2 ..23 A5
Sefton Park Cotts SL2 .23 A4
Segrave CI RG4 ....60 E2
Segsbury Gr RG12 ..118 F5
Selborne RG12 ......118 B6
Selborne CI GU17 ...150 C6
Selborne CI 2 RG1 ..86 C7
Selborne Gdns RG30 .58 A1
Selby Rd TW15 ......98 C2
Selcourt CI RG5 ......87 D8
Selim Ct 4 SL1 ......43 A4
Sellafield Way RG6 ..87 C2
Selsdon Ave RG5 ....87 F8
Selsey Way RG6 .....114 B8
Selva Ct 6 RG1 .....86 C6
Selwood CI TW19 ....70 C1
Selwood Gdns TW19 ..70 C1
Selwyn CI SL4 ....66 E5
Selwyn Dr GU46 ....149 B6
Selwyn PI SL1 ....41 F6
Sen CI RG42 ....91 C2
Send Rd RG4 ....59 C1
Sermed Ct SL2 ....43 C5
Servite Ho SL6 ....40 B8
Setley Way RG12 ...118 F6
Seton Dr RG31 ....84 F5
Sett The GU46 ......149 B5

Setter Cl RG42 ....91 D2
Settrington Cl **2** RG6 ...87 E2
Sevenoaks Dr RG7 ....113 B3
Sevenoaks Rd RG6 .....87 B3
Seventh Ave RG31 ......84 B6
Seventh St SL1 ....131 F5
Severalls The SN8 ....126 D3
Severn Cl
  Sandhurst GU47 ......150 C8
  Thatcham RG18 ......106 B5
Severn Cres SL3 ....69 B8
Severn Way RG30 ......84 F6
Sewell Ave RG41 .....116 A8
Sewell Cl RG18 ....79 B1
Seymour Ave RG2 ....113 E5
Seymour Cl SL6 ....39 B3
Seymour Court La SL7 ..1 B5
Seymour Court Rd SL7 ..1 C4
Seymour Ct RG45 .....142 E7
Seymour Dr GU15 .....152 B7
Seymour Ho SL3 ....43 E4
Seymour Park Rd SL7 ...1 D3
Seymour Plain SL7 .....1 C5
Seymour Rd SL1 ....42 D4
Seymour Way TW16 ....98 E1
Shackleton Cl **6** TW19 ..70 E1
Shackleton Rd SL1 .....42 F6
Shackleton Way RG5 ...88 A7
Shafer Ct RG14 ......105 A1
Shaftesbury Cl RG12 ..118 D4
Shaftesbury Cres TW18 .97 D1
Shaftesbury Ct
  Maidenhead SL6 ......39 E5
  6 Slough SL1 ....42 E4
  Wokingham RG40 ....116 D7
Shaftesbury Mount
  GU17 ....150 D3
Shaftesbury Rd
  Bisley GU24 ....153 F3
  Reading RG30 ....85 B8
Shaggy Calf La SL2 ....43 A6
Shakespeare Cl RG4 ...59 D5
Shakespeare Lodge SL1 .41 F5
Shakespeare Rd RG18 .106 C4
Shakespeare Way RG42 118 D5
Shalbourne Cl RG17 ...100 B5
Shalbourne Rise GU15 .151 D5
Sharney Ave SL3 ....44 B3
Sharnwood Dr RG31 ...84 F5
Sharonelle Ct RG40 ...116 B6
Sharpthorpe Ct **2** RG6 .87 B1
Shaw Ct SL4 ....68 A2
Shaw Farm Rd RG14 ..105 B6
Shaw Hill RG14 ......105 E3
Shaw Mill RG14 ......105 B5
Shaw Pk RG45 ....143 B3
Shaw Rd Newbury RG14 105 B4
  Reading RG30 ....85 F5
Shaw The SL6 ....19 E6
Shaw-Cum-Donnington
  Parochial Prim Sch
  RG14 ....105 A6
Shears Ct TW16 ....98 E1
Sheehy Way SL2 ....43 B6
Sheep Fair Way RG17 ..25 B2
Sheep Leaze La RG20 ..29 D2
Sheep Wlk Caversham RG4 59 B4
  Littleton TW17 ......125 A4
Sheepcote La
  Holyport SL6 ....64 C4
  Wooburn SL1 ....3 F1
Sheepcote Rd Eton SL4 .42 A1
  Windsor SL4 ....66 E5
Sheepdown RG20 ......30 E7
Sheepdrove Rd RG17 ..25 C3
Sheephouse Rd SL6 ....20 B2
Sheephouse Way RG4 ..49 A6
Sheepridge La SL7,HP10 ..2 C7
Sheeps Ditch Cl TW18 .97 A1
Sheepwalk TW17 .....124 F3
Sheepwash RG20 .....131 A2
Sheepways La RG4 ....58 B8
Sheerlands Rd RG2 ...140 F7
Sheet St SL4 ....67 D6
Sheet Street Rd SL4 ...94 A7
Sheffield Rd
  Harlington TW14,TW6 .71 C2
  Slough SL1 ....42 C7
Sheffield Way TW14,TW6 71 D2
Shefford CE Prim Sch
  RG17 ....48 B4
Shefford Cres RG40 ..116 D8
Shefford Lodge **3**
  RG14 ....105 A2
Sheldon Gdns RG2 ....86 C1
Shelgate Wlk RG5 .....87 C7
Shelley Ave RG12 ....118 E7
Shelley Cl
  Medmenham SL7 ......17 D7
  Slough SL3 ....43 F1
  Wooburn Green HP10 ..3 E8
  Woodley RG5 ....87 E4
Shelley Ct
  Camberley GU15 .....151 C5
  Reading RG1 ....86 D6
Shelley Rd **12** Marlow SL7 ..1 F3
  Thatcham RG18 ......106 C4
Shelley Wlk GU46 ....149 B5
Shellfield Cl TW19 ....70 A2
Shelson Ave TW13 .....98 F4
Shelton Cl SL3 ....43 C3
Shenston Ct **18** SL4 ...67 D6
Shenstone Cl RG40 ...142 A8
Shenstone Dr SL1 .....21 D1
Shenstone Pk SL5 ....121 E5

Shenstone Rd RG2 .....86 B4
Shepherd's Hill RG20 ..76 E4
Shepherd's House La
  RG6 ....87 A8
Shepherds Ave RG6 ....87 B8
Shepherds Chase GU19 .145 E2
Shepherds Cl Hurley SL6 .17 F3
  Shepperton TW17 ...125 B3
Shepherds Ct SL4 .....66 E5
Shepherds Hill
  Bracknell RG12 .....118 C8
  Compton RG20 ....31 E3
  Earley RG6 ....87 C8
  Hurley SL6 ....17 E4
Shepherds La
  Bracknell RG42 ......91 B1
  Caversham RG4 ....58 D6
  Hurley SL6 ....17 E4
Shepherds Mount RG20 .31 E3
Shepherds Rise RG20 ..31 E4
Shepherds Way RG45 .142 E4
Shepherds Wlk RG6 ...87 C8
Shepley Dr Reading RG30 .85 C4
  Wentworth SL5 ......121 D3
Shepley End SL5 .....121 D4
Sheppee Rdbt RG42 ...91 E1
Shepperton Bsns Pk
  TW17 ....125 C4
Shepperton Court Dr
  TW17 ....125 B4
Shepperton Ct TW17 .125 B3
Shepperton Rd TW17,
  TW18 ....124 D5
Shepperton Sta TW17 .125 C4
Shepperton Studios
  TW17 ....124 F6
Sheraton Cl GU17 ....150 E4
Sheraton Dr RG31 .....57 B1
Sherborne Cl SL3 .....69 E6
Sherborne Ct SL6 .....39 E6
Sherborne Rd TW14 ...98 D7
Sherbourne Dr
  Maidenhead SL6 ......39 C3
  Wentworth SL5 .....121 D4
  Windsor SL4 ....66 F3
  Woodley RG5 ....87 F8
Sherbourne Gdns TW17 125 C2
Sherbourne Wlk SL2 ...22 C8
Sherfield Cl RG2 ......86 D4
Sherfield Dr RG2 ......86 D4
Shergold Way SL6 .....19 E6
Sheridan Ave RG4 .....59 A4
Sheridan Cres RG26 ..134 E1
Sheridan Ct
  Maidenhead SL6 ......40 B8
  Newbury RG14 ......105 C2
  Slough SL1 ....41 E6
Sheridan Grange SL5 .121 A3
Sheridan Way RG41 ..115 C5
Sheringham Ct **3** RG1 .86 C5
Sherman Rd Reading RG1 .86 B6
  Slough SL1 ....42 E8
Sherrard Mead RG14 .105 B5
Sherring Cl RG42 .....91 C1
Sherwood Cl
  Bracknell RG12 .....119 A7
  Slough SL3 ....43 E3
Sherwood Ct
  Colnbrook SL3 ....69 D7
  Slough SL3 ....43 F1
Sherwood Dr SL6 ......39 A6
Sherwood Gdns RG9 ..35 C8
Sherwood Ho **8** RG1 ...85 E5
Sherwood Pl RG8 .....57 B4
Sherwood Rd RG41 ....88 C2
Sherwood Rise RG8 ...57 B5
Sherwood St RG30 ....85 C8
Shetland Rd TW6 ......71 C1
Shield Rd TW15 ....98 C4
Shifford Cres SL6 .....19 E3
Shildon Cl GU15 .....152 D3
Shilling Cl RG30 ......85 B6
Shinfield Inf Sch RG2 .113 E4
Shinfield Rd Earley RG2 .113 E8
  Reading RG2 ....86 E3
Shinfield Rise RG2 ....86 E1
Shinfield St Mary's CE Jun
  Sch RG2 ....113 F4
Shiplake CE Sch RG9 ..35 E2
Shiplake Coll RG9 .....35 F1
Shiplake Ho Bourne End SL8 ..3 B4
  Bracknell RG12 .....118 F5
Shiplake Sta RG9 ......36 B4
Shipley Cl RG5 ....61 A1
Shipton Cl RG31 ......57 C2
Shire Cl GU19 ....145 C2
Shire Cotts RG7 .....108 F6
Shire's Head Cl RG30 ..85 D5
Shires The RG41 .....115 D4
Shires Way GU46 ....149 D7
  Windsor SL4 ....66 F6
Shirley Ave Reading RG2 .113 C7
Shirley Rd SL6 ....39 C5
Shoesmiths Ct **6** RG1 ..86 A8
Sholto Rd TW6 ....71 A2
Shooter's Hill RG8 ....56 B7
Shooters Way RG2 ...112 F8
Shop La
  Leckhampstead RG20 ..49 D5
  Newbury RG14 ......104 E6
Shoppenhanger's Rd SL6 39 E4
Shoppenhangers Rd SL6 .39 C3
Shoreham Rd (E) TW6 ..70 E2
Shoreham Rd (W) TW6 .70 E2
Shoreham Rise SL2 ....21 D1
Shorland Oaks RG42 ..91 C2
Short La TW15,TW19 ..97 F7
Short Rd TW6 ....70 E1
Short St Caversham RG4 .59 B2

Short St continued
  Pangbourne RG8 ......56 D5
  Reading RG1 ....86 B6
Short The RG8 ....57 D5
Shortfern SL2 ....43 C7
Shortheath La RG7 ...110 E3
Shortlands UB3 ....71 E8
Shortlands Hill OX10 ..13 D4
Shortwood Ave TW18 ..97 B5
Shortwood Inf Sch TW18 97 B5
Shrewsbury Rd TW14,
  TW6 ....71 D1
Shrewsbury Terr RG14 104 E1
Shrivenham Cl **3** GU47 150 D8
Shropshire Gdns RG42 ..91 F1
Shrubbs Hill La SL5 ..121 C3
Shrubland Dr RG30 ....85 A4
Shrublands Dr RG30 ...85 A4
Shute End RG40,RG41 116 B6
Shyshack La RG26 ....134 F1
Sibley Park Rd RG6 ...87 A2
Sibson RG6 ....87 C2
Sidbury Cl RG31 ......121 A4
Sidestrand Rd RG14 ..130 E8
Sidings The TW18 .....97 B4
Sidmouth Ct **6** RG1 ...86 C7
Sidmouth Grange Cl RG6 87 B7
Sidmouth Grange Rd
  RG6 ....87 B7
Sidmouth St RG1 ......86 C7
Sidney Rd Staines TW18 .97 A4
  Windsor SL4 ....66 C4
Silbury Cl RG31 ....84 B4
Silchester CE Prim Sch
  RG7 ....136 B1
Silchester St TW15 ....97 E4
Silchester Ho SL6 .....40 B8
Silchester House Sch
  SL6 ....40 D7
Silchester Rd
  Reading RG30 ....85 C4
  Tadley RG26 ....135 D1
Silco Dr SL6 ....39 E6
Silver Birches RG41 ..115 D3
Silver Cl SL6 ....39 A5
Silver Dr GU16 ......152 C3
Silver Fox Cres RG5 ..87 D6
Silver Hill GU47 .....150 E8
Silver La RG7 ....136 B8
Silver St RG1 ....86 B6
Silver Street Flats **10**
  RG1 ....86 B6
Silverbeck Way TW19 .70 A2
Silverdale Rd Earley RG6 87 C3
  Tadley RG26 ....135 B1
  Wargrave RG10 ......36 E1
Silverglades GU46 ...149 C4
Silverthorne Dr RG4 ..58 E6
Silvertrees Dr SL6 ....39 A5
Silverwood Dr GU15 .152 A7
Silwood RG12 ....117 E1
Silwood Cl SL5 ......120 D7
Silwood Park (Imperial Coll)
  SL5 ....120 F6
Silwood Rd SL5 ......120 F5
Simkins Cl RG42 ......92 B2
Simmonds Cl RG42 ..117 E8
Simmonds Malthouse **5**
  RG1 ....86 A6
Simmonds St RG1 .....86 A7
Simmons Cl **6** SL3 ...44 A2
Simmons Field RG18 .106 F4
Simmons Fields RG10 ..61 B3
Simmons Pl TW18 .....96 E3
Simmons Rd RG9 ......15 D3
Simms Farm La RG7 ..136 F4
Simod Ct **3** RG30 ....85 C7
Simons Cl RG31 ....57 C4
Simons La RG41 .....115 D8
Simons Wlk TW20 .....95 C1
Simpson Cl SL6 ....40 B8
Simpsons Way SL1 ....42 E5
Sinclair Rd SL4 ....67 C4
Sindle Cl RG41 ....88 B2
Sindlesham Rd RG2 ..114 E3
Singer La RG9 ....15 E1
Singers Cl RG9 ....35 E8
Singers Ct RG9 ....35 E8
Sinhurst Rd GU15 ...151 B4
Sipson Cl UB7 ....71 A8
Sipson La UB3,UB7 ...71 B8
Sipson Rd UB7 ....71 A8
Sipson Way UB7 ......71 A7
Sir Henry Peeks Dr SL2 .22 A6
Sir Sydney Camm Ho
  SL4 ....67 B6
Sir William Borlase's Gram
  Sch SL7 ....1 C1
Sir William Perkin's Sch
  KT16 ....123 F1
Sirius Cl RG41 ......115 F6
Sirl Cotts SL5 ....120 C5
Six Acre La RG17 ....126 A5
Sixth Ave RG31 ....84 B6
Sixth St SL19 ....131 F5
Skarries View RG4 ....58 D8
Skeffling Ct **3** RG6 ...87 E2
Skelmerdale Way RG7 .87 B5
Skelton Fields RG42 ..91 C1
Skerries Ct **5** SL3 ...44 A2
Skerritt Way RG8 .....57 D4
Skillman Dr RG19 ...106 F3
Skilton Rd RG31 ......57 C3
Skimpedhill La RG12 .118 B7
Skinners Green La
  RG14 ....130 B7
Skippons Cl RG14 ...130 C6
Sky Bsns Pk TW20 ...123 C7

Skydmore Path SL2 ....21 F2
Skye Cl RG31 ....84 E4
Skylings RG14 ......105 C4
Skyport Dr UB7 ....70 D7
Skyway 14 Trad Est SL3 .69 F4
Slade Hill Gdns RG20 129 F2
Slaidburn Gn RG12 ..118 C2
Slanting Hill RG18 ....79 B4
Sledmere Ct TW14 ....98 E7
Slim Rd GU15 ....151 C7
Sloane Cl RG8 ....34 C6
Slopes The RG4 ....59 D2
Slough & Eton CE Sch
  SL1 ....42 D3
Slough Gram Sch SL3 .43 B3
Slough Mus★ SL1 .....43 A4
Slough Rd Datchet SL3 .68 B8
  Eton SL4 ....42 E2
Slough Sta SL1 ....42 F5
Slough Trad Est SL1 ...42 B7
Smalley Cl RG41 .....115 E4
Smallholdings TW15 ..98 B4
Smallmead
  Burghfield Common RG2 85 D1
  Reading RG2 ....86 A1
Smallridge RG14 ....130 C4
Smallwood Dr RG26 .135 B1
Smeaton Ct RG14 ...104 F4
Smewins Rd RG10,SL6 ..63 D5
Smith Sq RG12 ......118 D7
Smith's Hill OX12 ......6 F5
Smitham Bridge Rd
  RG17 ....100 C5
Smithfield Cl SL6 .....38 F3
Smithfield Rd SL6 ....39 A3
Smiths La SL4 ....66 E6
Smithy's Gn GU20 ...146 D4
Snake La RG20 ......104 A7
Snape Spur SL1 ......42 E7
Snelsmore Common Ctry
  Pk★ RG14 ....77 D2
Snipe La RG20 ......131 F2
Snowball Hill
  Maidenhead SL6 ......39 A1
  White Waltham SL6 ..64 B8
Snowberry Cl RG41 ..115 F5
Snowden Cl SL4 ......66 D3
Snowden Dr RG31 ....84 A6
Snowdon Cl RG19 ...106 D2
Snowdon Rd TW6 .....71 C1
Snowdrop Copse RG18 106 F4
Snowdrop Gr RG41 ...88 C3
Snows Paddock GU20 146 B7
Snows Ride GU20 ....146 B6
Soane End RG4 ....59 A7
Soham Cl RG6 ....114 C8
Soho Cres HP10 ....3 D4
Soho Mills Ind Est HP10 ..3 D4
Soke Rd RG7 ....135 C3
Soldiers Rise RG40 ..142 D7
Solent Ct **2** RG1 ....86 B6
Somerford Cl SL6 .....40 B8
Somersby Cres SL6 ...39 E3
Somerset Cl
  Hungerford RG17 ...100 C5
  Wokingham RG41 ..115 D6
Somerset Gr RG42 ...115 A4
Somerset Hospl SN8 ..99 B5
Somerset Lodge **3** SL6 .39 F6
Somerset Way SL0 ....44 F4
Somerset Wlk RG31 ..84 B6
Somerstown Ct RG1 ..85 F7
Somerton Gdns RG6 ..87 A2
Somerton Gr RG19 ..106 C2
Somerville Cl RG41 ..115 D4
Somerville Cres GU46 149 E4
Somerville Rd SL4 ....42 C1
Songbird Cl RG2 ....113 C6
Sonning CE Prim Sch
  RG4 ....60 D3
Sonning Gate RG4 ....60 C2
Sonning La RG4 ......60 C2
Sonning Mdws RG4 ...60 C1
Sonninge Ct GU47 ...150 D8
Sopwith Cl RG5 ......88 A7
Sorrel Cl
  Burghfield Common RG7 111 B3
  Newbury RG14 ......105 D5
  Wokingham RG40 ..116 E8
Sorrel Dr GU18 .....152 F7
Sospel Ct SL2 ....22 C3
South Ave Egham TW20 .96 C2
  Henley-On-T RG9 ....35 E8
South Bank RG8 ......14 C3
South Cl Burnham SL1 ..41 D6
  Medmenham SL7 .....17 D7
  Wokingham RG40 ..116 C4
South Dr Reading RG2 ..86 F2
  Sonning RG4 ....60 C1
  Sulhamstead RG7 ..110 D7
  Wentworth GU25 ...122 A2
  Wokingham RG40 ..116 C5
South End Rd RG7 ....82 B2
South Farm La GU19 .146 A2
South Field Ct SL4 ...41 B8
South Gate Ave TW13 .98 D4
South Gn SL1 ....42 E6
South Gr KT16 ......123 F3
South Groves RG17 ...73 A2
South Hill Rd RG12 ..118 B6
South Lake Cres RG5 .87 E5
South Lake Inf Sch RG5 .87 E5
South Lake Prim Sch
  RG5 ....87 D5
South Lynn Cres RG12 118 B4
South Mdw RG45 ....143 D5
South Meadow La SL4 .67 C8
South Oak Way RG2 .112 F7

South Path SL4 ....67 C3
South Pl Marlow SL7 ...1 E1
  Wokingham RG40 ...116 C6
South Rd Bisley GU24 153 F3
  Bracknell RG40,RG12 117 C1
  Crowthorne RG45 ..143 E3
  Englefield Green TW20 .95 D2
  Maidenhead SL6 ......39 E6
South Row Chilton OX11 ..D7
  Fulmer SL3 ....23 E8
South St Blewbury OX11 .12 A8
  Caversham RG4 ....59 B2
  Reading RG1 ....86 C7
  Staines TW18 ....96 F3
South Stoke Prim Sch
  RG8 ....14 B4
South Terr SL4 ....67 E6
South View
  Bracknell RG12 .....117 D6
  Cookham Rise SL6 ...19 E7
South View Ave RG4 ..59 C2
South View Gdns **9**
  RG14 ....105 B4
South View Pk RG4 ...59 C2
Southampton Cl GU17 150 C6
Southampton Rd TW6 .70 F1
Southampton St RG1 ..86 B6
Southbank Gdns RG17 .25 C2
Southbourne Dr SL8 ...3 A3
Southcote Ave TW13 ..98 F6
Southcote Dr GU15 ..152 A5
Southcote Farm La RG30 85 D4
Southcote La RG30 ...85 D4
Southcote Lodge RG30 .85 A4
Southcote Prim Sch
  RG30 ....85 C4
Southcote Rd RG30 ...85 D6
Southcroft
  Englefield Green TW20 .95 B3
  Slough SL2 ....22 B1
Southdown Rd
  Caversham RG4 ....59 B5
  Tadley RG26 ....135 A1
  Thatcham RG18 ....105 F4
Southend RG18 ......106 D6
Southern Cotts TW19 .70 A2
Southern Ct **9** RG1 ...86 B7
Southern Gate Pk RG2 113 A8
Southern Hill RG1 ....86 D5
Southern Ind Area
  RG12 ....117 F6
Southern Perimeter Rd
  East Bedfont TW6 ....71 B1
  Harlington TW14,TW6 .71 D2
  Stanwell TW19,TW6 ..70 D2
Southern Rd GU15 ..151 C6
Southerndene Ct RG31 .57 C2
Southfield Gdns SL1 ..41 B8
Southfield Sch RG40 .116 D5
Southfields Boxford RG20 .76 C3
  Chieveley RG20 ......78 B8
Southfields Ave TW15 .98 B2
Southgate Ho SL6 ....39 F7
Southglade RG2 .....113 D8
Southlake Ct RG5 .....87 D5
Southlands Cl RG40 ..116 D5
Southlands Rd RG40 .116 D4
Southlea Rd SL3 ......68 B5
Southside KT16 .....124 A6
Southview Cl RG10 ...61 E6
Southview Rd SL7 .....1 E4
Southville Cl TW14 ...98 E7
Southville Cres TW14 .98 E7
Southville Jun & Inf Schs
  TW14 ....98 E7
Southville Rd TW14 ...98 E8
Southwark Cl GU46 ..149 C6
Southway GU15 .....151 B4
Southwell Park Rd
  GU15 ....151 C5
Southwick GU19 ....145 E1
Southwick Ct RG12 ..118 E3
Southwold RG12 ....117 C5
Southwold Cl RG6 ....87 D1
Southwold Spur SL3 ..44 C4
Southwood RG40 ....116 D4
Southwood Gdns
  Burghfield Common RG7 111 A3
  Cookham Rise SL6 ...19 E5
Southwood Rd
  Cookham Rise SL6 ...19 E5
  Yateley GU17 ......149 E1
Sovereign Beeches SL2 .22 B6
Sovereign Ct **4** SL5 .121 B2
Sovereign Dr GU15 ..152 B7
Sovereign Ho TW15 ...97 E4
Sovereign Pk **3** RG31 .84 B8
Sovereign Way RG31 .84 C5
Sovoy Ct GU15 .....151 C5
Sowbury Pk RG20 ....79 A8
Spa Meadow Cl RG19 131 C8
Spackman Cl RG19 ..106 D2
Spackmans Way SL1 ..42 D3
Spade Oak Farm SL8 ...2 E3
Spade Oak Mdw SL8 ...2 E4
Span Hill RG4 ....60 B7
Sparrow Cl RG41 ....115 C5
Sparrowbill RG20 .....28 E2
Sparvell Way GU15 ..151 C6
Speedbird Way UB7 ...70 C7
Speedwell Way RG18 106 F4
Speen Hill Cl RG14 ..104 E4
Speen La RG14 ......104 D4
Speen Lodge Ct RG14 104 E4
Speen Pl RG14 ......104 E4
Speenhamland Ct **5**
  RG14 ....105 A4

Speenhamland Prim Sch
RG14 ....104 F4
Spelthorne Coll TW15 ...97 F4
Spelthorne Gr TW16 ....98 F1
Spelthorne Inf Sch TW15 98 E2
Spelthorne Jun Sch
TW15 ....98 D2
Spelthorne La TW15,
TW17 ....125 C8
Spelthorne Mus★ TW18 .96 E3
Spencer Cl
Silchester RG26 ....135 E1
Wokingham RG41 ....115 D6
Spencer Gdns TW20 ....95 D3
Spencer Rd
Bracknell RG42 ....117 F8
Newbury RG14 ....130 D6
Reading RG2 ....113 B7
Slough SL3 ....43 F3
Spencers Cl SL6 ....39 D8
Spencers Ct RG7 ....113 A3
Spencers La SL6 ....19 E7
Spencers Rd SL6 ....39 D8
Spenwood Cl RG7 ....113 B2
Sperling Rd SL6 ....19 F1
Spey Rd RG30 ....85 A7
Spinfield La SL7 ....1 B2
Spinfield La W SL7 ....1 C1
Spinfield Mount SL7 ....1 B1
Spinfield Pk SL7 ....1 C1
Spinfield Sch SL7 ....1 B2
Spinis RG12 ....117 F1
Spinner Gn RG12 ....118 B4
Spinners Wlk Marlow SL7 ..1 C1
Windsor SL4 ....67 C6
Spinney SL1 ....42 B5
Spinney Cl RG4 ....59 B7
Spinney Dr TW14 ....98 C8
Spinney La SL4 ....93 B7
Spinney The Ascot SL5 ..120 E4
Frimley GU15 ....152 C6
Reading RG31 ....84 E4
Wokingham RG40 ....141 F8
Yateley GU46 ....149 C7
Spinningwheel La RG42 .90 C8
Spires Ct KT16 ....124 A3
Spitfire Cl SL3 ....44 A2
Spitfire Way RG5 ....88 A7
Spittal St SL7 ....1 D2
Splash The RG42 ....91 B2
Spode Cl RG30 ....84 E8
Spout La TW19 ....70 A3
Spout La N TW19 ....70 B3
Spray La RG20 ....28 C1
Spray Rd SN8,RG17 ....126 E3
Spriggs Cl RG19 ....106 D2
Spring Ave TW20 ....95 F2
Spring Cl Maidenhead SL6 .19 F2
Pangbourne RG8 ....55 D5
Spring Cnr TW13 ....98 F5
Spring Farm Mews RG8 .14 C1
Spring Gdns Ascot SL5 ..120 B5
Bourne End SL8 ....3 A4
Frimley GU15 ....152 A5
Marlow SL7 ....1 E3
Newbury RG20 ....130 B3
Shinfield RG7 ....113 B2
Theale RG7 ....83 D3
Wooburn Green HP10 ....3 E8
Spring Gr RG1 ....86 B6
Spring Hill SL6 ....39 E3
Spring La
Aldermaston RG7 ....135 C6
Aston Tirrold OX11 ....12 E8
Caversham RG4 ....60 B5
Cold Ash RG18 ....106 C8
Cookham Dean SL6 ....19 C5
Farnham Common SL2 ....22 C5
Mortimer RG7 ....137 A6
Riseley RG7 ....139 A4
Slough SL1 ....41 F5
Spring Mdw RG12 ....118 D8
Spring Mdws RG17 ....48 B4
Spring Meadows Bsns Ctr
RG10 ....36 F5
Spring Rd TW13 ....98 F5
Spring Rise TW20 ....95 E2
Spring Terr 5 RG1 ....86 B5
Spring Wlk RG10 ....36 D1
Spring Wood La RG7 ....111 A2
Spring Woods
Sandhurst GU47 ....143 C1
Virginia Water GU25 ....122 B5
Springate Field SL3 ....43 E4
Springcross Ave GU17 ..150 D4
Springdale Earley RG6 ....87 B2
Wokingham RG40 ....141 E8
Springfield
Lightwater GU18 ....153 D8
Slough SL1 ....43 A3
Springfield Cl SL4 ....67 B5
Springfield Ct
Maidenhead SL6 ....40 B7
Twyford RG10 ....61 E5
Springfield End RG8 ....34 C8
Springfield Gr TW16 ....125 F8
Springfield La RG14 ....131 B8
Springfield Mews RG4 ....59 B4
Springfield Pk
Maidenhead SL6 ....40 C1
Twyford RG10 ....61 E4
Springfield Prim Sch
Reading RG31 ....84 B7
Sunbury TW16 ....125 F7
Springfield Rd
Ashford TW15 ....97 F3
Bracknell RG12 ....117 C8
Brands Hill SL3 ....69 B7
Springfield Rd *continued*
Frimley GU15 ....152 B5
Silchester RG26 ....135 E1
Windsor SL4 ....67 B5
Springfields Cl KT16 ....124 B1
Springhill Ct RG12 ....118 B5
Springhill Rd RG8 ....34 C8
Springmead Ct GU47 ....143 E1
Spruce Ct 1 SL1 ....42 F3
Spruce Dr GU18 ....153 A7
Spruce Rd RG5 ....88 A6
Spur The Slough SL1 ....41 D8
Wargrave RG10 ....36 E3
Spurcroft Prim Sch
RG19 ....106 D2
Spurcroft Rd RG19 ....106 D2
Square The
Bagshot GU19 ....145 E3
Bracknell RG12 ....118 E5
Earley RG6 ....114 A8
Harmondsworth TW6 ....70 B6
Lightwater GU18 ....146 C1
Newtown RG19 ....132 A4
Pangbourne RG8 ....56 D6
Shinfield RG7 ....113 B2
Yattendon RG18 ....53 E1
Squire's Bridge Rd
TW17 ....125 A6
Squire's Rd TW17 ....125 A5
Squires Bridge Rd KT17 124 F5
Squires Ct
Camberley GU15 ....151 C3
Chertsey KT16 ....124 B1
Squires Wlk TW15 ....98 D1
Squirrel Cl GU47 ....150 B8
Squirrel Dr SL4 ....93 B7
Squirrel Rise SL7 ....1 D6
Squirrel Wlk RG41 ....115 F7
Squirrels Drey RG45 ....142 F5
Squirrels Way RG6 ....87 B2
Stable Cl RG7 ....111 A3
Stable Cotts SL7 ....18 C5
Stable Croft GU19 ....145 D2
Stable Ct RG14 ....105 B6
Stable View GU46 ....149 D7
Stables Ct SL7 ....1 B1
Stables The SL5 ....121 B1
Stacey's Ind Est RG26 ..135 C1
Staddlestone Cl RG31 ....57 C2
Stadium Way RG30 ....58 B1
Staff College Rd GU15 .151 B6
Stafferton Way SL6 ....40 A6
Stafford Ave SL2 ....22 C1
Stafford Cl Burnham SL6 ..41 B7
Woodley RG5 ....87 F7
Stafford Lake GU21,
GU24 ....153 F1
Staffordshire Cl RG30 ....84 F8
Staffordshire Croft RG42 .91 F2
Stag Hill RG17 ....73 A2
Stainash Cres TW18 ....97 B3
Stainash Par TW18 ....97 B3
Staines By-Pass TW15,
TW18 ....97 C3
Staines La KT16 ....124 A3
Staines Lane Cl KT16 ....123 F4
Staines Prep Sch TW18 ..97 A3
Staines Rd
Chertsey KT16 ....124 A5
East Bedfont TW14 ....98 D8
Laleham TW18 ....124 B7
Wraysbury TW19 ....95 F7
Staines Rd W TW15 ....98 D1
Staines Sta TW18 ....97 A3
Stainford Cl TW15 ....98 D3
Stamford Ave GU16 ....151 F1
Stamford Rd SL6 ....39 C6
Stanbrook Cl RG7 ....82 A2
Stanbury Gate RG7 ....113 A3
Stanfield RG26 ....135 B1
Stanford Dingley Circular
Wlks★ RG18 ....80 E7
Stanham Rd RG30 ....84 F8
Stanhope Heath TW19 ..70 C1
Stanhope Rd
Camberley GU15 ....150 F4
Reading RG2 ....86 D3
Slough SL1 ....41 D7
Stanhope Way TW19 ....70 C1
Stanlake La RG10 ....61 F4
Stanley Cl SL7 ....1 F3
Stanley Cotts SL2 ....42 F5
Stanley Gn E SL3 ....43 F2
Stanley Gn W SL3 ....43 F2
Stanley Gr 1 RG1 ....85 F7
Stanley Ho SL4 ....68 A2
Stanley Rd Ashford TW15 .97 E3
Newbury RG14 ....105 B2
Wokingham RG40 ....116 E6
Stanley Spencer Art Gal★
SL6 ....20 B7
Stanley St RG1 ....85 F8
Stanmore Cl SL5 ....120 A5
Stanmore Gdns RG7 ....136 F5
Stanmore Rd RG20 ....30 C2
Stanshawe Rd RG1 ....86 A8
Stansted Rd TW6 ....70 F1
Stanton Cl RG6 ....87 C4
Stanton Way SL3 ....43 E2
Stanway Cotts RG1 ....86 F6
Stanwell Cl TW19 ....70 D1
Stanwell Gdns TW19 ....70 D1
Stanwell Moor Rd
Harmondsworth TW19,TW6,
UB7 ....70 B4
Stanwell TW19 ....70 B4
Stanwell New Rd TW18 ..97 B5
Stanwell Rd Ashford TW15 97 E3
Stanwell Rd *continued*
East Bedfont TW14,TW19,
TW6 ....98 B8
Horton SL3 ....69 C4
Stapleford Rd RG30 ....85 C4
Staplehurst RG12 ....117 E2
Stapleton Cl Marlow SL7 ...1 F4
Newbury RG14 ....130 C6
Star La Knowl Hill RG10 ....37 E4
Reading RG1 ....86 B7
Star Post Rd GU15 ....151 F8
Star Rd RG4 ....59 C2
Starling Cl RG41 ....115 F5
Starlings Dr RG31 ....84 B6
Starmead Dr RG40 ....116 E5
Starting Gates RG14 ....105 C1
Startins La SL6 ....19 C8
Starwood Ct SL3 ....43 C3
Statham Ct RG42 ....117 E8
Station App Ashford TW15 97 F4
Blackwater GU17 ....150 E4
Maidenhead SL6 ....39 F6
Marlow SL7 ....1 E1
Reading RG1 ....86 A8
Shepperton TW17 ....125 C4
Staines TW18 ....97 A3
Virginia Water GU25 ....122 D5
Station Cres TW15 ....97 E4
Station Hill Ascot SL5 ..120 A5
Cookham Rise SL6 ....19 F7
Hampstead Norreys RG18 ..52 F6
Reading RG1 ....86 A8
Station Ind Est RG40 ....116 B6
Station Par Ashford TW15 .97 F4
Cookham Rise SL6 ....19 F6
Sunningdale SL5 ....121 A2
Thorpe GU25 ....122 E4
Station Path TW18 ....96 F4
Station Rd Ashford TW15 ..97 F4
Bagshot GU19 ....145 E4
Ball Hill RG20 ....130 A3
Bourne End SL8 ....3 A3
Bracknell RG12 ....118 B7
Chertsey KT16 ....124 A1
Cookham Rise SL6 ....19 F7
Earley RG6 ....87 C4
East Garston RG17 ....47 C6
Egham TW20 ....96 A3
Frimley GU16 ....151 C1
Goring RG8 ....34 C6
Great Shefford RG17 ....48 A3
Henley-On-T RG9 ....15 E1
Hungerford RG17 ....100 D6
Kintbury RG17 ....102 B2
Lambourn RG17 ....25 B2
Marlow SL7 ....1 E1
Mortimer RG7 ....137 E5
Newbury RG14 ....105 A2
Newbury,Speen RG14 ....104 D5
1 Pangbourne RG8 ....56 C6
Reading RG1 ....86 B8
Shepperton TW17 ....125 C4
Shiplake RG9 ....36 A4
Slough SL1 ....41 E7
Slough,Langley SL3 ....44 A4
Sunningdale SL5 ....121 A4
Taplow SL6 ....40 F7
Thatcham RG19 ....106 E2
Theale RG7 ....83 E3
Twyford RG10 ....61 D4
Wargrave RG10 ....36 C1
Wokingham RG40 ....116 B6
Woolhampton RG7 ....108 C2
Wraysbury TW19 ....69 A1
Station Rd N 5 TW20 ....95 F3
Station Rise SL7 ....1 E2
Station Road Ind Est
RG19 ....106 F1
Station Terr RG10 ....61 E4
Station Way RG12 ....118 C7
Station Yard Ind Est
RG17 ....100 E5
Staunton Rd SL2 ....42 D8
Staveley Rd TW15 ....98 D2
Staverton Cl
Bracknell RG42 ....91 B1
Wokingham RG40 ....116 F6
Staverton Rd RG2 ....86 D3
Stayne End GU25 ....122 A5
Steam Farm La TW14 ....71 F3
Steeple Point SL5 ....120 B6
Steeple Wlk RG6 ....113 F8
Steerforth Copse GU47 ..143 E2
Steggles Cl RG5 ....87 D8
Stepgates KT16 ....124 B2
Stepgates Cl KT16 ....124 B2
Stepgates Com Prim Sch
KT16 ....124 B2
Stephanie Chase Ct
RG40 ....116 D7
Stephen Cl Egham TW20 ..96 C2
Twyford RG10 ....61 F3
Stephens Cl RG7 ....136 F6
Stephens Firs RG7 ....136 F6
Stephens Rd RG7 ....136 F6
Stephenson Cl RG18 ....106 D4
Stephenson Ct
Newbury RG14 ....104 F4
13 Slough SL1 ....42 F4
Stephenson Dr SL4 ....67 B7
Stephenson Rd RG2 ....141 A7
Sterling Ave TW17 ....125 E6
Sterling Ctr The RG12 ..118 D6
Sterling Gdns GU47 ....150 E8
Sterling Ind Est RG14 ..105 B2
Sterling Way RG30 ....58 B1
Stern Ct KT16 ....124 C1
Stevens Hill GU46 ....149 E5
Stevenson Dr RG42 ....90 C3
Stewart Ave
Littleton TW17 ....125 A5
Slough SL1 ....42 F8
Stewart Cl SL6 ....65 D6
Stewarts Dr SL2 ....22 B8
Stewarts Way SL7 ....1 D7
Stile Rd SL3 ....43 D3
Stilton Cl RG6 ....87 E2
Stilwell Cl GU46 ....149 E6
Stirling Cl Caversham RG4 59 D6
Frimley GU16 ....151 E2
Windsor SL4 ....66 D5
Stirling Gr SL6 ....39 B8
Stirling Ho 15 RG1 ....86 B6
Stirling Rd Slough SL1 ....42 B8
Stanwell TW6 ....70 F1
Stirling Way RG18 ....106 C4
Stirrup Cl RG14 ....131 B7
Stockbridge Way GU46 .149 D4
Stockbury Cl RG6 ....87 B1
Stockcross CE Sch
RG20 ....103 E6
Stockdales Rd SL4 ....41 F2
Stockton Rd RG2 ....86 C1
Stockwells SL6 ....20 D1
Stockwood Rise GU15 ..151 F5
Stoke Common Rd SL3 ..23 B8
Stoke Court Dr SL2 ....22 F4
Stoke Gdns SL1 ....42 F5
Stoke Gn SL2 ....23 A1
Stoke Park Ave SL2 ....22 C2
Stoke Poges La SL1, SL2 .42 E7
Stoke Poges Sch
Stoke Poges SL2 ....22 F5
Stoke Poges SL2 ....23 B5
Stoke Rd SL2 ....42 F7
Stoke View SL1 ....42 F5
Stoke Wood SL2 ....22 F8
Stokeford Cl 5 RG12 ....118 F4
Stokes Farm RG40 ....116 F8
Stokes La RG26 ....134 C1
Stokes View RG8 ....56 C5
Stokesay SL2 ....42 F6
Stokesley Rise HP10 ....3 E8
Stomp Rd SL1 ....41 C8
Stompits Rd SL6 ....65 C8
Stone Copse RG14 ....105 E7
Stone Cres TW14 ....98 F8
Stone House La SL6 ....2 C1
Stone St RG30 ....58 B1
Stone's Wlk RG7 ....111 A3
Stonea Cl RG6 ....114 C8
Stonebridge Field SL4 ..42 B1
Stonecroft Ave SL0 ....44 E7
Stonefield Pk SL6 ....39 C7
Stonegate GU15 ....152 C6
Stoneham Cl RG30 ....85 A6
Stonehaven Dr RG5 ....88 A6
Stonehill Gate SL5 ....120 D3
Stonehill Rd GU18 ....146 A1
Stonehouse Rise GU16 ..151 E1
Stoneleigh Ct
Frimley GU16 ....151 F1
Theale RG7 ....83 D2
Stoney Cl GU46 ....149 D4
Stoney La Burnham SL2 ..22 A4
Newbury RG14,RG18 ....105 D6
Thatcham RG19 ....106 E3
Stoney Meade SL1 ....42 B5
Stoney Rd RG42 ....118 A8
Stoney Ware SL7 ....18 E8
Stoney Ware Cl SL7 ....18 D8
Stoneyfield RG7 ....109 A6
Stoneyland Ct 6 TW20 ....95 F3
Stoneylands Rd TW20 ....95 F3
Stony La RG17 ....46 D3
Stookes Way GU46 ....149 B4
Stornaway Rd SL3 ....44 C2
Stour Cl Reading RG30 ....85 A8
Slough SL1 ....42 B3
Stovell Rd SL4 ....67 B7
Stowe Rd SL1 ....41 E6
Strachey Cl RG8 ....56 C2
Straight Bit HP10 ....3 B8
Straight La RG17 ....46 F4
Straight Mile The
Hurst RG10,RG40 ....89 D6
Waltham St Lawrence RG10 62 E1
Straight Rd SL4 ....68 B1
Strand Way RG6 ....87 C1
Strande La SL6 ....19 F5
Strande Pk SL6 ....19 F5
Strande View Wlk SL6 ....19 F5
Stranraer Gdns SL1 ....42 E5
Stranraer Way 1 TW6 ....70 E1
Stratfield RG12 ....117 E1
Stratfield Ct SL6 ....40 B8
Stratfield Rd SL1 ....43 A4
Stratford Cl SL2 ....21 D1
Stratford Dr HP10 ....3 D4
Stratford Gdns SL6 ....39 C4
Stratford Rd TW6 ....71 C2
Stratford Way RG31 ....84 A6
Strathcona Cl HP10 ....3 C7
Strathcona Way HP10 ....3 C7
Strathearn Ave UB3 ....71 F7
Stratheden Pl 6 RG1 ....85 F8
Strathmore Ct 3 GU15 ..151 D5
Strathmore Dr RG10 ....61 A4
Strathy Cl RG30 ....85 B8
Stratton Gdns RG2 ....86 C1
Stratton Rd TW16 ....125 F7
Strawberry Hill
Newbury RG14 ....104 F4
Newell Green RG42 ....91 E2
Streamside SL1 ....41 F5
Streatley & Goring Bridge
RG8 ....34 B6
Streatley CE Sch RG8 ....33 F6
Streatley Farm Cotts
RG8 ....34 A8
Streatley Hill RG8 ....33 F6
Street The
Aldermaston RG7 ....135 A7
Englefield RG7 ....83 B5
Mortimer RG7 ....137 D5
Moulsford OX10 ....14 A6
South Stoke RG8 ....14 B3
Swallowfield RG7 ....139 C6
Tidmarsh RG8 ....56 D2
Waltham St Lawrence RG10 63 A6
Streets Heath GU24 ....153 F7
Stretton RG7 ....82 A1
Stretton Cl RG7 ....82 A1
Strode St TW20 ....96 A4
Strode's Coll TW20 ....95 F3
Strode's Cres TW18 ....97 C3
Strodes College La TW20 95 F3
Stroller Cl RG19 ....105 F4
Stroma Ct SL1 ....41 D6
Strongrove Hill RG17 ...100 C6
Strood La SL5 ....93 C2
Stroud Cl
Aldermaston RG26 ....135 E1
Windsor SL4 ....66 D4
Stroud Farm Rd SL6 ....65 B8
Stroud La GU17 ....150 A4
Stroud Way TW15 ....98 B2
Stroude Rd Egham TW20 ..96 A1
Thorpe GU25,TW20 ....122 E6
Strouds Mdw RG18 ....106 C7
Strouds The RG7 ....108 F6
Stuart Cl Caversham RG4 ..59 B5
Windsor SL4 ....66 F5
Stuart Ho RG42 ....117 F8
Stuart Rd RG14 ....130 D6
Stuart Way Staines TW18 .97 B2
Virginia Water GU25 ....122 A5
Windsor SL4 ....66 F5
Stubbles RG8 ....54 C6
Stubbles La SL6 ....19 B6
Stubbs Folly GU47 ....150 D7
Studios Rd TW17 ....124 F6
Studland Cl RG2 ....113 C7
Studland Ind Est RG20 .129 B3
Sturbridge Cl RG6 ....87 C1
Sturdee Cl GU16 ....151 E1
Sturges Rd RG40 ....116 D5
Sturgis Ct RG40 ....116 D5
Sturt Gn SL6 ....64 E8
Styventon Pl KT16 ....123 F2
Suck's La RG8 ....54 D3
Suffolk Cl Bagshot GU19 .145 E2
Slough SL1 ....41 E7
Wokingham RG41 ....115 D6
Suffolk Combe RG42 ....91 F1
Suffolk Ct 2 SL6 ....39 F8
Suffolk Rd
Maidenhead SL6 ....39 D4
Reading RG30 ....85 D7
Sulham La RG8 ....56 E3
Sulham Wlk RG30 ....85 B4
Sulhamstead & Ufton Nervet
CE Prim Sch RG7 ....110 C4
Sulhamstead Hill RG7 ..110 C6
Sulhamstead Rd
Burghfield Common RG7,
RG30 ....111 B5
Ufton Nervet RG7 ....110 D4
Sullivan Rd GU15 ....151 A5
Sullivans Reach KT12 ..125 F2
Sumburgh Way SL1 ....42 E8
Summer Gdns GU15 ....152 C5
Summerfield Cl RG41 ....88 F1
Summerfield Rise RG8 ..34 D7
Summerhouse La UB7 ...70 D8
Summerlea SL1 ....42 B5
Summerleaze Rd SL6 ....20 B1
Summers Rd SL1 ....21 C2
Summit Cl RG40 ....141 F7
Summit Ctr UB7 ....70 D7
Sun Cl SL4 ....67 D8
Sun Gdns RG7 ....111 A1
Sun Hill RG7 ....108 F2
Sun La Maidenhead SL6 ....39 F7
Riseley RG7 ....139 B2
Sun Pas 14 SL4 ....67 D6
Sun Ray Est GU47 ....150 A8
Sun St RG1 ....86 D7
Sunbury Cres TW13 ....98 F4
Sunbury Cross Ctr 9
TW16 ....98 F1
Sunbury Ct SL4 ....67 D8
Sunbury Int Bsns Ctr
TW16 ....125 E8
Sunbury Manor Sch
TW16 ....125 F8
Sunbury Rd Eton SL4 ....67 D8
Feltham TW13 ....98 F4
Sunderland Cl RG5 ....88 B8
Sunderland Ct 11 TW19 ..70 E1
Sunderland Pl RG18 ....106 C4
Sunderland Rd SL6 ....39 B8
Sundew Cl
Lightwater GU18 ....153 D8
Wokingham RG40 ....116 E7
Sundial Cl RG30 ....85 A6
Sundon Cres GU25 ....122 C4
Sundown Rd TW15 ....98 C3
Sunley Cl RG14 ....130 D6
Sunmead Rd TW16 ....125 F6

Sunning Ave SL5 ....120 E2
Sunning Ho Ascot SL5 ..120 C5
Windlesham GU20 ....146 F8
Sunningdale Park (Civil Service Coll) SL5 .....120 F4
Sunningdale Sch SL5 ...120 F3
Sunningdale Sta SL5 ...121 A2
Sunninghill Cl SL5 .....120 D5
Sunninghill Ct SL5 .....120 D5
Sunninghill Lodge
Ascot SL5 ....120 C7
Ascot SL5 ....120 D5
Sunninghill Rd
Ascot SL5 ....120 D5
Windlesham GU20 ....146 A7
Winkfield SL4,SL5 ....93 E2
Sunnybank Ascot SL5 ...120 A5
Marlow SL7 ....1 D4
Sunnymeads Sta TW19 ..68 E4
Sunnymede Cotts SL6 ...20 B1
Sunnyside RG14 ....104 E6
Sunrise Hill RG20 ....30 F7
Superity Cotts RG20 .....31 D6
Surbiton Rd GU15 .....145 A1
Surley Row RG4 ....59 A5
Surly Hall Wlk SL4 ......66 F6
Surrey Ave
Camberley GU15 ....151 A4
Slough SL2 ....22 C1
Surrey Ct RG42 ....91 F1
Surrey Heath Mus*
GU15 ....151 D6
Surrey Rd RG2 ....86 B4
Surridge Ct GU19 ....145 E2
Sussex Cl SL1 ....43 B4
Sussex Gdns RG5 ....87 E7
Sussex Ho SL2 ....22 C6
Sussex Keep SL1 ....43 B4
Sussex La RG7 ....113 C1
Sussex Lodge 7 SL6 ......39 F6
Sussex Pl SL1, SL3 ....43 B3
Sutcliffe Ave RG6 ....87 D3
Sutherland Ave TW16 ..125 F7
Sutherland Chase SL5 ..119 E7
Sutherland Gdns TW16 .125 F7
Sutherland Gr RG31 ......84 E4
Sutherland Grange SL4 ..66 D7
Sutherlands RG14 ......130 E7
Sutherlands Ave RG1 .....86 C5
Sutton Ave SL3 ....43 C4
Sutton Cl Cookham SL6 ...20 B7
Maidenhead SL6 ....39 C5
Sutton La Brands Hill SL3 .69 B8
Slough SL3 ....44 C2
Sutton Pl SL3 ....69 B8
Sutton Rd
Camberley GU15 ....145 A1
Cookham SL6 ....20 B6
Newbury RG14 ....104 D5
Sutton Wlk RG1 ....86 C5
Suttons Park Ave RG6 ...86 E8
Swabey Rd SL3 ....44 A2
Swainstone Rd RG2 ......86 B5
Swaledale RG12 ....118 A4
Swallow Cl Reading RG31 .84 C6
Staines TW18 ....96 F4
Yateley GU46 ....149 B6
Swallow Field Gdns RG7 .83 E4
Swallow Ho SL7 ....2 A2
Swallow St SL0 ....44 D8
Swallow Way RG41 .....115 E5
Swallowfield TW20 ....95 B2
Swallowfield Dr RG2 ...113 C6
Swallowfield Pk* RG7 .139 E7
Swallowfield Rd
Arborfield RG2 ....114 D2
Swallowfield RG7 ....139 F6
Swallowfield St RG7 ...139 C7
Swallows Croft RG1 ......85 E5
Swan Ct RG14 ....104 F3
Swan Dr RG7 ....109 C3
Swan Ho GU47 ....150 B7
Swan La GU17,GU47 ....150 B7
Swan Pl 5 RG1 ....86 A7
Swan Rd SL0 ....44 F7
Swan Terr SL4 ....67 B7
Swan Wlk TW17 ....125 E2
Swanbrook Ct SL6 ....40 A7
Swancote Gn RG12 .....118 B4
Swandrift TW18 ....96 F1
Swangate RG17 ....100 D7
Swanholm Gdns RG31 ....84 F4
Swanmore Cl RG6 ....87 E1
Swanscourt RG10 ....61 E3
Swansdown Wlk RG19 ..106 B3
Swansea Rd
Harlington TW14,TW6 .....71 D1
Reading RG1 ....59 A1
Swansea Terr RG31 ....57 D1
Swanston Field RG8 .....56 D7
Sweeps La TW20 ....95 F3
Sweet Briar Dr RG31 .....84 C4
Sweetbriar RG45 ....143 A7
Sweetzer's Piece RG7 ..136 E6
Swepstone Cl RG6 ....87 C2
Swift Cl RG41 ....115 E5
Swift Ho SL7 ....2 A2
Swift La GU19 ....145 F3
Swinbrook Cl RG31 ......57 D3
Swindon Rd TW6 ....71 C2
Swinley Prim Sch SL5 ..120 A4
Swinley Rd SL5 ....119 C4
Swinnerton Ho RG9 ......15 E3
Swiss Cottage Cl RG31 ..84 C8
Swiss Ct GU17 ....150 C4
Switchback Cl SL6 ....19 D2
Switchback Rd N SL6 ....19 E3
Switchback Rd S SL6 ....19 D2
Switchback The SL6 .....19 D2
Swithin Chase RG42 .....91 E1
Sycamore Cl
8 Bourne End SL8 ....3 B3
Burghfield Common RG30 .111 B4
Frimley GU16 ....151 E1
Maidenhead SL6 ....39 C3
Sandhurst GU47 ....150 B8
Woodley RG5 ....87 C5
Sycamore Ct
Pangbourne RG8 ....56 C6
Windsor SL4 ....67 C4
Sycamore Dr
Frimley GU16 ....151 E1
Marlow Bottom SL7 ....1 D5
Twyford RG10 ....61 E5
Sycamore Lodge 7
TW16 ....98 F1
Sycamore Rd RG2 ....86 E2
Sycamore Rise
Bracknell RG12 ....118 D6
Newbury RG14 ....105 C5
Sycamore Wlk
Englefield Green TW20 ....95 B2
Slough SL3 ....43 E7
Sycamores The GU17 ...150 B5
Sydings The RG14 ......104 D5
Sydney Cl
Crowthorne RG45 ....143 C7
Thatcham RG19 ....106 E3
Sydney Cres TW15 ....98 B2
Sydney Gr SL1 ....42 C7
Sydney Loader Pl GU17 150 A5
Sydney Lodge RG19 ....106 E3
Syke Cluan SL0 ....44 E4
Syke Ings SL0 ....44 F4
Sykes Dr TW18 ....97 B3
Sykes Rd SL1 ....42 B7
Sylvan Ridge GU47 .....143 A1
Sylvan Wlk RG30 ....85 C4
Sylvanus RG12 ....117 F2
Sylverns Ct RG42 ....91 D1
Sylvester Cl
Newbury RG14 ....104 E5
Winnersh RG41 ....88 D3
Sylvester Rd SL6 ....19 E2
Symondson Mews RG42 .90 C4
Sympson Rd RG26 .....135 D1

T

Tachbrook Rd TW14 ......98 F8
Tadcroft Wlk RG31 ....84 E3
Tadham Pl RG19 ....106 C2
Tadley Common Rd
RG26 ....135 C1
Tadmor Cl TW16 ....125 F5
Taff Way RG30 ....85 A7
Tag La RG10 ....37 A1
Talbot Ave SL3 ....43 F4
Talbot Cl Caversham RG4 .59 D2
Newbury RG14 ....104 E5
Talbot Ct 2 Reading RG1 .86 A7
Windsor SL4 ....67 B4
Talbot Pl Bagshot GU19 .145 E4
Datchet SL3 ....68 C6
Talbot Rd TW15 ....97 E3
Talbot Way RG31 ....57 C3
Talbots Dr SL6 ....39 B6
Talfourd Ave RG6 ....87 A5
Talisman Cl RG45 ......142 D5
Tall Trees SL3 ....69 E6
Tallis La RG30 ....85 D4
Tamar Ct RG30 ....85 D6
Tamar Gdns RG2 ....86 C3
Tamar Way Slough SL3 ...44 B2
Wokingham RG41 ....115 E7
Tamarind Ct 3 TW20 .....95 F3
Tamarind Way RG6 ....86 F1
Tamarisk Ave RG2 ....86 E1
Tamarisk Ct RG18 ......106 F4
Tamarisk Rise RG40 ....116 C7
Tamarisk Way SL1 ....42 A5
Tamesa Ho TW17 ....125 A2
Tamesis Pl RG4 ....59 B1
Tamworth RG12 ....118 D2
Tamworth Cl 2 RG6 ......87 C1
Tangier Ct SL4 ....67 D8
Tangier La SL4 ....67 D8
Tanglewood RG40 ......142 A7
Tanglewood Ride GU24 .153 D7
Tangley Dr RG41 ......116 B4
Tanglyn Ave TW17 .....125 B4
Tanhouse La RG41 .....116 A5
Tank Rd GU15 ....150 F5
Tanner Ct RG14 ....105 A4
Tanners Cl RG7 ....110 F1
Tanners La RG4 ....58 F8
Tanners Yd GU19 ......145 E3
Tape La RG10 ....88 F8
Tapestries The SL4 ......68 A2
Taplow Common Rd SL1 .21 A3
Taplow Rd SL6 ....41 A7
Taplow Sta SL6 ....40 F7
Tarbat Ct 6 GU47 ......150 D8
Tarbay La SL4 ....66 B5
Target Cl TW14 ....71 E1
Target Hill RG42 ....91 D1
Targett Ct RG41 ....88 B2
Tarlton Ct RG30 ....84 F6
Tarmac Way UB7 ....70 B7
Tarn Howes Cl RG19 ...106 A3
Tarn La RG14 ....130 F8
Tarnbrook Way RG12 ...118 E2
Tarragon Cl
Bracknell RG42 ....91 D1
Earley RG6 ....86 F1
Tarragon Way RG7 .....111 B3
Tarrant Gn RG42 ....91 C1
Tarrant's Hill RG17 ....100 D5
TASIS-The American Sch in England TW20 ....123 C6
Tasker Cl UB7 ....71 C7
Tasman Ct TW16 ....98 E1
Tatchbrook Cl SL6 ......40 A8
Tattersall Cl RG40 .....116 E5
Tavistock Cl
Maidenhead SL6 ....39 A8
Staines TW18 ....97 D1
Tavistock Ind Est RG10 ..61 F5
Tavistock Rd RG2 ....86 B3
Tawfield RG12 ....117 E2
Tay Rd RG30 ....85 A7
Taylor Ct 7 RG1 ....85 E7
Taylor's Cl SL7 ....1 F2
Taylors Ct SL6 ....39 B8
Taynton Wlk 8 RG1 .....86 B5
Tazewell Ct RG1 ....85 F6
Tealgate RG17 ....100 D7
Tebbit Cl RG12 ....118 D7
Teesdale Rd SL2 ....41 F8
Teikyo Sch (UK) SL3 ....23 D5
Tekels Ave GU15 ......151 D4
Tekels Ct GU15 ....151 E4
Tekels Way GU15 ......151 F3
Telford Ave RG45 ......143 C8
Telford Cres RG5 ....60 F1
Telford Ct RG14 ....104 F5
Telford Dr SL1 ....42 A4
Telston Cl SL8 ....3 A5
Tempest Rd TW20 ....96 C2
Templar Cl GU47 ......150 A8
Templars Pl 1 SL7 ....1 E1
Temple Gdns TW18 .....123 F8
Temple Ho RG9 ....15 E3
Temple La SL7 ....18 D6
Temple Mews RG5 ....87 F7
Temple Mill Cotts SL7 ...18 C5
Temple Mill Island SL7 ..18 C5
Temple Park Rdbt RG42 .90 F2
Temple Pk SL6 ....17 F3
Temple Pl 17 RG1 ....86 A6
Temple Rd SL4 ....67 D5
Temple Way
Bracknell RG42 ....90 E1
Farnham Common SL2 ....22 C7
Templecroft TW15 ......98 D2
Templedene Ave TW18 ...97 C2
Templeton Gdns RG2 ...86 C1
Templeton Ho RG9 ....35 F8
Templewood Gate SL2 ...22 C7
Templewood La SL2 .....22 D8
Ten Acre La TW20 .....123 C7
Tenaplas Dr RG8 ....54 F5
Tenby Ave RG4 ....59 D5
Tenby Dr SL5 ....120 D4
Tennyson Rd
Ashford TW15 ....97 E3
Thatcham RG18 ....106 C4
Woodley RG5 ....87 E4
Tennyson Way SL2 ......21 E1
Tensing Ct TW19 ....97 E7
Tenth Ave RG31 ....84 B6
Teresa Vale RG42 ....91 E2
Tern Cl RG30 ....85 A6
Terrace Rd N RG42 ......90 C4
Terrace Rd S RG42 ......90 C2
Terrace The Ascot SL5 ..120 D4
Camberley GU15 ....151 A5
Crowthorne RG45 ....143 D5
Maidenhead SL6 ....40 C3
Wokingham RG40 ....116 B6
Terrent Ct SL4 ....67 A5
Terrington Hill SL7 ....1 C2
Terry's La SL6 ....19 F8
Tesimond Dr GU46 .....149 A6
Tessa Rd RG1 ....58 F1
Test Cl RG30 ....85 A8
Testwood Rd SL4 ....66 D6
Tetbury Ct 8 RG1 ....85 E7
Teviot Rd RG30 ....84 E7
Thackery Lodge TW14 ...71 D1
Thakerays The RG19 ...106 D2
Thames Ave
Chertsey KT16 ....124 A6
Pangbourne RG8 ....56 D6
Reading RG1 ....59 A1
Windsor SL4 ....67 D7
Thames Bank RG8 ....34 B7
Thames Cl Bourne End SL8 .3 A4
Chertsey KT16 ....124 C2
Thames Cres SL6 ....20 B2
Thames Ct Goring RG8 ...34 B6
Reading RG1 ....59 B1
Thames Dr RG10 ....60 F7
Thames Edge Ct TW18 ...96 E4
Thames Ho RG9 ....15 E3
Thames Ind Est SL7 ......1 F2
Thames Mdw KT12,
TW17 ....125 E1
Thames Mead SL4 ....66 E6
Thames Rd Goring RG8 ..34 B6
Slough SL3 ....44 B3
Thatcham RG18 ....106 B5
Thames Reach
Medmenham SL7 ....17 D6
Purley On T RG8 ....57 D5
Thames Side
Henley-On-T RG9 ....15 E2
Laleham KT16,TW18 ....124 C4
Reading RG1 ....59 A1
Staines TW18 ....96 F2
Thames Side continued
Windsor SL4 ....67 D7
Thames Side Prom RG1 .59 A2
Thames St
Oatlands Park KT12 .....125 F2
Sonning RG4 ....60 D4
Staines TW18 ....96 F3
Windsor SL4 ....67 D7
Thames Valley Bsns Pk
RG6 ....60 B1
Thames Valley Com Inf Sch
SL1 ....42 D4
Thames Valley Nuffield Hospl
The SL3 ....23 C4
Thames Valley Univ SL1 .42 E5
Thamesbourne Mews SL8 .3 A3
Thamesfield Ct TW17 ..125 C2
Thamesfield Gdns SL7 ....1 E1
Thamesgate TW18 ......124 B8
Thameside Prim Sch
RG4 ....59 B2
Thameside Reach RG8 ..14 A4
Thamesmead Sch
TW17 ....125 D3
Thanington Way RG6 ....87 B2
Thatcham Nature Discovery
Ctr* RG19 ....106 A2
Thatcham Sta RG19 ....106 F1
Thatchers Dr SL6 ....39 A5
Theal Cl GU47 ....150 D8
Theale CE Prim Sch RG7 83 D3
Theale Green Com Sch
RG7 ....83 D3
Theale Rd RG30 ....111 C6
Theale Sta RG7 ....83 E2
Theobald Dr RG31 ......57 D4
Theobalds Way GU16 ..152 C3
Thetford Ho 7 RG1 .....85 E5
Thetford Mews RG4 .....59 D6
Thetford Rd TW15 ....97 E5
Thibet Rd GU47 ....150 C8
Thicket Gr SL6 ....38 F7
Thicket Rd RG30 ....84 E8
Thickthorne La TW18 ....97 C1
Third Ave Marlow SL7 .....1 F2
Reading RG31 ....84 B6
Tadley RG7 ....135 C2
Third Cres SL1 ....42 C8
Third St E RG19 ....132 A5
Thirkleby Cl SL1 ....42 C5
Thirlmere Ave
Burnham SL1 ....41 C8
Reading RG30 ....57 F1
Thirlmere Cl TW20 ......96 B1
Thirlmere Wlk GU15 ...152 D4
Thirtover RG18 ....79 B1
Thistledown RG31 ....57 C1
Thistleton Way RG6 .....87 E2
Thomas Ct SL6 ....39 A2
Thomas Dr RG42 ....91 E1
Thomas La RG40 ....141 E8
Thomas Merriman Ct
RG14 ....105 A2
Thomas Rd HP10 ....3 D4
Thompkins La SL2 ......22 A5
Thompson Cl
Hermitage RG18 ....78 F6
Slough SL3 ....44 A2
Thompson Dr RG19 ....106 E2
Thompsons Yd 13 RG1 ..86 B6
Thomson Wlk RG31 .....84 E4
Thorburn Chase GU47 ..150 E6
Thorn Cl RG41 ....115 C3
Thorn Dr SL3 ....43 E7
Thorn La 2 RG1 ....86 B7
Thorn St RG1 ....86 A7
Thornaby Pl HP10 ....3 E8
Thornbank Cl TW19 .....70 A2
Thornbers Way RG10 ....61 B5
Thornbridge Rd RG2 ...113 B8
Thornbury Cl RG45 ....143 B5
Thornbury Gn RG10 .....61 D5
Thorncroft TW20 ....95 C1
Thorndike SL2 ....42 B8
Thorndown La GU20 ...146 D3
Thorne Cl
Crowthorne RG45 ....143 A7
Henley-On-T RG9 ....35 B8
Littleton TW15 ....98 C1
Thorney Cl RG6 ....87 E2
Thorney La N SL0 ....44 F6
Thorney La S SL0 ....44 F5
Thornfield RG19 ....132 D3
Thornfield Gn GU17 ....150 F3
Thornford Rd RG19 ....132 E3
Thornhill RG12 ....118 E5
Thornhill Way TW17 ...125 A4
Thorningdown OX11 .....10 D8
Thornton Mews
Crowthorne RG45 ....143 C4
Reading RG30 ....85 C8
Thornton Rd RG30 ....85 C8
Thorp Cl RG42 ....90 C3
Thorpe By-Pass TW20 ..123 B6
Thorpe CE Inf Sch
TW20 ....123 B6
Thorpe Cl RG41 ....116 A3
Thorpe Ho 4 RG30 ......85 B7
Thorpe Ind Est TW20 ..123 C7
Thorpe Ind Pk TW20 ...123 C8
Thorpe Lea Prim Sch
TW20 ....96 D2
Thorpe Lea Rd TW20 ....96 C2
Thorpe Pk* TW20 ....123 E5
Thorpe Rd
Chertsey KT16 ....123 D4
Egham TW18,TW20 ....96 D3
Thorpeside Cl TW18,
TW20 ....123 E7
Thrale Mews RG30 ......85 B8
Three Acre Rd RG14 ....130 F8
Three Firs Way RG7 ....110 F1
Three Gables La RG8 ....34 A7
Three Post La 1 RG17 ...25 B2
Threshfield RG12 ......118 A4
Thrift La SL6 ....39 D1
Throgmorton Rd GU46 .149 A5
Thrush Cl RG7 ....111 B3
Thurlby Way SL6 ....39 D3
Thurlestone Cl TW17 ..125 C3
Thurlestone Gdns RG2 ..86 C2
Thurlestone Par TW17 .125 C3
Thurley Bsns Units RG7 112 C1
Thurley Cotts SL3 ....23 B3
Thurnscoe Cl RG6 .....113 F8
Thurso Cl RG30 ....85 A8
Thurston Rd SL1 ....42 E7
Thyme Cl RG6 ....87 A1
Tichborne Cl GU17 .....150 D5
Tichborne Cl GU16 .....151 F3
Tickenor Dr RG40 ......141 F7
Tickhill Cl RG6 ....113 F7
Tickleback Row RG42 ...91 B6
Tides End Ct GU15 .....151 F4
Tidmarsh Ct RG8 ....56 C1
Tidmarsh La RG8 ....56 B2
Tidmarsh Rd RG8 ....56 C4
Tidmarsh St 1 RG30 ....85 B8
Tidwells Lea RG12 .....118 E8
Tierney Ct 2 SL7 ....1 E1
Tiffany Cl RG41 ....115 D6
Tiger Cl RG5 ....88 B7
Tigerseye Cl RG41 .....115 D7
Tiggell Cl RG6 ....87 D4
Tilbury Cl RG4 ....59 C3
Tilbury Wlk SL3 ....44 B3
Tile Barn Row RG20 ...129 E1
Tilebarn Cl RG9 ....15 C1
Tilecotes Cl SL7 ....1 D2
Tilehurst La RG42 ....90 D3
Tilehurst Rd RG1,RG30 ..85 D7
Tilehurst Sta RG31 ......57 E3
Tilling Cl RG31 ....57 B2
Tilly's La TW18 ....96 F4
Tilney Way Earley RG6 .113 F8
Lower Earley RG6 ....114 A8
Tilstone Ave SL4 ....41 E2
Tilstone Cl SL4 ....41 E1
Timberley Pl RG45 .....142 E4
Timbers Wlk SL6 ....39 B5
Timline Gn RG12 ......118 F7
Timson Ct RG14 ....105 B3
Timsway TW18 ....96 F3
Tindal Cl GU46 ....149 D6
Tinkers La SL4 ....66 D5
Tinsey Cl TW20 ....96 B3
Tinsley Cl RG6 ....113 F8
Tintagel Dr 1 GU16 ...151 F1
Tintagel Ho SL1 ....42 C5
Tintagel Rd RG40 .....142 A8
Tintern Cl SL1 ....42 C3
Tintern Cres RG1 ....85 F5
Tinwell Cl RG6 ....87 E2
Tippett Rise RG2 ....86 B5
Tippings La RG5 ....88 A8
Tippits Mead RG42 ....117 D8
Tiptree Cl RG6 ....113 F8
Tiree Ho SL2 ....42 B8
Titan Ho RG7 ....134 E2
Titcombe Way RG17 ....102 A2
Tite Hill TW20 ....95 D3
Tithe Barn Dr SL6 ....40 E1
Tithe Cl Maidenhead SL6 .40 C1
Wentworth GU25 ....122 D3
Tithe Ct Slough SL3 .....44 A2
Wokingham RG40 ....116 C7
Tithe La TW19 ....69 A1
Tithe Mdws GU25 ......122 D3
Tithebarn Gr RG31 ......84 F4
Titlarks Hill Rd SL5 ...121 B1
Tiverton Cl RG5 ....60 E1
Tiverton Way GU16 ....151 F1
Toad La GU17 ....150 E4
Tocker Gdns RG42 ......91 B2
Tockington Ct GU46 ...149 D6
Tockley Rd SL1 ....21 B2
Tofrek Terr RG30 ....85 C7
Tokers Green La RG4 ...58 D7
Toll Gdns RG12 ....118 F6
Tollgate SL6 ....39 A6
Tolpuddle Way GU46 ...149 F5
Tomlin Cl RG19 ....106 E2
Tomlin Rd SL2 ....21 E1
Tomlins Ave GU16 .....151 F2
Tomlinscote Sch & Sixth
Form Coll GU16 ....152 A2
Tomlinscote Way GU16 .152 A2
Tomlinson Dr RG40 ....142 A7
Tonkins Dr RG19 ......106 E2
Toogood Pl RG42 ....91 D3
Top Comm RG42 ....91 D1
Topaz Cl Slough SL1 ....42 B5
Wokingham RG41 ....115 E7
Tope Cres RG2 ....140 F7
Tope Rd RG2 ....140 F8
Torcross Gr RG31 ....84 B4
Torin Ct TW20 ....95 C3
Torquay Spur SL2 ....22 B2
Torridge Rd SL3 ....69 B8
Torrington Rd RG2 ......86 C2
Toseland Way RG6 ......87 E3
Totale Rise RG42 ....91 B2
Totnes Rd RG2 ....86 C2
Tottenham Wlk GU47 ..143 D1
Totterdown RG7 ....110 F1

Toulouse Cl GU15 152 B7
Toutley Cl RG41 88 F1
Toutley Rd RG41 89 A1
Toutley Works RG41 89 A2
Tower Cl Caversham RG4 59 C8
Flackwell Heath HP10 3 C7
Tower Hill RG20 49 A8
Tower Ho Iver SL0 44 E7
Marlow SL7 1 B1
4 Slough SL1 42 E4
Towers Dr RG45 143 B4
Town Farm Prim Sch
TW19 97 D8
Town Farm Way TW19 97 D8
Town Hall (Mus)★
KT15 124 A2
Town La Stanwell TW19 97 D7
Wooburn HP10 3 D4
Town Mills 6 RG14 105 A3
Town Quay TW18 124 C6
Town Sq Bracknell RG12 118 C7
Camberley GU15 151 C6
9 Slough SL1 42 F4
Town Tree Rd TW15 98 A3
Townlands Hospl RG9 15 D2
Townsend Cl RG12 118 E4
Townsend Rd
Aldworth RG8 32 E3
Ashford TW15 97 E3
Streatley RG8 34 A7
Townside Pl GU15 151 D6
Tozer Wlk SL4 66 D4
Trafalgar Cl RG41 115 E6
Trafalgar Ct RG1 85 E6
Trafalgar Way GU15 150 F4
Trafford Rd RG1 58 E1
Transcend Osbourne Mews
7 SL4 67 C5
Trash Gn RG30 111 B7
Travic Rd SL2 21 F2
Travis Ct SL2 22 B2
Travis La GU47 150 C7
Treacher Ct RG10 61 E5
Treble Ho Terr OX11 12 A8
Tredegar Rd RG4 59 A6
Tree Cl RG30 84 D8
Tree Tops Ave GU15 152 B8
Trees Rd SL8 3 B3
Treesmill Dr SL6 39 C3
Treeton Cl RG6 113 F8
Trefoil Cl RG40 116 E7
Trefoil Dro RG18 106 F4
Treforgan RG4 58 F5
Trelawney Ave SL3 43 F3
Trelawney Dr RG31 57 B1
Trelleck Rd RG1 85 F5
Tremayne Wlk GU15 152 C4
Trenchard Rd SL6 65 B8
Trenches La SL0,SL3 44 A6
Trent Cl RG41 115 E7
Trent Cres RG18 106 B5
Trent Rd SL3 69 B8
Trent Villas Est SL3 68 B6
Trenthams Cl RG8 57 B5
Trenton Cl GU16 152 A1
Tresham Cres GU46 149 A6
Tressell The SL6 39 D6
Trevelyan RG12 117 E2
Trevelyan Mid Sch SL4 67 C3
Trevithick Cl TW14 98 F7
Trevor Ct TW19 70 A2
Trevor Ho 2 RG30 85 B7
Trevose Ho SL2 22 B1
Triangle The
Newbury RG14 131 B7
Reading RG30 84 D8
Trident Ho TW19 97 E8
Trident Ind Est SL3 69 E4
Trilakes Ctry Pk★ GU46,
GU47 149 E8
Trindledown RG42 91 A2
Tring Rd RG31 57 C2
Tringham Cotts GU24 153 F7
Trinity GU47 143 E2
Trinity Ave SL7 1 D3
Trinity CE Prim Sch RG9 15 D1
Trinity Cl TW19 70 C1
Trinity Cres SL5 121 A4
Trinity Ct Bracknell RG12 117 F7
Theale RG7 83 D3
Trinity Ho SL6 19 F6
Trinity Pl Reading RG1 85 F7
Windsor SL4 67 C5
Trinity Rd SL7 1 D2
Trinity Sch RG14 105 B5
Trinity St Stephens CE Fst
Sch SL4 67 B6
Triumph Cl Harlington UB7 71 C6
Woodley RG5 87 F5
Troon Ct Ascot SL5 120 C4
18 Reading RG1 86 D7
Troston Ct 10 TW18 96 F3
Trotsford Mdw GU17 150 C4
Trotsworth Ave GU25 122 E5
Trotsworth Ct GU25 122 D5
Trotwood Cl GU47 143 E2
Trout Cl Earley RG6 87 A8
Marlow SL7 18 C8
Trout Wlk RG14 105 C4
Troutbeck Cl Slough SL2 43 A6
Twyford RG10 61 D6
Troutbeck Wlk GU15 152 D3
Trowe's La
Beech Hill RG7 138 D4
Swallowfield RG7 139 D5
Trumbull Rd RG42 91 A1
Trumper Way SL1 41 F5
Trumps Green Ave
GU25 122 D3
Trumps Green Cl GU25 122 E4
Trumps Green Inf Sch
GU25 122 D3
Trumps Mill La GU25 122 F4
Trumpsgreen Rd GU25 122 D3
Truro Cl SL6 39 A7
Truss Hill Rd SL5 120 C4
Trust Cnr RG9 35 E8
Trusthorpe Cl RG6 87 E2
Tubbs Farm Cl RG17 25 B2
Tubwell Rd SL2 23 B4
Tudor Ave RG20 51 C4
Tudor Cl Ashford TW15 97 E4
Wokingham RG40 116 F5
Tudor Ct Maidenhead SL6 20 C2
3 Stanwell TW19 70 E1
Thatcham RG18 106 C4
Tudor Dr
Wooburn Green HP10 3 D7
Yateley GU46 149 D4
Tudor Gdns SL1 41 C8
Tudor Hall GU15 151 F6
Tudor Ho RG12 118 B4
Tudor La SL4 95 C8
Tudor Mill HP10 3 E5
Tudor Rd Ashford TW15 98 D2
Newbury RG14 105 A1
Reading RG1 86 A8
Tudor Way SL4 66 E6
Tull Way RG18 105 F5
Tunnel Link Rd TW6 71 A2
Tunnel Rd E TW6 71 B6
Tunnel Rd W TW6 71 B6
Tuns Hill Cotts RG6 87 A5
Tuns La Henley-On-T RG9 15 E2
Slough SL1 42 C4
Tupsley Rd RG1 85 F5
Turbary Gdns RG26 135 B1
Turf Hill Rd GU15 151 F8
Turing Dr RG12 118 A4
Turk's La RG7 137 A4
Turks Head Ct SL4 67 D7
Turmeric Cl RG6 86 F1
Turnberry RG12 117 E2
Turnberry Ct 15 RG1 86 D7
Turnberry Ho SL5 121 A1
Turnbridge Cl RG6 114 B8
Turner Pl GU47 150 D6
Turner Rd SL3 43 C4
Turners Cl TW18 97 B3
Turners Dr RG19 106 E2
Turnery The RG19 106 C3
Turnfields RG19 106 D3
Turnoak Pk SL4 66 E3
Turnpike Ind Est RG14 105 D5
Turnpike Rd
Bracknell RG42 117 D7
Newbury RG14,RG18 105 E4
Turnstone Cl RG41 88 B3
Turnstone End GU46 149 B6
Turnville Cl GU18 146 A1
Turpin Rd TW14 71 F1
Turpins Gn SL6 39 A5
Turpins Rise GU20 146 B6
Turton Way SL1 42 D3
Tuscam Way GU15 150 F4
Tuscan Cl RG30 57 E1
Tuscany Villas GU18 146 B1
Tuscany Way GU46 149 C4
Tuxford Mews RG30 85 B7
Tweed Ct RG30 85 B7
Tweed Rd SL3 69 B8
Twin Oaks RG4 59 B6
Twinches La SL1 42 B5
Twinwoods RG20 49 A4
Two Mile Dr SL1 41 E4
Two Rivers Sh Ctr TW18 96 E4
Two Rivers Way RG14 105 D3
Two Tree Hill RG9 35 B8
Twycross Rd RG40 116 E7
Twyford Orchards Cvn Pk
RG10 61 F7
Twyford Rd
Binfield RG10,RG42 90 C7
Waltham St Lawrence RG10 62 E6
Wokingham RG40 89 B2
Twyford Sta RG10 61 E4
Twynersh Ave KT16 123 F3
Twynham Rd SL6 39 B7
Tyberton Pl RG1 85 F5
Tydehams RG14 130 F7
Tyle Pl SL4 68 A2
Tyle Rd RG30 84 D8
Tyler Cl RG4 58 E5
Tyler Dr RG2 140 E7
Tyler Wlk SL3 43 F1
Tyler's La RG7 80 B1
Tylers Pl RG30 84 F8
Tylorstown RG4 58 F5
Tymawr RG4 58 F5
Tyne Way RG18 106 B5
Tyrell Gdns SL4 66 F4
Tyrrel Ct 9 RG1 86 C7
Tytherton RG12 118 C7

U

Uffcott Cl RG6 113 F7
Uffington Cl RG31 84 C8
Uffington Dr RG12 118 E5
Ufton Court Yd SL8 3 B4
Ufton Ct SL8 3 B4
Ullswater RG12 117 F2
Ullswater Cl Burnham SL1 41 C8
Lightwater GU18 146 B1
Ullswater Cl *continued*
Thatcham RG19 106 A3
Ullswater Dr RG31 57 D3
Ullswater Rd GU18 146 B1
Ulster Cl RG4 59 D5
Umberville Way SL2 21 F2
Underhill OX10 14 A4
Underhill Cl SL6 39 E6
Underwood RG12 117 E3
Underwood Cotts RG8 33 F6
Underwood Ct RG42 90 C1
Underwood Rd RG30 85 A4
Union Cl GU47 143 E2
Union Rd RG7 82 D4
Union St RG1 86 A8
Unity Cl RG4 59 B6
Unity Ct RG4 59 B6
Univ of Reading
Earley RG6 87 B6
Reading RG1 86 C6
Reading,Whiteknights RG6 86 F4
Unwin Ave TW14 71 D2
Upavon Dr RG1 85 F6
Upavon Gdns RG12 118 F4
Upcroft SL4 67 B4
Upcroft Prim Sch RG30 84 F8
Updown Hill GU20 146 D4
Upland Rd GU15 151 D7
Uplands Hungerford RG17 100 C5
Marlow Bottom SL7 1 D6
Uplands Cl GU47 150 B8
Uplands Prim Sch GU47 150 B8
Uplands Rd RG4 58 E5
Upper Bray Rd SL6 40 C3
Upper Broadmoor Rd
RG45 143 D5
Upper Charles St GU15 151 C6
Upper Chobham Rd
GU15 152 B4
Upper College Ride
GU15 151 E8
Upper Crown St RG1 86 B6
Upper Eddington RG17 100 E7
Upper End RG20 49 A8
Upper Gordon Rd GU15 151 D5
Upper Halliford Rd
TW17 125 E5
Upper Halliford Sta
TW16 125 E7
Upper Lambourn Rd
RG17 25 A3
Upper Lees Rd SL2 22 B2
Upper Meadow Rd RG2 86 D2
Upper Nursery SL5 121 A4
Upper Park Rd GU15 151 E6
Upper Raymond Almshouses
14 RG14 104 F2
Upper Red Cross Rd RG8 34 C7
Upper Redlands Rd RG1 86 E5
Upper Terr RG41 115 B8
Upper Ventnor Cotts SL6 19 C8
Upper Verran Rd GU15 151 D3
Upper Village Rd SL5 120 D4
Upper Warren Ave RG4 58 D3
Upper Wlk GU25 122 E5
Upper Woodcote Rd RG4 58 D5
Uppingham Dr RG5 60 F1
Uppingham Gdns RG4 59 D6
Upshire Gdns RG12 118 F5
Upton Cl Henley-On-T RG9 15 E1
Slough SL1 42 F3
Upton Court Rd SL3 43 B2
Upton Hospl SL1 42 F3
Upton House Sch SL4 67 C5
Upton Lea Par SL2 43 B6
Upton Pk SL1 42 F3
Upton Rd Reading RG30 85 B7
Slough SL1,SL3 43 A3
Urquhart Rd RG19 106 E2
Usk Rd RG30 84 F6
Uxbridge Rd SL1,SL2,SL3 43 C6

V

Vachel Rd RG1 86 A8
Vale Cres RG30 57 E1
Vale Gr SL1 42 E3
Vale Rd Camberley GU15 151 A4
Windsor SL4 66 F6
Vale View RG10 61 B4
Vale View Dr RG7 138 D5
Valentia Cl RG30 85 D8
Valentia Rd RG30 85 D8
Valentine Cl RG6 86 F1
Valentine Cres RG4 59 C4
Valley Cl Caversham RG4 59 A4
Goring RG8 34 C6
Valley Cres RG41 116 A8
Valley End SL3 23 C1
Valley Gdns★ TW20 121 E7
Valley Rd
Burghfield Common RG7 111 A3
Henley-On-T RG9 35 B8
Newbury RG14 130 E8
Frimley GU16 152 C1
Valley Road Sch RG9 35 C8
Valley View GU47 150 A7
Valley Vineyards★ RG10 62 A3
Valley Way RG26 135 E1
Valon Rd RG2 140 F8
Valpy St RG1 86 B8
Valroy Cl GU15 151 D6
Vanbrugh Ct 1 RG1 86 E7
Vandyke RG12 117 E3
Vanguard Ho 5 TW19 70 E1
Vanguard Way TW6 71 E5
Vanlore Way RG31 84 C5
Vanners La RG20 129 D5
Vansittart Est SL4 67 C6
Vansittart Rd Bisham SL7 18 E7
Windsor SL4 67 B6
Vantage Rd SL1 42 B5
Vanwall Bsns Pk SL6 39 C5
Vanwall Rd SL6 39 C4
Vastern Rd RG1 59 B1
Vaughan Almshouses 1
TW15 98 B3
Vaughan Copse SL4 42 D2
Vaughan Gdns SL4 41 F2
Vaughan Way SL2 21 E1
Vauxhall Dr RG5 88 A6
Vegal Cres TW20 95 C3
Veitch Cl TW14 98 F8
Venetia Cl RG4 59 C7
Venning Rd RG2 140 F8
Ventnor Rd RG31 57 D1
Venture Ho TW18 97 A4
Venus Cl RG41 115 F6
Verbena Cl RG41 88 A3
Verdon Ct SL2 22 B2
Verey Cl RG10 61 F3
Verica Gdns RG26 135 E2
Vermont Rd SL2 21 F1
Vermont Woods RG40 141 E7
Verney Cl SL7 1 D2
Verney Mews RG30 85 C7
Verney Rd SL3 44 A2
Vernon Cl TW19 97 E7
Vernon Cres RG2 113 B7
Vernon Dr SL5 119 E7
Vernon Rd TW13 98 F6
Verran Rd GU15 151 D3
Vibia Cl TW19 97 D8
Viburnum Ct GU24 153 E6
Vicarage Ave TW20 96 B3
Vicarage Cl Cookham SL6 20 B7
Wokingham RG40 141 F6
Vicarage Cres TW20 96 B3
Vicarage Ct
East Bedfont TW14 98 C8
Egham TW20 96 B2
Shinfield RG2 113 D5
Vicarage Dr SL6 40 C4
Vicarage Flats SL4 67 D8
Vicarage Gdns
Ascot SL5 120 A4
White Waltham SL6 63 F8
Vicarage La
Cold Ash RG18 106 C8
Laleham TW18 124 C6
Wraysbury TW19 95 F7
Yateley GU46 149 C7
Vicarage Rd Ashford TW16 98 F2
Bagshot GU19 145 C3
Blackwater GU17 150 E4
Egham TW20 96 B3
Henley-On-T RG9 35 E8
Maidenhead SL6 39 F8
Reading RG2 86 C5
Staines TW18 96 E5
Yateley GU46 149 C7
Vicarage Way SL3 69 D7
Vicarage Wlk SL6 40 C4
Vicarage Wood Way
RG31 57 B1
Vickers Cl Shinfield RG2 113 F4
Woodley RG5 88 B7
Vickers Ct 9 TW19 70 E1
Victor Cl SL6 39 B8
Victor Pl RG7 108 C2
Victor Rd Thatcham RG19 106 E3
Windsor SL4 67 C4
Victor Way RG5 88 A7
Victoria Ave GU15 151 A5
Victoria Cres SL0 44 F6
Victoria Ct Bagshot GU19 145 E1
Camberley GU15 151 A5
Henley-On-T RG9 15 E1
2 Marlow SL7 1 E2
Slough SL1 42 E5
Victoria Dr
Blackwater GU17 150 C4
Burnham SL1,SL2 21 F6
Victoria Gdns Marlow SL7 1 E2
Newbury RG14 105 A4
Victoria Ho SL4 68 A2
Victoria La UB7 71 D8
Victoria Mews RG30 85 C7
Victoria Rd Ascot SL5 120 A4
Caversham RG4 59 A3
Eton SL4 41 F1
Farnham Common SL2 22 C6
Marlow SL7 1 E2
Mortimer RG7 136 F6
Reading RG31 84 D8
Sandhurst GU47 143 E1
Slough SL2 43 B5
Staines TW18 96 E5
Wargrave RG10 36 E2
Victoria St
Englefield Green TW20 95 C2
Reading RG1 86 D7
10 Slough SL1 42 F4
Windsor SL4 67 D6
Victoria Way 3 RG1 86 D7
Victory Cl TW15,TW19 97 E7
Victory Rd KT16 124 A1
Vigo La GU46 149 C3
Viking RG12 117 E4
Villa Mews 2 RG1 86 E7
Villa Pl RG7 139 C6
Village Cl RG2 113 B6
Village Ct SL5 120 C4
Village Gate TW17 125 B4
Village Mews SL5 120 C5
Village Rd Dorney SL4 41 B3
Thorpe TW20 123 C6
Village Sh Ctr The 5
SL1 42 F4
Village The
Finchampstead RG40 141 E3
Old Windsor SL4 94 B5
Village Way Ashford TW15 98 A4
Yateley GU46 149 D7
Villiers Ct SL4 67 B7
Villiers Mead RG41 116 A6
Villiers Rd SL2 42 D8
Villiers Way RG14 130 C6
Villiers Wlk RG14 130 C6
Vincent Cl Chertsey KT16 123 E2
Harmondsworth UB7 71 A8
Woodley RG5 87 F6
Vincent Dr TW17 125 E6
Vincent Ho 8 RG1 85 F8
Vincent Rd
Chertsey KT16 123 E2
Thatcham RG18 106 E4
Vincent Rise RG12 118 E6
Vine Cl TW19 70 A2
Vine Cres RG30 85 A4
Vine Ct Newbury RG14 105 B1
Stoke Poges SL2 23 A6
Vine Rd SL2 22 F6
Vineries Cl UB7 71 A8
Vinery The RG10 36 D2
Vines The RG41 115 C3
Vineyard Dr SL8 3 A5
Vinter Ct TW17 125 A4
Vinters Ho RG31 57 D1
Viola Ave TW19 97 E7
Viola Croft RG42 118 F8
Violet Gr RG18 106 E5
Virginia Ave GU25 122 C4
Virginia Beeches GU25 122 C6
Virginia Cl TW18 124 C6
Virginia Ct Ashford TW15 97 E4
Virginia Water GU25 122 D5
Virginia Dr GU25 122 C5
Virginia Water★ SL5 121 E6
Virginia Water Sta
GU25 122 E4
Virginia Way RG30 85 B5
Viscount Ct SL4 67 C6
Viscount Ind Est SL3 69 E4
Viscount Rd TW19 97 E7
Viscount Way Hatton TW6 71 E3
Woodley RG5 88 A7
Vivien Cl SL6 19 F6
Vivienne Ho TW18 97 A3
Vo-Tec Ctr RG14 105 E2
Voller Dr RG31 84 C6
Volunteer Rd RG7 83 D2
Vulcan Cl
Sandhurst GU47 150 A7
Woodley RG5 61 B1
Vulcan Ct GU47 150 A7
Vulcan Ho RG7 134 E2
Vulcan Way GU47 150 B7

W

Waborne Rd SL8 3 B4
Wade Dr SL1 42 A5
Wadham GU47 143 F1
Wadham Cl TW17 125 C2
Wagbullock Rise RG12 118 C3
Waggoners Hollow
GU19 145 E2
Wagner Cl SL6 38 F3
Wagtail Cl RG10 61 E4
Waingel's Copse Sch
RG5 61 A2
Waingels Rd RG5,RG10 61 A2
Wainscott SL5 120 F3
Wainwright Cl RG40 117 A6
Wakefield Cres SL2 22 F6
Wakeford Cl RG26 135 E1
Wakeford Ct RG26 135 E2
Wakelins End SL6 19 E7
Wakeman Rd SL8 3 A3
Wakemans RG8 55 D4
Walbury RG12 118 E5
Waldeck Rd SL6 40 A7
Waldeck St RG1 86 B5
Waldegrave Pl RG14 105 A3
Walden Ave RG2 114 C3
Waldens Cl SL8 3 A3
Waldorf Hts GU17 150 D3
Waldron Hill RG12 118 F8
Waldrons The RG17 47 C6
Waleys Pl 2 RG4 59 C2
Walgrove Gdns SL6 63 E7
Walk The Ashford TW16 98 F1
Eton SL4 42 A1
Walker Cl TW14 98 F8
Walker Ct SL6 39 D7
Walker Rd SL6 40 A4
Walker's La RG17 25 B3
Walker's Ridge GU15 151 E5
Walkers Pl RG30 85 C7
Wall La RG7 136 D2
Wallace Cl Marlow SL7 1 F4
Upper Halliford TW17 125 D5
Woodley RG5 87 D5
Wallace Gr RG7 113 A4
Wallace Wlk SL4 42 F1
Wallcroft Cl RG42 90 E1
Walled Gdn The RG10 36 D2
Waller Ct RG4 59 B2

Waller Dr RG14 ....105 E5
Wallingford Cl RG12 ...118 E5
Wallingford Rd
Compton RG20 ....31 E5
Moulsford RG8,OX10 ....14 A1
South Stoke RG8,OX10 ....14 C5
Streatley RG8 ....34 A7
Wallington Rd GU15 ...145 A1
Wallingtons Rd RG17 ...101 F1
Wallis Ct SL1 ....43 A4
Wallner Way RG40 ....116 E5
Walmer Cl
Crowthorne RG45 ....143 C5
Reading RG30 ....85 A6
Walmer Rd RG5 ....60 F1
Walnut Cl
Thatcham RG18 ....106 C4
Wokingham RG41 ....115 F5
Yateley GU46 ....149 D4
Walnut Ct RG40 ....116 C6
Walnut Gr HP10 ....3 E6
Walnut Lo SL1 ....42 D3
Walnut Mews RG42 ....117 F8
Walnut Tree Cl
Bourne End SL8 ....3 B2
Twyford RG10 ....61 F6
Walnut Tree Cotts RG20 .75 D8
Walnut Tree Ct RG8 ....34 C6
Walnut Tree Rd TW17 ..125 C7
Walnut Way Bourne End SL8 3 B2
Reading RG30 ....84 D8
Walpole Rd
Old Windsor SL4 ....95 B8
Slough SL1 ....41 D7
Walrus Cl RG5 ....88 B7
Walsh Ave RG42 ....91 E1
Walter Inf Sch RG41 ...116 A6
Walter Rd RG41 ....115 E7
Walters Cl RG18 ....106 C8
Waltham Cl
Maidenhead SL6 ....38 F2
Sandhurst GU47 ....143 D1
Waltham Ct RG8 ....34 C8
Waltham Rd
Maidenhead SL6 ....38 F1
Twyford RG10 ....61 E4
Twyford,Ruscombe RG10 ....62 B5
Waltham St Lawrence Prim Sch RG10 ....62 F3
Walton Ave RG9 ....35 E8
Walton Bridge Rd KT12, TW17 ....125 E2
Walton Cl RG5 ....87 C7
Walton Dr SL5 ....119 F8
Walton Gdns TW13 ....98 F4
Walton La Burnham SL2 ...21 F3
Lower Halliford TW17 ....125 D2
Oatlands Park KT12 ....125 E1
Walton Lodge KT12 ....125 F1
Walton Manor KT12 ....125 F2
Walton Way RG14 ....105 C4
Wandhope Way RG31 ....57 C2
Wansey Gdns RG14 ....105 D5
Wanstraw Gr RG12 ....118 E2
Wantage Cl RG12 ....118 E4
Wantage Rd
Great Shefford RG17 ....48 C5
Lambourn RG17 ....25 C5
Reading RG30 ....85 C7
Sandhurst GU47 ....150 D8
Streatley RG8 ....33 F8
Wapshott Rd TW18 ....96 E3
War Meml Pl RG9 ....35 E7
Waram Cl RG17 ....100 E7
Warbler Cl RG31 ....84 B6
Warbler Dr RG6 ....87 B1
Warborough Ave RG31 ...84 B8
Warborough Rd OX12 ....7 A7
Warbreck Dr RG31 ....57 B3
Warbrook La RG27 ....141 A1
Ward Cl Iver SL0 ....44 F7
Wokingham RG40 ....116 D8
Ward Gdns SL1 ....41 E6
Ward Royal 5 SL4 ....67 C6
Ward Royal Par 2 SL4 ...67 C6
Wardle Ave RG31 ....57 D1
Wardle Cl GU19 ....145 E3
Wards Cotts TW19 ....97 F8
Wards Pl TW20 ....96 C2
Wards Stone Pk RG12 ...118 E2
Wareham Rd RG12 ....118 F4
Warehouse Rd RG19 ....131 F5
Warfield CE Prim Sch RG42 ....91 E1
Warfield Rd
Bracknell RG12,RG42 ....91 C1
East Bedfont TW14 ....98 E8
Warfield Rdbt RG42 ....91 C2
Warfield St RG42 ....91 D3
Wargrave Hill RG10 ....36 D2
Wargrave Rd
Henley-On-T RG9,RG10 ....36 B8
Twyford RG10 ....61 D5
Wargrave Sta RG10 ....36 C1
Wargrove Dr GU47 ....150 D8
Waring Cl RG6 ....114 C8
Warings The RG7 ....109 A7
Warley Rise RG31 ....57 C3
Warner Cl Harlington UB3 .71 D7
Slough SL1 ....41 E5
Warner Ct GU47 ....150 E7
Warners Hill SL6 ....19 C8
Warnford Rd RG30 ....84 F7
Warnham La RG20 ....31 B2
Warnsham Cl 1 RG6 ....87 B1
Warren Cl
Burghfield Common RG7 ..111 A3
Sandhurst GU47 ....150 A8
Slough SL3 ....43 E3
Wokingham RG40 ....141 F6
Warren Ct Caversham RG4 .58 F2
Farnham Common SL2 ....22 C7
Warren Down RG42 ....117 E8
Warren Farm RG17 ....26 B8
Warren Ho RG4 ....58 F2
Warren House Ct RG4 ...58 F2
Warren House Rd RG40 116 D8
Warren La RG40 ....141 E5
Warren Rd Ashford TW15 .98 E1
Newbury RG14 ....130 D6
Woodley RG4,RG5 ....60 D1
Warren Rise GU16 ....151 F3
Warren Row SL5 ....119 D7
Warren Row Rd
Knowl Hill RG10 ....37 C6
Wargrave RG10 ....36 F7
Warren The RG4 ....58 D3
Warrington Ave SL1 ....42 C7
Warrington Spur SL4 ....95 B8
Warwick RG12 ....118 E3
Warwick Ave Slough SL2 ..22 C1
Staines TW18 ....97 C2
Thorpe TW20 ....123 C8
Warwick Cl Frimley GU15 152 B3
Maidenhead SL6 ....39 B4
Warwick Ct 3 SL4 ....67 C5
Warwick Dr RG14 ....105 B1
Warwick Ho RG2 ....86 C4
Warwick Rd Ashford TW15 97 E3
Reading RG2 ....86 C4
Warwick Villas TW20 ...123 C8
Wasdale Cl GU47 ....143 D2
Wash Hill HP10 ....3 E3
Wash Hill Lea HP10 ....3 E4
Wash Hill Mobile Home Pk HP10 ....3 E3
Wash Water RG20 ....130 B3
Washbury Ho RG14 ....130 E7
Washington Ct Marlow SL7 2 A2
Thatcham RG19 ....106 A3
Washington Dr
Slough SL1 ....41 D6
Windsor SL4 ....66 E4
Washington Gdns RG40 142 A8
Washington Rd RG4 ....59 B2
Wasing La RG7 ....134 D6
Watchetts Dr GU15 ....151 C2
Watchetts Jun Sch GU15 ....151 B2
Watchetts Lake Cl GU15 ....151 D3
Watchetts Rd GU15 ....151 B4
Watchmoor Pk GU15 ....151 B4
Watchmoor Rd GU15 ....151 A4
Watchmoor Trade Ctr GU15 ....151 A3
Water La RG19 ....131 C7
Water Oakley Cotts SL4 ..65 F8
Water Oakley Farm Cotts SL4 ....65 F8
Water Rd RG30 ....85 B7
Water St RG18 ....52 F6
Waterbeach Cl SL1 ....42 D7
Waterbeach Rd SL1 ....42 D7
Waterfall Cl GU25 ....122 A6
Waterford Way RG40 ...116 C6
Waterham Rd RG12 ....118 B3
Waterhouse Mead GU47 ....150 D7
Waterloo Cl
Camberley GU15 ....152 B7
East Bedfont TW14 ....98 F7
Moulsford OX10 ....14 A7
Waterloo Cres RG40 ....116 E4
Waterloo Rd
Crowthorne RG45 ....143 B4
Reading RG2 ....86 B5
Wokingham RG40 ....116 F5
Waterloo Rise RG2 ....86 B4
Waterman Ct SL1 ....41 E5
Waterman Pl RG1 ....59 A1
Waterman's Rd RG9 ....35 E8
Watermans Way RG10 ...36 C1
Watermead TW14 ....98 E7
Watermeadows The RG14 ....105 B4
Watermill Ct RG7 ....108 C2
Waters Dr TW18 ....96 F4
Watersfield Cl 4 RG6 ...87 B1
Waterside HP10 ....3 E7
Waterside Cotts RG4 ....60 B4
Waterside Ct
Newbury RG14 ....105 B3
Twyford RG10 ....61 C5
Waterside Dr Langley SL3 .43 F4
Purley On T RG8 ....57 D5
Theale RG7 ....83 F3
Waterside Gdns 4 RG1 ..86 A7
Waterside Lodge SL6 ....40 C8
Watersplash La
Ascot SL5 ....120 E8
Newell Green RG42 ....91 B2
Watersplash Rd TW17 ..125 A5
Watery La Chertsey KT16 123 D2
Kintbury RG20 ....128 F5
Wooburn Green HP10 ....3 E8
Watkins Cl RG40 ....141 E7
Watlington St RG1 ....86 C7
Watmore La RG41 ....88 D2
Watson Cl RG40 ....115 F1
Watt's La OX11 ....12 A8
Wavell Cl RG2 ....86 F1
Wavell Gdns SL2 ....21 F2
Wavell Rd SL6 ....39 B6
Wavendene Ave TW20 ...96 C1
Waverley RG12 ....117 E4
Waverley Cl GU15 ....151 F4
Waverley Ct 18 RG30 ....85 D6
Waverley Dr
Camberley GU15 ....151 F5
Virginia Water GU25 ....122 A5
Waverley Rd
Bagshot GU19 ....145 E3
Reading RG30 ....85 C7
Slough SL1 ....42 C8
Waverley Sch RG40 ....115 E1
Waverley Way RG40 ....115 F1
Waverleys The RG18 ...106 D4
Wawcott Farm Cotts RG20 ....102 C4
Waybrook Cres RG1 ....86 F6
Wayewood GU15 ....151 E6
Wayland Cl RG12 ....118 F5
Waylands TW19 ....68 E1
Waylands Cl RG7 ....82 D4
Waylen St RG1 ....85 F7
Ways End GU15 ....151 E4
Waysend Ho GU15 ....151 E4
Wayside Cotts GU20 ....146 F6
Wayside Mews SL6 ....39 F8
WC Lee's Resthouses GU20 ....146 D4
Weald Rise RG30 ....57 F2
Wealden Way RG30 ....84 F8
Weardale Cl RG2 ....86 D4
Weather Way RG12 ....118 C7
Weathervane Cotts RG17 ....100 C5
Weaver Moss GU47 ....150 B7
Weavers Ct
22 Reading RG1 ....86 D7
Wokingham RG40 ....116 C6
Weavers La RG17 ....127 C6
Weavers Way RG10 ....61 D4
Weavers Wlk 2 RG14 ...105 A3
Webb Cl Bagshot GU19 ...145 E1
Bracknell RG42 ....90 E1
Slough SL3 ....43 D2
Webb Ct RG40 ....116 E8
Webb's Cl RG1 ....85 F6
Webbs Acre RG19 ....106 F2
Webbs La RG7 ....109 B7
Webster Cl SL6 ....39 A5
Wedderburn Cl RG41 ....88 D2
Wedgewood Way RG30 ...57 F1
Weedon Cl OX10 ....14 A8
Weekes Dr SL1 ....42 B4
Weighbridge Row RG1 ...58 F1
Weir Cl RG31 ....84 F4
Weir Pl TW18 ....123 E8
Weir Pool Ct RG10 ....61 C4
Weir Rd KT16 ....124 B2
Weirside Ct 1 RG1 ....86 D7
Welbeck RG12 ....117 E4
Welbeck Rd SL6 ....39 D5
Welby Cl SL6 ....39 A4
Welby Cres RG41 ....88 B1
Weldale St RG1 ....85 F8
Welden SL2 ....43 C7
Welford & Wickham CE Prim Sch RG20 ....75 D4
Welford Pk RG20 ....75 E7
Welford Rd
Wickham RG20 ....75 D4
Woodley RG5 ....88 A8
Well Cl GU15 ....151 B4
Well End Cotts SL8 ....2 F5
Well House La RG27 ....140 B3
Well Mdw RG14 ....105 B5
Welland Cl Brands Hill SL3 69 B8
Reading RG31 ....57 C1
Wellbank SL6 ....20 E1
Wellburn Cl GU47 ....150 B7
Wellcroft Rd SL1 ....42 B5
Weller Dr Barkham RG40 .141 A6
Camberley GU15 ....151 C3
Weller's La RG42 ....91 C7
Wellesley Ave SL0 ....44 F4
Wellesley Cl GU19 ....145 C3
Wellesley Ct SL0 ....44 F4
Wellesley Dr RG45 ....142 E5
Wellesley Ho SL4 ....67 B6
Wellesley Path SL1 ....43 A4
Wellesley Rd SL1 ....43 A4
Welley Ave TW19 ....68 E3
Welley Rd TW19 ....68 E3
Wellfield Cl RG31 ....84 C7
Wellhill Rd OX12 ....27 C6
Wellhouse La RG18 ....79 E6
Wellhouse Rd SL6 ....19 E2
Wellington Ave
Reading RG2 ....86 D4
Virginia Water GU25 ....122 B4
Wellington Bsns Pk RG45 ....142 F4
Wellington Cl
Maidenhead SL6 ....39 B8
Newbury RG14 ....105 C5
Oatlands Park KT12 ....125 F1
Sandhurst GU47 ....150 C8
Wellington Coll RG45 ...143 A3
Wellington Cotts
Ball Hill RG20 ....129 B2
Knowl Hill RG10 ....37 C6
Wellington Cres RG26 ..134 D1
Wellington Ct
Ashford TW15 ....97 E3
Shinfield RG7 ....113 A3
Stanwell TW19 ....97 E8
Wellington Ctry Pk★ RG7 ....139 D1
Wellington Dr RG12 ....118 E4
Wellington Gdns RG7 ...82 A1
Wellington Ind Est RG7 .113 A1
Wellington Lodge SL4 ....93 B6
Wellington Rd
Ashford TW15 ....97 E3
Crowthorne RG45 ....143 C4
Hatton TW14 ....71 E2
Maidenhead SL6 ....39 D7
Sandhurst GU47 ....150 C8
Wokingham RG40 ....116 B5
Wellington St SL1 ....43 A4
Wellington Terr GU47 ...150 D8
Wellingtonia Ave RG45, RG40 ....142 C3
Wellingtonia Rdbt RG45 142 E4
Wellingtonias RG42 ....92 A1
Wells Cl SL4 ....67 A7
Wells La SL5 ....120 B5
Welsh La RG7,RG7 ....139 A2
Welshman's Rd RG7 ...136 A5
Welwick Cl RG6 ....87 E2
Welwyn Ave TW14 ....71 F1
Wendan Rd RG14 ....130 F8
Wendover Ct TW18 ....96 C3
Wendover Dr GU16 ....152 C3
Wendover Pl TW18 ....96 D3
Wendover Rd
Bourne End SL8 ....3 A5
Burnham SL1 ....41 B8
Egham TW18,TW20 ....96 D3
Wendover Way RG30 ....84 D7
Wenlock Edge RG10 ....61 B4
Wenlock Way RG19 ....106 D2
Wensley Cl RG10 ....61 D5
Wensley Rd RG1 ....85 E5
Wensleydale Dr GU15 ..152 D5
Wentworth Ave
North Ascot SL5 ....119 C7
Reading RG2 ....113 D8
Slough SL2 ....22 A2
Wentworth Cl
Ashford TW15 ....98 B4
Crowthorne RG45 ....142 F6
Yateley GU46 ....149 D5
Wentworth Cres SL6 ....39 C6
Wentworth Ct RG14 ....105 B1
Wentworth Dr GU25 ....121 F5
Wentworth Golf Club GU25 ....122 A4
Wentworth Lodge RG14 104 E2
Wentworth Way SL5 ...119 C7
Wescott Inf Sch RG40 ...116 D6
Wescott Rd RG40 ....116 D6
Wesley Dr TW20 ....96 A2
Wesley Pl SL4 ....93 B6
Wessex Cl RG17 ....100 C5
Wessex Ct 4 TW19 ....70 E1
Wessex Gdns RG10 ....61 E3
Wessex Inf Sch SL6 ....39 B4
Wessex Jun Sch SL6 ....39 B4
Wessex Rd Bourne End SL8 .3 B2
Harmondsworth TW19,TW6 .70 E4
Wessex Road Ind Est SL8 .3 B2
Wessex Way SL6 ....39 B4
Wessons Hill SL6 ....19 C7
West Berkshire Community Hospl RG14 ....105 E4
West Berkshire Mus★ RG14 ....105 A3
West Cl Ashford TW15 ....97 E4
Medmenham SL7 ....17 D7
West Cres SL4 ....66 F6
West Ct Maidenhead SL6 ..40 C4
Sonning RG4 ....60 E2
West Dean SL6 ....39 F8
West Dr Reading RG31 ....84 E5
Sonning RG4 ....60 D1
Wentworth GU25,SL5 ....121 E2
West End Ct SL2 ....22 F4
West End Ho RG14 ....105 B5
West End La
Harlington UB7 ....71 C7
Newell Green RG42 ....91 B3
Stoke Poges SL2 ....22 E4
West End Rd RG7 ....136 F5
West Fryerne GU46 ....149 D8
West Gn GU46 ....149 B7
West Green Ct RG1 ....85 F5
West Hill RG1 ....86 B6
West Ilsley Ho RG20 ....10 A1
West La RG9 ....15 D2
West Lawn RG41 ....115 A7
West Mead SL6 ....19 F2
West Mead Sch RG40 ....116 E6
West Mills RG14 ....104 F3
West Mills Yd RG14 ....104 F3
West Point SL1 ....41 D5
West Ramp TW6 ....71 A6
West Rd Bracknell RG40 .117 D2
Camberley GU15 ....151 D5
East Bedfont TW14 ....98 D8
Maidenhead SL6 ....39 E7
West Ridge SL8 ....3 B4
West Sq SL0 ....44 F7
West St Henley-On-T RG9 .15 D2
Maidenhead SL6 ....39 F7
Marlow SL7 ....1 D1
Newbury RG14 ....104 F3
Reading RG1 ....86 A7
West Surrey Estates TW15 ....125 C8
West View
East Bedfont TW14 ....98 C8
Peasemore RG20 ....50 C7
West View Cotts RG18 ....52 F6
West Way TW17 ....125 D3
Westacott Bsns Ctr SL6 ..38 E2
Westacott Way SL6 ....38 D4
Westborough Ct SL6 ....39 C6
Westborough Rd SL6 ....39 C6
Westbourne Rd
Feltham TW13 ....98 F5
Sandhurst GU47 ....150 E7
Staines TW18 ....97 B1
Westbourne Terr
3 Newbury RG14 ....105 A4
Reading RG30 ....85 C7
Westbrook SL6 ....40 E1
Westbrook Cl RG17 ....100 C5
Westbrook Gdns RG12 ..118 D8
Westbrook Gn OX11 ....11 F8
Westbrook Rd
Reading RG30 ....58 C1
2 Staines TW18 ....96 F3
Westbrook St OX11 ....11 F8
Westbury Cl
Crowthorne RG45 ....143 B6
Shepperton TW17 ....125 B3
Westbury La RG8 ....57 A6
Westcoign Ho SL6 ....40 B8
Westcombe Cl RG12 ....118 E2
Westcote Rd RG30 ....85 D6
Westcotts Gn RG42 ....91 D1
Westcroft SL2 ....22 B1
Westdene Cres RG4 ....58 E4
Westende RG40 ....116 D6
Westende Jun Sch RG40 ....116 D6
Westerdale RG19 ....106 D3
Westerdale Dr GU16 ....152 B3
Westerham Wlk 9 RG1 ..86 B5
Western Ave
Chertsey KT16 ....124 A6
Henley-On-T RG9 ....35 E8
Newbury RG14 ....104 E4
Thorpe TW20 ....123 B6
Woodley RG5 ....60 E1
Western Cl
Chertsey KT16 ....124 A6
Henley-On-T RG9 ....35 E8
Western Ctr The RG12 ..117 F7
Western Dr
Shepperton TW17 ....125 D3
Wooburn Green HP10 ....3 E5
Western Elms Ave RG30 .85 E7
Western End RG14 ....104 E2
Western House Inf Sch SL1 ....41 F6
Western Ind Area RG12 .117 F7
Western Oaks RG31 ....57 E2
Western Perimeter Rd TW19,TW6,UB7 ....70 B5
Western Perimeter Rd Rdbt TW19 ....70 C2
Western Rd
Bracknell RG12 ....117 F7
Henley-On-T RG9 ....35 E8
Reading RG1 ....85 E6
Westfield Bglws SL7 ....16 F6
Westfield Cotts SL7 ....16 F6
Westfield Cres
Shiplake RG9 ....36 B3
Thatcham RG18 ....106 B4
Westfield Rd
Camberley GU15 ....151 B2
Caversham RG4 ....59 B2
Cholsey OX10 ....13 D6
Maidenhead SL6 ....39 B7
Slough SL2 ....22 B1
Thatcham RG18 ....106 B5
Winnersh RG41 ....88 B2
Westfield Sch SL8 ....3 B4
Westfield Way RG14 ....104 E2
Westfields Compton RG20 .31 D4
Kintbury RG20 ....128 A3
Westfields Jun & Inf Sch GU46 ....149 B5
Westgate Cres SL1 ....41 F6
Westgate Ct RG14 ....104 E1
Westgate Rd RG14 ....104 E2
Westgate Sch The SL1 ...42 A5
Westhatch Cnr RG42 ....91 C5
Westhatch La RG42 ....91 C5
Westhead Dr RG14 ....131 A8
Westhorpe Park Cvn Site SL7 ....2 B3
Westhorpe Rd SL7 ....1 F3
Westland RG18 ....106 B4
Westland Cl TW19 ....70 E1
Westlands Ave Earley RG2 86 E1
Slough SL1 ....41 C7
Westlands Cl SL1 ....41 C7
Westleigh Ho RG31 ....84 B7
Westley Mill Binfield RG42 90 E8
Holyport RG42 ....63 F1
Westlyn Rd RG26 ....135 E1
Westmacott Dr TW14 ....98 F7
Westmead SL4 ....67 B4
Westminster Way RG6 ...87 C1
Westmorland Cl RG41 ..115 D6
Westmorland Dr
Bracknell RG42 ....91 F1
Frimley GU15 ....152 B3
Westmorland Rd SL6 ....39 D6
Weston Gr GU19 ....145 F2
Weston Rd SL1 ....41 F8
Weston's RG20 ....51 D8
Westonbirt Dr RG4 ....58 E3
Westridge Ave RG8 ....57 C5
Westside Ct GU24 ....153 E6
Westview Dr RG10 ....61 E6
Westward Rd RG41 ....115 F7
Westwates Cl RG12 ....118 D8
Westway RG8 ....34 C8

Westwood Farm Jun & Inf
 Schs RG31 . . . . .57 C3
Westwood Glen RG31 . .57 C1
Westwood Gn SL6 . . . . .19 F6
Westwood Rd Marlow SL7 . .1 C1
 Newbury RG14 . . . . . . .105 B4
 Reading RG31 . . . . .57 D1
 Windlesham GU20 . . . .146 E6
Westwood Row RG31 . . .57 C2
Wetherby Cl RG4 . . . . . .59 C6
Wetherby Ho GU15 . . . .151 D7
Wethered Pk SL7 . . . . . . .1 D1
Wethered Rd Marlow SL7 . .1 D2
 Slough SL1 . . . . .41 B8
Wetton Pl TW20 . . . . . . .95 F3
Wexford Ct SL6 . . . . . . .40 B7
Wexham Park Hospl SL3 .23 C1
Wexham Park La SL3 . . .23 C1
Wexham Pl SL3 . . . . . . .23 D6
Wexham Prim Sch SL3 . .43 C7
Wexham Rd SL1,SL2 . . . .43 B6
Wexham St SL3 . . . . . . .43 C8
Wexham St SL3 . . . . . . .23 B3
Wexham Woods SL3 . . . .43 C8
Wey Ave KT16 . . . . .124 A6
Wey GU15 . . . . .151 B5
Weybridge Mead GU46 .149 E7
Weycrofts RG42 . . . . . . .90 F1
Weymead Cl KT16 . . . . .124 C1
Whaley Rd RG40 . . . . . .116 D8
Wharf La SL8 . . . . .3 A3
Wharf Rd Newbury RG14 .105 A3
 Wraysbury TW19 . . . . . .95 D8
Wharf St RG14 . . . . . . .105 A3
Wharf The RG14 . . . . . .105 A3
Wharfe La RG9 . . . . .15 E2
Wharfedale Rd RG41 . . . .88 A3
Wharfside RG7 . . . . . . .109 C3
Whatley Gn RG12 . . . . .118 B3
Whatmore Cl TW19 . . . . .70 A1
Wheat Ho TW19 . . . . . . .97 E2
Wheatbutts The SL4 . . . .41 F2
Wheatfield Cl SL6 . . . . . .39 A4
Wheatfields Rd RG2 . . .113 E5
Wheatlands Cl RG31 . . . .84 E4
Wheatlands La RG14 . . .130 B6
Wheatlands Rd SL3 . . . . .43 C3
Wheatley RG12 . . . . . . .117 E4
Wheatley Cl RG2 . . . . . . .86 E1
Wheatsheaf La
 Newbury RG14 . . . . . .105 B4
 Staines TW18 . . . . .96 F1
Wheatsheaf Par SL4 . . . .68 A2
Wheatstone Cl 10 SL3 . . .43 A3
Wheble Dr RG5 . . . . .87 D8
Wheeler Cl
 Burghfield Common RG7 .111 B3
 Wokingham RG41 . . . . .115 F5
Wheeler Ct RG31 . . . . . .57 E1
Wheelers Green Way
 RG19 . . . . .106 A3
Wheelton Cl RG6 . . . . . .87 E3
Wheelwrights Pl SL6 . . . .69 C7
Whins Cl GU15 . . . . . . .151 B4
Whins Dr GU15 . . . . . . .151 B4
Whinshill Ct SL5 . . . . . .121 A1
Whistler Gr GU47 . . . . .150 D6
Whistlers La RG7 . . . . .136 B1
Whistley Cl RG12 . . . . .118 E6
Whistley Court Farm
 RG10 . . . . .61 E1
Whitakers Cl RG18 . . . .106 B4
Whitamore Row RG9 . . . .35 E8
Whitby Cl RG4 . . . . .59 D6
Whitby Dr 1 RG1 . . . . . .86 C5
Whitby Gn RG4 . . . . .59 D6
Whitby Rd SL1 . . . . .42 C6
Whitchurch Cl SL6 . . . . .19 E3
Whitchurch Prim Sch
 RG8 . . . . .56 E7
Whitchurch Rd RG8 . . . .56 D6
White Bridge Cl TW14 . .71 F1
White City RG45 . . . . . .143 D5
White Cl Hermitage RG18 .78 D4
 Slough SL1 . . . . .42 D5
White Gates RG20 . . . . .75 D5
White Hart Ind Est
 GU17 . . . . .150 E4
White Hart Rd
 2 Maidenhead SL6 . . . .39 F7
 Slough SL1 . . . . .42 D3
White Hart Row KT16 . .124 A2
White Hermitage SL4 . . .68 C2
White Hill
 Ashampstead RG8 . . . . .54 D6
 Remenham Hill RG9 . . . .16 A2
 Shiplake RG9 . . . . .35 A5
 Windlesham GU20 . . . .146 B6
 Wooburn Moor HP9 . . . . .3 F8
White Horse La RG40 . .141 D5
White Horse Rd SL4 . . . .66 D5
White House Gdns
 GU46 . . . . .149 C7
White House La
 Beech Hill RG7 . . . . . .138 F8
 Swallowfield RG7 . . . . .139 A8
White House Prep Sch
 RG41 . . . . .116 A3
White House Rd OX10 . .14 F8
White Lilies Island SL4 .67 B7
White Lion Way GU46 . .149 D7
White Lodge Cl
 Marlow Bottom SL7 . . . . .1 C6
 Purley On T RG31 . . . . .57 B3
White Paddock SL6 . . . . .39 A2
White Rd Chilton OX11 . .10 D8
 Sandhurst GU47 . . . . .150 F6
White Rock SL6 . . . . . . .20 B1

White Shoot OX11 . . . . .12 A5
White Waltham CE Prim Sch
 SL6 . . . . .63 D7
White's Hill RG7 . . . . . .110 D5
Whiteacres Dr SL6 . . . . .40 C1
Whitebeam Cl RG41 . . .115 D3
Whitefields Cotts RG14 .104 F7
Whiteford Rd SL2 . . . . . .42 E8
Whitegates La RG6 . . . . .87 A7
Whitegrove Prim Sch
 RG42 . . . . .91 F1
Whitegrove Rdbt RG42 . .91 D2
Whitehall SL6 . . . . .20 B1
Whitehall Dr RG2 . . . . .140 E8
Whitehall Farm La
 SL3 . . . . .122 E6
Whitehall La Egham TW20 .95 F1
 Wraysbury TW19 . . . . . .69 A1
Whitehart La RG7 . . . . . .83 E4
Whitehaven SL1 . . . . . . .42 F6
Whitehill Cl
 Camberley GU15 . . . . .151 D7
 Marlow SL7 . . . . .1 C6
Whitehill Pl GU25 . . . . .122 E4
Whitehills Gn RG8 . . . . .34 C6
Whitehouse Way SL3 . . .43 D3
Whiteknights Prim Sch
 RG6 . . . . .86 F1
Whiteknights Rd RG6 . . .86 F5
Whitelands Dr SL5 . . . .119 D8
Whitelands Park Prim Sch
 RG18 . . . . .106 C3
Whitelands Rd RG18 . . .106 D4
Whiteley SL4 . . . . .66 E7
Whitelocke Inf Sch
 RG40 . . . . .116 D7
Whitelocks Piece RG17 . .73 A2
Whitemoor La
 Lower Basildon RG8 . . . .34 C1
 Upper Basildon RG8 . . . .54 E5
Whitepit La HP10 . . . . . . .3 D7
Whites La Beenham RG7 .109 B7
 Datchet SL3 . . . . .68 B8
Whitestone Cl RG6 . . . . .87 E3
Whitewalls Cl RG20 . . . .31 E5
Whiteways Ct TW18 . . . .97 B1
Whitewell Cl RG2 . . . . .114 E2
Whitley Cl TW19 . . . . . . .70 E1
Whitley Park Inf Sch
 RG2 . . . . .86 B2
Whitley Park Jun Sch
 RG2 . . . . .86 B2
Whitley Park La RG2 . . . .86 D4
Whitley Rd GU46 . . . . . .149 D4
Whitley St RG2 . . . . .86 B5
Whitley Wood La RG2 . . .86 C7
Whitley Wood Rd RG2 . .113 C7
Whitmoor Rd GU19 . . . .145 F2
Whitmore Cl GU47 . . . .143 D1
Whitmore La SL5 . . . . . .121 D4
Whitstone Gdns RG2 . . . .86 C1
Whittaker Rd SL2 . . . . . .21 E1
Whittenham Cl SL2 . . . . .43 A5
Whittle Cl
 Sandhurst GU47 . . . . .143 A1
 Wokingham RG40 . . . . .141 E7
Whittle Parkway SL1 . . .41 D7
Whitton Cl 2 RG6 . . . . .87 D1
Whitton Rd RG12 . . . . .118 F6
Whitworth Rd RG2 . . . .141 A7
Whurley Way SL6 . . . . . .19 E2
Whybrow Ct RG18 . . . . .106 D3
Whynstones Rd SL5 . . .120 A4
Whyteladyes La SL6 . . . .19 E6
Wick Hill Ho RG12 . . . .118 C8
Wick Hill La RG40 . . . . .142 A5
Wick La TW20 . . . . .94 F3
Wick Rd TW20 . . . . .95 B1
Wickens Cnr RG7 . . . . .109 A6
Wickets The
 Ashford TW15 . . . . .97 E4
 Maidenhead SL6 . . . . . .39 C7
Wickford Way RG6 . . . .113 F8
Wickham La TW20 . . . . .96 A1
Wickham Rd
 Camberley GU15 . . . . .151 E8
 Earley RG6 . . . . .87 C1
Wickham Vale RG12 . . .117 E3
Wickhurst Cotts SL6 . . . .38 B5
Wicks Gn RG42 . . . . .90 B3
Wicks La RG10 . . . . .62 E2
Widbrook Rd SL6 . . . . . .20 B3
Widecroft Rd SL0 . . . . . .44 E7
Widmere La SL7 . . . . .1 A6
Wield Ct RG6 . . . . .87 E1
Wiggett Gr RG42 . . . . . .90 C2
Wiggington Ho SL4 . . . .67 D7
Wigmore La Reading RG30 .58 B1
 Reading RG30 . . . . .58 C1
 Theale RG7 . . . . .83 C1
Wigmore Rd RG26 . . . . .134 F1
Wilberforce Mews SL6 . .39 F7
Wilberforce Way RG12 .118 D4
Wilcox Gdns SL1 . . . . . .41 F7
Wild Briar RG40 . . . . . .141 F7
Wild Cl RG6 . . . . .114 C8
Wildcroft Dr RG40 . . . .116 A1
Wilde Theatre RG12 . . .118 C2
Wilder Ave RG8 . . . . . . .56 E5
Wilderness Ct RG6 . . . . .87 A4
Wilderness Rd Earley RG6 .87 A4
 Frimley GU16 . . . . .151 E2
Wilders Cl Bracknell RG42 .91 A1
 Frimley GU16 . . . . .151 E3
Wildgreen N 1 SL3 . . . .44 A2
Wildgreen S 2 SL3 . . . .44 A2
Wildoaks TW18 . . . . .97 B3

Wildridings Prim Sch
 RG12 . . . . .118 A5
Wildridings Rd RG12 . .118 A5
Wildridings Sq RG12 . .118 A5
Wildwood Dr RG42 . . . .134 D1
Wildwood Gdns GU46 . .149 C4
Wilford Rd SL3 . . . . .43 F2
Wilfred Way RG19 . . . . .107 A3
Wilfrids Wood Cl HP10 . . .3 B6
Willant Cl SL6 . . . . .38 F7
Willats Cl KT16 . . . . . . .124 A2
William Byrd Sch UB7 . . .71 D8
William Ellis Cl SL4 . . . .68 A1
William Hartley Yd SL3 . .23 B1
William Penn Sch The
 SL2 . . . . .22 D1
William Sim Wood RG42 .92 B2
William St Reading RG1 . .85 F8
 Slough SL1 . . . . .42 F5
 Windsor SL4 . . . . .67 D6
Williams Ct RG17 . . . . .100 D5
Williamson Cl RG41 . . . .88 B3
Willington Cl GU15 . . . .151 B6
Willink Sch The RG7 . . .110 F2
Willis Cl RG18 . . . . .79 B3
Willoners SL2 . . . . .42 A7
Willoughby Rd
 Bracknell RG12 . . . . . .117 F6
 Slough SL3 . . . . .44 A3
Willow Bank SL1 . . . . . . .1 D5
Willow Bank Jun & Inf Schs
 RG5 . . . . .60 F1
Willow Cl
 Burghfield Common RG30 .111 B5
 Colnbrook SL3 . . . . . . .69 C7
 Flackwell Heath HP10 . . .3 C6
 Newbury RG14 . . . . . .104 F1
Willow Cotts OX10 . . . . .13 F5
Willow Court La OX10 . . .13 F5
Willow Ct
 2 Ashford TW16 . . . . . .98 E1
 Frimley GU16 . . . . .151 D1
 Wokingham RG41 . . . . .116 B6
Willow Dr
 Bracknell RG12 . . . . . .118 C8
 Maidenhead SL6 . . . . . .40 B2
 Twyford RG10 . . . . .61 D6
Willow Gdns
 Purley On T RG31 . . . . .57 B2
 Reading RG2 . . . . .86 E1
Willow Gn GU24 . . . . . .153 F6
Willow La
 Blackwater GU17 . . . . .150 D4
 Wargrave RG10 . . . . . . .36 C4
Willow Lodge 6 SL6 . . . .19 F5
Willow Par SL4 . . . . .44 A3
Willow Pk SL2 . . . . .23 A5
Willow Pl SL4 . . . . .67 C8
Willow Rd
 Bishops Green RG20 . . .131 F2
 Poyle SL3 . . . . .69 E5
Willow St 3 RG1 . . . . . .86 A6
Willow Tree Glade RG31 .84 C4
Willow Way GU47 . . . . .142 F1
Willow Wlk
 Chertsey KT16 . . . . . . .124 B2
 Englefield Green TW20 . .95 C3
Willow Wood Cl SL1 . . . .21 B3
Willowbrook SL4 . . . . . .42 D2
Willowbrook Rd TW19 . .97 E6
Willowdale RG40 . . . . . .141 F8
Willowford GU46 . . . . . .149 D6
Willowherb Cl RG40 . . .116 E7
Willowmead TW18 . . . .124 B8
Willowmead Cl
 10 Marlow SL7 . . . . .1 F3
 Newbury RG14 . . . . . .130 C5
Willowmead Gdns SL7 . . .1 F3
Willowmead Rd 8 SL7 . . .1 F3
Willowmead Sq 9 SL7 . . .1 F3
Willows Ct 2 RG8 . . . . . .56 C6
Willows End GU47 . . . . .150 B8
Willows Rd SL8 . . . . .3 B4
Willows Riverside Pk The
 SL4 . . . . .66 C7
Willows The
 9 Bourne End SL8 . . . . .3 B3
 1 Bracknell RG12 . . . .118 F5
 Caversham RG4 . . . . . . .59 A2
 Lightwater GU18 . . . . .146 C1
 Windsor SL4 . . . . .66 D7
Willowside RG5 . . . . . . .60 F1
Willson Rd TW20 . . . . . .95 B3
Wilmington Cl RG5 . . . . .87 F8
Wilmot Cl RG42 . . . . . . .90 C2
Wilmot Rd SL1 . . . . .21 B2
Wilmot Way GU15 . . . . .151 F3
Wilmot Wlk RG14 . . . . .130 C6
Wilsford Cl RG6 . . . . . .113 E7
Wilson Ave RG9 . . . . . . .35 E8
Wilson Cl RG20 . . . . . . .31 E4
Wilson Ct RG41 . . . . . . .88 B1
Wilson Prim Sch RG30 . .85 C7
Wilson Rd RG30 . . . . . . .85 C2
Wilson Valkenburg Ct
 RG14 . . . . .104 E4
Wilstrode Ave RG42 . . . .90 F1
Wilton Cl UB7 . . . . .70 D8
Wilton Cres SL4 . . . . . . .66 D4
Wilton Rd
 Camberley GU15 . . . . .151 B1
 Reading RG30 . . . . .85 D3
Wiltshire Ave
 Crowthorne RG45 . . . . .143 B5
 Slough SL2 . . . . .22 C1
Wiltshire Cl RG17 . . . . .100 C5
Wiltshire Dr RG40 . . . . .116 D7

Wiltshire Gr RG42 . . . . .91 F2
Wiltshire Lodge 2 SL6 . .39 F6
Wiltshire Rd Marlow SL7 . .1 F4
 Wokingham RG40 . . . . .116 C7
Wiltshire Wlk RG31 . . . .84 B6
Wilwood Rd RG42 . . . . .117 E8
Wilwyne Cl RG4 . . . . . . .59 C4
Wimbledon Cl GU15 . . .144 F1
Wimbledon Rd GU15 . . .144 F1
Wimblington Dr RG6 . . .114 C8
Wimbourne Gdns RG30 . .58 A1
Wimbushes RG40 . . . . .141 D6
Winbury Ct SL6 . . . . . . .39 E7
Winbury Sch SL6 . . . . . .40 B4
Wincanton Rd RG2 . . . .113 C7
Winch Cl RG42 . . . . .90 C3
Winch Terr SL4 . . . . . . .66 D5
Winchbottom La SL7 ,HP10 .2 B6
Winchcombe Jun & Inf Schs
 RG14 . . . . .105 A4
Winchcombe Rd
 Newbury RG14 . . . . . .105 A2
 Twyford RG10 . . . . .61 E4
Winchester Cl SL3 . . . . .69 E6
Winchester Dr SL6 . . . . .39 B3
Winchester Ho 5 RG14 .105 A2
Winchester Rd
 Harlington UB3 . . . . . . .71 E7
 Reading RG2 . . . . .86 C4
Winchester Way GU17 . .150 C6
Winchgrove Rd RG42 . . .91 A1
Winchstone Cl TW17 . . .124 F5
Wincroft Rd RG4 . . . . . .58 E5
Windermere Cl
 East Bedfont TW14 . . . . .98 F7
 Stanwell TW19 . . . . . . .97 D6
 Thorpe Lea TW20 . . . . . .96 B1
 Winnersh RG41 . . . . . . .88 C3
Windermere Rd
 Lightwater GU18 . . . . .146 B1
 Reading RG2 . . . . .86 D3
Windermere Way
 Slough SL1 . . . . .41 C7
 Thatcham RG19 . . . . . .106 A3
Windermere Wlk GU15 .152 D5
Winding Wood Dr GU15 .152 B3
Windle Cl GU20 . . . . . . .146 D4
Windlebrook Gn 3
 RG42 . . . . .118 A8
Windlesham Ct GU20 . .146 C6
Windlesham Rd
 Bracknell RG42 . . . . . .117 F8
 West End GU24 . . . . . .153 F7
Windlesham Village Inf Sch
 GU20 . . . . .146 B6
Windmill Ave RG42 . . . .115 E8
Windmill Bsns Village
 TW16 . . . . .125 E8
Windmill Cl
 Charlton TW16 . . . . .98 E1
 Windsor SL4 . . . . .67 B5
 Wokingham RG41 . . . . .115 E8
Windmill Cnr RG7 . . . . .137 A6
Windmill Ct RG7 . . . . . .137 A6
Windmill Field GU20 . . .146 D4
Windmill La RG7 . . . . . .108 A5
Windmill Lodge TW16 . .125 E8
Windmill Rd
 Bracknell RG42 . . . . . .118 A8
 Charlton TW16 . . . . . . .125 E8
 Cookham Rise SL6 . . . . .19 E6
 Fulmer SL3 . . . . .23 D7
 Mortimer RG7 . . . . . . .137 A6
 Slough SL1 . . . . .42 D5
Windmill Rd W TW16 . .125 E8
Windmill Shott TW20 . . .95 F2
Windmill Terr TW17 . . .125 E2
Windrush Ave SL3 . . . . . .44 B3
Windrush Ct 5 RG30 . . .85 B7
Windrush Ho SL8 . . . . . . .3 A4
Windrush Hts GU47 . . . .150 B8
Windrush Way
 Maidenhead SL6 . . . . . .39 F8
 Reading RG30 . . . . .85 B7
Windsor & Eton Central Sta
 SL4 . . . . .67 D6
Windsor & Eton Riverside Sta
 SL4 . . . . .67 D7
Windsor Boys' Sch The
 SL4 . . . . .67 B6
Windsor Bsns Ctr The
 SL4 . . . . .67 C7
Windsor Castle★ SL4 . . .67 E7
Windsor Cl SL1 . . . . .21 C1
Windsor Ct
 Camberley GU15 . . . . .151 C5
 Newbury RG14 . . . . . .105 B2
 9 Reading RG1 . . . . . . .85 E7
Windsor Dr TW15 . . . . . .97 D4
Windsor Forest Ct SL5 .119 D8
Windsor Girls' Sch SL4 . .67 C3
Windsor Great Pk★ SL4 .94 D4
Windsor Hill HP10 . . . . . .3 F5
Windsor Ho
 4 Egham TW20 . . . . . .96 A3
 Henley-On-T RG9 . . . . . .35 E8
Windsor La SL1 . . . . .21 C1
Windsor Park Rd UB3 . . .71 F7
Windsor Pl KT16 . . . . . .124 A3
Windsor Rd Datchet SL3 . .68 A7
 Englefield Green SL4,TW19,
 TW20 . . . . .95 C6
 Fulmer SL2 . . . . .23 A8
 Maidenhead SL6 . . . . . .40 C1
 North Ascot SL5 . . . . . .120 A8
 Oakley Green SL4 . . . . .66 A7
 Slough SL1 . . . . .42 E4
 Wraysbury TW19 . . . . . .68 E1

Windsor Ride
 Bracknell SL5 . . . . . . .119 C4
 Sandhurst GU15 . . . . .151 A8
 Wokingham RG40 . . . . .142 A7
Windsor Rise RG14 . . . .131 C8
Windsor Sq 11 RG1 . . . .86 B5
Windsor St KT16 . . . . . .124 A3
Windsor Way RG31 . . . . .84 B4
Wing Cl SL7 . . . . .1 C1
Wingate Rd SL7 . . . . . . .87 E6
Wingfield Gdns GU16 . .152 D3
Wingrove Rd RG30 . . . . .85 C6
Winkfield Cl RG41 . . . . .116 B3
Winkfield La SL4 . . . . . . .92 D7
Winkfield Rd Ascot SL5 .120 D7
 Windsor SL4 . . . . .66 E2
Winkfield Row RG42 . . . .92 B3
Winkfield St SL4 . . . . . . .92 C6
Winkfield St Mary's CE Prim
 Sch RG42 . . . . .92 B3
Winkworth La RG7,RG26 135 C2
Winnersh Gate RG41 . . . .88 D2
Winnersh Gr RG41 . . . . .88 C1
Winnersh Prim Sch
 RG41 . . . . .88 D3
Winnersh Sta SL4 RG41 . .88 D2
Winnersh Triangle Ind Est
 RG41 . . . . .88 B3
Winnersh Triangle Sta
 RG41 . . . . .88 A3
Winscombe RG12 . . . . .117 E4
Winser Dr RG30 . . . . . . .85 D5
Winslett Pl RG30 . . . . . .58 B1
Winston Cl RG7 . . . . . . .113 D2
Winston Ct SL6 . . . . .39 B8
Winston Way
 Purley On T RG8 . . . . . .57 B5
 Thatcham RG19 . . . . . .105 A3
Winter Hill SL6 . . . . .2 C1
Winter Hill Rd SL6 . . . . .19 A4
Winterberry Way RG4 . . .58 E6
Winterbourne Ct RG12 . .118 D7
Winterbourne Rd RG20 . .76 E4
Winterton Dr RG14 . . . .104 D5
Winton Cres GU46 . . . . .149 D5
Winton Rd RG2 . . . . . . .113 D8
Wintoun Path SL2 . . . . . .21 E1
Wintringham Way RG8 . .57 D5
Winvale SL1 . . . . .42 E3
Winwood Slough SL2 . . . .43 C7
 Windsor SL4 . . . . .66 F6
Wisdom Ct 14 RG30 . . . .85 D6
Wise's Firs RG7 . . . . . . .110 D3
Wishmoor Cl GU15 . . . .151 E8
Wishmoor Rd GU15 . . . .151 E8
Wispington Cl RG6 . . . . .87 D2
Wistaria La GU46 . . . . .149 C5
Wisteria Cl RG41 . . . . . .115 F5
Wiston Terr RG1 . . . . . . .86 B8
Witcham Cl RG6 . . . . . .114 D8
Withey Cl SL4 . . . . .66 E6
Witheygate Ave TW18 . . .97 B2
Withy Cl Lightwater GU18 146 C1
 Reading RG31 . . . . .84 C5
Withybed La RG17 . . . . .101 E3
Withybed Way RG18 . . .106 E5
Withycroft SL3 . . . . .43 E7
Withys The RG18 . . . . . .53 E1
Wittenham Ave RG31 . . .84 B8
Wittenham Rd RG12 . . .118 F8
Wittington Cotts SL7 . . . .17 D6
Woburn Cl Caversham RG4 58 E4
 Frimley GU16 . . . . .152 A1
Woburn Ho SL5 . . . . . . .121 A1
Wokefield Row RG7 . . . .137 D8
Wokingham Hospl
 RG41 . . . . .116 A6
Wokingham Rd
 Bracknell RG42 . . . . . .117 F8
 Earley RG6 . . . . .87 C4
 Hurst RG10 . . . . .88 F8
 Sandhurst RG45,GU47 . .142 E2
Wokingham Sta RG40 . .116 B6
Wolf La SL4 . . . . .66 E4
Wolseley St RG1 . . . . . . .86 A6
Wolsey Rd Ashford TW15 . .97 E4
 Ashford,Felthamhill TW16 .98 C1
 Caversham RG4 . . . . . . .59 B2
Wolsingham Way RG19 .106 D2
Wondesford Dale RG42 . .90 C4
Wooburn Grange HP10 . . .3 D3
Wooburn Manor Pk HP10 . .3 E6
Wooburn Mead HP10 . . . .3 E5
Wooburn Mews HP10 . . . .3 E5
Wooburn Town HP10 . . . .3 D4
Wood Cl SL4 . . . . .67 C3
Wood End RG45 . . . . . .142 F4
Wood Gn RG2 . . . . .113 D8
Wood Green Cl RG30 . . .85 E7
Wood La Arborfield RG41 .114 F3
 Beech Hill RG7 . . . . . .138 E5
 Binfield RG42 . . . . .90 D1
 Bracknell RG42 . . . . . .117 E8
 Iver SL0 . . . . .44 C8
 Slough SL1 . . . . .42 A4
Wood Rd
 Camberley GU15 . . . . .151 B1
 Littleton TW17 . . . . . . .125 A5
Wood Ridge RG14 . . . . .130 C7
Woodavon Gdns RG18 . .106 D5
Woodberry Cl RG4 . . . . .59 B3
 Sandhurst GU47 . . . . .150 F6
Woodbine Cl Earley RG6 . .87 C1
Woodbine Cotts TW20 . . .95 F2
Woodbine La RG20 . . . .130 F1

Woodbourne Cl GU46 149 D6
Woodbridge Dr GU15 151 D7
Woodbridge Manor GU15 151 D7
Woodbridge Rd
Blackwater GU17 150 B5
Reading RG31 84 B6
Woodbury RG17 25 C1
Woodbury Cl SL8 3 C4
Woodbury Ct RG7 140 D4
Woodby Dr SL5 120 F2
Woodcock Ct RG7 113 A4
Woodcote SL6 39 D6
Woodcote House Sch GU20 146 B5
Woodcote Pl SL5 119 F8
Woodcote Rd
Caversham RG4 58 E4
South Stoke RG8 14 E4
Woodcote Way RG4 58 D5
Woodcott Ho RG26 135 A1
Wooden Hill Prim Sch RG12 117 E2
Woodend GU15 152 A7
Woodend Cl SL5 119 E8
Woodend Dr SL5 120 B4
Woodenhill RG12 117 E1
Woodfield Cotts RG8 34 A6
Woodfield Dr SL6 39 A6
Woodfield Way RG7 83 E4
Woodford Cl RG4 58 E4
Woodford Gn RG12 118 F5
Woodford Way SL2 22 A2
Woodhall La SL5 146 E8
Woodhaw TW20 96 B4
Woodhouse La RG19 133 E2
Woodhouse St RG42 90 E1
Woodhurst La RG41 115 F8
Woodhurst Rd SL6 20 B1
Woodhurst S SL6 20 C1
Woodies Cl RG42 90 C1
Woodland Ave Slough SL1 42 D6
Windsor SL4 66 F3
Woodland Cl SL7 1 E4
Woodland Cres RG42 91 C1
Woodland Dr RG30 84 D7
Woodland Way SL7 1 E4
Woodlands GU46 149 D4
Woodlands Ave
Burghfield Common RG7 111 A3
Wokingham RG41 115 E8
Woodley RG5 87 C7
Woodlands Bsns Pk SL6 39 A2
Woodlands Cl Ascot SL5 119 F3
Curridge RG18 78 D5
Farnborough GU17 150 E1
Woodlands Cotts SL2 22 C7
Woodlands Ct GU47 143 F1
Woodlands Gr RG4 59 D4
Woodlands La GU20, GU24 146 E3
Woodlands Par TW15 98 C2
Woodlands Park Ave SL6 39 A2
Woodlands Park Prim Sch SL6 39 A1
Woodlands Park Rd SL6 39 A2
Woodlands Rd
Camberley GU15 151 B5
Harpsden RG9 35 E4
Tadley RG26 134 D1
Virginia Water GU25 122 C5
Woodlands Rd E GU25 122 C5
Woodlands Rd W GU25 122 C5
Woodlands Ride SL5 120 A3
Woodlands The RG41 115 D4
Woodlands Wlk GU17 150 E1
Woodlark Glade GU15 151 D7
Woodlee Cl GU25 122 C7
Woodleigh Mans SL5 120 E4
Woodley CE Prim Sch RG5 88 B8
Woodley Gn RG5 87 F8
Woodley Park Est RG5 87 D8
Woodman Cl RG2 113 C6
Woodman's La RG7 110 F3
Woodmancott Cl RG12 118 F3
Woodmere RG12 118 E5
Woodmere Cl RG6 87 B2
Woodmill Ct SL5 119 D6
Woodmoor RG40 141 F2
Woodmoor End SL6 20 B7
Woodpecker Cl RG10 61 E3
Woodpecker Wlk RG41 115 F5
Woodpeckers RG12 118 B5
Woodridge Cl RG12 118 C6
Woodridge Ho
Bracknell RG12 118 C6
Newbury RG14 130 E7
Woodrow Ct RG4 58 F2
Woodrow Dr RG40 116 F6
Woods Rd RG4 59 E4
Woodsend Cl RG6 113 E8
Woodshore Cl GU25 122 B3
Woodside
Blackwater GU17 150 C3
Cold Ash RG18 79 C1
Flackwell Heath HP10 3 C6
Newbury RG14 130 D7
Sandhurst GU15 150 F7
Woodside Ave HP10 3 C7
Woodside Bsns Pk RG2 113 B7
Woodside Cl
Bucklebury RG7 107 C5
Mortimer RG7 137 A6
Wokingham RG40 141 E8
Woodside Dr RG18 79 B6
Woodside La SL4 93 C3
Woodside Rd SL4 93 B2
Woodside Way
Reading RG2 113 D7
Virginia Water GU25 122 B6
Woodstock RG40 116 C6
Woodstock Ave SL3 43 D2
Woodstock Cl SL6 19 F1
Woodstock St RG1 86 E7
Woodthorpe Rd TW15 97 D4
Woodview Rd RG8 56 D5
Woodville Cl GU17 150 B5
Woodward Cl RG41 88 D1
Woodway GU15 151 B5
Woodway Rd OX11 12 A7
Woodwaye RG5 87 D7
Woodyer Cl RG5 87 E5
Woolacombe Dr RG6 86 F2
Woolf Dr RG40 116 C7
Woolf Meml Cotts RG40 116 C7
Woolford Cl RG42 92 C1
Woolhampton CE Prim Sch RG7 108 D4
Woolhampton Hill RG7 108 C3
Woolhampton Way RG12 118 D4
Woolley Firs SL6 38 E5
Woolton Lodge Gdns RG20 129 F2
Woosehill RG41 115 E6
Woosehill Ct RG41 115 F7
Woosehill La RG41 115 F6
Wootton Cl RG31 84 C8
Wootton Dr HP10 3 E8
Wootton Rd RG9 35 C8
Wootton Way SL6 39 C6
Worcester Cl
Maidenhead SL6 39 D3
Reading RG30 85 A5
Worcester Ct 4 TW15 98 B3
Worcester Dr TW15 98 B3
Worcester Gdns SL1 42 D4
Worcestershire Lea RG42 91 F1
Wordsworth RG12 117 F4
Wordsworth Ave GU46 149 B4
Wordsworth Ct RG4 59 C7
Wordsworth Rd
Slough SL2 21 D1
Thatcham RG18 106 C4
World Bsns Ctr TW6 71 C6
Worlds End Hill RG12 118 F3
Wormersley Rd RG19 131 D7
Worple Ave TW18 97 B2
Worple Rd TW18 97 B1
Worple The TW19 68 F1
Worrall Way RG6 113 F8
Worsley Pl RG7 83 E4
Worster Rd SL6 19 E6
Worton Dr RG2 113 A8
Worton Grange Ind Est RG2 113 A8
Wrabness Way TW18 124 B8
Wraysbury Gdns TW18 96 E4
Wraysbury Prim Sch TW19 68 E1
Wraysbury Rd TW18, TW19 96 C5
Wraysbury Sta TW19 69 A1
Wren Cl
Burghfield Common RG7 111 B3
Wokingham RG41 115 E5
Yateley GU46 149 B6
Wren Ct Egham TW20 96 A3
Slough SL3 44 A3
Wrenfield Dr RG4 58 F5
Wrens Ave TW15 98 C4
Wrensfield SL7 1 C2
Wrenswood Cl RG2 113 B7
Wright SL4 66 C4
Wright Cl RG5 88 A7
Wright Gdns TW17 125 A4
Wright Sq SL4 66 C4
Wright Way SL4 66 C4
Wroxham RG12 117 F4
Wroxham Rd RG5 87 D8
Wulwyn Ct RG45 142 F5
Wyatt Rd Staines TW18 97 A3
Windsor SL4 66 D4
Wychcotes RG4 58 F3
Wychelm Rd
Lightwater GU18 153 C8
Shinfield RG2 113 E5
Wychwood Ave RG12 118 F5
Wychwood Cl RG6 86 F2
Wychwood Cres RG6 86 F2
Wychwood Pl GU15 152 B8
Wycombe La HP10 3 E7
Wycombe Rd Marlow SL7 1 E4
Marlow Bottom SL7 1 E6
Wye Cl Ashford TW15 98 B4
Reading RG30 84 F6
Wye Ct SL8 3 A3
Wye Rd HP10 3 D8
Wye Valley Sch The SL8 3 B4
Wykeham Cl UB7 71 A8
Wykeham Rd RG6 87 A6
Wylam RG12 117 F4
Wylands Rd SL3 44 A2
Wyld Court Hill RG18 53 B5
Wyldewood SL5 120 D3
Wymers Cl SL1 21 B3
Wymers Wood Rd SL1 21 A3
Wyncote Cl RG2 86 F1
Wyndale Cl RG9 15 E1
Wyndham Cl GU46 149 D7
Wyndham Cres
Burnham SL1 21 B3
Woodley RG5 60 D1
Wyndham Rd RG14 105 D5
Wynford Cl RG30 85 C4
Wynnstay Gdns SL7 1 E5
Wynsham Way GU20 146 B6
Wyre Ct RG31 57 C3
Wyresdale RG12 118 F2
Wythegate TW18 96 F1
Wythemede RG42 90 B2
Wyvern Cl RG12 118 A5
Wyvern Ct TW15 97 E5

Y

Yale Cl GU47 143 F2
Yard Mead TW20 96 A5
Yardley RG12 117 F4
Yarmouth Rd SL1 42 C6
Yarnold Cl RG40 116 F7
Yarnton Cl RG4 59 C6
Yarrow Cl RG18 106 D5
Yateley Common Ctry Pk★ GU17,GU46 149 F3
Yateley Inf Sch GU46 149 D6
Yateley Manor Sch GU46 149 D6
Yateley Rd GU47 149 F8
Yateley Sch GU46 149 C5
Yates Copse RG14 105 E5
Yattendon CE Prim Sch RG18 53 F2
Yattendon Ct RG18 53 F2
Yattendon La RG8,RG18 54 D2
Yattendon Rd RG18 79 C7
Yaverland Dr GU19 145 D2
Ye Meads SL6 40 F5
Ye Meads Cotts SL6 40 F5
Yelverton Rd RG2 86 C3
Yeoman Dr TW15 97 E7
Yeoman Pl RG5 87 C7
Yeomans La RG20 131 A1
Yeomans Way GU15 151 E5
Yeosfield RG7 139 C3
Yeoveney Cl TW19 96 D6
Yeovil Ent Ctr SL1 41 F8
Yeovil Rd
Sandhurst GU47 143 E1
Slough SL1 41 E8
Yew Cl Newell Green RG42 92 A1
Wokingham RG41 115 F5
Yew Cnr RG12 118 C6
Yew Gate RG14 104 F6
Yew La RG1 85 F5
Yew Tree Cl SL6 39 E8
Yew Tree Ct RG8 34 C6
Yew Tree Mews RG20 31 E4
Yew Tree Rd SL1 43 A3
Yew Tree Rise RG31 84 C5
Yew Tree Stables RG20 31 E4
Yew Tree Wlk GU16 151 F1
Yew Trees TW17 124 F5
Yewhurst Cl RG10 61 D6
Yews The TW15 98 B4
Yewtrees TW20 123 C6
Yield Hall La 1 RG1 86 B7
Yield Hall Pl RG1 86 B7
Yockley Cl GU15 152 D3
Yoreham Cl RG6 87 E1
York Ave Slough SL1 42 D7
Windsor SL4 67 B5
York Cl RG14 105 B2
York Ho Bracknell RG42 117 F8
Reading RG31 84 B4
York Pl GU15 151 D7
York Rd Binfield RG42 90 D3
Camberley GU15 151 D7
Henley-On-T RG9 15 D2
Hungerford RG17 100 D4
Maidenhead SL6 40 A7
Marlow SL7 1 D2
Newbury RG14 105 B2
Reading RG1 59 A1
Windsor SL4 67 B5
York Terrace La GU15 151 A5
York Town Ind Est GU15 151 A5
York Way GU47 150 B8
Yorkshire Pl RG42 91 F2
Yorktown Rd
Sandhurst GU47 150 C7
Sandhurst GU47 150 E7
Youlden Cl GU15 152 A5
Youlden Dr GU15 152 B6
Young Cres RG19 131 D8
Young's Ind Est RG7 134 F4

Z

Zealand Ave UB7 70 E7
Zenith Ct GU47 143 E1
Zephyr Ho RG7 134 E2
Zetland Ct SL6 40 B8
Zinnia Cl RG41 115 D7
Zinzan St RG1 85 F7
Zodiac Ho RG7 134 E2

Addresses

Name and Address	Telephone	Page	Grid reference

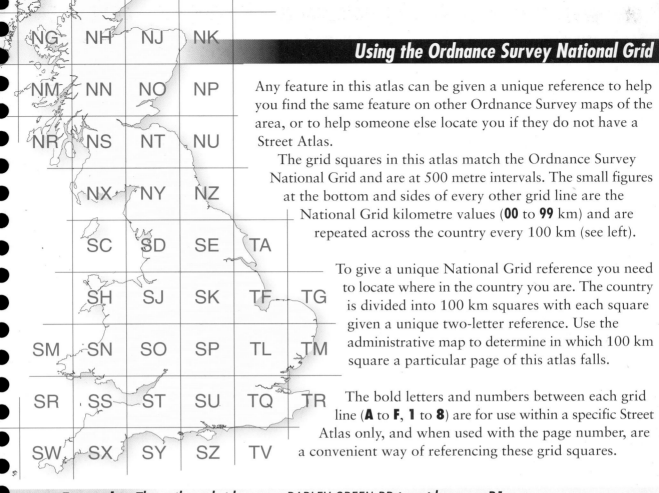

Any feature in this atlas can be given a unique reference to help you find the same feature on other Ordnance Survey maps of the area, or to help someone else locate you if they do not have a Street Atlas.

The grid squares in this atlas match the Ordnance Survey National Grid and are at 500 metre intervals. The small figures at the bottom and sides of every other grid line are the National Grid kilometre values (**00** to **99** km) and are repeated across the country every 100 km (see left).

To give a unique National Grid reference you need to locate where in the country you are. The country is divided into 100 km squares with each square given a unique two-letter reference. Use the administrative map to determine in which 100 km square a particular page of this atlas falls.

The bold letters and numbers between each grid line (**A** to **F**, **1** to **8**) are for use within a specific Street Atlas only, and when used with the page number, are a convenient way of referencing these grid squares.

Example *The railway bridge over DARLEY GREEN RD in grid square B1*

Step 1: Identify the two-letter reference, in this example the page is in **SP**

Step 2: Identify the 1 km square in which the railway bridge falls. Use the figures in the southwest corner of this square: Eastings **17**, Northings **74**. This gives a unique reference: **SP 17 74**, accurate to 1 km.

Step 3: To give a more precise reference accurate to 100 m you need to estimate how many tenths along and how many tenths up this 1 km square the feature is (to help with this the 1 km square is divided into four 500 m squares). This makes the bridge about **8** tenths along and about **1** tenth up from the southwest corner.

This gives a unique reference: **SP 178 741**, accurate to 100 m.

Eastings (read from left to right along the bottom) come before Northings (read from bottom to top). If you have trouble remembering say to yourself "Along the hall, THEN up the stairs"!

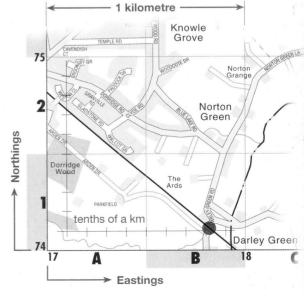

PHILIP'S MAPS
the Gold Standard for drivers

◆ Philip's street atlases cover every county in England, Wales, Northern Ireland and much of Scotland

◆ Every named street is shown, including alleys, lanes and walkways

◆ Thousands of additional features marked: stations, public buildings, car parks, places of interest

◆ Route-planning maps to get you close to your destination

◆ Postcodes on the maps and in the index

◆ Widely used by the emergency services, transport companies and local authorities

BEST BUY • BEST BUY Auto EXPRESS *BEST BUY • BEST BUY*

For national mapping, choose **Philip's Navigator Britain** the most detailed road atlas available of England, Wales and Scotland. Hailed by Auto Express as 'the ultimate road atlas', the atlas shows every road and lane in Britain.

'The ultimate in UK mapping'
The Sunday Times

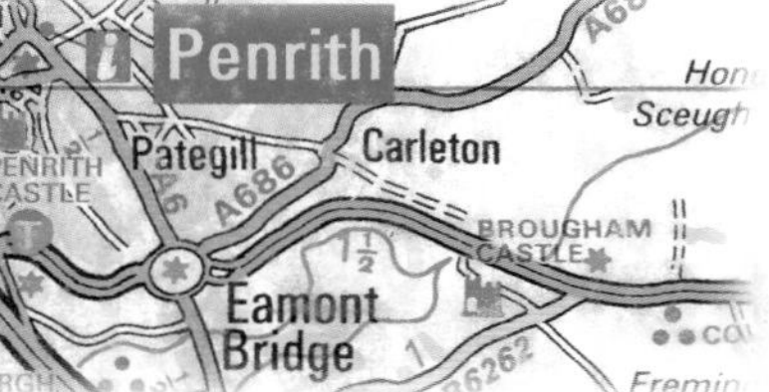

Street atlases currently available

England

Bedfordshire	East Sussex
Berkshire	West Sussex
Birmingham and West Midlands	Tyne and Wear
Bristol and Bath	Warwickshire
Buckinghamshire	Birmingham and West Midlands
Cambridgeshire	Wiltshire and Swindon
Cheshire	Worcestershire
Cornwall	East Yorkshire Northern Lincolnshire
Cumbria	North Yorkshire
Derbyshire	South Yorkshire
Devon	West Yorkshire
Dorset	
County Durham and Teesside	**Wales**
Essex	Anglesey, Conwy and Gwynedd
North Essex	Cardiff, Swansea and The Valleys
South Essex	Carmarthenshire, Pembrokeshire and Swansea
Gloucestershire	
Hampshire	Ceredigion and South Gwynedd
North Hampshire	
South Hampshire	Denbighshire, Flintshire, Wrexham
Herefordshire Monmouthshire	Herefordshire Monmouthshire
Hertfordshire	
Isle of Wight	Powys
Kent	
East Kent	**Scotland**
West Kent	Aberdeenshire
Lancashire	Ayrshire
Leicestershire and Rutland	Dumfries and Galloway
Lincolnshire	Edinburgh and East Central Scotland
London	Fife and Tayside
Greater Manchester	Glasgow and West Central Scotland
Merseyside	Inverness and Moray
Norfolk	Lanarkshire
Northamptonshire	Scottish Borders
Northumberland	
Nottinghamshire	**Northern Ireland**
Oxfordshire	County Antrim and County Londonderry
Shropshire	County Armagh and County Down
Somerset	
Staffordshire	Belfast
Suffolk	County Tyrone and County Fermanagh
Surrey	

How to order

Philip's maps and atlases are available from bookshops, motorway services and petrol stations. You can order direct from the publisher by phoning **0207 531 8473** or online at **www.philips-maps.co.uk**
For bulk orders only, e-mail philips@philips-maps.co.uk